Philosophy, Science and Theology of Mission
in the 19th and 20th Centuries
A Missiological Encyclopedia
Part I: The Philosophy and Science of Mission

STUDIEN ZUR INTERKULTURELLEN GESCHICHTE DES CHRISTENTUMS
ETUDES D' HISTOIRE INTERCULTURELLE DU CHRISTIANISME
STUDIES IN THE INTERCULTURAL HISTORY OF CHRISTIANITY

begründet von / fondé par / founded by
Hans Jochen Margull†, Hamburg

herausgegeben von / édité par / edited by

Richard Friedli · Walter J. Hollenweger · Theo Sundermeier
Université de Fribourg · University of Birmingham · Universität Heidelberg

Jan A. B. Jongeneel
Universiteit Utrecht

Band 92

PETER LANG
Frankfurt am Main · Berlin · Bern · New York · Paris · Wien

Jan A. B. Jongeneel

Philosophy, Science, and Theology of Mission in the 19th and 20th Centuries

A Missiological Encyclopedia
Part I: The Philosophy and
Science of Mission

PETER LANG
Europäischer Verlag der Wissenschaften

Die Deutsche Bibliothek - CIP-Einheitsaufnahme

Jongeneel, Jan A. B.:

Philosophy, science, and theology of mission in the 19th and
20th centuries : a missiological encyclopedia / Jan A. B.
Jongeneel. - Frankfurt am Main ; Berlin ; Bern ; New York ;
Paris ; Wien : Lang.
NE: HST

Pt. 1. The philosophy and science of mission. - 1995
    (Studies in the intercultural history of Christianity ; Bd. 92)
    ISBN 3-631-48312-0
NE: Studien zur interkulturellen Geschichte des Christentums

ISSN 0170-9240
ISBN 3-631-48312-0

© Peter Lang GmbH
Europäischer Verlag der Wissenschaften
Frankfurt am Main 1995

Printed in Germany 1 2 3 4   6 7

To the president and members of the:
-International Association for Mission Studies
-American Society of Missiology
-Deutsche Gesellschaft für Missionswissenschaft

To the memory of:
-Alexander Duff (1806-1878), Edinburgh
-Gustav Warneck (1834-1910), Halle
-François E. Daubanton (1853-1920), Utrecht

FOREWORD

This encylopedia or handbook is the result of ten years research at the Department of Church History, in the Faculty of Theology, at Utrecht University.

Utrecht University is a very good place to do mission studies. Voetius, the 17th century founder of the University, was the first Protestant theologian to develop a comprehensive missiology. And in the 20th century famous predecessors like Daubanton, Van Ruler, and Hoekendijk helped me to make missiology an attractive and very crucial discipline in the theological education of students.

Several colleagues in the Faculty were willing to contribute to my work in one form or another. For instance, Prof.Dr. Jannes Reiling was willing to read the New Testament section of this study and Prof.Dr. Luke van den Brom commented to the sections on the Philosophy of Mission. Most helpful was Dr. Peter Staples who works in the Department of Church History. He is not only a good scholar in contemporary church history, but also a competent corrector of the 'poor' and 'stereotype' English written by Dutch theologians. I acknowledge my thanks to him as *collega proximus*.

I also would like to thank Mr. Peter Pit, my assistant, who helped me both in checking the bibliographies and in preparing the indices. My thanks also goes to my son, Ir. Christian J.B. Jongeneel, who assisted me in making the whole manuscript camera-ready.

The second volume, dealing with the theology of mission and missionary theology, will hopefully be published in 2 years after this publication. The Dutch text of this second volume is already available as a book but will largely be revised.

I dedicate my study to the president and the members of the International Association for Mission Studies (IAMS), the American Society of Missiology (ASM), and the Deutsche Gesellschaft für Missionswissenschaft (DGM) with whom I share a basic commitment. I am aware that all contemporary mission studies, by IAMS-members, ASM-members, DGM-members, and others, are based on the endeavours of our 'ancestors' in the field, of whom I mention here only Duff, Warneck, and Daubanton. However, this study also makes very clear that missiology is greatly indebted to a large group of missionary theologians, missionaries, and missiologists -both man and woman, black and white- in six continents. Only in the course of this century, missiology developed from a western (Ger.: *West*) discipline to a world-wide (Ger.: *Welt*) discipline: with a new spirituality, new insights, new methods, and new activities.

Hopefully this study will help many colleagues and students in six continents to find their way in the broad and complex field of the philosophical, empirical, and theological studies of mission in the 19th and 20th centuries. In the

21th century, both the theological faculties and colleges and the churches need many missionary theologians, missionaries, and missiologists who are well equipped to face the enormous challenges of the third millennium of our Lord Jesus Christ.

Utrecht, August 1994
Jan A.B. Jongeneel

ABBREVIATIONS AND SYMBOLS

abbr.	abbreviation, abbreviated
abr.	abridged, abridgment
AD	*Anno Domini* (=in the year of the Lord)
Amer.	America(n)
AMZ	*Allgemeine Missions-Zeitschrift* (Gütersloh, 1874-1923)
anon.	anonymous
app(s).	appendix(es)
art(s).	article(s)
Aufl.	*Auflage* (=edition)
b.	born
Belg.	Belgian, Belgium
bibliog.	bibliographer, bibliographical, *Bibliographie, bibliographisch*, bibliography
biog.	biographer, biographical, *Biographie, biographisch*, biography
c.	*circa* (=about)
cap.	*caput* (=chapter), *capita* (=chapters)
cf.	*confer* (=compare)
chap(s).	chapter(s)
co.	company
comp(s).	compiled by, compiler(s)
CWME	Commission on World Mission and Evangelism of the World Council of Churches
d.	died
DH	*De Heerbaan* (Amsterdam, 1948-1971)
diss.	dissertation
dr.	*druk* (=edition)
ed(s).	edited (by), edition(s), editor(s)
éd.	*édition* (=edition)
EFMA	Evangelical Foreign Missions Association/Evangelical Fellowship of Mission Agencies
e.g.	*exempli gratia* (=for example)
EMM	*Evangelisches Missionsmagazin. Neue Folge.* (Basel, 1857-1974)
EMQ	*Evangelical Missions Quarterly* (Washington, & Wheaton, 1964-...)
EMZ	*Evangelische Missions-Zeitschrift* (Stuttgart, 1940-1974)
enc.	encyclopedia
Eng.	England, English

enl.	enlarged
ER	*The Ecumenical Review* (Geneva, 1948-...)
erw.	*erweitert(e)* (=enlarged)
esp.	especially
et al.	*et alii* (=and others)
etc.	*et cetera* (=and so forth)
f(f).	(and the) following
Fr.	France, French
Ger.	German(y)
Gk	Greek
herz.	*herzien(e)* (=revised)
HM	*Het Missiewerk* (Nijmegen, 1919-1971)
hrsg.	*herausgegeben* (=edited), *Herausgeber* (=editor)
IAMS	International Association for Mission Studies
ibid.	*ibidem* (=in the same place)
IBMR	*International Bulletin of Missionary Research* (Ventnor, 1981-...)
i.e.	*id est* (=that is)
IFMA	Interdenominational Foreign Mission Association
IIMO	Interuniversity Institute for Missiological and Ecumenical Research (Utrecht & Leiden)
IMC	International Missionary Council
introd.	introduced (by), introduction
IRM	*International Review of Mission(s)* (London, later: Geneva, 1912-...)
It.	Italian, Italy
Jr	Junior
Lat.	Latin
LCWE	Lausanne Committee for World Evangelization
lit.	literary, literature
Med.	*Mededeelingen (van wege het Nederlandsche Zendelinggenootschap)* (Rotterdam, 1857-1943)
misc.	miscellaneous
MR	*Missionswissenschaft und Religionswissenschaft* (Münster in Westfalen, 1938-1941, 1947-1949)
MRL	Missionary Research Library (New York)
ms(s).	manuscript(s)
NAMZ	*Neue Allgemeine Missionszeitschrift* (Gütersloh, 1924-1939)
n.d.	no date
no(s).	number(s)
Nor.	Norway, Norwegian
n.p.	no place, no publisher

NT	New Testament
NZM	*Neue Zeitschrift für Missionswissenschaft* (Schöneck, & Beckenried, 1945-...)
OBMR	*Occasional Bulletin of Missionary Research* (Ventnor, 1974-1980)
OT	Old Testament
p(p).	page(s)
par(s).	paragraph(s)
Port.	Portugal, Portuguese
pref.	preface
pseud.	pseudonym
pt(s)	part(s)
publ(s).	publication(s), published (by), publisher(s)
repr.	reprint, reprinted (by)
resp.	respectively
Rev.	Reverend
rev.	revised (by), revision
ser.	series
Sp.	Spain, Spanish
Sr	Senior
Swed.	Sweden, Swedish
theol.	theologian, theological, theology
tr(s).	translated (by), translation(s), translator(s)
Übers.	*Übersetzer* (=translator), *übersetzt* (=translated), *Übersetzung* (=translation)
univ.	university
v(v).	verse(s)
verb.	*verbeterd(e)*, *verbessert(e)* (=revised)
verm.	*vermeerderd(e)*, *vermehrt(e)* (=enlarged)
vert.	*vertaald* (=translated), *vertaler* (=translator), *vertaling* (=translation)
viz.	*videlicet* (=namely)
vol(s).	volume(s)
UN	United Nations
USA	United States of America
WCC	World Council of Churches
WenZ	*Wereld en Zending* (Amsterdam, 1972-...)
ZM	*Zeitschrift für Missionswissenschaft* (Münster in Westfalen, 1911-1937)
ZMiss.	*Zeitschrift für Mission* (Basel, & Stuttgart, 1975-...)
ZMkR	*Zeitschrift für Missionskunde und Religionswissenschaft* (Berlin, 1886-1939)

ZMR	*Zeitschrift für Missionswissenschaft und Religionswissenschaft* (Münster in Westfalen, 1949-...)
&	and, *und*, *en*, *et*

Postscript:
Bible books and Roman Catholic orders/congregations are abbreviated in the usual way.

REFERENCE WORKS

ANDERSON. 1961.
   *ANDERSON, GERALD H. (ed.). The theology of the Christian mission. New York, Toronto, & London, 1961.
BIBLIOGRAFIA MISSIONARIA. 1933-...
   *ROMMERSKIRCHEN, JOHANNES, OMI, et al. Bibliografia missionaria. Roma, 1933-... I-...
BIBLIOTHECA MISSIONUM. 1916-1974.
   *STREIT, ROBERT, OMI (und JOHANNES DINDINGER OMI; fortgesetzt von JOHANNES ROMMERSKIRCHEN OMI, und JOSEF METZLER OMI).Bibliotheca missionum. Münster in Westfalen, 1916-1974. 30 vols.
   I (1916): Grundlegender und allgemeiner Teil.
   XXII (1963): Grundlegender und allgemeiner Teil 1910-1935 und Nachtrag zu Band I.
   XXIII (1964): Grundlegender und allgemeiner Teil 1936-1960.
BOSCH. 1991.
   *BOSCH, DAVID J. Transforming mission: paradigm shifts in theology of mission. New York, 1991.
CONCISE DICTIONARY. 1971.
   *NEILL, STEPHEN C., GERALD H. ANDERSON, and JOHN F.B. GOODWIN (eds.). Concise dictionary of the Christian world mission. London, 1971.
   *Ger. tr.: NEILL, STEPHEN C., NIELS-PETER MORITZEN, and ERNST SCHRUPP (eds.). Lexikon zur Weltmission. Wuppertal, & Erlangen, 1975.
DAUBANTON. 1911.
   *DAUBANTON, FRANÇOIS E. Prolegomena van Protestantsche zendingswetenschap. Utrecht, 1911.
DEM. 1991.
   *LOSSKY, NICHOLAS, JOSÉ M. BONINO, JOHN S. POBEE, et al. (eds.). Dictionary of the ecumenical movement. Geneva, & Grand Rapids, 1991.
DICTIONARY CATALOG. 1968.
   *DICTIONARY CATALOG OF THE MISSIONARY RESEARCH LIBRARY NEW YORK. Boston, 1968. 17 vols.
HOLSTEN. 1953.
   *HOLSTEN, WALTER. Das Kerygma und der Mensch: Einführung in die Religions- und Missionswissenschaft. München, 1953.

LM. 1992.
  *RZEPKOWSKI, HORST, SVD. Lexikon der Mission: Geschichte, Theologie, Ethnologie. Graz, Wien, & Köln, 1992.
LMG. 1987.
  *MÜLLER, KARL, SVD, and THEO SUNDERMEIER (eds.). Lexikon missionstheologischer Grundbegriffe. Berlin, 1987.
MULDERS. 1962.
  *MULDERS, ALPHONSUS J.M. Missiologisch bestek: inleiding tot de katholieke missiewetenschap. Hilversum, & Antwerpen, 1962.
MYKLEBUST. 1955-1957.
  *MYKLEBUST, OLAV G. The study of missions in theological education: an historical inquiry into the place of world evangelisation in Western Protestant ministerial training with particular reference to Alexander Duff's chair of evangelistic theology. Oslo, 1955-1957. 2 vols.
  I : to 1910.
  II : 1910-1950.
OHM. 1962.
  *OHM, THOMAS, OSB. Machet zu Jüngern alle Völker: Theorie der Mission. Freiburg im Breisgau, 1962.
  Fr. tr.: Faites des disciples de toutes les nations: théorie de la mission. Paris, 1964-1967. 3 vols.
PHILLIPS and COOTE. 1993.
  *PHILLIPS, JAMES M., and ROBERT T. COOTE (eds.). Toward the 21st century in Christian mission: essays in honor of Gerald H. Anderson. Grand Rapids, 1993.
RGG. 1957-1965.
  *GALLING, KURT (ed.). Die Religion in Geschichte und Gegenwart: Handwörterbuch für Theologie und Religionswissen-schaft: dritte, völlig neu bearbeitete Aufl. Tübingen, 1957-1965. 7 vols.
  First ed.: Tübingen, 1909-1913. 5 vols.
SANTOS HERNANDEZ. 1961.
  *SANTOS HERNANDEZ, ANGEL, SJ. Misionologia: problemas introductorios y ciencias auxiliares. Santander, 1961.
SCHMIDLIN. 1925.
  *SCHMIDLIN, JOSEPH. Einführung in die Missionswissenschaft: zweite Aufl. Münster in Westfalen, 1925.
  First ed.: Münster in Westfalen, 1917.
SCHOMERUS. 1935.
  *SCHOMERUS, HILKO W. Misssionswissenschaft. Leipzig, 1935.
SCIENTIA MISSIONUM ANCILLA. 1953.
  *LOFFELD, ÉDOUARD, CSSp., and JOHN WILS (eds.). Scientia missionum ancilla: clarissimo doctori Alphonso I.M. Mulders ... hunc

librum dedicant amici occasione sexagesimi eius anniversarii. Nijmegen, & Utrecht, 1953.
SEUMOIS. 1952.
   *SEUMOIS, ANDRÉ V., OMI. Introduction à la missiologie. Schöneck, & Beckenried, 1952.
   *Sp. tr.: Introduccion a la misionologia: Roma, 1953-1954: versión y adaptación por el alumno Pbro. Benito López Velarde. México, 1960.
TDNT. 1964-1976. Ger. ed.: TWNT. 1933-1978.
   KITTEL, GERHARD (and GERHARD FRIEDRICH) (ed.). Theological dictionary of the New Testament: tr. and ed. by Geoffrey W. Bromiley. Grand Rapids, 1964-1976. 10 vols.
   *Ger. ed.: KITTEL, GERHARD (und GERHARD FRIEDRICH) (ed.). Theologisches Wörterbuch zum Neuen Testament. Stuttgart, 1933-1978. 10 vols.
VRIENS. 1960.
   *VRIENS, LIVINUS, OFMCap. Critical bibliography of missiology: with the collaboration of Anastasius Disch OFMCap. (Mission law) and John Wils (Linguistics): Eng. ed. Nijmegen, 1960.
   *Ger. tr.: Kritische Bibliographie der Missionswissenschaft. Nijmegen, 1961.
   Fr. tr.: Bibliographie analytique de la missiologie. Nijmegen, 1962.
WAGNER. 1989.
   *WAGNER, C. PETER (ed.), with WIN ARN and ELMER L. TOWNS. Church growth: state of the art: third printing. Wheaton, 1989.
   First ed.: Wheaton, 1986.
WARNECK. 1892-1903.
   *WARNECK, GUSTAV. Evangelische Missionslehre: ein missionstheoretischer Versuch. Gotha, 1892-1903. I-III/3 vols.
WCE. 1982.
   *BARRETT, DAVID B. (ed.). World Christian encyclopedia: a comparative study of churches and religions in the modern world AD 1900-2000. Nairobi, Oxford, & New York, 1982.

CONTENTS

Foreword   vii

Abbreviations and symbols   ix

Reference works   xiii

1. Introduction   1
   1.1. Mission studies   1
   1.2. Structure of the study   3
   1.3. Sources of the study   4
        1.3.1. Bibliographies   4
        1.3.2. Encyclopedias and dictionaries   7
        1.3.3. Glossaries   9
        1.3.4. Periodicals   9
        1.3.5. Reference works   10
   1.4. Final introductory questions   12

2. Names of missiology   15
   2.1. Names   15
   2.2. Minor names   16
        2.2.1. Halieutics   16
        2.2.2. Keryktics   18
        2.2.3. Matheteutics   20
        2.2.4. Auxanics   22
        2.2.5. Prosthetics   24
        2.2.6. Propagandics   24
        2.2.7. Conclusion   27
   2.3. Evangelistic theology, evangelistics, evangelistology,
        the theology of evangelism, the theology of evangelization   27
        2.3.1. *Euangelizein, euangelion, euangelistes*   27
        2.3.2. Evangelistic theology, evangelistics   28
        2.3.3. Evangelistology   31
        2.3.4. The theology of evangelism   31
               2.3.4.1. Evangelism   31
               2.3.4.2. The theology of evangelism   41
        2.3.5. The theology of evangelization   42
               2.3.5.1. Evangelization   42
               2.3.5.2. The theology of evangelization   48
        2.3.6. Conclusion   49

2.4. Apostolics, apostolo(lo)gy, theology of the apostolate   50
    2.4.1. *Apostellein, apostole, apostolos*   50
    2.4.2. Apostolics   51
    2.4.3. Apostolo(lo)gy   52
    2.4.4. Theology of the apostolate   52
        2.4.4.1. Apostolate   52
        2.4.4.2. Theology of the apostolate   56
    2.4.5. Conclusion   57
2.5. Missionics, missio(no)logy, the philosophy of mission,
the science of mission, the theology of mission, missionary
theology   58
    2.5.1. *Mittere, missio(nes), missionarius*   58
    2.5.2. Missionics   62
    2.5.3. Missio(no)logy   63
    2.5.4. The philosophy of mission, the science of mission,
        and the theology of mission   67
    2.5.5. Missionary theology   67
    2.5.6. Conclusion   69
2.6. Conclusion   69

3. **Concepts of missiology**   71
3.1. Concepts   71
3.2. The philosophy of mission   72
    3.2.1. Introduction   72
    3.2.2. The philosophy of mission (*Missionsphilosophie*)   72
    3.2.3. The philosophy of mission and the philosophy of
        religion (*Religionsphilosophie*)   76
    3.2.4. Conclusion   77
3.3. The science of mission   77
    3.3.1. Introduction   77
    3.3.2. The science of mission (*Missionswissenschaft*)   79
    3.3.3. The science of mission and the science of religion
        (*Religionswissenschaft*)   84
    3.3.4. Conclusion   86
3.4. The theology of mission   87
    3.4.1. Introduction   87
    3.4.2. The theology of mission (*Missionstheologie*)   88
        3.4.2.1. Introduction   88
        3.4.2.2. Biblical theology of mission
                [introduction; mission in the Bible;
                the Bible in mission; the missionary
                significance of the division of the Bible

into the Old and New Testament; mission
in the Old Testament; *shalach, shaliach*;
the law of Moses (*thora*); the prophets
(*nebiim*); the writings (*ketubim*); the
gentiles (*goiim*); the Old Testament in
mission; mission in the New Testament;
apostellein, apostolos, apostole; Jesus;
the gospels; the Acts of the Apostles;
Peter; Paul; the epistles; the Revelation
of John; the gentiles (*ethne*); the New
Testament in mission]   98

3.4.2.3. Ecclesiastical theology of mission
[introduction; Hebrew Christian theology
of mission; Eastern Orthodox theology of
mission; Roman Catholic theology of
mission; Protestant theology of mission;
Ecumenical theology of mission;
Evangelical theology of mission;
Pentecostal and Charismatic theology of
mission]   136

3.4.2.4. Corporate theology of mission
[introduction; missionary orders and
societies]   159

3.4.2.5. Individual theology of mission
[introduction; missionary theologians;
missionaries; missiologists]   162

3.4.3. The theology of mission and the theology of
religion (*Religionstheologie*)   168

3.4.4. Conclusion   170

3.5. Conclusion   171

4. **Methods of missiology**   175
4.1. Methods   175
4.2. Metaphysics and empiricism   176
4.3. Deductive and inductive methods   177
4.4. Descriptive and normative missiology   178
4.5. Missiology from above and missiology from below   180
4.6. Conclusion   182

5. **Branches of missiology**   185
5.1. Branches   185
5.2. The philosophy of mission (*Missionsphilosophie*)   185

5.2.1.	Introduction	185
5.2.2.	The epistemology of mission	186
	5.2.2.1. Introduction	186
	5.2.2.2. History	187
	5.2.2.3. The knowledge of Christian mission	187
5.2.3.	The phenomenology of mission	188
	5.2.3.1. Introduction	188
	5.2.3.2. History	190
	5.2.3.3. The appearance of Christian mission	191
	5.2.3.4. The comparison of Christian mission with other missions [the mission and propaganda of non-Christian religions and worldviews; the comparison of Christian mission with other missions]	192
	5.2.3.5. The phenomenology of Christian mission, the phenomenology of religion, and comparative theology	196
5.2.4.	The ontology of mission	197
	5.2.4.1. Introduction	197
	5.2.4.2. History	197
	5.2.4.3. The essence of Christian mission	198
5.2.5.	The axiology of mission	199
	5.2.5.1. Introduction	199
	5.2.5.2. History	200
	5.2.5.3. The value of Christian mission [the moral value of Christian mission; the aesthetic value of Christian mission]	200
5.2.6.	Conclusion	202
5.3.	The science of mission (*Missionswissenschaft*)	202
5.3.1.	Introduction	203
	5.3.1.1. Introduction	203
	5.3.1.2. History	203
	5.3.1.3. Branches of the science of mission	204
5.3.2.	The linguistics of Christian mission	207
	5.3.2.1. Introduction	207
	5.3.2.2. History	208
	5.3.2.3. The linguistics and philology of Christian mission	209
	5.3.2.4. Missionary language	211
	5.3.2.5. The science of translating and interpreting [Christian terminology; Bible translation; Bible interpretation]	213

5.3.2.6.	The linguistics of Christian mission and the linguistics of religion	218
5.3.2.7.	Conclusion	218
5.3.3.	The history of Christian mission	219
5.3.3.1.	Introduction	219
5.3.3.2.	History	223
5.3.3.3.	Chronology	226
5.3.3.4.	The history of Christian mission (general)	229
5.3.3.5.	The history of Roman Catholic mission	236
5.3.3.6.	The history of Protestant mission	240
5.3.3.7.	The history of missionary orders and societies	244
5.3.3.8.	Missionary biographies (collective works)	245
5.3.3.9.	Surveys of world-wide mission	249
5.3.3.10	The history of Christian mission and world history, the history of religion, church history, and the history of conversions [mission history and world history; mission history and the history of religion; mission history and church history; mission history and the history of conversions]	250
5.3.3.11	Conclusion	257
5.3.4.	The geography of Christian mission	258
5.3.4.1.	Introduction	258
5.3.4.2.	History	258
5.3.4.3.	The geography and cartography of Christian mission	261
5.3.4.4.	Missionary atlases and maps [General; Roman Catholic; Protestant]	262
5.3.4.5.	Mission fields and mission stations	268
5.3.4.6.	Missionary travels	269
5.3.4.7.	The geography of Christian mission and the geography of religion	270
5.3.4.8.	Conclusion	272
5.3.5.	The statistics of Christian mission	272
5.3.5.1.	Introduction	272
5.3.5.2.	History	274
5.3.5.3.	The statistics of Christian mission	275
5.3.5.4.	The statistics of Roman Catholic mission	278
5.3.5.5.	The statistics of Protestant mission	280
5.3.5.6.	The statistics of Christian mission and the statistics of religion	282

5.3.5.7. Conclusion 284
5.3.6. The ethnology and cultural anthropology of Christian
mission, missionary anthropology 284
5.3.6.1. Introduction 284
5.3.6.2. History 286
5.3.6.3. Ethnology and Christian mission 288
5.3.6.4. Cultural anthropology and Christian
mission 291
5.3.6.5. Missionary anthropology 294
5.3.6.6. Conclusion 296
5.3.7. The sociology of Christian mission 297
5.3.7.1. Introduction 297
5.3.7.2. History 298
5.3.7.3. The sociology of Christian mission 300
5.3.7.4. The sociology of Christian mission and
the sociology of religion 304
5.3.7.5. Conclusion 305
5.3.8. The law of Christian mission 306
5.3.8.1. Introduction 306
5.3.8.2. History 307
5.3.8.3. Human rights and Christian mission 308
5.3.8.4. Religious liberty, missionary freedom
[United Nations, associations, churches] 310
5.3.8.5. The law of Christian mission and national
and international law 316
5.3.8.6. Conclusion 319
5.3.9. The economics of Christian mission 320
5.3.9.1. Introduction 320
5.3.9.2. History 320
5.3.9.3. The economics of Christian mission 323
5.3.9.4. Missionary finance 325
5.3.9.5. Self-supporting churches 327
5.3.9.6. Mission, poverty and affluence 329
5.3.9.7. The economics of Christian mission and
world economy 331
5.3.9.8. Conclusion 333
5.3.10 The psychology of Christian mission 333
5.3.10.1 Introduction 333
5.3.10.2 History 334
5.3.10.3 The psychology of Christian mission and
missionary poimenics (=missionary care) 335

5.3.10.4 The psychology of Christian mission
[mission boards; missionaries; missionary
work]   336
5.3.10.5 The psychology of the Christian encounter
with non-Christian religions and
worldviews [the psychology of non-
Christian religions and worldviews; the
psychology of conversion and other
reactions to Christian mission]   340
5.3.10.6 The psychology of Christian mission and
the psychology of religion   343
5.3.10.7 Conclusion   344
5.3.11 The pedagogics of Christian mission   345
5.3.11.1 Introduction   345
5.3.11.2 History   346
5.3.11.3 The pedagogics of Christian mission and
missionary catechetics   349
5.3.11.4 Missionary education [catechesis; mission
schools; missionary participation in
people's education]   350
5.3.11.5 Missionary methods   355
5.3.11.6 The pedagogics of Christian mission and
the pedagogics of religion   356
5.3.11.7 Conclusion   357
5.3.12 Conclusion   357

Indices   361
1. Index of personal names   361
2. Index of subjects   381

1. INTRODUCTION

1.1. MISSION STUDIES

This book is a comprehensive survey and analysis of the main philosophical, scientific (or empirical), and theological studies of mission in the 19th and 20th centuries, with the brief title: THE PHILOSOPHY, SCIENCE, AND THEOLOGY OF MISSION IN THE 19TH AND 20TH CENTURIES: A MISSIOLOGICAL ENCYCLOPEDIA.

From the beginning of the 19th century missiology has been studied and still is studied primarily in theological colleges, seminaries and faculties; however, in the course of time, other institutions have occupied themselves with it as well. The object of its research, i.e. *mission* (Lat.: *missio*), is, after all, not only a religious, but also a linguistic, historical, social, and cultural phenomenon. From time to time linguists, historians, cultural anthropologists, sociologists, and other scholars in the social sciences have devoted as much attention to mission as theologians and missiologists; but their approach is usually more empirical. Because of this broad interest in mission as a many-sided phenomenon, publications by theologians and missiologists, as well as papers by authors from other faculties and disciplines, are catalogued, classified, described, and analysed in this 'encyclopedia'.

Missiology is now dependent on non-theological faculties and disciplines, which it also influences in turn. Over the centuries, missionaries have used the results of research by various non-theologians; and they have at the same time performed pioneer work in the field of the latter. Missionaries baptized people and founded churches overseas. Prior to and often at the same time as they carried out such purely religious activities, they wrote travel reports about countries hitherto unknown; made maps; compiled dictionaries and grammars; studied traditional religions and oriental cultures; etc. In many cases, they were the pioneers in those fields. It was not a diplomat or a tradesman, but the Italian missionary Matteo Ricci SJ (1552-1610) who was the first Westerner in modern history to travel from the Portuguese colony of Macao through the vast Chinese empire and to reach eventually the Chinese emperor in Beijing (=Peking). It was not a geographer or an ethnologist, but rather the Scottish missionary David Livingstone (1813-1873), in the service of the London Missionary Society, who was the first white man to travel across great parts of Central Africa. For these and other reasons, it was possible for Thomas Laurie in the USA to write his important book *The Ely Volume: or, the Contributions of Our Foreign Missions to Science and Human Well-being* (1881) in commemoration of the Rev. Alfred Ely (1778-1866), in which he pointed out the inestimable contribution of missionaries to the study of geography, geology, meteorology, natural science, archeology, cabinets and cuneiform inscriptions, philology, ethnography, general literature, periodical literature, music, Bible translations, religious beliefs, contributions to history, education, medical science, commerce and the arts, the wines of the Bible, national regeneration, and philanthropy.

Missiology studies in philosophical, empirical and theological ways the comprehensive phenomenon of mission in all its religious and non-religious aspects. It examines not only 'the expansion of Christianity' (Latourette) as a religious phenomenon, but also seeks what could be called 'the secular meaning of mission' which today manifests itself in the service of the Red Cross, the struggle for human rights (cf. Amnesty International), etc. Therefore missiology is important not only for the present and the future of Christianity and the church, but also for the so-called 'progress' of humanity in general. In missiology, the basic question is which call has been fulfilled and should be fulfilled by each human being and in particular each Christian, and by the church as a religious community and all mankind as creation - *in the sight of God* (Lat.: *coram Deo*).

So it is very clear that this study is not a handbook on *mission(s)*, but on *mission studies* (Ger.: *Missionsstudien*), i.e. *missiology*. It does not provide a comprehensive survey of mission(s), but rather a comprehensive view of the philosophical, empirical and theological study of mission(s). In other words: it is not primarily interested in the phenomenon of mission(s) as such, its foundation, purposes, methods, and organization, but in the way in which this phenomenon has been studied and still is studied philosophically, empirically, and theologically.

LÜCKE, G.C. FRIEDRICH. Missionsstudien oder Beyträge zur Missionswissenschaft. Göttingen, 1841.

PLATH, CARL H.C. Missions-Studien. Berlin, 1870.

*LAURIE, THOMAS. The Ely volume: or, the contributions of our foreign missions to science and human well-being. Boston, 1881.
   Second rev. ed.: Boston, 1885.

*GRUNDEMANN, PETER R. Missions-Studien und Kritiken in Verbindung mit einer Reise nach Indien. Gütersloh, 1894.

*GRUNDEMANN, PETER R. Missions-Studien und -Kritiken: zweite Reihe. Gütersloh, 1898.

LA ROCHE, FR. Rückwirkung des Missionsstudiums auf das theologische Denken. Basel, 1912.

PFEIFFER, EDWARD. Mission studies: historical survey and outlines of missionary principles and practice...: second rev. and enl. ed. Columbus, 1912.
   First ed.: Columbus, 1908.

TRAGELLA, GIOVANNI B., PIME. Avviamento allo studio delle missioni. Milano, 1930.
   Fr. tr.: 1934. Port. tr.: 1940.

*LATOURETTE, KENNETH S. A history of the expansion of Christianity. New York1937-1945.
   7 vols.

*MÜLLER, KARL, SVD (ed.). Missionsstudien. Kaldenkirchen, 1962.

*CONCISE DICTIONARY. 1971.
   P. 408-410: Mission studies in theological education (Marcus Ward, and eds.).

*MISSION STUDIES: journal of the International Association for Mission Studies (IAMS). 1984-...
   Nr.1-...

*CHEESMAN, GRAHAM. Mission today: an introduction to mission studies. Belfast, 1989.

1.2. STRUCTURE OF THE STUDY

Theological studies are either *material* or *formal* (Doedes 1876:2-3; Kuyper 1894:I,41-42). The same can be stated about mission studies. *Material mission studies* concentrate on the materials, i.e. the subject matters of mission: the (1) who, (2) what, (3) when, and (4) how of *mission* (cf. Kritzinger, Meiring, and Saayman 1984); whereas *formal mission studies* call attention to the forms, i.e. the structure of mission studies: the (1) who, (2) what, (3) when, and (4) how of *mission studies*. Formal mission studies deal with the branches of mission studies, the way in which these branches constitute missiology as a discipline, the connection between missiology as an independent discipline and other theological and non-theological disciplines and faculties, etc.

Gustav Warneck (1834-1910), professor of mission at Halle and founder of missiology as an academic discipline, developed material mission studies. He divided his excellent handbook *Evangelische Missionslehre* (1892-1903), after an introductory chapter, into three sections:

1. the basis (Ger.: *Begründung*) of mission;
2. the agencies (Ger.: *Organe*) of mission; and
3. the enterprise (Ger.: *Betrieb*) of mission (my tr.).

Our predecessor at the University of Utrecht, François E. Daubanton (1853-1920), however, can be seen as the first scholar who studied mission formally: in his famous book *Prolegomena van Protestantsche Zendingswetenschap* (1911), he discussed, after two introductory chapters, the following issues:

1. the structure of the science of mission;
2. the name of the science of mission;
3. the history of the science of mission;
4. the place of the science of mission in the theological encyclopedia;
5. the science of mission and 'the auxiliary sciences'; and
6. the methodology of the science of mission (my tr.).

Some missiologists (e.g. Ohm 1962) have followed, consciously or unconsciously, the example of Warneck; other missiologists (e.g. Schmidlin 1925; Schomerus 1935; Seumois 1952; Holsten 1953; Santos Hernandez 1961; Mulders 1962), however, the example of Daubanton.

This encyclopedia is *a formal study*. It deals with (1) the names, (2) the concepts, (3) the methods, and (4) the branches of missiology. Therefore, it concludes with four chapters after this introductory chapter. In these four chapters I only deal with (1) the history of mission studies, (2) the place of these studies in the whole field of theology and other disciplines, and (3) the so-called

4

'auxiliary sciences' (cf. Daubanton 1911), in passing. The 'auxiliary sciences' (Ger.: *Hilfsdisziplinen*) of mission studies (cf. Schmidlin 1925:167-179), for instance, will be discussed in chapter 5.3.1.2.

*DOEDES, JACOBUS I. Encyclopedie der christelijke theologie. Utrecht, 1876.
     P. 2-3: De formele encyclopedie.
*WARNECK. 1892-1903.
KUYPER, ABRAHAM. Encyclopedia of sacred theology... New York, 1898.
     *Dutch ed.: Encyclopaedie der heilige godgeleerdheid. Amsterdam, 1894. 3 vols.
     I, p. 41-42: Bloot formeel.
*DAUBANTON. 1911.
*SCHMIDLIN. 1925.
     P. 167-179: Hilfsdisziplinen.
*SCHOMERUS. 1935.
*SEUMOIS. 1952.
*HOLSTEN. 1953.
*SANTOS HERNANDEZ. 1961.
*MULDERS. 1962.
*OHM. 1962.
*KRITZINGER, J.J. (DONS), PIET G.J. MEIRING, & WILLEM A. SAAYMAN. You will be my witnesses: an introduction to methods of mission. Pretoria, 1984.

1.3. SOURCES OF THE STUDY

This encyclopedia -a revised and enlarged edition of my Dutch handbook *Missiologie: I. Zendingswetenschap; II. Missionaire Theologie* (1986-1991)- is based on the scholarly work of other people.

In this introductory chapter I refer to the most important general sources used in this study: bibliographies, encyclopedias and dictionaries, glossaries, periodicals, and reference works.

1.3.1. BIBLIOGRAPHIES

Among the useful *missiological bibliographies* are not only simple lists of books on special missionary topics, suitable for special purposes/groups (cf. Bliss 1894; Weitbrecht 1913; and Hering 1935), but also very extensive and well-documented surveys (cf. Bibliotheca missionum 1916-1974). Some of those works cover the whole field of missiology (cf. Vriens 1960), others only parts (cf. Anderson 1966). Further distinctions can be made regarding their annotation: some are (partly) annotated (e.g. Anderson 1961), while others are not annotated (e.g. Person 1961; Bürkle 1979).

    Robert Streit OMI (cf. Streit 1907; 1910; 1911; 1925) and Johannes Rommerskirchen OMI are undoubtly the most important bibliographers of

5

mission. They initiated the publication in Rome of the largest bibliographies of our time: *Bibliotheca missionum* in 30 volumes, and *Bibliografia missionaria*, which has been published annually since 1933 and which is now under the direction of Willie Henkel OMI and Josef Metzler OMI (cf. LM 1992:76-77). The former contains almost exclusively Roman Catholic literature, while the latter, influenced by Vatican II, to an increasing extent also covers Protestant literature. On the Protestant side, the Missionary Research Library in New York has in particular been instrumental in bibliographical work (cf. Person 1961; Anderson 1966; Dictionary Catalog 1968). Since the foundation of the IAMS, bibliographical projects of an interconfessional nature have also been established: I have in mind the *IAMS Bibliography Project on Missiology*, directed by Norman E. Thomas. Furthermore, a variety of bibliographical materials can also be found in several leading missiological journals (especially in IBMR, IRM, *Missiology*, and *Missionaria*). For a preliminary survey of the problems arising in the field of the bibliography of missiology we refer to both dictionaries (Concise Dictionary 1971:59-60) and reference books (Schmidlin 1925: Sachregister; Seumois 1952:468-469; Mulders 1962:123-124).

In each chapter of this study, I include the relevant bibliographical data. As a rule they are presented in the form of a 'selected bibliography'. Of course the given data correspond to the subjects discussed. Especially the *Bibliotheca missionum*, *Bibliografia missionaria*, *Dictionary Catalog*, and the bibliographies compiled by Samuel M. Jackson (1891), Emil Strümpfel (1898), Joseph Masson SJ (1945), Livinus Vriens OFMCap (1960), Gerald H. Anderson (1961; 1966), Angel Santos Hernandez SJ (1965), and Horst Bürkle (1979) have been used extensively. In the bibliographical surveys I refer to the bibliographies used, by inserting the abbreviation *Bibliog.* behind the title involved.

DOBBINS, FRANK S. A foreign missionary manual: geographical, synoptical, statistical, and bibliographical. Philadelphia, 1881.
  P. 102-197: A guide to missionary reading: being a classified list of books of travels, missions, and non-Christian religions, together with a list of missionary periodicals.
*BLISS, EDWIN M. (ed.). The encyclopaedia of missions: descriptive, historical, biographical, statistical... New York, London, & Toronto, 1891.
  I, p. 575-661: A bibliography of foreign missions: being a list of books and pamphlets upon missionary work and workers, and upon the religions, ethnology, topography, and geography of missionary lands down to the close of 1890 (comp. by Samuel M. Jackson; assisted by George W. Gilmore).
JACKSON, SAMUEL M. (comp.). A bibliography of foreign missions. New York, 1891.
  Repr. from: Bliss. 1891.
*BLISS, EDWIN M. (comp.). Descriptive catalogue of books on missions and mission lands, suitable for Church or Sunday-school libraries or for private use. Philadelphia, 1894.
*STRÜMPFEL, EMIL (ed.). Wegweiser durch die wissenschaftliche und pastorale Missionslitteratur... Berlin, 1898.
STREIT, ROBERT, OMI. Die deutsche Missionsliteratur. Paderborn, 1907.

STRÜMPFEL, EMIL (ed.). Neuer Wegweiser durch die deutsche Missionsliteratur... Berlin, 1908.

*STREIT, ROBERT, OMI. Die Missions-Geschichte in ihrer gegenwärtigen Lage und der Plan einer Missions-Bibliographie ... Freiburg im Breisgau, 1910.

*STREIT, ROBERT, OMI. Führer durch die deutsche katholische Missionsliteratur. Freiburg im Breisgau, 1911.

*WEITBRECHT, HERBERT U. (ed.). A bibliography for missionary students. London, & Edinburgh, 1913.

*BIBLIOTHECA MISSIONUM. 1916-1974. 30 vols.

MURRAY, J. LOVELL (comp.). A selected bibliography of missionary literature: rev. ed. New York, 1920.

    First ed. : New York, 1912.

HERING, HOLLIS W. (comp.). Recommended titles on missions and related subjects. New York, 1925.

*SCHMIDLIN. 1925.

    Sachregister: Missionsbibliographie.

*STREIT, ROBERT, OMI. Die katholische deutsche Missionsliteratur; die geschichtliche Entwicklung der katholischen Missionsliteratur in deutschen Landen von Beginn des 19. Jahrhunderts bis zur Gegenwart: ein Beitrag zur Geschichte des heimatlichen Missionslebens. Aachen, & Immensee, 1925.

SCHLUNK, MARTIN. Eine Wanderung durch die deutsche Missionsliteratur... Stuttgart, 1926.

*ZENTRALSTELLE FÜR MISSIONSLITERATUR IN STUTTGART UND BASEL (ed.). Wegweiser durch das Schrifttum der evangelischen Mission: unter Mitarbeit von Martin Schlunk: zweite Ausgabe. Stuttgart, & Basel, 1927.

    First ed.: Stuttgart, & Basel, 1924.

HERING, HOLLIS W. (comp.). A selected bibliography of recent books significant for the understanding of missions and mission problems. New York, 1928.

*MULDERS, ALPHONSUS J.M. Iets over missiebibliographie. In: HM, XIII (1931/32), p. 17-27.

BROWN, STEPHEN J.M., SJ (ed.). Bibliographie des missions catholiques. Dublin, 1932.

*BIBLIOGRAFIA MISSIONARIA. 1933-...

HERING, HOLLIS W. A worldwide Christian outlook: a selected bibliography prepared for the Student Volunteer Movement convention... New York, 1935.

*MASSON, JOSEPH, SJ. Bibliographie missionnaire moderne: choix classé de 1400 titres et notes d'histoire. Tournai, Paris, & Louvain, 1945.

*DIFFENDORFER, RALPH E. (ed.). Christian literature in the mission world: progress report. New York, 1946.

*SEUMOIS. 1952.

    P. 468-469: Instruments bibliographiques.

*ENIGE FRATRES VAN HET THEOLOGICUM DER PATERS MINDERBROEDERS TE ALVERNA (comp.). Moderne missie-bibliografische handleiding. Alverna, 1954.

LIST OF THESES in foreign missions and related subjects accepted by universities and theological schools in the United States 1950-1958. New York, 1958.

*VRIENS. 1960.

*ANDERSON. 1961.

    P. 315-336: Bibliography.

*PERSON, LAURA (comp.). Cumulative list of doctoral dissertations and Masters' theses in foreign missions and related subjects as reported by the Missionary Research Library in the 'Occasional Bulletin' 1950 to 1960. New York, 1961.

*MULDERS. 1962.

    P. 123-124: Bibliografie.

*SANTOS HERNANDEZ, ANGEL, SJ. Bibliografia misional. Santander, 1965. 2 vols.

    I: Parte doctrinal. II: Parte historica.

*ANDERSON, GERALD H. (comp.). Bibliography of the theology of missions in the twentieth
century: third ed., rev. and enl. New York, 1966.
*First ed.: New York, 1958.
*DICTIONARY CATALOG. 1968.
XI, p. 83-89: Missions - Bibliography.
XIII, p. 630-631: Roman Catholic church - Missions - Bibliography.
*CONCISE DICTIONARY. 1971.
P. 59-60: Bibliographies (Burton L. Goddard).
*DEUTSCHE GESELLSCHAFT FÜR MISSIONSWISSENSCHAFT (ed.). Literaturschau zu Fragen der
Weltmission. Stuttgart, 1971-...
Beiheft der Evangelischen Missions-Zeitschrift (EMZ).
*FACELINA, RAYMOND. Evangelization and mission: international bibliography 1972 indexed by
computer/Evangelisation et mission: bibliographie internationale 1972 établie par
ordinateur. Strasbourg, 1973.
*KRAUS, JOHANN, SVD. Missionswissenschaftliche Themen in Festschriften aus den Jahren
1960-1971. Immensee, 1974.
STUDIES IN MISSIONS; an index of theses on missions. Monrovia, 1974.
*BÜRKLE, HORST. Missionstheologie. Stuttgart, Berlin, Köln ..., 1979.
P. 193-205: Literaturverzeichnis.
*CERDIC. Evangelisation and mission: international bibliography 1975-1982/Evangelisation et
mission: bibliographie internationale 1975-1982. Strasbourg, 1982.
CERDIC=Centre de recherche et de documentation des institutions chrétiennes (=Center
of research and documentation of Christian institutions).
*WCE. 1982.
P. 857-861: Bibliography: selective world bibliography of Christianity.
*PETERSON, PAUL D. (ed.). Missions and evangelism: a bibliography selected from the ATLA
religion database: rev. ed. N.p., 1985.
ATLA=American Theological Library Association.
*LM. 1992.
P. 76-77: Bibliografia missionaria: Bibliotheca missionum.

1.3.2. ENCYCLOPEDIAS AND DICTIONARIES

So far *twelve encyclopedias and dictionaries* have been published which are
entirely or partly devoted to mission. In one way or another, they all have the
word *mission(s)* in their title, with one exception (the recent encyclopedia of
Barrett uses the term *World Christianity*). None of these encyclopedias and
dictionaries has the word *missiology* in the title. This does not imply, however,
a neglect of missiology as a philosophical, empirical, and theological discipline
in their articles.

Most of the encyclopedias and dictionaries mentioned in the bibliography
contain information on the history, geography, and statistics of mission (cf. the
encyclopedias of Aikman 1860; Newcomb 1860; Lacroix, and De Djunkovskoy,
in: Migne 1863-1864: vol. LIX-LX; Moister 1872; Dwight, Tupper Jr, and Bliss
1904; WCE 1982), as well as information on missionary societies and mission
agencies (cf. Gründler 1961; and Goddard 1967); they are, therefore, completely

8

in the field of the empirical study of mission. Some of them have gone beyond that by dealing with the theological study of mission as well (cf. Birkeli, Bjerkrheim, Ski, et al. 1965-1967; Concise Dictionary 1971; LM 1992; and, especially, LMG 1987). None of them, however, has paid any serious attention to the philosophical study of missions. And none of them has dealt systematically and comprehensively with the whole field of the philosophical, empirical, and theological study of mission as we are trying to do here.

Wherever this study makes use of missiological encyclopedias and dictionaries, this is always mentioned in the bibliography.

*AIKMAN, J. LOGAN. Cyclopaedia of Christian missions: their rise, progress, and present position. London & Glasgow, 1860.
   Second ed.: London, 1861.
*NEWCOMB, HARVEY. A cyclopedia of missions: containing a comprehensive view of missionary operations throughout the world: with geographical descriptions, and accounts of the social, moral, and religious condition of the people: second rev. ed. New York, 1860.
   First ed.: New York, 1854.
*MIGNE, JACQUES PAUL (ed.). Troisième et dernière encyclopédie théologique... Tome cinquante-neuvième et soixantième...: LACROIX, M., & ÉTIENNE DE DJUNKOVSKOY. Dictionnaire des missions catholiques... Paris, 1863-1864. 2 vols.
   I: Dictionnaire des missionnaires.
   II: Dictionnaire des missions catholiques.
(MOISTER, WILLIAM). The missionary world: being an encyclopaedia of information, facts, incidents, sketches, and anecdotes, relating to Christian missions, in all ages and countries, and of all denominations... New York, 1872.
*DWIGHT, HENRY O., H. ALLEN TUPPER Jr, and EDWIN M. BLISS (eds.). The encyclopedia of missions: descriptive, historical, biographical, statistical: second ed. New York, & London, 1904.
   First ed.: BLISS, EDWIN M. (ed.). The encyclopaedia of missions: descriptive, historical, biographical, statistical: with a full assortment of maps, a complete bibliography, and lists of Bible versions, missionary societies, mission stations, and a general index. New York, London, & Toronto, 1891. 2 vols.
   Repr.: Detroit, 1975.
*GRÜNDLER, JOHANNES. Lexikon der christlichen Kirchen und Sekten, unter Berücksichtigung der Missionsgesellschaften und zwischenkirchlichen Organisationen. Wien, Freiburg, & Basel, 1961. 2 vols.
*BIRKELI, FRIDTJOV, TRYGVE BJERKRHEIM, MARTIN SKI, et al. (eds.). Norsk misjonsleksikon: utgitt med tilslutning fra Norsk Misjonsrad og de misjoner dette representerer. Stavanger, 1965-1967. 3 vols.
*GODDARD, BURTON L. (ed.). The encyclopedia of modern Christian missions: the agencies: a publication of the Faculty of Gordon Divinity School. Camden, London, & Toronto, 1967.
*CONCISE DICTIONARY. 1971.
*WCE. 1982.
*LMG. 1987.
*LM. 1992.

1.3.3. GLOSSARIES

From the beginning of last century *only very few glossaries* have been produced. Here I only draw attention to the recent glossaries of WCE (1982) and C. Peter Wagner (1989), which are very helpful both to missionaries and missiologists. The first one is general, the last one, however, special, because it is related to the Church growth school. Both of them are used frequently in this study.

*WCE. 1982.
    P. 813-848: Dictionary: survey dictionary of world Christianity.
*WAGNER. 1989.
    P. 279-302: A glossary of church growth terms.

1.3.4. PERIODICALS

During the 19th and 20th centuries, *thousands of mission magazines* have been published. More than 500 titles of Protestant missionary periodicals have been catalogued in the Dutch language area alone (Jongeneel 1990). *Bibliotheca missionum* (1964) and *Dictionary Catalog* (1968) have made the most extensive inventories. Further I call attention to the compilations made by Bernard Arens SJ (1925), John T. Ma (1961), and Paul A. Byrnes (1972).

Most of the periodicals concerned deal with missions, and not with missiology. Therefore we do not have to take them into account. In my bibliography only data taken from missiologically-oriented periodicals are mentioned: AMZ, DH, EMM, EMQ, EMZ, ER, *Evangelikale Missiologie*, HM, IBMR, IRM, *Med.*, *Missiology*, *Missionaria*, MR, NAMZ, NZM, WenZ, ZM, ZMiss, ZMkR, and ZMR (cf. the list of 'Abbreviations'). I have used all these periodicals very selectively; only the articles published in IRM on missiological subjects are systematically included in the literature surveys.

For a preliminary survey of problems occurring in the field of missiological periodicals I refer both to dictionaries (Concise dictionary 1971: 312-313), and reference books (Warneck 1892:I,50-52; Schmidlin 1925:48,106-107; Seumois 1952:470-471; Mulders 1962: 129-133; Ohm 1962:112-113,120-121).

DOBBINS, FRANK S. A foreign missionary manual: geographical, synoptical, statistical, and bibliographical. Philadelphia, 1881.
    P. 102-197: A guide to missionary reading: being a classified list of books of travels, missions, and non-Christian religions, together with a list of missionary periodicals.
*WARNECK. 1892-1903. 3 vols.
    I, p. 50-52: Missionszeitschriften.
*STREIT, ROBERT, OMI. Führer durch die deutsche katholische Missionsliteratur. Freiburg im Breisgau, 1911.
    P. 103-109: Missionszeitschriften.

*ARENS, BERNARD, SJ. Manuel des missions catholiques: éd. française. Louvain, Paris, &
Bruxelles, 1925.
P. 352-417: Les revues des missions.
*Ger. ed.: Handbuch der katholischen Missionen: zweite, vollständig neubearbeitete
Aufl. Freiburg im Breisgau, 1925.
*First Ger. ed.: Freiburg im Breisgau, 1920.
*SCHMIDLIN. 1925.
P. 48: Missionszeitschriften.
P. 106-107: Zeitschriften.
*BIBLIOGRAFIA MISSIONARIA. 1933-...
I (1933) -...: 1. Bibliografia missionaria: Nuovi periodici.
*SEUMOIS. 1952.
P. 470-471: Répertoire des revues missionnaires.
*MYKLEBUST. 1955-1957.
I, p. 434-438: Periodicals.
II, p. 386-388: Periodicals.
*VRIENS. 1960.
P. 26-32: Periodicals.
*ANDERSON. 1961.
P. 315-317: Journals (with publishing addresses).
MA, JOHN T. (comp.). Current periodicals in the Missionary Research Library: alphabetical list
and indexes: second and rev. ed. New York, 1961.
*MULDERS. 1962.
P. 129-133: Tijdschriften.
*OHM. 1962.
P. 112-113, 120-121: Zeitschriften (katholische, evangelische).
*BIBLIOTHECA MISSIONUM. 1964.
XXIII, p. 596-668: Zeitschriften (1872 Titel).
*SANTOS HERNANDEZ, ANGEL, SJ. Bibliografia misional. Santander, 1965. 2 vols.
I, p. 143-160: Revistas.
*DICTIONARY CATALOG. 1968.
XVII, p. 1-303: Periodicals.
*CONCISE DICTIONARY. 1971.
P. 312-313: Journals for mission studies (Gerald H. Anderson).
*BYRNES, PAUL A. (comp.). Current periodicals in the Missionary Research Library: a subject
list. New York, 1972.
*JONGENEEL, JAN A.B. Protestantse zendingsperiodieken uit de negentiende en twintigste eeuw
in Nederland, Nederlands-Indië, Suriname, en de Nederlandse Antillen: een
bibliografische catalogus met inleiding. Utrecht, & Leiden, 1990.
*LM. 1992.
P.455-458: Zeitschriften.

I.3.5. REFERENCE WORKS

The main reference books which have been used are listed separately: *Reference
works*. In that list three categories are mentioned.

First, those encyclopedias, dictionaries, and bibliographies have been
classified here which cover either the whole field of the philosophical, empirical,

and theological study of mission:

1. *Bibliotheca missionum*. 1916-1974. 30 vols.
2. *Bibliografia missionaria*. 1933-...
3. *Critical Bibliography of Missiology*, by Livinus Vriens OFMCap. 1960.
4. *Dictionary Catalog*. 1968. 17 vols.
5. *Concise Dictionary*. 1971.
6. *WCE*. 1982.
7. *LMG*. 1987.
8. *LM*. 1992.

In addition to these missiological works I also refer to the following three dictionaries:

1. *RGG*.   1957-1965. 7 vols.
2. *TDNT*.   1964-1976/*TWNT*. 1933-1978. 10 vols.
3. *DEM*.   1991.

Although these works are not composed as missiological books at all, they should have a place in the list of reference works because of their great importance for (1) the study of mission in the context of Christian theology and the scientific study of religion, (2) the study of the origin of many missionary terms in the New Testament, and (3) the study of mission in connection with the ecumenical movement.

Secondly, the following introductions to, and handbooks of missiology have been classified here:

1. Warneck. 1892-1903. 3 vols.
2. Daubanton. 1911.
3. Schmidlin. 1925.
4. Schomerus. 1935.
5. Seumois. 1952.
6. Holsten. 1953.
7. Santos Hernandez. 1961.
8. Mulders. 1962.
9. Ohm. 1962.

This study links up with all these works (because of the strict formal character of my study I have the least methodological affinity with the handbooks of Warneck and Ohm).

Thirdly, I have also included here six books of special significance (both monographs and collective works):

1. *Scientia missionum ancilla.* 1953.
   Édouard Loffeld CSSp and John Wils (eds.) published this study, which is mainly a collection of scientific articles about several branches of missiology.
2. Myklebust. 1955-1957. 2 vols.
   The Study of Missions in Theological Education can be regarded as the best historical account of Protestant missiology.
3. Anderson. 1961.
   The Theology of the Christian Mission is a collection of 25 theological articles dealing with the biblical basis and the historical development of mission, Christianity and other faiths, and the theory of mission.
4. Wagner. 1989.
   Church Growth has an important glossary.
5. Bosch. 1991.
   Transforming Mission deals in a comprehensive way with the paradigm shifts in the theology of mission, leading to an ecumenical missionary paradigm.
6. Phillips and Coote. 1993.
   Toward the 21st Century in Christian Mission is a collection of 28 articles about 'Christian families in mission', 'Christian mission by region', 'foundational disciplines of mission', and 'special challenges in mission'.

These studies have been extensively used as well. Not only these six works, but all the above-mentioned publications have always been quoted in the indicated abridged form.

1.4. FINAL INTRODUCTORY QUESTIONS

At the end of this general introduction, I should clarify some special questions.

First, I emphasize that this encyclopedia has both a historical and a systematic character since, on the one hand, it aims at mapping the whole field of mission studies, while, on the other, it intends to provide insight into the historical developments of missiology as a discipline and of all its branches. In each chapter and each section as much attention as possible is given both to the history and contemporary situation of that particular field, and to the various problems occurring in that specific area. Since most branches of missiology only came into existence in the 19th century, most analyses, descriptions, and bibliographies do not go back beyond 1800 (for the study of the history of mission, however, it is necessary to take into account developments before 1800). As far as issues are concerned, it is also necessary to draw the line firmly: the interrelation and interdependence between mission and meteorology, mission and natural science, and mission and literature (cf. the afore-mentioned work of Thomas Laurie) have been omitted.

Furthermore, I point out that I only discuss and document 'general' problems. Those who want to find data about the missionary work of the Moravians in Greenland in the 18th century will search in vain. For data about particular missionaries (e.g. Francis Xavier, or William Carey), particular missionary societies (e.g. London Missionary Society, or Overseas Missionary Fellowship), particular countries and continents (Iran, or Africa), etc. I refer to the above mentioned encyclopedias of Stephen C. Neill, et al., and David B. Barrett. This silence about 'particular' subjects does not imply that I am not interested in those matters. On the contrary! In this encyclopedia, however, I concentrate on general matters.

In addition, I draw attention to the fact that the titles from works, other than the reference works, are cited as fully as possible (the publisher, however, is not mentioned). When more editions have been published and/or several translations have been made, this is usually mentioned. If a particular monograph, symposium, or article is quoted more than once, the extra information is usually not repeated. Sometimes long titles are given in an abbreviated form. When a German or other non-English original has been translated into English, the translated version takes preference above the original title. *Publications marked by an asterisk (*)* were available to the author. The bibliographical data of other publications, however, are taken from secondary sources. If I was not quite sure about the correctness of a title, taken from a secondary source, I marked the *publication with a question-mark (?)*.

Finally, the list of works cited at the end of each section is arranged chronologically. In each section -for instance, section 5.3.4.: 'The geography of Christian mission'- the titles are put in the most relevant part of that section -for instance, subsection 5.3.4.1.-. However, the book cited is used in the whole section. To avoid repetitions in the list of works cited, the title of the book is not repeated if the quotation occurs in another part of the same section -for instance, subsection 5.3.4.2.-. If in a special case it is difficult to recover the source of a quotation, the reader can go back to the Index of persons for finding the relevant data.

This handbook, renewing the seventy years old tradition of comprehensive mission studies -from Gustav Warneck (1892-1903) to Alphonsus J.M. Mulders and Thomas Ohm OSB (both 1962)- is a guide through the whole field of missiology: no more, no less. It can be compared to a railway-timetable which gives information about all the stations which can be visited. Those who want to study a particular field more closely, will be put on the right lines: but they will have to proceed further alone. Both the text of this encyclopedia and the corresponding bibliographies will lead the way.

2. NAMES OF MISSIOLOGY

2.1. NAMES

In this second chapter I discuss *the different names* which, in the course of last century and this century, are given to the study of missions.

I start my survey with a reference to the famous German theologian Friedrich E.D. Schleiermacher (1768-1834), who, influenced by the Moravians, reluctantly put mission studies as a discipline in the curriculum of the theology. In 1830 he wrote about the *theory of mission* (Lat.: *theoria missionis*; Ger.: *Theorie des Missionswesens*) and connected it with catechetics as a well-known part of practical theology: '... the theory of missions might also find a point of connexion here; a theory which, up to the present time, is as good as altogether wanting' (section 298; my tr.).

After Schleiermacher, we find in most theological encyclopedias and handbooks on practical theology a section on mission. Some of these works speak like Schleiermacher about 'theory of mission', but others about *doctrine of mission* (Ger.: *Missionslehre*). In Germany the term 'doctrine of mission' became popular with the publication of Warneck, *Evangelische Missionslehre* (1892-1903) (cf. Warneck, in: AMZ 1877:443-458; Schmidlin 1923; Richter 1927). In English, however, the title of the book of Schmidlin, *Katholische Missionslehre*, was not translated as 'Catholic Mission Doctrine', but as 'Catholic Mission Theory' (the German word *Lehre* is not fully synonymous with the English noun 'doctrine').

The different names of missiology can be divided into minor and major names. Firstly, I deal with the minor names (2.2.); and thereafter, I explain the major names (2.3.-2.5.). In both cases, I start with names of Greek derivation, and conclude with names of Latin derivation.

SCHLEIERMACHER, FRIEDRICH E.D. Brief outline of the study of theology. Edinburgh, 1850.
*Ger. ed.: Kurze Darstellung des theologischen Studiums zum Behuf einleitender Vorlesungen: zweite Aufl. Berlin, 1830.
First Ger. ed.: Berlin, 1811.
*WARNECK, GUSTAV. Die Missionslehre als 'Keryktik'. In: AMZ, IV (1877), p. 443-458.
*WARNECK. 1892-1903.
I, p. 20-23: Begriff und Name.
JÖRGENSEN, S.E. Missionslaere: et udkast. Kristiana, 1899.
*DAUBANTON. 1911.
P. 224-238: Benaming der zendingswetenschap.
SCHMIDLIN, JOSEPH. Missionstheorie... Münster in Westfalen, 1924.
*RICHTER, JULIUS. Evangelische Missionslehre: zweite erw. und umgearbeitete Aufl. Leipzig, 1927. 2 vols.
First ed.: Leipzig, 1920.
SCHMIDLIN, JOSEPH. Catholic mission theory. Techny, 1931.

*Ger. ed.: Katholische Missionslehre im Grundriss: zweite, verb. Aufl. Münster in Westfalen, 1923.
First Ger. ed.: Münster in Westfalen, 1919.
*SCHOMERUS. 1935.
P. 62-121: Missionstheorie: die Lehre vom Missionsbetrieb.
*SEUMOIS. 1952.
P. 85-103: Les divers termes employés et les diverses appréciations.
*BAVINCK, JOHAN H. An introduction to the science of missions. Philadelphia, 1960.
P. XVI-XVIII: A question of terminology.
*Dutch ed.: Inleiding in de zendingswetenschap. Kampen, 1954.
*MULDERS. 1962.
P. 139-140: Benaming.
*VERKUYL, JOHANNES. Contemporary missiology: an introduction. Grand Rapids, 1978.
P. 1-2: The term 'missiology'.
*Dutch ed.: Inleiding in de nieuwere zendingswetenschap. Kampen, 1975.
*Second Dutch ed.: 1985.

2.2. MINOR NAMES

Here I will describe *six minor names* separately: (1) halieutics; (2) keryktics; (3) matheteutics; (4) auxanics; (5) prosthetics; and (6) propagandics.

In passing I mention *four other minor names*, which did not have any real impact:

1. *thetics* - on the 'thesis' (Gr.: *tithenai*=to put) of mission (Daubanton 1911:203-205; Paventi 1949:40; Santos Hernandez 1961: 206);
2. *organics* - on the 'organs' or agencies of mission (Daubanton 1911: 206-207; Paventi 1949:40; Santos Hernandez 1961:206);
3. *agrics* - on the 'fields' (Gr.: *agros*=field) of mission (Daubanton 1911:207-209, 226; Paventi 1949:40; Santos Hernandez 1961:206);
4. *plethunics* - on the 'large numbers' (Gr.: *plethos*=large number, crowd, multitude) of mission (Paventi 1949:40; Santos Hernandez 1961:206).

*DAUBANTON. 1911.
P. 202-209: Thetiek, organiek, agriek.
*PAVENTI, SAVERIO. La chiesa missionaria: manuale di missionologia dottrinale. Roma, 1949.
P. 39-40: Etimologia.
*SANTOS HERNANDEZ. 1961.
P. 199-223: Misiologia o misionologia?

2.2.1. HALIEUTICS

The name *halieutics* is derived from the Greek verb *halieuein*=to (catch) fish, which occurs only once in the New Testament: 'Simon Peter said to them, "I am going *fishing*"' (John 21:3). The Greek noun *haleeus*=fisher(man), however, occurs five times: 'And he [Jesus] said to them, "Follow me, and I will make you *fish* for people"' (=*fishers of men*; Matt. 4:19; Mark 1:17; cf. Matt. 4:18; Mark 1:16; Luke 5:2).

The name 'halieutics' means: theory of fishing (Daubanton 1911: 232), or doctrine of 'fishers of men' (Warneck 1892:I,20). This name was introduced by Gustav A.F. Sickel (1829), who equated homiletics with halieutics: preaching is fishing. Alexander Schweitzer (1836:43), however, associated halieutics with mission studies: doing mission is fishing. E. Gustav Bring (1846:25ff.,45,54f.), Johannes H.A. Ebrard (1854:186-198), Johann P. Lange (1877:216f.), Jacobus I. Doedes (1883:241-250), and Johannes J. van Oosterzee (1898:II,349-367) have done the same. In his definition of halieutics, Doedes, on the one hand, did not use fishing terminology, but van Oosterzee, on the other hand, referred to 'the sea of the non-Christian world' (1898:II,349; my tr.), in which the church is fishing.

Warneck (1892:I,20-21), Abraham Kuyper (1894:III,518-519), and Daubanton (1911:232-233) have criticized the term 'halieutics'. Thereafter this name is no longer in circulation (cf. Wüllner 1967:8). I also reject this name as being too narrow and symbolic. The biblical expression 'fishers of men', however, is still useful. In missionary and other publications of both Roman Catholic authors (Charles 1929) and Protestant authors (Wüllner 1967; Stoll 1982) it still comes to the fore.

SICKEL, GUSTAV A.F. Grundriss einer christlichen Halieutik. Leipzig, 1829.
SCHWEITZER, ALEXANDER. Über Begriff und Eintheilung der praktischen Theologie. Leipzig, 1836.
BRING, E. GUSTAF. De principio theologiae practicae. Lund, 1846.
*EBRARD, JOHANNES H.A. Vorlesungen über praktische Theologie. Königsberg, 1854.
   P. 186-198: Die Halieutik oder Missionsthätigkeit.
LANGE, JOHANN P. Grundriss der theologischen Encyklopädie mit Einschluss der Methodologie. Heidelberg, 1877.
*DOEDES, JACOBUS I. Encyclopedie der christelijke theologie: tweede verm. dr. Utrecht, 1883.
   P. 241-250: Christelijke halieutiek.
   First ed.: Utrecht, 1876.
OOSTERZEE, JOHANNES J. VAN. Practical theology: a manual for theological students: second ed. London, 1889.
   First Eng. tr.: London, 1878.
   *Dutch ed.: Practische theologie: een handboek voor jeugdige Godgeleerden: tweede ... herz. en verm. dr. Utrecht, 1894-1898. 2 vols.
   II, p. 349-367: De christelijke halieutiek.
   First Dutch ed.: Utrecht, 1877-1878. 2 vols.
   Ger. tr.: 1878-1879. 2 vols.
   Danish tr.: 1881. 2 vols.
*WARNECK. 1892-1903.
   I, p. 20-21: Halieutik.

KUYPER, ABRAHAM. Encyclopedia of sacred theology: its principles. New York, 1898.
  *Dutch ed.: Encyclopaedie der heilige godgeleerdheid. Amsterdam, 1894. 3 vols.
SCHOLEY,CHARLES H. The prodigal's prayer and fishers of men. New York, Chicago..., 1899.
*DAUBANTON. 1911.
    P. 232-233: Halieutiek.
SIRCAR, BIPIN C. Fishers of men: being Bible studies in personal work in imitation of Jesus
    Christ ... specially in connection with the 'Evangelistic campaign'. Madras, 1919.
CHARLES, PIERRE, SJ. Fishers of men. London, 1929.
    *Fr. ed.: Pêcheurs d'hommes: méditations. Louvain, 1924.
    *Dutch tr.: 1925. Ger. tr.: 1929.
*WÜLLNER, WILHELM H. The meaning of 'Fishers of men'. Philadelphia, 1967.
*STOLL, DAVID. Fishers of men or founders of empire? The Wycliffe Bible Translators in
    Latin America. London, 1982.

2.2.2. KERYKTICS

The name *keryktics* (or: *kerygtics, kerygmatics*) is derived from the Greek verb *keryssein*=to announce, to make known, to proclaim (as a herald), to preach, which occurs 61 times in the New Testament. Here I quote only the following texts: 'Go into all the world and *proclaim* the good news to the whole creation' (Mark 16:15); 'Philip went down to the city of Samaria and *proclaimed* the Messiah to them' (Acts 8:5); 'And immediately he [Paul] began to *proclaim* Jesus in the synagogues, saying, "He is the Son of God"' (Acts 9:20). The Greek noun *kerygma*=announcement, proclamation, preaching, message, however, occurs only 8 times in the New Testament: 'God decided, through the foolishness of our *proclamation*, to save those who believe' (1Cor. 1:21); '... that through me [Paul] the *message* might be fully proclaimed and all the gentiles might hear it' (2Tim. 4:17); etc. And here the Greek noun *keryx*=announcer, preacher, herald, is used three times: 'I [Paul] was appointed a *herald* and an apostle and a teacher' (2Tim. 1:11); etc.

In 1830 Rudolf Stier introduced the term 'keryktics'. He associated homiletics with keryktics. At the same time he drew attention to the 'biblical mission - keryktics' (1844:95-146; my tr.). A few decennia later Carl A.G. von Zezschwitz (1876:169) identified mission studies with keryktics. He understood mission as *kerygma*, i.e. as the proclamation of the gospel to the nations. In his view, mission is *the invitation* (Ger.: *Einladung*) of the nations; catechesis is *the introduction* (Ger.: *Einführung*) of the nations; and baptism is their *implantation* (Ger.: *Einpflanzung*) (my tr.). Warneck (AMZ 1877:450; cf. 1892:I,21) crisised this name clearly: 'Keryktics is a very important part of the mission theory, but just not more than that' (my tr.). Abraham Kuyper (1894:III,518-519) and Daubanton (1911:233-235) also dissociated themselves from the opinions of Stier and von Zezschwitz. I share their criticisms.

The name 'keryktics' is not used anymore. The matter of the *kerygma*, however, is still very important. Charles H. Dodd (1944:7) rightly gave the following missionary definition of *kerygma*: 'the public proclamation of Christianity to the non-Christian world'. In the dialectical theology of Karl Barth (1886-1968) and Rudolf Bultmann (1884-1976) the 'proclamation (*kerygma*) of Jesus Christ' (Rom. 16:25) holds the centre. These systematic theologians influenced several missiologists: we refer to *The Christian Message in a non-Christian World* (1938) by Hendrik Kraemer, on the one hand, and *Das Kerygma und der Mensch* (1953) by Walter Holsten, on the other hand. Both Kraemer and Holsten (cf. Andersen, in: EMZ 1954:29-37) base mission on the *kerygma*, i.e. on the proclamation of Jesus Christ, which demands unquestioning obedience of the hearers.

In contemporary mission studies *kerygma* is widely known as the first part of the formula *kerygma - koinonia - diakonia*, which was coined by Johannes C. Hoekendijk (IRM 1950:171): 'These three aspects, *kerygma*, *koinonia*, and *diakonia*, should be integrated in our work of evangelism. Only so are our methods of evangelism justified'. Time and time again this formula is quoted, although Hoekendijk himself moved away from putting emphasis on *kerygma* to underlining *diakonia* as the most essential missionary task. Theodore O. Wedel (ER 1956/57:228) summarized and evaluated the purpose of this concept of evangelism as follows: '... the mission of the church involves at least three forms of communication: (1) *kerygma*: the gospel must be proclaimed; (2) *koinonia*: the gospel must be lived and its power made visible in the actual life of the community which embodies the new covenant relationship; and (3) *diakonia*: the gospel must be demonstrated in humble service. These three forms of communication are, of course, not the only ones. Biblical theologians usually set alongside the *kerygma*, or proclamation, the ethical teaching, or *didache*, of the New Testament'. Therefore, the formula *kerygma - koinonia - diakonia* is questionable.

*STIER, RUDOLF. Grundriss einer biblischen Keryktik: oder einer Anweisung durch das Wort Gottes sich zur Predigtkunst zu bilden: mit besonderer Beziehung auf Mission und Kirche...: zweite berichtigte und sehr verm. Aufl. Halle, 1844.
P. 95-146: Biblische Missions-Keryktik.
First ed.: Halle, 1830.
*ZEZSCHWITZ, CARL A.G. VON. System der praktischen Theologie. Leipzig, 1876.
P. 153-177: Die Keryktik.
*WARNECK, GUSTAV. Die Missionslehre als 'Keryktik'. In: AMZ, IV (1877), p.443-458.
*WARNECK. 1892-1903.
I, p. 21: Keryktik.
*KUYPER, ABRAHAM. Encyclopaedie der heilige godgeleerdheid. Amsterdam, 1894. 3 vols.
*DAUBANTON. 1911.
P. 233-235: Keryktiek.

*KRAEMER, HENDRIK. The Christian message in a non-Christian world. London, 1938.
    *Ger. tr.: 1940.

*DODD, CHARLES H. The apostolic preaching and its developments: three lectures...: new ed. London, 1944.
    First ed.: London, 1936. Several reprints.
    French tr.: 1964.
    *Dutch tr.: n.d.

*HOEKENDIJK, JOHANNES C. The call to evangelism. In: IRM, XXXIX (1950), p. 162-175.

*HOLSTEN. 1953.

*ANDERSEN, WILHELM. Die kerygmatische Begründung der Religions- und Missionswissenschaft: ein kritischer Bericht über Walter Holstens Buch 'Das Kerygma und der Mensch'. In: EMZ, XI (1954), p. 29-37.

*WEDEL, THEODORE O. Evangelism's threefold witness: kerygma, koinonia, diakonia. In: ER, IX (1956/57), p. 225-239.

*OHM. 1962.
    P. 556-562: Die Proklamation.

*TDNT. 1964-1976.
    III, p. 712: Sending and proclamation (Gerhard Friedrich).
    *Ger. ed.: TWNT. 1933-1978.
    III, p. 712: Sendung und Verkündigung (Gerhard Friedrich).

*COSTAS, ORLANDO E. The integrity of mission: the inner life and outreach of the church. New York, Hagerstown, San Francisco..., 1979.
    P. 1-12: Mission as proclamation.

*SPINDLER, MARC R., & PETER R. MIDDELKOOP (eds.). Bible and mission: a partially annotated bibliography 1960-1980. Leiden, & Utrecht, 1981. Bibliog.
    P. 17-19: Theology of proclamation.

*ABRAHAM, WILLIAM J. The logic of evangelism. Grand Rapids, 1989.
    P. 40-69: Proclamation.

*LM. 1992.
    P. 240-241: Kerygma.

2.2.3. MATHETEUTICS

The name *matheteutics* is derived from the Greek verb *matheteuein*=to make *mathetai*=disciples, pupils, learners, followers. Both the Greek verb (4 times) and the Greek noun (262 times) occur in the New Testament. We refer here only to the Great Commission, which since William Carey (1761-1834) became very central to Protestant missionary thinking: 'Go therefore and *make disciples* of all nations, baptizing them in the name of the Father and of the Son and of the Holy Spirit' (Matt. 28:19). In the Gospel according to John (John 8:31; 13:35; 15:8) *mathetes* is often simply used as an alternative for 'Christian'.

    The term 'matheteutics' was introduced by Abraham Kuyper (1894: III,518-519), and criticized by Daubanton (1911:235). As a name it does not make sense anymore. As a theological item, however, it is still as crucial as *kerygma*. Many exegetical studies on Matt. 28:16-20 (see chapter 3.4.2.2.: Barth 1945; Michel, in: Evangelische Theologie 1950/51:16-26; Lohmeyer, in:

Schmauch 1951:22-49; Bornkamm, in: Dinkler 1964:171- 191; Matthey, in: IRM 1980:161-173; Bosch, in: Shenk 1983:218-248; et al.) explain the significance of the Great Commission. Today 'discipling the nations' is not only a key issue in Protestant, but also in Roman Catholic missiological literature (Murphy 1958; Ohm 1962).

We can distinguish between several concepts of matheteutics. On the one hand, there are people who write about discipleship *and apostolate* (Schuurman 1920; Vicedom 1965:77-80), making discipleship a condition of doing mission; and, on the other hand, there are those who propagate discipleship as a goal of mission (Costas 1979:13-24). Alfred C. Krass (1974:87-115) speaks about 'the ministry of making *and equipping* disciples' (my italics), whereas W. Charles Arn (Wagner 1989:57-67) highlights some important differences between evangelism and disciple making.

In contemporary literature *discipling* is seen as the first stage of Christianization. In the Church Growth Movement two stages are discerned: (1) discipling, i.e. bringing persons or groups to commitment to Christ; and (2) perfecting, i.e. nurturing them in their faith and bringing about ethical change (Wagner 1989:288). WCE (1982:824) even distinguishes three stages: (1) discipling; (2) baptizing; and (3) perfecting. I am not willing to follow these authors in their co-ordination of these topics, because I take the view that in the Great Commission baptizing and teaching (in Greek participles!) are fully subjected to discipling.

Very popular is discipling in the DAWN literature. As acronym DAWN means: *discipling a whole nation*. Jim Montgomery (1990:12), who belongs to the Church Growth Movement, has developed a whole DAWN strategy: 'DAWN aims at mobilizing the whole body of Christ in whole countries in a determined effort to complete the Great Commission in that country by working toward the goal of providing an evangelical congregation for every village and every neighborhood of every class, kind and condition of people in the whole country'.

*KUYPER, ABRAHAM. Encyclopaedie der heilige godgeleerdheid. Amsterdam, 1894. 3 vols.
*DAUBANTON. 1911.
    P. 235: Matheteutiek.
*KRAEMER, HENDRIK, DRYO MESTOKO, CARL W. NORTIER, et al. (eds.). Over alle bergen: geschriften van Dr. B(arend) M. Schuurman, zendeling-leraar op Java... 's-Gravenhage, 1952.
    P. 100-113: Discipelschap en apostolaat (1920).
*MATHEWS, BASIL J. Disciples of all nations: the story of Christian expansion. London, New York, & Toronto, 1952.
    Amer. ed.: Forward through the ages. New York, 1951.
MURPHY, EDWARD L., SJ. Teach ye all nations: Matth. 28:19: the principles of Catholic missionary work. New York, Boston, Cincinnati..., 1958.
*OHM. 1962.

*VICEDOM, GEORG F. The mission of God: an introduction to a theology of mission. Saint Louis, 1965.
P. 77-80: Discipleship and apostolate.
*Ger. ed.: Missio Dei; Einführung in eine Theologie der Mission I: zweite unveränderte Aufl. München, 1960.
First Ger. ed.: München, 1958.
*KRASS, ALFRED C. Applied theology I: 'go... and make disciples'. London, 1974.
RIDDER, RICHARD R. DE. Discipling the nations: a biblical basis for missions. Grand Rapids, 1975.
*COSTAS, ORLANDO E. The integrity of mission: the inner life and outreach of the church. New York, Hagerstown, San Francisco..., 1979.
P. 13-24: Mission as disciple making.
*WCE. 1982.
P. 824: Discipling.
*GREENWAY, ROGER S. (ed.). Discipling the city: theological reflections on urban mission: third printing. Grand Rapids, 1986.
First ed.: Grand Rapids, 1979.
*COLEMAN, ROBERT E. The master plan of discipleship. Old Tappan, 1987.
*WAGNER. 1989.
P. 57-67: Evangelism or disciple making? (W. Charles Arn).
P. 288: Discipling - perfecting.
*WANG, THOMAS (ed.). Countdown to AD 2000... Pasadena, 1989.
P. 166-167: Discipling a whole nation (Jim Montgomery).
*MONTGOMERY, JIM. DAWN 2000: 7 million churches to go: the personal story of the DAWN strategy for world evangelization. Crowborough, 1990.
*BOSCH. 1991.
P. 56-83: Matthew: mission as disciple-making.

2.2.4. AUXANICS

The term *auxanics* is derived from the Greek verb *aux(an)ein*=to (cause to) grow, to increase, to spread (out), to multiply, to advance, which occurs 22 times in the New Testament. In the Acts of the Apostles we read: 'The word of God continued to *spread*; the number of the disciples increased greatly in Jerusalem' (Acts 6:7); 'But the word of God continued to *advance* and gain adherents' (Acts 12:24); 'So the word of the Lord *grew* mightily and prevailed' (Acts 19:20); etc. The Greek noun *auxesis*= increase, growth, however, occurs only two times in the New Testament (Eph. 4:16; Col. 2:19).

Abraham Kuyper (1894:III,518-519) proposed 'auxanics', but Daubanton (1911:228) rejected this term. Thereafter nobody has used this name anymore.

The idea of 'growth', however, is still current. After the Tambaram missionary conference (1938) produced a whole volume on 'the growing church', Donald A. McGavran (1959; 1965; 1990) became the missiologist who has propagated 'church growth' intensively. His Church Growth Movement distinguishes at least two types of church growth: (1) internal growth of Christians in grace (*spiritual growth*); and (2) external growth of the local congregations and the churches (*numerical growth*) (Wagner 1989:285). Charles E. van Engen (1981:183) has made clear in his dissertation on church growth ecclesiology that the New Testament not only emphasized spiritual growth, but also numerical growth: 'Luke portrays in his entire narrative a lively interest in the matter of numerical growth. This is because the element of numerical growth was such an astounding, dominant feature of the early church' (cf. Acts 2:42-47).

*KUYPER, ABRAHAM. Encyclopaedie der heilige godgeleerdheid. Amsterdam, 1894. 3 vols.
*DAUBANTON. 1911.
    P. 228: Auxaniek.
*IMC. Tambaram series. Oxford, & London, 1939.
    II: The growing church.
*PAYNE, ERNEST A. The growth of the world church: the story of the modern missionary movement. London, 1955.
*McGAVRAN, DONALD A. How churches grow: the new frontiers. London, 1959.
*BAVINCK, JOHAN H. Alzoo wies het Woord: een studie over den voortgang van het evangelie in de dagen van Paulus: tweede dr. Baarn, 1960.
    First ed.: Baarn, 1941.
*McGAVRAN, DONALD A. (ed.). Church growth and Christian mission. New York, Evanston, & London, 1965.
BRADSHAW, MALCOLM R. Church growth through evangelism-in-depth. Pasadena, 1969.
*CONCISE DICTIONARY. 1971.
    P. 110-111: Church growth (Stephen C. Neill).
KASDORF, HANS. Gemeindewachstum als missionarisches Ziel: ein Konzept für Gemeinde- und Missionsarbeit. Bad Liebenzell, 1976.
*VERKUYL, JOHANNES. Contemporary missiology: an introduction. Grand Rapids, 1978.
    P. 188-192: The goal of church growth.
*COSTAS, ORLANDO E. The integrity of mission: the inner life and outreach of the church. New York, Hagerstown, San Francisco..., 1979.
    P. 37-60: Mission as integral growth.
KRAUS, NORMAN C. (ed.). Missions, evangelism, and church growth. Scottdale, & Ontario, 1980.
*ENGEN, CHARLES E. VAN. The growth of the true church: an analysis of the ecclesiology of church growth theory. Amsterdam, 1981. Diss. V.U. Amsterdam.
*NOORDEGRAAF, ALBERT. Creatura Verbi: de groei van de gemeente volgens de Handelingen der Apostelen. 's-Gravenhage, 1983. Diss. Utrecht.
    P. 110-146: Alzo wies het Woord.
*LMG. 1987.
    P. 211-214: Kirchenwachstum, Gemeindewachstum (Herwig Wagner).
*ABRAHAM, WILLIAM J. The logic of evangelism. Grand Rapids, 1989.
    P. 70-91: Church growth.
*WAGNER. 1989.
    P. 285: Types of church growth.
*McGAVRAN, DONALD A, & C. Peter Wagner. Understanding church growth: third ed. Grand Rapids, 1990.
    First ed.: Grand Rapids, 1970.

24

2.2.5. PROSTHETICS

The name *prosthetics* is derived from the Greek verb *prostithenai*=to give in addition, to add (to the community), to incorporate (into a society), which occurs 18 times in the New Testament. Luke writes: 'So those who welcomed his message were baptized, and that day about three thousand persons were *added*' (Acts 2:41); 'And day by day the Lord *added* to their number those who were being saved' (Acts 2:47); 'Yet more than ever believers were *added* to the Lord, great numbers of both men and women' (Acts 5:14); 'And a great many people were brought[=*added*] to the Lord' (Acts 11:24).

Abraham Kuyper (1894:III,518-519) not only introduced 'auxanics' and 'matheteutics', but also 'prosthetics'. He himself preferred the last term. Daubanton (1911:236-238) also refused to accept the name 'prosthetics'. Nobody has followed Kuyper at this point. Even Johan H. Bavinck (1960: XVII) openly critised this name: 'The science of missions is not concerned with "adding" but with our calling to preach the gospel of Christ down through the ages'. According to Bavinck, the 'adding' is God's work alone; it is not at all the task of the missionaries and the mission agencies.

The Church Growth Movement has taken the biblical concept of *adding* as seriously as that of 'growing'. However, 'adding' and 'growing' (God's work) are not in the same way key words in mission studies as 'preaching' and 'discipling' (church work). In practice, as key issues they are only underlined and propagated by the Church Growth Movement at Fuller Theological Seminary, School of World Mission at Pasadena, California, which seems to have neglected the serious warning of Bavinck (1960:XVII): 'It is clearly evident that this "adding" does not lie within the capacity of man, but is exclusively a holy and secret operation of God's free good pleasure'.

*KUYPER, ABRAHAM. Encyclopaedie der heilige godgeleerdheid. Amsterdam, 1894.
    III, p.518-524: De prosthetiek.
*DAUBANTON. 1911.
    P. 236-238: Prosthetiek.
*BAVINCK, JOHAN H. An introduction to the science of missions. Philadelphia, 1960.
    P. XVII: Prosthetics.
*NOORDEGRAAF, ALBERT. Creatura Verbi: de groei van de gemeente volgens de Handelingen der Apostelen. 's-Gravenhage, 1983.
    P. 20-77: De toevoeging tot de gemeente.

2.2.6. PROPAGANDICS

Finally we refer to *propagandics*, which is derived from the Latin verb *propagare*=to propagate. It has no direct biblical roots.

Johannes Tideman (1863:58,78) introduced the name 'propagandics', but Daubanton refused it (1911:235-236). Thereafter nobody has defended it anymore.

The term 'propagandics' has its background in the Middle Ages, which used the following expressions: to propagate (Christian) faith (Lat.: *fidem propagare*); to propagate (Roman) Catholic religion (Lat.: *catholicam religionem propagare*); the propagation of the gospel (Lat.: *propagatio evangelii*); the propagation of the Christian religion (Lat.: *propagatio christianae religionis*); etc.

In 1622 Pope Gregory XV founded the Sacred Congregation for the Propagation of the Faith (Lat.: *Sacra congregatio de propaganda fide*), which recently changed its name: Sacred Congregation for the Evangelization of the Peoples. In Roman Catholic missions and mission studies 'propaganda' has always had a clear and concrete meaning.

In Protestant circles the word 'propaganda' is adopted as well. In the United Kingdom, the Society for the Propagation of the Gospel in New England (1649) and the Society for the Propagation of the Gospel in Foreign Parts (1701) were established. In his inaugural address at Edinburgh, Alexander Duff dealt with 'the course and method of Gospel propagation' (1868:21-23).

In Germany people started to make a very sharp distinction between mission and propaganda. Karl Axenfeld (1904:1-80) set Jewish propaganda against early Christian mission; Julius Richter (Axenfeld 1904:129-185) Muslim propaganda against modern Christian mission; and Martin Kähler (cf. Frohnes 1971:XXVII-XXX,108-116) Roman Catholic propaganda against Protestant mission. Therefore, Heinrich Frick (1927) posed the question: mission *or* propaganda? Thereafter, people like Johannes C. Hoekendijk (1948: 32-40), Walter Holsten (1953:61-63), Hans J. Margull (1959:70-71), and Hans-Werner Gensichen (1971:Sachregister) play off mission against propaganda. Anne van der Meiden (1972:121), however, has strongly criticized this distinction: 'All constructed contrasts between apostolate and propaganda are due to either a wrong understanding of the phenomenon propaganda, or an unjust interpretation of the missionary mandate, or both' (my tr.). I prefer to take a middle position. On the one hand, I view the missionary enterprise as propaganda, on the other hand, *God's mission* (Lat.: *missio Dei*) as far more than propaganda.

Because of the negative connotation of the word 'propaganda', today this term is no longer central in mission and mission studies. Even the Roman Catholic church has abandoned it. The bridging term *missionary propaganda* (Concise dictionary 1971:497-498; de Ridder 1971:113) is not helpful.

*TIDEMAN, JOHANNES. Theologische studiën. Amsterdam, 1863.
*DUFF, ALEXANDER. Evangelistic theology: an inaugural address delivered in the Common Hall

of the New College, Edinburgh, on Thursday, 7th November 1867. Edinburgh, 1868.

*AXENFELD, KARL, GUSTAV MÜLLER, CARL PAUL, et al. (eds.). Missionswissenschaftliche Studien: Festschrift zum 70. Geburtstag des Herrn Prof.D.Dr. Gustav Warneck... Berlin, 1904.

P. 1-80: Die jüdische Propaganda als Vorläuferin und Wegbereiterin der urchristlichen Mission (Karl Axenfeld).

P. 129-185: Die Propaganda des Islam als Wegbestreiterin der modernen Mission (Julius Richter).

?HAUSSLEITER, JOHANNES. Propaganda und Mission im Lichte des Neuen Testaments. 1908.

*DAUBANTON. 1911.

P. 235-236: Propagandiek.

*FRICK, HEINRICH. Mission oder Propaganda? Giessen, 1927.

*LÜTGERT, WILHELM. Reich Gottes und Weltgeschichte. Gütersloh, 1928.

P. 47-53: Mission und Propaganda (1924).

*RICHTER, JULIUS. Mission und Propaganda. In: NAMZ, V (1928), p. 257-260.

*HOEKENDIJK, JOHANNES C. Kerk en volk in de Duitse zendingswetenschap. Amsterdam, 1948. Diss. Utrecht.

P. 32-40: 'Zending en propaganda' (1874-1914).

*Ger. tr.: 1967.

*HOLSTEN. 1953.

*MARGULL, HANS J. Hope in action: the church's task in the world. Philadelphia, 1962.

*Ger. ed.: Theologie der missionarischen Verkündigung: Evangelisation als oekumenisches Problem. Stuttgart, 1959.

P. 70-71: Die Absage an die Propaganda.

*OHM. 1962.

P. 758-761: Mission und Propaganda.

*CONCISE DICTIONARY. 1971.

P. 497-498: Missionary propaganda (R. Pierce Beaver).

*FROHNES, HEINZGÜNTER (ed.). Martin Kähler: Schriften zu Christologie und Mission: Gesamtausgabe der Schriften zur Mission: mit einer Bibliographie. München, 1971.

P. 108-116: Was heisst Mission? (1908).

*GAZALBA,SIDI. Dialog antara propagandis Kristen dan logika. Djakarta, 1971.

*GENSICHEN, HANS-WERNER. Glaube für die Welt: theologische Aspekte der Mission. Gütersloh, 1971.

*RIDDER, RICHARD R. DE. The dispersion of the people of God: the covenant basis of Matthew 28:18-20 against the background of Jewish, pre-Christian proselyting and diaspora, and the apostleship of Jesus Christ. Kampen, 1971.

P. 110-120: The propaganda.

*HOF, IZAÄK P.C. VAN 'T. Op zoek naar het geheim van de zending: in dialoog met de wereldzendingsconferenties 1910-1963. Wageningen, 1972. Diss. Leiden.

P. 45-46: De zending als propaganda.

*MEIDEN, ANNE VAN DER. Mensen winnen: een verkenning van de relatie tussen ethiek, propaganda, en apostolaat. N.p., 1972. Diss. Utrecht.

P. 102-122: Apostolaat en propaganda.

2.2.7. CONCLUSION

The first five minor names of mission studies have very relevant biblical roots. In essence, halieutics is 'theology of fishing'; keryktics 'theology of proclamation' (cf. Spindler, & Middelkoop 1981:17-19); matheteutics 'theology of discipling (the nations)'; auxanics 'theology of (church) growth'; and prosthetics 'theology of adding (to the Christian community)'. Missiology as a discipline, however, is much broader than just 'theology of fishing', 'theology of proclamation', etc. (cf. chapter 3).

'Propagandics' also has a limited significance. Since 1622 it has been especially associated with the Roman Catholic organization of mission, but today this is not anymore the case. Today the word 'propaganda' is primarily connected with the whole world of politics, business, and advertisement (propaganda by government departments for public health, better driving, etc.), and therefore unsuitable to function as a synonym of 'mission' (missionary politics, missionary business, missionary propaganda, etc. is no more than just a small part of 'mission'; cf. 5.4.5.).

*SPINDLER, MARC R., & PETER R. MIDDELKOOP (eds.). Bible and mission: a partially annotated bibliography 1960-1980. Leiden, & Utrecht, 1981. Bibliog.
P. 17-19: Theology of proclamation.

2.3. EVANGELISTIC THEOLOGY, EVANGELISTICS, EVANGELISTOLOGY, THE THEOLOGY OF EVANGELISM, THE THEOLOGY OF EVANGELIZATION

2.3.1. EUANGELIZEIN, EUANGELION, EUANGELISTES

The first major name of mission studies is derived from the Greek verb *euangelizein/euangelizesthai*, which occurs 54 times in the New Testament. It means: to announce the *euangelion*, to proclaim, to preach. In the Acts of the Apostles we read: 'And every day in the temple and at home they did not cease to teach and *proclaim* Jesus as the Messiah' (Acts 5:42); 'Then Philip began to speak, and starting with this scripture, he *proclaimed* to him the good news about Jesus' (Acts 8:35); 'But among them were some men of Cyprus and Cyrene who, on coming to Antioch, spoke to the Hellenists also, *proclaiming* the Lord Jesus' (Acts 11:20).

The *euangelion* (76 times in the New Testament) is the good news, the gospel. It is often used in a missionary context: 'that I [Peter] should be the one through whom the gentiles would hear the message of the *good news* and become believers' (Acts 15:7); 'For I [Paul] am not ashamed of the *gospel*; it is the power of God for salvation to everyone who has faith, to the Jew first and also to the Greek' (Rom. 1:16).

The *euangelistes* (3 times in the New Testament) is the announcer or proclaimer of the *euangelion*, the evangelist. In the New Testament the evangelist is clearly distinguished from the apostle: he is engaged in both church leadership (2Tim. 4:5) and missionary work (Acts 21:8).

The terms 'evangelistic theology', 'evangelistics', 'evangelistology', 'the theology of evangelism', and 'the theology of evangelization' are more related to *euangelizein* and *euangelion* than to *euangelistes*, which is a special ministry in the early church (Eph. 4:11). At that time, and also afterwards, not only the evangelists, but also the apostles -and others- were -and are- called to preach the *euangelion*: the subject of *euangelizein* is much wider than the *euangelistes* in the New Testament.

DAY, ALBERT E. The evangel of a new world. Nashville, 1939.
TDNT. 1964-1976.
II, p. 707-737: Euangelizomai, euangelion, proeuangelizomai, euangelistes (Gerhard Friedrich).
*TWNT. 1933-1978.
II, p. 705-735: Euangelizomai, euangelion, proeuangelizomai, euangelistes (Gerhard Friedrich).

2.3.2. EVANGELISTIC THEOLOGY, EVANGELISTICS

The names *evangelistic theology* and *evangelistics* were coined in last century.

Alexander Duff (1806-1878), who worked in India from 1829-1863, advocated 'evangelistic theology'. In a letter, sent in 1844 from Calcutta to Robert Gordon, the first Convener of the Foreign Missions Committee of the Free Church of Scotland, he made a plea for a new professorship of 'Missions and Education' (Myklebust 1955:I,173). Ten years later, he was chosen as the chair person of the Union Missionary Conference at New York, which passed a resolution 'that for the due preparation of candidates for the foreign field, it were very desirable that provision were made in our theological seminaries generally, for bringing the nature, history, and obligations of the missionary enterprise before the minds of the students, or what may be briefly designated a course of *Evangelistic theology*' (Myklebust 1955:I,156). Subsequently, in 1867, the first full time chair of mission studies, i.e. 'evangelistic theology', was established. Duff was appointed as the first professor of this chair. He accepted his academic duties by delivering an inaugural address, *Evangelistic Theology* (1868:19), which he regarded as 'only another name for the vast and comprehensive subject of Christian missions, considered in all their varied and multiplied bearings, in relation alike to God and man, time and eternity'. To Duff the adjective 'evangelistic' had the same meaning as 'missionary'. As object of evangelistic theology he regarded '(the evangelization of) the great world outside the pale of professed belief in the Bible ... with its at least eight hundred millions of unevangelized heathen' (ibid.:32-33).

On the continent of Europe, Karl Graul (1814-1864), the distinguished director of the Leipzig Mission, used the German term *Evangelistik* (1864: 9ff.). He equated this term with the 'theory of missions' in the theology of Schleiermacher. At the same time, Carl H.C. Plath (1829-1901), who was a disciple of Graul and a correspondent of Duff, wrote a chapter on 'Evangelistik' in the large theological handbook of Otto Zöckler, in which he described this new discipline as an explanation of 'the essential missionary function of the church producing effect in the world' (Zöckler 1890:IV,41: *missionarischen Wesensfunktion kirchlicher Selbstauswirkung in der Welt*; my tr.). Theodosius Harnack (1877:I,54ff.), Gustav Warneck (AMZ 1877:IV,157), and Henry W. Tottie (1892) discussed this term as well. Olav G. Myklebust (1955:I,190) analysed the writings of these three European theologians and concluded: 'All of these, however, use *Evangelistik* as a designation for the theory of missions only, not for the subject as a whole'.

In the United States of America, Philipp Schaff (1819-1893) was influenced by Duff. This famous professor of Union Theological Seminary at New York produced a theological encyclopedia in which he explained 'evangelistic' as an important part of practical theology (1893:517): this discipline can be described as *'science of missions* (Ger.:*Missionswissenschaft*), that is, of the propagation of Christianity at home and abroad. It is a new branch of theological learning, demanded by the growing zeal in missions. Christianity is a missionary religion...'.

In 1909, the year before the first World Missionary Conference at Edinburgh, Duff's famous chair of evangelistic theology was discontinued. This had a negative effect on the use of the term 'evangelistic theology'. The Edinburgh Conference did not deal with 'evangelistic theology', but with 'science and history of missions'. However, the *Encyclopaedia of Religion and Ethics* (1921:XII,299) declared: 'Evangelistic theology, or theory of missions, deals with the best methods of propagating the Christian religion at home and among heathen peoples abroad'. And the WCE (1982:826) recently described evangelistics as 'the science of the propagation of the gospel'.

In Germany Warneck (1892:I,22-23) moved away from the term 'evangelistics'. And in the Netherlands this term was critized by Abraham Kuyper (1894:III,518-519), Johannes J. van Oosterzee (1898:II,349), and Daubanton (1911:228-232). Thereafter, Netherlands Reformed theologians have dissociated themselves from this term (with the exception of Johannes C. Hoekendijk in 1954-1960). Theologians of the Reformed Churches in the Netherlands, however, have maintained the above mentioned vocabulary. Up to the present both the Free University of Amsterdam and the Theological

Universities of Kampen maintain evangelistics as a discipline which is co-ordinately linked with missiology. Duff, Harnack, Warneck, Tottie, Schaff, and the *Encyclopaedia of Religion and Ethics* have identified mission studies (theory of mission, science of mission) with evangelistics, but both Johannes Verkuyl and Jochem Douma distinguish them very sharply (cf. Andrew N. Somerville, who in 1874 published his lectures on 'missions *and evangelism*'; my italics): Verkuyl (1978:11) typifies mission studies as the discipline which analyses the communication of the gospel to persons 'who are strangers to the gospel' (my tr.), and evangelistics as the discipline which reflects on the communication of the gospel to persons 'who are alienated from the gospel' (my tr.); whereas Douma (1982:6) maintains the old geographical distinction between mission studies as a subject related to 'far away' and evangelistics as a subject related to 'the neighbourhood' (my tr.).

Also in South-Africa the name 'evangelistics' is still in use: J.J. de Klerk (1979:17) declares that evangelistics as discipline deals with 'the restoration of the covenant'.

GRAUL, KARL. Über Stellung und Bedeutung der christlichen Mission im Ganzen der Universitätswissenschaften. Erlangen, 1864.
*DUFF, ALEXANDER. Evangelistic theology. Edinburgh, 1868.
SOMERVILLE, ANDREW N. Lectures on missions and evangelism. Edinburgh, 1874.
HARNACK, THEODOSIUS. Praktische Theologie. Erlangen, 1877-1878. 2 vols.
WARNECK, GUSTAV. Das Studium der Mission auf der Universität. Gütersloh, 1877.
    *First ed.: AMZ, IV (1877), p. 145-164.
*ZÖCKLER, OTTO (ed.). Handbuch der theologischen Wissenschaften in encyklopädischer Darstellung mit besonderer Rücksicht auf die Entwicklungsgeschichte der einzelnen Disziplinen: dritte, sorgfältig durchgesehene, teilweise neu bearbeitete Aufl. München, 1890.
    IV, p. 39-100: Evangelistik (Carl H.C. Plath).
TOTTIE, HENRY W. Evangelistik. Uppsala, 1892.
*WARNECK. 1892-1903. 3 vols.
    I, p. 22-23: Evangelistik.
*SCHAFF, PHILIPP. Theological propaedeutic: a general introduction to the study of theology, exegetical, historical, systematic, and practical, including encyclopaedia, methodology, and bibliography: a manual for students. New York, 1893.
    P. 517-518: Evangelistic.
*KUYPER, ABRAHAM. Encyclopaedie der heilige godgeleerdheid. Amsterdam, 1894. 3 vols.
*OOSTERZEE, JOHANNES J. VAN. Practische theologie... Utrecht, 1894-1898. 2 vols.
GIBSON, J. CAMPBELL. Mission problems and mission methods in South China: lectures on evangelistic theology... Edinburgh, & London, 1901.
EKLUND, JOHAN A. Teologisk encyklopedi. Uppsala, 1902.
    P. 244 ff., 269, 274: (Evangelistik).
*DAUBANTON. 1911.
    P. 228-232: Evangelistiek.
*ENCYCLOPAEDIA OF RELIGION AND ETHICS. Edinburgh, & New York, 1921.
    XII, p. 293-300: Theology (David S. Adam).

SWIGCHEM, DOUWE VAN. Handboekje voor de evangelistiek. Kampen, 1950.
*HOEKENDIJK, JOHANNES C. Aanloop naar de evangelistiek. In: Woord en dienst, III (1954), p. 194-195, 214-215, 230, 242, 250-251, 258-259; IX (1960), p. 100-101.
*MYKLEBUST. 1955-1957.
    I, p. 158-242: Alexander Duff's chair of evangelistic theology (established in 1867).
JONG, PETER Y. DE. A theology of evangelistic concern. Nashville, 1963.
*VERKUYL, JOHANNES (met medewerking van OKKE JAGER). Inleiding in de evangelistiek. Kampen, 1978.
*KLERK, J.J. DE (ed.). Evangelistiek. Pretoria, 1979.
*DOUMA, JOCHEM. Evangelistiek: college-dictaat. Kampen, 1982. *WCE. 1982.
    P. 826: Evangelistics.
*JONGENEEL, JAN A.B. De 'Inleiding in de evangelistiek' van Verkuyl-Jager na 12 jaar. In: Kerk en theologie, XLI (1990), p. 307-310.

2.3.3. EVANGELISTOLOGY

In passing I mention here the term *evangelistology*, which did not obtain much support (cf. Paventi 1949:40; Seumois 1952:91,93; Santos Hernandez 1961: 206). As a name it is parallel to 'missiology', and for that reason broader than 'evangelistic theology' and 'theology of evangelism/ evangelization'.

*PAVENTI, SAVERIO. La chiesa missionaria: manuale di missionologia dottrinale. Roma, 1949.
*SEUMOIS. 1952.
*SANTOS HERNANDEZ. 1961.

2.3.4. THE THEOLOGY OF EVANGELISM

2.3.4.1. EVANGELISM

> Evangelism is not a type of work.
> It is a type of living.
> *Edward T. Perry (IRM 1933:68).*

The term *evangelism* is eventually derived from the Greek noun *evangelismos*, which has the following distinct meanings: (1) glad tidings, or the preaching of the gospel; (2) annunciation; and (3) evangelization (Barrett 1987:21). It was coined in the 17th century, but was never widely used until the middle of the last century.

    The first theologian who put 'evangelism' on a par with missions is perhaps Willem Muurling (1860:593-598). Thereafter, in 1868, the United Presbyterian Church appointed Andrew N. Somerville as lecturer in 'missions *and evangelism*' (my italics). He published a book about this subject (1874) which directly or indirectly made a great impact: we encounter his co-ordination both in the missiological literature (Bosch 1980:11-20; idem, in: ZMR 1984:161-191; cf. RGG 1960:IV,999-1001), and in the vocabulary of the WCC (Amsterdam 1948ff.), especially in the name of its Commission on World Mission *and Evangelism* (my italics), with its publication: *Mission and Evangelism - an Ecumenical Affirmation* (1982); etc. I disagree with this terminology, because I experience it as both belonging to the 19th century and as contrary to the theology of St. Paul: 'For Christ did not *send* (Greek: *apostellein*; Latin: *mittere*) me to baptize but to *proclaim the gospel* (Greek: *euangelizesthai*)' (1Cor. 1:17). Here 'evangelism' is not parallel to, but subjected to mission: evangelism is the primary goal of the mission of the church.

Since the 1930s there is a plethora of literature on *evangelism*, and *world evangelism* (Zwemer 1934; Niles 1957; Johnston 1974; 1978; Gurganus 1976; Kim-Sai Tan 1981), especially in the Ecumenical Movement. The second World Missionary Conference at Jerusalem (1928), and especially the third World Missionary Conference at Tambaram (1938), contributed to the advent of this plethora. John R. Mott (1865-1955), the founder and first chair-person of the International Missionary Council (1921ff.), asked in 1938: *What is Evangelism?* He published the results of this enquiry (125 replies) both in the conference report (IMC 1939:III, 45-57), and separately. We get the following impressions from this world-wide enquiry: at that time many people (1) did not connect 'evangelism' with the western world, and 'missions' with the non-western world; and (2) did not put 'evangelism' on a par with 'missions', but rather identified the one with the other. I quote here only a few definitions, at that time given by some (western and non-western) Christians in the third world, which implicitly reject the above mentioned co-ordination:

Toyohiko Kagawa (Japan):
> *Evangelism* means conversion of people from worldliness to Christ-like godliness.

Yoshimune Abe (Japan):
> *Evangelism* is the imparting of the Christian experience in all its implication from one life to another.

J.S. Ryang (Korea):
> *Evangelism* is a passion to share Christ with others.

Samuel B. Boon-Itt (Thailand):
> *Evangelism* means living, doing, and talking for Christ.

Daniel T. Niles (Sri Lanka):
> *Evangelism* means to me primarily the proclamation of the good news - the gospel.

Puthenveetre O. Philip (India):
> Evangelism is, primarily, making known the love of God which is at the center of the universe and persuading men to adopt the way of love as revealed by Jesus Christ, in all human relationships.

Bishop William J. Thompson (Iran):
> Evangelism, put very concisely, is a conscious desire and longing to bring others in contact with Christ.

Davidson T. Jabavu (South-Africa):
> Evangelism means the preachment of the gospel by word and deed in such a way as to convince others.

G. Baez Camargo (Mexico):
> Evangelism signifies to me the endeavor of the church, assisted by the Holy Spirit and through her witnessing in life, words, and service, to bring all men in touch with the redeeming power of Christ.

In fact, the 19th century terms 'evangelistic (theology)' and 'evangelistics' are replaced here by 'evangelism', although the term 'evangelism' is not a discipline, but the object of a discipline.

A remarkable feature is that most books on evangelism refer rarely or not at all to older publications on this subject. This implies a lot of unknown repetition, on the one hand, and a lack of reflected continuity, on the other hand. Nevertheless, we can observe some progress in both vocabulary and thinking. Here I refer to the following new terms in chronological order:

- *new evangelism*: Henry Drummond (1899: 'The new evangelism, in a word, is the gospel for the age...'); Elmer T. Clark (1915); Jesse M. Bader (1937); and Ronald H. Nash (1963); cf. Robert Smith (IRM 1944:304-311; IRM 1945:412-420); Alan Walker (1977); and Virginia R. Mollenkott (IRM 1983:32-40);
- *itinerant evangelism*: Samuel M. Zwemer (1944:79-88);
- *expectant evangelism*: Enlarged Meeting of the IMC at Whitby 1947; Second Assembly of the WCC at Evanston 1954 (cf. Margull 1959:20-23);
- *effective evangelism*: George E. Sweazey (1953); Arthur E. Graf (1965); Lewis A. Drummond (1972:133-183; 1975:114-158); Floyd McClung Jr, et al. (1988); and Donald A. McGavran (1988);
- *personal evangelism*: Joseph C. Macauley, & Robert H. Belton (1956); H. Cecil Pawson (1968); WCE (1982:838: 'evangelistic witnessing and sharing by a Christian with other individuals'); and C. Peter Wagner (1989:47-49);
- *evangelism-in-depth* (Sp.: *evangelismo a fondo*; Ger.:*Tiefen-evangelisation*): R. Kenneth Strachan (1961); Ray S. Rosales (1968);

Malcolm R. Bradshaw (1969); WCE (1982:826: 'a programme and philosophy of mobilizing the total membership and resources of the churches of an area for proclamation of the gospel to non-Christians'; initiated in 1960 in Latin America, later on other continents); DEM (1991:139: R. Kenneth Strachan, the founder of evangelism-in-depth); and LM (1992:149-150);

- *saturation evangelism*: Clyde W. Taylor and Wade T. Coggins (1969: VII: 'saturation or in-depth evangelism'); George W. Peters (1970); and Wade T. Coggins (1975:50-58);
- *secular evangelism*: Fred Brown (1970); and William J. Abraham (1989:191-200);
- *engagement evangelism*: Gabriel J. Fackre (1973:54: 'Engagement evangelism is a telling inextricably bound up with a doing');
- *cross-cultural evangelism*: Marvin K. Mayers (1974); and C. Peter Wagner (1989:286: 'extending evangelistic efforts beyond cultural, racial, social, or linguistic boundaries');
- *mass evangelism*: Michael Cassidy (IRM 1976:202-215); William Thomas (1977:21-108,249-286); and WCE (1982:833);
- *service evangelism*: Richard S. Armstrong (1979);
- *agape evangelism*: Richard G. Korthals (1980);
- *incarnational evangelism*: Lester Comee, & Darrell Guides (1981);
- *power evangelism*: John Wimber (1985); John Wimber, & Kevin Springer (1986); C. Peter Wagner (1989:223-224,297); and F. Douglas Pennoyer, & C. Peter Wagner (1990);
- *contagious evangelism*: George G. Hunter III (Wagner 1989:69-81);
- *crusade evangelism*: Elmer L. Towns (Wagner 1989:49-50,286: 'that method of reaching people with the gospel in the context of a public meeting place in which an evangelist delivers a message and people are asked to respond, with follow-up being the responsibility of the local churches');
- *lifestyle evangelism*: Jim Petersen (1989).

This list of terms is not at all limitative, but enuntiative. Here we can also notice some new distinctions:

- two forms of evangelism, expressed by Lewis R. Misselbrook (1956:49-51) as: (1) *personal evangelism*; and (2) *church evangelism*; by George W. Target (1968:13-110) as: (1) *public evangelism* and (2) *personal evangelism*; and by David L. Watson (IBMR 1983:6-9) as: (1) *prophetic evangelism*; and (2) *personal evangelism*;
- three approaches to evangelism: (1) *presence evangelism* (winning a hearing); (2) *proclamation evangelism* (making the gospel of Christ

known); and (3) *persuasion evangelism* (motivating 'the unsaved' to respond to the gospel) (Wagner 1989:43-46,296-297).

A critical analysis of the whole literature on evangelism is an urgent task in the field of mission studies. It must be an analysis of at least the following issues (in chronological order):

-   the relation mission (overseas?) and evangelism (at home?) (Somerville 1874; RGG 1960:IV,999-1001; Bosch 1980:11-20; idem, in: ZMR 1984:161-191; idem, in: 1991:409-420; Kraus 1980);
-   the goals of evangelism (Zwemer 1934);
-   the message of evangelism (Zwemer 1934; 1944; 1948; Bader 1937; Watson 1977:64-82);
-   the motives of evangelism (Zwemer 1934; 1948; Watson 1977:83-97);
-   the methods of evangelism (Bader 1937; Zwemer 1944; Scott 1957; Taylor 1964; Woodson 1973);
-   the relation evangelism and social witness/social service/social action/social justice/social responsibility/social involvement (Temple 1943; Wiser, & Thomas 1950; Richardson 1977; Sider 1977; Conn 1982; Nicholls 1985; Miles 1986);
-   the dynamics of evangelism (Zwemer 1948; Borchert 1976);
-   the principles of evangelism (Scott 1957);
-   the plans/strategies of evangelism (Coleman 1968; Mayers 1974; Dayton 1978).

Especially the issues raised, the terms given, and the distinctions made by (1) the Church Growth Movement; (2) the school of Power Evangelism within the Church Growth Movement, led by John Wimber (Abraham 1989:157,159); and (3) Evangelism Explosion, developed by D. James Kennedy (1972), need a thorough investigation. Kenneth S. Latourette (IRM 1937:309-321), M. Taylor (1964), William Thomas (1977), David L. Watson (IBMR 1983:6-9), David J. Bosch (ZMR 1984:161-191; 1991:409-420), and especially David B. Barrett (1987), have initiated serious research into this wide and complex field. I quote Barrett (1987:78): '"Evangelize" and cognates are key words and key concepts in Christian theology. If the terms themselves become, or have become, overused, overexposed, debased, discredited, or devalued in any way, in any circles, this does not mean that they should be abandoned or replaced. Instead, they must be revalued or recredited drawing upon their inherent richness of meaning and usage throughout history'.

ADAMS, CHARLES. Evangelism in the middle of the nineteenth century. Boston, 1850.
*MUURLING, WILLEM. Practische godgeleerdheid, of beschouwing van de evangeliebediening voor namelijk in de Nederlandsche Hervormde Kerk: een handboek bij de academische

lessen: tweede, verb. uitgave. Groningen, 1860.

    P. 593-598: Onderscheid en verhouding tusschen de zending en de evangeliebediening: derzelver object, werkkring, subject, en meer bepaald doel.

    First ed.: Groningen, 1851-1857. 3 vols.

SOMERVILLE, ANDREW N. Lectures on missions and evangelism. Edinburgh, 1874.

DRUMMOND, HENRY. The new evangelism: and other papers. London, 1899.

    First ed.: London, 1892.

KILPATRIC, THOMAS B. New Testament evangelism. London, 1911.

CLARK, ELMER T. The new evangelism. Nashville, 1915.

FRENCH, ERNEST A. (ed.). Evangelism: a re-interpretation. London, 1921.

*CONANT, JUDSON E. Every-member evangelism: rev. ed. New York, & London, 1922.

*IMC. Reports of the meeting ... at Jerusalem, Easter 1928. London, Melbourne, Cape Town..., 1928.

    VIII, p. 121-137: The power of evangelism (John A. Mackay, James H. Linton, E. Stanley Jones).

FERGUSON, ROBERT. The meaning of evangelism for today: our new approach to the old task. London, 1930.

RATTENBURY, J. ERNEST. Evangelism: its shame and glory. London, 1932.

*PERRY, EDWARD T. Evangelism: a type of work or a quality of living?

    In: IRM, XXII (1933), p. 63-68.

*ZWEMER, SAMUEL M. Thinking missions with Christ: some basic aspects of world-evangelism, our message, our motive, and our goal. Grand Rapids, 1934.

HOCKING, WILLIAM E. Evangelism: an address on permanence and change in church and mission. N.p., 1935.

BAILEY, AMBROSE M. Evangelism in a changing world. New York, 1936.

BADER, JESSE M. (ed.). The method and message of the new evangelism: a joint statement of the evangelistic mission of the Christian church. New York, 1937.

*EVANGELISM FOR OUR DAY: reporting the Council on Evangelism, East Northfield, Massachusetts, June 1937. East Northfield, 1937.

*LATOURETTE, KENNETH S. Pre-nineteenth century evangelism: its outstanding characteristics. In: IRM, XXVI (1937), p. 309-321.

*MOTT, JOHN R. (ed.). Evangelism for the world today: as interpreted by Christian leaders throughout the world. New York, & London, 1938.

PATON, WILLIAM (ed.). Studies in evangelism. London, 1938.

*IMC. Tambaram series. Oxford, & London, 1939.

    III, p. 1-444: Evangelism.

    VII, p. 52-72: Evangelism: opportunities and difficulties.

BLACKWOOD, ANDREW W. Evangelism in the home church. New York, & Nashville, 1942.

*BRYAN, DAWSON C. Building church membership through evangelism. New York, & Nashville, 1942.

TEMPLE, WILLIAM. Social witness and evangelism. London, 1943.

*MOTT, JOHN R. The larger evangelism... New York, & Nashville, 1944.

SMITH, ROBERT. The new dimension in evangelism. In: IRM, XXXIII (1944), p. 304-311.

*ZWEMER, SAMUEL M. Evangelism today: message not method. New York, London, & Edinburgh, 1944.

*BRYAN, DAWSON C. A workable plan of evangelism. New York, & Nashville, 1945.

*SMITH, ROBERT. Evangelism in the new age. In: IRM, XXXIV (1945), p. 412-420.

JESSOP, THOMAS E. Evangelism and education: the presentation of religion to adults. London, 1947.

*DILLISTONE, FREDERICK W. Revelation and evangelism. London, & Redhill, 1948.

?MONSMA, M., et al. Reformed evangelism. Grand Rapids, 1948.

ZWEMER, SAMUEL M. Evangelism today: its message, its motive, its dynamic. Grand Rapids, 1948.

*ARCHIBALD, ARTHUR C. New Testament evangelism: how it works today: fourth printing. Philadelphia, Chicago, & Los Angeles, 1949.
    First ed.: 1946.

DODDS, J.L. Friendship evangelism. Lucknow, 1950.

*HOEKENDIJK, JOHANNES C. The call to evangelism. In: IRM, XXXIX (1950), p. 162-175.
    *Dutch tr.: 1964.

LAUBACH, FRANK C. Literacy as evangelism... New York, 1950.

WISER, WILLIAM H., & C.L. HOWELL THOMAS. Evangelism and social service in the Church of Christ in India. Lucknow, 1950.

*GREEN, BRYAN. The practice of evangelism... London, 1951.

HOEKENDIJK, JOHANNES C. New forms of evangelism? Preparatory material for the European Layman's conference. Genève, 1951.

*HOEKENDIJK, JOHANNES C. Evangelism - the raison d'être of the church. In: ER, IV (1951/52), p. 431-435.

LEAVELL, ROLAND Q. Evangelism: Christ's imperative commission. Nashville, 1951.

*SWEAZEY, GEORGE E. Effective evangelism: the greatest work in the world. New York, 1953.

TAYLOR, VINCENT. Doctrine and evangelism. London, 1953.

*STUDY DEPARTMENT WCC. Evangelism - the mission of the church to those outside her life: an ecumenical survey prepared under the auspices of the WCC. New York, 1954.

MACAULEY, JOSEPH C., & ROBERT H. BELTON. Personal evangelism. Chicago, 1956.

*MISSELBROOK, LEWIS R. Winning the people for Christ: an experiment in evangelism. London, 1956.

*WEDEL, THEODORE O. Evangelism's threefold witness: kerygma, koinonia, diakonia. In: ER, IX (1956/57), p. 225-239.

*NILES, DANIEL T. (ed.). World evangelism today: a series. London, 1957.

*RGG. 1957-1965.
    II, p. 795: Evangelism (Hans J. Margull).
    IV, p. 999-1001: Mission und Evangelisation (Hans-Werner Gensichen).

*SCOTT, ROLAND W. (ed.). Ways of evangelism: some principles and methods of evangelism in India. Mysore City, 1957.
    First ed.: 1953.

*TEMPLETON, CHARLES B. Evangelism for tomorrow. New York, 1957.

?BRYAN, DAWSON C. A handbook of evangelism for layman. 1958.

FERM, ROBERT O. Cooperative evangelism: is Billy Graham right or wrong? are his policies supported by Scripture and the great evangelists of history? Grand Rapids, 1958.

AUTREY, C.E. Basic evangelism. Grand Rapids, 1959.

*PACKER, JAMES I. Evangelism and the sovereignty of God. Chicago, 1961.
    Several reprints.

*STRACHAN, R. KENNETH (ed.). Evangelism-in-depth: experimenting with a new type of evangelism: as told by team members of the Latin America Mission. Chicago, 1961.

*MARGULL, HANS J. Hope in action... Philadelphia, 1962.
    *Ger. ed.: Theologie der missionarischen Verkündigung: Evangelisation als oekumenisches Problem. Stuttgart, 1959.
    P. 20-23: 'Expectant evangelism'.

NASH, RONALD H. The new evangelism. Grand Rapids, 1963.

*VERWER, GEORGE. Literature evangelism: a manual. Kansas City, 1963.

*KETTNER, ELMER A. Adventures in evangelism. Saint Louis, 1964.

TAYLOR, MENDELL. Exploring evangelism: history, methods, theology. Kansas City, 1964.
*WEBSTER, DOUGLAS. What is evangelism? London, 1964.
    *First ed.: London, 1959.
GRAF, ARTHUR E. The church in the community: an effective evangelism program for the
    Christian congregation. Grand Rapids, 1965.
*SCHARPFF, PAULUS. History of evangelism: three hundred years of evangelism in Germany,
    Great Britain, and the United States of America. Grand Rapids, 1966.
    *Ger. ed.: Geschichte der Evangelisation: dreihundert Jahre Evangelisation in
    Deutschland, Grossbrittannien und USA. Giessen, & Basel, 1964.
HENRY, CARL F.H., & W. STANLEY MOONEYHAM (eds.). One race, one gospel, one task: World
    Congress on Evangelism, Berlin, 1966. Minneapolis, 1967.
    Ger. tr.: 1967.
*COLEMAN, ROBERT E. The master plan of evangelism: sixth printing. Westwood, 1968.
    First ed.: Westwood, 1963.
*MASSON, JOSEPH, SJ. Mission, missions, and evangelism. In: ER, XX (1968), p. 131-137.
*PAWSON, H. CECIL. Personal evangelism. London, 1968.
*POTTER, PHILIP. Evangelism and the WCC. In: ER, XX (1968), p. 171-182.
*ROSALES, RAY S. The evangelism in depth program of the Latin America Mission:
    a description and evaluation. Mexico, 1968.
*TARGET, GEORGE W. Evangelism Inc. London, 1968.
    P. 13-82: Public evangelism; p. 83-110: Personal evangelism.
*THOMSON, DAVID P. Aspects of evangelism. Crieff, 1968.
BRADSHAW, MALCOLM R. Church growth through evangelism-in-depth. Pasadena, 1969.
*TAYLOR, CLYDE W., & WADE T. COGGINS (eds.). Mobilizing for saturation evangelism. Wheaton,
    1969. BROWN, FRED. Secular evangelism. London, 1970.
*GREEN, MICHAEL. Evangelism in the early church. London, 1970.
    *Dutch tr.: 1979. Fr. tr.: 1981.
PETERS, GEORGE W. Saturation evangelism. Grand Rapids, 1970.
    Ger. tr.: 1977.
*CONCISE DICTIONARY. 1971.
    P. 199-200: Evangelism (Stephen C. Neill).
JAFFRAY, GEORGE R., Jr. Explosive evangelism. N.p., 1972.
*KENNEDY, D. JAMES. Evangelism explosion: eighth ed. Wheaton, 1972.
    First ed.: Wheaton, 1970.
*KIRBY, GILBERT W. (ed.). Evangelism alert: official reference volume: European congress on
    evangelism. Amsterdam, 1971. London, 1972.
*POULTON, JOHN. A today sort of evangelism. Aylesbury, 1972.
*WOOLSEY, RAYMOND H. Evangelism handbook. Washington, 1972.
*FACKRE, GABRIEL J. Do and tell: engagement evangelism in the '70s. Grand Rapids, 1973.
*WOODSON, LESLIE H. Evangelism for today's church: meaning, motivation, method,
    mobilization. Grand Rapids, 1973.
*FRANCIS, JOHN E. (ed.). Contemporary evangelism. Birmingham, 1974. Unpublished.
JOHNSTON, ARTHUR P. World evangelism and the Word of God: foreword by Billy Graham.
    Minneapolis, 1974.
MAYERS, MARVIN K. Christianity confronts culture: a strategy for cross-cultural
    evangelism. Grand Rapids, 1974.
*BRIA, ION. The church's role in evangelism: icon or platform? In: IRM, LXIV (1975),
    p. 243-250.
*COGGINS, WADE T. So that's what missions is all about. Chicago, 1975.
    P. 50-58: Saturation evangelism.

*COLEMAN, ROBERT E. Evangelism in perspective. Harrisburg, 1975.

LANEY, JAMES T. (ed.). Evangelism: mandates for action. New York, 1975.

PONDER, JAMES A. (comp.). Evangelism men: proclaiming the doctrines of salvation. Nashville, 1975.

*BORCHERT, GERALD L. Dynamics of evangelism. Waco, 1976.

*CASSIDY, MICHAEL. Limitations of mass evangelism and its potentialities. In: IRM, LXV (1976), p. 202-215.

*GURGANUS, GEORGE P. (ed.). Guidelines for world evangelism. Abilene, 1976.

*HOLLENWEGER, WALTER J. Evangelism today: good news or bone of contention. Belfast, 1976.

    *Ger. ed.: Evangelisation gestern und heute. Stuttgart, 1973.

*McDILL, WAYNE. Evangelism in a tangled world. Nashville, 1976.

*MILLER, HERB. Evangelism's open secrets. St. Louis, 1977.

*RICHARDSON, WILLIAM J. Social action vs. evangelism. South Pasadena, 1977.

SIDER, RONALD J. Evangelism, salvation, and social justice: with a response by John R.W. Stott. Bramcote, 1977.

    *First ed.: Evangelism, salvation, and social justice: definitions and interrelationships. In: IRM, LXIV (1975), p. 251-267.

*THOMAS, WILLIAM. An assessment of mass meetings as a method of evangelism - case study of Eurofest'75 and the Billy Graham crusade in Brussels. Amsterdam, 1977. Diss. V.U. Amsterdam.

*WALKER, ALAN. The new evangelism. Belfast, & Dublin, 1977.

*WATSON, DAVID C.K. I believe in evangelism. Grand Rapids, 1977.

    First ed.: London, 1976.

DAYTON, EDWARD R. Planning strategies for evangelism: a workbook: sixth ed. Monrovia, 1978.

*JOHNSTON, ARTHUR P. The battle for world evangelism. Wheaton, 1978.

KRASS, ALFRED C. Five lantarns at Sundown: evangelism in a chastened mood. Grand Rapids, 1978.

*SMITH, BAILEY E. Real evangelism... exposing the subtle substitutes for that evangelism. Nashville, 1978.

STEPHENS, KEN. Discipleship evangelism: a manual for evangelism through home Bible studies. Scottdale, 1978.

*STEWART, MARJORIE. Women in neighborhood evangelism. Springfield, 1978.

*ARMSTRONG, RICHARD S. Service evangelism. Philadelphia, 1979.

*GREEN, MICHAEL. Evangelism - now and then. Leicester, 1979.

*HOEKSTRA, HARVEY T. Evangelism in eclipse: world mission and the WCC. Exeter, 1979.

*McPHEE, ARTHUR G. Friendship evangelism: the caring way to share your faith: third printing. Grand Rapids, 1979.

    First ed.: Grand Rapids, 1978.

*SISSON, RICHARD. Training for evangelism. Chicago, 1979.

*BOSCH, DAVID J. Witness to the world: the Christian mission in theological perspective. London, 1980.

    P. 11-20: Mission and evangelism.

KORTHALS, RICHARD G. Agape evangelism: roots that reach out. Wheaton, 1980.

KRAUS, NORMAN C. (ed.). Missions, evangelism, and church growth. Scottdale, & Ontario, 1980.

?COMEE, LESTER, & DARRELL GUIDES (eds.). Incarnational evangelism. Colorado Springs, 1981.

*TAN, KIM-SAI. The great digression: world evangelism since 1910: the ecumenical digression and evangelical response. Petaling Jaya, 1981.

ARMSTRONG, JAMES. From the underside: evangelism from a third world vantage point. New York, 1982.

40

CONN, HARVIE M. Evangelism, doing justice, and preaching grace. Grand Rapids, 1982.
*WCE. 1982.
    P. 826: Evangelism-in-depth.
    P. 833: Mass evangelism.
    P. 838: Personal evangelism.
MILES, DELOS. Introduction to evangelism. Nashville, 1983.
*MOLLENKOTT, VIRGINIA R. New age evangelism. In: IRM, LXXII (1983), p. 32-40.
*SAMUEL, VINAY, & CHRIS SUGDEN (eds.). Evangelism and the poor: a third world study guide:
    rev. ed. Bangalore, 1983.
    First ed.: Bangalore, 1982.
*WATSON, DAVID L. Evangelism: a disciplinary approach. In: IBMR, VII/1 (1983), p. 6-9.
*WCC. Mission and evangelism - an ecumenical affirmation. Geneva, 1983.
    *First ed.: IRM, LXXI (1982), 427-451.
    Ger. tr.: 1982.
    *Dutch tr.: 1983.
*BOSCH, DAVID J. Mission and evangelism: clarifying the concepts. In: ZMR, LXVIII (1984),
    p. 161-191.
*CALVER, CLIVE, DEREK COPLEY, BOB MOFFETT, & JIM SMITH (eds.). A guide to evangelism.
    Basingstoke, 1984.
    P. 82-103: Presence evangelism.
*NICHOLLS, BRUCE J. (ed.). In word and deed: evangelism and social responsibility. Exeter,
    1985.
WIMBER, JOHN. Power evangelism: signs and wonders today. London, 1985.
*COLEMAN, ROBERT E. (ed.). Evangelism on the cutting edge. Old Tappan, 1986.
?MILES, DELOS. Evangelism and social involvement. Nashville, 1986.
*STOTT, JOHN R.W. Christian mission in the modern world. Eastbourne, 1986.
    P. 35-57: Evangelism.
    First ed.: 1975.
    Ger. tr.: 1976.
    *Dutch tr.: 1978.
WIMBER, JOHN, & KEVIN SPRINGER. Power evangelism. San Francisco, 1986.
*BARRETT, DAVID B. Evangelize! A historical survey of the concept. Birmingham, 1987.
*BOSCH, DAVID J. Evangelism: theological currents and cross-currents today. In: IBMR, XI
    (1987), p. 98-103.
*McCLUNG, FLOYD, Jr, with GEOFF and JANET BENGE. Effective evangelism: a guide to
    friendship evangelism. London, 1988.
McGAVRAN, DONALD A. Effective evangelism: a theological mandate. Phillipsburgh, 1988.
*ABRAHAM, WILLIAM J. The logic of evangelism. Grand Rapids, 1989.
*PETERSEN, JIM. Living proof. Colorado Springs, 1989.
    P. 133-214: Practical guidance in lifestyle evangelism.
    First eds.: Evangelism as a lifestyle. 1980; and: Evangelism for our generation.
    1983.
*WAGNER. 1989.
    P. 43-55: Evangelism: the why and how (Elmer L. Towns).
    P. 57-67: Evangelism or disciple making? (W. Charles Arn).
    P. 69-81: The bridges of contagious evangelism: social networks (George G. Hunter
    III).
    P. 223-224: The biblical mandate: power evangelism.
    P. 286: Cross-cultural evangelism: crusade evangelism.
    P. 296: Persuasion evangelism.

P. 297: Power evangelism: proclamation evangelism.
*GREEN, MICHAEL. Evangelism through the local church. London, Sydney, Auckland..., 1990.
?PENNOYER, F. DOUGLAS, & C. PETER WAGNER (eds.). Understanding power evangelism. Ventura, 1990.
*BOSCH. 1991.
　　　P. 409-420: Mission as evangelism.
*DEN. 1991.
　　　P. 137-140: Central America.
　　　P. 396-400: Evangelism (Emilio Castro).
*LM. 1992.
　　　P. 149-150: Evangelism in depth (Tiefenevangelisation).
MURRAY, IAIN. El obstaculo al evangelismo... Cochabamba, n.d.

2.3.4.2. THE THEOLOGY OF EVANGELISM

The *theology of evangelism* has 'evangelism' as its object. This new term is the real partner or successor of the older names 'evangelistic (theology)' and 'evangelistics'.

The term 'theology of evangelism' was coined both in the International Missionary Council and elsewhere (cf. Johnston 1969:178-190: the theology of the larger evangelism; Shivute 1980). Henry Cook (1951) seems to have been the first theologian to use this term in the title of a book.

Soon after the Amsterdam Assembly of the World Council of Churches in 1948, the Secretary for Evangelism issued a questionnaire with comments, entitled *A Theology of Evangelism*. However, the first full discussion on what evangelism is only took place after the Evanston Assembly of 1954. In 1958 a major consultation was held at Bossey: it produced the first draft of *A Theology for Evangelism*. Thereupon the draft was revised in the light of the criticisms and comments received, and published by the Department on Evangelism. It opens with the following statement: 'Evangelism, defined in terms of its end result, is simply and only the work of God. Only God can save men from their sins, and only He can give to men the grace of saving faith' (Division of Studies WCC 1959:5). In this way the World Council of Churches has greatly contributed to the rise and progress of a 'theology of evangelism'. However, in both this publication of the World Council of Churches and in other publications on the same subject (for instance: Kantonen 1954) we do not find any definition of this discipline.

Our working definition of the 'theology of evangelism' is as follows: the theology of evangelism is that part of missionary theology which deals with the communication of *evangel* thoughts and values to non-Christians (being the primary goal of mission). In this sense it is totally parallel to a missionary 'theology of social witness/social service/social justice/social responsibility/

42

social involvement' and a missionary 'theology of healing', which are other
important branches of a missionary theology.

*COOK, HENRY. The theology of evangelism: the gospel in the world of to-day. London, 1951.
LEWIS, EDWIN. Theology and evangelism. Nashville, 1952.
*KANTONEN, TAITO A. The theology of evangelism: second printing. Philadelphia, 1954.
?BILHEIMER, ROBERT S. Concerning 'theology for evangelism'. 1955.
*HARTT, JULIAN N. Toward a theology of evangelism. New York, & Nashville, 1955.
*DIVISION OF STUDIES WCC. A theological relection on the work of evangelism. Geneva, 1959.
JONG, PIETER DE. Evangelism and contemporary theology: a study of the implications for
    evangelism in the thoughts of six modern theologians. Nashville, 1962.
TAYLOR, MENDELL. Exploring evangelism: history, methods, theology. Kansas, 1964.
AUTREY, C.E. The theology of evangelism. Nashville, 1966.
*JOHNSTON, ARTHUR P. A study of the theology of evangelism in the IMC 1921-1961. 1969.
    Thèse Strasbourg.
    P. 178-190: The theology of the larger evangelism (Madras 1938).
?AMAYA, ISMAEL E. Teologia biblica del evangelismo. Miami, 1970.
PICKERING, ERNEST D. The theology of evangelism. Clarks Summit, 1974.
*DRUMMOND, LEWIS A. Leading your church in evangelism. Nashville, 1975.
    P. 35-58: A theology of evangelism.
    *First ed.: Evangelism - the counter-revolution. London, 1972.
    P. 41-66: A theology of evangelism.
*FACKRE, GABRIEL J. Word in deed: theological themes in evangelism. Grand Rapids, 1975.
*KUIPER, RIENK B. God-centered evangelism: a presentation of the scriptural theology of
    evangelism. Edinburgh, & Carlisle, 1978.
    First ed.: Grand Rapids, 1961.
*SHIVUTE, TOMAS. The theology of mission and evangelism in the IMC from Edinburgh to New
    Delhi. Helsinki, 1980. Diss. Helsinki.
*KOLB, ROBERT. Speaking the gospel today: a theology for evangelism. St. Louis, 1984.

2.3.5. THE THEOLOGY OF EVANGELIZATION

2.3.5.1. EVANGELIZATION

> Evangelization is the test of our ecumenical vocation.
> *Philip A. Potter (Anderson, & Stransky 1975:175).*

The term *evangelization*, in common with the term 'evangelism', was already
used in last century (Gaume 1879; Broomhall 1887; Cust 1894; Oehler, in:
EMM 1894:177-188; Märker 1896; Schneider 1897). It was formed from the
Latin noun *evangelizatio* and coined in the 17th century. In 1889 it became
well-known by the watchword of the Student Volunteer Movement for Foreign
Missions in the U.S.A. (1886) which eventually was invented by the Protestant
Bible expositor Arthur T. Pierson (1837-1911): *the evangelization of the world*

in this generation (Speer 1902:510-526; Jansen Schoonhoven, in: DH 1954: 1-16; Hoekendijk, in: IRM 1970:23-31; Lotz 1970; Robert, in: IBMR 1986: 146-149; Barrett 1987:26-30). In 1897 Warneck attacked this watchword as smacking of Anglo-Saxon eschatological optimism (AMZ 1897:305-325), but John R. Mott rallied to its defence: 'The evangelization of the world in this generation means the giving to all men an adequate opportunity of knowing Jesus Christ as their Saviour and of becoming His real disciples' (1904:4-5).

Here we note that after the Second World War 'evangelization' as a term is clearly propagated by both the Lausanne Committee for World Evangelization (however, without rejecting the term 'evangelism'!), and the Roman Catholic Church. Following the Second Vatican Council (1962- 1965), the *Sacra congregatio de propaganda fide* was renamed: *Sacra congregatio pro gentium evangelizatione* (=Sacred Congregation for the Evangelization of the Peoples) (1967). Thereafter many Roman Catholic publications on 'evangelization' have appeared. The 1974 Synod of Roman Bishops met on the topic 'Evangelization in the modern world'. And Pope Paul VI promulgated the Apostolic Exhortation *Evangelii nuntiandi* (1975:18) which states: 'evangelizing means bringing the good news into all the strata of humanity, and through its influence transforming humanity from within and making it new'. At the same time we testify that both the *Concise Dictionary* (1971), Wagner (1989), and DEM (1991) do not offer articles on 'evangelization' (in addition to their articles on 'evangelism').

We are confronted with two problems. Firstly, both in Dutch and in German there is only one word: *evangelisatie* (Dutch) and *Evangelisation* (German). Continentals can live without the plurality of terms which is available in English. Usually they translate both 'evangelism' and 'evangelization' by the word *evangelisatie/Evangelisation*. At the same time they are surprised that sometimes translations of continental publications into English use the word 'evangelism' instead of the expected word 'evangelisation'. For instance, Paulus Scharpff's *Geschichte der Evangelisation* (1964) was not published as *History of Evangelisation*, but as *History of Evangelism* (1966).

Secondly, in English literature I observe a confusion of the the terms 'evangelism' and 'evangelisation'. Among the few authors who have recently reflected on the convergencies and divergencies of both terms are WCE, David B. Barrett, William J. Abraham, Edward R. Dayton, & David A. Fraser, and David J. Bosch. They have done it each in their own way. Here I refer to the very essence of their diverse interpretations. WCE (1982:826) gives two definitions, without making a clear link between them: *evangelism* is described as the activities involved in spreading the gospel; and *evangelization* as: (1) the whole process of spreading the good news of the kingdom of God; (2) the extent to which the good news has been spread; and (3) the extent of awareness of Christianity, Christ and the gospel. Barrett concludes (1987:78): 'In English, these two nouns *evangelization* and *evangelism* are not exact synonyms but have clear differentia. *Evangelism* is usually used only in reference to human evangelistic activity. *Evangelization* has a broader meaning and refers to the whole range of evangelizing activity, both human and divine, as well as the overall situation and status produced by all such ativities'. Abraham (1989:40-41) states that historically the two terms mean much the same thing: 'People prefer the word *evangelization* because it gives them more freedom to change the meaning of the term and because it cuts them loose from the negative associations of the word *evangelism*. In my view nothing much hangs on the distinction'. Dayton, & Fraser (1990:55), however, underline the importance of this distinction: '*Evangelization* is the total process of announcing the gospel and bringing people into discipleship. In this sense evangelization is a process to enhance rather than an event or goal to happen. In contrast, *evangelism* refers to specific actions and methods associated with the process of evangelization'. Bosch (1991:409), referring to WCE (1982: 826), clearly tries to distinguish both terms, but finally concludes: 'It remains difficult, however, to determine precisely what authors mean by evangelism or evangelization'. As a continental I prefer the term 'evangelization'. However, I am also open to use the Anglo-Saxon term 'evangelism'. I am inclined to compare the terms under consideration with the terms humanism/humanization and secularism/ secularization and to propose the following definitions: *evangelism* is *the view* (or, theory/principle/belief) emphasizing 'evangel' thoughts and values; and *evangelization* is *the process* (or, action/practice) of making society and human beings 'evangel' (cf. WCE 1982:826; Dayton, & Fraser 1990:50).

In the literature under consideration the definitions of *evangelization* and *world evangelization* (Barton 1908; Jenks 1926; McLeish 1934; Hillis 1965; Douglas 1975; Glasser 1976; Bouw 1982; Underwood 1988; Dayton, & Fraser 1990) are nearly the same as those of 'evangelism' and 'world evangelism'. However, here I like to notice some new terms and distinctions as well. For example: Orlando E. Costas (1989) introduces the term 'contextual evangelization'; whereas Duraisamy S. Amalorpavadass (1971), Samuel Rayan SJ (Anderson, & Stransky 1975:99; cf. Barrett 1987:64) and other Roman Catholic theologians distinguish between 'direct evangelization' (verbal presentation of the gospel) and 'indirect evangelization' (presentation through works that liberate people, develop society, and promote humanization). Other new terms proposed by Roman Catholic and/or Protestant authors are 'preevangelization' (Häring 1974:43-44: 'what prepares more or less directly for evangelization'); 'co-responsible evangelization' (cf. Barrett 1987:64); 'ongoing evangelization', or 'catechesis' (cf. Barrett 1987:68); 'integral evangelization', and 'inculturated evangelization' (cf. Barrett 1987:73); and 'new evangelization' (Fr.: *nouvelle évangélisation*; cf. Champagne, in: Mission 1994:95-135).

GAUME, JEAN-JOSEPH. L'évangelisation apostolique du globe, preuve péremptoire et trop peu connue de la divinité du Christianisme. Paris, 1879.

BROOMHALL, BENJAMIN (comp.). The evangelisation of the world: a missionary band: a record of consecration, and an appeal: second ed. London, 1887.
>First ed.: Missionary band ... London, 1886.

*WARNECK. 1892-1903.
>III/1, p. 233-243: Evangelisierung.

CUST, ROBERT N. Essay on the prevailing methods of the evangelization of the non-Christian world... London, 1894.

*OEHLER, THEODOR. Gedanken über Evangelisation und Mission. In: EMM, XXXVIII (1894), p. 177-188.

MÄRKER, O. Die Evangelisation. Stuttgart, 1896.

SCHNEIDER, J. Evangelisation und Gemeinschaftspflegen. Gütersloh, 1897.

*WARNECK, GUSTAV. Die moderne Weltevangelisations-Theorie. In: AMZ, XXIV (1897), p. 305-325.

*SPEER, ROBERT E. Missionary principles and practice: a discussion of Christian missions and of some criticisms upon them. New York, Chicago, & Toronto, 1902.
>P. 510-526: The evangelization of the world in this generation.
>Several reprints.

MOTT, JOHN R. The evangelization of the world in this generation. New York, 1904.
>*First ed.: New York, 1900. Reprinted: 1972.
>*Ger. tr.: 1901.
>Also Fr., Japanese, Nor., Swed. trs.

BARTON, JAMES L. The unfinished task of the Christian church: introductory studies in the problem of the world's evangelization. New York, 1908.

WHITLEY, WILLIAM T. Missionary achievement: a survey of world-wide evangelisation... New York, Chicago..., 1908.

*JENKS, DAVID. A study of world evangelisation. London, 1926.

*IMC. Reports of the meeting ... at Jerusalem, Easter 1928. London, Melbourne, Cape Town..., 1928.
>I, p. 459-476: A statement of the case for evangelization (The Bishop of Manchester).

PASSERI, VINCENZO. Evangelizazzione antica e moderna. Sora, 1930.

*RICHTER, JULIUS. Mission und Evangelisation im Orient: zweite Aufl. Gütersloh, 1930.
>First ed.: Gütersloh, 1908.

*BIBLIOGRAFIA MISSIONARIA. 1933-...
>XLII (1978) - ...: 6. Pastorale missionaria (...Evangelizzazione...). Bibliog.

*McLEISH, ALEXANDER. Jesus Christ and world evangelization: missionary principles: Christ's or ours? London, 1934.

*GROSHEIDE, FREDERIK W., T.J. HAGEN, & J. MULDER (eds.). Handboek voor gereformeerde evangelisatie. Kampen, 1939.

*HOEKENDIJK, JOHANNES C. The evangelisation of man in modern mass society. In: ER, II (1949/50), p. 133-140.

*STUDY DEPARTMENT WCC. The evangelisation of man in modern mass society: an ecumenical enquiry. Geneva, 1949.

46

*JANSEN SCHOONHOVEN, EVERT. De evangelisatie van de wereld in onze generatie. In: DH, VII (1954), p.1-16.

ULRICH, HEINRICH H. Die Kirche und ihre missionarische Aufgabe: Tatsachen und Probleme der Evangelisation in Deutschland. Berlin, 1955.

*RGG. 1957-1965.

    II, p. 770-775: Evangelisation und Volksmission (Heinrich Rendtorff).

    IV, p. 999-1001: Mission und Evangelisation (Hans J. Margull).

*WELTKIRCHENLEXIKON: Handbuch der Ökumene. Stuttgart, 1960.

    P. 378-384: Evangelisation (Johannes C. Hoekendijk).

*MARGULL, HANS J. Hope in action... Philadelphia, 1962.

    *Ger. ed.: Theologie der missionarischen Verkündigung; Evangelisation als oekumenisches Problem. Stuttgart, 1959.

HILLIS, DON W. (ed.). The scriptural basis of world evangelization. Grand Rapids, 1965.

*BEYREUTHER, ERICH. Kirche in Bewegung: Geschichte der Evangelisation und Volksmission. Berlin, 1968.

*ABINENO, JOHANNES L.C. Sekitar theologia praktika. Jakarta, 1969. 2 vols.

    II, p.133-215: Evangelisasi gereja.

*BRAUER, WILHELM. Evangelisation als biblische Forderung. Giessen, & Basel, 1970.

*HOEKENDIJK, JOHANNES C. Evangelisation of the world in this generation. In: IRM, LIX (1970), p. 23-31.

LOTZ, DENTON. 'The evangelization of the world in this generation': the resurgence of a missionary idea among the Conservative Evangelicals. 1970. Diss. Hamburg.

*BLENK, C., W.M.M. MOONEN, & BASTIAAN J. WIEGERAAD. Evangelisatie in Europa: verslag van een congres. Amersfoort, 1972.

AVILA, RAFAEL. Teología, evangelización y liberación. Bogotá, 1973.

*FACELINA, RAYMOND. Evangelization and mission: international bibliography 1972 indexed by computer... Strasbourg, 1973. Bibliog.

PATHRAPANKAL, JOSEPH, CMI (ed.). Service and salvation: Nagpur theological conference on evangelization. Bangelore, 1973.

*ARNOLD, WALTER (ed.). Evangelisation im ökumenischen Gespräch: Beiträge eines Symposiums (Genf 1973) zwischen Bangkok 1973 und Lausanne 1974. Erlangen, 1974.

HÄRING, BERNARD. Evangelization today. Slough, 1974.

*AMALORPAVADASS, DURAISAMY S. (ed.). Evangelisation of the modern world (synod of bishops, Rome, 1974). Bangalore, 1975.

*ANDERSON, GERALD H., & THOMAS F. STRANSKY CSP (eds.). Mission trends. No. 2: Evangelization. New York, Paramus, Toronto..., 1975.

?COOK, GUILLERMO. Profundidad en la evangelización: reflexiones sobre la evangelización a la luz de la Biblia y de la ciencia de la comunicación. Costa Rica, 1975.

*DHAVAMONY, MARIASUSAI, SJ (ed.). Evangelisation. Roma, 1975.

*DOUGLAS, JIM D. (ed.). Let the earth hear his voice: international congress on world evangelization Lausanne, Switzerland: official reference volume: papers and responses. Minneapolis, 1975.

*LAURENTIN, RENÉ. L'évangélisation après le quatrième synode. Paris, 1975.

GLASSER, ARTHUR F., et al. (eds.). Crucial dimensions in world evangelization. Pasadena, 1976.

*HOFINGER, JOHANNES, SJ. Evangelization and catechesis. New York, Paramus, & Toronto, 1976.

*LAAN, D.W. VAN DER. Enkele lijnen in de geschiedenis van de gereformeerde evangelisatie. Leusden, 1976.

PONTIFICIA UNIVERSITA URBANIANA. Evangelizzazione e culture: atti del congresso internazionale scientifico di missiologia, Roma, 5-12 Ottobre 1975. Roma, 1976. 3 vols.

?WIESKE, GÜNTER. Persönliche Evangelisation... Wuppertal, & Kassel, 1977.
First ed.: Wuppertal, 1974.

GREINACHER, NORBERT, & ALOIS MÜLLER (eds.). Evangelization in the world today. New York, 1979.

?SCHULTE, ANTON. Evangelisation praktisch. Moers, 1979.

*RIVIERE, L. LA (ed.). Evangelisatie. Kampen, 1980.

*BERTSCH, LUDWIG, & FELIX SCHLÖSSER (eds.). Evangelisation in der dritten Welt: Anstösse für Europa. Freiburg, Basel, & Wien, 1981.

*BOUW, W.J. (ed.). Evangelisatie: wat verstaan we er onder? ... Kampen, 1981.

*BOUW, W.J. Evangelisatie in de tachtiger jaren: het Pattaya-beraad over wereldevangelisatie en de betekenis daarvan voor Nederland. Amersfoort, 1982.

*CERDIC. Evangelisation and mission: international bibliography 1975-1982/ Evangelisation et mission: bibliographie internationale 1975-1982. Strasbourg, 1982. Bibliog.
CERDIC=Centre de recherche et de documentation des institutions chrétiennes.

*THEOLOGISCHE REALENZYKLOPÄDIE. 1982.
X, p. 636-641: Evangelisation (Walter J. Hollenweger).

WALSH, JOHN, MM. Evangelization and justice: new insights for Christian ministry. New York, 1982.

*WCE. 1982.
P. 117-121: Evangelization: quantifying the concept of evangelization.
P. 826: Evangelization.

ARIAS, MORTIMER. Announcing the reign of God: evangelization and the subversive memory of Jesus. Philadelphia, 1984.

*ROBERT, DANA L. The origin of the Student Volunteer watchword: 'The evangelization of the world in this generation'. In: IBMR, X (1986), p. 146-149.

*BARRETT, DAVID B. Evangelize! ... Birmingham, 1987.

*LMG. 1987.
P. 102-105: Evangelisation, Evangelisierung (David J. Bosch).

*BARRETT, DAVID B., & JAMES W. REAPSOME. Seven hundred plans to evangelize the world: the rise of a global evangelization movement. Birmingham, 1988.

?UNDERWOOD, B.E. Sixteen New Testament principles for world evangelization. Franklin Springs, 1988.

*ABRAHAM, WILLIAM J. The logic of evangelism. Grand Rapids, 1989.
P. 40-41: Evangelism, evangelization.

*COSTAS, ORLANDO E. Liberating news: a theology of contextual evangelization. New York, 1989.

*MUGAMBI, JESSE N.K. The biblical basis for evangelization: theological reflections based on an African experience. Nairobi, 1989.

*DAYTON, EDWARD R., & DAVID A. FRASER. Planning strategies for world evangelization; rev. ed. Grand Rapids, & Monrovia, 1990.
First ed.: 1980.

*BOSCH. 1991.
P. 409: Evangelism, evangelization.

POPE-LEVISON, PRISCILLA. Evangelization from a liberation perspective. New York, Bern, Frankfurt am Main..., 1991.

*WIJSSEN, FRANS (ed.). Evangelisatie in nieuw perspetief. Heerlen, 1991.

?BOFF, LEONARDO. New evangelization: good news to the poor. New York, 1992.

*LM. 1992.
P. 148-149: Evangelisierung.

48

*CHAMPAGNE, CLAUDE, OMI. La nouvelle évangélisation chez les épiscopats des églises du Premier-Monde. In: Mission, I (1994), p. 95-135.
*BEMMEL, HENDRIK A. VAN, & C. VAN BART. De nieuwe theologie en de evangelisatie-arbeid. Amersfoort, n.d.

2.3.5.2. THE THEOLOGY OF EVANGELIZATION

The name *theology of evangelization* is younger and less wide-spread than the name 'theology of evangelism'. Today, however, both Protestant authors (Hoekendijk, in: Revue de l'évangélisation 1959: 227-240; Costas 1973; 1989), and Roman Catholic authors (Amalorpavadass 1971; Dhavamony et al. 1972), use this term: normally without offering a definition.

I did not encounter any publication which has made a clear distinction between a 'theology of evangelism' and a 'theology of evangelization'. I prefer the last term, but am willing to use the first term as well. In the case of maintaining both terms, we can follow David B. Barrett and interpret the former as a theology of 'human evangelistic activity' (cf. Barrett 1987:78), and the latter as a theology of 'the whole range of evangelizing activity, both human and divine, as well as the overall situation and status produced by all such activities' (cf. Barrett 1987:78). However, I myself (cf. 2.3.5.1.) am inclined to interpret the former as a systematic theological discipline that is concerned with '*the view* emphasizing *evangel* thoughts and values', and the latter as a practical theological discipline that is concerned with '*the process*, or action, of making human beings and society *evangel*'.

*KANTONEN, TAITO A. Evangelium und Evangelisation: eine theologische Grundlegung christlichen Zeugendienstes. Berlin, 1957.
HOEKENDIJK, JOHANNES C. Plan d'étude sur la théologie de l'évangélisation et de la mission. In: Revue de l'évangélisation, LXXXIV (1959), p. 227-240.
*ÖKUMENISCHER RAT DER KIRCHEN. Salz der Erde: eine theologische Besinnung über die Evangelisation: zweite, überarbeitete Aufl. Genf, 1963.
POETSCH, HANS L. Theologie der Evangelisation. Bremen, 1967.
AMALORPAVADASS, DURAISAMY S. The theology of 'indirect evangelisation'. Bangalore, 1971.
*DHAVAMONY, MARIASUSAI, SJ (ed.). Evangelization, dialogue, and development: selected papers of the International Theological Conference, Nagpur (India) 1971. Roma, 1972.
      P. 21-39: The theology of evangelization in the Asian context (A.S. Amalorvapavadass).
      P. 41-53: Biblical theology of evangelization (Matthew Vellanickal).
      P. 105-116: Vatikan II and post conciliar theology of evangelization (Joseph Masson SJ).
*AMALORPAVADASS, DURAISAMY S. Theology of evangelisation in the Indian context. Bangalore, 1973.
COSTAS, ORLANDO E. (comp.). Hacia una teologia de la evangelización. Buenos Aires, 1973.
DAGRAS, MICHEL. Théologie de l'évangélisation. Paris, 1976.

BIFET, J. ESQUERDA. Teologia della evangelizzazione. Roma, & Brescia, 1980.
*HACKER, PAUL. Theological foundations of evangelization. St. Augustin, 1980.
*HANSEN, JOHANNES, & CHRISTIAN MÖLLER (eds.). Evangelisation und Theologie: Texte einer Begegnung. Neukirchen, 1980.
HOLMES, URBAN T. Turning to Christ: a theology of renewal and evangelization. New York, 1981.
*BARRETT, DAVID B. Evangelize!... Birmingham, 1987.
*COSTAS, ORLANDO E. Liberating news: a theology of contextual evangelization. Grand Rapids, 1989.

2.3.6. CONCLUSION

Although I have made it clear that the first full chair of mission studies was established as a chair in 'evangelistic theology', I can not recommend this first major name of mission studies - or one of its synonyms: 'evangelistics', 'theology of evangelism', 'theology of evangelization' - as a good one.

I have three main reasons for rejecting these names as relevant names to the whole of mission studies: 1. All four terms derived from the Greek verb *euangelizein* are in the field of 'theology' (cf. the first five minor names mentioned in 2.2.), and not in the field of 'science', and/or 'philosophy'. Missiology as a discipline, however, is much broader than '(evangelistic) theology', 'theology of evangelism', etc. (cf. next chapter). 2. The relations between the four terms derived from the Greek verb *euangelizein* are unclear. Are the nineteenth century terms 'evangelistic (theology)' and 'evangelistics' replaced nowadays by the twentieth century terms 'theology of evangelism' and 'theology of evangelization'? And if so, how can we make a good choice between 'theology of evangelism' and 'theology of evangelization'? Or, must we support both terms? 3. There is no unanimous opinion about the relation between mission and evangelism: are they on a par (WCC, et al.), or is evangelism/ evangelization the primary goal of mission (my own view)? And as a consequence: are 'mission studies' and 'evangelistics' on the same level (Free University of Amsterdam, Theological Universities of Kampen), or is 'evangelistics' not more than just a thorough part of 'missiology' (my own view)?

However, the already mentioned derivations from the Greek verb *euangelizein* are still important. Firstly, it is impossible to develop a comprehensive missiology by ignoring the existence and importance of the phenomena of 'evangelism' and 'evangelization'. And secondly, the widely-known terms 'theology of evangelism' and/or 'theology of evangelization' can still be used in the broader framework of missiology: i.e. as a thorough description of that important part of missionary theology which reflects on the primary goal of mission: i.e. 'to proclaim the gospel (Greek: *euangelizesthai*)' (1Cor. 1:17), in principles and practice, to our neighbours.

2.4. APOSTOLICS, APOSTOLO(LO)GY, THEOLOGY OF THE APOSTOLATE

2.4.1. APOSTELLEIN, APOSTOLE, APOSTOLOS

The second major name of mission studies is derived from the Greek verb *apostellein*=to send (out/forth), which occurs 131 times in the New Testament. Here I quote a few texts: 'These twelve Jesus *sent out*' (Matt. 10:5); 'See, I [Jesus] am *sending* you *out* like sheep into the midst of wolves' (Matt. 10:16); 'When I [Jesus] *sent* you *out* without a purse, bag, or sandals, did you lack anything?' (Luke 22:35); 'And how are they to proclaim him [Christ] unless they are *sent*?' (Rom. 10:15); 'For Christ did not *sent* me [Paul] to baptize but to proclaim the gospel' (1Cor. 1:17).

The Greek noun *apostole*=apostolate, apostleship, (com)mission, occurs 4 times in the New Testament. In Acts we read: 'Show us which one of these two you have chosen to take the place in this ministry and *apostleship* from which Judas turned aside to go to his own place' (Acts 1:24-25; cf. Rom. 1:5; 1Cor. 9:2; Gal. 2:8).

The Greek noun *apostolos* which occurs 79 times in the New Testament means: one who is sent, i.e. envoy, ambassador, delegate, messenger, missionary, apostle. Here I mention the following texts: 'With great power *the apostles* gave their testimony to the resurrection of the Lord Jesus' (Acts 4:33); 'Now I [Paul] am speaking to you gentiles. Inasmuch then as I am *an apostle* to the gentiles, I glorify my ministry' (Rom. 11:13).

In the Middle Ages people did not only use the Latin terms *propagatio evangelii*, *propagatio fidei* and *propagatio christianae religionis* (cf. 2.2.6.), but also the Latin terms *praedicatio apostolica* (=apostolic preaching) and *apostolatus* (=apostolate). In fact the modern noun 'apostolate' is a direct derivation of the Latin word *apostolatus*, which in turn is known as the Vulgate translation of *apostole*=(com)mission in the Greek New Testament.

*DAUBANTON. 1911.
      P. 48-50: Apostellein.
TDNT. 1964-1976.
      I, p. 398-447: Apostello (pempo), exapostello, apostolos, pseudapostolos, apostole (Karl H. Rengstorf).
      *TWNT. 1933-1978.
      I, p. 397-446: Apostello (pempo), exapostello, apostolos, pseudapostolos, apostole (Karl H. Rengstorf).

2.4.2. APOSTOLICS

Johan T.L. Danz (1832:362-366) introduced the German term *Apostolik*. Others (Schweitzer 1836:44; Hinkel 1843-1845; Von Zezschwitz 1876:169) followed him. Willem Muurling (1860:573) defined this new discipline as 'the science of mission'.

This term was criticized by Abraham Kuyper (1894:III,518-519), François E. Daubanton (1911:227-228), Johan H. Bavinck (1960:XVI-VII), and Johannes Verkuyl (1978:1-2). Kuyper, on the one hand, recognized the term 'apostolics' as suitable to express the notion of missions in general, but, on the other hand, feared that the use of this term would bring us almost automatically to the conviction of Adrianus Saravia (1531-1613) that the mission mandate fully rests in the church, i.e. in the apostolic succession (the episcopal system). Thereupon Bavinck declared: 'The terms *apostolate* and *apostolic* are easily misunderstood and must therefore be used with caution, but this does not warrant their rejection. Calvin has noted that both the apostolate and the office of the evangelist are not permanent; they were utilized by Christ to establish his church. Nevertheless God can subsequently raise apostles or evangelists for a special task. Such cases are very unusual, however, and do not lend themselves to the construction of a science'. And finally Verkuyl has objected that the term 'apostolics' erases the necessary difference between the disciplines of missiology and evangelistics. My own view differs from that of Verkuyl: I look at the eradication of this difference as an advantage of the term at issue. The objections of Kuyper and Bavinck, however, are far more serious. If the use of the words 'apostolate' and 'apostolic' entail the acceptance of the apostolic succession (episcopalism), these terms must be avoided. However, I really think that this is not the case.

After the Second World War the term 'apostolics' was only used by Johannes Severijn (1948:87) at Utrecht: he holds the broad view that 'the science of mission' is a part of 'apostolics' (cf. the famous article on 'the apostolate of the church' in the 1951 church order of the Netherlands Reformed Church to which I refer in 2.4.4.1.).

DANZ, JOHANN T.L. Encyklopaedie und Methodologie der theologischen Wissenschaften. Weimar, 1832.
SCHWEITZER, ALEXANDER. Über Begriff und Eintheilung der praktischen Theologie. Leipzig, 1836.
HINKEL, KARL A.F. Die Bekehrung der Welt zu Jesus Christus und das christliche Missionswerk: ein Beitrag zur Apostolik und Apologetik des Christenthums, nach den Worten der Heiligen Schrift und den Zeugnissen der Reichsgeschichte. Berlin, 1843-1845. 3 vols.
*MUURLING, WILLEM. Practische godgeleerdheid ... Groningen, 1860.
    P. 573-637: Apostoliek.
*ZEZSCHWITZ, CARL A.G. VON. System der praktischen Theologie. Leipzig, 1876.

*KUYPER, ABRAHAM. Encyclopaedie der heilige godgeleerdheid. Amsterdam, 1894. 3 vols.
*DAUBANTON. 1911.
    P. 227-228: Apostoliek.
*SEVERIJN, JOHANNES. Encyclopaedie der theologische wetenschap. Haarlem, 1948.
*BAVINCK, JOHAN H. An introduction to the science of missions. Philadelphia, 1960.
    P. XVI-XVII: Apostolics.
*VERKUYL, JOHANNES. Contemporary missiology... Grand Rapids, 1978.

2.4.3. APOSTOLO(LO)GY

In passing I mention the term *apostolo(lo)gy*, which is a synonym of the term 'missio(no)logy' (2.5.3.; cf. the term 'evangelistology' in 2.3.3.).

This correct name obtained very little support. However, some Roman Catholic and Protestant authors were ready to support it. Here I only mention Lucien-Mary Dewailly OP in 1947 (Seumois 1952:91,93,100; cf. Paventi 1949:40; Santos Hernandez 1961:206,211) and the Netherlands reformed theologian Hendrik Berkhof who used this word at the same time (NThT 1947/48:152).

*BERKHOF, HENDRIK. De apostoliciteit van de kerk. In: Nederlands theologisch tijdschrift, II (1947/48), p. 146-160.
*PAVENTI, SAVERIO. La chiesa missionaria: manuale di missionologia dottrinale. Roma, 1949.
*SEUMOIS. 1952.
*SANTOS HERNANDEZ. 1961.

2.4.4. THEOLOGY OF THE APOSTOLATE

2.4.4.1. APOSTOLATE

> ... the term *apostolate* ... is, in fact,
> as old as the church ...
> *Johannes C. Hoekendijk (Wieser 1966:37-38).*

C. Peter Wagner (1989) does not mention the term 'apostolate' at all. David B. Barrett (WCE 1982:816), however, does mention it, but he suggests that 'apostolate' is a distinct Roman Catholic term: 'the service of souls and spread of the faith, discharged by bishops, priests, religious and laity'. He is not quite right in doing so: because (1) this term dates back to the early church (Vulgate translation of the Bible); and (2) Protestants, especially in the Netherlands, have used and are using this term as well. In Roman Catholic literature we frequently find expressions like the 'mission(ary) apostolate' (de Pressensé 1879; Bühlmann, in: NZM 1954:81- 95; Seumois 1961; Ohm 1962:39;

Richardson 1965; da Nembro 1968) and the 'lay apostolate' (Specker, & Bühlmann 1961; cf. WCE 1982:816), which do not make sense in Protestantism. However, some Protestants have adopted the term 'lay apostolate' (Schram, in: DH 1965:210-216), which on close inspection is a supplement of the term 'hierarchical apostolate' (Ohm 1962:372,458; DEM 1991:583-584). The expression 'mission(ary) apostolate' is a tautology, and therefore totally 'inappropriate' (Ohm 1962:37).

Especially the Netherlands Reformed Church and its theologians have propagated the term 'apostolate' in a very broad sense. In the new church order of this church (1951) a key article is dedicated to 'the apostolate of the church', i.e. to: 1. the dialogue with Israel; 2. the missionary work; and 3. the spread of the gospel, and the continuing work on the Christianization of the life of the people in the Reformation sense (my tr.; cf. Jansen Schoonhoven, in: Hermelink, & Margull 1959:278-284). Arnold A. van Ruler at Utrecht is still known as one of the main architects of this article. Other Netherlands reformed theologians have adopted this term as well (Schuurman 1920; Jansen Schoonhoven 1951; Pop 1967; Hoedemaker, in: NThT 1976:141-154; idem 1978; cf. Brisbois 1972 on Kraemer, Hoekendijk, and Van Leeuwen). However, theologians of the Reformed Churches in the Netherlands (De apostolische kerk 1954:98-133; Verkuyl 1978:1-2) were never open to the reception of this new name (they experienced it as an eradication of the distinction between 'mission' and 'evangelism').

Outside the Netherlands, Protestant theologians like R. Pierce Beaver (Anderson 1961:263-265), Johannes L.C. Abineno (1969:II,7-132), and Eugène Mallo (Markhoff 1971:121-139) have frequently used the term 'apostolate'. Here I quote only Beaver, who has developed a view on apostolate which is nearly as broad as the formulation of the above- mentioned church order of the Netherlands Reformed Church: 'There are two supplementary and complementary parts to the apostolate which can be separated or the one of them neglected only to the hurt of the church's health and to the disobedience to the great commission. One is the local apostolate, *evangelism*... The other aspect of the apostolate is the *sending* - mission in the more traditional sense. It is the evangelistic outreach beyond the congregation and home locality... Evangelism and mission are the two poles of the apostolate'.

In the literature at issue, especially in Roman Catholic publications, several new terms are proposed and new distinctions are made. Here I only call attention to the terms 'heathen apostolate' (Thauren 1927; Schmidlin 1929), 'universal apostolate' (Trueblood 1972:69-71), and 'last apostolate' (Durrwell 1973:135-160); and to the following distinctions: (1) 'apostolate' and 'implantation of the church' (Seumois 1952:218-219); and (2) 'direct apostolate' and 'indirect apostolate' (Seumois 1952:335-339). This last

54

distinction must, of course, be related to the distinction mentioned in the previous section 2.3.5.1.: 'direct evangelization' and 'indirect evangelization'.

DALLY, NICOLAS. Histoire de l'apostolat... Paris, 1846.

PRESSENSÉ, EDMOND D. DE. L'apostolat missionnaire... Paris, 1879.

SEUFERT, WILHELM. Der Ursprung und die Bedeutung des Apostolates in der christlichen Kirche der ersten zwei Jahrhunderte... Leiden, 1887.

HAUPT, ERICH. Zum Verständniss des Apostolats im Neuen Testament. Halle, 1896.

*GRÖSZEL, WOLFGANG. Die Mission und die evangelische Kirche im 17. Jahrhundert. Gotha, 1897.

   P. 68-69: Die Lehre vom Apostolat.

MONNIER, HENRI. La notion de l'apostolat, des origines à Irénée. Paris, 1903.

*THAUREN, JOHANNES, SVD. Die Akkomodation im katholischen Heidenapostolat: eine missionstheoretische Studie. Münster in Westfalen, 1927.

MUSEUM LESSIANUM, SECTION MISSIOLOGIQUE. Obstacles à l'apostolat: compte rendu de la septième semaine de missiologie de Louvain (1929). Louvain, 1929.

SCHMIDLIN, JOSEPH. Das gegenwärtige Heidenapostolat im Fernen Osten. Münster in Westfalen, 1929.

*JANSEN SCHOONHOVEN, EVERT. Het apostolaat der kerk en de uitwendige zending. Oegstgeest, 1951.

*KRAEMER, HENDRIK, DRYO MESTOKO, CARL W. NORTIER, et al. (eds.). Over alle bergen: geschriften van Dr. B(arend) M. Schuurman, zendeling-leraar op Java... 's-Gravenhage, 1952.

   P. 100-113: Discipelschap en apostolaat (1920).

*SEUMOIS. 1952.

   P. 218-219: L'apostolat, l'implantation.

   P. 335-337: Apostolat direct.

   P. 337-339: Apostolat indirect.

CHAVASSE, ANTOINE, HENRI DENIS, JEAN FRISQUE, et al. Église et apostolat. Paris, & Tournai, 1953.

ROCHE, ALOYSIUS. In the track of the gospel: an outline of the Christian apostolate from Pentecost to the present. London, 1953.

*DE APOSTOLISCHE KERK: theologische bijdragen ter gelegenheid van het honderdjarig bestaan der Theologische Hogeschool van de Gereformeerde Kerken in Nederland aangeboden door de hoogleraren. Kampen, 1954.

   P. 98-133: 'Het apostolaat van de kerk' in deze tijd (Gerrit Brillenburg Wurth).

*BÜHLMANN, WALBERT, OFMCap. Science missionnaire et apostolat missionnaire. In: NZM, X (1954), p. 81-95.

*RENGSTORF, KARL H. Apostolat und Predigtamt... Stuttgart, & Köln, 1954.

?WYK, J. ALEX. VAN. Die apostolaat van die kerk: 'n studie oor sekere nuwere gedagtes in verband met die roeping van die kerk tot evangelisasie en sending. Morija, 1958.

*HERMELINK, JAN, & HANS J. MARGULL (eds.). Basileia: Walter Freytag zum 60. Geburtstag. Stuttgart, 1959.

   P. 278-284: Der Artikel 'Vom Apostolat der Kirche' in der Kirchenordnung der Niederländischen Reformierten Kirche (Evert Jansen Schoonhoven).

*ANDERSON. 1961.

   P. 258-268: The apostolate of the church (R. Pierce Beaver).

SEUMOIS, ANDRÉ V., OMI. L'anima dell'apostolato missionario: seconda ed. Bologna, Milano, Parma..., 1961.

First ed.: Bologna, Milano, Parma..., 1958.

*SPECKER, JOHANN, SMB, & WALBERT BÜHLMANN OFMCap. (eds.). Das Laienapostolat in den Missionen: Festschrift Prof.Dr. Johannes Beckmann SMB zum 60. Geburtstag dargeboten... Schöneck, & Beckenried, 1961.

KLOSTERMANN, FERDINAND. Das christliche Apostolat. Innsbrück, Wien, & München, 1962.

*OHM. 1962.

    P. 37-43: Bezeichnungen für das Werk der Glaubensverbreitung.

    P. 39: Missionsapostolat.

    P. 372, 458: Hierarchisches Apostolat, Apostolat der Laien.

    P. 542-546: Das Apostolat des christlichen Anlitzes.

*DANKBAAR, WILLEM F., & MARINUS DE JONGE (eds.). Inleiding tot de theologische studie... Groningen, 1965.

    P. 185-200: Apostolaat (Evert Jansen Schoonhoven).

*RICHARDSON, WILLIAM J., MM (ed.). The modern mission apostolate: a symposium. New York, 1965.

*SCHRAM, PETER L. Lekenapostolaat. In: DH, XVIII (1965), p. 210-216.

THOMAS, JOSEPH, SJ. L'apostolat de l'église: interrogations actuelles. Paris, 1966.

*WIESER, THOMAS (ed.). Planning for mission: working papers on the new quest for missionary communities. New York, 1966.

    P. 37-48: Notes on the meaning of mission(ary) (Johannes C. Hoekendijk).

    First ed.: Concept, special issue, V (1963), p. 11-19.

    Ger. tr.: 1965.

    Fr. tr.: 1966.

*ALEXANDER, CALVERT, SJ. The missionary dimension: Vatican II and the world apostolate. Milwaukee, 1967.

*POP, FRANÇOIS J. Zo is God bij de mensen: profiel van het apostolaat. 's-Gravenhage, 1967.

NEMBRO, METODIO DA, OFMCap. Un contributo all' apostolato missionario. Roma, 1968.

*ABINENO, JOHANNES L.C. Sekitar theologia praktika. Djakarta, 1969. 2 vols.

    II, p. 7-132: Apostolat geredja.

AMALORPAVADASS, DURAISAMY S. Approaches in our apostolate among non-Christians. Bangalore, 1970.

*CONCISE DICTIONARY. 1971.

    P. 28-29: Apostolate (Stephen C. Neill).

*MARKHOFF, GÉRARD (ed.). Manuel de théologie pratique. Yaoundé, 1971.

    P. 121-139: L'apostolat (Eugène Mallo).

*BRISBOIS, JACQUES, SJ. Apostolat, religion, eschatologie dans la théologie de la mission selon H. Kraemer, J.C. Hoekendijk, A.T. van Leeuwen. Paris, 1972. Thèse Faculté de Théologie de l'Institut Catholique de Paris.

*MEIDEN, ANNE VAN DER. Mensen winnen: een verkenning van de relatie tussen ethiek, propaganda, en apostolaat. N.p., 1972. Diss. Utrecht.

*SEDOS (ed.). Foundations of mission theology: second printing. New York, 1972.

    P. 63-86: The apostolate to non-Christians (Duraisamy S. Amalorpavadass).

    First Fr. ed.: 1969.

    SEDOS=Servizio Documentazione e Studi.

*TRUEBLOOD, ELTON. The validity of the Christian mission. New York, Evanston, & San Francisco, 1972.

*DURRWELL, FRANÇOIS X., CSSR. The apostolate and the church. London, & New York, 1973.

    First ed.: Le mystère pascal, source de l'apostolat. Paris, 1970.

*JANSEN SCHOONHOVEN, EVERT. Variaties op het thema 'zending'. Kampen, 1974.

    P. 34-47: Apostolaat en eschatologie (1955).

*HOEDEMAKER, LIBERTUS A. De oorspronkelijkheid van het apostolaat: een paar kanttekeningen bij het werk van Hans Hoekendijk. In: Nederlands theologisch tijdschrift, XXX (1976), p. 141-154.

*HOEDEMAKER, LIBERTUS A. Met Christus bij anderen: opmerkingen over dialoog en apostolaat. Baarn,1978.

*VERKUYL, JOHANNES. Contemporary missiology... Grand Rapids, 1978. *WCE. 1982.
      P. 816: Apostolate.

*WAGNER. 1989.

*DEM. 1991.
      P. 583-584: The lay apostolate in the Roman Catholic Church.

*LM. 1992.
      P. 43-44: Apostolat/apostolisch.

*SCHRAM, PETER L. (ed.). Alledaags geloven: gedachten over het lekenapostolaat. Kampen, n.d.

2.4.4.2. THEOLOGY OF THE APOSTOLATE

Both Roman Catholic and Protestant theologians have developed a *theology of the apostolate* which as a term emerged before the Second World War (cf. Charles, in: Nouvelle revue théologique 1940:385-396). Neither Arnold A. van Ruler (1953) nor Léon-Joseph Suenens (1953) has offered a definition of this discipline which has the *apostolate* or *world apostolate* (Association of Professors of Missions 1964; Alexander 1967) as its object.

Georg F. Vicedom (1965:68-70), Marc R. Spindler (1967:82-93), and David J. Bosch (1980:176-178) have commented on the Netherlands Reformed theology of the apostolate. Bosch writes about the stimulus of the 1947 World Missionary Conference in Whitby on post-war missionary thinking: 'in Dutch missiology it led to the unfolding of the theology of the apostolate. This latter development meant that, in addition to Tambaram's distinction between a church-centric and a society-centric mission, there now emerged the concept of a mission-centric church'.

John Bolt has not translated Van Ruler's Dutch term *Theologie van het Apostolaat* as 'theology of the apostolate', but as 'theology of mission', which in his view (1989:199) is 'the more conventional theological usage'. I regret this eradication of distinct language, although I cordially agree with Bolt that the name 'theology of the apostolate' is unconventional in the U.S.A. Here I suggest that the terms 'theology of the apostolate' and 'theology of mission' are essentially interchangable. Many theologians (Arnold A. van Ruler, R. Pierce Beaver, et al.), however, consider 'theology of the apostolate' as a much broader term than 'theology of mission'.

CHARLES, PIERRE, SJ. Tactique missionnaire ou théologie de l'apostolat. In: Nouvelle revue théologique, LXVII (1940), p. 385-396.

SUENENS, LÉON-JOSEPH. Theology of the apostolate of the Legion of Mary, with letter of papal approbation. Techny, 1953.

*Fr. ed.: Théologie de l'apostolat: commentaire doctrinal de la promesse légionnaire. Bruges, 1951.

Ger. tr.: 1952.

Sp. tr.: 1954.

*Dutch tr.: n.d.

CONGAR, YVES M.J., OP. Theology of the apostolate. In: Worldmission, VII/3 (1956), p. 283-294.

*ARNOLD, FRANZ X. Pour une théologie de l'apostolat: principes et histoire. Tournai, 1961.

First ed.: Grundsätzliches und Geschichtliches zur Theologie der Seelsorge: das Prinzip des Gott-Menschlichen. Freiburg im Breisgau, 1949.

SEUMOIS, ANDRÉ V. Apostolat: structure théologique. Rome, 1961.

Sp. tr.: 1968.

ASSOCIATION OF PROFESSORS OF MISSIONS. The theology of the world apostolate: common ground for Protestant - Catholic consideration, held at Eastern Baptist Theological Seminary, Philadelphia, 1964. N.p., 1964.

*VICEDOM, GEORG F. The mission of God: an introduction to a theology of mission. Saint Louis, 1965.

P. 68-70: The theology of the apostolate.

*SPINDLER, MARC R. La mission, combat pour le salut du monde. Neuchâtel, 1967. Thèse Strasbourg.

P. 82-93: La théologie de l'apostolat.

*BOSCH, DAVID J. Witness to the world: the Christian mission in theological perspective. London, 1980.

P. 176-178: Theology of the apostolate.

*RULER, ARNOLD A. VAN. Calvinist trinitarianism and theocentric politics: essays toward a public theology: tr. John Bolt. Lewistin, Queenston, & Lampeter, 1989.

P. 199-226: A theology of mission.

*Dutch ed.: Theologie van het apostolaat. Nijkerk, 1953.

*Ger. tr.: 1954.

2.4.5. CONCLUSION

The second major name of mission studies is derived from the Greek verb *apostellein*=to send, and therefore much more appropriate than the first major name, which is derived from the verb *euangelizein*.

In fact, derivations of *apostellein* are the best names we can find. I prefer the contemporary term 'apostology' to the nineteenth century term 'apostolics'. I regard this contemporary term as a synonym of the term 'missiology' which will be dealt with in the next section. In that section I will also explain why this study is not entitled 'apostology', but 'missiology'.

The term 'apostolate' (of Greek origin) has exactly the same meaning and purpose as the term 'mission' (of Latin origin). Some missiologists, however, have wrongly used the former in a very broad sense, and the latter in a very narrow sense: on the one hand, they call attention to *'mission and evangelism'*, and, on the other hand, they refuse to speak about *'apostolate and* evangelism'. In my view, 'evangelism' is always included in both 'apostolate' and 'mission'. Therefore I consider 'theology of evangelism' as an important part of the 'theology of the apostolate' which must be treated as a synonym of the 'theology of mission'.

The use of the term 'apostology' and/or the term '(theology of the) apostolate' must especially be recommended to Christians and churches in countries (for instance Islamic countries) where Christian 'mission' is either put under restraint, or is totally forbidden.

2.5. MISSIONICS, MISSIO(NO)LOGY, THE PHILOSOPHY OF MISSION, THE SCIENCE OF MISSION, THE THEOLOGY OF MISSION, MISSIONARY THEOLOGY

The third and last major name of mission studies is derived from the Latin verb *mittere*, which is frequently used in the Vulgate translation of the Bible. However, the Latin nouns *missio* (plural: *missiones*) and *missionarius* do not occur in the Vulgate (Seumois 1952:66 has stated that the latter noun has only been used since 1625).

The terms 'missionics' and 'missio(no)logy' are derived from the noun *missio(nes)* which only in modern times became a *terminus technicus*. The terms 'philosophy of mission', 'science of mission', 'theology of mission', and 'missionary theology' go back to the same Latin noun.

*SEUMOIS. 1952.

2.5.1. MITTERE, MISSIO(NES), MISSIONARIUS

> Mission as applied to the work of the church
> means the *specific intention* of bearing witness
> to the gospel of salvation in Jesus Christ
> at the borderline between faith and unbelief.
> *James A. Scherer (1987:37).*

In the Vulgate the word *mittere* occurs as translation of the Greek verbs *apostellein* and *pempein* which also means 'to send (out/forth)'. The famous saying of Jesus: 'Peace be with you. As the Father has *sent* (Greek: *apostellein*) me, so I *send* (Greek: *pempein*) you', is translated in the Vulgate by using the verb *mittere* twice: 'Sicut *misit* me Pater, et ego *mitto* vos' (John 20:21). Therefore we must conclude: *apostellein*=*mittere*; so we can state: *apostole*=*apostolate*=*missio*; *apostolics*=*missionics*; etc.

In the 16th century the term *missio(nes)* was introduced by the *Societas Jesu* (1534) as a key term. Ignace of Loyola (1491-1556) published *Constititiones circa missiones* (1544/45), which state that all members of the Society must be willing to be sent to their special fields, i.e. to their 'divisions' or 'missions'. Here the term 'missions' means both the 'destinations', and the 'territories' to which the people were sent by their superiors. Thereafter this new term is also used to convey in language both 'going' to the territories involved, and the 'tasks' (or 'functions') to be performed at the places of destination. In 1588 José de Acosta SJ (1540-1600) published at Salamanca *De natura novi orbis libri duo, et de promulgatione evangelii apud barbaros, sive de procuranda Indorum salute libri sex*, in which he defined 'missions' as 'the expeditions and voyages which in all towns are attempted for the sake of the divine Word' (liber V, caput 21; my tr.). Other Jesuits have connected these expeditions with concrete destinations in both Asia and Africa: *Brevis et compendiosa narratio missionum* (1592), is concerned about India, Japan, Ethiopia, Peru, and Mexico, whereas Luis de Guzman SJ, *Historia de las missiones* (Alcala 1601), has dealt with India, China, and Japan.

Other Roman Catholic authors have followed in the footsteps of the Jesuits. Here I only mention three publications which also have used the plural *missiones*: Joannes a Jesu Maria OCD, *Tractatus quo asseruntur missiones, et rationes adversae refelluntur: votum, seu consilium pro missionibus, quo ad nova objecta respondetur* (1604); idem, *Instructio missionum* (1605); and Thomas a Jesu OCD, *Stimulus missionum, sive de propaganda a religiosis per universum orbem fide* (1610). Afterwards the singular *missio* occurs in the vocabulary of Juan Lopez OP: *Mision en el Iapon* (1621).

The *Sacra congregatio de propaganda fide* (1622) received the term *missio(nes)* with thanks to the Jesuits. In its first letter (15 January 1622) to the apostolic nuncios, the *Congregatio* already used this term 4 times. Pope Gregory XV determined the tasks of the *Congregatio* in his constitution *Inscrutabili divinae* (22 June 1622), in which the term *missiones* also occurs: 'With regard to all *missions* who are called to preach and teach the gospel, they [i.e. the leaders of the *Congregatio*] must watch the Catholic doctrine, and appoint and transfer the necessary personnel' (cf. Seumois 1952:73; my tr.). André V. Seumois (1952:61-84), Édouard Loffeld CSSp (1956:357-370), Angel Santos Hernandez SJ (1961:9-67), et al. provide us with many more details about the use of the term *missio(nes)* in the 17th and subsequent centuries.

In Roman Catholic law, liturgy (cf. Braam, in: MR 1941:207-216; 1949:131-133), and literature we can find several special terms and distinctions. I mention here the term *missio canonica* (RGG 1960:IV,969; Riedel-Spangenberger 1991), and the following distinctions: (1) mission countries (=*terrae missionis*) and church provinces (=*provinciae eclesiasticae*);

and (2) holy missions (=*sacrae missiones*) and missions *ad gentes* (=*missiones exterae*).

Protestants have translated the Latin word *missio* into German, Dutch, and English: *Sendung*, *zending* and *sending* respectively. In Germany Gustav Warneck used this noun to define the three main sections of his *Evangelische Missionslehre* (1892-1903): (1) the basis of *sending*; (2) the agencies of *sending*; and (3) the enterprise of *sending*. In Germany people also created the expression: *Sammlung und Sendung*, i.e. 'gathering and sending' (cf. Freytag 1959). In the Netherlands the noun *zending* is more domesticated than *Sendung* in Germany and *sending* in the United Kingdom and the U.S.A.: both Johannes C. Neurdenburg (1879), François E. Daubanton (1911), Johan H. Bavinck (1954), and Johannes Verkuyl (1975) entitled their missiological handbooks: *zendingswetenschap* (=mission science) (see the bibliography of 3.3.2.). And in English we encounter the following statement of R. Pierce Beaver: '...*sending* is intimately bound up with *evangelism*. When the *sending* to the "ends of the earth" is neglected, the wellsprings of evangelism dry up' (Anderson 1961:264). Outside the Netherlands, however, Protestants use the noun 'mission' much more than the just mentioned translations of this word in the Germanic languages.

In Protestant literature we also meet new terms and distinctions. The Latin term *missio Dei* (=God's mission) was remarkably not put into contemporary circulation by a famous Roman Catholic author, but by the Protestant Karl W. Hartenstein and the World Missionary Conference of Willingen 1952 (Rosin 1972:23), in order 'to find a basis for missionary activity of the Protestant Christian world in the activity of the Triune God himself' (Concise dictionary 1971:387). Hereafter the Latin terms *missio Christi* (=Christ's mission), *missio ecclesiae* (=the mission of the church), and *missio hominum* (=the mission of all human beings), came into being. The traditional distinction between 'mission at home' (=home mission), and 'mission in foreign countries' (=foreign mission) still exists, but has become irrelevant since the influential World Missionary Conference of Mexico City (1963) introduced the concept of 'mission in six continents': Christians in all six continents are now bound to 'the common witness of the whole church, bringing the whole gospel to the whole world' (Orchard 1964:175).

Here I can present a long list of definitions of the term 'mission(s)' (cf. the list of definitions on 'evangelism' in 2.3.4.1.), but I will resist this temptation. I agree with the following statement by James A. Scherer (1987:243) about definitions: 'Discourse about mission is hampered by a growing lack of preciseness about what any given speaker means when speaking of mission. Clearer definitions of the scope, content, and goal of each of these terms, biblically grounded and related to the meaning of *missio Dei*, are needed to guide the church's activity'. Scherer's definition of 'mission' is excellent: 'the total activity of the church in preaching, teaching, healing, nurturing Christian communities, and witnessing to the kingdom, including advocacy of justice and service to humanity' (:244). However, Scherer appended to this new formulation an old-fashioned definition of 'evangelization': 'the specific task of awakening or reawakening faith in Jesus Christ where it no longer exists or has ceased to exist'.

We have observed that the plural *missiones* became a *terminus technicus* prior to the singular *missio*. In the same way, the plural 'missions' became popular before the singular 'mission'. However, the situation has changed remarkably: today the singular *missio Dei* is considered to be of primary importance, and the plural *missiones ecclesiae* of secondary importance. After a long discussion, the International Missionary Council had the courage to change the name of its periodical: from *International Review of Missions* to *International Review of Mission*. Stephen C. Neill (1986:477) stated: 'The age of missions ended. The age of mission began'. And David J. Bosch (1991:391) added: 'It follows that we have to distinguish between mission and missions. We cannot without ado claim that what we do is identical to the *missio Dei*; our missionary activities are only authentic insofar as they reflect participation in the mission of God'. I whole-heartedly follow this new trend of missionary thinking, which originates from the World Missionary Conference of Willingen (1952). And therefore I adopt the term *world mission* (singular) as well, which became widely known by the existence and publications of the Commission on *World Mission* and Evangelism (CWME; my italics) in the World Council of Churches.

*WARNECK. 1892-1903.
    I, p. 1-8: Begriff der Mission.
GRENTRUP, THEODORUS, SVD. Die Definition des Missionsbegriffes. In: ZM, III (1913), p. 265-274.
RIJCKEVORSEL, LUDWIG J. VAN, SJ. Missie en missieactie: tweede dr. Nijmegen, 1917.
    *First ed.: Nijmegen, 1915.
*SCHMIDLIN. 1925.
    P. 11-24: Grundbegriffe.
*SCHOMERUS. 1935.
    P. 1-4 : Die Bedeutung des Wortes 'Mission'.
    P. 4-6 : Die begriffliche Definition von 'Mission'.
*BRAAM, JOHANN, MSC. 'Missio' und 'Missionarius' im römischen Brevier: ein Beitrag zur Geschichte des Proprium Sanctorum und der katholischen Missionsterminologie. In: MR, IV (1941), p. 207-216; no series number (1949), p. 131-133 (Nachtrag).
*SEUMOIS. 1952.
    P. 61-84: Le terme 'mission'.
*LOFFELD, ÉDOUARD, CSSp. Le problème cardinal de la missiologie et des missions catholiques. Rhenen, 1956. Diss. Nijmegen.
    P. 357-370: Le mot 'mission'.
*RGG. 1957-1965.

IV, p. 969: Missio canonica (Hans Barion).

*ANDERSON. 1961.

    P. 258-268: The apostolate of the church (R. Pierce Beaver).

*HERMELINK, JAN, & HANS J. MARGULL (eds.). Walter Freytag: Reden und Aufsätze. München, 1961. 2 vols.

    I, p. 150-155: Sammlung und Sendung: von der Kirche unter den Völkern (1959).

*SANTOS HERNANDEZ. 1961.

    P. 9-67: El término 'Misíon'.

*OHM. 1962.

    P. 33-57: Missionsbegriff.

*ORCHARD, RONALD K. (ed.). Witness in six continents: records of the meeting of the CWME of the WCC held in Mexico City, December 8th to 19th, 1963. London, 1964.

*VICEDOM, GEORG F. The mission of God... Saint Louis, 1965.

*WIESER, THOMAS (ed.). Planning for mission... New York, 1966.

    P. 37-48: Notes on the meaning of mission(ary) (Johannes C. Hoekendijk).

*CONCISE DICTIONARY. 1971.

    P. 387: Missio Dei (Georg F. Vicedom).

*WINSEN, GERARDUS A.C. VAN, CM. Missio 1900-1970: fasen van Rooms-katholieke bezinning op een kerngedachte. Leiden, 1971.

*ROSIN, HELLMUT H. 'Missio Dei': an examination of the origin, contents, and function of the term in Protestant missiological discussion. Leiden, 1972.

    *Dutch ed.: Missio Dei: term en functie in de zendingstheologische discussie. Leiden, 1971.

*NEILL, STEPHEN C. A history of Christian missions: rev. for the second ed. by Owen Chadwick. Harmondsworth, 1986.

*STOTT, JOHN R.W. Christian mission in the modern world. Eastbourne, 1986.

    P. 15-34: Mission.

*SCHERER, JAMES A. Gospel, church, and kingdom: comparative studies in world mission theology. Minneapolis, 1987.

    P. 243-244: What is mission today?

*BOSCH. 1991.

    P. 389-393: Mission as missio Dei.

*RIEDEL-SPANGENBERGER, ILONA. Sendung in der Kirche: die Entwicklung des Begriffs 'missio canonica' und seine Bedeutung in der kirchlichen Rechtssprache. Paderborn, München, Wien..., 1991.

2.5.2. MISSIONICS

Parallel to the terms 'evangelistics' and 'apostolics', the term *missionics* has also been proposed. I do not know the name of any missiologist who has propagated this name. Daubanton (1911:235) discussed this term, but did not refer to any previous author who used it. He rejected this 'Roman' name. Thereafter nobody is known to have supported this term.

    'Missionics' is essentially a synonym of 'apostolics', and as strong and as weak as 'apostolics'. However, the last term is more frequently used than its Latin parallel.

*DAUBANTON. Prolegomena. 1911.
    P. 235: Missioniek.

2.5.3. MISSIO(NO)LOGY

The term *missiology* was coined by Ludwig J. van Rijckevorsel SJ (1915:57).
Thereafter it is frequently used by both Roman Catholic and Protestant writers.
    In Roman Catholic mission literature two points are debated. The first
question is whether the term under consideration must be spelled as
'missiology' (van Rijckevorsel, et al.), or 'missionology' (Mioni 1921, et al.).
In this case I prefer the haplography (cf. the term 'apostology' instead of
'apostolology'), although we speak about 'climatology' (instead of
'climalogy'), 'ontology' (instead of 'onlogy'), and 'ornithology' (in stead of
'ornology') (cf. Seumois 1952:85-106; Santos Hernandez 1961:199-223).
    Secondly, Joseph Schmidlin (1925:117) equated 'missiology' with
'practical mission theory' (Ger.: *praktische Missionstheorie*). This narrow
concept of 'missiology' (cf. DEM 1991:689: 'the systematic consideration of
the nature of the Christian mission'), has been overruled by those authors who
accept 'missiology' as a term which covers the whole field of mission studies
(cf. DEM 1991:689: 'the whole range of studies appropriate to the
understanding of mission, its context and practical application'). Today this last
and broad interpretation of the term 'missiology' is generally accepted in both
Roman Catholic and Protestant circles.
    From the very beginning, Protestants had a negative attitude towards
'missiology' (cf. 'missionics'). For instance, Raoul S.P. Allier declared in his
review of the Report of the Sixth Missiological Week at Louvain in 1928: 'I
cannot approve of the word *missiology*, which, being half Latin and half
Greek, has a barbarous appearance. Its structure is as bad as that of *sociology*,
and has the same defects. This unnatural marriage of Latin and Greek hurts
one's ears' (IRM 1929:282). However, after the Second World War a more
positive attitude has developed. Whereas Johan H. Bavinck (1954) was still
silent about 'missiology', his successor at the Theological University of
Kampen, Hendrik Bergema, has convincingly defended this term in his
inaugural address (1956). And Hugo du Plessis (1960), Johannes Verkuyl
(1965, 1978), Marc R. Spindler (1967), Arie de Kuiper (1968), Orlando E.
Costas (1976), Edward C. Pentecost (1982), WCE (1982:834), Alan R. Tippett
(1987), and C. Peter Wagner (1989:293), are other Protestants who have
already used the word 'missiology' in their publications.
    Many definitions of 'missiology' exist. I refer here only to some recent
examples:

WCE (1982:834):

> *Missiology* is the science of missions, missionary history, missionary thought, and missionary methods.

Alan R. Tippett (1987:XIII):

> *Missiology* is the academic discipline or science which researches, records, and applies data relating to the biblical origin, the history (including the use of documentary materials), the anthropological principles and techniques, and the theological base of the Christian mission.

C. Peter Wagner (1989:293):

> *Missiology* is the study of cross-cultural communication of the Christian faith.

Especially Wagner's definition is weak, because missiology is also concerned about the study of the communication of the gospel within the frame-work of a specific (western or non-western) culture. I add to this small enumeration of definitions my own preferred formulation:

> *Missiology* is the academic discipline which, from a philosophical, empirical, and theological point of view, reflects on the history, theory and practice of Christian world mission as a means for both preaching the gospel, healing the sick, and casting out 'evil spirits' (active in idolatry and immorality), for the glory of God and the well-being of all human beings.

This definition will be explained in the following chapters (starting with the next chapter which deals with the philosophy of mission, the science of mission, and the theology of mission as concepts of mission studies).

Finally I mention here three arguments which support my preference for the term 'missiology' compared with the term 'apostology':

1. the biblical argument: both terms are rooted in the Bible - the one in the Greek text, the other in the Latin translation -, and therefore they are fully equal;
2. the historical argument: 'missiology' is the older name, in fact the logical end of a process which started in the 16th century when *missio(nes)* became *terminus technicus*, primarily in Roman Catholic circles, thereafter also in Protestant circles; and
3. the secular argument: the term 'missiology' can easily be understood by non-religious people because in our modern world of 'diplomatic missions', 'parliamentary missions', 'commercial missions', 'goodwill missions', etc. it is not strange to speak about an academic discipline

which researches 'mission(s)' in general, and 'Christian mission(s)' in particular.

The last two arguments are the main reasons for calling this academic mission study 'missiology', instead of 'apostology', which basically has the same meaning and purpose (first argument).

RIJCKEVORSEL, LUDWIG J. VAN, SJ. Missie en missieactie... Nijmegen, 1917.
  *First ed.: Nijmegen, 1915.
MIONI, UGO. Manuale di missionologia. Milano, 1921.
*SCHMIDLIN. 1925.
  P. 117-139: Grundlegende Missionstheorie (Missiologie).
*ALLIER, RAOUL S.P. Book review of: L'âme des peuples à évangéliser: compte-rendu de la sixième semaine de missiologie de Louvain (1928). Louvain, 1928. In: IRM, XVIII (1929), p. 282-284.
CARMINATI, CESARE, SCJ. Compendio di missiologia: 3a ed. Bergamo, 1929.
  *First ed.: Bergamo, 1925.
MONDREGANES, PIO M. DE, OFMCap. El movimiento misionológico en la actualidad y sus orientaciones científicas. Asis, 1934.
TRAGELLA, GIOVANNI B., PIME. Introduction à la missionologie. 1934.
PERBAL, ALBERT, OMI. What is missiology? Trichinopoly, 1935.
MULDERS, ALPHONSUS J.M. Missiologie en Oostersche theologie. Nijmegen, & Utrecht, 1936. Inaugural address.
CHARLES, PIERRE, SJ. Les dossiers de l'action missionnaire: manuel de missiologie: deuxième ed., entièrement refondue et augmentée. Louvain, & Bruxelles, 1938.
  First ed.: Louvain, & Bruxelles, 1926. Reprint: Louvain, 1948.
  Sp. tr.: 1954.
BARBERO, GIUSEPPE, SSP. Le missioni: compendio di missionologia dottrinale - descrittiva et operativa. Alba, & Roma, 1939.
*CHARLES, PIERRE, SJ. Missiologie: études - rapports: conférences: I. Louvain, Bruxelles, & Paris, 1939.
CARMINATI, CESARE, SCJ. Il problema missionario: manuale di missionologia: parte prima: principi e aspetti dottrinali. Roma, 1941.
*PAVENTI, SAVERIO. La chiesa missionaria: manuale di missionologia dottrinale. Roma, 1949.
*JETTÉ, FERNAND, OMI. Qu'est-ce que la missiologie? De l'unité scientifique en missiologie. Ottawa, 1950.
MONDREGANES, PIO M. DE, OFMCap. Manual de misionología: tercera ed. corregida y aumentada. Madrid, 1951.
  First ed.: Vitoria, 1933.
  It. tr.: 1950.
*SEUMOIS. 1952.
  P. 85-106: Le terme 'missiologie'.
*SCIENTIA MISSIONUM ANCILLA. 1953.
  P. 6-45: La raison d'être de la missiologie (Édouard Loffeld CSSp.).
  P. 284-299: Das Verhältnis der Mission und Missiologie zu den Profanwissen-schaften (Max Bierbaum).
*BERGEMA, HENDRIK. Universaliteit en eigen kring in de missiologie. Kampen, 1956.
*CHARLES, PIERRE, SJ. Études missiologiques. Louvain, 1956.

66

KASBAUER, SIXTA, SSpS. Missionskenntnis, Missionsliebe, Missionstat: missiologisches Lehrbuch für Missionsschwestern, nach älteren und neueren Missiologen zusammengestellt. Maria Sorg bei Salzburg, & Steyl, 1956.

OSPINA, EDUARDO, SJ. Manual de misiología católica: segunda ed. Bogotà, 1957.
First ed.: Bogotà, 1941.

SANTOS HERNANDEZ, ANGEL, SJ. Una misionología Española. Bilbao, 1958.

?PLESSIS, HUGO DU. Die missiologie as 'n teologiese wetenskap. Potchefstroom, 1960.

UNCITI, MANUEL DE. Misionologia doctrinal: 2a ed. Vitoria, 1960.
First ed.: Vitoria, 1956.

HATTON, DESMOND J. (ed.). Missiology in Africa today: thought-provoking essays by modern missionaries. Dublin, 1961.

NEMBRO, METODIO DA, OFMCap. Missionologia. Roma, 1961.

*SANTOS HERNANDEZ. 1961.
P. 199-223: Misiologia o misionologia?

SILVA REGO, ANTONIO DA. Liçoes de missionologia. Lisboa, 1961.
First ed.: Curso de missionologia. Lisboa, 1956.

*MULDERS. 1962.

MULDERS, ALPHONSUS J.M. Missiologie: inzicht en inzet. Utrecht, & Nijmegen, 1963.

CRACCO, AMEDEO, OFM. Breve corso di missionologia: 2a ed. ampliata e aggiornata. Padova, 1964.
*First ed.: Padova, 1960.

*VERKUYL, JOHANNES. De taak der missiologie en der missionaire methodiek in het tijdperk van saecularisatie en saecularisme. Kampen, 1965. Inaugural address.

*BERGEMA, HENDRIK. De missiologie in nieuwe banen. In: DH, XX (1967), p. 198-212.

*SPINDLER, MARC R. La mission, combat pour le salut du monde. Neuchâtel, 1967.
First ed.: Méthode et principes d'une missiologie protestante. 1967. Thèse Strasbourg.

*GLAZIK, JOSEF, MSC. The meaning and place of missiology today. In: IRM, LVII (1968), p. 459-467.

*KUIPER, ARIE DE. Missiologia (ilmu pekabaran indjil). Djakarta, 1968.
Several reprints.

*RAHNER, KARL, SJ, with CORNELIUS ERNST OP and KEVIN SMITH (eds.). Sacramentum mundi: an encyclopedia of theology. London, 1968-1970. 6 vols.
IV, p. 86-88: Missiology (Edward L. Murphy).
*Ger. ed.: Sacramentun mundi: theologisches Lexikon für die Praxis. Freiburg im Breisgau, Basel, & Wien, 1967-1969. 4 vols.
III, p. 477-482: Missiologie (Edward L. Murphy).

*CONCISE DICTIONARY. 1971.
P. 387-389: Missiology (Josef Glazik MSC).

*COSTAS, ORLANDO E. Theology of the crossroads in contemporary Latin America: missiology in mainline protestantism: 1969-1974. Amsterdam, 1976. Diss. V.U. Amsterdam.

*VERKUYL, JOHANNES. Contemporary missiology: an introduction. Grand Rapids, 1978.

*VERSTRAELEN, FRANS J. Missiologie onderweg: een auto-bibliografie in kontekst. Leiden, 1980.

*DHAVAMONY, MARIASUSAI, SJ (ed.). Prospettive di missiologia, oggi: volume commemorativo del 5oo anniversario della Facoltà di Missiologia. Roma, 1982.

*PENTECOST, EDWARD C. Issues in missiology: an introduction. Grand Rapids, 1982.

*WCE. 1982.
P. 834: Missiology.

*TIPPETT, ALAN R. Introduction to missiology. Pasadena, 1987.
*VERSTRAELEN, FRANS J., et al. (eds.). Oecumenische inleiding in de missiologie: teksten en konteksten van het wereldchristendom. Kampen, 1988.
*WAGNER. 1989.
    P. 293: Missiology.
*DEM. 1991.
    P. 689-690: Missiology (Andrew Walls).

2.5.4. THE PHILOSOPHY OF MISSION, THE SCIENCE OF MISSION, AND THE THEOLOGY OF MISSION

Both the *philosophy of mission(s)*, the *science of mission(s)*, and the *theology of mission(s)* will be thoroughly discussed in the next chapter. Here I only mention these disciplines as names of mission studies, which were coined either in last century or in this century: William Orme (1828) maybe the first author to have used the term 'philosophy of missions', Johann T.L. Danz (1832) the first writer to have propagated the German term *Missionswissenschaft* (=science of mission), and Gustav Warneck (1877) the first scholar to advocate the term *Missionstheologie* (=theology of mission).

These three names are only useful as names of the main concepts of mission studies, not as names for the whole field. However, some missiologists have supported one of them as the term which is capable of embracing the whole field. In this way they have reduced missiology to one of its concepts, either by making this discipline more or less 'secular': a *Missionswissenschaft* which refuses to deal with theological questions; or by making it more or less 'sacred': a *Missionstheologie* which considers 'empirical mission studies' as a matter of secondary importance. In my own view, missiology must be an academic discipline which always tries to avoid the absolutizing of one of its three concepts, at the cost of the others.

Bibliography: see 3.2., 3.3., and 3.4.

2.5.5. MISSIONARY THEOLOGY

Although many missiologists do not distinguish 'theology of mission' from *missionary theology*, I like to make a clear distinction between both.

The term 'missionary theology' was coined in last century (White 1869). However, in this century it became a generally respected term, especially in the Roman Catholic Church (Lazzarini 1929; Perbal 1937; 1961; Raguin 1947; Seumois 1952; idem, in: Scientia missionum ancilla 1953:54-65; idem 1973-1978; Rétif 1963; et al.). The Protestant Johannes C. Hoekendijk, however, has contributed more to its profile than anybody else: he moved

68

away from 'theology of mission' to 'missionary theology' (cf. the title of the study of Coffele 1976). Hoekendijk was not at all satisfied with a 'theology of mission', which only functions as a part of systematic and practical theology, i.e. being on a par with dogmatics, ethics, pastoral care, etc. According to Hoekendijk, Christian theology as a whole (both systematic and practical theology) must be 'missionary'. I fully agree with this view of my predecessor at Utrecht University, but at the same time I like to correct his one-sidedness: in all its expressions, Christian theology must not only be 'missionary' (cf. Hoekendijk), but also - and at the same time - 'communal' and 'adoring', because Christians are living both in relation with God (adoration), with one another (church, congregation, communion of saints), and with the world (mission outside the gates).

The term 'missionary theology' is essential in my theological thinking (cf. the second volume of this study). However, for two reasons it is unsuited to serve as name for the whole field of mission studies: on the one hand, this name does not include philosophical analysis and empirical research (and therefore is too narrow), and, on the other hand, it deals with a considerable number of systematic and practical questions which in the proper sense do not belong to mission studies (and therefore is too broad).

WHITE, EDWARD. Missionary theology, considered in its two doctrines of endless misery... London, 1869.
TURNER, FREDERICK S. The missionary problem: a reply to 'Missionary theology', an article by Edward White... London, 1870.
*MACKICHAN, DUGALD. A present-day phase of missionary theology. In: IRM, III (1914), p. 243-254.
?LAZZARINI, D.M. PALERMO, SJ. Theologia missionaria... Roma, 1929.
*BIBLIOGRAFIA MISSIONARIA. 1933-...
        XLII (1978)-....: 2. Teologia missionaria (biblica, patristica). Bibliog.
PERBAL, ALBERTO, OMI. Premières leçons de théologie missionnaire. Paris, 1937.
        First ed.: Paris, 1935.
        It. tr.: 1941.
RAGUIN, YVES, SJ. La théologie missionnaire de l'Ancien Testament. Paris, 1947.
*SEUMOIS. 1952.
        Index analytique, sub voce: Théologie missionnaire.
*SCIENTIA MISSIONUM ANCILLA. 1953.
        P. 54-65: L'évolution de la théologie missionnaire au vingtième siècle (André V. Seumois OMI).
PERBAL, ALBERTO, OMI. La teologia misional. Barcelona, 1961.
RÉTIF, ANDRÉ V., SJ. La mission: éléments de théologie et de spiritualité missionnaire. Paris, 1963.
        It. tr.: 1965.
*SEUMOIS, ANDRÉ V., OMI. Théologie missionnaire. Rome, 1973-1978. 4 vols.
*LEIPOLD, HEINRICH. Missionarische Theologie: Emil Brunners Weg zur theologischen Anthropologie. Göttingen, 1974.

*COFFELE, GIANFRANCO, SDB. Johannes Christiaan Hoekendijk: da una teologia della missione ad una teologia missionaria. Roma, 1976.
*WEISS, G. CHRISTIAN. The heart of missionary theology. Chicago, 1977.
NEWBIGIN, J.E. LESSLIE. The open secret: sketches for a missionary theology. London, 1978.
?UNION PONTIFICALE MISSIONNAIRE. Elements de theologie missionnaire. Roma, 1978.
*DUNN, EDMOND J. Missionary theology: foundations in development. Lanham, 1980.
*BOSCH. 1991.
    P. 492-496: From a theology of mission to a missionary theology.

2.5.6. CONCLUSION

The third major name of mission studies is derived from the Latin noun *missio(nes)*, which became a *terminus technicus* at the beginning of the colonial period. 'Missiology' as term was born at the end of the colonial period, but can be propagated in the post-colonial period as well.

The name 'missiology' must be prefered to both 'apostology' and 'missionics'. As an academic discipline, 'missiology' must not be reduced to one of its three concepts: philosophy of mission(s), science of mission(s), or theology of mission(s). 'Missionary theology', not being identical with 'theology of mission(s)', is as discipline both narrower and broader than 'missiology'. In the second volume of this study I will make intensive use of this term, but not as a name for the whole field of mission studies.

2.6. CONCLUSION

I conclude this chapter on the names of mission studies by making a chronological table of the minor and major names discussed, and by making some final observations.

I start with the presentation of the list of years in which the minor and major names are mentioned for the first time (the four crucial names are printed in italics):

1828: PHILOSOPHY OF MISSION(S) (WILLIAM ORME)
1829: *Halieutik*=Halieutics (Gustav A.F. Sickel)
1830: *Theorie des Missionswesens*=Theory of mission(s) (Friedrich E.D. Schleiermacher)
1830: *Keryktik*=Keryktics (Rudolf Stier)
1832: *Apostolik*=Apostolics (Johann T.L.Danz)
1832: *MISSIONSWISSENSCHAFT*=SCIENCE OF MISSION(S) (JOHANN T.L. DANZ)
1854: Evangelistic theology (Alexander Duff)
1863: *Propagandiek*=Propagandics (Johannes Tideman)

1864: *Evangelistik*=Evangelistics (Karl Graul)
1869: Missionary theology (Edward White)
1877: *Missionslehre*=Doctrine of mission(s) (Gustav Warneck)
1877: *MISSIONSTHEOLOGIE*=THEOLOGY OF MISSION(S) (GUSTAV WARNECK)
1894: *Auxaniek*=Auxanics (Abraham Kuyper)
1894: *Matheteutiek*=Matheteutics (Abraham Kuyper)
1894: *Prosthetiek*=Prosthetics (Abraham Kuyper)
1911: *Missioniek*=Missionics (François E. Daubanton)
1915: *MISSIOLOGIE*=MISSIOLOGY (LUDWIG J. VAN RIJCKEVORSEL SJ)
1940: *Théologie de l'apostolat*=Theology of the apostolate (Pierre Charles SJ)
1947: *Apostologie*=Apostolo(lo)gy (Lucien-Mary Dewailly OP)
1949: *Evangelistologia*=Evangelistology (Saverio Paventi)
1951: Theology of evangelism (Henry Cook; cf. questionnaire WCC)
1959: *Théologie de l'évangelisation*=Theology of evangelization (Johannes C. Hoekendijk).

This list can be revised, because I do not claim to have all the data available for making a final compilation of the birth-years of the names of mission studies.

The main lines and issues of this chapter are very clear. At the end of this chapter I like to declare that nearly all names under consideration make sense in one way or another. However, the names 'auxanics' and 'prosthetics' are the least satisfatory, because they confuse God's missionary work (growth as gift) and the missionary work of the Christians. In fact, missiology as an academic discipline must start with, and focus on the human side. We cannot reflect upon *missio Dei* in the same way as we can reflect upon *missio ecclesiae* and *missio hominum*. Nevertheless, *missio Dei* is the universal and unique (back)ground of *missio ecclesiae* and *missio hominum*.

At the moment the name *missiology*(=*apostology*) is the most satisfactory one. However, tomorrow the situation may well change. We must always be open to consider new terms. Stanley J. Samartha has already proposed that we should speak about *witnessology*, which of course, being half English and half Greek, 'has a barbarous appearance... and ... hurt one's ears' (Allier, in: IRM 1929:282). Although I agree with Samartha that more attention must be given to *witness* (Greek: *martyria*) as a topic in mission studies, I still consider for the time being *martyriology* (in the same way as 'evangelistology') as only a small but crucial part of 'missiology'.

*ALLIER, RAOUL S.P. Book review. In: IRM, XVIII (1929), p. 282-284.
SAMARTHA, STANLEY J. Christian concern for dialogue in India. In: Current dialogue, IX (december 1985), p. 6.

3. CONCEPTS OF MISSIOLOGY

3.1. CONCEPTS

In this third chapter I discuss what in missiological literature is known as the problem of the 'definition' (Warneck 1892:I,20-23; Schmidlin 1925: 1-11; Mulders 1962:139-152; Ohm 1962:58-59), the 'character' (Schmidlin 1925: 1-11), the 'nature' (Seumois 1952:19-161), or the 'meaning' (Verkuyl 1978: 2-6) of mission studies. I prefer to speak about the *concepts* of missiology.

I distinguish *three 'concepts' of missiology: the philosophical, the scientific, and the theological.* Each will be discussed in a separate section of this chapter.

The 'philosophy of mission(s)' is treated first, because of both historical and systematic reasons. This term emerged before the terms 'science of mission(s)' and 'theology of mission(s)' came into being. And as a concept of missiology the 'philosophy of mission(s)' largely precedes the other ones. Although it must be recognised that this concept of missiology reflects *a posteriori* upon the whole process of doing missiology, and also upon the results of mission studies as a discipline, it must be emphasized that this concept is of primary importance to mission studies because it reflects *a priori* upon the structure of missiology as an independent academic discipline: its names, its concepts, its methods, and its branches.

The 'science of mission(s)' is put in the middle of this spectrum. This term is not as old as the term 'philosophy of mission(s)', but is indeed older than the term 'theology of mission(s)'. However, the main reason for treating the 'science of mission(s)' in the second place is a systematic one: this concept is the key form of missiology. It is only preceded by the 'philosophy of mission(s)' as far as this discipline reflects *a priori* upon the conditions for doing empirical mission studies successfully. And it is completed by systematic thinking about the results of empirical mission studies: the normative theological reflection upon mission does not belong to the 'science of mission(s)', but goes *a posteriori* 'beyond' its proper empirical field.

Christians consider the 'theology of mission(s)'/'missionary theology' as the third, last, and ultimate concept of doing mission studies. This term is the latest of the three terms under consideration. Systematically it must be stated that this term points to the ultimate reality of normative Christian thinking about mission which, of course, cannot be detached from Christian missionary experience.

After the explanation of each of these three concepts of mission studies, this chapter will be closed by a conclusion.

Finally, I note that Chapter 5 also deals with the philosophy, the science, and the theology of mission(s)/missionary theology. This third chapter, however, has a wider scope. Chapter 5 is limited to an explanation of the branches of mission studies, whereas this third chapter tries to analyse what is involved in philosophical, scientific, and theological studies of mission.

*WARNECK. 1892-1903.
    I, p. 20-23: Begriff und Name.
*DAUBANTON. 1911.
    P. 124-135: Zendingswetenschap.
*SCHMIDLIN. 1925.
    P. 1-11: Begriff, Charakter, Gegenstand, und Stellung der Missionswissenschaft.
*SEUMOIS. 1952.
    P. 19-161: Nature de la missiologie.
*MULDERS. 1962.
    P. 139-152: Begrip en bestaansrecht.
*OHM. 1962.
    P. 58-59: Begriff und Aufgabe.
*VERKUYL, JOHANNES. Contemporary missiology: an introduction. Grand Rapids, 1978.
    P. 2-6: Meaning of the term.

3.2. THE PHILOSOPHY OF MISSION

3.2.1. INTRODUCTION

As the first concept of mission studies, the *philosophy of mission(s)* (Ger.: *Missionsphilosophie*) will be discussed under two headings: it will be explained as (1) a discipline in its own right; and (2) a discipline which is closely related to the *philosophy of religion(s)* (Ger.: *Religionsphilosophie*).

In the well-known handbooks of Warneck (1892-1903), Daubanton (1911), Schmidlin (1925), Schomerus (1935), and others, no attention is paid to the 'philosophy of mission(s)'. Some special mission studies, however, mention this discipline.

3.2.2. THE PHILOSOPHY OF MISSION (MISSIONSPHILOSOPHIE)

The term 'philosophy of missions' was coined during the last century. Olav G. Myklebust (1955:I,358) has made clear that this happened in its first part: 'It would appear that the term *the philosophy of missions* was originally coined by William Orme, see his *Memoirs of John Urquhart* (1828), Vol. I, pp. 91f. Cf.

W. Swan's *Letters on Mission* (second ed., 1843), p. XVII (Preface by Orme)'. However, Myklebust has not clarified in which way Orme used this particular term.

In the Anglo-Saxon world, especially in the USA, the terms *philosophy of missions* (Slater 1882; Mabie 1910; Mills 1932; Baker 1934:281-318; van Dusen, in: Foreign missions conference of North America 1938: 139-147; Lindsell 1949; McGavran 1959:67), *philosophy of mission* (Soper 1943; McGavran 1959:67-76; Lindsell, in: Anderson 1961:239-249; Wead, in: Gasque, & La Sor 1978:176-186), and *missionary philosophy* (Dye, in: Whiteman 1983:215-228; Tippett 1987:48), became very popular. I agree with the following observation of Myklebust (1955:I,28): 'In America, the designation in common use for the theory of missions is *the philosophy of missions*'. I would like to refer to the following definition of this term by Donald A. McGavran (1959:67): 'An arrangement of convictions or theories about "what mission correctly is" we call a philosophy of missions'. And I would like to illustrate this crucial point by quoting Harold Lindsell (Anderson 1961:239-249): 'Every moment is undergirded by a basic philosophy whether that philosophy is known and expressed or unknown and unarticulated. The missionary activities of those who are wedded to a conservative theological viewpoint are founded on a basic philosophy which is generally known to them and which, while it has not appeared in print too often, has been adequately articulated in the minds of those who accept it. Although it is impossible here to delineate all of the presuppositions undergirding conservative missionary endeavor, there are five which are worthy of mention:

1.   The infallible Word of God...
2.   The gospel of Christ...
3.   Man's condition, need, and destiny...
4.   The inadequacy of the non-Christian religions...
5.   The church in the plan of God...

These are the five basic presuppositions which underlie a conservative philosophy of the Christian mission'.

On the continent of Europe, the terms *Missionsphilosophie* (German) and *zendingsfilosofie* (Dutch) are not as popular as the term *philosophy of mission(s)* in the Anglo-Saxon world. This has to do with the meaning of the term involved. From a linguistic point of view, 'of mission(s)' in the term 'philosophy of mission(s)' can be understood both as an objective and as a subjective genitive. In the Anglo-Saxon world, this word is interpreted as a subjective genitive: the philosophy developed by mission boards, missiologists, and others: for instance, by conservative Christians (cf. Lindsell, in: Anderson 1961:239-249). I have fundamental objections to this interpretation and use of

74

the term 'philosophy of mission(s)'. In my view it only makes sense to use this term if 'of mission(s)' is understood as an objective genitive: the philosophy which reflects upon mission as a phenomenon. Every missiologist recognizes the genitive in the terms 'science of mission(s)' and 'theology of mission(s)' as an objective genitive; why shall we make an odd exception for the term 'philosophy of mission(s)'? I agree with those European missiologists who hesitate to use the term 'philosophy of mission'. This term must either be dropped or be reinterpretated as 'the philosophical analysis of the phenomenon *mission* in all its religious and secular aspects'. I endorse the latter.

Only a few philosophers have developed thorough ideas about mission. Here I refer to Nicolaus Cusanus (1401-1464), Blaise Pascal (1623-1662), and Gottfried W. von Leibniz (1646-1716) at the end of the Middle Ages and the beginning of modern history. Especially the works of Leibniz are full of 'missionary thoughts' (Plath 1869; cf. Merkel, 1920; idem, in: IRM 1920:399-410; Zangger 1973). The philosophy of the Enlightenment, however, has either neglected mission or dealt with it in a negative way. Sometimes post-Enlightenment philosophers have developed a positive attitude towards mission. Kenneth S. Latourette (1971:V,104) writes about Darwin (1809-1882), the father of the evolution theory, as follows: 'Charles Darwin was so impressed with the achievements registered among peoples whom he had regarded as hopelessly degraded that he became a regular contributor to the funds of the society'.

The primary task of 'the philosophy of mission' (I prefer the singular) is the critical analysis of missiology as a discipline: its structure, its methods, etc. This discipline also reflects upon the branches of the philosophy of mission: i.e. the knowledge of the mission (epistemology); the appearance of the mission (phenomenology); the essence of the mission (ontology); and the value of the mission (axiology), including both the ethics of the mission and the esthetics of the mission. In chapter 5.2. these last subjects will be explained one by one as the branches of the philosophical study of mission.

The titles (not the contents!) of some German publications explain exactly what is involved in the philosophy of mission: Hermann Gundert (EMM 1865:14-50,90-100,123-132,152-196) speaks about 'mission in front of the judgement-seat of the immanence' (my tr.; Ger.: *Die Mission vor dem Richterstuhl der Immanenz)'*, whereas Adolf Dyroff (1922) calls attention to 'mission in the light of philosophical reflection' (my tr.; Ger.: *Die Mission im Lichte philosophischer Betrachtung)*.

*GUNDERT, HERMANN. Die Mission vor dem Richterstuhl der Immanenz. In: EMM, IX (1865), p. 14-50, 90-100, 123-132, 152-196.
PLATH, CARL H.C. Die Missionsgedanken des Freiherrn von Leibnitz. Berlin, 1869.
*SLATER, THOMAS E. The philosophy of missions: a present-day plea. London, 1882.
MABIE, HENRY C. The task worth while: or, the divine philosophy of missions.

Philadelphia, Boston..., 1910.
*MERKEL, FRANZ R. Christentum und Mission im Urteil eines neueren Philosophen. In: ZMR, XXXV (1920), p. 173-184.
MERKEL, FRANZ R. G.W. von Leibniz und die China-Mission... Leipzig, 1920.
*MERKEL, FRANZ R. The missionary attitude of the philosopher G.W. von Leibnitz. In: IRM, IX (1920), p. 399-410.
*OLDHAM, JOSEPH H. A philosophical interpretation of the missionary idea. In: IRM, X (1921), p. 63-76.
*DYROFF, ADOLF. Die Mission im Lichte philosophischer Betrachtung. Aachen, 1922.
*LUMEN CAESIS: Festschrift zum silbernen Amts-Jubiläum des Hochwürdigsten Herrn Dr. Norbert Weber OSB ... St. Ottilien, 1928.
    P. 84-111: Die Philosophie im Dienste des Heidenapostolates (Rupert Klingseis OSB).
*KOHNSTAMM, PHILIPP A. The necessity for a new philosophy and its bearing on missionary work. In: IRM, XIX (1930), p. 161-173, 321-332.
MILLS, WILSON P. Suggestions towards a philosophy of missions... New York, 1932. M.Th. thesis Union Theological Seminary New York.
*BAKER, ARCHIBALD G. Christian missions and a new world culture. Chicago, & New York, 1934.
    P. 281-318: Toward a philosophy of missions.
*RICHTER, JULIUS. Eine Missionsphilosophie. In: NAMZ, VI (1929), p. 353-363.
*WHITE, HUGH V. A theology for Christian missions. New York, & Chicago, 1937.
    Appendix: John Dewey on a common faith.
FOREIGN MISSIONS CONFERENCE OF NORTH AMERICA. Report of the forty-fifth meeting. Toronto, 1938.
    P. 139-147: New emphases in the philosophy of missions (Henry P. van Dusen).
*SOPER, EDMUND D. The philosophy of the Christian world mission. New York, & Nashville, 1943.
LINDSELL, HAROLD. A Christian philosophy of missions. Wheaton, 1949.
    *Rev. ed.: An evangelical theology of missions. Grand Rapids, 1970.
*MYKLEBUST. 1955-1957.
*McGAVRAN, DONALD A. How churches grow: the new frontiers of mission. London, 1959.
    P. 67-76: Current philosophies of mission.
*ANDERSON. 1961.
    P. 239-249: Fundamentals for a philosophy of the Christian mission (Harold Lindsell).
*DICTIONARY CATALOG. 1968.
    XI, p. 173: Missions and philosophy. Bibliog.
*LATOURETTE, KENNETH S. A history of the expansion of Christianity. New York, 1971. 7 vols.
    First ed.: New York, 1937-1945. 7 vols.
*ZANGGER, CHRISTIAN D. Welt und Konversation: die theologische Begründung der Mission bei Gottfried Wilhelm Leibniz. Zürich, 1973. Diss. Basel.
*GASQUE, W. WARD, & WILLIAM S. LA SOR (eds.). Scripture, tradition, and interpretation: essays presented to Everett F. Harrison by his students and colleagues in honor of his 75th birthday. Grand Rapids, 1978.
    P. 176-186: The centripetal philosophy of mission (David W. Wead).
*HESSELGRAVE, DAVID J. (ed.). Theology and mission ... Grand Rapids, 1978.
    P. 241-257: Some philosophical perspectives on missionary dialogue (Norman L. Geisler).
*WHITEMAN, DARRELL L. (ed.). Missionaries, anthropologists, and cultural change. Williamsburg, 1983.
    P. 215-228: A missionary philosophy of development (T. Wayne Dye).

*TIPPETT, ALAN R. Introduction to missiology. Pasadena, 1987.
*KANE, J. HERBERT. Understanding Christian missions: fourth ed. Grand Rapids, 1988.
    P. 454-455: Philosophy of missions. Bibliog.
*WAGNER. 1989.
    P. 95-96, 296: Philosophy of ministry.

3.2.3. THE PHILOSOPHY OF MISSION AND THE PHILOSOPHY OF RELIGION (RELIGIONSPHILOSOPHIE)

Most philosophers of religion neglect mission as an item. Either they ignore mission totally (Mourant 1970), or they mention it only in passing (Trillhaas 1972 refers to mission five times in passing). This is regrettable. So I hereby invite philosophers of religion to reflect upon the subject of Christian and non-Christian mission in the same way as they are already reflecting upon the existence of God, the freedom of the will, the immortality of the soul, etc.

Most missiologists ignore the *philosophy of religion* (Ger.: *Religions-philosophie*). This is also regrettable; because I believe that in a serious dialogue with the philosophers of religion missiologists can only grow in maturity. Myklebust (1957:II,297) has mentioned that Oberlin College at Oberlin, Ohio, once had a chair of 'Philosophy of Religion and Christian Missions', but this is indeed an exception.

'Philosophy of mission' is both a branch of the philosophy of religion and a branch of missiology. Ronald W. Hepburn (Richardson 1972:258-259) has offered the following definition of the 'philosophy of religion': 'Philosophy of religion is the logical study of religious and theological concepts, arguments, language: the scrutiny of various interpretations of religious experiences and activities'. In a parallel way 'philosophy of mission' can be defined as 'the logical study of missionary and missiological concepts, arguments, language: the scrutiny of various interpretations of missionary experiences and activities'. Other definitions can be proposed and defended as well. For instance, WCE (1982:838) describes this discipline as follows: 'The search for the underlying causes and principles of reality in religion through logical reasoning rather than revelation'. We can, therefore, treat the 'philosophy of mission' as a 'search for the underlying causes and principles of reality in mission through logical reasoning rather than revelation'. My own definition of the 'philosophy of mission' is as follows: 'the discipline which, from a logical point of view, reflects systematically upon mission as an empirical and theological phenomenon'.

The lack of serious philosophical reflection upon mission so far has made missiology and the philosophy of religion unrelated disciplines. Missiology has suffered from this lack more than the philosophy of religion. It is primarily the task of missiologists to bridge this gulf and to link the philosophy of mission with the philosophy of religion.

*NIPPOLD, FRIEDRICH W. Missionswissenschaft und Religionsphilosophie. In: ZMR, V (1890), p. 232-245.
*PFLEIDERER, OTTO. Religionsphilosophie auf geschichtlicher Grundlage: dritte, neu bearbeitete Aufl. Berlin, 1896.
     P. 730-736: Die Kirche neben und über der Gesellschaft.
*LÜTGERT, WILHELM. Reich Gottes und Weltgeschichte. Gütersloh, 1928.
     P. 1-12: Mission und Geschichtsphilosophie (1914).
*SCIENTIA MISSIONUM ANCILLA. 1953.
     P. 176-177: Religionsphilosophie (Johannes P. Steffes).
*MYKLEBUST. 1955-1957.
*MOURANT, JOHN A. Readings in the philosophy of religion. New York, 1970.
*RICHARDSON, ALAN (ed.). A dictionary of Christian theology: second impression. London, 1972.
     P. 258-259: Philosophy of religion (Ronald W. Hepburn).
     First ed.: London, 1969.
*TRILLHAAS, WOLFGANG. Religionsphilosophie. Berlin, & New York, 1972.
*WCE. 1982.
     P. 838: Philosophy of religion.
*LAUBE, JOHANNES. Dialektik der absoluten Vermittlung: Hajime Tanabes Religionsphilosophie als Beitrag zum 'Wettstreit der Liebe' zwischen Buddhismus und Christentum... Freiburg, Basel, & Wien, 1984.

3.2.4. CONCLUSION

Although I regard *the philosophy of mission* as the first 'concept' of missiology, I conclude that this discipline is much more 'underdeveloped' than the science of mission and the theology of mission.

As long as missiologists neglect their duty to develop fully the philosophy of mission as an essential form of mission studies, they will be regarded by philosophers as 'childish' because of their lack of reflection upon the nature of their own discipline: its names, forms, methods, branches, etc. I plead for a swift and radical change in this unfortunate situation, so that academic circles will generally accept missiology as a *philosophically* mature discipline.

3.3. THE SCIENCE OF MISSION

3.3.1. INTRODUCTION

The *science of mission(s)* (Ger.: *Missionswissenschaft*) is the second concept of missiology. Here I will deal with this concept as (1) a discipline in its own right; and (2) a discipline which is closely connected with *religious studies* or the *science of religion(s)* (Ger.: *Religionswissenschaft*).

The main missiological handbooks devote considerable attention to 'the science of mission(s)', both in their booktitles and in their texts. The Dutch missiologist Johan C. Neurdenburg (1879) was the first author who used this term (Dutch: *zendingswetenschap*) in the title of a missiological handbook. Others in the Netherlands and in Germany who were academic scholars followed: Daubanton (1911), Schmidlin (1925), Schomerus (1935), Mulders (1950; 1962), Holsten (1953), Bavinck (1954), and Verkuyl (1975). In France, Spain, and the Anglo-Saxon world, however, this term did not appear in the titles of handbooks, with the exception of the translation of the Dutch handbook of Bavinck (1960). The translator of the Dutch handbook of Verkuyl actually replaced this term by the more modern term 'missiology' (1978).

Besides these handbooks, we also have at our disposal many monographs and articles in journals which deal with the science of mission(s).

*NEURDENBURG, JOHAN C. Proeve eener handleiding bij het bespreken der zendingswetenschap. Rotterdam, 1879.
*WARNECK. 1892.
  I, p. 8-19: Die wissenschaftliche Missionskunde.
*DAUBANTON. 1911.
*SCHMIDLIN. 1925.
*SCHOMERUS. 1935.
*MULDERS, ALPHONSUS J.M. Inleiding tot de missiewetenschap: tweede om- en bijgewerkte dr. Bussum, 1950.
  First ed.: 's-Hertogenbosch, 1937.
*SEUMOIS. 1952.
  P. 127-161: Caractère scientifique de la missiologie.
*HOLSTEN. 1953.
  P. 24-34: Missionswissenschaft.
*BAVINCK, JOHAN H. An introduction to the science of missions. Philadelphia, 1960.
  *Dutch ed.: Inleiding in de zendingswetenschap. Kampen, 1954.
*SANTOS HERNANDEZ. 1961.
  P. 225-281: Es una sciencia propria la misionologia?
*MULDERS. 1962.
*OHM. 1962.
  P. 58-62: Missionswissenschaft.
  P. 832-834: Der Dienst der Missionswissenschaft.

*VERKUYL, JOHANNES. Contemporary missiology. Grand Rapids, 1978.
*Dutch ed.: Inleiding in de nieuwere zendingswetenschap. Kampen, 1975.

3.3.2. THE SCIENCE OF MISSION (MISSIONSWISSENSCHAFT)

The science of missions has come, and no man should go into
our ministry of to-day without being versed in that science.
Oswald E. Brown (World Missionary Conference 1910:VI,315).

Whereas the term 'philosophy of mission(s)' was coined in the Anglo-Saxon
world, the term *science of mission(s)* was invented on the continent of Europe.
Johannes C. Hoekendijk (1948:31) stated that G.C. Friedrich Lücke (1841)
was the first person to use this term. However, others had done so before.
Olav G. Myklebust (1955:I,88-89) has rightly called attention to the German
church historian Johann T.L. Danz (1769-1851): 'J.T.L. Danz, as early as
1832, explicitly mentions *die christliche Missionswissenschaft* or *Apostolik*,
although as yet only a science in being, as one of the subjects to be treated in
connection with Practical Theology'.

Although Myklebust (1955:I,280) considered Gustav Warneck to be 'the
real founder of the science of missions', I regard him as 'the real founder of
the theology of missions'. I treat François E. Daubanton (1911), on the
Protestant side, and Joseph Schmidlin (1910; idem, in: ZM 1911:10-21,106-
122; 1916:11-21; 1919; 1924; 1925; idem, in: ZM 1925:1-9; cf. Müller
1989), as well as Robert Streit OMI (1909; 1928:161-183; cf. Pietsch 1952),
on the Roman Catholic side, as the real founders of the science of mission(s) as
an empirical discipline. These authors used the technical term *Missionswissenschaft* more frequently than Warneck, and clearly preferred induction as a
method to deduction which prevails in the classic work of Warneck (1892-
1903). After the publications of Daubanton and Schmidlin - and Streit - the
term under consideration took precedence in Europe. It appeared not only in
the titles of several handbooks (cf. 3.3.1.), but also in the names of famous
journals (e.g. MR 1938-1941, 1947-1949; NZM 1945-...; ZM 1911-1937;
ZMR 1949-...; cf. Baumgartner 1970), of well-known collective works and
series (Missionswissenschaftliche Abhandlungen und Texte 1917-1929;
Missionswissenschaftliche Forschungen 1920ff.), of important societies and
institutes (for instance: Deutsche Gesellschaft für Missionswissenschaft
1918-...; das missionswissenschaftliche Institut Missio at Aachen, Germany),
etc.

In the Anglo-Saxon world this particular term became known via the
bad translation of a German study of Carl H.C. Plath (1868): the word
Missionswissenschaft (the singular 'Mission') was translated by L. Kirkpatrick
as 'science of missions' (the plural 'missions'). After that the last term was

indeed accepted by several missiologists in the Anglo-Saxon world but never became as popular as the term *Missionswissenschaft* on the continent of Europe. It not only came to the fore in translations of European studies (Bavinck 1960), but also in original English and American publications (Gall 1878; Schaff 1893:517; Speer 1902:43-68; Brown at the World Missionary Conference, Edinburgh 1910; Concise Dictionary 1971: 387-389; WCE 1982: 834). Myklebust (1955:I,389) observed that the term 'science of missions' was 'deliberately adopted and employed' by Robert E. Speer; and in addition he wrote that the Foreign Missions Conference of North America was founded in part 'to foster and promote a science of missions', bringing about the establishment and direction of the MRL in New York (1957:II,56). Dr. Harlan P. Beach, Professor of the Theory and Practice of Missions at Yale University, expressed his view to the World Missionary Conference at Edinburgh 1910 as follows: '... we can only put forward the high-sounding title of *The Science of Missions* as an aspiration and a challenge. We are glad, however, to note that the foundations for the superstructure have been laid with true German thoroughness and insight' (World Missionary Conference 1910:V,162).

I prefer the term *science of mission* (singular) to the term *science of missions* (plural), but I did not come across this term. Also I rarely encountered the term *missionary science* (cf. the French term: *la science missionnaire*). However, the Edinburgh Missionary Conference used this term in connection with the term 'the science of the home base (or the science of missionary societies)' (World Missionary Conference 1910:VI,250), whereas David H. Freeman mentioned this term as a synonym of the term 'science of missions' in his translation of the Dutch term *zendingswetenschap* in the missiological handbook of Johann H. Bavinck (1960:XIX-XXI).

Josef Glazik MSC (Concise dictionary 1971:387-389) and WCE (1982: 834) have more or less equated the term 'science of missions' with 'missiology'. I regard the last term as broader. I limit the use of the term 'science of mission' to the empirical study of mission, but realize that Glazik and WCE are not the only ones who take another stance. For decades the term *Missionswissenschaft* was used as the over-arching term; its replacement by the term 'missiology' dates largely from the sixties of the twentieth century. Just this replacement enables us now to consider the science of mission merely as a 'concept' of missiology.

As the philosophy of mission is not at all limited to a logical analysis of the Christian mission -over against the mission of the non-Christian religions and worldviews-, so the science of mission includes the empirical study of both Christian mission and Muslim mission, Buddhist mission, Communist propaganda, etc. In this study, however, I limit myself to the empirical study of the Christian mission.

The 'science of mission' is the empirical part of missiology. It includes a great variety of disciplines. First, there are the classical branches of the empirical study of mission: the linguistics of mission, with regard to the language of the Christian mission; the history of mission, with regard to the birth and growth of the Christian mission; the geography of mission, with regard to the spread of the Christian missionary enterprise; the statistics of mission, with regard to the numbers of Christian mission stations, missionaries, converts, etc.; whereas ethnology/cultural anthropolgy calls attention to the link between ethnic groups and the Christian mission. Second, new branches of empirical mission studies came to the fore. Here I mention the sociology, law, economics, psychology, and paedagogics of mission, which study the link between the Christian mission on the one hand, and social life, law, the financial system, the inner life of mankind, and education on the other hand. The methods used by these branches can be applied to mission generally, but are applied in this study to the Christian mission only. Each of these broad fields of mission studies will be explained historically and systematically in the separate sections of chapter 5.3.

Not only a few philosophers (cf. 3.2.3.), but also a few scientists -linguists, historians, geographers, etc.- have dealt with Christian mission in an empirical way. The famous historian Arnold J. Toynbee (1889-1975), the author of *Christianity among the Religions of the World* (1958), is one of them. However, he fundamentally transcends empiricism by agreeing much more with the basic attitude of the Asian religions than with the main principles of the monotheistic religions (Jewish religion, Christianity, and Islam), which in his view essentially are based upon the Old Testament concept of a 'jealous God'. Hendrik Kraemer (1963:292-294) is one of those missiologists who have answered the criticisms of Christian mission by Toynbee.

DANZ, JOHANN T.L. Encyklopädie und Methodologie der theologischen Wissenschaften. Weimar, 1832.

LÜCKE, G.C. FRIEDRICH. Missionsstudien oder Beyträge zur Missionswissenschaft. Göttingen, 1841.

PLATH, CARL H.C. Die Erwählung der Völker im Lichte der Missionsgeschichte: eine missionswissenschaftliche Studie. Berlin, 1867.

PLATH, CARL H.C. The subject of missions considered under three new aspects: the church and missions; the representation of the science of missions at the universities; commerce and the church...; tr. by L. Kirkpatrick... Edinburgh, 1873.

*Ger. ed.: Drei neue Missionsfragen (Kirche und Mission; die Vertretung der Missionswissenschaften auf der Universität; der Weltverkehr und die Kirche). Berlin, 1868.

*ZÖCKLER, OTTO. Mission und Wissenschaft. In: AMZ, IV (1877), p. 3-16, 49-61.

GALL, JAMES. The science of missions. Edinburgh, & London, 1878.

*PRINS, JOHANNES J. Over zendingwetenschap. In: Med., XXIII (1879), p. 308-312.

*LAURIE, THOMAS. The Ely volume: or, the contributions of our foreign missions to science and human well-being: second rev. ed. Boston, 1882.

82

*WARNECK, GUSTAV. Die Mission als Wissenschaft. In: AMZ, XVI (1889), p. 397-407, 448-457.

*WARNECK. 1892-1903.

SCHAFF, PHILIPP. Theological propaedeutic... New York, 1893.

*SPEER, ROBERT E. Missionary principles and practice... New York, Chicago, & Toronto, 1902.
   P. 43-68: The science of missions.
   *Repr. from Missionary review of the world, XXII (1899), p. 27-37.

*AXENFELD, KARL, et al. (eds.). Missionswissenschaftliche Studien: Festschrift zum 70. Geburtstag des Herrn Prof.D.Dr. Gustav Warneck... Berlin, 1904.

KEEN, WILLIAM W. The service of missions to science and society... Boston, 1906.

STREIT, ROBERT, OMI. Die theologisch-wissenschaftliche Missionskunde. Paderborn, 1909.

SCHMIDLIN, JOSEPH. Ein Hauptpostulat der katholischen Missionswissenschaft. Berlin, 1910.

*WORLD MISSIONARY CONFERENCE. Edinburgh, London, New York..., 1910.
   V, p. 162-164: The science and history of missions (Harlan P. Beach).
   VI, p. 249-257: The science of missionary societies.

*DAUBANTON. 1911.

SCHMIDLIN, JOSEPH. Die katholische Missionswissenschaft. In: ZM, I (1911), p. 10-21.

SCHMIDLIN, JOSEPH. System und Zweige der Missionswissenschaft. In: ZM, I (1911), p. 106-122.

*HEADLAND, ISAAC T. Some by-products of missions. Cincinnati, & New York, 1912.
   P. 35-46: By-products in science.

*MEINERTZ, MAX. Zur Bedeutung der Missionswissenschaft. In: ZM, IV (1914), p. 242-243.

GRUNDEMANN, PETER R. Unser heimatliches Missionswesen: Beiträge zu wissenschaftlicher Behandlung desselben. Leipzig, 1916.

SCHMIDLIN, JOSEPH (ed.). Missionswissenschaftlicher Kursus in Köln für den deutschen Klerus... Münster in Westfalen, 1916.
   P. 11-21: Missionswissenschaft (Joseph Schmidlin).

BERGMANN, LORENZ. Missionsvidenskaben paa universitetet. Copenhagen, 1918. Inaugural address.

SCHMIDLIN, JOSEPH. Missionswissenschaft und Missionspraxis. Aachen, 1919.

MERKEL, FRANZ R. Mission und Wissenschaft. Herrnhut, 1921.

CARALT, MIGUEL DE LOS SANTOS. Una nueva ciencia: las misiones catolicas. 1923.

SCHMIDLIN, JOSEPH. Katholische Missionswissenschaft. Münster in Westfalen, 1924.

*SCHMIDLIN. 1925.

SCHMIDLIN, JOSEPH. Probleme und Aufgaben der Missionswissenschaft. In: ZM, XV (1925), p. 1-9.

*STREIT, ROBERT, OMI. Die Weltmission der katholischen Kirche: Zahlen und Zeichen auf Grund der Vatik. Missionsausstellung 1925. Hünfeld, 1928.
   P. 161-183: Im Dienste der Wissenschaft.

*SCHÄRER, HANS. Die Begründung der Mission in der katholischen und evangelischen Missionswissenschaft. Zürich, 1944.

*MULDERS, ALPHONSUS J.M. Missie en wetenschap. Nijmegen, & Utrecht, 1946.

*HOEKENDIJK, JOHANNES C. Kerk en volk in de Duitse zendingswetenschap. Amsterdam, 1948. Diss. Utrecht.
   *Ger. tr.: 1967.

*JETTÉ, FERNAND, OMI. Qu'est-ce que la missiologie? De l'unité scientifique en missiologie. Ottawa, 1950.

*KNAK, SIEGFRIED. Ökumenischer Dienst in der Missionswissenschaft. In: Theologia viatorum, II (1950), p. 156-174.

ROMMERSKIRCHEN, JOHANNES, OMI, & NIKOLAUS KOWALSKY OMI (eds.). Missionswissenschaftliche Studien: Festgabe Prof.Dr. Johannes Dindinger OMI... Aachen, 1951.

BECKMANN, JOHANNES, SMB. Forderungen der gegenwärtigen Missionslage an die Missionswissenschaft. In: NZM, VIII (1952), p. 241-250.

*DOERNE, MARTIN (ed.). Grundriss des Theologiestudiums. Gütersloh, 1948-1952. 3 vols.

    III, p. 190-205: Die Missionswissenschaft (Carl Ihmels).

*PIETSCH, JOHANNES, OMI. P. Robert Streit OMI: ein Pionier der katholischen Missionswissenschaft. Schöneck, & Beckenried, 1952.

*EERENBEEMT, ANDRÉ VAN DEN, CICM. Missieactie en missieproblemen. Tilburg, 1953.

    P. 116-123: Missie en wetenschap.

*SCIENTIA MISSIONUM ANCILLA. 1953.

*KÖSTER, HERMANN, SVD. Vom Wesen und Aufbau katholischer Theologie. Kaldenkirchen, 1954.

    P. 65-122: Wissenschaftstheoretisches zur sogenannten Missionswissenschaft.

*MYKLEBUST. 1955-1957.

*BAVINCK, JOHAN H. An introduction to the science of missions. Philadelphia, 1960.

*KRAEMER, HENDRIK. World cultures and world religions: the coming dialogue... London, 1960.

    *Dutch tr.: 1963.

    P. 292-294: Toynbee - een Aziatische wijze.

*RGG. 1960.

    IV, p. 1012-1016: Missionswissenschaft (Gerhard Rosenkranz, & Thomas Ohm OSB).

*GLAZIK, JOSEF, MSC (ed.). 50 Jahre katholische Missionswissenschaft in Münster 1911-1961: Festschrift. Münster in Westfalen, 1961.

*VRIENS. 1961. Bibliog.

*FREITAG, ANTON, SVD. Mission und Missionswissenschaft... Kaldenkirchen, 1962.

*BOHREN, RUDOLF (ed.). Einführung in das Studium der evangelischen Theologie. München, 1964.

    P. 33-54: Missionswissenschaft und Ökumenik (Manfred Linz).

NEMBRO, METODIO DA, OFMCap. Temi e problemi di scienza delle missioni. Milano, 1964.

*ROSENKRANZ, GERHARD. Religionswissenschaft und Theologie: Aufsätze zur Evangelischen Religionskunde. München, 1964.

    P. 48-70: Missionswissenschaft als Wissenschaft (1956).

*BIRKELI, FRIDTJOV, TRYGVE BJERKRHEIM, MARTIN SKI... (eds.). Norsk misjonsleksikon... Stavanger, 1965-1967. 3 vols.

    III, p. 87-98: Misjonsvitenskap (Olav G. Myklebust).

*NEUHÄUSLER, ENGELBERT, & ELISABETH GÖSSMANN (eds.). Was ist Theologie? München, 1966.

    P. 369-384: Missionswissenschaft (Josef Glazik MSC).

*DICTIONARY CATALOG. 1968.

    XI, p. 174: Missions and science. Bibliog.

*SENDINGWETENSKAP VANDAG; 'N TERREINVERKENNING. Pretoria, 1968.

    P. 9-12: Die beoefening van die sendingwetenskap in Afrika (Willem J. van der Merwe).

    P. 13-44: Kaleidoskoop van die na-oorlogse sendingwetenskap (David J. Bosch).

*BAUMGARTNER, JAKOB, SMB. Missionswissenschaft im Dienste der Weltkirche: 25 Jahre Neue Zeitschrift für Missionswissenschaft: ihre Beziehungen zur Schweizerischen Missionsgesellschaft Bethlehem, Immensee. Schöneck, & Beckenried, 1970.

*CONCISE DICTIONARY. 1971.

    P. 387-389: Missiology (the science of missions) (Josef Glazik MSC).

*GENSICHEN, HANS-WERNER. Glaube für die Welt: theologische Aspekte der Mission. Gütersloh, 1971.

    P. 250-254: Missionswissenschaft.

*MANN, ULRICH (ed.). Theologie und Religionswissenschaft: der gegenwärtige Stand ihrer Forschungsergebnisse und Aufgaben im Hinblick auf ihr gegenseitiges Verhältnis.

Darmstadt, 1973.
P. 438-453: Oekumenische Theologie und Missionswissenschaft (Werner Schilling).
*KRAUS, JOHANN, SVD. Missionswissenschaftliche Themen in Festschriften aus den Jahren 1960-1971. Immensee, 1974. Bibliog.
*LINDE, JAN M. VAN DER. Gods wereldhuis: voordrachten en opstellen over de geschiedenis van zending en oecumene. Amsterdam, 1980.
P. 167-185: Honderd jaar zendingswetenschap in Nederland 1876/77-1975 (1977).
*WCE. 1982.
P. 834: Missiology.
*MÜLLER, KARL, SVD. Friedrich Schwager (1876-1929): Pionir katholischer Missionswissenschaft. Nettetal, 1984.
*LMG. 1987.
P. 323-327: Missionswissenschaft (H.-J. Findeis).
*CRAFFORD, DIONNE. Sendingwetenskap waarheen? Pretoria, 1989.
*MÜLLER, KARL, SVD. Josef Schmidlin (1876-1944): Papsthistoriker und Begründer der katholischen Missionswissenschaft. Nettetal, 1989.
*LM. 1992.
P. 305-307: Missionswissenschaft.

3.3.3. THE SCIENCE OF MISSION AND THE SCIENCE OF RELIGION (RELIGIONSWISSENSCHAFT)

Scholars, especially in Germany and the Netherlands, have thought, talked and written much more about the relation between the *science of mission* and the *science of religion* (Ger.: *Religionswissenschaft*) than about the relation between the 'philosophy of mission' and the 'philosophy of religion' (cf. 3.2.3.).

German scholars started the journal *Missionswissenschaft und Religionswissenschaft* (Münster in Westfalen 1938-1941, 1947-1949). And German universities established chairs of *mission studies and religious studies* (Ger.: *Missionswissenschaft und Religionswissenschaft*). Until quite recently 'mission studies' was given priority. In several new publications, however, 'religious studies' takes precedence (Holsten 1953; Andersen, in: EMZ 1954:29-37; Bürkle, in: Lohff, & Hahn 1974:62-70). At the state universities in the Netherlands (Leiden, Groningen, Utrecht and Amsterdam) we are confronted with yet another situation: both disciplines are separated from one another, leaving more room for 'religious studies' to go its own independent way. Because I agree with this division of fields and responsiblities at the Dutch state universities, I disagree with all those who in one way or another try to give a theological foundation to the science of religion (Holsten 1953; Andersen, in: EMZ 1954:29-37; Bürkle 1979:167-170). In my view, the science of religion is a totally secular discipline.

In missiological literature, 'religious studies' is primarily considered as an auxiliary discipline of 'mission studies' (Daubanton 1911:537-562;

Schmidlin 1925:174-178; Mulders 1950:250-258). I prefer to consider them as equals; because both religious studies and mission studies are empirical studies. The difference between them, however, is also clear: religious studies are nothing more than purely empirical studies, whereas missiology has both an empirical side and a theological, i.e. normative, dimension. Therefore missiology is rather more complicated: in the same way as religious studies it serves academic needs and maintains academic standards (the empirical study of mission), but in addition to this scientific task it also serves church needs and maintains church standards (the theological study of mission).

'Science of mission' is both a branch of the science of religion and a branch of missiology. The term 'science of religion' is used by Johannes G. Platvoet (1982:4) to 'indicate that the discipline should be a scientific one in which objective knowledge of religion and religions, based on empirical analysis, is sought'. This means that the science of mission can be defined as that academic discipline which seeks objective knowledge of mission and missions, based on empirical analysis. Although I acknowledge that other definitions of this science can be proposed and defended, I really prefer to equate the science of mission (Ger.: *Missionswissenschaft*) with the empirical study of mission.

*DAUBANTON. 1911.
P. 537-562: De zendingswetenschap en de godsdienstwetenschap.
*SPIETH, JACOB. Die Religionsforschung im Dienste der Mission. In: AMZ, XXXIX (1912), p. 249-257, 297-303.
GRÖSSER, MAX, PSM. Die Beziehungen der Missionswissenschaft und Missionspraxis zur Völker-, Sprachen- und Religionskunde. In: ZM, III (1913), p. 29-53.
?FRICK, HEINRICH. Allgemeine Religionswissenschaft und Missionskunde in ihrer organischen Verbundenheit. In: Theologische Blätter, (1922), p. 97-103.
*AUFHAUSER, JOHANN B. Missions- und Religionswissenschaft an der Universität: zweite verm. Aufl. Freiburg im Breisgau, 1925.
First ed.: Die Pflege der Missionswissenschaft an der Universität. Diessen vor München, 1920.
*SCHMIDLIN. 1925.
P. 174-178: Religionskunde.
SCHMIDLIN, JOSEPH. Missions- und Religionswissenschaft. In: ZM, XVIII (1928), p. 1-4.
TITIUS, ARTHUR (ed.). Deutsche Theologie: Bericht über den ersten deutschen Theologentag zu Eisenach (Herbst 1927). Göttingen, 1928.
P. 160-167: Missions- und Religionswissenschaft als theologische Disziplinen (Heinrich Frick).
*BIBLIOGRAFIA MISSIONARIA. 1933-...
XXIX (1965) - XLI (1977): 7. Scienza delle religioni e missione. Bibliog.
*STEFFES, JOHANNES P. Religionswissenschaftliche Überlegungen zur Mission der Gegenwart. In: MR, no series number (1947/48), p. 14-31.
*MULDERS, ALPHONSUS J.M. Inleiding tot de missiewetenschap... Bussum, 1950.
P. 250-258: Godsdienstwetenschap.

*HOLSTEN. 1953.
P. 34-42: Das Verhältnis von Religionswissenschaft und Missionswissenschaft zu einander.

*SCIENTIA MISSIONUM ANCILLA. 1953.
P. 173-179: Die Religionswissenschaft im Dienste der Mission (Johannes P. Steffes).

*ANDERSEN, WILHELM. Die kerygmatische Begründung der Religions- und Missionswissenschaft: ein kritischer Bericht über Walter Holstens Buch 'Das Kerygma und der Mensch'. In: EMZ, XI (1954), p. 29-37.

*WINSEN, GERARDUS A.C. VAN, CM. Meelevend begrijpen: een studie over het verband tussen de godsdienstwetenschap en de missiologie. Nijmegen, 1954. Diss. Nijmegen.

*VRIENS. 1960.
P. 103-114: The science of religion. Bibliog.

*LOHFF, WENZEL, & FERDINAND HAHN (eds.). Wissenschaftliche Theologie im Ueberblick. Göttingen, 1974.
P. 62-70: Die Religions- und Missionswissenschaft (Horst Bürkle).

*BÜRKLE, HORST. Missionstheologie. Stuttgart, Berlin, Köln..., 1979.
P. 167-170: Missionswissenschaft und Religionswissenschaft als theologische Disziplinen.

*PLATVOET, JOHANNES G. Comparing religions: a limitative approach... The Hague, Paris, & New York, 1982.
P. 4-6: Objectivity.

*LMG. 1987.
P. 411-422: Religion, Religionen (Theo Sundermeier).
P. 422-426: Religionswissenschaft (H.-J. Klimkeit).

3.3.4. CONCLUSION

The empirical study of mission, also known as *the science of mission*, being the second 'concept' of missiology, is already fairly developed as a discipline. I agree with the following observation of Edward C. Pentecost (1982:10): 'Missiology is, therefore, *a science* that is becoming recognized as *a science*, drawing from the fields of anthropology, sociology, psychology, and communications, as well as from the experience of those who have poineered various mission endeavors. Missiology is seen today as a vital field of study in its own right' (my italics). And I add to his statement: today anthropology, sociology, psychology, etc. also draw from the field of missiology.

The 'science of mission' is as empirical as the 'science of religion'. In the next section we will observe that the 'theology of mission' as a normative discipline certainly does not destroy the 'science of mission' as an empirical discipline: it presupposes and also perfects the empirical study of mission.

*PENTECOST, EDWARD C. Issues in missiology: an introduction. Grand Rapids, 1982.

3.4. THE THEOLOGY OF MISSION

3.4.1. INTRODUCTION

The *theology of mission(s)* (Ger.: *Missionstheologie*) is the third and last concept of mission studies. It is treated under two headings: as (1) a discipline in its own right; and (2) a discipline which is closely related to the *theology of religion(s)* (Lat.: *theologia religionum*; Ger.: *Religionstheologie*).

Most handbooks of missiology focus upon the 'theology of mission(s)' or 'theological study of mission'. Usually they pay more attention to this concept of mission studies than to the philosophy of mission, but less than to the science of mission. However, the well-known handbooks of Warneck (1892-1903), Ohm (1962), and Verkuyl (1978) concentrate on theological issues.

The theology of mission is not only described and analysed in missiological handbooks, but also in many monographs. In the following sections of this chapter I will refer to both categories of theological mission studies.

Although several theological mission studies speak about the *theology of missions* (plural), I like to follow Paul Tillich (Occasional bulletin of missionary research 1954) and later authors who prefer to write about *theology of mission* (singular), which runs parallel with the above-mentioned terms 'philosophy of mission' (singular) and 'science of mission' (singular).

As already explained (cf. 2.5.5.), contemporary missiology uses the term *missionary theology* in a totally different way from the term *theology of mission* (=*mission theology*). In this section I only deal with the theology of mission, whereas the second volume of this encyclopedia (5.4.) will make clear the essence and purpose of 'missionary theology'.

*WARNECK. 1892-1903.
TILLICH, PAUL. The theology of mission. In: Occasional bulletin of missionary research, V/10 (1954).
*OHM. 1962.
*VERKUYL, JOHANNES. Contemporary missiology. Grand Rapids, 1978.

3.4.2. THE THEOLOGY OF MISSION (MISSIONSTHEOLOGIE)

3.4.2.1. INTRODUCTION

> The development of mission theology is in its
> early stages and is still in the process of formation.
> *Ronan Hoffman OFMConv. (Campbell 1965:42).*

The *theology of mission* can be divided as follows: (1) the general theology of mission, which will be discussed in this section; and (2) the special theologies of mission, which will be dealt with thereafter: the biblical, ecclesiastical, corporate, and individual theology of mission. In fact the general theology of mission is based upon the special theologies of mission; therefore it is also defensible to put the general theology of mission as the 'concluding' discipline at the very end of this section 3.4.2.

The term 'theology of mission(s)' is rather more recent than the terms 'philosophy of mission(s)' and 'science of mission(s)'. It was coined in the last quarter of the nineteenth century: in Germany Gustav Warneck (1877:16) wrote about the 'practical theology of mission' (Ger.: *praktische Missionstheologie*), whereas in the Anglo-Saxon world George Smith (1884: 4-6) used the term *theology of missions*. This term, however, only became popular in the twentieth century, especially after the Second World War. In the period between the First and the Second World War, people such as John A. Mackay (IRM 1933:174-188), the successor of John Mott as President of the International Missionary Council, and Hugh V. White (1937), the Secretary of the American Board of Commissioners for Foreign Missions, already made use of this term.

The term *theology of mission(s)* replaces the older term *theory of mission(s)* which was introduced into the theological encyclopedia by Friedrich D.E. Schleiermacher, et al. Protestant missiologists were much more inclined to adopt this new term than Roman Catholic missiologists. In the Roman Catholic Church, Benno M. Biermann OP (MR 1949:138-142) discussed the significance of the terms *doctrine of mission* and *theology of mission*. Thereafter Alphonsus J.M. Mulders (1950:124-185) advocated this new term, but he was critisized by Thomas Ohm OSB (1962:67). In the end, however, nearly all Roman Catholic missiologists adopted the new term 'theology of mission(s)' cordially. Here I refer only to the studies of Danilo Catarzi SX (1958), and Antonin-Marcel Henry OP (1963).

Classical theology of mission deals with the following six questions formulated by my predecessor Gisbertus Voetius in the seventeenth century:

1. who does the sending (Lat.: *qui sint mittentes*)?
2. to whom are they sent (Lat.: *ad quos mittendi*)?
3. where are they sent (Lat.: *ad quid mittendi*)?
4. who and what sort of people are sent (Lat.: *qui et quales mittendi*)?
5. by what means and in what manner are they sent (Lat.: *qua via methodo et quo modo mittendi*)?
6. to what do missionaries need to devote their attention (Lat.: *quid missis et missionariis observandum*)? (my tr.; cf. Jongeneel, in: Calvin theological journal 1991:47-79).

Gustav Warneck (1892-1903) compiled and reshaped these six main questions under the following three heads:

1. the basis of mission (Ger.: *Die Begründung der Sendung*);
2. the mission agencies (Ger.: *Die Organe der Sendung*);
3. the missionary enterprise (Ger.: *Der Betrieb der Sendung*). (my tr.)

Also in contemporary theology of mission these traditional topics are debated. For instance, in their introductory survey of mission studies J.J.(Dons) Kritzinger, Piet G.J. Meiring, & Willem A. Saayman (1984) discussed in separate chapters the following four topics:

1. mission-who?
2. mission-what?
3. mission-where?
4. mission-how?

In modern theology of mission -both the general theology of mission and the special theologies of mission- we can discern several 'trends and factors' (Anderson 1961:4), 'viewpoints' (Dumas, in: Campbell 1965:79-108), 'new orientations' (Aring 1971; Rütti 1972), or 'models' (Kramm 1979; Bosch 1980:28-40). Here I only draw attention to those 'trends and factors', 'viewpoints', 'new orientations', or 'models' which have been substantially influential in both the past and the present theology of mission and missionary theology:

1. contextualization;
2. worldviews or -isms;
3. denominationalism; and
4. the focus of attention ('-centeredness').

First, in both mission theology and missionary theology *contextualization* is very important (cf. Evers 1974:158-182). I will discuss this topic in detail later (cf. 5.4.1.3.), but here I already refer to it. Although today 'contextualization' is discussed in all six continents, it is very crucial in the so-called 'third world' (mission) theology, which in Protestant circles came to the fore after the incorporation of the International Missionary Council into the World Council of Churches (New Delhi 1961).

The 'third world' does not yet produce theological mission studies to the same extent as the western world, but it has taken the lead in the world-wide process of contextualizing both missionary thinking and missionary activities. Here, I only draw attention to the fact that both the Commission for World Mission and Evangelism and the sub-unit on Dialogue with People of Living Faiths of the World Council of Churches have 'third world' theologians as their secretaries. In the Roman Catholic Church and the Lausanne Movement, however, contextualization is not yet as strong as in the World Council of Churches, and therefore the role of 'third world' theologies in shaping 'new orientations', 'models', etc. is more modest.

Second, I call attention to *the influence of worldviews or -isms* on the development of both the theology of mission and missionary theology. Here the main distinction is: liberalism-conservatism. J. Herbert Kane (1986:235) writes as follows about this distinction: 'Liberals and conservatives are divided into two separate and distinct camps. Though the former are outnumbered nine to one they are better educated, better organized, and certainly more vocal than the conservatives'. However, today the number of conservative missiological publications is increasing. A substantial number of people are inclined to consider Conciliar and Liberationist theologians of mission as 'liberals' on the one hand, and on the other Evangelical and Roman Catholic theologians of mission as 'conservatives'; but we must be very careful, because there are also conservatives in the Ecumenical Movement and non-liberationalist liberals in the Roman Catholic church.

Other influential worldviews or -isms in the theology of mission and missionary theology are imperialism, colonialism, nationalism, racism, etc. On the one hand, we must protest against the many publications of those scholars who 'persist in identifying the Christian mission with Western imperialism' (Glasser, & McGavran 1985:11), but, on the other hand, we must acknowledge that missiologists have not always taken a critical stance in ideological matters. In the past many missionary theologians and missionaries have, wholeheartedly or with a troubled conscience, served both Christ and colonialism, imperialism, nationalism, and/or racism. The well-known slogan 'Only German missionaries in German colonies' (cf. Bosch 1991:309) has its equals in other western countries.

At the same time we must recognize that worldviews not only in a (very) negative way, but also in a (very) positive way have influenced the Christian mission and its theology. Hendrik Kraemer (1938:86), for instance, advocated '(biblical) realism' (versus 'naturalism': eudaemonism, et al.). He wrote: 'The Christian ethic, as contained in Biblical realism, is neither eudaemonistic nor individualistic nor collectivistic'. Also I call attention to the Jewish philosopher Philip A. Kohnstamm, who was converted from agnosticism via idealism to '(biblical) personalism': basically he considered the non-Christian religions as impersonalistic religions, but Christianity as the religion which does not accept a doctrine, but a person -the living Christ- as the ultimate norm (Hofstee 1973).

In any case we must inquire about the influence of ideologies and -isms on missionary 'viewpoints', 'models', etc. A considerable number of old and new theologies of mission and missionary theologies ignore this crucial problem, although they themselves are influenced, consciously or unconsciously, by worldviews and -isms as well. This also applies to the biblical, ecclesiastical, corporate, and individual theology of mission as special theologies of mission. In the biblical theology of mission, for instance, both historicism and fundamentalism/biblicism are very strong.

Third, I deal with *denominationalism*, which is 'exported along with the gospel' (Kane 1986:281). The main distinction in Christian community life is: Jewish, & non-Jewish (Hebrew: *goiim*). Therefore the oldest type of mission theology is Hebrew Christian (cf. 3.4.2.3.). Thereafter came the Orthodox, Roman Catholic, and Protestant (Lutheran, Reformed, etc.) theologies of mission and missionary theologies, which are mainly produced, propagated, and practised by non-Jewish missiologists and missionaries. Today both the Orthodox, the Roman Catholic, and the Protestant theologies of mission as denominational theologies of mission are struggling to find their own identity. Gerald H. Anderson (1961:3-16) regarded as the main pioneer Protestant theologians of mission in the first half of this century: Karl W. Hartenstein (IRM 1931:210-227; 1933; EMM 1938:69-83), the noted Mission Director from Basel; William E. Hocking -cf. *Re-thinking Missions* issued by the Laymen's Foreign Missions Inquiry (1932)-; Archibald G. Baker (1934), Professor of Missions at the University of Chicago; Hugh V. White (1937), Secretary for the American Board of Commissioners for Foreign Missions; Hendrik Kraemer (1938), Professor of the History of Religions at Leiden University; Godfrey E. Phillips (1939), Professor of Missions at Selly Oak College in Birmingham; and Edmund D. Soper (1943), Professor of the History of Religion at Garrett Biblical Institute, Evanston; they belonged to different Protestant denominations. André V. Seumois OMI (Anderson 1961:122-134) mentioned as the leading Roman Catholic theologians of mission in the same period: Robert Streit OMI (1909), Théodorus Grentrup SVD (1925), Joseph Schmidlin (1925), and Pierre Charles SJ (1938).

After the establishment of the World Council of Churches (1948) on the Protestant side, after the entry of the Orthodox churches into the World Council of Churches (1961), and after the Second Vatican Council (1962-1965) on the Roman Catholic side, the situation has changed remarkably. The main contemporary Protestant theologians of mission who are members of different Protestant churches -Paul Tillich (Occasional Bulletin of Missionary Research 1954), Hans J. Margull (1962), Georg F. Vicedom (1965), Peter Beyerhaus (1972), Alan R. Tippett (1973), Carl E. Braaten (1977), Melvin L. Hodges (1977), David J. Bosch (1980; 1991), and Arthur F. Glasser, & Donald A. McGavran (1985), et al.- must now be classified as scholars who primarily represent either the Ecumenical, the Evangelical, or the Pentecostal movement (cf. 3.4.2.3.). On the one hand, David J. Bosch (1980:28-40) ignored the Orthodox, Roman Catholic, and Pentecostal theologies of mission, and, on the other, he analysed the Ecumenical and Evangelical views of mission as two 'contrasting missionary models'. Today the Roman Catholic theology of mission is nearly as diverse as the Protestant theology of mission: besides the various theologies of liberation in Latin America and elsewhere I refer to the mission theology of Ludwig Rütti SMB (1972), Yves M.J. Congar SJ (Theologische Revue 1973:353-360), Heinz R. Schlette (ZMR 1975:161-169), Joseph Comblin (1977), and Karl Müller SVD (1987) as leading missiologists who have developed their own different viewpoints (cf. 3.4.2.3.). Arthur F. Glasser, & Donald A. McGavran (1985:11) paid no attention to the mission theology of the Orthodox churches and the Pentecostals; for that reason they only distinguished between four major trends in the contemporary theology of mission: Conciliar (=Ecumenical), Evangelical, Roman Catholic, and Liberationist. They clearly linked their first and their fourth model on the one hand, and their second and their third model on the other hand: '... the answers depend exclusively on whether the Bible is regarded as God's one authoritative revelation ... or as simply one of many "revelations of God" or the religious insights of humans... Conciliar and liberationist theologies of mission are on one side of the watershed. Evangelical and Roman Catholic theologies of mission are on the other side' (:9-10). In one way or another denominationalism is either present in, or transcended by the Ecumenical, the Evangelical, the Pentecostal, and the Liberationist movement and its missionary trends and factors. *Interdenominationalism* is very strong especially in the Evangelical movement.

Fourth, I question *the focus of attention* in theological studies of mission. Gerald H. Anderson (1961:15) made the following survey of points of concentration or *-centeredness* in the contemporary Protestant theologies of mission and missionary theologies: 'There have been attempts from the culture-centered, man-centered, revelation-centered, eschatology-centered, kingdom-centered, Bible-centered, Church-centered, and Christ-centered points of view'. Anderson did not discuss all these models one by one, but he stated that Karl W. Hartenstein developed an eschatology- centered theology of mission, whereas Archibald G. Baker adopted a culture-centered approach (:9). He also referred to Hugh V. White, the chief supporter of an anthropocentric approach. According to Hendrik Kraemer (Bergema, in: DH 1963:9), the title of the study of White: *A Theology for Christian Missions* (1937), can easily be replaced by the title 'An Anthropology for Christian Missions'.

The above-mentioned catalogue of Anderson is not at all definitive. Inside and outside the Protestant world there are also important attempts to do mission theology from a God-centered, a Spirit-centered, a salvation- centered, a liberation-centered, and a dialogue-centered point of view. Georg F. Vicedom (1965), for instance, propagated theocentrism; Melvin L. Hodges (1977) and other Pentecostal theologians pneumatocentrism; Gustavo Gutierrez (1973) and other liberation theologians liberation- centrism; the Lausanne movement (1974) soteriocentrism; and Stanley J. Samartha and other dialogue theologians (cf. 5.4.11.) dialogue-centrism in their mission studies. Every biblical, ecclesiastical, corporate, and individual theology of mission also demonstrates in a clear or hidden way its own 'focus of attention' or '-centeredness'.

In conclusion, it can be stated that the theological mission studies of both the colonial period and the post-colonial period are influenced by one or more contextual 'factors': worldviews, denominationalism, etc. To many scholars the 'focus of attention' or '-centeredness' seems to be an uncontextual issue, but I disagree with them because this point also has its own 'trends' and 'new orientations'. In the next sections I hope to make clear that the biblical, ecclesiastical, corporate, and individual mission theologies also have their own context, their own 'viewpoints' and 'models', etc.

*WARNECK, GUSTAV. Das Studium der Mission auf der Universität. Gütersloh, 1877.
*SMITH, GEORGE. Short history of Christian missions from Abraham and Paul to Carey, Livingstone, and Duff. Edinburgh, 1884.
*WARNECK. 1892-1903.
BERGMANN, LORENZ. Missionens betydning for kirken og teologien... Kobenhavn, 1901.
STREIT, ROBERT, OMI. Die theologisch-wissenschaftliche Missionskunde. Paderborn, 1909.
LA ROCHE, FR. Rückwirkung des Missionsstudiums auf das theologische Denken. Basel, 1912.
*RICHTER, JULIUS. Weltmission und theologische Arbeit. Gütersloh, 1913. Habilitationsschrift Berlin.
LANGE, RENÉ, SJ. Le problème théologique des missions. Louvain, 1924.
GRENTRUP, THÉODORUS, SVD. Ius missionarium. Steyl, 1925.
*SCHMIDLIN. 1925.
*RICHTER, MARTIN. Dialektische Theologie und Mission. In: NAMZ, V (1928), p. 228-241.
THEOLOGY AND THE CHRISTIAN WORLD MISSION: a short report of a Conference on the preparation of the ministry, held at York, 2-5 April, 1929. London, 1929.
MULDERS, ALPHONSUS J.M. Kerk en missie in theologische en historische belichting... Nijmegen, & Utrecht, 1930.

*HARTENSTEIN, KARL W. The theology of the Word and missions. In: IRM, XX (1931), p. 210-227.

KÖBERLE, ADOLF. Die Neubesinnung auf den Missionsgedanken in der Theologie der Gegenwart. Leipzig, 1931.

*BARTH, KARL. Die Theologie und die Mission in der Gegenwart. In: Zwischen den Zeiten, X (1932), p. 189-215.
Repr.: 1957. Fr. tr.: 1932.

*KNAK, SIEGFRIED. Die Mission und die Theologie in der Gegenwart. In: Zwischen den Zeiten, X (1932), p. 331-355.

LAYMEN'S FOREIGN MISSIONS INQUIRY, COMMISSION OF APPRAISAL (William E. Hocking, chairman). Re-thinking missions... New York, 1932.

*HARTENSTEIN, KARL W. Die Mission als theologisches Problem: Beiträge zum grundsätzlichen Verständnis der Mission. Berlin, 1933.

*MACKAY, JOHN A. The theology of the Laymen's foreign missions inquiry. In: IRM, XXII (1933), p. 174-188.

*BAKER, ARCHIBALD G. Christian missions and a new world culture. Chicago, & New York, 1934.

BADLEY, BRENTON T. Laymen re-thinking theology: an examination of some theological views and implications of the Appraisal Commission's Report. Bombay, 1935.

*WHITE, HUGH V. A theology for Christian missions. New York, & Chicago, 1937.

CHARLES, PIERRE, SJ. Les dossiers de l'action missionnaire... Louvain, & Bruxelles, 1938.

*HARTENSTEIN, KARL W. Der Beitrag der Theologie zu den missionarischen Problemen der Gegenwart. In: EMM, LXXXII (1938), p. 69-83.

*KRAEMER, HENDRIK. The Christian message in a non-Christian world. London, 1938.

*HARKNESS, GEORGIA. The theological basis of the missionary message. In: IRM, XXVIII (1939), p. 518-526.

*PHILLIPS, GODFREY E. The gospel in the world: a re-statement of missionary principles. London, 1939.
Abridgment: 1947.

DURAND, ALEXANDRE, SJ. Le problème théologique des missions. St. Étienne, 1942.

ALLEN, GEOFFREY F. The theology of missions. London, 1943.

TEOLOGIA ET MISSIONI. Roma, 1943.

*SOPER, EDMUND D. The philosophy of the Christian world mission. New York, & Nashville, 1943.

*LUBAC, HENRI DE, SJ. Le fondement théologique des missions. Paris, 1946.
Reprints.
Port. tr.: n.d.

*MORGAN, EDMUND R., & ROGER LLOYD (eds.). The mission of the Anglican communion. London, 1948.
P. 1-17: The theology of missions (Norman J. Blow).

*WARD, MARCUS. Towards a theology of missions. In: IRM, XXXVII (1948), p. 249-255.

*BIERMANN, BENNO M., OP. Missionslehre oder Missionstheologie. In: MR, no series number (1949), p. 138-142.

*MULDERS, ALPHONSUS J.M. Inleiding tot de missiewetenschap... Bussum, 1950.
P. 124-185: Missietheologie.

*WIEBE, FRANZ (ed.). Mission und Theologie. Göttingen, 1953.

TILLICH, PAUL. The theology of mission. In: Occasional bulletin of missionary research, V/10 (1954).

*ANDERSEN, WILHELM. Towards a theology of mission: a study of the encounter between the missionary enterprise and the church and its theology. London, 1955.

*Second impression: 1956.

Ger. tr.: 1957. Second Ger. ed.: 1958.

*MYKLEBUST. 1955-1957.

I, p. 368-372: Missions and theology.

CATARZI, DANILO, SX. Teologia delle missioni estere: aspetti specifice. Parma, 1958.

Sp. tr.: 1961.

ANDERSON, GERALD H. The theology of missions: 1928-1958. Michigan, 1960. Thesis Boston University.

*ANDERSON. 1961.

*HERMELINK, JAN, & HANS J. MARGULL (eds.). Walter Freytag: Reden und Aufsätze. München, 1961. 2 vols.

II, p. 198-207: Theologische Ueberlegungen zur Mission (1946).

MARGULL, HANS J. Hope in action... Philadelphia, 1962.

*Ger. ed.: Theologie der missionarischen Verkündigung: Evangelisation als oekumenisches Problem. Stuttgart, 1959.

*OHM. 1962.

*BERGEMA, HENDRIK. Theocentrische tendenzen in de Amerikaanse zendingswetenschap. In: DH, XVI (1963), p. 1-14.

HENRY, ANTONIN-MARCEL, OP. A mission theology... Notre Dame, 1963.

*Fr. ed.: Esquisse d'une théologie de la mission. Paris, 1959.

Sp. tr.: 1962.

*Ger. tr.: 1963.

*BOCKMÜHL, KLAUS. Die neuere Missionstheologie: eine Erinnerung an die Aufgabe der Kirche. Stuttgart, 1964.

*LINZ, MANFRED. Anwalt der Welt: zur Theologie der Mission. Stuttgart, & Berlin, 1964.

*CAMPBELL, ROBERT E., MM (ed.). The church in mission. New York, 1965.

P. 42-78: The development of mission theology in the twentieth century (Ronan Hoffman OFMConv.).

P. 79-108: Viewpoints on mission theology: external and internal missions (N. Dumas).

TILSON, EVERETT (ed.). Papers on the theology of mission... New York, 1965.

*VICEDOM, GEORG F. The mission of God: an introduction to a theology of mission. Saint Louis, 1965.

*First ed.: Missio Dei... München, 1960.

*ANDERSON, GERALD H. (comp.). Bibliography of the theology of missions in the twentieth century: third ed. rev. and enl. New York, 1966. Bibliog.

First ed.: New York, 1958.

?DOURNES, JACQUES, MEP. Teologia existencial de la mision. Madrid, 1966.

*ANDERSON, GERALD H. (ed.). Christian mission in theological perspective: an inquiry by Methodists. Nashville, & New York, 1967.

*DICTIONARY CATALOG. 1968.

XI, p. 177-178: Missions and theology. Bibliog.

*WAGNER, FALK. Über die Legitimität der Mission: wie ist die Mission der Christenheit theologisch zu gründen? München, 1968.

*CONCISE DICTIONARY. 1970.

P. 594-595: Theology of mission (Gerald H. Anderson).

*LINDSELL, HAROLD. An evangelical theology of missions: rev. ed. Grand Rapids, 1970.

First ed.: A Christian philosophy of missions. Wheaton, 1949.

*PIET, JOHN H. The road ahead: a theology for the church in mission. Grand Rapids, 1970.

*SHORTER, AYLWARD, WF. Theology of mission. Cork, 1970.

*ARING, PAUL G. Kirche als Ereignis: ein Beitrag zur Neuorientierung der Missionstheologie. Neukirchen, & Vluyn, 1971.
First ed.: 1969. Diss. Prag.

*FROHNES, HEINZGÜNTER (ed.). Martin Kähler: Schriften zu Christologie und Mission: Gesamtausgabe der Schriften zur Mission: mit einer Bibliographie. München, 1971.
P. 184-221: Mission und Theologie (1908).

*GENSICHEN, HANS-WERNER. Glaube für die Welt: theologische Aspekte der Mission. Gütersloh, 1971.

*POWER, JOHN, SMA. Mission theology today: second printing. New York, 1971.
*First ed.: Dublin, 1970.

SCHMITZ, JOSEF. Die Weltzuwendung Gottes: Thesen zu einer Theologie der Mission. Freiburg, & Nürnberg, 1971.

*AMSTUTZ, JOSEF, SMB. Kirche der Völker: Skizze einer Theorie der Mission. Freiburg, Basel, & Wien, 1972.

*BEYERHAUS, PETER. Allen Völkern zum Zeugnis: biblisch-theologische Besinnung zum Wesen der Mission. Wuppertal, 1972.

*BEYERHAUS, PETER. Shaken foundations: theological foundations for mission. Grand Rapids, 1972.

*RICHARDSON, ALAN (ed.). A dictionary of Christian theology: second impression. London, 1972.
P. 217-220: Theology of mission (Robert M.C. Jeffery).

*RÜTTI, LUDWIG, SMB. Zur Theologie der Mission: kritische Analysen und neue Orientierungen. München, & Mainz, 1972. Diss. Münster.

*SEDOS (ed.). Foundations of mission theology: second printing. New York, 1972.
Fr. ed.: Spiritus, XXXIX (1969), p. 321-351.
SEDOS = Servizio documentazione e studi.

*TRUEBLOOD, ELTON. The validity of the Christian mission. New York, Evanston, San Francisco..., 1972.

?AAGAARD, JOHANNES. Missionsteologi og oekumenisk teologi. Aarhus, 1973.

*CONGAR, YVES M.J., SJ. Zur Theologie der Mission. In: Theologische revue, LXIX (1973), p. 353-360.

*GUTIÉRREZ, GUSTAVO. A theology of liberation: history, politics, and salvation. New York, 1973.
First ed.: Teología de la liberación... Lima, 1971.
*Dutch tr.: 1974.
Also other trs.

*HOFSTEE, HARM, Pzn. Het bijbels personalisme van Prof.Dr. Ph.A. Kohnstamm: onstaan en grondslagen. Assen, 1973. Diss. Groningen.

*TIPPETT, ALAN R. Verdict theology in missionary theory; second ed. South Pasadena, 1973.
First ed.: Lincoln, 1969.

*ANDERSON, GERALD H., & THOMAS F. STRANSKY CSP (eds.). Mission trends. No. 1: Crucial issues in mission today. New York, Paramus, Toronto..., 1974.
P. 23-36: Guidelines for a new theology of mission (William B. Frazier MM).

*BOCKMÜHL, KLAUS. Was heisst heute Mission? Entscheidungsfragen der neueren Missionstheologie. Giessen, & Basel, 1974.

*EVERS, GEORG. Mission, nichtchristliche Religionen, weltliche Welt. Münster, 1974.
P. 3-83: Die theologische Besinnung auf die Mission.
P. 158-182: Der Wandel des theologischen Kontextes der Mission.

*HOECKMAN, RÉMI. Unité de l'église - unité du monde: essai d'une théologie oecuménique de la mission. Berne, & Francfort/M., 1974.

*KRAUS, JOHANN, SVD. Missionswissenschaftliche Themen in Festschriften aus den Jahren 1960-1971. Immensee, 1974. Bibliog.
  P. 11-18: Theologische Ueberlegungen.
*SCHLETTE, HEINZ R. Bemerkungen zur Theologie der Mission - im Anschluss an L. Rütti. In: ZMR, LIX (1975), p. 161-169.
*BRAATEN, CARL E. The flaming center: a theology of the Christian mission. Philadelphia, 1977.
*COMBLIN, JOSEPH. The meaning of mission: Jesus, Christians, and the wayfaring church. New York, 1977.
  ?First ed.: Teologia de la mision. Buenos Aires, 1974.
HODGES, MELVIN L. A theology of the church and its mission: a Pentecostal perspective. Springfield, 1977.
*ROSENKRANZ, GERHARD. Die christliche Mission: Geschichte und Theologie. München, 1977.
*BASSHAM, ROGER C. Seeking a deeper theological basis for mission. In: IRM, LXVII (1978), p. 329-337.
*HESSELGRAVE, DAVID J. (ed.). Theology and mission: papers and responses prepared for the consultation on theology and mission Trinity Evangelical Divinity School, School of World Mission and Evangelism March 22-25, 1976. Grand Rapids, 1978.
*VERSTEEG, JOHANNES P., CORNELIS GRAAFLAND, et al. Gij die eertijds verre waart...: een overzicht van de geschiedenis en taken van de zending. Utrecht, 1978.
  P. 61-137: Theologische hoofdlijnen (Cornelis Graafland).
*BÜRKLE, HORST. Missionstheologie. Stuttgart, Berlin, Köln..., 1979.
*KRAMM, THOMAS. Analyse und Bewährung theologischer Modelle zur Begründung der Mission: Entscheidungskriterien in der aktuellen Auseinandersetzung zwischen einem heilsgeschichtlich-ekklesiologischen und einem geschichtlich-eschatologischen Missionsverständnis. Aachen, 1979.
*BOSCH, DAVID J. Witness to the world: the Christian mission in theological perspective. London, 1980.
*SHIVUTE, TOMAS. The theology of mission and evangelism in the IMC from Edinburgh to New Delhi. Helsinki, 1980.
*SUNDERMEIER, THEO (ed.). Fides pro mundi vita: Missionstheologie heute: Hans-Werner Gensichen zum 65. Geburtsdag: in Verbindung mit Hans-Jürgen Becken und Bernward H. Willeke OFM hrsg. Gütersloh, 1980.
*GEFFRÉ, CLAUDE, OP. Theological reflections on a new age of mission. In: IRM, LXXI (1982), p. 478-492.
KÖSTER, HEINRICH M., & MANFRED PROBST (eds.). Wie mich der Vater gesandt hat, so sende ich euch; Beiträge zur Theologie der Sendung. Limburg, 1982.
*BRIA, ION. Reflections on mission theology and methodology. In: IRM, LXXIII (1984), p. 66-72.
?CONN, HARVIE M. Eternal Word and changing worlds: theology, anthropology, and mission in trialogue. Grand Rapids, 1984.
*KRITZINGER, J.J.(DONS), PIET G.J. MEIRING, & WILLEM A. SAAYMAN. You will be my witnesses: an introduction to methods of mission. Pretoria, 1984.
*GLASSER, ARTHUR F., & DONALD A. McGAVRAN. Contemporary theologies of mission: second printing. Grand Rapids, 1985.
  First printing: 1983.
*KANE, J. HERBERT. Understanding Christian missions: fourth ed. Grand Rapids, 1986.
  First ed.: 1978.
*LMG. 1987.
  P. 470-495: Theologie der Mission (Theo Sundermeier).

98

*MÜLLER, KARL, SVD (ed.). Mission theology: an introduction... Nettetal, 1987.
    *Ger. ed.: Missionstheologie: eine Einführung... Berlin, 1985.
*BOSCH. 1991.
*JONGENEEL, JAN A.B. The missiology of Gisbertus Voetius: the first comprehensive
    Protestant theology of missions. In: Calvin theological journal, XXVI (1991), p.
    47-79.

3.4.2.2. BIBLICAL THEOLOGY OF MISSION

INTRODUCTION

André V. Seumois (1952:187; cf. Santos Hernandez 1962; 1965) distinguished
'biblical missiology' from 'patristic missiology'. I prefer to distinguish between
biblical theology of mission and *ecclesiastical theology of mission*, which will
be dealt with in 3.4.2.3.

    In this section 3.4.2.2. I put the 'biblical theology of mission' as
general discipline at the beginning, but in fact it is based upon the 'Old
Testament theology of mission' and the 'New Testament theology of mission'
as special disciplines. Therefore, it is also defensible to put the 'biblical
theology of mission' as the 'concluding' discipline at the very end of this
section 3.4.2.2.

*DAUBANTON. 1911.
    P. 478-484: Exegeze.
*SCHMIDLIN. 1925.
    P. 131-139: Biblisch-traditionelle Missionstheorie.
*SCHOMERUS. 1935.
    P. 16-18: Die Missionsapologetik und die biblischen und systematischen Disziplinen.
*SEUMOIS. 1952.
    P. 187-191: Missiologie biblique.
*HOLSTEN. 1953.
    P. 120-126: Die biblische Begründung der Mission.
*MULDERS. 1962.
    P. 166-200: Bijbelse missieleer.
*OHM. 1962.
    P. 137: Missionsexegese (der Missionsgedanke in der Bibel).
SANTOS HERNANDEZ, ANGEL, SJ. Teología biblico-patristica de las missiones. Santander, 1962.
*SANTOS HERNANDEZ, ANGEL, SJ. Bibliografia misional. Santander, 1965. 2 vols.
    I, p. 167-224: Teologia biblica misional. Bibliog.

MISSION IN THE BIBLE

From cover to cover the Bible is a missionary book...
Robert H. Glover (1946:14).

The following names are given to the 'biblical theology of mission': *biblical missiology* (Seumois 1952:187-191); *biblical mission theory* (Vriens 1960:37-39); *biblical theology of (holistic) mission(s)* (Blauw 1962; Santos Hernandez 1962; Peters 1974; Dyrness 1983); *biblical theology of evangelism* (Amaya 1970); and *biblical theology of evangelization* (Vellanickal, in: Dhavamony 1972:41-53).

The 'biblical theology of mission' belongs to both biblical theology and missiology. Therefore, both biblical theologians and missiologists are dealing with this discipline, which is concerned about *the view* of the law of Moses (Hebrew: *thora*), the prophets (Hebrew: *nebiim*), and the writings (Hebrew: *ketubim*) (in the Old Testament), and of Jesus, the apostles and evangelists (in the New Testament) on the mission of God, of Israel, of Christ, of the Holy Spirit, of Christians, and of the church in the world. Here I use the noun *view* (cf. di Gangi 1979), although most publications speak either about the biblical *basis/foundation* of mission(s) (Kolmodin 1920; Richter 1927:II,7-33; Simon 1935; Inter-Varsity Christian Fellowship 1949; Studiecommissie Nederlandsche Zendingsraad, in: DH 1951:197-211; Albright 1957; Bavinck 1960:9-76; Anderson 1961:317-319; idem, 1966: 3-16; Blackman 1961; Beyerhaus, in: IRM 1964:393-407; Hillis 1965; de Kuiper 1968:13-49; Glover 1969; Kraus 1974:6-11; Lum, & Lum 1976; Tippett 1976; Versteeg 1978:9-60; Bosch 1980:41-83; Senior, & Stuhlmüller 1983; Mugambi 1989), or about the missionary *message* of the Bible (Carver 1921; Cook 1924; Love 1941; Raen 1979), or the *witness* of the Bible (Martin 1927).

Biblical theology of mission was born in the last century. In 1841, G.C. Friedrich Lücke, a friend of Friedrich D.E. Schleiermacher, had already dealt with missions in the context of his Biblical lecture courses (Myklebust 1955:I,75). However, it was only at the turn of the century that a large stream of publications began to emerge. Here I call attention to the following monographs which, in one way or another, initiated the biblical theology of mission as an independent discipline: Paul von Zychlinski (1884) and B. Kleinpaul (1901) on the whole Bible; Alfred Bertholet (1896) and Max R.H. Löhr (1896) on the Old Testament; and Theodor Zahn (1886) and Erich Haupt (1895) on the New Testament. Most of the 20th century publications are the result of private initiatives. The well-known study of the Dutch scholar Johannes Blauw, however, was commissioned by both the International Missionary Council and the World Council of Churches. He wrote in the Introduction to his study: 'This little book is not intended to present a new biblical theology of missionary work but a "critical survey" of what has been said about the subject by others in the past thirty years' (1962:11). Blauw referred in passing also to the just mentioned studies of Kleinpaul (1901), Bertholet (1896), and Löhr (1896), which do not belong to the 'past thirty years'.

In the Roman Catholic Church, biblical mission studies began later than in Protestantism, but they have developed very well. Robert Streit OMI (1909), Max Meinertz (1916), Charles O'Connor Sloane STJ, SSL, & Wendell S. Reilly SS (1944), Johannes P.M. van der Ploeg OP (1949), André Rétif SJ (1955; 1960), Gauthier A. Hamman OFM (1956), Angel Santos Hernandez SJ (1962), Adrianus de Groot SVD (1964), John Power SMA (1970), Félix Asensio Nieto SJ (1974), Donald Senior CP, & Carroll Stuhlmüller CP (1983), et al. brought them to prosperity. The last mentioned publication, which did not refer to most of the biblical mission studies catalogued in our bibliography (even the book of Blauw is absent!), concluded: '... the biblical data remain unique and crucial. The biblical witness has been and will be the ultimate catalyst for the universal mission of the church. The biblical call to *go to the end of the earth* will ring in the ears of heroic Christians even if our communal reflection on why we should do so may cause hesitation' (:339).

In most mission studies we read that some Bible-books (Ruth; Deutero-Isaiah; Jonah; The Acts of the Apostles) and some Bible-chapters (Ps. 67; Ps. 87; Matt. 10 and parallels; Matt. 28 and parallels) are more missionary than others. A few authors, however, protested against this splitting of the whole Bible into a mission-relevant and mission-irrelevant part; because they really believed that mission is not only in the Bible, but the whole Bible is mission(ary). Paul von Zychlinski (1884), Robert F. Horton (1908), John H. Ritson (IRM 1922:390-400), Henry A. Lapham (1925), Hugh Martin (1927), John B. Lawrence (1936), Axel Hjeressen (1944), Evert Jansen Schoonhoven (1955), and Robert H. Glover (1969) considered the Bible in its totality as a *mission(ary) (hand)book*. Here I only quote three of these authors. Lapham (1925:4), who under the Baptist Missionary Society served in Ceylon (now Sri Lanka), wrote: 'The earlier of its two volumes, the Old Testament, recounts the age-long preparation of a missionary nation, which, however, never rose to the full height of its intended destiny. Its second volume, the New Testament, is from end to end a missionary story, the most marvellous missionary story in all literature, whose heroes are a few not very gifted men, transformed into world-subduers by a new missionary message, *God was in Christ* (2 Cor. 5:19), and by a new missionary motive, *the love of Christ constraineth us* (2 Cor. 5:14)'. Martin (1927:IX) said: 'The Bible is a missionary book, not because it contains isolated texts with a missionary flavour, but because the main line of argument that binds together all its volumes is the exposition, the unfolding, and the gradual execution of a missionary purpose. The Bible is the book of the world'. And Jansen Schoonhoven (1955:20), retired Professor of Mission at Leiden University, added to this the following: '...the Bible is a missionary book and only an exegesis which does justice to this missionary viewpoint does justice to the text, and only a preaching which is driven by a missionary passion is a preaching close to the Bible' (my tr.). In this clearly non-selective approach to the whole Bible as a missionary book, biblical theology is in the same way identical with missionary theology as Heinzgünter Frohnes, Hans-Werner Gensichen, & Georg Kretschmar (1974-1978) identified church history with mission history (Ger.: *Kirchengeschichte als Missionsgeschichte*; cf. 5.3.3.).

Several authors have also drawn attention to the missionary aspects of the relation between the Old Testament and the New Testament. Most of them strongly emphasize the continuity between both Testaments, stating that this continuity does not mean identity. Others, however, separated the New Testament from the Old Testament. Robert F. Horton (1908:33-35), for instance, belongs to the last mentioned group: 'The Old Testament is only missionary in the sense, that it issues in the New ... The Old Testament in itself has never had a missionary message to the world... The Old Testament is only a missionary book in the sense that it represents a race, a religious institution, and a great expectation, as the necessary preparation for the event which constitutes a missionary message to mankind. Painful as it sounds to Jewish ears, it is yet historically true that the Old Testament has no significance for the human race, except in so far as it has issued in the New'. Contrary to Horton, Henry A. Lapham (1925: 4), for example, emphasized the continuity: '... the missionary idea was taken over by the New Testament from the Old. It was not born in New Testament times. At that time it was revivified by the supply of the new message and the new motive...'.

*ZYCHLINSKI, PAUL VON (ed.). Missions-Bibel... Gütersloh, 1884.

*KLEINPAUL, B. Die Mission in der Bibel. Leipzig, 1901.

POST, GEORGE E. The missionary as a student of the Bible: an address delivered before the third Brummana conference of foreign missionary workers, August 3, 1904. N.p., 1904.

McLEAN, ARCHIBALD. Where the book speaks: or, mission studies in the Bible... New York, Chicago..., 1907.

WARNECK, GUSTAV. Die Mission im Lichte der Bibel: 5. Aufl. Gütersloh, 1907.
      *Dritte verm. Aufl.: Missionsstunden. I. Gütersloh, 1888.

*HORTON, ROBERT F. The Bible, a missionary book: new ed. Edinburgh, & London, 1908.
      First ed.: Edinburgh, 1904.

STREIT, ROBERT, OMI. Die Mission in Exegese und Patrologie. Paderborn, 1909.

WATSON, CHARLES R. God's plan for world redemption: an outline study of the Bible and missions. Philadelphia, 1911.

WEISMANN, GOTTHILF. Biblische Missions-Grundgedanken. Basel, 1913.

*BEETS, HENRY. Triumfen van het kruis: schetsen der christelijke zending van alle eeuwen en allerlei landen ... Kampen, 1914.

P. 7-30: De zending in de Heilige Schrift (Herman Bavinck).

?MEINERTZ, MAX. Die Heilige Schrift und die Mission. Münster in Westfalen, 1916.

CARVER, WILLIAM O. All the world in all the Word: twelve Bible studies in missions. Nashville, 1918.

RHINELANDER, PHILIP M. The gospel of the kingdom: an outline for missionary study of the Bible. Philadelphia, 1918.

KOLMODIN, ADOLF. Världsmissionens bibliska grund. Uppsala, 1920.

MONTGOMERY, HELEN B. The Bible and missions. West Medford, 1920.

*CARVER, WILLIAM O. The Bible a missionary message: a study of activities and methods. New York, Chicago, Toronto..., 1921.

*RITSON, JOHN H. The Bible: an unfettered missionary. In: IRM, XI (1922), p. 390-400.

COOK, EDMUND F. The missionary message of the Bible. Nashville, 1924.

STORR, VERNON F. The missionary genius of the Bible. London, 1924.

*LAPHAM, HENRY A. The Bible as missionary handbook. Cambridge, 1925.

*MARTIN, HUGH. The kingdom without frontiers: the witness of the Bible to the missionary purpose of God: fourth ed. London, 1927.

First ed.: London, 1924. Reprints.

*RICHTER, JULIUS. Evangelische Missionskunde: zweite erw. und umgearbeitete Aufl. Leipzig, 1927.

II, p. 7-33: Die biblische Begründung.

*SCHLUNK, MARTIN. Gott und die Völker: eine Einführung in die Missionsgedanken der Bibel: zweite Aufl. Berlin, 1930.

*First ed.: Berlin, 1930.

LAWRENCE, JOHN B. Missions in the Bible. Atlanta, 1931.

*BIBLIOGRAFIA MISSIONARIA. 1933-...

XLIX (1978)-...: 2 Teologia missionaria (Biblica, Patristica).

*SIMON, GOTTFRIED. Beiträge zur biblischen Begründung der Mission. Bethel, 1935.

Sonderdruck aus dem Jahrbuch der Theol. Schule Bethel, VI (1935), p. 69-96.

LAWRENCE, JOHN B. The Bible, a missionary book. Atlanta, 1936.

BURKHART, I.E. The world goal of Bible missions: prepared under the direction of the mission study course committee of the Mennonite Board of Missions and Charities. Scottdale, 1940.

LOVE, JULIAN P. The missionary message of the Bible. New York, 1941.

DETWEILER, CHARLES S. The Bible and missions: six compelling studies. Philadelphia, 1944.

GOERNER, HENRY C. 'Thus it is written': the missionary motif in the Scriptures. Nashville, 1944.

HJERESSEN, AXEL. Bibelen, kirkens missionsbog. Kobenhavn, 1944.

O'CONNOR SLOANE, CHARLES, STJ, SSL, & WENDELL S. REILLY SS. Holy Scripture and missionary endeavor. New York, 1944.

*HOEKENDIJK, JOHANNES C. Kerk en volk in de Duitse zendingswetenschap. Amsterdam, 1948. Diss. Utrecht.

P. 223-228: De bijbelse context van de zending.

ZWEMER, SAMUEL M. How rich is the harvest? Studies in Bible themes and missions. New York, 1948.

INTER-VARSITY CHRISTIAN FELLOWSHIP. Therefore go: the Bible basis of missions. Chicago, 1949.

PLOEG, JOHANNES P.M. VAN DER, OP. Missiegedachten in de Heilige Schrift. Hilversum, 1949.

*BLAUW, JOHANNES. Goden en mensen: plaats en betekenis van de heidenen in de Heilige Schrift. Groningen, 1950. Diss. V.U. Amsterdam.

*MEINERTZ, MAX. Bibel und Mission. In: ZMR, XXXIV (1950), p. 14-23.

CARVER, WILLIAM O. Missions in the plan of the ages: Bible studies in missions. Nashville, 1951.
   First ed.: New York, 1909.
SOPER, EDMUND D. The biblical background of the Christian world mission. New York, 1951.
   *First ed.: The philosophy of the Christian world mission. New York, & Nashville, 1943, p. 19-88. Reprint.
*STUDIECOMMISSIE NEDERLANDSCHE ZENDINGSRAAD. Rapport... inzake 'de bijbelse grondslagen van de zending'. In: DH, IV (1951), p. 197-221.
*SEUMOIS. 1952.
*MANSON, WILLIAM. The biblical doctrine of mission. In: IRM, XLII (1953), p. 257-265.
*JANSEN SCHOONHOVEN, EVERT. De Bijbel als missionair boek. Oegstgeest, 1955.
*MYKLEBUST. 1955-1957. 2 vols.
?RÉTIF, ANDRÉ, SJ. Bible et mission. Paris, 1955.
SCHICK, ERICH. Mission und Missionsverantwortung im Licht der Bibel. Basel, 1955.
*WIERSINGA, HENDRIK A. Bijbel en zending. Kampen, 1955.
?GÉLIN, P. ALBERT. L'idée missionnaire dans la Bible. 1956.
HAMMAN, GAUTHIER A., OFM. L'apostolat du chrétien: réflexion sur les données bibliques. Paris, 1956.
ALBRIGHT, LELAND S. The biblical basis of missions. Toronto, 1957.
KVIST, GUSTAV. Intet annat namn, missionen i bibelns ljus... Helsingfors, 1957.
*McGAVRAN, DONALD A. How churches grow: the new frontiers of mission. London, 1959.
   P. 60-66: What do the Scriptures say of mission?
*BAVINCK, JOHAN H. An introduction to the science of missions. Philadelphia, 1960.
   P. 9-76: The foundation of missions.
*RÉTIF, ANDRÉ, SJ. Initiation à la mission: Bible - doctrine - liturgie. Paris, 1960.
*VRIENS. 1960.
   P. 37-39: Biblical mission theory. Bibliog.
*ANDERSON. 1961.
   P. 317-319: The biblical basis for the Christian mission. Bibliog.
*BLACKMAN, CYRIL. The biblical basis of the Church's missionary enterprise. London, 1961.
THE BIBLE AND GOD'S MISSION: an adventure in study to rediscover and rethink some biblical motivations for the Christian mission in our world today. New York, 1962. Symposium.
*BLAUW, JOHANNES. The missionary nature of the church: a survey of the biblical theology of mission. New York, Toronto, & London, 1962.
   *Ger. ed.: Gottes Werk in dieser Welt: Grundzüge einer biblischen Theologie der Mission. München, 1961.
   Fr. tr.: 1968.
SANTOS HERNANDEZ, ANGEL, SJ. Misionologia... Santander, 1962. 2 vols.
   I, p. 165-223: Teologia biblico-patristica de las misiones.
*BEYERHAUS, PETER. The three selves formula: is it built on biblical foundations? In: IRM, LIII (1964), p. 393-407.
BRANNON, T. LEO. The Bible and evangelism. Nashville, 1964.
*GROOT, ADRIANUS DE, SVD. De Bijbel over het heil der volken. Roermond, & Maaseik, 1964.
HILLIS, DON W. (ed.). The scriptural basis of world evangelization. Grand Rapids, 1965.
*ANDERSON, GERALD H. (ed.). Bibliography of the theology of missions in the twentieth century: third ed., rev. and enl. New York, 1966.
   P. 3-16: Biblical basis. Bibliog.
*WEBSTER, DOUGLAS. Unchanging mission: biblical and contemporary: second impression. London, 1967.

*First ed.: London, 1965.

*DICTIONARY CATALOG. 1968.

    II, p. 467-473: Bible and missions. Bibliog.

*KUIPER, ARIE DE. Missiologia (ilmu pekabaran indjil). Djakarta, 1968.

    P. 13-49: Dasar alkitabiah.

    Several reprints.

GLOVER, ROBERT H. The Bible basis of missions... Chicago, 1969.

    *First ed.: Chicago, 1946.

*MÜLLER, JOSEF. Wozu noch Mission? Eine bibeltheologische Überlegung. Stuttgart, 1969.

?AMAYA, ISMAEL E. Teología bíblica del evangelismo. Miami, 1970.

*POWER, JOHN, SMA. Mission theology today. Dublin, 1970.

    P. 59-96: Missions - an Old Testament ideal; the New Testament - a missionary mandate.

?WEBSTER, DOUGLAS. Bible and mission. London, 1970.

*CONCISE DICTIONARY. 1971.

    P. 56-57: The Bible as a missionary force (Harold K. Moulton).

*BEYERHAUS, PETER. Allen Völkern zum Zeugnis: biblisch-theologische Besinnung zum Wesen der Mission. Wuppertal, 1972.

*DHAVAMONY, MARIASUSAI (ed.). Evangelization, dialogue, and development: selected papers of the International Theological Conference, Nagpur (India) 1971. Roma, 1972.

    P. 41-53: Biblical theology of evangelization (Matthew Vellanickal).

ASENSIO NIETO, FÉLIX, SJ. Horizonte missional a lo largo del Antiguo y Nuevo Testamento. Madrid, 1974.

GRANT, COLIN A. The heart of mission: a survey of what the Bible teaches about world mission. London, 1974.

*KRAUS, JOHANN, SVD. Missionswissenschaftliche Themen in Festschriften aus den Jahren 1960-1971. Immensee, 1974.

    P. 6-11: Biblische Grundlagen. Bibliog.

*PETERS, GEORGE W. A biblical theology of missions: second printing. Chicago, 1974.

    *First ed.: Chicago, 1972.

?ASHCRAFT, MORRIS (ed.). National seminar on support of missions... biblical and doctrinal foundations of support of missions. Nashville, 1976.

*KANE, J. HERBERT. Christian missions in biblical perspective. Grand Rapids, 1976.

LUM, ADA, & GINNEY LUM. World mission: twelve studies on the biblical basis. Downers Grove, 1976.

TIPPETT, ALAN R. Church growth and the Word of God: the biblical basis of the Church growth viewpoint. Grand Rapids, 1976.

    First ed.: 1960.

*VERSTEEG, JOHANNES P., CORNELIS GRAAFLAND, et al. (eds.). Gij die eertijds verre waart...: een overzicht van de geschiedenis en taken van de zending. Utrecht, 1978.

    P. 9-60: De bijbelse fundering van het zendingswerk (Johannes P. Versteeg).

*BÜRKLE, HORST. Missionstheologie... Stuttgart, Berlin, Köln..., 1979.

    P. 196-197: Die Mission in der Bibel. Bibliog.

GANGI, MARIANO DI. I believe in mission: a biblical view of the church as a going and growing concern. Phillipsburg, 1979.

GOERNER, HENRY C. All nations in God's purpose: what the Bible teaches about missions. Nashville, 1979.

RAEN, GUTTORM. Bibelens misjonsbudskap. Oslo, 1979.

*BOSCH, DAVID J. Witness to the world: the Christian mission in theological perspective. London, 1980.

P. 41-83: The biblical foundation of mission.
*SPINDLER, MARC R., & PETER R. MIDDELKOOP (eds.). Bible and mission: a partially annotated bibliography 1960-1980. Leiden, & Utrecht, 1981. Bibliog.
TESTA, EMMANUELE, OFM. La missione e la catechesi nella Bibbia. Roma, & Brescia, 1981.
*BRÜGGEMANN, WALTER. The Bible and mission: some interdisciplinary implications for teaching. In: Missiology, X (1982), p. 397-412.
*DUBOSE, FRANCIS M. God who sends: a fresh quest for biblical mission. Nashville, 1983.
?DYRNESS, WILLIAM A. Let the earth rejoice! A biblical theology of holistic mission. Westchester, 1983.
*SENIOR, DONALD, CP, & CARROLL STUHLMÜLLER CP. The biblical foundations for mission. London, 1983.
     It. tr.: 1985.
*BOSCH, DAVID J. Mission in biblical perspective. In: IRM, LXXIV (1985), p. 531-538.
*LMG. 1987.
     P. 50-53: Bibel (Marc R. Spindler).
LEGRAND, LUCIEN. Le Dieu qui vient: la mission dans la Bible. Paris, 1988.
*MUGAMBI, JESSE N.K. The biblical basis for evangelization: theological reflections based on an African experience. Nairobi, 1989.
*BOSCH. 1991.
     P. 20-24: Bible and mission.

THE BIBLE IN MISSION

Every missionary used the Bible in his own missionary work. Some people, however, used the Bible more than others. M.A. Adriani (1906:6) pointed out that a missionary without a Bible is really 'unimaginable'.

Protestants have translated the Bible into more languages than Roman Catholics. Nevertheless, Roman Catholic missionaries also had a positive attitude towards the use of the Bible in their own missionary work (cf. Beckmann, Bühlmann, & Specker 1966).

Robert P. Wilder (1897) was one of the first to reflect in a monograph upon the relation between the Bible and foreign missions. Arthur M. Chirgwin (1954:107) wrote -at the invitation of the United Bible Societies- a very stimulating book about the place of the Bible in evangelism, both in 'individual work' and in 'concerted efforts'. He quoted the following testimony in a Muslim paper called *The Moslem Censor*: 'The trouble with these books (i.e. the Christian Scriptures) is not in any special passage, but that everyone who reads them wants to become a Christian'. And at the end of his study, he concluded:

1. The Bible has always been used in evangelism;
2. The Bible is the best evangelistic tool there is;
3. The Bible gives the cutting edge;
4. The Bible is for everyman;
5. The Bible is being fruitfully used in evangelism; and
6. The challenge is now to the churches and their leaders (:149-162).

106

Gerrit H. Wolfensberger (1968:24), who was the United Bible Society Study Secretary, working in Geneva, stated: '... the printed Gospel is the best missionary we have in these modern times of population explosion and increasing literacy'.

*COOLSMA, SJOERD. De Bijbel en de evangelische zending. Amsterdam, 1878.
*ZAHN, FRANZ M. Die Bibel in der Mission. In: AMZ, XIX (1892), p. 393-411.
*WILDER, ROBERT P. The Bible and foreign missions: fifth ed. London, 1897.
    Several reprints.
OBER, CHARLES K. Bible studies in missions ... New York, 1899.
?BORNEMANN, FRIEDRICH W.B. Die Bibel und die Mission. Heidelberg, 1901.
*ADRIANI, M.A. Bijbel en zending. Rotterdam, 1906.
*PLATT, W.J. The place of the Bible in evangelism. In: IRM, XLII (1953), p. 184-193.
*CHIRGWIN, ARTHUR M. The Bible in world evangelism. London, 1954.
*BÜHLMANN, WALBERT, OFMCap. Die Bibel in der katholischen Weltmission. In: NZM, XVI (1960),
    p. 1-26.
*BECKMANN, JOHANNES, SMB, in Verbindung mit WALBERT BÜHLMANN OFMCap., & JOHANNES SPECKER
    SMB (ed.). Die Heilige Schrift in den katholischen Missionen: gesammelte Aufsätze.
    Schöneck, & Beckenried, 1966.
*WOLFENSBERGER, GERRIT H. Die Bibel im heutigen Asien und Afrika. Stuttgart, 1966.
*WOLFENSBERGER, GERRIT H. Multiplying the loaves: the Bible in mission and evangelism.
    London, & Glasgow, 1968.

THE MISSIONARY SIGNIFICANCE OF THE DIVISION OF THE BIBLE INTO THE OLD AND NEW TESTAMENT

The decision of the Early Church in the second and third century after Christ to canonize 66 books as 'Bible' and to divide them into two parts -the (Hebrew) *Old* Testament (cf. 2 Cor. 3:14; Gk.: *he palaia diatheke*) and the (Greek) *New* Testament (cf. Jer. 31:31; Marc. 14:24; Luc. 22:20; 1 Cor. 11:25; 2 Cor. 3:6; Hebr. 8:8; 9:15; 12:24; Gk.: *he kaine diatheke*)- is a missionary decision of primary importance. However, Jesus, the apostles, and the evangelists used only the law of Moses (Hebrew: *thora*), the prophets (Hebrew: *nebiim*), and the writings (Hebrew: *ketubim*) as Bible.

Paul considered Christ crucified as 'a stumbling block to the Jews' and as 'a foolishness to gentiles' (1 Cor. 1:23). We also can use this vocabulary in connection with the canon. On the one hand, we can value the fundamental missionary decision of the Early Church to divide the Bible in an Old Testament and a New Testament as a 'stumbling block' to the Jews who do not recognize the *New* Testament and therefore do not speak about the law of Moses, the prophetical books, and the writings as the *Old* Testament. And, on the other hand, we can value its decision as a 'foolishness' to the non-Jews who -in cases of non-oral cultures- have their own 'sacred books' (cf. Hinduism, Buddhism, Confucianism, and Taoism) and who prefer these books

-instead of the Jewish Old Testament- as their own preparation for the gospel (Lat.: *preparatio evangelica*).

MISSION IN THE OLD TESTAMENT

> ... if there is a missionary in the Old Testament,
> it is God himself.
> *David J. Bosch (1991:19).*

In many biblical mission studies, passages from the Old Testament are mentioned and quoted. Some scholars placed all these passages in a historical framework (Sellin, in: NAMZ 1925:33-45, 66-72; de Liagre-Böhl, in: Med. 1929:215-237; idem, in: Baumgartner 1950:77-96; Eichrodt, in: EMM 1942: 129-145; Paterson, in: Anderson 1946:1-10; Hempel, in: ZAW 1954:244-272; Vriezen, in: DH 1954:98-110; Wright, in: Anderson 1961:17-30; Martin-Achard 1962; et al.), whereas others (totally) failed to contextualize these Scripture materials.

On the one hand, some missiologists were not really interested in Old Testament studies and their criticisms, especially their Pentateuchal criticisms. On the other hand, many evolutionist Old Testament scholars neglected the theme of mission in the Old Testament. Johannes Blauw, however, actually specialized in both Old Testament studies and mission studies. In his afore-mentioned book he critisized both the biblicism and the evolutionist scheme of 'monotheism-polytheism-universalism-mission' (1962:29-30), which he considered as inadequate to describe the Old Testament message of 'universalism' (versus 'particularism') as missionary and messianic message. And he agreed with Robert Martin-Achard (1962), who closed his investigation into the missionary perspective of the Old Testament with the following words: '... the evangelization of the world is not a matter of words or of activity, but of presence: the presence of the people of God in the midst of humanity, the presence of God among His people. It is not without purpose that the Old Testament brings this to the recollection of the church' (1959:71-72; tr. Blauw).

Already before the Second World War, Bengt G.M. Sundkler in his study on Jesus and the gentiles (Sundkler, & Fridrichsen 1937:1-38) clearly distinguished between the *centripetal* and the *centrifugal* 'interpretation' of Bible passages. After the War, John Paterson (Anderson 1946:1,8) indicated -without referring to Sundkler- that centrifugal and centripetal 'tendencies' were at work in the history of Israel. Thereupon Johannes Blauw -with a reference to Sundkler- renewed this vocabulary by writing about the centripetal missionary 'consciousness' in the Old Testament and the centrifugal missionary 'consciousness' in the New Testament. He also wrote: 'I believe that those who advocate a missionary exegesis of Deutero-Isaiah and Jonah are right in so far as they understand that these passages of Scripture are concerned with more than universalism... On the other hand, I believe that those who reject such a missionary exegesis are right in so far as they understand that there is no thought of mission in the Old Testament in the centrifugal sense in which it comes to the fore in the New Testament' (1962:34-35; cf. 40-41, 146, 149). Hans-Werner Gensichen (1971:60), however, criticized Blauw, because he considers 'centripetal mission' as a *contradictio in adiecto*.

*RIEHM, EDUARD K.A. Der Missionsgedanke im Alten Testament. In: AMZ, VII (1880), p. 453-465.

*WARNECK. 1892.
I, p. 136-149: Die missionarischen Wurzeln im Alten Testament.

*LÖHR, MAX R.H. Der Missionsgedanke im Alten Testament: ein Beitrag zur alttestamentlichen Religionsgeschichte. Freiburg im Breisgau, & Leipzig, 1896.

JORDAN, WILLIAM G. The song and the soil: or, the missionary idea in the Old Testament. New York, 1913.
First ed.: Edinburgh, 1912.

*WEISMANN, GOTTHILF. Die Mission im Alten Testament. In: EMM, LXI (1917), p. 288-298.

*SELLIN, ERNST. Der Missionsgedanke im Alten Testament. In: NAMZ, II (1925), p. 33-45, 66-72.

STAERK, WILLY. Ursprung und Grenzen der Missionskraft der alttestamentlichen Religion. In: Theologische Blätter, IV (1925), p. 25-37.

*DE LIAGRE-BÖHL, FRANZ M.TH. Oud-Israël en de zending. In: Med., LXXIII (1929), p. 215-237.

*SCHOMERUS. 1935.
P. 6: Das Alte Testament als missionswissenschaftliches Buch.

ROWLEY, HAROLD H. Israel's mission to the world. London, 1939.

*EICHRODT, WALTHER. Gottes Volk und die Völker. In: EMM, LXXXVI (1942), p. 129-145.

*ROWLEY, HAROLD H. The missionary message of the Old Testament. London, 1944.
Reprint: London, 1955.

*ANDERSON, WILLIAM K. (ed.). Christian world mission. Nashville, 1946.
P. 1-10: From nationalism to universalism in the Old Testament (John Paterson).

*RAGUIN, YVES, SJ. La théologie missionnaire de l'Ancien Testament. Paris, 1947.

*BAUMGARTNER, WALTER, OTTO EISSFELDT, KARL ELLIGER, et al. (eds.). Festschrift Alfred Bertholet zum 80. Geburtstag... Tübingen, 1950.
P. 77-96: Missions- und Erwählungsgedanke in Alt-Israël (Franz M.Th. de Liagre-Böhl).

*KOPER, JACOB. Het Oude Testament en de zending. In: DH, VI (1953), p. 89-105.

*COOK, HAROLD R. An introduction to the study of Christian missions. Chicago, 1954.
P. 44-58: The Old Testament and missions.

*HEMPEL, JOHANNES. Die Wurzeln des Missionswillens im Glauben des Alten Testaments. In: Zeitschrift für die alttestamentliche Wissenschaft, LXVI (1954), p. 244-272.

*VRIEZEN, THEODORUS C. De zending in het Oude Testament. In: DH, VII (1954), p. 98-110.

*WIERSINGA, HENDRIK A. Zendingsperspectief in het Oude Testament. Baarn, 1954.

*BOSCH, DAVID J. Der alttestamentliche Missionsgedanke. In: EMM, C (1956), p. 174-188.

*OESTERLEY, WILLIAM O.E., & THEODORE H. ROBINSON. Hebrew religion: its origin and development. London, 1957.
First ed.: London, 1930.

JACOB, EDMOND. Theology of the Old Testament. London, 1958.
  *Fr. ed.: Théologie de l'Ancien Testament. Neuchâtel, & Paris, 1955.
  P. 176-181: La mission.
  Deuxième éd. revue et augmentée: Neuchâtel, 1968.
*BLAUW, JOHANNES. Het geding om de wereld: bijbelse hoofdlijnen ten dienste van het studieprogramma 'The life and mission of the church'. Zeist, 1959.
  I: Oude Testament.
*ANDERSON. 1961.
  P. 17-30: The Old Testament basis for the Christian mission (G. Ernest Wright).
*DOBBIE, ROBERT. The biblical foundation of the mission of the church: I: Old Testament. In: IRM, LI (1962), p. 196-205.
MARTIN-ACHARD, ROBERT. A light to the nations: a study of the Old Testament conception of Israel's mission to the world. Edinburgh, & London, 1962.
  *Fr. ed.: Israël et les nations: la perspective missionnaire de l'Ancien Testament. Neuchâtel, & Paris, 1959.
*OHM. 1962.
  P. 218-228: Das Alte Testament.
*GENSICHEN, HANS-WERNER. Glaube für die Welt: theologische Aspekte der Mission. Gütersloh, 1971.
  P. 57-63: Das Alte Testament und die Grundlage der Mission.
*HUPPENBAUER, HANS W. Missionarische Dimensionen des Gottesvolkes im Alten Testament. In: ZM, III (1977), p. 37-47.
SHENK, WILBERT R. (ed.). Exploring church growth. Grand Rapids, 1983.
  ?P. 171-180: The Old Testament roots of mission (Richard R. de Ridder).
*BOSCH. 1991.
  P. 16-20: Mission in the Old Testament.

SHALACH, SHALIACH

Although many Old Testament mission studies mention the verb *shalach* and/or the noun *shaliach*, they fail to make a serious study of their meaning.

Karl H. Rengstorf (TDNT 1964:I,400), however, corrected this omission. He pointed out that *shaliach* is a technical term for 'the sending of a messenger with a special task; the messenger does not have to be named. In other words, the emphasis rests on the fact of sending in conjunction with the one who sends, not on the one who is sent'.

The verb *shalach* is frequently used in the Old Testament. In the following observations on the views of the law of Moses, the prophetical books, and the writings on mission I include references to some basic *shalach* texts in the Old Testament which are quoted by missiologists and/or by Old Testament scholars writing on mission in the Old Testament.

TDNT. 1964-1976.
  I, p. 400-403: Apostello and pempo in the LXX (OT) and Judaism (Karl H. Rengstorf).
  *Ger. ed.: TWNT. 1933-1978.
  I, p. 399-402: Apostello und pempo in LXX (AT) und Judentum (Karl H. Rengstorf).

THE LAW OF MOSES (THORA)

In the literature under consideration I encountered authors who emphasized the missionary importance of the primeval history (Ger: *Urgeschichte*) (Gen. 1-11); authors who emphasized the call of Abraham (Gen. 12); and authors who paid special attention to the vocation of Moses (Ex. 3).

Johannes Blauw (1962:17-19) agreed with Karl W. Hartenstein that the first chapters of Genesis are of special significance for a theology of mission. He pointed out that '... it becomes clear that the whole history of Israel is nothing but the continuation of God's dealings with the nations, and that therefore the history of Israel is only to be understood from the unsolved problem of the relation of God to the nations'.

The Old Testament scholar Franz M.Th. de Liagre de Böhl (Baumgartner 1950:77-96; cf. Jansen Schoonhoven 1955:9), however, considered Abraham and his 318 servants (Gen. 14:14) to be the proper beginning of Israel's mission. And Johannes Blauw added (1962:22): 'That the call of Abraham (and thus implicitly that of Israel) must be seen in the light of God's revelation to the nations, is especially to be gleaned from Gen. 12:3'.

Harold H. Rowley (1944:11,15), who as a missionary taught Old Testament at the Shantung Christian University in China, pointed out that not Abraham, but Moses (thirteenth century BC) was 'the real founder of Old Testament religion' and 'the first missionary of whom we have any knowledge. JHWH sent him to the Israelites in Egypt not alone to save them and to lead them out, but to bring them to worship Him'. This view is, of course, more historically based than the just mentioned views of Blauw and de Liagre de Böhl.

Although the verb *shalach* is incidentally used in Genesis -cf. Gen. 45:5,7-8: the sending of Joseph as a prelude to the sending of Moses (and Aaron)- it occurs five times in the famous third chapter of Exodus on the revelation of the name JHWH and the call of Moses (none of these verses are quoted by Blauw or by Rowley): '"So come, I [the Lord] will *send* you to Pharaoh... and this shall be the sign for you that it is I who *sent* you"... But Moses said to God, "If I come to the Israelites and say to them, The God of your ancestors has *sent* me to you; and they ask me, What is his name? what shall I say to them?" God said to Moses, "I AM WHO I AM". He said further, "Thus you shall say to the Israelites, I AM has *sent* me to you". God also said to Moses, "Thus you shall say to the Israelites, The Lord, the God of your ancestors, the God of Abraham, the God of Isaac, and the God of Jacob, has *sent* me to you: This is my name forever, and this is my title for all generations"' (Ex. 3:10-15).

In other parts of the law of Moses, which received its final form in the post-exile period, there are also references to sending: God *sends* not only

Moses and Aaron (Lev. 16:28-29; cf. Ps. 105:17,26), but also angels to destroy Sodom (Gen. 19:13), to guard Israel on its way (Ex. 23:20), and to bring it out of Egypt (Num. 20:16). In his systematic interpretation of these and other *thora*-texts, Francis M. DuBose (1983:42) spoke about the missionary significance of 'God's providential guidance of his people and his judgment upon their enemies'. A historical perspective must be added to justify and clarify these philological observations.

*BÄCHLI, OTTO. Israël und die Völker: eine Studie zum Deuteronomium. Zürich, & Stuttgart, 1962.

THE PROPHETS (NEBIIM)

> The prophets were first and foremost men
> whom God had *sent*.
> *Francis M. DuBose (1983:46).*

The noun *shalach* as *terminus technicus* is also frequently used in the prophets (*nebiim*), which either originate from the eighth century (Amos, Isaiah, Micah, et al.), or the seventh century (Jeremiah et al.), or the period of the exile (Deutero-Isaiah, et al.), or the Persian and Greek period (Jonah, et al.).

Here I draw attention to Isaiah's vocation: 'Then I heard the voice of the Lord saying, "Whom shall I *send*, and who will go for us?" And I said, "Here am I; *send* me"' (Is. 6:8; cf. Jer. 14:14-15; Ez. 2:3-4; et al.). Johannes Blauw did not quote this text, but Francis M. DuBose (1983:46) referred to it as 'the dramatic call and sending of Isaiah'. And John Paterson (Anderson 1946:4-5) summarized the message of this early prophet as follows: 'There is here no thought of Israel's missionary function but only of the glory and preeminence of Israel. To him Jerusalem is the centre of the universe... JHWH is now the God of international relations'.

Other relevant prophetic texts on mission are the following: 'For I [the Lord] brought you up from the land of Egypt, and redeemed you from the house of slavery; and I *sent* before you Moses, Aaron, and Miriam' (Micah 6:4); 'They in their turn said to Jeremiah, "May the Lord be a true and faithful witness against us if we do not act according to everything that the Lord your God *sends* us through you. Whether it is good or bad, we will obey the voice of the Lord our God to whom we are *sending* you"' (Jer. 42:5-6). John Paterson (Anderson 1946:5-6) called Jeremiah (cf. Jer. 29) 'the most Christlike of the prophets', and 'the founder of foreign missions and the first man to teach prayer for one's enemies'.

The great prophet who is known as Deutero-Isaiah is considered as a great missionary. Here I quote only Isaiah 61:1-2: 'The spirit of the Lord God is upon me, because the Lord has anointed me; he has *sent* me to bring good news to the oppressed, to bind up the brokenhearted, to proclaim liberty to the captives, and release to the prisoners; to proclaim the year of the Lord's favor, and the day of vengeance of our God; to comfort all who mourn'. Here I also refer to some views on 'mission' in Deutero-Isaiah. Harold H. Rowley (1944:76) pointed out that this prophet emphasized the God-given mission of the suffering Servant (Is. 48:16; 66:19) and 'believed that Israel was called to be a missionary people'. John Paterson (Anderson 1946:7) wrote: 'Here we have proclaimed for the first time the program of a missionary religion (Is. 42:1-4)'. G. Ernest Wright (Anderson 1961:19- 20) added: 'It is in Second Isaiah... that the finest missionary texts in the Old Testament appear'. And Johannes Blauw (1962:39) summarized the whole recent discussion on Deutero-Isaiah as follows: '... we have already seen that a missionary significance to these Biblical passages is both accepted (Sellin, Volz, Eichrodt, Vriezen, Rowley, Jacob) and rejected (De Boer, Snaith, Martin-Achard)... I think that it is difficult to oppose the missionary character of such declarations as Isa. 42:4; 45:22-23; 49:6; 53:11 - for they clearly say that salvation shall reach the coastlands; that the nations shall see the light of the Servant of YHWH; that the ends of the earth are called to turn to YHWH'.

Theodorus C. Vriezen (DH 1954:109) refers to Jonah only in passing. John Paterson (Anderson 1946:9), however, called the book of Jonah 'the finest missionary tract ever written', and stated: 'Jonah is a missionary sermon written with a missionary purpose by a man whose mind was bigger than his church, big as the world'. And G. Ernest Wright (Anderson 1961:19) added: 'The deepest penetration into the methods of the mission appears in the Books of Jonah and the Second Isaiah. The former undoubtedly sees in the figure of the unwilling prophet the Chosen People herself who attempt to escape from God's calling of them for an important responsibility in the redemption of the world'.

Already Henry A. Lapham (1925:6-11) placed the prophets in the framework of the 'development of the missionary idea in the history of Israel' and 'the progressive revelation of God in the Old Testament and its significance for the study of missionary methods'. Thereafter, Franz M.Th. de Liagre de Böhl (Rowley 1950:77-96) described the 'prophetic movement' in Israel as a 'missionary movement'. This can especially be applied to such great prophets as Isaiah, Jeremiah, and Deutero-Isaiah. The book Jonah, however, is a special case, with its 'sense of a universal mission' (Oesterley, & Robinson 1957:415).

DAHLE, LARS N. Der Heidenmissionar des Alten Bundes: der Prophet Jona, seine Person und Zeit, seine Aufgabe und Sendung... Berlin, 1899.

WARMAN, FREDERIC S.G. Missions and the minor prophets: a series of Bible studies... London, 1909.

*DÖLLER, JOHANNES. Jonas als Heidenmissionar. In: ZM, IV (1914), p. 173-176.

*FELDMANN, FRANZ. Die Bekehrung der Heiden im Buche Isaias. Aachen, 1919.

AICH, JOHANN A. Die Mission der kleinen Propheten. Aachen, & Immensee, 1924.

?VOLZ, PAUL. Jesaja II, übersetzt und erklärt... Leipzig, 1932.

*ROWLEY, HAROLD H. (ed.). Studies in Old Testament prophecy: presented to Professor Theodore H. Robinson... Edinburgh, 1950.

  P. 187-200: The servant of the Lord in Deutero-Isaiah (Norman H. Snaith).

*BOER, PIETER A.H. DE. Second Isaiah's message. Leiden, 1956.

  P. 80-101: The limits of Second-Isaiah's message.

RÉTIF, ANDRÉ, SJ. Les prophètes et la mission... Paris, 1956.

THE WRITINGS (KETUBIM)

The verb *shalach* is also used in the writings (*ketubim*). For instance, we read in the historical books: 'Then I [Nehemiah] perceived that God had not *sent* him [Shemaiah] at all' (Neh. 6:12). This verse, which is neither quoted by Johannes Blauw (1962), nor quoted by Donald Senior CP, & Carroll Stuhlmüller CP (1983), makes clear that *shalach* in the Old Testament is primarily not a geographic term -crossing the borders of Israel: Elijah and the widow of Zarephath (1 Kings 17:8-24), Elisha and Naaman (2 Kings 5), Jonah, et al.- but a relational term: it is used to express the relation between the one who sends (God) and the one who is sent (His messenger).

In the book of Psalms which was studied by Franz Feldmann (1919), Joseph Schmitt (1934), and Albert Ströbel OMI (1950), we encounter the idea that Jerusalem is the great religious centre of the whole world, to which all nations will come to share Israel's faith and to worship Israel's God (Ps. 86: 9f.; 102:15ff.,21f.). Also Robert Martin-Achard (1962:58) paid attention to the hymnody in the Jerusalemite temple: 'The sole purpose of the writers of the psalms is to praise the God of Israel... YHWH deserves the praise of the whole creation; this is the thought that is voiced in more than one psalm. It is not only the nations that are to be summoned by the faithful among the chosen people. The heavens, the earth, the rivers, and even the sea must applaud the God of Israel. It is by reason of their belonging to the realm of creation and not because they are called to share Israel's faith, that the heathen must glorify God'.

Francis M. DuBose (1983:45) also calls attention to the Psalter which highlights 'the providential *sending* through the role of the forerunner Joseph, the salvific *sending* through the role of the emancipators Moses and Aaron, and the judgmental *sending* through the place of judgment and justice in the event':

He had *sent* a man ahead of them, Joseph, who was sold as a slave.

He *sent* his servant Moses and Aaron whom he had chosen.

He *sent* darkness, and made the land dark; they rebelled against his words (Ps. 105:17,26,28).

*FELDMANN, FRANZ. Laudate Dominum omnes gentes: Missionsgedanken im Buche der Psalmen. Aachen, 1919.

SCHMITT, JOSEPH. L'idée missionnaire dans le Psautier. 1934. Supplément à la revue l'Union missionnaire du clergé.

STROBEL, ALBERT, OMI. La conversion des gentils dans les psaumes. Paris, 1950. Thèse de doctorat présentée à l'Institut Biblique Pontifical de Rome.

THE GENTILES (GOIIM)

Goiim can be translated in different ways. Johannes Blauw pointed out that *(gentile) nations* is a good term to describe the meaning of *goiim*. He wrote: 'The designation *nations* is identical with *heathen*; in other words, the designation *nations* (*goiim*) does not have a political or national, but a religious meaning' (1962:25).

Already in 1896 the Old Testament scholar Alfred Bertholet drew attention to the relation of Israel to the *goiim*. Others have followed his steps: Paul Heinisch (1916), Robert Martin- Achard (1962), André Rétif SJ, & Paul Lamarche SJ (1966), et al. Martin- Achard (cf. the title of his study in 1962) stipulates that Israel is *a light to the nations* (cf. Is. 42:6; 49:6), but Johannes Blauw (1962:51, 145-146) relates this expression first of all to 'the Messiah as the one to whom the nations look forward and for whom he shall be a light'. According to Blauw (:26), the nations are 'also created (Ps. 86:9) and summoned by their relation to Israel to praise (i.e. to recognize) the God of the whole earth (Exod. 19:5; Deut. 32:8: Psalms *passim*)'.

Jean Daniélou SJ (1957) emphasized that the Old Testament does not limit holiness to Israel; the nations have their own holy men and women ('holy pagans'). And Terence L. Donaldson (Journal for the study of the Pseudepigrapha 1990:27) referred to the proselytes or 'righteous gentiles' in the literature of the period between the Old and the New Testament: 'Those gentiles who abandoned their idols and streamed to Zion in the last days to worship the God of Israel would have a share in the blessings of the age to come, but without being fully incorporated into the covenant community of Israel'.

*BERTHOLET, ALFRED. Die Stellung der Israeliten und der Juden zu den Fremden. Freiburg im Breisgau, & Leipzig, 1896.

*SIEFFERT, FRIEDRICH. Die Heidenbekehrung im Alten Testament und im Judentum. Berlin, 1908.

*HEINISCH, PAUL. Die Idee der Heidenbekehrung im Alten Testament. Münster in Westfalen, 1916.

*ROSEN, GEORG. Juden und Phönizier: das antike Judentum als Missionsreligion und die Entstehung der jüdischen Diaspora: neu bearbeitet und erw. ... Tübingen, 1929.

*DALBERT, PETER. Die Theologie der hellenistisch-jüdischen Missions-Literatur unter Ausschluss von Philo und Josephus. Hamburg, & Volksdorf, 1954.

DANIÉLOU, JEAN, SJ. Holy pagans of the Old Testament... London, & New York, 1957.
  Fr. ed.: Les saints païens de l'Ancien Testament: la sainteté des infidèles. Paris,
  1956.
RÉTIF, ANDRÉ, SJ., & PAUL LAMARCHE SJ. The salvation of the gentiles and the prophets.
  Baltimore, & Dublin, 1966.
  ?Fr. ed.: Le salut des nations: universalisme et perspectives missionnaires dans
  l'Ancien Testament. Paris, 1959.
  *Ger. tr.: 1960.
*MITTERHÖFER, JAKOB, SVD. Thema Mission. Wien, Freiburg, & Basel, 1974.
  P. 15-35: Israels Dienst an den Völkern.
*DONALDSON, TERENCE L. Proselytes or 'righteous gentiles'? The status of gentiles in
  eschatological pilgrimage patterns of thought. In: Journal for the study of the
  Pseudepigrapha, VII (1990), p. 3-27.

THE OLD TESTAMENT IN MISSION

Gerrit H. Wolfensberger (n.d.:7) wrote about the 'indispensable' Old Testament as the 'Holy Scripture for the apostles and the early church'.

The Old Testament not only developed a missionary outlook, but also plays its own part in missionary processes. After Jewish scholars had finished the translation of the Hebrew Old Testament into Greek (Septuagint), the Christians took initiatives to translate not only the New Testament, but also the Old Testament into other languages. The Christian mission made the law, the prophets, and the writings known to nearly all nations and civilizations.

Some missionaries and missiologists have a negative view of the contribution of the Old Testament to mission processes. Others, however, approach the Old Testament (very) positively. Here I refer to the studies of Emil Brunner (1934), Karl W. Hartenstein (Mission und Pfarramt 1934), Werner Kessler (1935), Walter Freytag (1936; cf. Hermelink, & Margull 1961:I,193-209), Theodor Devaranne (1938), and Godfrey E. Phillips (IRM 1938:662-666; IRM 1940:382-390; 1942) as having a positive attitude. Brunner (1934), for instance, made clear that without the Old Testament there is no Jesus Christ in the New Testament; the missionary significance of the cross is completely incomprehensible apart from the Old Testament.

The missionary relevance of the Old Testament to the nations is especially clear in its universalism (versus particularism); its ethical monotheism (ethical decalogue, etc.); its linear theory of history (versus circular or cyclical theory of history); and its prophetic critique of idol worship. John Paterson (Anderson 1946:1) emphasized not only Old Testament universalism but also joined David S. Cairns (1937) in saying that 'in the Bible we have the linear theory. Not that we need think of a straight line but rather a spiraling line, moving backward at times and then again forward on a higher level. Thus the Old Testament is full of dreams and hopes and messianic expectations'. And G. Ernest Wright (Anderson 1961:21; cf. IRM 1951:265-276) wrote that

116

'the Old Testament is the church's bulwark against the "natural" powers that invade and weaken, where they do not destroy, her faith'.

*BRUNNER, EMIL. Die Unentbehrlichkeit des Alten Testaments für die missionierende Kirche... Stuttgart, & Basel, 1934.
?HARTENSTEIN, KARL W. Das Alte Testament in der ausseren Mission. In: Mission und Pfarramt, Heft 3/4, 1934.
KESSLER, WERNER. Das Alte Testament in der Mission. Herrnhut, 1935.
CAIRNS, DAVID S. The riddle of the world. London, 1937.
DEVARANNE, THEODOR. Das Alte Testament und seine Verwendung in der Mission. Berlin, 1938.
*PHILLIPS, GODFREY E. The Old Testament in the life of the younger churches. In: IRM, XXVII (1938), p. 662-666.
*PHILLIPS, GODFREY E. The use of the Old Testament in India. In: IRM, XXIX (1940), p. 382-390.
*PHILLIPS, GODFREY E. The Old Testament in the world church: with special reference to the younger churches. London, & Redhill, 1942.
*WRIGHT, GEORGE E. The Old Testament, a bulwark of the church against paganism. In: IRM, LX (1951), p. 265-276.
*HERMELINK, JAN, & HANS J. MARGULL (eds.). Walter Freytag: Reden und Aufsätze. München, 1961. 2 vols.
    I, p. 193-209: Das Alte Testament und die junge Kirche (1936).
*WOLFENSBERGER, GERRIT H. The indispensable Old Testament. N.p., n.d.

MISSION IN THE NEW TESTAMENT

New Testament mission studies deal both with the whole field of the New Testament mission views (e.g. Hahn 1965) and with special mission views in the separate New Testament books. Instead of mission *views* people also speak about mission *problems* (cf. Schneemelcher 1958), mission *foundation* (cf. Dobbie, in: IRM 1962:281-290), mission *perspective(s)* (cf. Nissen 1984; Wiersinga n.d.), or mission *principles* (Underwood 1988).

New Testament mission studies which cover the whole field of the New Testament deal with a large variety of topics. Here I only mention chronologically the following topics which have received special attention from scholars: missionary methods (Zahn 1886; idem, in: AMZ 1898:385-403; Oehler 1901; Liechtenhan 1946; Honig 1951); the origin and growth of the Christian mission (Warneck 1892:I,63-93; Weinel 1907; Würz 1922; Liechtenhan 1946; Kuhn, in: EMZ 1954:161-168; Schille 1967; Kasting 1969; Hengel, in: NTS 1971/72:15-38; Beyerhaus 1975; Pesch, in: Kertelge 1982:11-70); Jewish proselytism as preparation for the early Christian mission (Axenfeld, in: Axenfeld, et al. 1904:1-80); missionary message/thought/ preaching (Heim, in: IRM 1928:133-144; Sundkler, & Fridrichsen 1937; Dodd 1944; Lemaître 1944; Schrenk 1954:131-148); missionary motives (Shillito 1936; Liechtenhan 1946); missionary consciousness (Joubert 1939); missionary texts/words (Knak, in: Theologia viatorum 1954:27-50; Moulton 1956); mission and hospitality/salary/ poverty (Rusche 1958; Theissen, in: NTS 1975:192-221; Nissen 1984); mission and eschatology (Cullmann, in: Anderson 1961:42-54); and proselytism (Lerle 1961). Gerd Theissen (NTS 1975:192-221; 1977) was one of the first scholars who placed these topics into a socio-political framework.

David W. Wead (Gasque, & La Sor 1978:176-186) distinguished between two philosophies of world missions within the early church: the centrifugal philosophy of mission 'which most have come to emphasize', and the centripetal philosophy of mission which 'placed the emphasis upon the discipleship rather than on being thrust into a new environment for the purpose of evangelism'.

The New Testament, 'a post-resurrection collection' (Warren 1979:17-21), is a *missiological/missionary document* (Schomerus 1935:6-7; Bosch 1991:15-55). In his explanation of this thesis, David J. Bosch (1991:16) cordially agreed with the famous German theologian Kähler: 'Contemporary New Testament scholars are... affirming what the systematic theologian Martin Kähler said eight decades ago: Mission is "the mother of theology" (Kähler [1908] 1971:190). Theology, said Kähler, began as "an accompanying manifestation of the Christian mission" and not as "a luxury of the world-dominating church" (:189). The New Testament writers were not scholars who had sufficient leisure to research the evidence before they put pen to paper. Rather, they wrote in the context of an "emerging situation", of a church which, because of its missionary encounter with the world, was *forced* to theologize (:189)'.

*WARNECK, GUSTAV. Die apostolische und die moderne Mission: eine apologetische Parallelle. Gütersloh, 1876.
*ZAHN, THEODOR. Missionsmethoden im Zeitalter der Apostel: zwei Vorträge im akademischen Missionsverein zu Erlangen gehalten. Erlangen, 1886.
*WARNECK. 1892-1903. 3 vols.
    I, p. 63-93: Der Ursprung der christlichen Mission.
HAUPT, ERICH. Zum Verständnis des Apostolats im Neuen Testament. Halle, 1895.
*ZAHN, FRANZ M. Giebt das Neue Testament für alle Zeiten bindende Vorschriften über die Methode der christlichen Mission? In: AMZ, XXV (1898), p. 385-403.
*OEHLER, THEODOR. Enthält das Neue Testament bindende missions-methodische Vorschriften? Basel, 1901.
*AXENFELD, KARL, GUSTAV MÜLLER, CARL PAUL, et al. (eds.). Missionswissenschaftliche Studien: Festschrift zum 70. Geburtstag des Herrn Prof.D.Dr. Gustav Warneck... Berlin, 1904.
    P. 1-80: Die jüdische Propaganda als Vorläuferin und Wegbereiterin der urchristlichen Mission (Karl Axenfeld).
*WEINEL, HEINRICH. Die urchristliche und die heutige Mission: ein Vergleich. Tübingen, 1907.
?HAUSSLEITER, JOHANNES. Propaganda und Mission im Lichte des Neuen Testaments. 1908.

118

BEACH, HARLAN P. New Testament studies in missions. New York, 1911.
First ed.: New York, 1899.

KILPATRIC, THOMAS B. New Testament evangelism. London, 1911.

*SCHLATTER, ADOLF. Die Gemeinde in der apostolischen Zeit und im Missionsgebiet. Gütersloh, 1912.

*WÜRZ, FRIEDRICH. Die Mission der ersten Christen. Stuttgart, 1922.

*HEIM, KARL. The message of the New Testament to the non-Christian world. In: IRM, XVII (1928), p. 133-144.
?Ger. ed.: Die Botschaft des Neuen Testaments an die Heidenwelt, in: Glaube und Leben: gesammelte Aufsätze und Vorträge. Berlin, 1928, p. 737-757.

*MICHAELIS, WILHELM. Geist Gottes und Mission nach dem Neuen Testament. In: EMM, LXXVI (1932), p. 5-16.

*SCHOMERUS. 1935.
P. 6-7: Das Neue Testament als missionswissenschaftliches Buch.

SHILLITO, EDWARD. The way of the witnesses: a New Testament study in missionary motive. London, 1936.

*SUNDKLER, BENGT G.M., & ANTON FIDRICHSEN (eds.). Contributions à l'étude de la pensée missionnaire dans le Nouveau Testament. Uppsala, 1937.

BRUNDIN, GUNNAR. Missionen Herrens verk. Stockholm, 1938.

JOUBERT, HENDRIK L.N. Die roeping, sending en sendingsbewussyn van die Nuwe-Testamentiese apostel: met spesiale verwysing na die sendingsbewussyn van die Ou-Testamentiese profete en van Jesus Christus. Amsterdam, 1939. Diss. V.U. Amsterdam.

*DODD, CHARLES H. The apostolic preaching and its developments: three lectures...: new ed. London, 1944.

LEMAITRE, AUGUSTE. L'universalité du message Chrétien: comment Jésus et les apôtres ont-ils envisagé la tâche missionnaire de l'église? Genève, 1944.

*LIECHTENHAN, RUDOLF. Die urchristliche Mission: Voraussetzungen, Motive und Methoden. Zürich, 1946.

HAY, ALEXANDER R. The New Testament order for church and missionary: second ed., rev. and enl. Temperley, 1947.

*ARCHIBALD, ARTHUR C. New Testament evangelism... Philadelphia, Chicago, & Los Angeles, 1949.

*HONIG, ANTON G. Bijdrage tot het onderzoek naar de fundering van de zendingsmethode der comprehensive approach in het Nieuwe Testament. Kampen, 1951. Diss. Kampen.

*COOK, HAROLD R. An introduction to the study of Christian missions. Chicago, 1954.
P. 19-43: The New Testament and missions.

*KNAK, SIEGFRIED. Neutestamentliche Missionstexte nach neuerer Exegese. In: Theologia viatorum, V (1954), p. 27-50.

*KUHN, KARL G. Das Problem der Mission in der Urchristenheit. In: EMZ, XI (1954), p. 161-168.

*RIDDERBOS, HERMAN N. De zending in het Nieuwe Testament. In: DH, VII (1954), p. 133-142.

SCHRENK, GOTTLOB. Studien zu Paulus. Zürich, 1954.
?P. 131-148: Urchristliche Missionspredigt im 1. Jahrhundert.

MOULTON, HAROLD K. The mission of the church: studies in the missionary words of the New Testament. London, 1956.

RUSCHE, HELGA. Gastfreundschaft in der Verkündigung des Neuen Testaments und ihr Verhältnis zur Mission. Münster, 1958.

SCHNEEMELCHER, WILHELM. Missionsprobleme im apostolischen und nachapostolischen Zeitalter. Tübingen, 1958.

*BLAUW, JOHANNES. Het geding om de wereld: bijbelse hoofdlijnen ten dienste van het studieprogramma 'The life and mission of the Church'. Zeist, 1960.
  II: Nieuwe Testament.
*ANDERSON. 1961.
  P. 42-54: Eschatology and missions in the New Testament (Oscar Cullmann).
  First ed.: Eschatologie und Mission im Neuen Testament. In: EMM, LXXXV (1941), p. 98-108.
LERLE, ERNST. Proselytenwerbung und Urchristentum. Berlin, 1961.
*DOBBIE, ROBERT. The biblical foundation of the mission of the church; II: The New Testament. In: IRM, LI (1962), p. 281-290.
*OHM. 1962.
  P. 228-231: Das Neue Testament.
HAHN, FERDINAND. Mission in the New Testament. Naperville, 1965.
  *Ger. ed.: Das Verständnis der Mission im Neuen Testament. Neukirchen, & Vluyn, 1963.
*SCHILLE, GOTTFRIED. Die urchristliche Kollegialmission. Zürich, & Stuttgart, 1967.
*KASTING, HEINRICH. Die Anfänge der urchristlichen Mission: eine historische Untersuchung. München, 1969.
*FROHNES, HEINZGÜNTER (ed.). Martin Kähler: Schriften zu Christologie und Mission: Gesamtausgabe der Schriften zur Mission... München, 1971.
  P. 3-43: Der Menschensohn und seine Sendung an die Menschheit (1893).
  P. 44-67: Die richtige Beurteilung der apostolischen Gemeinden nach dem Neuen Testament (1894).
  P. 184-221: Mission und Theologie (1908).
*HENGEL, MARTIN. Die Ursprünge der christlichen Mission. In: New Testament Studies, XVIII (1971/72), p. 15-38.
LEGRAND, LUCIEN, MEP, JOSEPH PATHRAPANKAL CMI, & MATTHEW VELLANICKAL. Good news and witness; the New Testament understanding of evangelization. Bangalore, 1974.
*MITTERHÖFER, JAKOB, SVD. Thema Mission. Wien, Freiburg, & Basel, 1974.
  P. 37-64: Sendung zu allen Völkern.
*BEYERHAUS, PETER. Mission in urchristlicher und endgeschichtlicher Zeit. Giessen, & Basel, 1975.
*THEISSEN, GERD. Legitimation und Lebensunterhalt: ein Beitrag zur Soziologie urchristlicher Missionare. In: New Testament Studies, XXI (1975), p. 192-221.
*THEISSEN, GERD. Soziologie der Jesusbewegung: ein Beitrag zur Entstehungsgeschichte des Urchristentums. München, 1977.
*GASQUE, W. WARD, & WILLIAM S. LA SOR (eds.). Scripture, tradition, and interpretation: essays presented to Everett F. Harrison by his students and colleagues in honor of his seventy-fifth birthday. Grand Rapids, 1978.
  P. 176-186: The centripetal philosophy of mission (David W. Wead).
*WARREN, MAX A.C. I believe in the great commission. Grand Rapids, 1979.
  P. 15-55: The New Testament spells it out.
*KERTELGE, KARL (ed.). Mission im Neuen Testament. Freiburg, Basel, & Wien, 1982.
*NISSEN, JOHANNES. Poverty and mission: New Testament perspectives on a contemporary theme. Leiden, & Utrecht, 1984.
?UNDERWOOD, B.E. Sixteen New Testament principles for world evangelization. Franklin Springs, 1988.
*BOSCH. 1991.
  P. 15-55: Reflections on the New Testament as a missionary document.
*WIERSINGA, HENDRIK A. Perspectief in het Nieuwe Testament. Baarn, n.d.

APOSTELLEIN, APOSTOLOS, APOSTOLE

In chapter 2.4. on 'Apostolics, apostolo(lo)gy, theology of the apostolate' we already dealt with *apostellein, apostole, apostolos*. Here I only quote Karl H. Rengstorf (TDNT 1964:I,404) who wrote: 'At any rate we can say in general that when *pempein* is used in the NT the emphasis is on the sending as such, whereas when *apostellein* is used it rests on the commission linked with it, no matter whether the one who sends or the one who is sent claims prior interest'. *Apostellein* is the divine act of sending people out to serve in the kingdom of God.

Although there is a connection between the Christian *apostolos* and the Jewish *shaliah*, there is no likeness, because the apostle in the New Testament represents something new, quite outside the Jewish sphere. The Christian apostolate is bound up with the duty of missionary work among both the Jews and the gentiles (*goiim*).

In the New Testament *apostole*=apostolate, apostleship, and (com)mission, indicates a missionary function, not an office in the church.

TDNT. 1964-1976. 10 vols.
    I, p. 403-406: Apostello and pempo in NT (Karl H. Rengstorf).
    *Ger. ed.: TWNT. 1933-1978. 10 vols.
    I, p. 402-405: Apostello und pempo in NT (Karl H. Rengstorf).

JESUS

> Without Jesus Christ there would be
> no Christian world mission.
> *Edmund D. Soper (1943:37).*

In New Testament mission studies, Jesus of Nazareth is typified in different ways. Gustav Warneck (1892:I,158), for instance, spoke about him as the 'representative of humanity'. William O. Carver (1921:103,109) described him as the founder of the Christian missionary enterprise which had two motives: to glorify God and to save all people. Hugh Martin (1927:57) wrote: 'Jesus is too great a Saviour for anything less than the whole race'. Schomerus (1935:31) considered Jesus' breaking through Jewish particularism as his main missionary concern. And Martin Hengel (NTS 1971/72:35-37) referred to Jesus as the 'original missionary' (Ger.: *Urmissionar*; my tr.).

In the 19th century there was a great debate about the 'historic mission' of Jesus to the gentiles or 'non-Jews' (Manson 1955). Johannes Blauw (1962: 152-153), Ferdinand Hahn (1965), and other scholars described and analysed the development of this debate. They claimed that various 19th century authors developed an evolutionary concept: Jesus gradually moved from a particularistic view to an universalistic conviction. However, Gustav Warneck (1892:I, 149-194; AMZ 1903:57-67), in line with Martin Kähler (cf. AMZ 1893:149-178), criticized this concept. In 1902 Adolf von Harnack defended the thesis that Jesus indeed preached an 'intensive universalism', but kept mission beyond his own horizon. Friedrich Spitta (1909) protested against this view, stating that Jesus himself preached beyond the borders of Israel. Max Meinertz (ZM 1911:21-41; 1925; 1926) followed Spitta: he advocated the 'explicit universalism' of Jesus. Albert Schweitzer, however, emphasized the eschatological character of Jesus' universalism: 'Jesus thought universalistically and acted particularistically' (1910). Bengt G.M. Sundkler (Sundkler, & Fridrichsen 1937:1-38) excoriated the -false- alternative between 'particularism' and 'universalism', and turned our attention to the eschatological significance of Zion, Jerusalem, and especially the temple as the reintegration of the world. Helene Stoevesandt (1943) and Joachim Jeremias (1958) followed Sundkler; however, without accepting his theory on the significance of the temple. Jeremias (1958:11-39) identified three important negative conclusions:

1. Jesus pronounces a stern judgement upon the Jewish mission;
2. Jesus forbade his disciples during his lifetime to preach to non-Jews; and
3. Jesus limited his own activity to Israel.

And he added three important positive conclusions:

1. Jesus removes the idea of vengeance from the eschatological expectation;
2. Jesus promises the gentiles a share in salvation; and
3. The redemptive activity and lordship of Jesus includes the gentiles.

In Jesus' sayings about the gentiles, especially in Matt. 8:11-12/ Luke 13:28-29, Jeremias found a solution to the just mentioned contradiction of negative and positive elements. David J. Bosch (Beyerhaus, & Hallencreutz 1969:3-19; 1991:25-41) reviewed the latest developments in this debate and concluded: 'For a long time New Testament scholars tended to deny the fundamental missionary dimension of Jesus' earthly ministry... scholars are today far more ready to credit Jesus himself with laying the foundations for the gentile mission' (1991:30). He mentioned as salient missionary features of Jesus' person and all-inclusive ministry: Jesus and the reign of God; Jesus and the law (Hebrew: *thora*); Jesus and his disciples; and the significance of the Easter event.

Rudolf Pesch (Kertelge 1982:11-70) not only connected the mission of Jesus and the mission of John the Baptist (John 1:6: 'a man *sent* from God'), but also mentioned the 'presuppositions of the early Christian gentile mission':

1. the missionary concerns of Judaism about the gentiles;
2. the attitude of Jesus of Nazareth towards the gentiles and their reception;
3. the attitude of Jesus of Nazareth towards the law (Hebr.: *thora*) and its reception;
4. the universal interpretation of the expiatory death of Jesus;
5. the relativization of circumcision through the baptism;
6. the development of christology; and
7. the missionary concept of the gentile mission (:33; my tr.).

*WARNECK. 1892-1903. 3 vols.
   I, p. 149-194: Die Mission in den Reden Jesu.
*KÄHLER, MARTIN. Der Menschensohn und seine Sendung an die Menschheit. In: AMZ, XX (1893), p. 149-178.
*BORNHÄUSER, KARL B. Wollte Jesus die Heidenmission? Eine moderne theologische Frage für die Missionsgemeinde beantwortet. Gütersloh, 1903.
*WARNECK, GUSTAV. Jesus Christus und die Weltmission nach den Evangelien. In: AMZ, XXX (1903), p. 57-67.
BROWN, OSWALD E. Jesus as a missionary. N.p., 1905.
MAUNU, J.A. Jeesus ja pakanalähetys (=Jesus and missions to the heathen). 1905. Diss. Helsinki.
MONNIER, HENRI. La mission historique de Jésus. Paris, 1906.
   Rev. ed.: Paris, 1914.
*BORNHÄUSER, KARL B. Jesus und die Heidenmission. In: EMM, LIII (1909), p. 461-468.
SPITTA, FRIEDRICH. Jesus und die Heidenmission. Giessen, 1909.
FISCHER, HERMANN, SVD. Our Lord's last will and testament: thoughts on foreign missions. London, 1910.
   Ger. ed.: Jesu letzter Wille: Stiftung und Stellung der katholischen Heidenmission: neue Bearbeitung. Steyl, 1923.
   *Fünfte Aufl.: Steyl, 1912.
   Amer. ed.: 1915. Reprint: 1929.
   Dutch tr.: 1913.
   Sp. tr.: 1922; reprints.
   Hungarian tr.: n.d.
MEINERTZ, MAX. Jesus als Begründer der Heidenmission. In: ZM, I (1911), p. 21-41.
LINDBLOM, JOHANNES. Jesu missions- och dopbefallning: Matt. 28: 18-20: tillika en studie över det kristna dopets ursprung. Stockholm, 1919.
*MEINERTZ, MAX. Jesus und die Heidenmission: zweite neubearbeitete Aufl. Münster in Westfalen, 1925.
   *First ed.: Münster in Westfalen, 1908.
*MEINERTZ, MAX. Wie Jesus die Mission wollte. Münster in Westfalen, 1926.
   First ed.: ZM, XV (1925), p. 237-257.

*McLEISH, ALEXANDER. Jesus Christ and world evangelization: missionary principles: Christ's or ours? London, 1934.

*SCHOMERUS. 1935.

P. 29-35: Jesus und die Mission.

*SUNDKLER, BENGT G.M., & ANTON FRIDRICHSEN (eds.). Contributions... Uppsala, 1937.

P. 1-38: Jésus et les païens (Bengt G.M. Sundkler).

MAJOR, HENRY D.A., THOMAS W. MANSON, & CHARLES J. WRIGHT. The mission and message of Jesus: an exposition of the gospels in the light of modern research. New York, 1938.

First ed.: London, 1937.

*CADOUX, CECIL J. The historic mission of Jesus: a constructive re-examination of the eschatological teaching in the synoptic gospels. London, & Redhill, 1941.

LEIPOLDT, JOHANNES. Jesu Verhältnis zu Griechen und Juden. Leipzig, 1941.

*SOPER, EDMUND D. The philosophy of the Christian world mission. New York, & Nashville, 1943.

P. 37-50: Jesus Christ and the world mission.

?STOEVESANDT, HELENE. Jesus und die Heidenmission. 1943. Diss. Göttingen. Unpublished.

*ANDERSON, WILLIAM K. (ed.). Christian world mission. Nashville, 1946.

P. 11-19: The universal gospel of Jesus (Wyatt A. Smart).

*STÄHLIN, GUSTAV. Die Endschau Jesu und die Mission. In: EMZ, VII (1950), p. 97-105, 134-147.

CURTIS, ARTHUR H. The vision and mission of Jesus: a literary and critical investigation based specially upon the baptismal and temptation narratives and their Old Testament background. Edinburgh, 1954.

FULLER, REGINALD H. The mission and achievement of Jesus: an examination of the presuppositions of New Testament theology. Chicago, 1954.

SCHWEITZER, ALBERT. The quest of the historical Jesus: a critical study of its progress from Reimarus to Wrede. London, 1954.

First Eng. ed.: London, 1910.

*Ger. ed.: Geschichte der Leben Jesu Forschung. Tübingen, 1906.

Many reprints.

MANSON, THOMAS W. Jesus and the non-Jews. London, 1955.

*JEREMIAS, JOACHIM. Jesus' promise to the nations. London, 1958.

*First ed.: Jesu Verheissung für die Völker. Stuttgart, 1956.

*ALLAN, DEREK W. Christ's teaching about missions. In: IRM, XLVIII (1959), p. 157-167.

*BOSCH, DAVID J. Jesus, die lydende Messias, en ons sendingmotief. Bloemfontein, 1961.

HARNACK, ADOLF VON. The mission and expansion of Christianity in the first three centuries. New York, 1961.

First Eng. ed.: London, 1904-1905. 2 vols.

*Ger. ed.: Die Mission und Ausbreitung des Christentums in den ersten drei Jahrhunderten: dritte neu durchgearbeitete und verm. Aufl... Leipzig, 1915. 2 vols.

I, p. 35-44: Jesus Christus und die Weltmission.

First Ger. ed.: Leipzig, 1902.

*BOSCH, DAVID J. Die Heidenmission in der Zukunftsschau Jesu: eine Untersuchung zur Eschatologie der synoptischen Evangelien. St. Augustin, 1967.

First ed.: Zürich, 1959.

*BEYERHAUS, PETER, & CARL F. HALLENCREUTZ (eds.). The church crossing frontiers: essays on the nature of mission: in honour of Bengt Sundkler. Lund, 1969.

P. 3-19: 'Jesus and the gentiles' - a review after thirty years (David J. Bosch).

*CONCISE DICTIONARY. 1971.

P. 307-309: Jesus Christ (J. Lesslie Newbigin).

124

*GENSICHEN, HANS-WERNER. Glaube für die Welt: theologische Aspekte der Mission. Gütersloh, 1971.
P. 66-71: Jesus und die Heiden.
*LOHFINK, GERHARD. Wie hat Jesus Gemeinde gewollt? Zur gesellschaftlichen Dimension des christlichen Glaubens. Freiburg, Basel, & Wien, 1982.
*ABESAMIS, CARLOS H. The mission of Jesus and good news to the poor: biblico-pastoral considerations for a church in the third world. Quezon City, 1987.
*LMG. 1987.
P. 194-200: Jesus (W. Stegemann).
*BOSCH. 1991.
P. 31-41: Salient features of Jesus' person and ministry.
*MEIJER, BEN F. Master builder and copestone of the portal: images of the mission of Jesus. In: Toronto journal of theology, IX (1993), p. 187-209.

THE GOSPELS

> The gospel not only contains the missionary idea,
> but it is the missionary idea and nothing else.
> *Robert F. Horton (1908:62).*

All four gospels were written from the perspective of Easter (cf. Rudolf Bultmann). Each of them 'represents a sub-paradigm of the early Christian missionary paradigm' (Bosch 1991:54).

The gospel of *Matthew* is known as the gospel which emphasizes both the exclusive mission to Israel before Easter (Matt. 10:1-16; 15:24) and the gentile mission after Easter. The missionary view of this gospel, and especially of the Great Commission at the end of the gospel (Matt. 28: 16-20), has recently been studied by scholars such as Karl Barth (1945; cf. Anderson 1961:55-71), Otto Michel (Evangelische Theologie 1950/51:16- 26), Ernst Lohmeyer (Schmauch 1951:22-49), Günther Bornkamm (Dinkler 1964:171-191), Jacques Matthey (IRM 1980:161-173), and David J. Bosch (Shenk 1983: 218-248). Richard R. de Ridder (1971) laid the emphasis upon the covenant basis of the Great Commission, whereas Edward C. Pentecost (1982:37) explained the essence of the *spiritual mandate* (Matt. 28:19-20; Mark 16:15; Luke 24:46-48) over against the *cultural mandate* (Gen. 1:26- 28; 2:15). And David J. Bosch (1991:56-83) highlighted Matthew's paradigm as 'missionary discipleship'.

Most scholars neglect the study of the missionary dimension in the gospel of *Mark* (Mark 13:9-11; 16:14-20; et al.). Johannes Blauw (1962: 88), however, compared the first and the second gospel and concluded: '... Mark accentuates more the intensive, comprehensive authority of Jesus (as superior power over unbelief, powers, sickness)'. George D. Kilpatrick (Nineham 1955: 145-158) and Zenji Kato (1986) explored the concept of 'gentile mission' in the second gospel, whereas Klemens Stock SJ (Kertelge 1982:130-144) presented an outline of its theology of mission from the perspective of 'the fishers-of-men missionaries' (my tr.).

The mission concept in the gospel of *Luke* (Luke 24:36-49; et al.) is studied by several scholars (Haussleiter 1904; Lohse, in: Theologische Zeitschrift 1954:1-13; Mathews 1959; Bieder 1964; Wilson 1973). David J. Bosch (1991:84-122) considered the Lukan missionary concept as the paradigm of 'practicing forgiveness and solidarity with the poor'. He emphasized the importance of Luke because this author demonstrated in his gospel and in Acts 'the essential unity between the mission of Jesus and that of the early church' (:55).

The mission concept in the gospel of *John* (John 20:19-23; et al.) has often been studied (Bornhäuser 1928; Oehler 1936, 1941; Fridrichsen, in: Sundkler, & Fridrichsen 1937:39-45; Oepke, in: EMZ 1941:4-26; Bieder 1964; Kuhl 1967; Miranda 1977; Winn 1981), but is ignored by David J. Bosch (1991). Johannes Blauw (1962:88) pointed out that John 20:21-23 emphasized 'the continuity of the sending of Jesus Christ by the Father and the sending of the disciples by Jesus', whereas Ferdinand Hahn (1963:136,142) underlined that in the view of the fourth gospel mission can only be realized where the disciples are conscious of their contrast with the world; their message in the world is a message of 'salvation universalism' (Ger.: *Heilsuniversalismus*).

The four gospels are 'resurrection gospels' (Robson 1908 against Adolf von Harnack) and as such they are missionary gospels; because 'it is the exalted Christ who draws all people to him (cf. John 12:32; cf. also the hymn which Paul quotes in 1Tim. 3:16 and which likewise links Easter with mission)' (Bosch 1991:40).

*WARNECK, GUSTAV. Jesus Christus und die Weltmission nach den Evangelien. In: AMZ, XXX (1903), p. 57-67.

HAUSSLEITER, JOHANNES. Der Missionsgedanke im Evangelium des Lukas. Barmen, 1904.

PAUNU, UNO. Lähetysaate synoptisissa evankeliumeissa (=The missionary idea in the synoptic gospels). 1904.

ROBSON, JOHN. The resurrection gospel: a study of Christ's great commission. Edinburgh, & London, 1908.

LILLEY, JAMES P. Four apostles: the training of Christian missionaries. London, & New York, 1912.

*BORNHÄUSER, KARL B. Das Johannesevangelium: eine Missionsschrift für Israël. Gütersloh, 1928.

OEHLER, WILHELM. Das Johannesevangelium: eine Missionsschrift für die Welt. Gütersloh, 1936.

*SUNDKLER, BENGT G.M., & ANTON FRIDRICHSEN (eds.). Contributions... Uppsala, 1937.
P. 39-45: La pensée missionnaire dans le quatrième évangile (Anton Fridrichsen).

OEHLER, WILHELM. Zum Missionscharakter des Johannesevangeliums. Gütersloh, 1941.

*OEPKE, ALBRECHT. Das missionarische Christuszeugnis des Johannesevangeliums. In: EMZ, II (1941), p. 4-26.

126

MICHEL, OTTO. Der Abschluss des Matthäusevangeliums. In: Evangelische Theologie, X (1950/51), p. 16-26.

SCHMAUCH, WERNER (ed.). In memoriam Ernst Lohmeyer. Stuttgart, 1951.
> P. 22-49: 'Mir ist gegeben alle Gewalt!' Eine Exegese von Matt. 28,16-20 (Ernst Lohmeyer).

LOHSE, EDUARD. Missionarisches Handeln Jesu nach dem Evangelium des Lukas. In: Theologische Zeitschrift, X (1954), p. 1-13.

NINEHAM, DENNIS E. (ed.). Studies in the gospels: essays in memory of Robert H. Lightfoot. Oxford, 1955.
> P. 145-158: The gentile mission in Mark 13:9-11 (George D. Kilpatrick).

MATHEWS, JAMES K. To the end of the earth: a study in Luke-Acts on the life and mission of the church. Nashville, 1959.

CERFAUX, LUCIEN. Apostle and apostolate, according to the gospel of St. Matthew. New York, 1960.
> *Fr. ed.: L'évangile de Saint Matthieu: discours de mission. Tournai, 1956.
> *Dutch tr.: 1958.
> It. tr.: 1962.

*ANDERSON. 1961.
> P. 55-71: An exegetical study of Matthew 28:16-20 (Karl Barth).
> First ed.: Die Auslegung von Matthäus 28:16-20. Basel, 1945.
> P. 85-93: The gospel according to St. John and the Christian mission (Francis N. Davey).

*BIEDER, WERNER. Gottes Sendung und der missionarische Auftrag der Kirche nach Matthäus, Lukas, Paulus und Johannes. Zürich, 1964.

*DINKLER, ERICH (ed.). Zeit und Geschichte: Dankesgabe an Rudolf Bultmann zum 80. Geburtstag. Tübingen, 1964.
> P. 171-191: Der Auferstandene und der Irdische. Mt. 28,16-20 (Günther Bornkamm).

*KUHL, JOSEF, SVD. Die Sendung Jesu und der Kirche nach dem Johannes-Evangelium. St. Augustin, 1967.

*RIDDER, RICHARD R. DE. The dispersion of the people of God: the covenant basis of Matthew 28:18-20 against the background of Jewish, pre-Christian proselyting and diaspora, and the apostleship of Jesus Christ. Kampen, 1971. Diss. V.U. Amsterdam.

WEBER. HANS-RUEDI. The invitation: Matthew in mission. Cincinnati, 1971.
> *Dutch tr.: 1972.

WILSON, STEPHEN G. The gentiles and the gentile mission in Luke-Acts. London, 1973.

WEBER, HANS-RUEDI. ... was ich euch ins Ohre sage, das predigt auf den Dächern: Mission im Matthäus-Evangelium. Kassel, 1975.

MIRANDA, JUAN P. Die Sendung Jesu im vierten Evangelium: religions- und theologiegeschichtliche Untersuchungen zu den Sendungsformeln. Stuttgart, 1977.

*MATTHEY, JACQUES. The great commission according to Matthew. In: IRM, LXIX (1980), p. 161-173.

WINN, ALBERT C. A sense of mission: guidance from the gospel of John. Philadelphia, 1981.

*PENTECOST, EDWARD C. Issues in missiology: an introduction. Grand Rapids, 1982.
> P. 37-51: The cultural and spiritual mandates.

SHENK, WILBERT R. (ed.). Exploring church growth. Grand Rapids, 1983.
> P. 218-248: The structure of mission: an exposition of Matthew 28:16-20 (David J. Bosch).

*KATO, ZENJI. Die Völkermission im Markusevangelium: eine redaktionsgeschichtliche Untersuchung. Bern, Frankfurt am Main, & New York, 1986.

*BANKS, WILLIAM L. In search of the great commission: what did Jesus really say? Chicago, 1991.

*BOSCH. 1991.
    P. 56-83: Matthew: mission as disciple-making.
    P. 84-122: Luke-Acts: practicing forgiveness and solidarity with the poor.

THE ACTS OF THE APOSTLES

Roland Allen (1917) was one of the first scholars to investigate the link between pneumatology (Acts 2: Pentecost) and mission in the Acts of the Apostles. He influenced many people. Werner Bieder (1960) called attention to the history of the interpretation of Acts as a missionary book, whereas Ulrich Wilckens (1974; cf. Buss 1980) researched the missionary speeches of Peter, Paul, and others in Acts. Thereafter Beverly R. Gaventa (Missiology 1982:416) made clear that in Acts 'witness' becomes the appropriate term for 'mission'. And David J. Bosch (1991:121) emphasized that in Acts 'the journey of the church-in-mission parallels that of Jesus to Jerusalem'.

In the Acts of the Apostles - 'the story of Christ's first missioners' (Penstone, & Hughes n.d.) and at the same time the story of church growth (Noordegraaf 1983)- the route is from Jerusalem, the centre of Israel, to Rome, the centre of the world. It is, however, a route which includes Africa: the first non-Jewish person who was baptized came from Ethiopia (Acts 8:26-40).

The Acts of the Apostles is *the first history of mission*, and consequently *the first church history*. Rudolf Pesch (Kertelge 1982:11-70) used this book mainly to construct the history of the early Christian mission:

Jewish mission:
1.   mission in Jerusalem;
2.   Jewish mission in Palestine;
3.   Jewish mission outside Palestine;
4.   the hypothesis of Galilean congregations from the very beginning;
5.   the hypothesis of Galilean congregations which were not affected by the Easter experience; and
6.   the development of Jewish mission after the appearance of the gentile mission.

Gentile mission:
1.   the launching of the gentile mission by the Hellenists;
2.   Paul as missionary to the gentiles;
3.   the development of the gentile mission without circumcision;
4.   the decision of Jerusalem;
5.   the conflict in Antioch; and
6.   the concept of a world-wide gentile mission (my tr.).

128

?HARPER. Lessons regarding the missionary enterprise which may be derived form the Acts of the Apostles. 1861.
Source: Myklebust. 1955. I, p. 130.

*BUCHNER, C. Die Bedeutung der Apostelgeschichte für unsere heutige Missionszeit. In: AMZ, XXV (1898), p. 304-315.

WALKER, THOMAS. Missionary ideals: missionary studies in the Acts of the Apostles... London, 1913.
?First ed.: London, 1911. Reprint: London, 1953.

*ALLEN, ROLAND. Pentecost and the world: the revelation of the Holy Spirit in 'the Acts of the Apostles'. London, 1917.

*KELLERHALS, EMMANUEL. Das neue Gottesvolk: ein Missions-Bibelstudium über Gemeinde und Mission in der Apostelgeschichte. Stuttgart, & Basel, 1938.

*HOLSTEN, WALTER. Das Evangelium und die Völker: Beiträge zur Geschichte und Theorie der Mission. Berlin, & Friedenau, 1939.
P. 139-147: Apostelgeschichte und Missionsbericht (1938).

*RÉTIF, ANDRÉ, SJ. Foi au Christ et mission d'après les Actes des Apôtres. Paris, 1953.

*BIEDER, WERNER. Die Apostelgeschichte in der Historie: ein Beitrag zur Auslegungsgeschichte des Missionsbuches der Kirche. Zürich, 1960.

AUTREY, C.E. Evangelism in the Acts. Grand Rapids, 1964.

*WILCKENS, ULRICH. Die Missionsreden der Apostelgeschichte: form- und traditions-geschichtliche Untersuchungen: dritte, überarbeitete und erw. Aufl. Neukirchen, 1974.
First ed.: Neukirchen, 1961.

*BUSS, MATTHÄUS F.J. Die Missionspredigt des Apostels Paulus im Pisidischen Antiochien: Analyse von Apg. 13,16-41 im Hinblick auf die literarische und thematische Einheit der Paulusrede. Stuttgart, 1980.

*GAVENTA, BEVERLY R. 'You will be my witnesses': aspects of mission in the Acts of the Apostles. In: Missiology, X (1982), p. 413-425.

*NOORDEGRAAF, ALBERT. Creatura Verbi: de groei van de gemeente volgens de Handelingen der Apostelen. 's-Gravenhage, 1983. Diss. Utrecht.

?PENSTONE, M.M., & M.V. HUGHES. The story of Christ's first missioners: biographical lessons on the Acts of the Apostles, intended for use with scholars between the ages of eleven and fourteen. London, n.d.

PETER

Especially Roman Catholic scholars (cf. Seumois 1953:14-46) are interested in the missionary role of Peter, who used the sending motif in his sermons: '... he [God] may *send* the Messiah appointed for you, that is, Jesus... When God raised up his servant, he *sent* him first to you, to bless you by turning each of you from your wicked ways' (Acts 3:20,26). Nevertheless, it was a Protestant scholar who wrote about 'the missionary work of Peter and the early church' (Hahn 1963:37-43; my tr.).

SEUMOIS, ANDRÉ V., OMI. La papauté et les missions au cours des six premiers siècles: méthodologie antique et orientations modernes. Paris, 1953.
P. 14-46: Saint Pierre.

PAUL

> ... the theology that supported Paul's ministry
> was born in mission and produced by mission.
> *Dean S. Gilliland (1983:10).*

The monographs on 'Paul and the mission' (Alcott 1834; 1835) started earlier than the monographs on 'Jesus and the mission' (Bornhäuser 1903). Some of these studies are good, others are weak. Dieter Zeller (Kertelge 1982:164) characterised the studies of Karl Pieper (1929) and Anton Freitag SVD (1952) as 'naïve' and 'uncritical'.

Many topics are discussed in the publications on 'Paul and the mission'. Here I mention five issues:

First, I refer to publications on the missionary call of Paul. The Korean Seyoon Kim (1981:65; cf. Warneck 1870) pointed out that 'at the Christophany on the Damascus road Paul received his call to the gentile mission as well as his gospel'.

Secondly, the (three) missionary journeys of Paul are dealt with by several authors, especially in the nineteenth century (Alcott 1834; 1835; Briggs 1864).

Thirdly, we also possess special studies of the missionary work of Paul (Ostwald 1850; Browne 1864; Schmitz, in: Titius 1928:167-174; Pieper 1929; Haas 1971); of his mission theology (Warneck 1892:I,194-251: Dahl 1977; Gilliland 1983); of his missionary preaching (Oepke 1920; Pieper 1921; Bussmann 1971); of his missionary thought/message (Rabanos Espinosa 1947; Baird 1960; Gardini 1963); of his missionary methods (Gregory von Breda, in: Scientia missionum ancilla 1953:84-101; Allen 1962 [1912]; Grassi 1965; Jeffery, in: Concise dictionary 1971:476-477; Haas 1971); of his missionary strategy (Bosch 1991:129-131); et al.

Fourthly, scholars have also studied Paul's converts (Lees 1910) and his missionary colleagues (Gramberg 1931; Ollrog 1978).

Finally, scholars called attention to the titles of Paul as 'missionary' (Brune 1896; Cone 1898; Minor 1921; Pieper 1925; Schlunk 1937; Taylor 1962; Pak 1991): the 'missionary of the gentiles' (Ger.: *Heidenmissionar*) (Wernle 1899; Weber 1946); the 'apostle of the gentiles' (Ger.: *Apostel der Heiden*) (Nösgen 1908; Tricot 1930; Bosch 1991:55); the 'apostle of the nations' (Ger.: *Völkerapostel*) (Müller, in: Studia missionalia 1956:5-33; Becker 1989); and the 'apostle of the non-Jews' (Ger.: *Apostel der Nichtjuden*) (Dabelstein 1981:38); et al.

David J. Bosch (1991:124) discussed both classical and recent studies on Paul. He concluded: 'It is today widely acknowledged that Paul was the first Christian theologian precisely because he was the first Christian missionary'. And he typified the missionary paradigm of Paul as an 'invitation to join the eschatological community' (1991:123-178).

ALCOTT, WILLIAM A. A first foreign mission: or, journey of Paul and Barnabas to Asia Minor... Boston, 1834.

ALCOTT, WILLIAM A. The second foreign mission: or, journey of Paul, Silas, Luke, and Timothy to Europe ... Boston, 1835.

?OSTWALD, THEODOR. Das Missions-Werk des Apostel Paulus. Langensalza, 1850.

BRIGGS, FREDERICK W. Missions apostolic and modern: an exposition of the narrative of St. Paul's first journey in relation to the Protestant missions of the present century. London, 1864.

BROWNE, EDWARD H. The mission work of St. Paul... Cambridge, 1864.

WARNECK, GUSTAV. Pauli Bekehrung: eine Apologie des Christentums. Gütersloh, 1870.

FABER, ERNST. Paul, the apostle in Europe: a guide to our mission work in Asia. Shanghai, 1891.

*WARNECK. 1892-1903. 3 vols.

    I, p. 194-251: Die Missionstheologie des Paulus.

BRUNE, R. St. Paulus als Missionar. Berlin, 1896.

*STOSCH, JOHANN E.G. Paulus als Typus für die evangelische Mission. In: AMZ, XXIII (1896), p. 345-357, 393-405.

BEACH, HARLAN P. St. Paul and the gentile world: or, missions in the light of Acts and the gentile epistles. New York, 1898.

CONE, ORELLO. Paul, the man, the missionary, and the teacher. London, 1898.

WERNLE, PAUL. Paulus als Heidenmissionar. Freiburg im Breisgau, Leipzig, & Tübingen, 1899.

    Second ed.: Tübingen, 1909.

BROWN, OSWALD E. Paul as a missionary. N.p., 1905.

?NÖSGEN, KARL F. Paulus der Apostel der Heiden. Gütersloh, 1908.

LEES, HARRINGTON C. St. Paul and his converts: a series of studies in typical New Testament missions... London, 1910.

*OEPKE, ALBRECHT. Die Missionspredigt des Apostels Paulus: eine biblisch-theologische und religionsgeschichtliche Untersuchung. Leipzig, 1920.

?MINOR, ERNEST. Paulus als Missionar. Wandesbeck, 1921.

*PIEPER, KARL. Die Missionspredigt des heiligen Paulus: ihre Fundstellen und ihr Inhalt: ein biblisch-theologische Untersuchung. Paderborn, 1921.

*WARNECK, JOHANNES G. Paulus im Lichte der heutigen Heidenmission: 3. und 4. Aufl. Berlin, 1922.

    *First ed.: Berlin, 1913.

?PIEPER, KARL. Paulus als Missionar. 1925.

TITIUS, ARTHUR (ed.). Deutsche Theologie: Bericht über den ersten deutschen Theologentag zu Eisenach (Herbst 1927). Göttingen, 1928.

    P. 167-174: Die Briefe des Paulus als integrierende Bestandteile seiner Missionsarbeit (Otto Schmitz).

CAVE, SYDNEY. The Gospel of St. Paul: a reinterpretation in the light of the religion of his age and modern missionary experience. New York, 1929.

PIEPER, KARL. Paulus: seine missionarische Persönlichkeit und Wirksamkeit: zweite und dritte, neubearbeitete und verm. Aufl. Münster in Westfalen, 1929.

    *First ed.: Münster in Westfalen, 1926.

    Polish tr.: 1929.

*RICHTER, JULIUS. Die Briefe des Apostels Paulus als missionarische Sendschreiben. Gütersloh, 1929.

TRICOT, ALPHONSE E. St. Paul, the apostle of the gentiles. London, Edinburgh, & St. Louis, 1930.

    *Fr. ed.: Saint Paul, apôtre des gentils. Paris, 1927.

*GRAMBERG, Th.W.B.G. Zendings-dienst: figuren uit den kring van Paulus: Tychicus, Phebe, Epaphroditus. Hoenderloo, 1931.

*SIMON, GOTTFRIED. Mission heute? Eine Besinnung auf die Mission des Paulus. Bad Salzuflen, 1935.

*SCHLUNK, MARTIN. Paulus als Missionar. Gütersloh, 1937.

KRISTOFFERSEN (LIER), ALF. Äpenbaringstanke og misjonsforkynnelse hos Paulus. Stavanger, 1938.

*DIBELIUS, MARTIN. Paulus auf dem Areopag. Heidelberg, 1939.

?WEBER, HANS E. Paulus: der Heidenmissionar und sein Ruf an uns. Leipzig, 1946.

RABANOS ESPINOSA, RICARDO, CM. El pensamiento misionero de San Pablo. Madrid, 1947.

RENAUD, ROSAIRE, SJ. Saint Paul missionnaire. Montréal, 1947.

FREITAG, ANTON, SVD. Paulus baut die Weltkirche: ein Missionsbuch. Mödling bei Wien, 1952.

*SCIENTIA MISSIONUM ANCILLA. 1953.

    P. 84-101: Missionsmethodische Richtlinien nach den Schriften des Hl. Paulus (Gregory von Breda OFMCap.).

?MÜLLER, KARL, SVD. Das universale Heilsdenken des Völkerapostles nach dem Galater- und Römerbrief. In: Studia missionalia, IX (1956), p. 5-33.

BAIRD, WILLIAM. Paul's mission and message. New York, 1960.

*ANDERSON. 1961.

    P. 72-84: Pauline motives for the Christian mission (Donald G. Miller).

*ALLEN, ROLAND. Missionary methods: St. Paul's or ours? a study of the church in the four provinces. Grand Rapids, 1962.

    First ed.: London, 1912.

    *Reprinted: Grand Rapids, 1989.

TAYLOR, WILLIAM M. Paul, the missionary. Grand Rapids, 1962.

    First ed.: New York, 1881.

GARDINI, WALTER, SX. Il messagio missionario di San Paolo. Parma, 1963.

    Sp. tr.: 1963.

GRASSI, JOSEPH A. A world to win: the missionary methods of Paul the apostle. New York, 1965.

*BUSSMANN, CLAUS. Themen der Paulinischen Missionspredigt auf dem Hintergrund der spätjüdisch-hellenistischen Missionsliteratur. Bern, & Frankfurt am Main, 1971.

    Second ed.: 1975.

*CONCISE DICTIONARY. 1971.

    P. 476-477: Paul's missionary methods (Robert M.C. Jeffery).

*HAAS, ODO. Paulus der Missionar: Ziel, Grundsätze und Methoden der Missionstätigkeit des Apostels Paulus nach seinen eigenen Aussagen... Münsterschwarzach, 1971.

STENDAHL, KRISTER. Paul among Jews and gentiles. Philadelphia, 1976.

*DAHL, NILS A. (assisted by PAUL DONAHUE). Studies in Paul: theology for the early Christian mission. Minneapolis, 1977.

*OLLROG, WOLF-HENNING. Paulus und seine Mitarbeiter: Untersuchungen zu Theorie und Praxis der paulinischen Mission. Neukirchen, 1978.

BEKER, J. CHRISTIAAN. Paul the apostle: the triumph of God in life and thought. Philadelphia, 1980.

*DABELSTEIN, ROLF. Die Beurteilung der 'Heiden' bei Paulus. Frankfurt am Main, Bern, &
    Cirencester/U.K., 1981.
*KIM, SEYOON. The origin of Paul's gospel. Tübingen, 1981.
?MONLOUBOU, LOUIS. Saint Paul et la prière: prière et évangelisation. 1982.
*GILLILAND, DEAN S. Pauline theology and mission practice. Grand Rapids, 1983.
*LMG. 1987.
    P. 369-375: Paulus (Karl Kertelge).
*BECKER, JÜRGEN. Paulus: der Apostel der Völker. Tübingen, 1989.
*BOSCH. 1991.
    P. 123-178: Mission in Paul: invitation to join the eschatological community.
*PAK, JAMES YEONG-SIK. Paul as missionary: a comparative study of missionary discourse in
    Paul's epistles and selected contemporary Jewish texts. Frankfurt am Main, Bern,
    New York..., 1991.
BERKHOF, LOUIS. Paul the missionary. Grand Rapids, n.d.

THE EPISTLES

We find 'mission theology' in the letters of Paul and other letters of the New
Testament: each of them conveying different theological and missiological
perspectives.

Some mission studies deal with several New Testament letters whereas
others only focus on one epistle. Here I mention the following studies on
particular epistles:

-   the epistle to the Romans (Colenso 1861; Weber 1905; Schrenk 1954:
    81-106; Müller, in: Studia missionalia 1956:5-33; Minear, in:
    Hermelink 1959:42-48; Zeller 1973);
-   the epistles to the Corinthians (Bishop 1949; Linssen 1952; Danbolt
    1956; Baum 1977);
-   the epistle to the Galatians (Steinmann 1908; Warren 1955; Müller, in:
    Studia missionalia 1956:5-33);
-   the epistle to the Ephesians (Roels 1962; van Bemmel 1967; Meyer
    1977; 1979);
-   the epistle to the Colossians (Stein 1894; Schmidt 1950);
-   the epistle to the Thessalonians (Müller, in: Axenfeld 1904:81-102);
-   the epistles of Peter (Bieder 1950; van Swigchem 1955; Gilhuis 1979).

These studies make clear that each letter has its own 'contextual' theology of
mission: the epistles of Paul differ in missionary view from the epistles of
Peter; as the letters to Christians in towns (Rome, Corinth, Ephesus, et al.) are
different from the letters to Christians in rural areas (Galatia, et al.).

We also encounter mission theology in the New Testament letters which
do not appear in the afore-mentioned list. For instance, the first epistle of John
is really a missionary letter which is waiting for missiological exploration in a

monography. We read in this letter: 'God *sent* his only Son into the world so that we might live through him... he loved us and *sent* his Son to be the atoning sacrifice for our sins... And we have seen and do testify that the Father *sent* his Son as the Savior of the world' (1 John 4:9-10,14).

COLENSO, JOHN W. St. Paul's Epistle to the Romans: newly translated and explained from a missionary point of view. Cambridge, 1861.

*STEIN, P.E. Das Missions-Sendschreiben St. Pauli an die Kolosser in Missionsbetrachtungen für Missionsfreunde ausgelegt und durch Beispiele aus der Missionsgeschichte illustriert. Gütersloh, 1894.

*AXENFELD, KARL, GUSTAV MÜLLER, CARL PAUL, et al. (eds.). Missionswissenschaftliche Studien: Festschrift zum 70. Geburtstag des Herrn Prof.D.Dr. Gustav Warneck... Berlin, 1904.
    P. 81-102: Die missionarische Tätigkeit des Apostel Paulus in Thessalonich: eine Studie über die Thessalonicherbriefe (Gustav Müller).

WEBER, HANS E. Die Beziehungen von Römer 1-3 zur Missionspraxis des Paulus... Gütersloh, 1905.

STEINMANN, ALPHONS A. Der Leserkreis des Galaterbriefes: ein Beitrag zur urchristlichen Missionsgeschichte. Münster in Westfalen, 1908.

BISHOP, ERIC F.F. Missionary studies in the Epistles to the church at Corinth. Beirut, 1949.

*BIEDER, WERNER. Grund und Kraft der Mission nach dem 1. Petrusbrief. Zürich, 1950.

SCHMIDT, OTTO H. Saint Paul shows us how: the pastor and missionary worker looks at his task in the light of St. Paul's Epistle to the Colossians. St. Louis, 1950.

*LINSSEN, GERARDUS, CICM. Het apostolaat volgens St. Paulus: een bijbels-theologische studie van 1 Kor. IX. Nijmegen, 1952. Diss. Nijmegen.

?SCHRENK, GOTTLOB. Studien zu Paulus. Zürich, 1954.
    P. 81-106: Der Römerbrief als Missionsdokument.

*SWIGCHEM, DOUWE VAN. Het missionair karakter van de christelijke gemeente volgens de Brieven van Paulus en Petrus. Kampen, 1955. Diss. V.U. Amsterdam.

*WARREN, MAX A.C. The gospel of victory: a study in the relevance of the Epistle to the Galatians for the Christian mission to-day. London, 1955.

DANBOLT, ERLING G. Forste Korintierbrev i lys av misjonen. Stavanger, 1956.

MÜLLER, KARL, SVD. Das universale Heilsdenken des Völkerapostels nach dem Galater- und Römerbrief. In: Studia missionalia, IX (1956), p. 5-33.

*HERMELINK, JAN, & HANS J. MARGULL (eds.). Basileia: Walter Freytag zum 60. Geburtstag. Stuttgart, 1959.
    P. 42-48: Gratitude and mission in the Epistle to the Romans (Paul S. Minear).

*ROELS, EDWIN D. God's mission: the Epistle to the Ephesians in mission perspective. Franeker, 1962. Diss. V.U. Amsterdam.

*BEMMEL, H.A. VAN. Het grote geheimenis; een Bijbelstudie over Efeziërs 3:6 ten dienste van kerk en zending. Zeist, 1967.

*ZELLER, DIETER. Juden und Heiden in der Mission des Paulus: Studien zum Römerbrief. Stuttgart, 1973.

*BAUM, HORST, SVD. Mut zum Schwachsein - in Christi Kraft: theologische Grundelemente einer missionarischen Spiritualität anhand von 2 Kor. Sankt Augustin, 1977.

MEYER, REGINA P.M. Kirche und Mission im Epheserbrief. Stuttgart, 1977.

GILHUIS, JAN C. '... ik zag een kerk': de missionaire gemeente onder het gehoor van Petrus. Kampen, 1979.

?MEYER, REGINA P.M. Universales Heil, Kirche und Mission: Studien über die ekklesial-missionarischen Strukturen in der Theologie Karl Rahners und im Epheserbrief. Sankt Augustin, 1979. Diss. Münster.

THE REVELATION OF JOHN

The last Bible book, which like other apostolic letters was written in the mission field, 'uses the language of the sending to convey a variety of theological ideas' (DuBose 1983:52). We read about God who *sent* his angel to his servant John (Rev. 1:1), and about Jesus who *sent* his angel 'with this testimony for the churches. I am the root and the descendant of David, the bright morning star' (Rev. 22:16), etc.

We possess one special study on mission in the last Bible book. It emphasizes the commission of being God's witnesses to the churches and to the world (du Preez 1979:223-224):

-       Witnessing by means of a life wholly dedicated to God;
-       Witnessing by the offering of verbal testimony;
-       Witnessing through the offering of suffering;
-       Witnessing through the offering of prayer (supplication and intercession); and
-       Witnessing through the offering of prayer (thanksgiving and praise).

*PREEZ, JANNIE DU. Die koms van die Koninkryk volgens die Boek Openbaring (sendingperspektief in die laaste Bybelboek). Kaap, 1979. Diss. Stellenbosch.
*DUBOSE, FRANCIS M. God who sends... Nashville, 1983.
       P. 51-52: The Epistles and Revelation.

THE GENTILES (ETHNE)

There are not only special studies on the gentile nations in the Old Testament, but also on their place in the New Testament (Rengstorf 1936; Schlier, in: EMZ 1942:166-182,208-212; Dabelstein 1981). These studies make clear that the position of the gentile nations (Hebrew: *goiim*) in the Old Testament is totally different from their position in the New Testament because the (early) church is not at all an ethnic community (cf. the Jewish synagoge), but a fellowship of Christian Jews (who originate from the Jewish mission) and Christian 'non-Jews' (who originate from the gentile mission) in one -interracial and international- body. Hospitality (Koenig 1985) is one of the main characteristics of this new body.

135

RENGSTORF, KARL H. Die Mission unter den Heiden im Lichte des Neuen Testaments. Hermannsburg, 1936.
*SCHLIER, HEINRICH. Die Entscheidung für die Heidenmission in der Urchristenheit. In: EMZ, III (1942), p. 166-182, 208-212.
*DABELSTEIN, ROLF. Die Beurteilung der 'Heiden' bei Paulus. Frankfurt am Main, Bern, & Cirencester/U.K., 1981.
*KOENIG, JOHN. New Testament hospitality: partnership with strangers as promise and mission. Philadelphia, 1985.

THE NEW TESTAMENT IN MISSION

The New Testament has already been translated into nearly all the languages of the world, and has a tremendous 'impact' (Ting, in: IRM 1948:129-137) on world history. However, some of its parts made a deeper impression than others. The epistles of Paul had a great influence in Christian theology (Augustine, Luther, Karl Barth, et al.). The four gospels, however, went time and time again beyond the boundaries of Christianity. Especially the Sermon on the Mount (Matt. 5-7) and the Great Commandment (Matt. 22: 34-40; Mark 12:28-34; cf. Luke 20:25-37) were and are respected by many non-Christians, for instance by Mahatma Gandhi in India.

Nobody was more influential in world history than the person of Jesus Christ who -as the sent one and the sending one- is the real centre of the whole -missionary- New Testament. The -missionary- church accepted him as Lord and Saviour of the whole universe, whereas people outside the church respect him in their own unbound way. The Jewish philosopher Martin Buber, for instance, called him 'his brother'; the Muslim novelist Naguib Mahfuz drew more attention to his crucifixion and death in his book *The Children of Our Quarter* (1959) than is usual in the world of Islam; and the Hindu Gandhi loved the well-known Christian hymn: 'When I survey the wondrous cross' (Wessels 1990:31,55,137).

*TING, KWANG HSUN. The impact of the New Testament on the non-Christian. In: IRM, XXXVII (1948), p. 129-137.
*WESSELS, ANTON. Images of Jesus: how Jesus is perceived and portrayed in non-European cultures. Grand Rapids, 1990.
    Dutch ed.: Jezus zien: hoe Jezus is overgeleverd in andere culturen. Baarn, 1986.

3.4.2.3. ECCLESIASTICAL THEOLOGY OF MISSION

> ... different ecclesiastical traditions.
> *David J. Bosch (Van Engen 1993:89).*

INTRODUCTION

Theology of mission is not only imlicitly or explicitly expressed in the Bible, but also in 'ecclesiastical documents' (cf. Ohm 1962:21-23: *kirchliche Dokumente*), or 'church documents'. *Ecclesiastical theology of mission(s)* -a term which I did not encounter in the missiological literature- is the discipline which deals with *church mission* (Ger.: *Kirchenmission*; cf. Daubanton 1911:9-13; Schomerus 1935:67-69) from the theological (i.e. ecclesiological) point of view, and which includes the study of missionary statements by churches, church bodies, and other ecclesiastical institutions at the global, the regional, and the national level.

Ecclesiastical engagement in mission, i.e. the engagement of the church as church in mission, already starts in the New Testament and in the early church. The so-called Council of Jerusalem (Acts 15; Gal. 2) already dealt with the missionary problem of the circumcision of non-Jewish Christians, whereas the Council of Nicea (325) took a decision to delegate the task of doing mission in Asia to the patriarchate of Antioch. Although missionary problems were also on the agenda of the church throughout the Middle Ages, it was the foundation of the *Sacra congregatio de propaganda fide* (1622) which really paved the way for the growth and flourishing of an ecclesiastical theology of mission. In modern history, Protestant missiologists were generally less in favour of an ecclesiastical theology of mission than their Roman Catholic and also their Eastern Orthodox counterparts.

In the strict sense of the word, we only can speak about 'ecclesiastical theology of mission' or 'traditional theology of mission' (Schmidlin 1925:131-139; Mulders 1950:140-161) if we can refer to activities and documents which are drafted and officially promulgated by churches, church bodies, and other ecclesiastical institutions, i.e. by the Pope, the councils, the synods, the assemblies, etc. However, in a broader sense we also can speak about this form of mission theology if we can refer to sources which in one way or another are 'church-related'. In this section I will use the term under consideration in both senses of the word. The Hebrew Christian, the Ecumenical, the Evangelical, and the Charismatic theology of mission can only be typified as 'ecclesiastical' if we use this term in the broader sense. For their theology of mission is not as *denominational* as that of the Eastern Orthodox, the Roman Catholic, the Lutheran, the Reformed, the Anabaptist, the Anglican, and the Methodist theology of mission. In other words: their theology of mission is basically *interdenominational* or *transdenominational*.

*WARNECK. 1892-1903. 3 vols.
    I, p. 251-272: Die kirchliche Begründung.
*DAUBANTON. 1911.
    P. 9-13: De kerkelijke zending.
*SCHMIDLIN. 1925.
    P. 131-139: Biblisch-traditionelle Missionstheorie.
*SCHOMERUS. 1935.
    P. 67-69: Bedenken gegen direkte Kirchenmission.
*MULDERS, ALPHONSUS J.M. Inleiding tot de missiewetenschap. Bussum, 1950.
    P. 140-161: Overgeleverde missietheologie.
*OHM. 1962.
    P. 21-23: Kirchliche Dokumente.
SANTOS HERNANDEZ, ANGEL, SJ. Téologia biblico-patristica de las misiones. Santander, 1962.
*SANTOS HERNANDEZ, ANGEL, SJ. Bibliografia misional. Santander, 1965. 2 vols.
    I, p. 165-233: Teologia biblico-patristica de las misiones. Bibliog.
*BASSHAM, RODGER C. Mission theology: 1948-1975 years of worldwide creative tension Ecumenical, Evangelical, and Roman Catholic. Pasadena, 1979.
*BOSCH, DAVID J. Witness to the world: the Christian mission in theological perspective. London, 1980.
*GLASSER, ARTHUR F., & DONALD A. McGAVRAN. Contemporary theologies of mission. Grand Rapids, 1985.
*SCHERER, JAMES A. Gospel, church, and kingdom: comparative studies in world mission theology. Minneapolis, 1987.
*BOSCH. 1991.
*JONGENEEL, JAN A.B., et al. (eds.). Pentecost, mission and ecumenism; essays on intercultural theology: Festschrift in honour of Professor Walter J. Hollenweger. Frankfurt am Main, Bern, New York..., 1992.
    P. 231-246: Ecumenical, Evangelical and Pentecostal/Charismatic views on mission as a movement of the Holy Spirit (Jan A.B. Jongeneel).
*SCHERER, JAMES A., & STEPHEN B. BEVANS SVD (eds.). New directions in mission and evangelization I: basic statements 1974-1991. New York, 1992.
*ENGEN, CHARLES VAN, DEAN S. GILLILAND, & PAUL PIERSON (eds.). The good news of the kingdom: mission theology for the third millennium. New York, 1993.
    P. 89-95: God's reign and the rulers of the world (David J. Bosch).
*PHILLIPS, JAMES M., & ROBERT T. COOTE (eds.). Toward the twenty-first century in Christian mission. Grand Rapids, 1993.
    P. 7-53: Christian families in mission.

HEBREW CHRISTIAN THEOLOGY OF MISSION

First, I call attention to the *Hebrew Christian theology of mission(s)*, or *Jewish Christian theology of mission(s)*, which was not only developed during the first centuries of church history -i.e. the period from the New Testament to Constantine the Great- but also in the 19th and 20th centuries.

Here I refer to the writings of contemporary Jewish Christian (missionary) scholars such as Philip A. Kohnstamm (1875-1951), and to (missionary) statements formulated by Hebrew Christians as a group. However, Hebrew Christians not only attend ecumenical and evangelical conferences and consultations, but also take part in the formulation of their statements. For instance, the Fourth International Conference of the Lausanne Consultation on Jewish Evangelism, which met in Zeist, the Netherlands, August 5-9, 1991, implored the churches 'to stand with us against powers that promote anti-Semitism and to affirm the urgency of Jewish evangelism' (Scherer, & Bevans 1992:306-314). In both Roman Catholic theology of mission and Ecumenical theology of mission, we also encounter the struggle against anti-Semitism, but they do not call upon their members to evangelize the Jews. In fact, they replace *Jewish evangelism* by dialogue with the synagogue.

Hebrew Christians are very divided on this issue. Some Hebrew Christians evangelize their fellow Jews and/or take part in global missionary activities among Jews, whereas other Hebrew Christians (vehemently) reject these activities. Therefore, Hebrew Christian theology of mission is really pluriform, as pluriform as non-Jewish theology of mission.

In missiological literature, the Hebrew Christian theology of mission is totally neglected. Such writings seem to treat the biblical distinction between Jews and non-Jews as entirely irrelevant to contemporary missions. In my view, however, the Jewish Christians must be recognised both in missions and in the church as the *primi inter pares*. The 'missionary paradigm' (David Bosch 1991) of the Hebrew Christians is the primary missionary paradigm of Christianity.

*KOHNSTAMM, PHILIP A. The necessity for a new philosophy and its bearing on missionary work. In: IRM, XIX (1930), p. 161-173, 321-332.

EASTERN ORTHODOX THEOLOGY OF MISSION

The Eastern Orthodox churches became member-churches of the World Council of Churches (WCC) at the New Delhi assembly (1961). In this way they relate themselves to the Commission on World Mission and Evangelism (CWME) which, as the successor of the International Missionary Council, was founded at the same time. This link with the WCC and its CWME was prepared by Bishop Anastasios Yannoulatos. He founded an Orthodox missionary society -*Porefthentes (=Go out)*- and an Orthodox missionary journal. In fact, he caused a renewal of the *Eastern Orthodox theology of mission(s)/Eastern Orthodox mission theology* (Stamoolis 1986), or *Eastern Orthodox missiology* (Stamoolis 1980; Scherer, & Bevans 1992:XIII-XVI), which can ultimately be traced back to the missionary concepts and activities from Byzantium among the Goths, Huns, and Slavs during the fourth to the eleventh centuries.

After the New Delhi assembly, the Orthodox churches established a Bureau of Orthodox Theology and Relations within the CWME of the WCC. First Bishop Anastasios (1970-1973), and thereafter Professor Ion Bria (1973ff.), served in this office. In this way Orthodox theologians not only influenced the WCC, and especially its CWME, but also the local Orthodox churches. Since 1974 annual conferences have been held at the local level in order to clarify Orthodox mission theory and practice. The Neapolis consultation (1988) on the theme 'Your Will Be Done - Orthodoxy in Mission' declared that 'the mission of the church has cosmic dimensions. Its aim is to embrace and to renew the whole world, to transfigure it into God's kingdom. Mission is to approach and draw near, to sanctify and to renew the world, to give new content to old ways of life, to accept local cultures and their ways of expression that do not contradict the Christian faith, transforming them into means of salvation' (Scherer, & Bevans 1992:233).

James A. Scherer and Stephen B. Bevans SVD published the texts of the following statements: *Go Forth in Peace: Orthodox Perspectives on Mission* (1986); *Final Report of CWME Consultation of Eastern Orthodox and Oriental Orthodox Churches* (1988); and *Final Report of CWME Orthodox Advisory Group* (1990). They also summarized the major principles underlying these documents:

1. A consistently trinitarian basis, fully involving each person of the Trinity in the mystery of salvation;
2. A cosmic eschatological perspective, which looks forward to the salvation of the entire creation as the goal of the kingdom;
3. The church, or Body of Christ, as the visible manifestation in the power of the Holy Spirit of the presence of Christ in human history;
4. The witness of the eucharistic community through doxology and liturgy as a primary expression of mission; and
5. The contextualization of faith in the language and culture of each local community (1992:XV).

After the New Delhi assembly of the WCC (1961), Anastasios Yannoulatos (IRM 1963:300-302), Ion Bria (1980; 1986; ER 1987:265-270), James J. Stamoolis (1980; 1986), Elias Voulgarakis (LMG 1987:355-360), and George Lemopoulos (1989; 1990) can be considered as leading missiologists in the Eastern Orthodox churches. At the end of his survey of Orthodox mission thinking, Stamoolis concluded that 'it is appropriate to make an evaluation of the success of the Orthodox in producing a missiology. Some who have read this study have questioned the use of the term *missiology*. Their opinion is that the Orthodox have, at best, some thinking about mission, but not a fully developed missiology. My reply is that there is some truth in their claim. We have yet to see a thorough study of the subject from an Orthodox perspective. Anastasios Yannoulatos admits that what is needed is "to start from the general presuppositions and principles of Orthodox theology and to meditate upon Orthodox soteriology, ecclesiology, and eschatology in the perspective of mission". More work needs to be done to draw out the richness of the Orthodox position' (1986:128).

*BOLSHAKOFF, SERGE. Orthodox missions today. In: IRM, XLII (1953), p. 275-284.
*HERMELINK, JAN, & HANS J. MARGULL (eds.). Basileia: Walter Freytag zum 60. Geburtstag. Stuttgart, 1959.
P. 76-80: The Orthodox concept of mission and missions (The Metropolitan James of Melita=Athanasius Coucouzes).
*ANDERSON. 1961.
P. 250-257: The missionary imperative in the Orthodox tradition (Alexander Schemann).
*WINSEN, GERARDUS A.C. VAN, CM, GERBEN J.F. BOURITIUS SCJ, & JAKOB BUYS SVD (eds.). Novella ecclesiae germina... Nijmegen, & Utrecht, 1963.
P. 13-23: L'implantation d'églises particulières ou l'idée de mission chez les Pères Grecs (André V. Seumois OMI).
*YANNOULATOS, ANASTASIOS. Orthodox spirituality and external mission. In: IRM, LII (1963), p. 300-302.
*CONCISE DICTIONARY. 1971.
P. 413-414: Orthodox missions (Josef Glazik MSC).
*ANDERSON, GERALD H., & THOMAS F. STRANSKY CSP (eds.). Mission trends. No. 1: Crucial issues in mission today. New York, Paramus, & Toronto..., 1974.
P. 59-71: The Orthodox church and mission: past and present perspectives (John Meyendorff).
STAMOOLIS, JAMES J. A selected bibliography of Eastern Orthodox mission theology. In: Occasional bulletin of missionary research, I/3 (1977), p. 24-27. Bibliog.
*BRIA, ION (ed.). Martyria/mission: the witness of the Orthodox churches today. Geneva, 1980.
?STAMOOLIS, JAMES J. An examination of contemporary Eastern Orthodox missiology. 1980.
*BRIA, ION (comp. and ed.). Go forth in peace: Orthodox perspectives on mission. Geneva, 1986.
*STAMOOLIS, JAMES J. Eastern Orthodox mission theology today. New York, 1986.
*BRIA, ION. Unity and mission from the perspective of the local church: an Orthodox view. In: ER, XXXIX (1987), p. 265-270.
*LMG. 1987.
P. 355-360: Orthodoxe Mission (Elias Voulgarakis).
*LEMOPOULOS, GEORGE (ed.). Your will be done: Orthodoxy in mission. Katerini, & Geneva, 1989.
LEMOPOULOS, GEORGE (ed.). The Holy Spirit and mission. Geneva, 1990.
*BOSCH. 1991.
P. 190-213: The missionary paradigm of the Eastern church.

ROMAN CATHOLIC THEOLOGY OF MISSION

The *Roman Catholic theology of mission(s)/Roman Catholic mission theology* (Bassham 1979:297-328), or *Roman Catholic missiology* (Scherer, & Bevans 1992:XII-XIII), can be divided into the period before and after the establishment of the *Sacra congregatio de propaganda fide* (1622), and the period before and after the Second Vatican Council (1962-1965) which, more than any previous council, dealt with missions. In several ways the 'medieval Roman Catholic missionary paradigm' (Bosch 1991:214-238) has now been updated by both the *Sacra congregatio de propagande fide* and the Second Vatican Council.

In 1622 Gregory XV established the *Sacra congregatio de propaganda fide* in his constitution *Inscrutabili divinae*. In the same year he described her responsibility by *motu proprio* in *Cum inter multiplices* (cf. 2.5.1.).

First of all we can find Roman Catholic theology of mission in the following (collections of) documents of the Vatican, especially of the *Sacra congregatio de propaganda fide* (cf. Stanghetti 1943):

- *Constitutiones apostolicae Sacrae Congregationis de Propaganda Fide,* 1642;
- *Constitutiones apostolicae, brevia, decreta, etc...,* 1676;
- *Constitutiones apostolicae et brevia ad usum Sacrae Congregationis de Propaganda Fide,* 1745;
- *Bullarium Pontificium Sacrae Congregationis de Propaganda Fide,* 1839-1841;
- *Iuris Pontificii de Propaganda Fide pars prima, complectens bullas, brevia, acta S. Sedis,* 1888-1897;
- *Collectanea S. Congregationis de Propaganda Fide, seu decreta, instructiones, rescripta pro apostolicis missionariis,* 1893, second ed. 1907;
- *Iuris Pontificii de Propaganda Fide pars secunda, complectens decreta, instructiones, encyclicas literas, etc.,* 1909;
- *Instructions au missionnaires de la S. Congrégation de la Propaganda; traduites par un missionnaire de la Congrégation du Coeur Immaculé de Marie (Scheut),* 1920, second ed. 1928;
- *Sylloge praecipuorum documentorum recentium summorum Pontificium et S. Congregationis de Propaganda Fide, necnon aliarum S.S. Congregationum Romanarum ad usum missionariorum,* 1939.

In the pre-Vatican period the following Roman Catholic documents are also important for missions:

1840: *Probe nostis* (encyclical letter of Gregory XVI);
1880: *Sancta civitas Dei* (encyclical letter of Leo XIII);
1894: *Christi nomen* (apostolic letter of Leo XIII);
1919: *Maximum illud* (apostolic letter of Benedict XV);
1926: *Rerum ecclesiae* (encyclical letter of Pius XI);
1943: *Mystici corporis Christi* (encyclical letter of Pius XII);
1951: *Evangelii praecones* (encyclical letter of Pius XII);
1957: *Fidei donum* (encyclical letter of Pius XII); and
1959: *Princeps pastorum* (encyclical letter of John XXIII).

These documents have been studied by many writers (Zameza 1945; Clark 1948; Burke 1957; Glazik 1961; Marmy, & auf der Maur 1961; Rétif 1963; Wanko 1968; et al.).

The latest of the afore-mentioned documents were influenced by the theories of two prominent missiological schools which came to the fore after the First World War: the so-called German school (Joseph Schmidlin at Münster) which emphasized mission as 'preaching the gospel among non-Christians', and the so-called Louvain school (Pierre Charles SJ at Louvain) which emphasized mission as the 'planting of the church' (Lat.: *plantatio ecclesiae*) (cf. Seumois, in: Rommerskirchen, & Kowalsky 1951:39-53).

Ronan Hoffman OFMConv. (Campbell 1965:43-78) also regarded both Josef Schmidlin (1925) and Pierre Charles SJ (1938) as the main founders of the modern Roman Catholic theology of mission. However, he also discussed the positions of René Lange SJ (1924), Henri de Lubac SJ (1941), Alexandre Durand SJ (1942), et al. And he disagreed with Angel Santos Hernandez SJ, who distinguished between 'the German school of Schmidlin; the Belgian school of Lange and especially of Charles; the French school of ... de Lubac, Durand, Daniélou, Perbal, and others; the Spanish school... This, however, seems rather premature, not only because these different directions complement one another, but also because these speculations are still in an elaborate stage in trying to establish a body of doctrine which is completely satisfactory' (:50-51).

At the Second Vatican Council (1962-1965) missionary ideas were expressed in a different context and in a new direction (Beckmann, in: IRM 1964:83-88; Alexander 1967; Gensichen, in: IRM 1967:291-309; Hogg, in: IRM 1967:281-290; auf der Maur, in: Stirnimann 1970:81-102; Kollbrunner, in: LMG 1987:520-525; et al.). Here, we only mention the documents of the council which, in one way or another, deal with mission:

1964: *Lumen gentium* (dogmatic constitution on the church);
1965: *Ad gentes* (decree on missionary activities);
1965: *Dignitatis humanae* (declaration on religious liberty);

1965: *Gaudium et spes* (pastoral constitution on the church in the modern world); and

1965: *Nostra aetate* (declaration on the relation of the church to non-Christian religions).

From the missiological point of view, *Ad gentes* (Rétif 1966; Schelbert 1968; Nunnenmacher 1984; et al.) is the most important statement of the council. This decree transcended the controversy between the so-called German school and the Louvain school by defining missions as those 'special undertakings in which preachers of the gospel, sent by the church, and going into the whole world, carry out the work of preaching the gospel and implanting the church among people who not yet believe in Christ'.

In the post-Vatican period -a period of 'greater inclusiveness' (Mary Motte, in: Phillips, & Coote 1993:38)- reflection on mission and its relation to the church and to non-Christian religions continues (Schütte 1967; Masson, in: Dhavamony 1972:105-116; et al.). In their survey of basic Roman Catholic texts promulgated between 1974-1991, James A. Scherer and Stephen B. Bevans SVD mention 14 documents of which the following are most important:

1975: *Evangelii nuntiandi* (apostolic exhortation of Paul VI on the evangelization in the modern world);

1990: *Redemptoris missio* (encyclical letter of John Paul II); and

1991: *Dialogue and proclamation* (Pontifical council for interreligious dialogue and Congregation for the evangelization of peoples).

Special studies exist of these ecclesiastical documents (e.g.: Rzepkowski 1976; International Journal of Frontier Missions 1991:99-105, which offers the text and 12 reflections on *Redemptoris missio*).

In the post-Vatican period, Latin American, African and Asian episcopal conferences have also dealt seriously with missions: e.g. the Puebla document of the Latin American bishops (CELAM III, 1979). In the same period, new Roman Catholic scholars have taken the lead in developing a contemporary theology of mission. Here I call attention to both the divergent publications of Ludwig Rütti SMB (1972), Yves M.J. Congar SJ (Theologische revue 1973:353-360), Heinz R. Schlette (ZMR 1975:161-169), Joseph Comblin (1977), and Karl Müller SVD (1987), and the collective works of Mariasusai Dhavamony SJ, et al. (1972), and Mary Motte FMM, & Joseph R. Lang MM, et al. (1982). They not only emphasize 'the missionary nature of the church' (Rweyemamu 1968), but also the significance of liberation and dialogue in present-day church life.

Finally we call attention to the Joint Working Group of the Roman Catholic Church (Secretariat for Promoting Christian Unity) and the World

144

Council of Churches (WCC: Commission on World Mission and Evangelism), which published *Common Witness: a Study Document* in 1984. James A. Scherer and Stephen B. Bevans SVD (1992) did not publish the text of this unique document in a separate section, but in the section on the WCC (:18-26). In this document we read: 'The church as a whole is the primary subject of Christian witness. As the church is one body of many members, Christian witness is by its nature communitarian. When one of the faithful acts in individual witness this is related to the witness of the whole Christian community. Even when the witness is given by Christians in separated churches it should be witness to the same Christ and necessarily has a communitarian aspect' (:20).

*ARENS, BERNARD, SJ. Papst Pius X und die Weltmission: mit einem Bild des Papstes. Aachen, 1919.

LANGE, RENÉ, SJ. Le problème théologique des missions. Louvain, 1924.

TRAGELLA, GIOVANNI B., PIME. Pio XI, papa missionario: ricordo del Giubelo sacerdotale del S. Padre (1879-1929). Milano, 1930.

DEL FOSSE ET D'ESPIERRES, ABBÉ. Documents sur l'activité missionnaire de S.S. Pie XI. Namur, 1937.
    Fascicule I, II, III.

PERBAL, ALBERTO, OMI. Premières leçons de théologie missionnaire: nouvelle éd. revue et augmentée. Paris, 1937.

CHARLES, PIERRE, SJ. Les dossiers de l'action missionnaire: manuel de missiologie... Louvain, & Bruxelles, 1938.

LUBAC, HENRI DE, SJ. Le fondement théologique des missions. Paris, 1941.

DURAND, ALEXANDRE, SJ. Le problème théologique des missions. St. Étienne, 1942.

*STANGHETTI, GIUSEPPE. Prassi della S.C. de Propaganda Fide. Roma, 1943.

*SCHÄRER, HANS. Die Begründung der Mission in der katholischen und evangelischen Missionswissenschaft. Zürich, 1944.

ZAMEZA, JOSÉ, SJ. Ecos de una gran encíclica: comentario misional de la encíclica Mystici Corporis Christi de S.S. Pio XII: cuarta ed. Bilbao, 1945.

GOULET, EDWARD, SJ. Holy See and the missions: a history of the missionary efforts of the papacy. New York, 1946.

CLARK, FRANCIS X., SJ. 'The purpose of missions': a study of mission documents of the Holy See, 1909-1946. New York, 1948.
    Doctoral diss. Pontifical Gregorian University.

DANIÉLOU, JEAN, SJ. The salvation of the nations. London, 1949.
    Fr. ed.: Le mystère du salut des nations. Paris, 1948.
    First ed.: Paris, 1946.
    Also Ger., It., and Port. trs.

AROZ, H. LÉON M. DE, & ENRIQUE PELACH. Pio XII Misionero... Burgos, 1950.

ROMMERSKIRCHEN, JOHANNES, OMI, & NIKOLAUS KOWALSKY OMI (eds.). Missionswissenschaftliche Studien. Aachen, 1951.
    P. 39-53: La mission 'implantation de l'église' dans les documents ecclésiastiques (André V. Seumois OMI).

RÉTIF, ANDRÉ, SJ. Introduction à la doctrine pontificale des missions. Paris, 1953.
    Sp. tr.: 1959.

*SEUMOIS, ANDRÉ V., OMI. La papauté et les missions au cours des six premiers siècles: méthodologie antique et orientations modernes. Paris, & Louvain, 1953.

DIRECCION NACIONAL DE LAS OBRAS MISIONALES PONTIFICIAS EN ESPANA. Documentos de la Santa Sede sobre organización y propaganda misional. Madrid, 1955.

BURKE, THOMAS J.M., SJ (ed.). Catholic missions: four great encyclicals... New York, 1957.

GARDINI, WALTER, SX. Pio XII per un'Africa cristiana: commento alla Fidei Donum. Parma, Bologna, Milano..., 1959.

?LE SIEGE APOSTOLIQUE ET LES MISSIONS: textes et documents pontificaux. I. Paris, & Lyon, 1959.

First ed.: Paris, & Lyon, 1956.

BALZARINI, MARIO, FSCJ, & A. ZANOTTO FSCJ (eds.). Comboniani le missioni nel pensiero degli ultimi pontefici: piccolo studio missionologico sui documenti pontifici... Milano, Roma, Bologna..., 1960.

*VRIENS. 1960.

P. 41-42: Teaching authority of the Church. Bibliog.

*ANDERSON. 1961.

P. 122-134: The evolution of mission theology among Roman Catholics (André V. Seumois OMI).

*First ed.: Scientia missionum ancilla. 1953.

P. 54-65: L'évolution de la théologie missionnaire au vingtième siècle (André V. Seumois OMI).

GLAZIK, JOSEF, MSC. Päpstliche Rundschreiben über die Mission von Leo XIII bis Johannes XXIII. Münsterschwarzach, 1961.

*MARMY, EMIL, & IVO AUF DER MAUR OSB (eds.). Geht hin in alle Welt...: die Missionsenzykliken der Päpste Benedikt XV, Pius XI, Pius XII und Johannes XXIII. Freiburg, 1961.

?PERBAL, ALBERTO, OMI. La teologia misional. Barcelona, 1961.

*SANTOS HERNANDEZ. 1961.

P. 113-152: La misionología católica.

BELTRAMI, SILVIO. Testamento missionario di Giovanni XXIII. Roma, 1963.

GHEDDO, PIERO, PIME, & DOMENICO COLOMBO PIME. L'opera missionaria ed ecumenica di Giovanni XXIII. Milano, 1963.

RÉTIF, ANDRÉ, SJ (ed.). Princeps pastorum: texte et commentaires. Tours, 1963.

*BECKMANN, JOHANNES, SMB. Roman Catholic missions in the light of the Second Vatican Council (1962-1963). In: IRM, LIII (1964), p. 83-88.

*CAMPBELL, ROBERT E., MM (ed.). The church in mission. New York, 1965.

P. 43-78: The development of mission theology in the 20th century (Ronan Hoffman OFMConv.).

*SANTOS HERNANDEZ, ANGEL, SJ. Bibliografia misional. Santander, 1965. 2 vols.

I, p. 137-142: Documentos del Magisterio eclesiastico. Bibliog.

RÉTIF, ANDRÉ, SJ. Les papes contemporains et la mission: en appendice: décret conciliaire sur la mission. Paris, 1966.

*SIEPEN, KARL (ed.). Das Konzil und die Missionstätigkeit der Orden. Köln, 1966.

*ALEXANDER, CALVERT, SJ. The missionary dimension: Vatican II and the world apostolate. Milwaukee, 1967.

*GENSICHEN, HANS-WERNER. The second Vatican Council's challenge to Protestant mission. In: IRM, LVI (1967), p. 291-309.

*HOGG, W. RICHEY. Some background considerations for Ad gentes. In: IRM, LVI (1967), p. 281-290.

SCHÜTTE, JOHANNES (ed.). Mission nach dem Konzil. Mainz, 1967.

*SECOND VATICAN COUNCIL. Decree on the church's missionary activity: promulgated ... December 7, 1965. In: IRM, LVI (1967), p. 267-280.
   Several tr.
   *Dutch tr.: 1968.

RWEYEMAMU, ROBERT. People of God in the missionary nature of the church: a study of concilian ecclesiology applied to the missionary pastoral in Africa. Rome, 1968.

SCHELBERT, GEORG, SMB. Das Missionsdekret des II. Vaticanums im Gesamtwerk des Konzils. Schöneck, & Beckenried, 1968.

?WANKO, PETER. Kirche, Mission, Missionen: eine Untersuchung der ekklesiologischen und missiologischen Aussagen von I. Vatikanum bis 'Maximum illud'. Münster in Westfalen, 1968.

STIRNIMANN, HEINRICH, CMM (ed.). Ökumenische Erneuerung in der Mission. Freiburg im Breisgau, 1970.
   P. 81-102: Die Aussagen des II. Vatikanischen Konzils über Mission und Ökumene (Ivo auf der Maur OSB).

*CONCISE DICTIONARY. 1971.
   P. 406-407: Mission encyclicals of the Popes (Josef Glazik MSC).
   P. 414-416: Roman Catholic missions (Peter J. Dirven MHM).

*CORDES, PAUL J. Sendung zum Dienst: exegetisch-historische und systematische Studien zum Konzilsdienst 'Vom Dienst und Leben der Priester'. Frankfurt am Main, 1972.

*DHAVAMONY, MARIASUSAI, SJ (ed.). Evangelization, dialogue, and development... Roma, 1972.
   P. 105-116: Vatikan II and post-conciliar theology of evangelization (Joseph Masson SJ).

*RÜTTI, LUDWIG, SMB. Zur Theologie der Mission: kritische Analysen und neue Orientierungen. Mainz, & München, 1972.

*CONGAR, YVES M.J., SJ. Zur Theologie der Mission. In: Theologische revue, LXIX (1973), p. 353-360.

*EVERS, GEORG. Mission, nichtchristliche Religionen, weltliche Welt. Münster in Westfalen, 1974.
   P. 3-83: Die theologische Besinnung auf die Mission.

*SCHLETTE, HEINZ R. Bemerkungen zur Theologie der Mission - im Anschluss an L. Rütti. In: ZMR, LIX (1975), p. 161-169.

*RZEPKOWSKI, HORST, SVD. Der Welt verpfichtet: Text und Kommentar des Apostolischen Schreibens Evangelii Nuntiandi über die Evangelisierung in der Welt von heute. Sankt Augustin, 1976.

*COMBLIN, JOSEPH. The meaning of mission... New York, 1977.

*ROSENKRANZ, GERHARD. Die christliche Mission: Geschichte und Theologie. München, 1977.
   P. 412-462: Die Römisch-katholische Mission.

*MOTTE, MARY, FMM, & JOSEPH R. LANG MM (eds.). Mission in dialogue: the Sedos research seminar on the future of mission... New York, 1982.

*JOINT WORKING GROUP OF THE ROMAN CATHOLIC CHURCH AND THE WORLD COUNCIL OF CHURCHES. Common witness: a study document. Geneva, 1984.

*NUNNENMACHER, EUGEN. Missionarisches Selbstverständnis nach dem Konzilsdekret 'Ad gentes' und nach persönlichen Äusserungen von Afrikamissionaren. Nettetal, 1984. Diss. Pontificia Universitas Urbaniana.

*ENGELEN, J.M. VAN. De zending van de kerk in onze tijd: een onderzoek naar de missievisie van onze paus Johannes Paulus II. 's-Hertogenbosch, 1985.

*LMG. 1987.
   P. 520-525: Vatikan II (Fritz Kollbrunner).

MOTTE, MARY, FMM. A critical examination of mission today: research project - phase one. Washington, 1987.
*MÜLLER, KARL, SVD. Mission theology: an introduction... Nettetal, 1987.
  *Ger. ed.: Missionstheologie... Berlin, 1985.
*BOSCH. 1991.
  P. 214-238: The medieval Roman Catholic missionary paradigm.
*INTERNATIONAL JOURNAL OF FRONTIER MISSIONS, VIII (1991), p. 69-112.
  Text and reflections on Redemptoris missio.

PROTESTANT THEOLOGY OF MISSION

It is much more difficult to present a survey of the *Protestant -ecclesiastical-theology of mission(s)*, or *Protestant missiology* (Spindler 1967), than to give a survey of the Roman Catholic theology of mission, because (1) Protestant theology of mission is not at all, or at least not in the same way, 'church-centred' as the Roman Catholic theology of mission (which ultimately is a theology of *missio canonica*), and (2) Protestantism is still divided into a great variety of denominations: Lutherans, Calvinists, Anabaptists (Littell, in: The Mennonite quarterly review 1947:5-17), Anglicans (Blow, in: Morgan, & Lloyd 1948:1-17), Methodists (Tilson 1965), et al. Nevertheless, we can start to fill in the picture by referring to synods of Protestant churches which have dealt with missions. For instance, the famous Reformed synod of Dordrecht in the Netherlands already (1618/19) gave an opinion upon the baptism of heathen children who were living in Christian families overseas (Kaajan 1914:221-259).

In his source book on German Protestant missions from the Reformation to the World Missionary Conference at Edinburgh (1910), Werner Raupp (1990) did not publish one single church document. In conclusion we can state that the 'missionary paradigm of the Protestant Reformation' (Bosch 1991:239-261) is developed much more theologically than ecclesiastically. The real lack of church interest in missions forced those Protestants who were deeply concerned about mission (cf. Van den Berg 1956), to go their own independent way. Since the end of the 18th century (William Carey), they established mission societies, i.e. 'para-church agencies'. However, we must also call attention to other developments. In the 18th century, the Moravians, under the leadership of Count Nicolaus L. von Zinzendorf (1700-1760), had already developed their own ecclesiastical theology of mission; whereas at the end of the 19th century (1896) the General synod of the Reformed Churches in the Netherlands, at the instigation of Abraham Kuyper (1837-1920), adopted a report on missions which made the local congregations responsible for doing mission. In the 20th century, under the influence of Karl Barth, Karl W. Hartenstein, and Hendrik Kraemer (cf. Richter, in: NAZM 1928:228-241; Wiedenmann 1965; Rosin 1972), several Protestant churches became more aware of their own missionary responsiblity. For example, after a long debate the Netherlands Reformed Church included in her new Church Order (1951) the article on 'the apostolate of the church' before the article on the confession (cf. Jansen Schoonhoven, in: Hermelink, & Margull 1959:278-284).

In the post-colonial period, some Protestant churches in Asia, Africa, and Latin America made mission a central concern in their church orders, and even in their official confessions. Here I only quote the *New Confession* of the Presbyterian Church in the Republic of Korea (1972), section VI/3 on 'the mission of the church' (Vischer 1982:83-84):

Mission is the commandment of Christ given to the church (Matt.28: 19-20; Acts 1:8) to go to all peoples and nations, proclaiming Christ to them in word and deed, baptizing them and teaching them to observe all that Christ has commanded.

Mission can take shape differently acccording to the time and the circumstances. Mission is gathering people together to hear the Word and praise God; but it is also going out into the world and working together in Christ.

In mission teaching takes an important position. Mission exists to change man and to save society by reforming it. Mission promotes truth and helps understand the world rightly, and it is pedagogical in nature.

The field of mission is the world, and the whole of society is its object. There are various methods of mission, which must change according to its object. Mission reaches into all fields of life - state institutions, social organizations, occupations, etc.- and especially so in the pluralistic society of today. Mission should also be carried out in the areas which the church has not yet reached. Mission knows 'whether we live or die' (Rom. 14:7-8). The age of mission continues until the end of human history.

Mission has a variety of methods all of which are relative and flexible in character. For mission we need to be like a Jew to the Jews and like a gentile to the gentiles (1Cor. 9:19-23). The basic means of mission is through individual contact. But since an individual does not exist apart from society, methods of witnessing to Christ to the whole of society must be found. To help the world meet Christ and thereby be transformed, we should not be enslaved by obsessive doctrinal bondage of any kind, but should be open to the everchanging society around us in the spirit of incarnation and love of neighbour.

Mission always renews the whole church, culture and the Christian life of each person. Contact with all cultures and with all religions is a necessity. We must open our minds and develop the power to understand the truth established by God the Creator. In meeting with other religions we will be cooperating in solving the problems of human existence and in furthering the welfare of humanity.

In chapter 3.4.2.1., we already encountered some important contemporary Protestant theologians of mission after New Delhi (1961): Hans J. Margull, Georg F. Vicedom, Peter Beyerhaus, Alan R. Tippett, Carl E. Braaten, Melvin L. Hodges, David J. Bosch, Donald A. McGavran, and Arthur F. Glasser; but other Protestant names can be added and are mentioned elsewhere in this handbook. Some of those scholars are primarily denominational, and others primarily interdenominational in their thinking. The Lutheran missiologist James A. Scherer (1987), for instance, belongs to the first category. He refers to relevant statements adopted by assemblies of the Lutheran World Federation, and also mentions the following 'six indications of current missiological trends in Lutheranism':

1. The kingdom of God as the goal of mission;
2. The church as instrument of God's mission;
3. The calling to mission and unity;
4. 'Salvation history' as a valid paradigm;
5. Justification by grace through faith as the Word of proclamation;
6. The correlation of creation and redemption in mission practice (:82-91).

However, Scherer ends his survey of Lutheran mission by stating his conviction, that 'Lutherans will benefit greatly from considering the missionary reflections of other Christians' (:92). This conviction is also expressed by other Protestants, who, in one way or another, prefer to maintain their own denominational identity within the broader framework of the Ecumenical Movement and/or the Evangelical Movement.

KESSELRING, HEINRICH. Die Aufgabe der protestantischen Kirche und Theologie in Bezug auf die äussere Mission... Zürich, 1884.
?ROEHRICH, HENRI. L'oeuvre des missions: tâche actuelle de l'église et de la theologie protestante. Genève, 1884.
*KAAJAN, HENDRIK. De pro-acta der Dordtsche Synode in 1618. Rotterdam, 1914. Diss. V.U. Amsterdam.
    P. 221-259: De doop der heiden-kinderen.
*RICHTER, MARTIN. Dialektische Theologie und Mission. In: NAMZ, V (1928), p. 228-241.
KÜBLER, OTTO. Mission und Theologie: eine Untersuchung über den Missionsgedanken in der systematischen Theologie seit Schleiermacher. Leipzig, 1929.
*SCHÄRER, HANS. Die Begründung der Mission in der katholischen und evangelischen Missionswissenschaft. Zürich, 1944.
LITTELL, FRANKLIN H. The Anabaptist theology of missions. In: The Mennonite quarterly review, XXI (1947), p. 5-17.

150

*MORGAN, EDMUND R., & ROGER LLOYD (eds.). The mission of the Anglican communion. London, 1948.
P. 1-17: The theology of missions (Norman J. Blow).

*BERG, JOHANNES VAN DEN. Constrained by Jesus' love: an inquiry into the motives of the missionary awakening in Great Britain in the period between 1698 and 1815. Kampen, 1956. Diss. Kampen.

*HERMELINK, JAN, & HANS J. MARGULL (eds.). Basileia: Walter Freytag zum 60. Geburtstag. Stuttgart, 1959.
P. 278-284: Der Artikel 'Vom Apostolat der Kirche' in der Kirchenordnung der Niederländischen Reformierten Kirche (Evert Jansen Schoonhoven).

*ANDERSON. 1961.
P. 95-111: The rise of protestant missionary concern, 1517-1914 (William R. Hogg).
P. 112-121: The free church view of missions (Franklin H. Littell).

*SANTOS HERNANDEZ. 1961.
P. 69-111: Misionología protestante.

*BEAVER, R. PIERCE. Ecumenical beginnings in Protestant world mission: a history of comity. Edinburgh, New York, & Toronto, 1962.

*ROOY, SIDNEY H. The theology of missions in the Puritan tradition: a study of representative Puritans... Delft, 1965. Diss. VU Amsterdam.

TILSON, EVERETT, et al. Papers on the theology of mission: essays on the aim of mission written by Methodist scholars... New York, 1965.

*WIEDENMANN, LUDWIG, SJ. Mission und Eschatologie: eine Analyse der neueren deutschen evangelischen Missionstheologie. Paderborn, 1965.

*SPINDLER, MARC R. La mission, combat pour le salut du monde. Neuchâtel, 1967.
First ed.: Méthode et principes d'une missiologie protestante. 1967. Thèse Strasbourg.

*HORNER, NORMAN A. Protestant crosscurrents in mission: the ecumenical-conservative encounter. Nashville, & New York, 1968.

*ROSIN, HELLMUT H. 'Missio Dei': an examination of the origin, contents, and function of the term in protestant missiological discussion. Leiden, 1972.

*VERKUYL, JOHANNES. Contemporary missiology... Grand Rapids, 1978.

*VISCHER, LUKAS (ed.). Reformed witness today: a collection of confessions and statements of faith issued by Reformed churches. Bern, 1982.
P. 69-85: Presbyterian Church in the Republic of Korea. New confession (1972). VI. The church and mission (3. The church's mission).
P. 201-218: United Presbyterian Church in the U.S.A. Confession of 1967. IIA. The mission of the church.
P. 229-265: Presbyterian Church in the United States. A declaration of faith (1976). VIII. The christian mission (1. God sends the church into the world. 2. God sends us to proclaim the gospel. 3. God sends us to strive for justice. 4. God sends us to exercise compassion. 5. God sends us to work for peace).
P. 419-448: Joint Commission on Church Union in New Zealand. Plan for union (1971). 2. The mission of the Church (God's mission; mission essential to the Church's life; the elements of mission; mission and the Church's structures).

*SCHERER, JAMES A. Gospel, church, and kingdom: studies in world mission theology. Minneapolis, 1987.
P. 51-92: Lutheran mission in historical perspective.

*RAUPP, WERNER (ed.). Mission in Quellentexten: von der Reformation bis zur Weltmissionskonferenz 1910. Erlangen, & Liebenzell, 1990.

*BOSCH. 1991.
P. 239-261: The missionary paradigm of the Protestant Reformation.

ECUMENICAL THEOLOGY OF MISSION

The term *ecumenical mission* came into use in the second half of the 1950s and was given prominence through the formation of an 'Asia Council on Ecumenical Mission' (1955) by some Asian churches and their associated mission boards (cf. Hayward, in: Hermelink, & Margull 1959:467-473; Orchard, in: Concise Dictionary 1971:180). Thereafter, the term *ecumenical theology of mission(s)* prevails over the term *theology of ecumenical mission(s)*.

The *ecumenical theology of mission(s)/ecumenical mission theology* (Bassham 1979:13-169; Dapper 1979), *conciliar theology of mission(s)*, or *conciliar ecumenical missiology* (Scherer, & Bevans 1992:X-XII), arose in Protestant circles, but in the meantime (since New Delhi 1961) has been adopted by Eastern Orthodox churches as well.

We must refer to the World Missionary Conferences as the main contexts in which this type of mission theology was born and has grown up:

1910:	Edinburgh:
1928:	Jerusalem;
1938:	Tambaram;
1947:	Whitby - Christian witness in a revolutionary world;
1953:	Willingen - The missionary obligation of the church;
1957/58:	Achimota/Ghana - The Christian mission at this hour;
1963:	Mexico City - God's mission and our task;
1973:	Bangkok - Salvation today;
1980:	Melbourne - Your kingdom come; and
1989:	San Antonio - Mission in Christ's way - Your will be done.

Edinburgh is the birth-place of the 'emerging ecumenical missionary paradigm' (Bosch 1991:368-510). Thereafter, the conferences at Jerusalem, Tambaram, Whitby, Willingen, and Achimota/Ghana were organized under the auspices of the International Missionary Council (IMC). The following conferences -after the integration of the IMC in the World Council of Churches (WCC) in 1961- were, however, organized by the WCC's Commission on World Mission and Evangelism (CWME). Therefore, the conferences after 1963 are, in one way or another, 'ecclesiastical'; whereas the previous conferences (1910-1957/58) can, at the most, be considered as 'church-related'. The ecumenical statements of these conferences -which, according the late Anglican Archbishop William Temple, 'carry only as much authority as they are entitled to have by virtue of their innate wisdom' (Scherer, & Bevans 1992:XII)- and other conference materials have been carefully studied by many contemporary scholars (e.g. Gillespie 1947; Latourette 1948; Freytag 1952; Sell 1967; Johnston 1969; Schulz-Ackermann 1969; Günther 1970; Van 't Hof 1972; Nissen 1972; van Lin 1974; Hoekstra 1979; Shivute 1980; Tan 1981; Wind 1984ff.). Moreover, a few others (Hogg 1952; Rouse, & Neill 1954) have focused in their studies on the history and context of these conferences.

During the periods between the world missionary conferences, the IMC and the CWME have taken several initiatives. CWME, for instance, published several documents: apart from the afore-mentioned *Common Witness* (1984) we must also refer to *Guidelines on Dialogue* (1979) and *Ecumenical Affirmation - Mission and Evangelism* (1982), which - together with several other documents- have been published by James A. Scherer and Stephen B. Bevans SVD (1992:1-88) under the heading: 'Conciliar Ecumenical Statements'. In the *Ecumenical Affirmation* (1982), we are confronted with 'an ecumenical perception of Christian mission expressed in the following convictions under which they covenant to work for the kingdom of God':

1. Conversion;
2. The gospel to all realms of live;
3. The church and its unity in God's mission;
4. Mission in Christ's way;
5. Good news to the poor;
6. Mission in and to six continents; and
7. Witness among people of living faiths.

We not only encounter ecumenical theology of mission at the global level, but also at the regional level (for instance the mission desk of the All Africa Council of Churches), and the national level (for instance the former Division of Overseas Ministries of the National Council of Churches of Christ in the USA). National and regional councils of churches are normally closely related to the WCC: on the one hand, they follow missiological trends in the WCC, and, on the other hand, they provide this Council with the fruits of their own ecumenical missionary reflections.

In the post New Delhi period (from 1961 onwards), the leading Ecumenical theologians of mission are no longer found only in the western world -Johannes Verkuyl (1978), David Bosch (1991), et al.- but also in Asia -Daniel T. Niles (1963), Raymond Fung (1992), et al.-, in Africa -John Gatu (who suggested a moratorium on western missionary involvement in the so-called third world), John S. Pobee (1987), et al.-, as well as in Latin America -Eugene L. Stockwell (1965), Emilio Castro (1985), et al. In this period, western ecumenical theology of mission became global ecumenical theology of mission. This global ecumenical theology is not only in constant dialogue with the Eastern Orthodox and Roman Catholic theology of mission, but also with the Evangelical theology of mission: for instance, a group of 'evangelical Ecumenicals' attending the San Antonio Conference (1989) addressed a special letter to the Manila Congress (1989) urging that future world missionary conferences will be organised together.

*GILLESPIE, RICHARD T. Edinburgh, Jerusalem, and Madras in the light of the Kingdom concepts... Nashville, 1947. Diss. Union Theological Seminary.

*LATOURETTE, KENNETH S., & WILLIAM R. HOGG. Tomorrow is here: the mission and work of the church as seen from the meeting of the IMC at Whitby, Ontario, July 5-24, 1947. New York, 1948.

*FREYTAG, WALTER (ed.). Mission zwischen Gestern und Morgen: vom Gestaltwandel der Weltmission der Christenheit im Licht der Konferenz des Internationalen Missionsrats in Willingen. Stuttgart, 1952.

*HOGG, WILLIAM R. Ecumenical foundations: a history of the IMC and its nineteenth-century background. New York, 1952.
   Ger. tr.: Mission und Oekumene. Stuttgart, 1954.

*ROUSE, RUTH, & STEPHEN C. NEILL (eds.). A history of the ecumenical movement 1517-1948. London, 1954.

*HERMELINK, JAN, & HANS J. MARGULL (eds.). Basileia: Walter Freytag zum 60. Geburtstag. Stuttgart, 1959.
   P. 467-473: The concept of ecumenical mission (Victor E.W. Hayward).

*KARLSTRÖM, NILS. Ökumene in Mission und Kirche: Entwicklungslinien der heutigen ökumenischen Bewegung. München, 1962.
   *Swed. ed.: Mission och ekumenisk... Stockholm, 1960.

*NILES, DANIEL T. Upon the earth: the mission of God and the missionary enterprise of the churches: second impression. London, 1963.
   First ed.: 1962.

*STOCKWELL, EUGENE L. Claimed by God for mission: the congregation seeks new forms. New York, 1965.

*PORTMANN, JOHN R. The concepts of mission and unity in the WCC: a study of the official documents of the Central Committee from its inception to the New Delhi Assembly, 1961. Rome, 1966. Diss. Rome.

SELL, CHARLES M. A critical survey of the theology of missions of the IMC. Dallas, 1967. Diss. Dallas Theological Seminary.

*JOHNSTON, ARTHUR P. A study of the theology of evangelism in the IMC 1921-1961. Strasbourg, 1969. Thèse Strasbourg. Unpublished.

*SCHULZ-ANKERMANN, FRIEDERIKE. Die Boten Christi und ihr nicht christliches Gegenüber auf den Weltmissionskonferenzen von 1910 bis 1963. Lübeck, 1969. Diss. Hamburg.

*GÜNTHER, WOLFGANG. Von Edinburgh nach Mexico City: die ekklesiologischen Bemühungen der Weltmissionskonferenzen (1910-1963). Stuttgart, 1970. Diss. Erlangen/ Nürnberg.

*CONCISE DICTIONARY. 1971.
   P. 133-138: World missionary conferences (W. Richey Hogg).
   P. 180: Ecumenical mission (Ronald K. Orchard).
   P. 289-291: The IMC (W. Richey Hogg).
   P. 657-660: The WCC (Willem A. Visser 't Hooft).

*HOF, IZAÄK P.C. VAN 'T. Op zoek naar het geheim van de zending: in dialoog met de wereldzendingsconferenties 1910-1963. Wageningen, 1972. Diss. Leiden.

154

NISSEN, KARSTEN. 'Mission og enhed': en undersogelse af de strukturelle, teologiske og politiske konsekvenser af det Internationale Missionsrads integration med Kirkernes Verdensrad i 1961. 1972. Diss. Aarhus.

*AAGAARD, JOHANNES. Trends in missiological thinking during the sixties. In: IRM, LXII (1973), p. 8-25.

*HOECKMAN, REMI. Unité de l'église - unité du monde: essai d'une théologie oecuménique de la mission. Berne, & Francfort/M., 1974.

*LIN, JOHANNES J.E. VAN. Protestantse theologie der godsdiensten: van Edinburgh naar Tambaran (1910-1938). Assen, 1974. Diss. Nijmegen.

*DAPPER, HEINZ. Mission - Glaubensinterpretation - Glaubensrealisation: ein Beitrag zur ökumenischen Missionstheologie. Frankfurt am Main, Bern, & Las Vegas, 1979.

*HOEKSTRA, HARVEY T. Evangelism in eclipse: world mission and the WCC. Exeter, 1979.

*SHIVUTE, TOMAS. The theology of mission and evangelism in the IMC from Edinburgh to New Delhi. 1980. Diss. Helsinki.

*TAN, KIM-SAI. The great digression: world evangelism since 1910: the ecumenical digression and evangelical response. Petaling Jaya, 1981.

*COMMISSION ON WORLD MISSION AND EVANGELISM. Mission and evangelism - an ecumenical affirmation. Geneva, 1983.

*WIND, ANNE. Zending en oecumene in de twintigste eeuw: handboek over de geschiedenis van zending en oecumene aan de hand van de grote conferenties en assemblées. Kampen, 1984-...
    I: Van Edinburgh 1910 tot en met Evanston 1954.
    IIA: Van Ghana 1957/58 tot en met Upssala 1968.

*CASTRO, EMILIO. Sent free: mission and unity in the perspective of the kingdom. Geneva, 1985.

POBEE, JOHN S. Who are the poor? The beatitudes as a call to community. Geneva, 1987.

*BOSCH. 1991.
    P. 368-510: Elements of an emerging ecumenical missionary paradigm.

?FUNG, RAYMOND. Evangelistically yours: ecumenical letters on contemporary evangelism. Geneva, 1992.

EVANGELICAL THEOLOGY OF MISSION

The *evangelical theology of mission(s)/evangelical mission theology* (Lindsell 1970; Bassham 1979:171-295; Glasser, in: IBMR 1985:9-13), or *evangelical missiology* (Cheesman 1989:81-109; Scherer, & Bevans 1992: XVI-XIX), has its roots in 19th century evangelical movements. Today it is especially associated with the World Evangelical Fellowship (1951), and the Lausanne Committee for World Evangelization (1974), and has -in the same way as the ecumenical or conciliar theology of mission- an interdenomina-tional character.

In the USA, the Interdenominational Foreign Mission Association (IFMA 1917) and the Evangelical Foreign Missions Association (EFMA 1945) -which changed its name in 1991 to the Evangelical Fellowship of Mission Agencies (EFMA)- paved the way for a renewal of the evangelical theology of mission. After the strong criticisms of the integration of the International Missionary Council (IMC) into the World Council of Churches at New Delhi

(1961) (cf. Harvey T. Hoekstra 1979; Kim-Sai Tan 1981), Evangelicals went their own way and created their own structures. They consider themselves to be the real continuation of (the evangelical wing in) the independent IMC and have expressed their evangelical theology of mission in the documents of the following international congresses:

1966: Wheaton - congress on the church's worldwide mission;
1966: Berlin - world congress on evangelism;
1974: Lausanne - international congress on world evangelization;
1980: Pattaya - consultation on world evangelization; and
1989: Manila - second international congress of evangelization.

The Lausanne congress produced the *Lausanne Covenant* (1974), which became 'the ongoing basis for evangelical cooperation' (Scherer, & Bevans 1992:XVIII). The *Manila Manifesto* (1989) is presented as 'an elaboration of the Lausanne Covenant 15 years later'. The *Manila Manifesto* also refers to several smaller consultations which, after the Lausanne Congress, have dealt with major topics such as Gospel and Culture; Evangelism and Social Responsiblity; Simple Lifestyle; the Holy Spirit; and Conversion. (Between 1974-1989, the Lausanne Committee for World Evangelization sponsored in total no less than 54 separate conferences and 11 national congresses.)

Billy Graham played an important role in the birth and growth of the so-called Lausanne Movement (as umbrella organization for all Evangelicals). Peter Beyerhaus (Bosch 1980:30) placed him in the first category of the no less than six distinguishable evangelical groupings (other classifications by Robert Webber and by Donald G. Bloesch, see: Phillips, & Coote 1993:11-12):

1.   The so-called 'new evangelicals' who, like Billy Graham, attempt to unite all evangelical forces;
2.   The separatist fundamentalists who joined hands in organisations such as the International Council of Christian Churches (versus the WCC);
3.   The so-called 'confessional evangelicals' (for instance, Peter Beyerhaus himself as a Lutheran evangelical);
4.   The Pentecostal and Charismatic evangelicals;
5.   The radical evangelicals (Latin Americans such as Samuel Escobar, René Padilla, and Orlando Costas); and
6.   The ecumenical evangelicals (for instance, Festo Kivengere in Africa).

This survey makes clear that, in the same way as the Ecumenicals, the Evangelicals do not constitute a monolithic block. The polemical *Frankfurt Declaration on the Fundamental Crisis of Mission* (1970), prepared under the leadership of Lutheran Evangelical Peter Beyerhaus, differs radically from the

156

irenic *Lausanne Covenant*, prepared under the leadership of the Anglican Evangelical John R.W. Stott.

Apart from the above-mentioned persons, we can consider as leading evangelical theologians of mission such figures as Arthur F. Glasser and Donald A. McGavran, who wrote together an evangelical textbook on mission (second printing 1985), David J. Hesselgrave (1978; 1980), and J. Herbert Kane (1986). Jim D. Douglas (1975; 1990), and Carl F.H. Henry and W. Stanley Mooneyham (1967) are well-known as editors of evangelical congress volumes. And Bruce J. Nicholls (1985) edited a symposium in which the Korean scholar J. Chongnahm Cho (:215-238) compared the theology of mission at the Berlin Congress (1966) and the Lausanne Congress (1974), and noted a distinct shift in emphasis from the individual Christian to the whole body of the church.

HENRY, CARL F.H., & W. STANLEY MOONEYHAM (eds.). One race, one gospel, one task: World Congress on Evangelism, Berlin 1966. Minneapolis, 1967.

*LINDSELL, HAROLD. An evangelical theology of missions: rev. ed. Grand Rapids, 1970.
   First ed.: A Christian philosophy of missions. Wheaton, 1949.

*DOUGLAS, JIM D. (ed.). Let the earth hear his voice: International Congress on World Evangelization, Lausanne, Switzerland: official reference volume: papers and responses. Minneapolis, 1975.

*HESSELGRAVE, DAVID J. (ed.). Theology and mission: papers and responses... Grand Rapids, 1978.

*HESSELGRAVE, DAVID J. (ed.). New horizons in world mission: Evangelicals and the Christian mission in the 1980s... Grand Rapids, 1980.

*GLASSER, ARTHUR F. The evolution of evangelical mission theology since World War II. In: IBMR, IX (1985), p. 9-13.

*GLASSER, ARTHUR F., & DONALD A. McGAVRAN. Contemporary theologies of mission: second printing. Grand Rapids, 1985.

*NICHOLLS, BRUCE J. (ed.). In word and deed: evangelism and social responsibility. Exeter, 1985.

*KANE, J. HERBERT. The Christian world mission: today and tomorrow: second printing. Grand Rapids, 1986.
   First printing: Grand Rapids, 1981.

*LMG. 1987.
   P. 115-118: Fundamentalismus (Evangelikale Mission) (Klaus Fiedler).

*TIPPETT, ALAN R. Introduction to missiology. Pasadena, 1987.

*CHEESMAN, GRAHAM. Mission today: an introduction to mission studies. Belfast, 1989.
   P. 81-109: Some aspects of modern evangelical missiology.

*PATE, LARRY D. From every people: a handbook of two-thirds world missions... Monrovia, 1989.

*DOUGLAS, JIM D. (ed.). Proclaim Christ until He comes: calling the whole church to take the whole gospel to the whole world: Lausanne II in Manila International Congress on World Evangelization, 1989. Minneapolis, 1990.

PENTECOSTAL AND CHARISMATIC THEOLOGY OF MISSION

> Since all believers can experience the
> Spirit-filled life, each one should
> also be an active witness for Christ.
> *Gary B. McGee (Dempster 1991:206).*

Peter Beyerhaus (cf. Bosch 1980:30) considered both the Pentecostal Movement -born in the first decade of this century in the USA (William J. Seymour; Charles F. Parham)- and the Charismatic Renewal -born after the Second World War- as part of the Evangelical Movement. However, other scholars are inclined to deal with these movements -and consequently with the *Pentecostal theology of mission(s)* (Pomerville 1985:XI) and the *Charismatic theology of mission(s)*- separately. Gary B. McGee (Phillips, & Coote 1993:41-53) is one of them. In his survey of Pentecostal and Charismatic missions he wrote: 'Missiological statements by Pentecostals, therefore, often represent traditional evangelical doctrines with the addition of Pentecostal theological distinctives. This is particularly evident in Hodges' *Theology of the Church and its Mission* (1977). Ironically, this identification with evangelical missiology (also characteristic of many charismatics) partially explains the neglect of Pentecostal perspectives in recent surveys of missiology (e.g., James A. Scherer's *Gospel, Church, and Kingdom* [1987])' (:43).

I prefer to deal with both the Pentecostal Movement and the -interdenominational- Charismatic Renewal in a separate section: *Pentecostal and Charismatic Theology of Mission*. They present a new way of doing mission and mission theology (dynamic pneumatology: glossolalia, miraculous healings, exorcisms, etc.). C. Peter Wagner (School of World Mission, Fuller Theological Seminary) adds to these movements a 'third wave' of 'the power of the Holy Spirit' in our century:

1. The Pentecostal Movement;
2. The Charismatic Renewal; and
3. The 'Third Wave' Evangelicals, who practice prayer for the sick, exorcise demons, and manifest spiritual gifts (e.g., prophecy) (cf. McGee, in: Phillips, & Coote 1993:41).

This 'Third Wave' of Wagner is very problematic. However, it advocates the view that the Pentecostal Movement and the Charismatic Renewal should be placed outside the framework of the Evangelical Movement.

Pentecostal participation in the Evangelical Movement was seriously debated at the meetings of the World Evangelical Fellowship (since 1951), and the congresses of the Lausanne Movement. At the evangelical congress

Lausanne II held at Manila (1989), the Pentecostal evangelist Jack W. Hayford had an opportunity to address the congress. Because some of the Evangelicals protested against his message, Leighton Ford, as chairman of the Lausanne Committee for World Evangelization, felt obliged to defend in public the decision made by the committee involved to invite Hayford as a congress speaker.

Hayford (Douglas 1990:108-115), when speaking at Manila about 'the power and work of the Holy Spirit', affirmed the statement of the Lausanne Covenant on the ministry of the Holy Spirit (article 14). In addition, he strongly emphasized 'baptism with the Spirit' and 'supernatural operations and manifestations of the Holy Spirit' in evangelism: i.e. signs and wonders. Miracles and miraculous growth belong together. Hayford advocated a ministry of the people of the fulness (Gr.: *pleroma*) of Christ. He stated : 'Perhaps *pleroma* is the word for a new millennium. As we stand on the threshold of the twenty-first century, could it be that this is the word -the ministry- he would give us; a ministry which breaks through in all Christ's fulness and power as we are filled and energized by the Holy Spirit?' (:114).

Today, the leading Pentecostal missionary theologians are Melvin L. Hodges (1977), Paul A. Pomerville (1985), L. Grant McClung Jr. (1986), and Gary B. McGee (Dempster 1991:203-224). The name of David Shibley can be added as far as the Charismatic Renewal is concerned. Shibley (1989:29) maintains that 'world evangelization can never be accomplished by Charismatics alone. Neither can it be realized without us'. Leading Charismatic (missionary) theologians are now present and active in both the Roman Catholic Church, mainline Protestant churches, and the free churches; whereas Pentecostal (missionary) theologians are found in their own -black and white-Pentecostal churches.

Not only in the Ecumenical Movement and in the Evangelical Movement, but also in the Pentecostal Movement we can note a great variety of opinions and strategies: some Pentecostal churches are members of the World Council of Churches and take part in Commission on World Mission and Evangelism, and others are not; and some 'modern' Pentecostal and Charismatic theologians, rejecting the terminology 'Trinity' and 'three persons', focus on the Oneness doctrine (cf. Gill, in: Jongeneel 1992:107-114), whereas others (e.g. Pomerville 1985) base their mission theory and practice upon the classical doctine of the early church and, in addition, agree with evangelical statements of faith.

*CONCISE DICTIONARY. 1971.
       P. 478-479: Pentecostal missions (R.T. McGlasson).
HODGES, MELVIN L. A theology of the church and its mission: a Pentecostal perspective.
       Springfield, 1977.

*POMERVILLE, PAUL A. The third force in missions: a Pentecostal contribution to contemporary mission theology. Peabody, 1985.
*McCLUNG, L. GRANT, Jr (ed.). Azusa Street and beyond: Pentecostal missions and church growth in the 20th century. South Plainfield, 1986.
*VACCARO DE PETRELLA, LIDIA S. The tension between evangelism and social action in the Pentecostal movement. In: IRM, LXXV (1986), p. 34-38.
WIMBER, JOHN, & KEVIN SPRINGER. Power evangelism. San Francisco, 1986.
GOFF, JAMES R., Jr. Fields white unto harvest: Charles F. Parham and the missionary origins of Pentecostalism. Fayetteville, 1988.
*SPITTLER, RUSSELL P. Implicit values in Pentecostal missions. In: Missiology, XVI (1988), p. 409-424.
*SHIBLEY, DAVID. A force in the earth: the charismatic renewal and world evangelism. Altamonte Springs, 1989.
*DEMPSTER, MURRAY A., BYRON D. KLAUS, & DOUGLAS PETERSON (eds.). Called and empowered: global mission in Pentecostal perspective. Peabody, 1991.
    P. 203-224: Pentecostal strategies for global mission: a historical assessment (Gary B. McGee).
*JONGENEEL, JAN A.B., et al. (ed.). Pentecost, mission and ecumenism... Frankfurt am Main, Bern, New York..., 1992.
    P. 107-114: The Oneness doctrine as a contextualized doctrine of the Trinity for Mexico (Kenneth D. Gill).
POUSSON, EDWARD K. Spreading the flame: charismatic churches and missions today. Grand Rapids, 1992.

3.4.2.4. CORPORATE THEOLOGY OF MISSION

INTRODUCTION

Because the Biblical theology of mission and the ecclesiastical theology of mission belong together, so do the corporate theology of mission and the individual theology of mission belong together. The terms *corporate theology of mission(s)*, or *communitarian theology of mission(s)*, and *individual theology of mission(s)*, or *personal theology of mission(s)*, are our own invention.

Officially, Roman Catholics mention the Bible and the tradition of the church as their sources of theology (including mission theology), and Protestants only the Bible (Lat.: *sola scriptura*); but in practice they use other sources as well. So it is very important to know both the order or society to which a (missionary) theologian belongs and the (missionary) theologian as an individual. Although both Franciscans and Jesuits affirm the Bible and the tradition of the church as the sources of their (mission) theology, they still differ greatly in (missionary) spirituality and activities. The same can be said about Protestants: although both Hans Egede (1686-1758) and the Moravians based their mission theory and practice on the Bible alone, they disagreed in Greenland, as the Franciscans and the Jesuits did in China and Japan in the same period. And, in addition, Roman Catholic orders and Protestant societies are not at all monolithic blocks: within these communities there is a great variety of opinions as well. Therefore, the individual aspect of doing (mission) theology can no more be ignored than its corporate aspect.

In this section, I emphasize the influence of societies on the theology of mission -*corporate mission theology*- whereas the next section will deal with the problem of individuality in the theology of mission -*individual mission theology*.

MISSIONARY ORDERS AND SOCIETIES

In the Middle Ages, mission theory and practice were renewed by two great *orders of friars* -the Franciscans and the Dominicans- which from the very beginning affirmed different aims and purposes. Stephen C. Neill (1986:99) described those differences as follows: 'Francis (1181-1226) lived to bring back simplicity and joy into the Christian world, and to release new forces for the service of the very poor. In the work of Dominic (1170-1221) there were from the beginning harsher traits. His order was to be intellectually competent, devoted to the conversion of heretics particularly through the work of preaching, as its official title the *Order of Preachers* indicates. But in each lived a genuine missionary impulse'. Neill (:127) also described the different (missionary) attitude of the 'modern' order of the Jesuits which had a considerable influence that can be compared with that of the afore- mentioned orders: 'this strange new body of men who were to be neither secular priests nor religious, who were to be bound by the most rigid vows of obedience, were to be utterly subject to the Pope, and were to be devoted to the reconversion of heretics, and the conversion of pagans, to the Catholic faith'.

Protestantism did not give birth to *(missionary) orders*, but it did create *(missionary) societies* (Ger.: *Missionsgesellschaften*). In 1792, the first missionary society was founded by the English Baptists. The 19th century became *the great age of societies* (Neill 1986:214). These societies had their own individual aims which were also incumbent upon their members. In 1797, the Netherlands Missionary Society was established as a conservative interdenominational society; but, in the middle of the 19th century, liberalism began to predominate. Although the liberals maintained the established missionary aims of the society, they lost many conservatives who, after their departure, created new orthodox societies with more strict doctrinal statements.

The doctrinal statements of missionary societies such as the Interdenominational Foreign Mission Association (IFMA), the Evangelical Fellowship of Mission Agencies (EFMA), and the Fellowship of Mission, are also very strict. Here I quote the doctrinal statement of the EFMA, which is much shorter than the statements of the IFMA and the Fellowship of Mission:

EFMA believes:
1. The Bible to be the inspired, the only infallible authorative Word of God;
2. That there is one God, eternally existent in three persons: Father, Son, and Holy Spirit;
3. In the deity of our Lord Jesus Christ, in his virgin birth, in his sinless life, in his miracles, in his vicarious and atoning death through his shed blood, in his bodily resurrection, in his ascension to the right hand of the Father, and in his personal return in power and glory;
4. That for the salvation of lost and sinful men regeneration by the Holy Spirit is absolutely essential;
5. In the present ministry of the Holy Spirit by whose indwelling the Christian is enabled to live a godly life;
6. In the resurrection of both the saved and the lost; they that are saved unto the resurrection of life and they that are lost unto the resurrection of damnation; and
7. In the spiritual unity of believers in our Lord Jesus Christ.

The Evangelical Missiological Society (EMS) requires in article IV on the doctrinal statement, that all members of EMS shall affirm the tenets of the Christian faith as set forth in the statements of the IFMA, the EFMA, or the Fellowship of Missions: statements which, strangely enough, say nothing at all about mission or evangelism...

Corporate theology of mission is that type of mission theology which not only intends to be obedient to the Bible (and to the tradition of the church), but also to the spiritual and doctrinal statements of orders and/or societies. Evangelicals are, much more than Ecumenicals, inclined to make such statements of faith obligatory: one must sign the Lausanne Covenant in order to be recognised as an Evangelical.

The corporate theology of mission has been less thoroughly researched than the biblical, ecclesiastical, and individual theology of mission.

*DAUBANTON. 1911.
     P. 13-15: De genootschappelijke zending.
*NEILL, STEPHEN C. A history of Christian missions: rev. for the second ed. by Owen Chadwick. Harmondsworth, 1986.
*LMG. 1987.
     P. 289-292: Missionsgesellschaften (Horst Rzepkowski SVD).

3.4.2.5. INDIVIDUAL THEOLOGY OF MISSION

INTRODUCTION

Individual theology of mission(s), or *personal theology of mission(s)*, is that type of mission theology which emphasizes the crucial role which individuals played -and are playing- in creating mission theology.

From the very beginning, individuals such as Paul were important in mission theory and practice. However, after the Enlightenment, their role became more prominent. Some scholars (cf. Kunze 1927; zur Nieden 1928; Kübler 1929) consider Friedrich D.E. Schleiermacher (1768-1834), who has grown up in a Moravian setting, to be the founding father of the 'individual theology of mission'; because he rejected biblicism, ecclesiasticism, and corporate thinking; and because he made both the human mind and the human experience his final authority. However, other scholars -including myself- state that the individual has not only shaped liberal missionary thinking, but also -in a different way- conservative missionary thinking. The Faith missions, as well as the Pentecostal missions, have all emphasized -and still continue to emphasize- the importance of being 'reborn' and having a personal 'call' to do mission and mission theology.

The official Roman Catholic mission theology is, as far as the Pope is not concerned, the most non-individualistic expression of mission theology. However, in modern Roman Catholic missionary thinking individuality is nearly as strong as in ecumenical and evangelical Protestant missionary thinking.

Here we discuss the different categories of people -missionary theologians, missiologists and missionaries- who, in their own individual way, have contributed to the birth and growth of mission theology. These categories have not only shaped their own identity, but also influenced each other. Some belong to more than one category: e.g. Hendrik Kraemer, Johannes C. Hoekendijk, and Arend Th. van Leeuwen can be subsumed both under the second and the third category.

*OOSTERZEE, JOHANNES J. VAN. Practische theologie. Utrecht, 1898. 2 vols.
    II, p. 352-354: Individuele zendingsarbeid.
*DAUBANTON. 1911.
    P. 5-9: De z.g. individuele zending.

MISSIONARY THEOLOGIANS

The first main category of people doing mission theology individually are *the missionary theologians*, i.e. *the individual missionary theologians*, who made mission an essential element in their own systematic and practical theologies.

This category is very diverse. First, we must subsume under this category virtually all of the theologians of the first three centuries (until Constantine 325) who lived in a really missionary situation: e.g. Justin Martyr (Kubik 1973). Second, we also must refer to some *corpus christianum* theologians: e.g. Ambrose of Milan (Mesot 1958), John Chrysostom (Andres 1935), Augustine (Walter 1921; Metzger 1936), and Thomas Aquinas (Ohm 1927; idem, in: Festschrift Grabmann 1935:735-748); and -after the Reformation- Philipp Nicolai (Hess 1962), Gisbertus Voetius (van Andel 1912; Jongeneel, in: Calvin theological journal 1991: 47-79), Johann A. Comenius (Geissler, in: EMZ 1957:74-82), Count Nicolaus L. von Zinzendorf (Beyreuther, in: EMZ 1960:65-76,97-113), and John Wesley (Schmidt 1958; Boraine 1969). Third, we should also mention the Nestorian and Monophysite theologians outside the *corpus christianum* in Asia and Africa, who did -and still do- theology in a non-Christian context. Fourth, most contemporary theologians in Asia, Africa, and Latin America must be recognised as 'missionary theologians': e.g. Emilio Castro (Ninomiya 1980). And, finally, a few contemporary western theologians also belong to this category: Martin Kähler (Heinzgünter Frohnes 1971: XX-XXXVI; Bosch, in: Theologia evangelica 1972:165-189), Karl Barth (Hartenstein 1928; Knak, in: Zwischen den Zeiten 1932:331-355; van 't Hof 1946; Manecke 1972; Scott 1978), Emil Brunner (Leipold 1974), and Karl Rahner SJ (Meyer 1976), who, in one way or another, accept that the end of the *corpus christianum* is the beginning of (renewed) 'mission in the West'.

*ANDEL, HUIBERT A. VAN. De zendingsleer van Gisbertus Voetius. Kampen, 1912. Diss. V.U. Amsterdam.

WALTER, GONSALVUS, OFMCap. Die Heidenmission nach der Lehre des heiligen Augustinus. Münster in Westfalen, 1921.

KUNZE, WILHELM. Der Missionsgedanke bei Schleiermacher und seinen Schülern. Gütersloh, 1927.

*OHM, THOMAS, OSB. Die Stellung der Heiden zu Natur und Übernatur nach dem hl. Thomas von Aquin: eine missionstheoretische Untersuchung. Münster in Westfalen, 1927.

*HARTENSTEIN, KARL W. Was hat die Theologie Karl Barths der Mission zu sagen? Zweite Aufl. München, 1928.
First ed.: Zwischen den Zeiten, VI (1928), p. 59-83.

NIEDEN, ERNST ZUR. Der Missionsgedanke in der systematischen Theologie seit Schleiermacher. Gütersloh, 1928.

*KÜBLER, OTTO. Mission und Theologie: eine Untersuchung über den Missionsgedanken in der systematischen Theologie seit Schleiermacher. Leipzig, 1929.

*KNAK, SIEGFRIED. Die Mission und die Theologie in der Gegenwart. In: Zwischen den Zeiten, X (1932), p. 331-355.

*ANDRES, PAUL, OMI. Der Missionsgedanke in den Schriften des heiligen Johannes Chrysostomus. Hünfeld, 1935.

*LANG, ALBERT, JOSEPH LECHNER, & MICHAEL SCHMAUS (eds.). Aus der Geisteswelt des Mittelalters: Studien und Texte Martin Grabmann zur Vollendung des 60. Lebensjahres von Freunden und Schülern gewidmet. Münster, 1935.
P. 735-748: Thomas von Aquin und die Heiden- und Mohammedanermission (Thomas Ohm OSB).

METZGER, GERHARD. Kirche und Mission in den Briefen Augustins. Gütersloh, 1936.

*HOF, IZAÄK P.C. VAN 'T. Het zendingsbegrip van Karl Barth. Oegstgeest, 1946.

*WINSEN, GERARDUS A.C. VAN, CM, GERBEN J.F. BOURITIUS SCJ, & JAKOB BUYS SVD (eds.). Novella ecclesiae germina. Nijmegen, & Utrecht, 1953.
P. 13-23: L'implantation d'églises particulières ou l'idée de mission chez les Pères Grecs (André V. Seumois OMI).

*GEISSLER, HEINRICH. Johann Amos Comenius als Wegbereiter evangelischen Missionsdenkens. In: EMZ, XIV (1957), p. 74-82.

*MESOT, JEAN, SMB. Die Heidenbekehrung bei Ambrosius von Mailand. Schöneck, & Beckenried, 1958.

SCHMIDT, MARTIN. The young Wesley: missionary and theologian of missions. London, 1958.
*First ed.: Der junge Wesley als Heidenmissionar und Missionstheologe. Gütersloh, 1955.

*BEYREUTHER, ERICH. Mission und Kirche in der Theologie Zinzendorfs. In: EMZ, XVII (1960), p. 65-76, 97-113.

*HOFFMAN, RONAN, OFMConv. Pioneer theories of missiology: a comparative study of the mission theories of Cardinal Brancati de Laurea OFMConv., with those of three of his contemporaries: Jose de Acosta SJ, Thomas a Jesu OCarm, and Dominicus de Gubernatis OFM... Washington, 1960.

*HESS, WILLY. Das Missionsdenken bei Philipp Nicolai. Hamburg, 1962. Diss. Münster in Westfalen.

*WIEDENMANN, LUDWIG, SJ. Mission und Eschatologie: eine Analyse der neueren deutschen evangelischen Missionstheologie. Paderborn, 1965.

BORAINE, ALEXANDER L. The nature of evangelism in the theology and practice of John Wesley. Madison, 1969. Diss. Drew University.

*FROHNES, HEINZGÜNTER (ed.). Martin Kähler: Schriften zu Christologie und Mission: Gesamtausgabe der Schriften zur Mission: mit einer Bibliographie. München, 1971.
P. XX-XXXVI: Zur Ortsbestimmung der Mission in Theologie und Leben Martin Kählers (Heinzgünter Frohnes).

BOSCH, DAVID J. Systematic theology and mission: the voice of an early pioneer. In: Theologia evangelica, V/3 (1972), p. 165-189.

*MANECKE, DIETER. Mission als Zeugendienst: Karl Barths theologische Begründung der Mission im Gegenüber zu den Entwürfen von Walter Holsten, Walter Freytag und Johannes Christiaan Hoekendijk. Wuppertal, 1972. Diss. Bonn.

?KUBIK, W. Universalität als missionstheologisches Problem: der Beitrag von Justin dem Märtyrer, Nicolaus Cusanus und Karl Heim zum Gespräch um Christus und die Mission. 1973. Diss. Heidelberg.

*LEIPOLD, HEINRICH. Missionarische Theologie: Emil Brunners Weg zur theologischen Anthropologie. Göttingen, 1974.

*SCOTT, WALDRON. Karl Barth's theology of mission. In: Missiology, III (1975), p. 209-224.
*Ger. tr.: Die Missionstheologie Karl Barths. Giessen, & Basel, 1977.

?MEYER, REGINA, P.M. Universales Heil, Kirche und Mission: Studien über die ekklesial-missionarischen Strukturen in der Theologie Karl Rahners und im Epheserbrief. Sankt Augustin, 1979. Diss. Münster.

*NINOMIYA, TADAHIRO. Pastorale Missiologie: die protestantische Theologie in Latein Amerika am Beispiel Emilio Castros. Frankfurt am Main, Bern, & Cirencester, 1980.

*JONGENEEL, JAN A.B. The missiology of Gisbertus Voetius: the first comprehensive Protestant theology of missions. In: Calvin theological journal, XXVI (1991), p.47-79.

MISSIONARIES

> *Missionary* is not a finished-product concept. It
> is a continuous-participation concept.
> *Kosuke Koyama (Anderson, & Stransky, 1974:129).*

The second important category of individuals who produce mission studies is that of *the missionaries*, i.e. *the individual missionaries* (cf. Hesselgrave 1980:83-84), who have their own -particular- mission field experience (cf. 5.3.3.8.).

Here, in fact, every missionary who since the apostle Paul expressed his or her own missionary ideas can be mentioned. However, the missionary thoughts of the 'great mission leaders of church history' (Martin Schlunk 1931) are very important: e.g. Boniface, Raymond Lull, Francis Xavier, Bartholomew Ziegenbalg, Henry Martyn, David Livingstone, J. Hudson Taylor, Alexander Duff, Jacob Spieth, Alexander Merensky, and Ludwig I. Nommensen. Also very important are the ideas of missionary martyrs such as Lull.

It is impossible to refer here to every study of the missionary theologies of individual missionaries. We can only mention several modern examples which have been researched very carefully: William Carey (Oussoren 1945); Bruno Gutmann (Weist 1940); Carl H. Hahn (Sundermeier 1962); Hendrik Kraemer (Menasce, in: NZM 1945:241-257; Conway 1966; Hallencreutz 1966; Brisbois 1972); Johannes C. Hoekendijk (Brisbois 1972; Manecke 1972; Coffele 1976; van Gurp 1989); and Arend Th. van Leeuwen (Brisbois 1972; Jeroense 1994).

*SCHLUNK, MARTIN. Grosse Missionsführer der Kirchengeschichte. Leipzig, 1931.

WEIST, HELLMUT. Die Theologie des Missionars Bruno Gutmann in kritischer Beurteilung. Halle, 1941. Diss. Halle, & Wittenberg.

*MENASCE, JEAN-PIERRE DE, OP. La théologie de la mission selon M. Kraemer. In: NZM, I (1945), p. 241-257.

*OUSSOREN, AALBERTINUS H. William Carey, especially his missionary principles. Leiden, 1945. Diss. V.U. Amsterdam.

SUNDERMEIER, THEO. Mission, Bekenntnis und Kirche: missionstheologische Probleme des 19. Jahrhundert bei C[arl] H. Hahn. Wuppertal, & Barmen, 1962.

WEBSTER, DOUGLAS. What is a missionary? Rev. ed. London, 1962.
First ed.: London, 1956.

*CONWAY, GERALD W. An exposition and critical analysis of the theology of the missions as proposed by Hendrik Kraemer. Winona, 1966.

*HALLENCREUTZ, CARL F. Kraemer towards Tambaram: a study in Hendrik Kraemer's missionary approach. Uppsala, 1966. Diss. Uppsala.

*BRISBOIS, JACQUES, SJ. Apostolat, religion, eschatologie dans la théologie de la mission selon H. Kraemer, J.C. Hoekendijk, A.T. van Leeuwen. Paris, 1972. Thèse Faculté de Théologie de l'Institut Catholique de Paris.

*ANDERSON, GERALD H., & THOMAS F. STRANSKY CSP (eds.). Mission trends. No. 1: Crucial issues in mission today. New York, Paramus, & Toronto..., 1974.
P. 111-153: The missionary (Kosuke Koyama).

*COFFELE, GIANFRANCO, SDB. Johannes Christiaan Hoekendijk: da una teologia della missione ad una teologia missionaria. Roma, 1976.

*HESSELGRAVE, DAVID J. (ed.). New horizons in world mission... Grand Rapids, 1980.

*GURP, PIETER VAN. Kerk en zending in de theologie van Johannes Christiaan Hoekendijk (1912-1975): een plaatsbepaling. Haarlem, 1989. Diss. Utrecht.

*JEROENSE, P. JEROEN G. Theologie als zelfkritiek: een onderzoek naar de missionaire theologie van Arend Th. van Leeuwen. Zoetermeer, 1994. Diss. Utrecht.

MISSIOLOGISTS

The third and last category of people doing mission theology individually consists of *the missiologists*, i.e. *the individual missiologists*, who, part-time or full-time, devoted themselves to mission studies.

In Germany scholars such as Gustav Warneck (Dürr 1947; Lefebvre, in: NZM 1955:15-29; Teinonen 1957; 1959; Kasdorf 1990), and Joseph Schmidlin (Lefebvre, in: NZM 1956:288-294); and in the Netherlands others such as François E. Daubanton (Jongeneel, in: NThT 1990:288-307), and Alphonsus J.M. Mulders belong to this category. They contributed substantially to the birth and growth of missiology as an academic discipline; although they never went to the so-called 'mission fields' in Asia, Africa, and Latin America. They recognised the significance of the contributions of the overseas missionaries. Warneck, for instance, based his missiology not only upon his own research, but also upon the findings of his son Johannes Warneck who worked in the Netherlands East Indies.

In this category, we must also include notable individuals such as Friedrich Fabri (Schmidt 1965), Franz M. Zahn (Schindelin 1936), Walter Freytag (Manecke 1972; Triebel 1976), and Walter Holsten (Manecke 1972) in Germany. Max A.C. Warren (Dillistone 1978), the famous leader of the Church Missionary Society in the United Kingdom, also belongs to this particular category.

Especially after the establishment of desks for mission studies in mission societies, and after the establishment of professorships of mission in universities and theological colleges, this category became considerably larger. Such institutions were not always able to appoint candidates who had overseas experience.

Also in the case of this third category, our list of literature can only constitute a small selection of what is actually available.

?SCHINDELIN, FRIEDA. Franz Michael Zahns Beitrag zur Missionstheorie. Bremen, 1936.

*DÜRR, JOHANNES. Sendende und werdende Kirche in der Missionstheologie Gustav Warneck's. Basel, 1947. Diss. Bern.

*LEFEBVRE, PIERRE, CICM. La théologie missionnaire de Gustav Warneck. In: NZM, XI (1955), p. 15-29.

*WEBSTER, DOUGLAS. P[eter] T. Forsyth's theology of missions. In: IRM, XLIV (1955), p. 175-181.

*LEFEBVRE, PIERRE, CICM. L'influence de Gustav Warneck sur la théologie missionnaire catholique. In: NZM, XII (1956), p. 288-294.

TEINONEN, SEPPO A. Gustav Warneck und Robert Pearsall Smith: eine Begegnung der deutschen neupietistischen Missionstheologie mit einer amerikanischen Heiligungsbewegung. Helsinki, 1957.

*TEINONEN, SEPPO A. Gustav Warneckin varhaisen lähetysteorian teologiset perusteet. Helsinki, 1959. Diss. Helsinki.

*ROOY, SIDNEY H. The theology of missions in the Puritan tradition: a study of representative Puritans: Richard Sibbes, Richard Baxter, John Eliot, Cotton Mather, and Jonathan Edwards. Delft, 1965. Diss. V.U. Amsterdam.

*SCHMIDT, WOLFGANG R. Mission, Kirche und Reich Gottes bei Friedrich Fabri. Wuppertal, & Barmen, 1965.

*TRIEBEL, JOHANNES. Bekehrung als Ziel der missionarischen Verkündigung: die Theologie Walter Freytags und das oekumenische Gespräch. Erlangen, 1976. Diss. Erlangen, & Nürnberg.

?DILLISTONE, FREDERICK W. The missionary theology of Max Warren... N.p., 1978.

*SCHWARZ, GEROLD. Mission, Gemeinde und Ökumene in der Theologie Karl Hartensteins. Stuttgart, 1980.

*SCHIRRMACHER, THOMAS. Theodor Christlieb und seine Missionstheologie. Wuppertal, 1985. Diss. Kampen.

*JONGENEEL, JAN A.B. De ethische zendingstheologie van François E. Daubanton (1853-1920)... In: Nederlands Theologisch Tijdschrift, XLIV (1990), p. 288-307.

*KASDORF, HANS. Gustav Warnecks missiologisches Erbe: eine biographisch-historische Untersuchung. Giessen, & Basel, 1990.

3.4.3. THE THEOLOGY OF MISSION AND THE THEOLOGY OF RELIGION (RELIGIONSTHEOLOGIE)

> No issue in missiology is more important, more
> difficult, more controversial, or more divisive
> for the days ahead than the theology of religions.
> *Gerald H. Anderson (van Engen 1993:200).*

As the philosophy of mission is related to the philosophy of religion (see 3.2.3.), and the science of mission is related to the science of religion or religious studies (see 3.3.3.), so *the theology of mission(s)* (Ger.: *Missionstheologie*) is related to *the theology of religion(s)* (Ger.: *Religionstheologie*; Lat.: *theologia religionum*). Although there is a Jewish theology of mission and religion, and a Muslim theology of mission and religion, we limit ourselves here to Christianity.

As the -Christian- theology of mission is both a systematic and a practical theological discipline, so the -Christian- theology of religion is developed both systematically and practically. For the theology of religion is concerned with 'truth' -e.g. the uniqueness of Christ- as well as concerned with actual affairs: religious pluralism, dialogue, etc.

David J. Bosch (1991:474) writes: 'The *theologia religionum*, the "theology of religions", is a discipline that has evolved only since the 1960s'. As far as the use of the term 'theologia religionum' is concerned, this is true: in the 1960s this term became popular; but, in 1951, Gerhard Rosenkranz had already published an 'Introduction to a Theological View of Religions' (Ger.: *Einführung in eine theologische Schau der Religionen*). However, the problem is older than the term: Gustav Warneck and Ernst Troeltsch, and subsequently Hendrik Kraemer and William E. Hocking, already disputed the whole question of the relation between Christian mission and the non-Christian religions. Hence the question: can we deal with the non-Christian religions apart from Christian mission? Warneck and Kraemer were unwilling to separate the two issues, but Troeltsch and Hocking clearly advocated the emancipation of the theology of religion (cf. Van Lin 1974). The modern theology of religion -John Hick, W. Cantwell Smith, Stanley J. Samartha, Raimund Panikkar, Paul F. Knitter, et al. (cf. Knitter 1985)- is basically in agreement with Troeltsch and Hocking.

Willem A. Visser 't Hooft wrote a famous book entitled *No Other Name* (1963), but Paul F. Knitter turned the indicative of Visser 't Hooft -without refering to the book of Visser 't Hooft- into a question: *No Other Name?* (1985). In *No Other Name?*, the non-Christian religions are no longer treated within the framework of the theology of mission; rather, Christian mission is elaborated in the framework of the theology of religion. As a

Christian, Knitter is willing to witness to Christ; but, at the same time, he declares: '... in the new ecclesiology and in the new model of truth, one admits also that all peoples should know of Buddha, of Muhammad, of Krishna. This, too, is part of the goal and inspiration for missionary work: to be witnessed to, in order that Christians might deepen and expand their own grasp of God's presence and purpose in the world. Through this mutual witnessing, this mutual growth, the work of realizing the kingdom moves on' (:222).

As I am willing to treat the philosophy of mission as a branch of the philosophy of religion, and the science of mission as a branch of religious studies, so I am also willing to treat the theology of mission as a branch of the theology of religion; because the theology of religion has a broader scope than the theology of mission. However, this does not necessarily mean that we should ultimately endorse the concepts of Hick, Smith, Samartha, Panikkar, Knitter, et al. Theology of religion can be pluralistic; but there are other models as well: exclusivism and inclusivism. Therefore, the theology of mission can also be placed within the framework of an exclusivistic or an inclusivistic treatment of the non-Christian religions. I certainly agree with the emancipation of the theology of religion from the tutelage of mission theology. The great problem of our time, however, is that the most important theologians of mission are not at all the great theologians of religion, and vice versa. I advocate a serious interaction between both disciplines in order to develop a mature theology of mission which can ultimately be respected by the theologians of religion.

?ROSENKRANZ, GERHARD. Einführung in eine theologische Schau der Religionen. 1951.

*HEINRICHS, MAURUS, OFM. Die Bedeutung der Missionstheologie aufgewiesen am Vergleich zwischen den abendländischen und Chinesischen Kardinaltugenden. Münster in Westfalen, 1954.

*FULTON, AUSTIN. The missionary nature of the church: reflections on the Christian faith and other religions. In: IRM, XLVIII (1959), p. 389-397.

*VISSER 'T HOOFT, WILLEM A. No other name. Philadelphia, 1963.

*MULDERS, ALPHONSUS J.M. Het missionair karakter van de kerk en het zicht op de niet-christelijke godsdiensten. In: HM, XLVI (1967), p. 2-20.

*EVERS, GEORG. Mission - nichtchristliche Religionen - weltliche Welt. Münster in Westfalen, 1974.
    P. 84-150: Die Missionstheologie und die Theologie der nichtchristlichen Religionen.

*LIN, JOHANNES J.E. VAN. Protestantse theologie der godsdiensten: van Edinburgh naar Tambaram (1910-1938). Assen, 1974.

*PANIKKAR, RAIMUND. The intrareligious dialogue. New York, 1978.

*VERKUYL, JOHANNES. Contemporary missiology... Grand Rapids, 1978.
    P. 341-372: Trends in the theology of religions: types of contemporary dialogue.

*ANDERSON, GERALD H., & THOMAS F. STRANSKY CSP (eds.). Mission trends. No. 5: Faith meets faith. New York, Ramsey, Toronto..., 1981.

P. 1-89: Mission and religious pluralism.

*SAMARTHA, STANLEY J. The lordship of Jesus Christ and religious pluralism: with responses by Arthur Glasser and Robert Schreiter and a reply by the author. Madras, 1981.

*SMITH, W. CANTWELL. Towards a world theology: faith and the comparative history of religion. London, & Basingstoke, 1981.

*HICK, JOHN. Problems of religious pluralism. London, & Basingstoke, 1985.

*KNITTER, PAUL F. No other name? A critical survey of Christian attitudes toward the world religions. London, 1985.

P. 220-223: Implications for religious experience and missionary activity.

*LMG. 1987.

P. 495-505: Theologie der Religionen (C.H. Ratschow).

*SWIDLER, LEONARD (ed.). Toward a universal theology of religion: second printing. New York, 1988.

First ed.: New York, 1987.

KISTE, REINHARD (ed.). Ansätze zu einer christlichen Theologie der Religionen... Stuttgart, 1989.

BERNHARDT, REINHOLD. Der Absolutheitsanspruch des Christentums: von der Aufklärung bis zur pluralistischen Religionstheologie. Gütersloh, 1990.

*D'COSTA, GAVIN (ed.). Christian uniqueness reconsidered: the myth of a pluralistic theology of religions. New York, 1990.

*BOSCH. 1991.

P. 474-489: Mission as witness to people of other living faiths.

*DEM. 1991.

P. 690, 801: Theology of religion.

*KLOOTWIJK, EEUWOUT. Commitment and openness: the interreligious dialogue and theology of religions in the work of Stanley J. Samartha. Zoetermeer, 1992. Diss. Utrecht.

*ENGEN, CHARLES VAN, DEAN S. GILLILAND, & PAUL PIERSON (eds.). The good news of the Kingdom: mission theology for the third millennium. New York, 1993.

P. 200-208: Theology of religions and missiology (Gerald H. Anderson).

3.4.4. CONCLUSION

The *theology of mission*, as continuation of the 'theory of mission', is certainly flourishing. The Bible, the tradition of the church, as well as the principles and statements of orders and societies, together with the ideas and experiences of individuals, are used as the principle sources of contemporary missionary thinking.

Both the churches as churches, and communities (orders and societies) and individuals (missionary theologians, missionaries and missiologists) are all involved in the shaping and reshaping of this third and last concept of missiology. The theology of mission is on the whole very well developed; however, the corporate theology of mission is still in its infancy.

The relation between the theology of mission and the theology of religion is still one of the most disputed questions in the theology of mission. Liberals have brought about the emancipation of the theology of religion; but conservatives can accept the theology of religion as the horizon of the theology of mission as well. A profound Christian theology of religion is certainly not a danger; it is, rather, a great blessing to the theology of mission.

3.5. CONCLUSION

This chapter has dealt with the three concepts of missiology. At the end of this third chapter I present a chronological table of the names of those concepts and their subdivisions which have been discussed:

1828: PHILOSOPHY OF MISSION(S) (WILLIAM ORME)
1910: Divine philosophy of missions (Henry C. Mabie)
1943: Philosophy of the Christian world mission (Edmund D. Soper)
1949: Christian philosophy of missions (Harold Lindsell)
1961: Conservative philosophy of the Christian mission (Harold Lindsell, in: Anderson 1961:239-249)
1978: Centripetal/centrifugal philosophy of mission (David W. Wead, in: Gasque 1978:176-188)
1983: Missionary philosophy (T. Wayne Dye, in: Whiteman 1983: 215-228)

1832: MISSIONSWISSENSCHAFT=SCIENCE OF MISSION(S) (JOHANN T.L. DANZ)
1892: *Wissenschaftliche Missionskunde*=scientific mission knowledge (Gustav Warneck)
1910: *Katholische Missionswissenschaft*=Catholic science of mission(s) (Joseph Schmidlin)
1910: Science of missionary societies (World Missionary Conference 1910:VI,249-257)
1910: *Theologisch-wissenschaftliche Missionskunde*=theological and scientific theory of mission(s) (Robert Streit OMI)
1944: *Evangelische Missionswissenschaft*=Evangelical science of mission(s) (Hans Schärer)

1877: MISSIONSTHEOLOGIE=THEOLOGY OF MISSION(S) (GUSTAV WARNECK)
1910: *Theologisch-wissenschaftliche Missionskunde*=theological and scientific theory of mission(s) (Robert Streit OMI)
1925: *Biblisch-traditionelle Missionstheorie*=biblical-traditional theory of mission(s) (Joseph Schmidlin)
1937: Theology for Christian missions (Hugh V. White)
1947: Anabaptist theology of mission (Franklin H. Littell)

1950: *Overgeverde missietheologie*=traditional theology of mission(s) (Alphonsus J.M. Mulders)

1952: *Missiology biblique*=biblical missiology (André V. Seumois OMI)

1958: *Teologia delle missioni estere*=theology of foreign mission(s) (Danilo Catarzi SX)

1959: *Theologie der missionarischen Verkündigung*=theology of the missionary preaching (Hans J. Margull)

1960: Biblical mission theory (Livinus Vriens OFMCap)

1961: *Biblische Theologie der Mission*=biblical theology of mission(s) (Johannes Blauw)

1961: *Misionologia protestante*=protestant missiology (Angel Santos Hernandez SJ)

1962: *Teología biblico-patristica de las misiones*=biblical-patristical theology of missions (Angel Santos Hernandez SJ)

1966: *Teologia existencial de la mision*=existential theology of mission(s) (Jacques Dournes MEP)

1970: *Teología bíblica del evangelismo*=biblical theology of evangelism (Israel E. Amaya)

1970: Evangelical theology of missions (Harold Lindsell)

1972: Biblical theology of evangelization, Post-conciliar theology of evangelization (respectively Matthew Vellanickal and Joseph Masson SJ, in: Dhavamony 1972: 41-53,105-116)

1974: *Théologie oecuménique de la mission*=ecumenical theology of mission(s) (Rémi Hoeckman)

1977: Theology of the Christian mission (Carl E. Braaten)

1979: Ecumenical/Conservative evangelical/Roman Catholic mission theology (Rodger C. Bassham)

1983: Biblical theology of holistic mission (William A. Dyrness)

1985: Pentecostal theology of mission (Paul A. Pomerville)

1986: Eastern Orthodox mission theology (James J. Stamoolis)

1990: *Ethische zendingstheologie*=ethical theology of mission (Jan A.B. Jongeneel)

1991: Comprehensive Protestant theology of mission (Jan A.B. Jongeneel)

1994: Ecclesiastical theology of mission, Corporate (or, communitarian) theology of mission, Individual (or, personal) theology of mission (Jan A.B. Jongeneel)

This list is not exhaustive because much research still remains to be done before a definitive account of the birth-years of the names of the concepts of missiology, i.e. the philosophy of mission, the science of mission, and the theology of mission -and their subdivisions- can be presented.

Secondly, I can now present a survey of all the disciplines involved in the philosophical, empirical, and theological study of mission:

PHILOSOPHY (general)	PHILOSOPHY OF RELIGION (general)	PHILOSOPHY OF MISSION (general)
1. Epistemology	1. Epistemology of r.	1. Epistemology of m.
2. Phenomenology	2. Phenomenology of r.	2. Phenomenology of m.
3. Ontology	3. Ontology of r.	3. Ontology of m.
4. Axiology	4. Axiology of r.	4. Axiology of m.

SCIENCE (general)	SCIENCE OF RELIGION (general)	SCIENCE OF MISSION (general)
1. Linguistics	1. Linguistics of r.	1. Linguistics of m.
2. History	2. History of r.	2. History of m.
3. Geography	3. Geography of r.	3. Geography of m.
4. Statistics	4. Statistics of r.	4. Statistics of m.
5. Etnology/ Sociology	5. Etnology of r.	5. Etnology of m.
6. Economy	6. Economy of r.	6. Economy of m.
7. Law	7. Law of r.	7. Law of m.
8. Psychology	8. Psychology of r.	8. Psychology of m.
9. Paedagogics	9. Paedagogics of r.	9. Paedagogics of m.

THEOLOGY (Christian)	THEOLOGY OF RELIGION (Christian)	THEOLOGY OF MISSION (Christian)
1. Ascetics		1. Missionary ascetics
2. Dogmatics		2. Missionary dogmatics
3. Ethics		3. Missionary ethics
4. Cybernetics		4. Missionary cybernetics
5. Catechetics		5. Missionary catechetics
6. Liturgics		6. Missionary liturgics
7. Homiletics		7. Missionary homiletics
8. Poimenics		8. Missionary poimenics
9. Diakonics		9. Missionary diakonics
10. Apologetics		10. Missionary apologetics

After chapter 4 we can deal systematically with the branches of the philosophy of mission, the science of mission, and the theology of mission.

The main lines and topics of this third chapter are now clear: the philosophical, the empirical, and the theological study of mission not only complement each other, but also connect missiology, in one way or another, with all the philosophical, theological, and other academic disciplines. Missiology is a very broad discipline which can never be studied in isolation. Missionary theologians, missionaries, and missiologists must always be willing to learn from others, and also to teach them. Ghettoism and doing mission and mission studies are mutually exclusive. Especially the missionary theologians, the missionaries, and the missiologists must enter into a dialogue with the philosophers of religion, the scientists of religion, and the theologians of religion who, by their profession, should never confine their thoughts exclusively to the well-known and much-cherished world of the Bible, the Christian faith, and the Church.

4. METHODS OF MISSIOLOGY

4.1. METHODS

Missiology as an academic discipline which embraces the philosophical, empirical, and theological study of mission, employs several methods.

Most missiological handbooks deal widely with the methods used in mission -for instance, the methods of presentation at the home base and the methods in the field (cf. 5.4.5.7.)- but only draw attention in passing to, or even are practically silent about, the methods used by missiology as a scientific discipline. François E. Daubanton (1911:563), however, warned us not to neglect the *missiological methodology*: 'If we travel without a method, we are, although we do not see it ourselves, on the way to the terminus called *Tohu-wabohu*. Methodological work -a requirement in the cultivating of every special science- is above all needed in mission studies which extend broadly in time and space' (my tr.).

Joseph Schmidlin (1925:44) pointed out that missiology has not one method, but a variety of methods which is closely allied to the variety of its branches (cf. next chapter). André V. Seumois (1952:362-370), however, divided *missionary methodology* (Fr.: *méthodology missionnaire*) into *methods of realisation* (Fr.: *méthodes de réalisation*) and *methods of cooperation* (Fr.: *méthodes de coopération*). These methods are used in mission.

Alphonsus J.M. Mulders (1962:154) insisted that missiology requires a methodology which is 'both scientific and ecclesiastical'. In essence I agree with the view of Mulders, but I prefer to speak about the philosophical, empirical, and theological methods of mission studies, which either have a *scientific* or a *metascientific* character.

*DAUBANTON. 1911.
P. 563-577: Methodologie der zendingswetenschap.
*SCHMIDLIN. 1925.
P. 44-52: Methode des missionswissenschaftlichen Studiums.
*STREIT, ROBERT, OMI. Die katholische deutsche Missionsliteratur... Aachen, & Immensee, 1925.
P. 178-179: Missionsmethodologische Schriften. Bibliog.
*SEUMOIS. 1952.
P. 362-370: Méthodologie missionnaire.
P. 467-482: Méthode de la missiologie.
*VRIENS. 1960.
P. 68-85: Mission methodology.
*SANTOS HERNANDEZ. 1961.
P. 276-277: Metodologia misionera.
*MULDERS. 1962.
P. 154: De methode van de missiologie.

176

*SPINDLER, MARC R. La mission, combat pour le salut du monde. Neuchâtel, 1967.
    First ed.: Méthode et principes d'une missiologie protestante. 1967.
*DUBOSE, FRANCIS M. God who sends: a fresh quest for biblical mission. Nashville, 1983.
    P. 27-29: A methodology for investigating the sending.
*BRIA, ION. Reflections on mission theology and methodology. In: IRM, LXXIII (1984),
    p. 66-72.
*TROMPF, GARRY W. Missiology, methodology and the study of new religious movements. In:
    Religious traditions: a journal in the study of religion, X (1987), p. 95-106.

4.2. METAPHYSICS AND EMPIRICISM

In missiological literature I scarcely encountered the term *metaphysics*. However, François E. Daubanton (1911:483) used this term: he wrote about the 'metaphysical basis' of mission. Others prefer to speak about the 'ontological basis' of mission (cf. 5.2.4.).

Although mission studies rarely use the terms *empiricism*, *empiric*, and *empirical*, they strongly support and practise what is implicated in these terms. This applies especially to the science of mission (Ger.: *Missionswissenschaft*): the linguistics, history, geography, statistics, ethnology, sociology, law, economics, psychology, and pedagogics of (Christian and non-Christian) mission (cf. 5.3.: *Empirical mission studies*).

Arnulf Camps OFM (Vox Theologica 1972:218-219) averred that 'until recently the study of the empiric was an auxiliary science of missiology... Only with difficulty can we therefore speak about *empirical missiology*' (my tr.). A.T. van Holten (Vox Theologica 1972:217), on behalf of the Editorial Board, expressed the following view: the board will contribute 'to the transformation of the prevailing image of missiology as a deductive and prescriptive science to that of a more inductive and empirical science with respect for, and attention of religious studies and social sciences to the real situations' (my tr.). These authors rightly criticize the priority of the theological study of mission over the empirical study of mission; but they also lose sight of the fact that as early as the 19th century the above-mentioned branches of the empirical study of mission -the linguistics, history, geography etc. of Christian mission- rejected theological control. Since that time, each of these branches has already developed its own empirical methodology.

Jacques Waardenburg (1973:528) quoted the following sentence of the analytical psychologist Carl G. Jung (1875-1961): 'I trust that it does not collide with the principles of scientific empiricism if one occasionally makes certain reflections which go beyond a mere accumulation and classification of experience'. In the same way, but more than occasionally, missionary theologians are going beyond the principles of *scientific empiricism*, which they, however, always respect in their empirical study of mission.

*CAMPS, ARNULF, OFM. Vier sleutelbegrippen voor een meer empirische missiologie. In: Vox theologica, XLII (1972), p. 218-231.
*HOLTEN, A.T. VAN. Religie en verandering buiten Europa: over zendingswetenschap en empirie. In: Vox theologica, XLII (1972), p. 217.
*WAARDENBURG, JACQUES. Classical approaches to the study of religion: aims, methods and theories of research. I. The Hague, & Paris, 1973.
*SPINDLER, MARC R., & JACQUES GADILLE (eds.). Sciences de la mission et formation missionnaire au XXe siècle: actes de la XIIe session du CREDIC... Lyon, & Bologna, 1992.
P. 27-41: Missiologie empirique et théologie de la mission (Jacques Gadille).

4.3. DEDUCTIVE AND INDUCTIVE METHODS

> A science of missions could not be
> deductively reasoned out.
> *Robert E. Speer (1902:45).*

Archibald G. Baker (1934:283) has already stated that 'the usual procedure has been to deduce the principles of missions from *a priori* principles and doctrines already held with conviction'. He dissociated himself from that procedure and used the 'unusual', i.e. inductive method, which does not start with axioms, but with concrete situations and contexts.

David J. Bosch equated the difference between the *deductive and inductive method* with the difference between the Ecumenicals and the Evangelicals. He wrote: 'Whereas Evangelicals seek to apply Scripture deductively - in other words, make Scripture their point of departure from which they draw the line(s) to the present situation - Ecumenicals follow the inductive method; the situation in which they find themselves becomes the hermeneutical key. Their thesis is: we determine God's will *from* a specific situation rather than *in* it. The nature and purpose of the Christian mission therefore has to be reformulated from time to time so as to keep pace with events. In the words of the Uppsala Assembly: The world provides the agenda' (1980:38). In my own view the difference between induction and deduction must not be connected primarily with the difference between groups of persons, but with the difference between the various types of mission studies: the empirical study of mission is mainly or only inductive, whereas the philosophical and theological studies of mission are mainly, or at least ultimately, deductive. Nevertheless, I certainly agree with Bosch that conservatives are more in favour of the deductive method (because of their ultimate concentration on the theological study of mission), whereas liberals are more in favour of the inductive method (because of their great interest in the innovation and adaptation of mission and mission studies to the modern way of life and thinking). In the Roman Catholic Church, conservatives repeatedly go back to the official missionary statements of the Pope, the *Congregatio de propaganda fide*, the councils, the bishops, etc.; whereas in Protestantism conservatives always go back to the Bible (Lat.: *sola scriptura*). The method of citing quotations from biblical and/or ecclesiastical sources is therefore more common in the publications of conservative missiologists in the Evangelical Movement than in those of liberal and modern missiologists in the Ecumenical Movement.

Both *deductive missiology* and *inductive missiology* (my terms) have their own rights. Missiology, as a scientific discipline, needs both induction and deduction. The advantage of the inductive method is that missiology can be as open as all other sciences, but its danger is to secularize missiology. And the advantage of deduction is that the biblical and ecclesiastical roots of mission and missionary theology are fully respected, but its danger is to lose contact with the contemporary world and its variety of religions and worldviews.

Missiologists as empiricists mainly use the inductive method, whereas missiologists as missionary theologians are familiar with the deductive method (Bible, church statements). David J. Bosch (1980:45) is quite right in stating that neither method should be practised 'in isolation from or over against one another'.

*SPEER, ROBERT E. Missionary principles and practice... New York, Chicago, & Toronto, 1902.
    P. 43-68: The science of missions.
*BAKER, ARCHIBALD G. Christian missions and a new world culture. Chicago, & New York, 1934.
*BOSCH, DAVID J. Witness to the world: the Christian mission in theological
    perspective. London, 1980.
    P. 43-45: Inductive or deductive?

4.4. DESCRIPTIVE AND NORMATIVE MISSIOLOGY

We can not only make a distinction between inductive missiology and deductive missiology, but also between *descriptive missiology* and *prescriptive missiology* or *normative missiology*. In missiological literature the terms 'inductive missiology' and 'deductive missiology' are new, but the terms 'descriptive missiology' and/or 'normative missiology' occur frequently (Barbero 1939; Seumois 1952:238-277,292,315; Santos Hernandez 1961:270-273; Mulders 1962:255-359; et al.). The term 'normative missiology' is even divided into 'internal normative missiology' (based upon church authority) and 'external normative missiology' (based upon national and international law).

Seumois (Anderson 1961:132) writes: 'Normative missiology, studying the juridical figure of mission organization in conformity with the norms of doctrine (being a study of theological order -*theologia rectrix*- like the whole of ecclesiastical law), is now being treated integrally'. However, he and other

Roman Catholic missiologists do not set up 'normative missiology' over against 'descriptive missiology', but they do set it up over against 'fundamental missiology'. I disagree with this usage, because the 'fundamental missiology' of Seumois, et al. is from the scientific point of view 'normative' and not at all 'descriptive'. Normative missiology does not only deal with the 'juridical figure of mission organization in conformity with the norms of doctrine' (Seumois), but with the whole field of the principles and practice of mission (cf. 5.4.). Missionary cybernetics (cf. 5.4.5.), which among other things deals with the 'juridical figure of mission organization' (Seumois), is only a small, but very crucial part of this whole field.

David J. Bosch (1980:87) also drew our attention to the problem of descriptive and normative missiology. Dealing with the theology of mission through the ages he wrote: 'Missiology, like any other branch of theology, always has a *critical* function. It is both normative and descriptive. In its normative function it provides guidelines for the way in which mission *ought* to be undertaken. In its descriptive function it critically evaluates the way in which mission has in fact been understood and carried out through the centuries. There is a temptation to regard this second function as unimportant. The two functions are, however, intimately related. It is impossible really meaningfully to discuss the way in which the Church ought to express her missionary calling without taking careful cognisance of the way in which she has in fact been doing this'. It is also the opinion of William J. Abraham (1989:11) that both methods should not be practised in isolation from or over against each other. He made the following fresh approach to the subject of evangelism: 'What we need is the kind of reflection that will take up these matters with one steady eye gazing both descriptively and normatively on the evangelistic activity of the church and the other eye firmly fixed on the relevant data and warrants that any scholar must draw on to deal with them satisfactorily'.

Description, of course, is very strong in empirical mission studies, especially when producing encyclopedias (Newcomb 1860; Dwight, Tupper, & Bliss 1904), catalogues (Bliss 1894), and atlases (Beach, & Fahs 1925), and presenting statistics (cf. WCE 1982). Prescription, however, prevails in systematic and practical missionary theology. The 'norm' of doing Christian mission and doing missionary theology is God's own missionary work in creation, redemption, and sanctification.

*NEWCOMB, HARVEY. A cyclopedia of missions: containing a comprehensive view of missionary operations throughout the world: with geographical descriptions ...: second rev. ed. New York, 1860.
*BLISS, EDWIN M. (comp.). Descriptive catalogue of books on missions and mission lands... Philadelphia, 1894.

*DWIGHT, HENRY O., H. ALLEN TUPPER Jr, & EDWIN M. BLISS (eds.). The encyclopaedia of missions: descriptive, historical, biographical, statistical: second ed. New York, & London, 1904.

*BEACH, HARLAN P., & CHARLES H. FAHS (eds.). World missionary atlas: containing a directory of missionary societies, classified summaries of statistics, maps showing the location of mission stations throughout the world, a descriptive account of the principal mission lands, and comprehensive indices... New York, 1925.

BARBERO, GIUSEPPE, SSP. Le missioni: compendio di missionologia dottrinale - descrittiva et operativa. Alba, & Roma, 1939.

*SEUMOIS. 1952.

    P. 238-277: Missiologie normative.

    P. 292, 315: Missiologie descriptive.

*ANDERSON. 1961.

    P. 122-134: The evolution of mission theology among Roman Catholics (André V. Seumois OMI).

*SANTOS HERNANDEZ. 1961.

    P. 270-273: Misionologia normativa.

*MULDERS. 1962.

    P. 255-359: Normatieve missieleer.

*BAARDA, TJITZE, et al. (eds.). Zending op weg naar de toekomst: essays aangeboden aan Prof.Dr. Johannes Verkuyl... Kampen, 1978.

    P. 203-213: Normatieve kerkgeschiedenis? (Johannes van den Berg).

*BOSCH, DAVID J. Witness to the world... London, 1980.

    P. 86-92: The historical perspective.

*WCE. 1982.

*ABRAHAM, WILLIAM J. The logic of evangelism. Grand Rapids, 1989.

WALSH, JAMES E. Description of a missioner. New York, n.d.

4.5. MISSIOLOGY FROM ABOVE AND MISSIOLOGY FROM BELOW

Wolfgang Pannenberg (1969:26-31) made a fundamental distinction between 'christology from above' (starting with the incarnation) and 'christology from below' (starting with the historical Jesus and his message), which had a strong impact on both western and non-western theology. In Asia, Stanley J. Samartha (1991:115-120) spoke about *helicopter christology* (from above) and *bullock-cart christology* (from below). He wrote: 'A helicopter christology, in its attempts to land on the religiously plural terrain of Asia, makes such a lot of missiological noise and kicks up so much theological dust that people around it are prevented from hearing the voice and seeing the vision of the descending divinity. A bullock-cart christology, on the other hand, always has its wheels touching the unpaved roads of Asia, for without continual friction with the ground, the cart cannot move forward at all. Moreover, a bullock-cart christology has the advantage of having its bullocks move on with a steady pace, even when the driver sometimes falls asleep'. Samartha prefers the bullock-cart christology, which comes first. I agree with Samartha, but I would like to ask whether it is better to speak on the one hand about a 'helicopter christology' which may have -or has- difficulties in landing and on the other hand about a 'helicopter christology' which may have -or has- difficulties in taking off again.

Not only in christology, but also in missiology we can make a distinction between below and above. Anton Wessels (Musschenga 1983:166-171) was probably the first missiologist to use the terms *missiology from below* and *missiology from above*. Others followed (Jongeneel, in: Verstraelen 1988; Bosch, in: Anderson, Phillips, & Coote 1991). I consider both God/Christ/ Spirit-centered, salvation history-centered, and church-centered missiologies as missiologies from above; whereas context-centered (humanizing, dialogical, liberationist, etc.) missiologies are missiologies from below (Verstraelen 1988:451-459). David J. Bosch (Anderson, Phillips, & Coote 1991:61) maintains a rather different position: 'At least since the time of Constantine, theology was conducted *from above* as an elitist enterprise (except in the case of minority Christian communities, traditionally referred to as *sects*); its main source (apart from Scripture and tradition) was *philosophy*, and its main interlocutor was the *educated nonbeliever*. Contextual theology, on the other hand, is theology *from below*; its main source (apart from Scripture and tradition) is the *social sciences*, and its main interlocutors are the *poor* and the *culturally marginalized*'. As far as I can see, missiology from above already starts in the Gospel according to John and in the Epistles of the apostle Paul, whereas missiology from below is mainly rooted in the Synoptic Gospels and in the Acts of the Apostles.

PANNENBERG, WOLFHART. Jesus, God and man. Philadelphia, 1968.
    *Ger. ed.: Grundzüge der Christologie: dritte Aufl. Gütersloh, 1969.
    P. 26-31: Die Methode der Christologie.
*MUSSCHENGA, ALBERT W. (ed.). De dialoog kritisch bezien: studies over de plaats van de waarheidsvraag in de dialoog met gelovigen uit andere kulturen. Baarn, 1983.
    P. 166-171: Missiologie van beneden (Anton Wessels).
*VERSTRAELEN, FRANS J., et al. (eds.). Oecumenische inleiding in de missiologie: teksten en konteksten van het wereldchristendom. Kampen, 1988.
    P. 451-459: Missiologieën van boven en van beneden (Jan A.B. Jongeneel).
*ANDERSON, GERALD H., JAMES M. PHILLIPS, & ROBERT T. COOTE (eds.). Mission in the nineteen 90s. Grand Rapids, & New Haven, 1991.
    P. 60-64: Toward a new paradigm of mission (David J. Bosch).
*SAMARTHA, STANLEY J. One Christ - many religions: toward a revised christology. New York, 1991.
    P. 115-120: Helicopter christology vs. bullock-cart christology.

4.6. CONCLUSION

This necessarily brief chapter on the methods of mission studies makes clear that there is a great variety of missiological methods. This variety is so important that mission studies, apart from the philosophical study of mission, must be divided into two basic types: the scientific or empirical study of mission (mainly inductive) and the theological study of mission (ultimately deductive). The empirical study of mission start and end 'on earth', whereas the theological study of mission start and/or end 'in heaven'. (Missiology from below, versus missiology from above, refuses to start in heaven.) Although liberal theologians and missiologists prefer a theology and missiology 'from below', they cannot deny that, like the conservatives, they ultimately depend also upon the 'above'; because the divine -God's revelation in Jesus Christ as the ultimate norm- comes finally from beyond human experiences and reflection.

In the past and at the present, the empirical study of mission is sometimes mixed with theological insights. For instance, Nicolas Poulain's study of the history of Christian mission (1867) not only deals descriptively with the historical matters of fact in mission, but also makes abundantly clear that God is mightily at work in human history. He interprets the history of Christian mission as the history of God's great works (Lat.: *magnalia Dei*). This normative interpretation of Christian mission in the framework of human history is a theological interpretation. Here I prescind from the serious question of whether or not this interpretation is also a metaphysical interpretation.

Here I conclude with a short list of dates in which the afore-said names of 'missiology from the methodological point of view' are mentioned for the first time:

1939: *Missionologia descrittiva*=descriptive missiology (Giuseppe Barbero SSP)
1952: *Missiologie normative*=normative missiology (André V. Seumois OMI) [Internal/external normative missiology]
1972: *Empirische missiologie*=empirical missiology (Arnulf Camps OFM)
1983: *Missiologie van beneden/van boven*=missiology from below/from above (Anton Wessels)
1994: Inductive/deductive missiology (Jan A.B. Jongeneel).

This list is necessarily provisional; because I do not possess all of the data for compiling a definitive draft of the birth-years of 'missiology from the methodological point of view'.

The problem of missiological methodology will not be dealt with again in the final chapter of this study. However, it is very clear that every branch of missiology which will be discussed in chapter 5, has its own methodological approach and problems. This chapter is a general introduction to the basic methodology of mission studies, which in the next chapter will be applied in every branch of the philosophical, empirical, and theological study of mission.

POULAIN, NICOLAS. L'oeuvre des missions évangéliques au point de vue de la divinité du christianisme. Genève, 1867.

5. BRANCHES OF MISSIOLOGY

5.1 BRANCHES

This chapter deals with the various branches (or divisions) of mission studies, i.e. of missiology. I have divided this discipline into three concepts: (1) the philosophical study of mission; (2) the empirical study of mission; and (3) the theological study of mission (cf. chapter 3). Each of these concepts has its own branches. Each of these branches will be explained in a separate section of this chapter (5.2., 5.3., and 5.4. respectively).

The order of the sections 5.2., 5.3., and 5.4. is determined by both historical and systematic considerations. Historically, the proposed order is in agreement with the chronological order of the birth-years of the names of the three concepts of mission studies already mentioned in chapter 2.6.:

1828: Philosophy of mission(s) (William Orme);
1832: *Missionswissenschaft*=science of mission(s) (Johann T.L. Danz);
1877: *Missionstheologie*=theology of mission(s) (Gustav Warneck).

Systematically, the general concepts of mission studies -philosophy and science- must be given priority, and the special one -Christian theology- should appear at the end. The various branches of mission studies are dealt with in this comprehensive frame.

The order of the branches of each form of mission studies will be discussed in the introduction of sections 5.2., 5.3., and 5.4. respectively. Thereafter these sections will explain each branch in its own particular context. At the very end of this chapter -the last chapter of this encyclopedia- a general 'conclusion' will be drawn concerning all the branches of the various forms of mission studies.Both section 5.4. and the concluding section 5.5. will be dealt with in the second volume of this study.

5.2. THE PHILOSOPHY OF MISSION (MISSIONSPHILOSOPHIE)

5.2.1. INTRODUCTION

Francis M. DuBose, Professor of Missions and Director of the World Missions Center, Golden Gate Baptist Theological Seminary, Mill Valley, California, USA, is one of the very few missiologists who has seriously reflected upon the structure of philosophical mission studies. He entitled the third part of his study

God Who Sends as follows: 'The Ultimacy of the Sending: Mission as Meaning' (1983:71-95), and divided it in four parts:

1. Epistemology: the Sending and How We Know;
2. Ontology: the Sending and Who We Are;
3. Ethics: the Sending and How We Live; and
4. Aesthetics: the Sending and What We Value.

I adopt the basic structure of DuBose's division. However, after epistemology, I deal first with phenomenology, which is absent in the reflections of DuBose. And, instead of dealing with ethics and aesthetics separately, I speak about axiology as a philosophical discipline which includes both ethics and aesthetics. Therefore, I also divide *the philosophy of mission* (Ger.: *Missionsphilosophie*) into four sections:

1. Epistemology: the knowledge of mission (both Christian and non-Christian);
2. Phenomenology: the phenomenon of mission (both Christian and non-Christian);
3. Ontology: the essence of mission (both Christian and non-Christan); and
4. Axiology: the ethical and aesthetical value of mission (both Christian and non-Christian).

*DUBOSE, FRANCIS M. God who sends: a fresh quest for biblical mission. Nashville, 1983.
    P. 71-95: The ultimacy of the sending: mission as meaning.

5.2.2. THE EPISTEMOLOGY OF MISSION

5.2.2.1. INTRODUCTION

Ronald W. Hepburn, Professor of Philosophy at the University of Edinburgh, offers the following definition of 'epistemology': '*Epistemology or theory of knowledge* is a part of philosophy that has great relevance to the theologian. It explores problems about knowing, believing, doubting, proving, about the probable and the improbable: the justification of claims to know, to be sure, to have good grounds; and the counter-claims of sceptics' (Richardson 1972:112).

Epistemology (from the Greek noun *episteme*=knowledge) also deals with religious knowledge, including missionary knowledge. In the framework of missiology, epistemology explores problems about missionary knowing, believing, doubting, proving, about the probable and the improbable in missions: the justification of missionary claims to know, to be sure, to have good grounds; and the counter-claims of sceptics (cf. Hepburn).

In the chapter 'Epistemology: the Sending and How We Know' of his already-mentioned book, Francis DuBose (1983:72-76) discusses the various systems of epistemology which have emerged over the centuries. He draws attention to two radically different views of religious knowledge: (1) the view of ultimate reality as transcendent (knowledge through reason); and (2) the view of ultimate reality as immanent (knowledge through meditation). He links the first view with Traditional Religions, Hinduism, and Buddhism; and the second view with Confucianism, Zoroastrianism, Gnosticism, Judaism, and Islam. Finally, he describes Christianity as a meaningful synthesis of transcendence and immanence (knowledge through revelation-faith).

Some religions and worldviews are missionary, others are not. Epistemology as part of the philosophical study of mission deals with the 'knowledge' of missionary religions and worldviews. Following the above-mentioned classification of DuBose, I observe that both immanentism (cf. Buddhism and contemporary Hinduism), and transcendentism (cf. Islam), and its synthesis (cf. Christianity) have developed missions. And adding to the observations of DuBose, I question whether all current approaches to knowledge (rationalism, empiricism, etc.) are helpful *to know* both the views and activities, and the claims of missionary religions and worldviews.

*RICHARDSON, ALAN (ed.). A dictionary of Christian theology. London, 1972.
    P. 112: Epistemology (Ronald W. Hepburn).
*DUBOSE, FRANCIS M. God who sends... Nashville, 1983.
    P. 72-76: Epistemology: the sending and how we know.

5.2.2.2. HISTORY

Epistemology of (Christian) mission as a discipline is still in its infancy.

As far as I know, no missiologist has yet seriously tackled the whole problem of knowledge with regard to Christian and non-Christian mission. In 1983 DuBose began to place 'the epistemology of the (Christian) mission' on the agenda of mission studies. Thereafter, Robert Kolb, Professor of Religion at Concordia College, St. Paul, Minnesota, and David J. Bosch made modest contributions; without, however, referring to DuBose.

5.2.2.3. THE KNOWLEDGE OF CHRISTIAN MISSION

DuBose sees the significance of epistemology in its relationship to Christian mission in 'the fact that the God of the Bible acts through the sending to make himself known in deeds of providential blessings and judgment and supremely in redemption' (1983:74).

The epistemology of Christian mission is concerned about *the knowledge* of the *missio Dei*; of the *missio Christi*; of the *missio ecclesiae*; and of the *missio hominum*. This epistemology includes both vertical relationships (knowledge of the missionary God) and horizontal relationships (knowledge of the missionary individual as well as knowledge of missionary communities). From one point of view, we need a thorough epistemology of Christian mission in order to confront the missionary challenges of our time, and from another point of view, Robert Kolb (1984:55) is right in stating the following: 'Believers need not be able to conduct a lengthy discourse on epistemology in order to present that objective truth which rests on God's promise rather than on human proof. Neither should they be intimidated by popular claims in behalf of empirically tested truth claims. They should be prepared to use logical argument and cultural common sense to destroy false systems of security and false sources of meaning and identity, and they should be able to make the faith as plausible as possible. At the same time, they must always remember that plausibility and proof without the Holy Spirit cannot effect acceptance of the promise in faith'.

David J. Bosch (1991:423-425) called attention to both the 'epistemo-logical break' and the new epistemology. He mentions as features of the new epistemology (versus the traditional western epistemology) the emphasis on theology 'from the underside of history' (cf. 4.5.: missiology from below), on the priority of praxis, and on commitment as 'the first act of theology'.

*DUBOSE, FRANCIS M. God who sends... Nashville, 1983.
    P. 72-76: Epistemology: the sending and how we know.
*KOLB, ROBERT. Speaking the gospel today: a theology for evangelism. St. Louis, 1984.
    P. 51-55: The epistemology of the gospel.
*BOSCH, DAVID J. Transforming mission... New York, 1991.
    P. 423-425: The epistemological break.

5.2.3. THE PHENOMENOLOGY OF MISSION

> Relatively little scholarly attention has been
> paid to the important and fascinating
> comparative religious topic of mission.
> *Frank Whaling (IRM 1981:314).*

5.2.3.1. INTRODUCTION

Phenomenology is a modern way of doing philosophy which, according to James Richmond (Richardson 1972:257), 'conducts a descriptive inquiry into the most fundamental structure of our experience, into those essences which are most immediately present to our consciousness' (cf. 5.2.4.1.: 'Ontology' is the discipline which, acording to Paul Tillich 1968:I,24, deals with 'those structures of being which we encounter in every meeting with reality').

Edmund Husserl (1859-1938), Max Scheler (1874-1928), et al., introduced the *phenomenological method* into philosophy. Rudolf Otto (1869-1937), Gerardus van der Leeuw (1890-1950), Friedrich Heiler (1892-1967), Gaston Berger (1896-1960), Joachim Wach (1898-1955), et al., used this method in the science of religion (Ger.: *Religionswissenschaft*). In 1957 Berger explained this method as follows: 'The phenomenological method may be able to help us, it seems, to take the right attitude and to understand religious life. It reminds us, first of all, that all meaning is based on a conscious intention and that thought and acts are in fact incomprehensible when they are isolated from the movement that constitutes them. It also teaches us that if we find it impossible to suppress our own beliefs and our own feelings when studying human material, we can at least put them into parantheses, so that they become suspended without our having to become unfaithful to them, and we can sympathize with other people's deepest emotions, without having to approve all acts into which those are translated. The phenomenologist thus stops confusing truth and meaning. He does not necessarily regard everything he describes as true or good, but through various examples, he applies himself to the task of discovering deep-lying structures, the meaning of which becomes clear to him' (Waardenburg 1973:665).

Phenomenology is the systematic study of *what appears* (Gr.: *phenomenon*). The phenomenology of religion therefore deals with religious phenomena. The phenomenology of mission as a branch of the philosophical study of mission deals with *the phenomenon of mission* (cf. Trueblood 1972: 1-22), or *the missionary phenomenon* (cf. Spindler, in: La revue réformée 1983:25-27: *le phénomène missionnaire*). Where missionary theology is primarily concerned with the question of *the truth* about the Christian mission, the phenomenology of mission seeks to understand *the meaning* of 'what appears' as mission in both Christianity and the non-Christian religions. Dean Gilliland (Missiology 1979:458) rightly concluded: 'Phenomenology can keep the Christian missionary from falling into absolutism'.

Furthermore Gilliland (Missiology 1979:452) made clear that he came to see 'how a careful use of the phenomenological method can be a valuable approach to missiological understanding'. He emphasized that, on the one hand, a careful use of this method avoids the 'dangers' of intellectualism, syncretism, and relativism; whilst, on the other hand, it takes 'advantage' of a creative and sympathetic approach to other religions (:457).

*RICHARDSON, ALAN (ed.). A dictionary of Christian theology. London, 1972.
    P. 257: Phenomenology (James Richmond).

190

*TRUEBLOOD, ELTON. The validity of the Christian mission. New York, Evanston, San Francisco..., 1972.
   P. 1-22: The phenomenon of mission.
*WAARDENBURG, JACQUES. Classical approaches to the study of religion: aims, methods, and theories of research. I. The Hague, & Paris, 1973.
*GILLILAND, DEAN. Phenomenology as mission method. In: Missiology, VII (1979), p. 451-459.
*SPINDLER, MARC R. Missiologie anonyme et missiologie responsable. In: La revue réformée, XXXIV (1983), p. 25-36.

5.2.3.2. HISTORY

Several modern missiologists have dealt with the *phenomenology of (Christian) mission*, which Johannes Severijn (1948:89), Professor of the Philosophy of Religion at Utrecht University, used to call the *comparative science of mission* (Dutch: *vergelijkende zendingswetenschap*).

In the 19th century, several scholars had already published comparative studies. Here I refer to the publications of Francis Wayland (1854), Theodor Christlieb (1876), Joseph B. Lightfoot (1888), and Jens Vahl (1892). However, only after the advent of the phenomenological school in the 20th century, can we speak about 'the phenomenology of the (Christian) mission' in its proper sense.

Samuel M. Zwemer taught 'comparative missionary biography' (Myklebust 1957:II,89), whereas Julius Richter considered the *comparative study of religions* as 'an integral part of missionary science' (Myklebust 1957:II,107). Nevertheless, in missiological literature I rarely encountered the terms *comparative study of missions* (Whaling, in: IRM 1981:314-333) and *comparative mission studies*. Although missiologists on the continent of Europe are already familiar with the German term *Religionsphänomenologie* (Dhavamony, in: ZMR 1986:222-231), they did not yet advocate and popularize the German term *Missionsphänomenologie*.

WAYLAND, FRANCIS. Comparative view of the means to be employed in foreign missions. N.p., 1854.
*CHRISTLIEB, THEODOR. Der Missionsberuf des evangelischen Deutschlands nach Idee und Geschichte: eine vergleichende Studie. Gütersloh, 1876.
   *First ed.: AMZ, II (1875), p. 193-210, 289-302, 337-354.
LIGHTFOOT, JOSEPH B. Comparative progress of ancient and modern missions: a paper... London, 1888.
   First ed.: London, 1874.
*VAHL, JENS. Der Stand der evangelischen Heidenmission in den Jahren 1845 und 1890: eine vergleichende missionsgeschichtliche und missionsstatistische Rundschau... Gütersloh, 1892.
*SEVERIJN, JOHANNES. Encyclopaedie der theologische wetenschap. Haarlem, 1948.
   P. 89: De vergelijkende zendingswetenschap.
*MYKLEBUST. 1955-1957. 2 vols.

5.2.3.3. THE APPEARANCE OF CHRISTIAN MISSION

The Christian mission is an astonishing phenomenon.
Elton Trueblood (1972:1).

In mission studies, the phenomenological method can be used in a twofold way: (1) to compare missionary 'appearances' or 'phenomena' inside Christianity (5.2.3.3.) - *internal comparison*; and (2) to compare Christian and non-Christian missionary phenomena (5.2.3.4.) - *external comparison*.

Within the Christian tradition, we can compare, for instance, ancient and modern mission (Lightfoot 1888; Weinel 1907), Roman Catholic and Protestant mission (Horner 1965), one type of Roman Catholic mission with another type (Hoffman 1960), one type of Protestant mission with another type (Oussoren 1945:250-269), etc. Here I refer only to the study of Norman A. Horner (1965:29,35,46,60): 'Roman Catholics are generally more concerned with liturgics than with homiletics... Roman Catholics in many parts of the world have a much more elaborate arrangement for urban work than Protestants... Catholic missions have been historically less dependent than Protestants on funds from the sending land... the nationality of Catholic missionary priests and sisters is usually less obtrusive than that of Protestants'.

Internally, we can also compare missionary means (Wayland 1854), missionary ideas/thoughts/principles/theories/theologies (Christlieb 1876; Cairns, in: IRM 1929:321-331; Oussoren 1945; Hoffman 1960; Scherer 1987), missionary progress (Lightfoot 1888), missionary statistics (Vahl 1892), missionary rights (Mabie 1908), missionary biography (Anonymous author 1905; Sailer 1929), missionary strategy (Horner 1965), etc. Externally these items can be compared as well.

WAYLAND, FRANCIS. Comparative view of the means to be employed in foreign missions. N.p., 1854.

*CHRISTLIEB, THEODOR. Der Missionsberuf des evangelischen Deutschlands nach Idee und Geschichte... Gütersloh, 1876.

LIGHTFOOT, JOSEPH B. Comparative progress of ancient and modern missions... London, 1888.

COMPARATIVE VIEW OF CHRISTIAN WORK IN THE HOME AND FOREIGN FIELDS. 1892.

*VAHL, JENS. Der Stand der evangelischen Heidenmission in den Jahren 1845 und 1890: eine vergleichende missionsgeschichtliche und missionsstatistische Rundschau... Gütersloh, 1892.

COMPARATIVE STUDIES IN MISSIONARY BIOGRAPHY. New York, 1905.

*WEINEL, HEINRICH. Die urchristliche und die heutige Mission: ein Vergleich. Tübingen, 1907.

MABIE, HENRY C. The divine right of missions: or, Christianity the world-religion and the right of the church to propagate it: a study in comparative religion. Philadelphia, Boston..., 1908.

SCHMIDLIN, JOSEPH (ed.). Missionswissenschaftlicher Kursus... Köln, 1916.
    P. 69-81: Die altchristliche und mittelalterliche Mission im Vergleich mit der gegenwärtigen (Andreas Bigelmair).
LENNOX, WILLIAM G. A comparative study of the health of missionary families in Japan and China, and a selected group in America. Denver, 1922.
*CAIRNS, DAVID S. The Christian message: a comparison of thought in 1910 and in 1928. In: IRM, XVIII (1929), p. 321-331.
SAILER, THOMAS H.P. Five missionary lives: a study in comparative biography for boys and girls of high school age, David Livingstone, Mary Slessor, Dr. Theodore Pennell, Jacob Riis, Booker T. Washington. New York, 1929.
*DESCAMPS, BARON EDOUARD E.F. (ed.). Histoire générale comparée des missions... Paris, Bruxelles, & Louvain, 1932.
*OUSSOREN, AALBERTINUS H. William Carey, especially his missionary principles. Leiden, 1945.
    P. 250-269: His missionary principles compared with those of the Pietists, especially the Moravians.
*HOFFMAN, RONAN, OFMConv. Pioneer theories of missiology: a comparative study of the mission theories of Cardinal Brancati de Laurea OFMConv., with those of three of his contemporaries: Jose de Acosta SJ, Thomas a Jesu OCarm., and Dominicus de Gubernatis OFM... Washington, 1960.
HORNER, NORMAN A. Cross and crucifix in mission: a comparison of Protestant - Roman Catholic missionary strategy. Nashville, 1965.
    *Dutch tr.: 1967.
*DICTIONARY CATALOG. 1968.
    XI, p. 89: Missions - comparative studies.
*TRUEBLOOD, ELTON. The validity of the Christian mission. New York, Evanston, San Francisco..., 1972.
*BARRETT, DAVID B. (ed.). World Christian encyclopedia: a comparative study of churches and religions in the modern world AD 1900-2000. Nairobi, Oxford, & New York, 1982.
*SCHERER, JAMES A. Gospel, church, and kingdom: comparative studies in world mission theology. Minneapolis, 1987.

5.2.3.4. THE COMPARISON OF CHRISTIAN MISSION WITH OTHER MISSIONS

> What does it mean to participate in
> God's continuing mission in the world today
> as we live together with our neighbours who belong to
> various faiths, cultures, and ideologies?
> *Stanley J. Samartha (Missiology 1975:143).*

Externally we can only compare the Christian mission with *non-Christian missions*, if we start to make serious study of the mission of non-Christian religions and worldviews. I note that this comparison has not yet been done systematically.

THE MISSION AND PROPAGANDA OF NON-CHRISTIAN RELIGIONS AND WORLDVIEWS

Several non-Christian religions and worldviews are missionary. A few case-studies have been made: here I refer to studies on the mission of Buddhism (Beckmann, in: Katholisches Missionsjahrbuch der Schweiz 1940/41:20-35; Humphreys 1969:35-36,60-61) and Islam (Antes, in: Waldenfels 1978:375-381) as religions, and on the mission/propaganda of Free-Thought (Russell 1922) and Communism (Evans 1955; Labin 1960; Clews 1964) as worldviews and ideologies. To illustrate this phenomenon, I only quote the following observation of Peter Gay (1968:9) on the Enlightenment philosophers: 'As a group, the philosophers were a solid, respectable clan of revolutionaries, with their *mission* continually before them' (my italics).

Phenomenological studies on the mission and propaganda of non-Christian religions and worldviews are non-normative. However, there are also normative studies written by the adherents of the missionary religions and worldviews involved (cf. Iqbal 1977).

RUSSELL, BERTRAND A.W. Free thought and official propaganda... London, 1922.

BECKMANN, JOHANNES, SMB. Der Buddhismus als Missionsreligion. In: Katholisches Missionsjahrbuch der Schweiz, VII/VIII (1940/41), p. 20-35.

*SEUMOIS. 1952.
  P. 426-429: Étude des mouvements missionnaires non catholiques.

EVANS, FRANK B. (ed.). Worldwide communist propaganda activities. New York, 1955.

BENZ, ERNST. Die gegenwärtige Mission und Ausbreitung asiatischer Religionen in Europa und den USA. In: Zeitschrift für Religions- und Geistesgeschichte, X/4 (1958), p. 297-400. Sonderheft.

VICEDOM, GEORG F. Die Mission der Weltreligionen. München, 1959.

LABIN, SUZANNE. The unrelenting war: a study of the strategy and techniques of communist propaganda and infiltration: ed. by Moshe Decter... New York, 1960.

*HUTTEN, KURT, & SIEGFRIED VON KORTZFLEISCH (eds.). Asien missioniert im Abendland. Stuttgart, 1962.

CLEWS, JOHN C. Communist propaganda techniques... New York, 1964.

*GAY, PETER. The Enlightenment: an interpretation: the rise of modern paganism. New York, 1968.

*HUMPHREYS, CHRISTMAS. Buddhism. Harmondsworth, 1969.
  P. 35-36: The first missionaries.
  P. 60-61: Buddhism as a missionary religion.
  First ed.: Harmondsworth, 1951.

?IQBAL, MUHAMMAD. The mission of Islam. New Delhi, 1977.

*WALDENFELS, HANS (ed.). '... denn Ich bin bei euch' (Mt. 28,20): Perspektiven im christlichen Missionsbewusstsein heute: Festgabe für Josef Glazik und Bernward Willeke... Zürich, Einsiedeln, & Köln, 1978.
  P. 375-381: 'Mission' im Islam (P. Antes).

KIRBY, RICHARD. The mission of mysticism. London, 1979.

*HUMMEL, REINHART. Indische Mission und neue Frömmigkeit im Westen: religiöse Bewegungen Indiens in westlichen Kulturen. Stuttgart, Berlin, Köln..., 1980.

194

*LMG. 1987.
      P. 274-277: Mission in den Religionen (P. Antes).

THE COMPARISON OF CHRISTIAN MISSION WITH OTHER MISSIONS

Rudolf Otto has already drawn our attention to the *parallels and convergences* of Christianity and the non-Christian religions, and the 'still more important task of comparing their content and value, to ascertain where the higher and fuller values may be found' (Waardenburg 1973:448,458). Christianity -including Christian mission- can be compared with either one other religion or worldview (White 1811; Dilger 1908; Goddard 1927; Schomerus 1931; Gensichen 1959; Masutani 1967); or two (or more) other religions or worldviews (Whaling, in: IRM 1981:314-333); or all other religions and worldviews (Speer 1911; Tisdall 1912; Daniélou 1962; Van der Leeuw 1964).

Walter J. Hollenweger (1973), for instance, compared the mission of Christianity with one other mission, i.e. that of the communist ideology. He considered as parallels the originally critical and prophetic mission of Karl Marx (1818-1883) and Simon Kimbangu (1889-1951), but looks at the Protestant principle of *sola gratia* as the point at which they took different roads.

Frank Whaling compared Christianity as a missionary religion with Buddhism and Islam as missionary religions. He concluded: 'So far we have found a reasonable congruence between Buddhist, Christian and Muslim mission... The parallels now begin to be less evident... Like the Buddha and Jesus he (=Muhammad, J.) too had received a vision of transcendent reality. Unlike them he was not content to limit his preaching to a minority of interested followers... Mission for Muhammad was not a purely spiritual matter, it was an integral combination of spiritual, social, political and even military matters... By comparison with Buddhist and Christian mission the political support came first rather than last... This worldview did not emerge slowly, like those of the Greek and Latin Christians or the Chinese Buddhists, by gradual interaction with another thought-world... This Arabic Quranic thought-world did not adapt to the worldview of the conquered lands as the Buddhist and Christian worldviews had adapted to China and Europe... By contrast with Christian and Buddhist spread, the process of penetration was not a religious advance into a politally alien world... but the advocacy of a given worldview within a politically dominant situation' (IRM 1981:330-333).

The most difficult task would be to compare the Christian mission with the mission of all other religions and worldviews; because such an unlimited comparison takes the risk of being too general, and therefore being inadequate. In the past this comprehensive approach was very popular, but today most scholars prefer a limited approach: the comparison of the Christian mission with a limited group of non-Christian missions.

WHITE, JOSEPH. A comparison of Mahometism and Christianity in their history, their evidence, and their effects: new ed. London, 1811.
First ed.: Oxford, 1784.
Ger. tr.: 1786.
DILGER, WILHELM. Salvation in Hinduism and Christianity: a comparison and a contrast... Mangalore, 1908.
*Ger. ed.: Die Erlösung des Menschen nach Hinduismus und Christentum: eine vergleichende Untersuchung auf Grund der beidenseitigen Urkunden. Basel, 1902.
SPEER, ROBERT E. The light of the world: a brief comparative study of Christianity and non-Christian religions. West Medford, 1911.
*TISDALL, WILLIAM St. CLAIR. Christianity and other faiths: an essay in comparative religion. London, 1912.
UNDERWOOD, ALFRED C. Conversion, Christian and non-Christian: a comparitive and psychological study. New York, 1925.
GODDARD, DWIGHT. Was Jesus influenced by Buddhism? a comparative study of the lives and thoughts of Gautama and Jesus. Thetford, 1927.
*SCHOMERUS, HILKO W. Buddha und Christus: ein Vergleich zweier grosser Weltreligionen. Halle-Saale, 1931.
P. 1-2: Die Verbreitung des Christentums und der Buddhismus.
*HEINRICHS, MAURUS, OFM. Die Bedeutung der Missionstheologie, aufgewiesen am Vergleich zwischen den abendländischen und chineschen Kardinaltugenden. Münster, 1954.
GENSICHEN, HANS-WERNER. Buddhistische Mission und christliches Zeugnis. Bad Salzuflen, 1959.
DANIÉLOU, JEAN, SJ. The advent of salvation: a comparative study of non-Christian religions and Christianity. New York, 1962.
*First ed.: Le mystère de l'Avent. Paris, 1948.
LEEUW, GERARDUS VAN DER. Religion in essence and manifestation: a study in phenomenology. London, 1964.
*First Eng. tr.: London, 1938.
*Ger. ed.: Phänomenologie der Religion. Tübingen, 1933.
P. 576-585: Dynamik der Religionen. Synkretismus. Mission.
*Rev. and enl. Ger. ed.: Tübingen, 1956.
*Fr. tr.: 1948; second ed.: 1970.
It. tr.: 1960.
MASUTANI, FUMIO. A comparative study of Buddhism and Christianity: fifth ed. Tokyo, 1967.
*First ed.: Tokyo, 1957.
*HOLLENWEGER, WALTER J. Marxist and Kimbanguist mission - a comparison. Birmingham, 1973.
*Ger. tr.: 1979.
*WAARDENBURG, JACQUES. Classical approaches to the study of religion... The Hague, & Paris, 1973.
*SAMARTHA, STANLEY J. Missions and movements of innovation. In: Missiology, III (1975), p. 143-154.
*WHALING, FRANK. A comparative religious study of missionary transplantation in Buddhism, Christianity, and Islam. In: IRM, LXX (1981), p. 314-333.
*PAK, JAMES YEONG-SIK. Paul as missionary: a comparative study of missionary discourse in Paul's epistles and selected contemporary Jewish texts. Frankfurt am Main, Bern, New York..., 1991.

5.2.3.5. THE PHENOMENOLOGY OF CHRISTIAN MISSION, THE PHENOMENOLOGY OF RELIGION, AND COMPARATIVE THEOLOGY

The *phenomenology of (Christian) mission* is part of the wider discipline called the *phenomenology of religion*. However, missionary theologians, missionaries, and missiologists have their own interest in phenomenological studies. Johannes P. Steffes (Scientia religionum ancilla 1953:177-178) made very clear that the science of religion, including the phenomenology of religion, must be put at the service of mission. He stated that missionaries need this discipline for two reasons: (1) to obtain as much as possible an all-round picture of the people who are living in their own mission field; and (2) to evaluate the relationship between Christianity and the non-Christian religions.

Today the relatively old term 'comparative religion' parts company with the term *comparative theology* (Ger.: *vergleichende Theologie*). Gerardus van der Leeuw (Waardenburg 1973:408) coined the term 'phenomenological theology', but the Roman Catholic theologian Adolf Exeler (Waldenfels 1978: 199-211; cf. Kramm, in: ZMR 1984:69-73) raised the provoking question whether to replace missiology with comparative theology, which must be assigned the following tasks: the promotion of understanding of the fact that the Christian faith and its modes of expression are culturally conditioned; intercultural and international theological dialogue; and interdisciplinary working procedures, even beyond the perimeters of theology. However, I accept the criticisms of this concept by Karl Müller SVD (1987:14), who doubts 'whether Exeler's alternative suggestion could solve the problems of missiology as a theological discipline', because 'the missionary commission, which has its source in the *missio Dei*, cannot appear only in the specifically theological sphere but also embraces liturgy, prayer, proclamation, communication of the faith in all its forms'.

*SCIENTIA MISSIONUM ANCILLA. 1953.
    P. 173-179: Die Religionswissenschaft im Dienste der Mission (Johannes P. Steffes).
*WAARDENBURG, JACQUES. Classical approaches to the study of religion... The Hague, & Paris, 1973.
*LEXIKON ZUR WELTMISSION. 1975.
    P. 574-575: Vergleichende Religionswissenschaft (Stephen C. Neill).
*WALDENFELS, HANS (ed.). '... denn Ich bin bei euch' (Mt. 28,20): Perspektiven im christlichen Missionsbewusstsein heute... Zürich, Einsiedeln, & Köln, 1978.
    P. 199-211: Vergleichende Theologie statt Missionswissenschaft? Provozierende Anfrage eines Nichtfachmanns (Adolf Exeler).
*KRAMM, THOMAS. Was ist von einer 'vergleichenden Theologie' zu erwarten? Adolf Exeler zum Andenken. In: ZMR, LXVIII (1984), p. 69-73.
*DHAVAMONY, MARIASUSAI. Klassische Religionsphänomenologie und Missiologie. In: ZMR, LXX (1986), p. 222-231.

*MÜLLER, KARL. Mission theology: an introduction. Nettetal, 1987.
  *Ger. ed.: Missionstheologie: eine Einführung. Berlin, 1985.

5.2.4. THE ONTOLOGY OF MISSION

5.2.4.1. INTRODUCTION

Ontology (from the Greek noun *to on*=being) is the philosophical discipline which deals with (the structures of) *ultimate reality or 'being' itself* (cf. 5.2.3.1.: 'Phenomenology', according to Richmond, in: Richardson 1972:257, deals with 'essences'). Here I quote Paul Tillich's definition of this discipline (1968:I,24): 'Ontology is not a speculative-fantastic attempt to establish a world behind the world; it is an analysis of those structures of being which we encounter in every meeting with reality'.

In one way or another missionary religions and worldviews relate their own mission to God, i.e. 'being' itself, ultimate reality. In the philosophical study of mission we research both the essence of mission and the properties of its existence, and the relation of mission to God, 'being' itself, ultimate reality. The study of DuBose contains a chapter on 'Ontology: the Sending and Who We Are' (1983:77-82), but it does not go into the ontological structure and significance of non-Christian missions. However, the very young discipline 'ontology of mission' can not avoid reflection on the essence of both Christian and non-Christian mission. For missionary religions and worldviews mission is a question of to be or not to be.

*TILLICH, PAUL. Systematic theology. Digswell Place, 1968. 3 vols.
*DUBOSE, FRANCIS M. God who sends... Nashville, 1983.
     P. 77-82: Ontology: the sending and who we are.

5.2.4.2. HISTORY

The *ontology of (Christian) mission* as a discipline is still in its infancy. As far as I know, only Paul Tillich and Francis M. DuBose have called for serious attention to this discipline.

In the first half of this century, however, well-known scholars such as Roland Allen (1913), Joseph H. Oldham (1920), and Frank Lenwood (1921) had, consciously or unconsciously, already used ontological terms in the titles and chapters of their missiological publications.

ALLEN, ROLAND. Essential missionary principles. New York, 1913.
OLDHAM, JOSEPH H. The essential qualifications of a missionary in view of present conditions in the mission field. London, 1920.
LENWOOD, FRANK. The essential meaning of the present missionary situation at home and abroad: a summary... Swanwick, 15th to 17th June 1921. N.p., 1921.

5.2.4.3. THE ESSENCE OF CHRISTIAN MISSION

Paul Tillich renewed Christian missionary thinking by proclaiming Jesus Christ as 'the New Being'. He wrote about '... the missionary principle that the New Being in Jesus as the Christ is the answer to the question asked implicitly and explicitly by the religions of mankind' (1968:I,44).

DuBose (1983:77-82) prefers another concept. He relates 'being' to 'sending' in the following three significant ways:

1. Being, the Old and New Adam, and the Sending;
2. Being, the Exodus Paradigm, and the Sending; and
3. Being, the Christ Paradigm, and the Sending.

First, he emphasizes the relationship between the *imago Dei* (image of God) and the *missio Dei* (mission of God). Second, he connects the language of being in the revelation of God's name 'I AM WHO I AM' (Exod. 3:14) with the missiological context in which this name was revealed. And, finally, he calls attention to the Fourth Gospel where 'Jesus' sense of being and sense of being sent were strongly linked... This sense of being and sense of mission, which have their source in the Father, reached climatic expression in the prayer of Jesus recorded in John 17. The prayer links the theme of being and the theme of sending' (:82).

I recognize the importance of both concepts. First, 'being' and 'being sent' cannot be separated. And second, through the centuries Christian mission is a dynamic reality -grounded in God as the ultimate dynamic reality and in Christ as 'the New Being'- which always requires thorough ontological reflection and analysis. To be (fully) missionary is to be (fully) alive.

*TILLICH, PAUL. Systematic theology. Digswell Place, 1968. 3 vols.
*DUBOSE, FRANCIS M. God who sends... Nashville, 1983.
        P. 77-82: Ontology: the sending and who we are.

5.2.5. THE AXIOLOGY OF MISSION

> Missiology is not a 'value-free' science.
> *Alfred C. Krass (Coote, & Stott 1980:255).*

5.2.5.1. INTRODUCTION

Axiology is the philosophical discipline which deals with *values* (Gr: *axios*= value): goodness, beauty, etc. This discipline is very broad: it includes both ethics (moral values) and aesthetics (aesthetic values). In fact, it is concerned about the justification for calling some things right and others wrong, and some things beautiful and others ugly.

In the framework of mission studies, axiology is concerned about the enduring value of Christian and non-Christian missions. First of all, it enquires in general into the 'religious values' (Waardenburg 1973:54) in their own right. Here I quote Hendrik Kraemer who dealt with the value of Christianity and non-Christian religions in the following way: 'To become more deeply aware of the stupendous richness and depth of religious life in *all* religions has made the question of value and truth in the non-Christian religions more, not less, acute. For many, it has made the question an agonizing one, as it is rightly felt that it has become impossible and utterly objectionable to dispose lightly of these religions in regard to their value and truth' (Waardenburg 1973:652). Second, it enquires especially into the 'missionary values' of both Christianity and the non-Christian religions: have missions value in their own right (intrinsic value), or have they only instrumental value (extrinsic value)?

Scholars must use their reason as well as their intuition to enquire into both the productive and the unproductive, and both the lasting and the transient value of Christian and non-Christian mission. As missiologists they must work empirically. However, they must also recognize that missionary theologians and missionaries are concerned about the normative axiology which tries to answer the fundamental question: what kind of missionary ideas and activities must be preached and practised as having basic 'value'?

*WAARDENBURG, JACQUES. Classical approaches to the study of religion... The Hague, & Paris, 1973.

*COOTE, ROBERT T., & JOHN R.W. STOTT (eds.). Down to earth: studies in Christianity and culture: the papers of the Lausanne consultation on Gospel and Culture. Grand Rapids, 1980.
P. 231-256: Mission as inter-cultural encounter - a sociological perspective (Alfred C. Krass).

5.2.5.2. HISTORY

The Edinburgh World Missionary Conference (1910), Joseph Schmidlin (1925), Helen B. Montgomery (1931), et al., already raised the question of the *value of (Christian) mission (studies)*. However, they did not initiate the *axiology of (Christian) mission* as an academic discipline.

DuBose (1983:83) is one of the few missiologists who consciously linked mission studies and 'axiology, which is the study of values'. And Russell P. Spittler (Missiology 1988:409-422) took the initiative to discuss the implicit values in Pentecostal missions: experience, orality, spontaneity, otherworldliness, and biblical authority. There are, of course, also explicit values in Christian mission.

*WORLD MISSIONARY CONFERENCE. Edinburgh, London, New York..., 1910.
  VI, p. 258-268: The fundamental value of missions to the church.
*SCHMIDLIN. 1925.
  P. 35-44: Wert und Nutzen der Missionswissenschaft.
MONTGOMERY, HELEN B. The preaching value of missions... Philadelphia, 1931.
*DUBOSE, FRANCIS M. God who sends... Nashville, 1983.
*SPITTLER, RUSSELL P. Implicit values in Pentecostal missions. In: Missiology, XVI (1988),
  p. 409-422.
TAFT, WILLIAM H. The value of foreign missions. New York, n.d.

5.2.5.3. THE VALUE OF CHRISTIAN MISSION

In *Report of Commission VI*, the afore-mentioned Edinburgh World Missionary Conference (1910) draw attention to the fundamental, educational *value* of foreign missions. Here I quote the following sentences of this Report: '... the foreign missionary work of the Church has been of immense value in giving to Christian people a wider outlook...'; 'This wider outlook has not merely an intellectual, but also a moral and spiritual value'; 'The value of missions to the remote nations of the earth can never be computed in human figures. It can be expressed only in terms of eternity' (VI,258-268).

In fact, Christian mission has both a theoretical and a practical value. DuBose (1983:137-160) concludes his above-mentioned book with an explanation of 'the practical value of mission as sending'.

I am inclined to consider Christian mission as a basic, productive, and enduring value; because it is grounded in the very nature of God as missionary God; it produces faith, hope, and love beyond existing racial, cultural, national, and ideological boundaries; and, once created or achieved, it continues to be valued.

*DUBOSE, FRANCIS M. God who sends... Nashville, 1983.
   P. 137-160: The practical value of mission as sending.

THE MORAL VALUE OF CHRISTIAN MISSION

Christian mission has both a 'moral' value (Christian ethics as discipline), and an 'aesthetic' value (Christian aesthetics as discipline).

In the chapter on missionary ethics (5.4.4.) I shall explain *the moral value of Christian mission*. Therefore I confine myself here to the view of DuBose (1983:83-87). He considers Christian ethics to be an ethic of relationships: the divine-human relationship; the interpersonal relationship; and the societal relationship. He describes the ethic of the sending as an ethic of relationships under the two headings: 'the apostolate of morality'; and 'the morality of the apostolate'. And he concludes: 'The ethic of the sending is the ultimate ethic because it is the morality of God sanctifying the morality of human affairs through a divinely inspired, redemptive relationship'.

*DUBOSE, FRANCIS M. God who sends... Nashville, 1983.
   P. 83-87: Ethics: the sending and how we live.

THE AESTHETIC VALUE OF CHRISTIAN MISSION

In this study *the aesthetic value of Christian mission* will not receive a chapter of its own, as does the moral value of the Christian mission. However, in the chapter on missionary liturgics (5.4.7.), I shall make some comments on the 'beauty' of the Christian mission.

I close this section with a few remarks on the significance of Christian aesthetics for mission. I observe that in their lives nearly all missionaries have not only experienced the burden, but also the beauty of their missionary work. However, in missiological literature only a few scholars draw our attention to the beauty of mission and mission studies. The only author who has seriously reflected upon the beauty of Christian mission is DuBose (1983:92-95). He wrote about 'the beauty of the sending purpose'. He divided this theme under two heads: 'the beauty of the missional vision', and 'the beauty of the missional task'. He considered 'the missional vision' as a call to 'the missional task'. And he concluded: 'To be on mission as God's messenger to bring his good news is a thing of beauty because it is participation in his redemptive purpose' (:95). This sentence makes very clear that Christian mission has aesthetic value, both in theory and in practice.

*DUBOSE, FRANCIS M. God who sends... Nashville, 1983.
   P. 88-95: Esthetics: the sending and what we value.

5.2.6. CONCLUSION

I conclude this section of chapter 5 on *the philosophy of mission* as the first concept of mission studies by making a chronological table of the names of its various branches, and by making some final observations.

I start with the presentation of a short list of the dates when the names of the various branches were mentioned for the first time:

1828: *PHILOSOPHY OF MISSION(S)* (WILLIAM ORME)
1948: *Vergelijkende zendingswetenschap*=comparative science of mission (Johannes Severijn)
1978: *Vergleichende Theologie*=comparative theology (Adolf Exeler)
1981: Comparative study of missions (Frank Whaling)
1983: Francis DuBose related missions to epistemology, ontology, (philosophical) ethics, and aesthetics, but did not speak about 'the epistemology of mission', 'the ontology of mission', 'the (philosophical) ethics of mission', and/or 'the aesthetics of mission'.

This small list is necessarily provisional. Much research still remains to be done before a definite account of the birth-years of the branches of philosophical mission studies can be presented.

The main lines and issues of this section of chapter 5 are very clear. At the end of this section I would like to say that, in fact, all branches of the philosophical study of mission are still badly discussed and poorly developed. The phenomenology of mission is the most developed discipline of the philosophical study of mission, but even this discipline is still weak. Of the three concepts of missiology -the philosophical, empirical, and theological study of mission- it is the philosophy of mission which urgently needs further exploration and development.

5.3. THE SCIENCE OF MISSION (MISSIONSWISSENSCHAFT)

In this section of chapter 5 we deal with the branches of *the empirical study of mission*, i.e. of *the science of mission(s)* (Ger.: *Missionswissenschaft*).

Each of its various branches will be discussed in a separate section of this part of chapter 5 (5.3.2.-5.3.11.). The first section (5.3.1.), however, is devoted to some general introductory problems, whereas the final section (5.3.12.) will draw a conclusion.

5.3.1. INTRODUCTION

This first section of chapter 5.3. is a general introduction to *the science of mission*, or *empirical study of mission*.

5.3.1.1. INTRODUCTION

The science of mission is that discipline which deals *empirically* with both the Christian and the non-Christian mission.

The use of the empirical method is the decisive factor in the second concept of mission studies. Here I refer to what I made clear in chapter 4.2. on 'metaphysics and empiricism'. Although linguistics, historiography, geography, statistics, etc. as academic disciplines all have their own methods, they have in common a rejection of metaphysics, on the one hand, and an orientation towards 'the principles of scientific empiricism' (Jung, in: Waardenburg 1973:528), on the other hand. To the extent that missionaries employ empirical methods, they can be regarded as '(scientific) researchers' (Ger.: *Forscher*) (Wolff 1920).

*WOLFF, LUDWIG, SCJ. Der Missionar als Forscher: Anleitung für Missionare zum Beobachten und Sammeln von Material... Aachen, 1920.
  Dutch tr.: n.d.
*WAARDENBURG, JACQUES. Classical approaches to the study of religion: aims, methods, and theories of research. I. The Hague, & Paris, 1973.

5.3.1.2. HISTORY

The age of Enlightenment gave birth to empirical studies. So the empirical study of mission is also the product of that era. At that time, 'the history of the Christian mission' was born as an empirical discipline. Thereafter -either in the 19th century or in the 20th century- the other branches of the empirical study of mission came into being.

The birth and growth of the empirical study of mission opened up a new way to look at other empirical disciplines. The term *auxiliary sciences* came about (Daubanton 1911; Schmidlin 1925:167-179; Mulders 1950: 232-258; Santos Hernandez 1961; et al.). François E. Daubanton (1911:502-562), for instance, looked at the following 'profane sciences' (Bierbaum, in: Scientia missionum ancilla 1953:284-299: *Profanwissenschaften*) as the 'auxiliary sciences' of missiology: ethnology, linguistics, and the science of religion (Ger.: *Religionswissenschaft*). Other scholars, however, mentioned other disciplines. Angel Santos Hernandez SJ (1961:283-291), for instance, also referred to ethnography and colonialistics, as well as to geography, anthropology, statistics, the psychology of religion, the philosophy of religion, the philosophy of cultures (Sp.: *filosofía de los pueblos*), cultural history, ethics and ontology, missiological bibliography, pagan mysticism, sociology, tropical hygiene, and the non-Catholic missionary movements.

I reject the term 'auxiliary sciences', however, because I consider these disciplines to be totally mature and independent disciplines. Therefore, I treat these disciplines as disciplines which can give assistance and support to missiology as a discipline, and vice versa. I also refuse to consider the statistics of mission and the geography of mission as merely 'auxiliary sciences of the history of mission' (Daubanton 1911:218). The statistics of mission and the geography of mission are as independent as the history of mission. All branches of the empirical study of mission are called in the same way to give mutual assistance to one another as the totality of empirical mission studies is called to assist and support other empirical disciplines, and vice versa.

*DAUBANTON. 1911.
    P. 502-562: De zendingswetenschap en hare hulpwetenschappen.
*SCHMIDLIN. 1925.
    P. 167-179: Hilfsdisziplinen.
*MULDERS, ALPHONSUS J.M. Inleiding tot de missiewetenschap... Bussum, 1950.
    P. 232-258: Hulpwetenschappen.
*SCIENTIA MISSIONUM ANCILLA. 1953.
    P. 284-299: Das Verhältnis der Mission und Missiologie zu den Profanwissenschaften
    (Max Bierbaum).
*SANTOS HERNANDEZ. 1961.
    P. 283-291: Las disciplinas auxiliares de la misionologia.
*MULDERS. 1962.
    P. 289-291: Hulpwetenschappen van het missierecht.

5.3.1.3. BRANCHES OF THE SCIENCE OF MISSION

The oldest branch of the empirical study of mission is the history of mission. Thereafter the other branches of empirical mission studies came into being. The number of these branches has increased progressively.

Daubanton (1911:136-223) mentioned three specific branches: the history of mission, the geography of mission, and the statistics of mission. Alphonsus J.M. Mulders (1962:153-154), however, divided the empirical study of mission into two branches: the history of mission and missiography; but subdivided missiography into the statistics of mission, the cartography of mission, the geography of mission, and the sociography of mission. This division and subdivision can also be found in the textbook of Angel Santos Hernandez SJ (1961:280). My own view, however, is not only broader than these concepts of Daubanton, Mulders, and Santos Hernandez SJ, but also more strict: I consider the term 'missiography' (Mulders; Santos Hernandez) as outmoded and no longer applicable. Altogether I recognize ten disciplines as independent branches of the empirical study of mission. Here follows a list of these branches and their objects:

1. Linguistics/philology: the language (and terminology) of the mission;
2. History: the past events (and chronology) of the mission;
3. Geography: the spreading over the earth (and mapping) of the mission;
4. Statistics: the numbers of the mission;
5. Ethnology/cultural anthropology: the tribal, racial, and cultural dimensions of the mission;
6. Sociology: the 'sociation' or 'structuration' of the mission;
7. Law: the rules (and rights) of the mission;
8. Economics: the finance of the mission;
9. Psychology: the 'soul', or 'mind', of the mission; and
10. Pedagogy: the teaching of the mission.

This list directly links the empirical study of mission with other empirical sciences. The ten branches of the 'science of mission' is not at all a 'holy' number. It is possible to shorten this list by dealing, for instance, with statistics in the frame of sociology; and to increase it by separating criminology from law or jurisprudence.

An important question is the precise structure of the ten catalogued branches. Daubanton (1911:140) considered the history of mission as the 'first main part of the science of mission'. I can understand this view very well (because of the seniority and substantial extent of the discipline involved), but I still disagree. The linguistics of the mission is of primary importance. There is no history of mission in town A or country B if there is no primordial teaching and preaching of the gospel in the language of that town or that country. We can state that as 'in the beginning was the Word' (John 1:1), so at the beginning of mission history 'the living voice' (Lat.: *viva vox*) comes as the creative power of all missionary processes and activities.

In the second place on my list I have put the history of mission. This does not require further explanation. In the third position I put the geography of mission; because mission is not only a phenomenon 'in time' but also 'in space'. The link between the second and third branch is very old, because in 1844 Johann C. Blumhardt had already written a 'small manual on mission history and mission geography' (Ger.: *Handbüchlein der Missionsgeschichte und Missionsgeographie*). The same can be said about the link between the third and fourth branch: in 1901 Peter R. Grundemann already published a 'small geography and statistics of mission' (Ger.: *Kleine Misssions-Geographie und -Statistik*). Historically it is very clear that the statistics of mission is not developed as a part of the -much younger- sociology of mission. The first four branches, therefore, deal with the numerical growth of Christianity (and of the church) as a response to the 'Word of God' in time and space.

Also very old is the link between ethnology and cultural anthropology, on the one hand, and the empirical study of mission, on the other. Therefore this discipline can be put in the fifth place on the list. I have added to it other disciplines such as sociology, law (jurisprudence), and economics, which, in one way or another, deal with the community and society. These disciplines focus primarily upon the *social* evidences of Christianity (the Church) as a response to 'the living voice' in time and space.

The *individual* evidences of Christianity (the Church) as a response to this 'voice', however, are primarily dealt with by the psychology and pedagogics of mission. Although I acknowledge the existence of social psychology and social pedagogics, I still consider these branches as disciplines which have a basic interest in the individual, in the *psyche* and the education of the individual. This is the main reason why I have put the psychology and pedagogics of the Christian mission at the very end of my list.

Further, I emphasize that empirical mission studies are done by both missiologists and specialists in other empirical sciences such as linguists, historians, geographers, ethnologists, cultural anthropologists, sociologists, etc. In some of these fields there is (much) more cooperation and mutual assistance than in other fields. This is not only an interdisciplinary, but also an intercultural problem; because both in the empirical study of mission and in other empirical studies western dominance is still apparent. As in section 5.2., so in section 5.3. I can only refer to a very few non-western publications. It is clear that the linguistics of the mission, the history of the mission, the geography of the mission, etc. must be rewritten to make them genuinely 'post-colonial' both in essence and in purpose.

Finally, I would claim that the empirical study of mission is certainly not limited to the study of the Christian mission. This study also deals with the study of non-Christian mission and propaganda. In the following sections, however, I largely confine myself to the empirical study of the language, the history, the global expansion, etc. of the Christian mission. I cannot do it fully because I cannot ignore the incidental interdependence and interaction of the Christian mission and the non-Christian mission and propaganda in language, history, geography, etc. For instance, we must acknowledge that, on the one hand, Islam depends upon Christianity as a missionary religion and that, on the other hand, Christians in Muslim nations propagate prayers to *Allah - Allah* being the translation of *El(ohim)* in the OT and *Theos* in the NT. Therefore, in the following sections I shall not advocate a total separation of the empirical study of the Christian mission and the empirical study of the mission and propaganda of non-Christian religions and worldviews.

*WARNECK. 1892.
>   I, p. 23-28: Inhalt und Gliederung.
*DAUBANTON. 1911.
>   P. 136-223: Organizeering der zendingswetenschap.
*SCHMIDLIN. 1925.
>   P. 1-11: Begriff, Charakter, Gegenstand, und Stellung der Missionswissenschaft.
*SCHOMERUS. 1935.
>   P. 13-22: Umfang und Einteilung der Missionswissenschaft, sowie ihre Stellung
>   innerhalb der theologischen Wissenschaft und ihre Abgrenzung anderen Wissenschaften
>   gegenüber.
*SEUMOIS. 1952.
>   P. 163-371: Répartition de la missiologie.
*BAVINCK, JOHAN H. An introduction to the science of missions. Philadelphia, 1960.
>   P. XXI: The division of missionary science.
*SANTOS HERNANDEZ. 1961.
>   P. 280: Nuestra estructura.
*MULDERS. 1962.
>   P. 153-154: Indeling.
*OHM. 1962.
>   P. 60-62: Einteilung.

5.3.2. THE LINGUISTICS OF CHRISTIAN MISSION

> Between missions and philology the connection is obvious and intimate
> In order to preach in a foreign language, missionaries must study it;
> and, to be masters of it, they must continue the study while they live.
> *Thomas Laurie (1882:184-185).*

5.3.2.1. INTRODUCTION

Missions and language belong together. In many parts of the world the missionaries were the people who transformed oral cultures into cultures of the book. Ulfilas (c. 311-383), for instance, 'reduced the Gothic language to writing and translated the Bible into it. This was the first time that a language of northern Europe became a literary language' (Neill 1986:48-49).

Mission studies and *the linguistics of Christian mission*, or *missionary linguistics*, also belong together (Daubanton 1911:520-537; Schmidlin 1925: 170-172; Mulders 1950:232-242; Santos Hernandez 1961:289-290,405-468). Karl Graul (1814-1864), the director of the Leipzig Mission, is one of the founders of this empirical branch of mission studies. Olav G. Myklebust summarized Graul's concept of mission studies as follows: 'The science of missions, as conceived by Graul, embraces the following subjects: history of missions, theory of missions, history of religions (Ger.: *Geschichte des Heidenthums*), comparative religion (Ger.: *Allgemeine Mythologik*), statistics of religion, and missionary linguistics' (1955:I,101).

*DAUBANTON. 1911.
    P. 93-95: De taal waarvan de zendeling zich bedient.
    P. 520-537: De zendingswetenschap en de taalwetenschap.
*SCHMIDLIN. 1925.
    P. 170-172: Sprachkunde.
*MULDERS, ALPHONSUS J.M. Inleiding tot de missiewetenschap: tweede om- en bijgewerkte dr. Bussum, 1950.
    P. 232-242: Taalwetenschap.
*MYKLEBUST. 1955-1957.
*SANTOS HERNANDEZ. 1961.
    P. 289-290, 405-468: Las misiones y la lingüistica.
*NEILL, STEPHEN C. A history of Christian missions: rev. for the second ed. by Owen Chadwick. Harmondsworth, 1986.

5.3.2.2. HISTORY

The problem of *missionary language* (cf. Warneck 1903:III/2,49-65: *missionarische Sprache*) was already dealt with by the apostles and evangelists in the New Testament and by the Early Church (cf. Bardy 1948; Mohrmann, in: ZMR 1954:103-111). In the Middle Ages, Raymond Lull (c. 1232-1315), Roger Bacon (c. 1214-1294), et al. contributed to the reflection of the church on the use of all sorts of languages in missionary processes. Thomas Laurie (1882:187) drew our attention to the situation at the end of this period: 'The earliest contributions to the modern science of language were made mainly by Papal missionaries; and the beginnings of comparative philology rose from a comparison of translations of the Lord's prayer in the 15th century'.

In modern times, further progress has been made. At the request of American missionaries who worked among the Indians, John Pickering (1777-1846) studied their languages and published *An Essay on a Uniform Orthography for the Indian Languages of North America* (1820). This book was very influential. Both Henry Venn, *Rules for Reducing Unwritten Languages to Writing in Roman Characters* (1848), and Richard Lepsius, *Standard Alphabet for Reducing Unwritten Languages and Foreign Graphic Systems to a Uniform Orthography in European Letters* (1855; second ed. 1863), derived considerable benefit from it. Many missionaries in Asia, Africa, and Latin America used these and similar studies to put the language of their mission field on paper (grammars, dictionaries, etc.).

The conviction of Kenneth S. Latourette (1971:IV-VI) that the 19th century is 'the great century' of the Christian mission also applies to the missionary linguistics. The number of grammars and language dictionaries produced by 19th century missionaries exceeds the number of these works throughout the whole of the previous eighteen centuries. François E.

Daubanton (1911:522) quoted the following assessment of F. Max Müller, the founder of the science of religion (Ger.: *Religionswissenschaft*), on the influence of the Christian mission on linguistics in modern times: 'the full extent of our knowledge of the dialects of primal peoples we owe mainly, if not exclusively, to the missionaries' (my tr.). The birth and progress of (missionary) linguistics as an academic discipline in Europe and the USA is closely related to the large number and high quality of such linguistic studies in the various mission fields.

François E. Daubanton (1911), Joseph Schmidlin (1925), Alphonsus J.M. Mulders (1950), John Wils (Scientia missionum ancilla 1953:243-253), et al., treated linguistics as an *auxiliary science* of mission studies. I already made clear that I disagree with these scholars (cf. 5.3.1.2.). As an academic discipline, linguistics is as independent as missiology.

*LAURIE, THOMAS. The Ely volume: or, the contributions of our foreign missions to science and human well-being. Boston, 1882.
    P. 184-196: Philology.
*WARNECK. 1892-1903. 3 vols.
    III/1, p. 17-26: Die sprachliche Verschiedenartigkeit des Missionsgebiets.
    III/2, p. 49-65: Die missionarische Sprache.
*BARDY, GUSTAVE. La question des langues dans l'église ancienne. Paris, 1948.
*SCIENTIA MISSIONUM ANCILLA. 1953.
    P. 243-253: The mission and linguistics (John Wils).
*MOHRMANN, CHRISTINE. Das Sprachenproblem in der frühchristlichen Mission. In: ZMR, XXXVIII (1954), p. 103-111.
*LATOURETTE, KENNETH S. A history of the expansion of Christianity. Exeter, & Grand Rapids, 1971. 7 vols.
    IV-VI: The great century (1800-1914 AD).

5.3.2.3. THE LINGUISTICS AND PHILOLOGY OF CHRISTIAN MISSION

Several names are given to this discipline. The most important names are: *mission(ary) linguistics* (Myklebust 1955:I,101; Wils, in: Vriens 1960:114-118) and *mission(ary) philology*. The latter is used by Max Bierbaum (Scientia missionum ancilla 1953:299), who advocated a good relation between missiologists and philologists as the basis of a 'mission philological movement' (Ger.: *missionsphilologische Bewegung*). I prefer the term *linguistics of Christian mission* which is parallel to the term 'history of Christian mission'.

After Graul, other missionary liguists established themselves. On the Protestant side, Carl Meinhof (1857-1944), Kenneth L. Pike (b. 1912), and Eugene A. Nida (b. 1914) must be mentioned; and, on the Roman Catholic side, Joseph Dahlmann SJ, André Rétif SJ, and John Wils.

Olav G. Myklebust (1957:II,119,313) mentioned the name of Carl Meinhof, but did not connect his work with missionary linguistics. However, Meinhof is the scholar who, more than many others, reflected upon the study of indigenous languages. On the one hand, he researched many African languages scientifically, and, on the other hand, he devoted himself to the 'Christianisation' of African languages (1905).

Pike is well-known as a Camp Wycliffe linguist who became the president of the Summer Institute of Linguistics (SIL) (cf. Pike, & Brend 1977). David Stoll (1982) evaluated the situation in this Institute before and after the arrival of Pike. He came to the following conclusion: '... some were forced to leave owing to theological differences, divorces or other affronts to fundamentalist sensibilities. Yet under the guidance of Kenneth Pike, now SIL's president emeritus, the professionals who remained made the Summer Institute a respected name in North American and European linguistics' (:251).

Nida, the Executive Secretary of the American Bible Society, who worked with missionaries on the solution of translation problems for decades, is the most influential contemporary linguist of the Christian mission. He treats linguistics as a discipline which not only deals with the empirical problem of the formal structures of languages, but also deals with the hermeneutical questions of meaning and communication: '... the communication of the gospel by its nature requires acceptance or rejection on the basis of a people's most keenly felt values' (1960:XIII).

Dahlmann (1891) researched the history of Roman Catholic missionary linguistics in modern times, while Rétif (1953) called attention to the problem of competence in linguistics. And Wils (Scientia missionum ancilla 1953:252) suggested as the ultimate goal of missionary linguistics 'the creation of a native Christian language, i.e. of a vehicle in which the gospel can reach without impediment and in a wholly adapted way the non-European people. The eternal Word of the Father has no language. The historical church, however, cannot do without. The church belongs to all languages, and unifies them'. The last part of Wils' statement clearly transcends 'the principles of scientific empiricism' (Jung, in: Waardenburg 1973:528). Mission linguistics as an academic discipline, however, is bound to accept these principles.

*ZÖCKLER, OTTO. Missionare als Sprach- und Religionsforscher. In: AMZ, IV (1877), p. 52-61.

DAHLMANN, JOSEPH, SJ. Die Sprachkunde und die Missionen: ein Beitrag zur Charakteristik der ältern katholischen Missionsthätigkeit (1500-1800). Freiburg im Breisgau, 1891.
It. tr.: 1892.
Sp. tr.: 1893.

*WALLROTH, E. Was hat die gegenwärtige Mission für die Sprachwissenschaft geleistet? In: AMZ, XVIII (1891), p. 322-339, 387-400, 449-465, 509-526; XX (1893), p. 26-37, 74-87, 117-137, 222-240, 408-421.

MEINHOF, CARL. Die Christianisierung der Sprachen Afrikas. Basel, 1905.

GRÖSSER, MAX, PSM. Die Beziehungen der Missionswissenschaft und Missionspraxis zur Völker-, Sprachen- und Religionskunde. In: ZM, III (1913), p. 29-53.

*BIBLIOGRAFIA MISSIONARIA. 1933-... XLII (1978)- ...: 6. Pastorale missionaria (... arte linguistica...). Bibliog.

*WILS, JOHN. De missionaris en de taalwetenschap. In: HM, XXV (1946), p. 32-45.

*RÉTIF, ANDRÉ, S.J. Introduction à la doctrine pontificale des missions. Paris, 1953.
    P. 115-118: La compétence en matière linguistique.

*SCIENTIA MISSIONUM ANCILLA. 1953.
    P. 284-299: Das Verhältnis der Mission und Missiologie zu den Profanwissenschaften (Max Bierbaum).

WALLIS, ETHEL E., & MARY A. BENNETT. Two thousand tongues to go: the story of the Wycliffe Bible Translators... New York, 1959.
    *Ger. tr.: 1964.

*NIDA, EUGENE A. Message and mission: the communication of the Christian faith. New York, Evanston, & London, 1960.

*VRIENS. 1960.
    P. 114-118: Mission linguistics (John Wils). Bibliog.

*SANTOS HERNANDEZ, ANGEL, SJ. Bibliografia misional. Santander, 1965. 2 vols.
    I, p. 101-105: La lingüistica. Bibliog.

*SMALLEY, WILLIAM A. (ed.). Readings in missionary anthropology. New York, 1967.
    P. 7-9: Missionary linguistics.

*CONCISE DICTIONARY. 1971.
    P. 349-350: Linguistics (Eugene A. Nida).
    P. 667-668: Wycliffe Bible Translators, Inc. (J. Herbert Kane).

*WAARDENBURG, JACQUES. Classical approaches to the study of religion... I. The Hague, & Paris, 1973.

*PIKE, KENNETH L., & RUTH M. BREND (eds.). The Summer Institute of Linguistics: its works and contributions. The Hague, 1977.

*STOLL, DAVID. Fishers of men or founders of empire? The Wycliffe Bible Translators in Latin America. London, 1982.

*SALAMONE, FRANK A. (ed.). Missionaries and anthropologists. Williamsburg, 1983. 2 vols.
    II, p. 93-116: The Summer Institute of Linguistics/Wycliffe Bible Translators in anthropological perspective (Robert B. Taylor).

5.3.2.4. MISSIONARY LANGUAGE

Missionary linguists are primarily interested in language as such. They study both vernacular languages and the *lingua franca*. Usually they prefer the former on biblical grounds: 'Parthians, and Medes, and Elamites, etc. ... we do hear them speak *in our tongues* the wonderful works of God' (Acts 2:9-11). This preference of 'the mother tongue' (Ger.: *Muttersprache*) can, however, entail conservatism; because vernacular languages are usually more rooted in the past than the *lingua franca* which, in most cases, is firmly connected with political ideology, commercial activity, and scientific exchange.

Missionary linguists are especially interested in the creation of *missionary language*, i.e. in the 'rooting' (Richter 1906; Ger.: *Einwurzelung*), 'incarnation' (cf. Nida 1966), or 'penetration' of biblical and Christian language into local language(s). In other words: they have a particular interest in what Gustav Warneck (1903:III/3,99) called the 'Christianisation of language' (Ger.: *Sprachchristianisierung*), i.e. the Christianisation of the so-called 'pagan' languages.

Finally, missionary linguists are concerned about the impact of missionary language on societies. The 'Christianisation of language' also influences the speech of non-Christians: both in the western and in the non-western world non-Christians are, consciously or unconsciously, influenced by Christian vocabulary.

For these reasons, missionaries, and also missiologists, are engaged in 'missionary language learning' (Smalley, in: IRM 1953:82-88; idem, in: Cultural anthropology 1956:5-12). They try to overcome 'language barriers' (Nida, in: Concise Dictionary 1971:332-333), in order to be able to communicate the gospel: teaching people to read the Bible in their own language(s) and to pray to God in their own mother-tongue(s).

*ZAHN, FRANZ M. Die Muttersprache in der Mission. In: AMZ, XXVIII (1895), p. 337-360.
*WARNECK. 1892-1903. 3 vols.
    III/2, p. 49-65: Die missionarische Sprache.
*RICHTER, JULIUS (ed.). Die Einwurzelung des Christentums in der Heidenwelt: Untersuchungen über schwebende Missionsprobleme... Gütersloh, 1906.
    P. 145-161: Die Einführung des Missionars in das Volkstum der Heiden durch die Sprache (Carl Meinhof).
MEINHOF, CARL. Die sprachliche Ausbildung des Missionars, nach einem Referat für die erste Missionslehrerkonferenz am 6 und 7 Juli 1908 in Berlin. Basel, 1909.
*HEADLAND, ISAAC T. Some by-products of missions. Cincinnati, & New York, 1912.
    P. 301-311: By-products in language and literature.
FOREIGN MISSIONS CONFERENCE OF NORTH AMERICA. Language study courses for missionaries: prepared for the Conference on language study for missionaries, The Inn, Buck Hill Falls, Pa., January 7-8, 1949... N.p., (1949).
*MELZER, FRISO. Unsere Sprache im Lichte der Christus-Offenbarung: zweite, neubearbeitete Aufl. Tübingen, 1952.
    First ed.: 1946.
NIDA, EUGENE A. How the Word is made flesh: communicating the gospel to aboriginal peoples. Princeton, 1952.
*SMALLEY, WILLIAM A. A programme for missionary language learning. In: IRM, XLII (1953), p. 82-88.
?SMALLEY, WILLIAM A. Missionary language learning. In: Cultural anthropology, III (1956), p. 5-12.
LANGUAGE PREPARATION AND THE COMMUNICATION OF THE GOSPEL: third annual conference of mission board secretaries to consider the improvement of language preparation of personnel engaged in the world mission of the church, April 26-28, 1956. Hartford, 1957.
*NIDA, EUGENE A. God's word in man's language: rev. ed. New York, 1966.
    First ed.: New York, 1952.
    *Ger. tr.: 1966.

*DICTIONARY CATALOG. 1968.
IX, p. 484-489: Language and languages. Bibliog.
*CONCISE DICTIONARY. 1971.
P. 332-333: Language barriers (Eugene A. Nida).
P. 333: Language study and language schools (Eugene A. Nida).
*GENSICHEN, HANS-WERNER. Glaube für die Welt: theologische Aspekte der Mission. Gütersloh, 1971.
P. 193-199: Sprache, Gesellschaft, Kultur.
*VERSTEEG, JOHANNES P., & CORNELIS GRAAFLAND, et al. Gij die eertijds verre waart...: een overzicht van de geschiedenis en taken van de zending. Utrecht, 1978.
P. 241-265: Taal, cultuur en zending (Christiaan Fahner).
*BÜRKLE, HORST. Missionstheologie. Stuttgart, Berlin, Köln..., 1979.
P. 89-91: Sprache.
*LMG. 1987.
P. 447-449: Sprache (Ernst Dammann).

5.3.2.5. THE SCIENCE OF TRANSLATING AND INTERPRETING

In recent years, a *science of translating* (Nida 1964) has been developed which deals with both 'the theory and practice of translating' (Nida, & Taber 1974): i.e. 'the theory of translation and its application to biblical texts' (Margot 1979: *la théorie de la traduction et son application aux textes bibliques*).

This science of translating includes reflection on both the Christian terminology and the Bible translation. The science of interpreting the Bible (biblical hermeneutics) is closely connected with this new discipline.

*NIDA, EUGENE A. Learning a foreign language: a handbook prepared especially for missionaries: rev. ed. New York, 1957.
P. 58-59: Missionary language.
First ed.: New York, 1950.
MOREAU, JULES L. Language and religious language: a study in the dynamics of translation. Philadelphia, 1961.
*NIDA, EUGENE A. Toward a science of translating: with special reference to pinciples and procedures involved in Bible translating. Leiden, 1964.
*CONCISE DICTIONARY. 1971.
P. 58-59: Bible translations and versions (Harold K. Moulton).
P. 604-605: Translation work (Harold K. Moulton).
NIDA, EUGENE A., & CHARLES R. TABER. The theory and practice of translating: photomechanical reprint. Leiden, 1974.
First ed.: Leiden, 1969.
MARGOT, JEAN CLAUDE. Traduire sans trahir: la théorie de la traduction et son application aux textes bibliques. Lausanne, 1979.

CHRISTIAN TERMINOLOGY

> ... the missionary has to face the problem of
> creating a new, Christian terminology in every
> language in which the message of God
> is to be preached.
> *Stanislaus N. Wald SVD (Müller 1962:228).*

The Bible and Christian theology have their own distinct language. Such key-concepts as 'gospel', 'baptism', 'eucharist', 'Trinity', etc. are unknown in many languages. How can we translate them -and other key-words-meaningfully?

And how should we deal with the literal and metaphorical meaning of words? For instance, there are people who do not eat 'bread'. From one point of view it is then allowed to replace 'bread' by the word 'fish', or 'rice', or 'food' (class-name) in the Lord's prayer: 'Give us this day our daily fish/rice/food'. But, from the other point of view, it is not helpful to do so because we lose sight of the link between 'bread' and 'the body of Christ' when celebrating the eucharist.

The greatest problem, however, is the proper translation of the name for God (cf. WCE 1982:984-987 lists 'the names for God in 900 languages'). In China, the proper translation of the words 'God' and 'Spirit' provoked controversies among the Protestant missionaries (Williams, in: Bibliotheca sacra 1878:732-778). The whole dissertation of Hellmut H. Rosin (1956) is devoted to the problem of the proper translation of the divine names. He concluded that the Old Testament and the New Testament 'exhibit a structure which does not leave the translating of the designations of God to our opinion and arbitrary judgment, nor to our philological insight or to our missionary intuition, but which on the contrary prescribes this translation. Therefore, preceding all translation work, this structure, i.e. the way of God in the testimony of his revelation, has to be discovered' (:4). Therefore, the key question is: how can people (1) discover and (2) translate meaningfully the tetragrammaton JHWH as the proper name of God in their own or other languages?

The creation of *Christian terminology* (Bühlmann 1950; Wald, in: Müller 1962:228-275), or *Christian vocabulary* (Mohrmann, in: Scientia missionum ancilla 1953:254-262), differs from context to context: in traditional cultures missionaries were confronted with spoken words only, while in South and East Asia they were confronted with written words as well. The creation of Christian terms is partly the transformation of oral and written language, and partly a *creatio ex nihilo*. The transformation of the meaning of existing terms is as difficult as the creation of new language: it is not at all easy to transform

Indian *advaita* language and Chinese *yin-yang* language into language which has a distinctive Christian character.

WILLIAMS, SAMUEL W. The controversy among the Protestant missionaries on the proper translation of the words God and Spirit into Chinese. In: Bibliotheca sacra, XXXV (1878), p. 732-778.
*BÜHLMANN, WALBERT, OFMCap. Die christliche Terminologie als missionsmethodisches Problem, dargestellt am Swahili und an andern Bantusprachen. Schöneck-Beckenried, 1950.
*SCIENTIA MISSIONUM ANCILLA. 1953.
    P. 254-262: Le problème du vocabulaire chrétien: expériences d'évangélisation Paléo-chrétiennes et modernes (Christine Mohrmann).
*ROSIN, HELLMUT H. The Lord is God: the translation of the divine names and the missionary calling of the church. Amsterdam, 1956.
*MÜLLER, KARL, SVD (ed.). Missionsstudien. Kaldenkirchen, 1962.
    P. 228-275: Christian terminology in Hindi (Stanislaus N. Wald SVD).
*SMALLEY, WILLIAM A. (ed.). Readings in missionary anthropology. New York, 1967.
    P. 61-64: Vocabulary and the preaching of the gospel (William A. Smalley).
*WCE. 1982.
    P. 984-987: The names for God in 900 languages.

BIBLE TRANSLATION

The problem of making a good Bible translation is already evident in the New Testament. Thereafter it is demonstrated repeatedly in all six continents. Emerito P. Nacpil (1968:92) therefore treats this problem as a continuing problem: 'When the mission moved beyond Jerusalem and Judea and Samaria, its future definitely depended upon the use of Greek. This meant translating the Aramaic traditions about Jesus' teaching and ministry and interpreting Hebrew mentality into common, everyday Greek. It meant appropriating Greek words and thought-forms and using them as vehicles of communication of the Christian *kerygma*. It meant the cultural accommodation of the Christian faith. The New Testament itself stands as incontrovertible proof of the success of this task of translation, interpretation, communication, and accommodation. Today this task of the mission has become more important and also more formidable simply because a huge hermeneutic gap has developed between the Bible and Christian faith and modern, scientific, technological man. The Christian community in Asia has only recently realized that it has a tremendous task of interpretation because of the heightened cultural self-awareness of the Asian peoples...'.

The African Lamin Sanneh, the D. Willis James Professor of Missions and World Christianity, criticized the widespread tendency in the West to treat Christian missionaries as the destroyers of non-western indigenous cultures. He considered the contemporary western missions-related guilt complex as really unfounded. By translating the Bible into the vernaculars of the non-western world, missionaries both damaged the colonial rule and stimulated populism. The western missionary movement is a 'powerful translation movement'. Therefore he concludes his article by saying 'that Christian missions are better seen as a translation movement, with consequences for vernacular revitalization, religious change and social transformation, than as a vehicle for western cultural domination' (World evangelization 1993/64:15-19).

The task of *translating the Word of God* (Beekman, & Callow 1974; Kathleen Callow 1974) is, from one point of view, nearly finished -we possess Bible translations in nearly all languages of the world- but, has, from another point of view, just started -in every language the Bible translation must be continually adapted to modern speech; and also accommodated to the latest findings of Old Testament and New Testament (mission) philology.

*LAURIE, THOMAS. The Ely volume... Boston, 1882.
    P. 228-256: Bible translations.
AMERICAN BIBLE SOCIETY. A guide for translators, revisers, and editors... New York, 1932.
*NIDA, EUGENE A. Bible translating: an analysis of principles and procedures, with special reference to aboriginal languages. New York, 1947.
*KOPER, JACOB. Enkele aspecten van het vraagstuk der missionaire Bijbelvertaling, in het bijzonder in Indonesië. N.p., 1956. Diss. Utrecht.
*NACPIL, EMERITO P. Mission and change. Manila, 1968.
BEEKMAN, JOHN, & JOHN CALLOW. Translating the Word of God: with Scripture and topical indexes. Grand Rapids, 1974.
CALLOW, KATHLEEN. Discourse considerations in translating the Word of God. Grand Rapids, 1974.
*WAARD, JAN DE, & EUGENE A. NIDA. From one language to another: functional equivalence in Bible translating. Nashville, Camden, & New York, 1986.
SANNEH, LAMIN. Translating the message: the missionary impact on culture. New York, 1989.
*SANNEH, LAMIN. A powerful translation movement: confronting the western missions-related guilt complex. In: World evangelization, XVIII/64 (1993), p. 15-19.

BIBLE INTERPRETATION

> ... without a faith-response to God
> all hermeneutics remains
> an exercise in scholarly futility.
> *Stanley J. Samartha (1987:50)*

Hermeneutics is 'the science and art of *interpretation*' (Richardson, in: Richardson 1972:154). C. Timothy Carriker (Van Engen, & Gilliland 1993:45) invented the term *missiological hermeneutic*, but I prefer the term *missionary hermeneutics*.

Philosophical hermeneutics (rationalism, historism, existentialism, Marxism, et al.) has certainly had a considerable impact on both biblical hermeneutics and missionary hermeneutics: especially in the Ecumenical Movement and the Roman Catholic theology of liberation. Such Evangelicals as Arthur F. Glasser and Donald A. McGavran (1985:97-99) encountered officials of the World Council of Churches who stated that 'to appeal to what the Bible says has become out of date'; they protested against this 'hermeneutical revolt'.

Pentecostal missiologist Paul A. Pomerville (1985:14) devoted a whole chapter of his book on mission theology to the hermeneutical task because 'the hermeneutical issue is central in a discussion of contemporary mission theology. Not only do the various approaches to contemporary mission issues reflect different hermeneutical methods, but the idea of contextualizing the Christian faith in non-western cultures and ethnotheology makes its discussion imperative'. This observation leads to the conclusion that the *science* and art of interpretation' (Richardson) cannot be separated from the *theology* of interpretation'. However, I consider (missionary) hermeneutics to be primarily an empirical discipline.

Linguistics and hermeneutics are closely related; but ultimately they are basically different. The former is only concerned about terminology and text; while the latter is also concerned about interpretation. These disciplines are 'missionary' as far as they try to solve both the problems posed by specific Christian terminology and the problems of Bible translation and Bible interpretation in the context of the Christian encounter with religious or secular non-Christians (cf. Larkin 1988).

Jacob Koper (1965) dealt with several aspects of the problem of missionary Bible translations and concluded: 'Real understanding, however, can only be effected in the act of proclamation, which also includes inter-pretation of the translated Scriptures. Hence, hermeneutical questions are more important with regard to missionary Bible translations than linguistic questions' (:164-165).

*RICHARDSON, ALAN (ed.). A dictionary of Christian theology. London, 1972.
    P. 154-155: Hermeneutics (Alan Richardson).
NIDA, EUGENE A., & WILLIAM D. REYBORN. Meaning across cultures. New York, 1981.
*GLASSER, ARTHUR F., & DONALD A. McGAVRAN. Contemporary theologies of mission. Grand Rapids, 1985.
    P. 97-98: The hermeneutical revolt.
*POMERVILLE, PAUL A. The third force in missions... Peabody, 1985.
    P. 121-124: The interpretive-theological task and the Spirit.
    P. 124-127: The interpretive-theological task and a dynamic concept of revelation.
*SAMARTHA, STANLEY J. The search for new hermeneutics in Asian Christian theology. Bangalore, 1987.
*BALZ, HEINRICH. Hermeneutik und Mission. In: ZM, XIV (1988), p. 206-220.
LARKIN, WILLIAM J. Culture and biblical hermeneutics: interpreting and applying the authoritative word in a relativistic age. Grand Rapids, 1988.

*BOSCH. 1991.
    P. 430: Hermeneutic of suspicion.
*ENGEN, CHARLES VAN, DEAN S. GILLILAND, et al. (eds.). The good news of the kingdom:
    mission theology for the third millennium. New York, 1993.
    P. 30-32: The hermeneutical circle of Liberation theology: critical hermeneutics
    through mission paradigms (Charles van Engen).
    P. 45-55: Missiological hermeneutic and Pauline apocalyptic eschatology (C. Timothy
    Carriker).

5.3.2.6. THE LINGUISTICS OF CHRISTIAN MISSION AND THE LINGUISTICS OF RELIGION

The problem of missionary language cannot be separated from the problem of *religious language* (Richardson, in: Richardson 1972:188-189). So the linguistics of Christan mission cannot be separated from the *the study of (Christian and non-Christian) religious language*, i.e. the linguistics of religion.

Christian language is influenced by non-Christian religious language and vice versa. However, Christian language is also influenced by secularism nowadays. The American theologian Paul van Buren wrote a famous book, *The Secular Meaning of the Gospel* (1963), in which he made a stand against religious language. His book can be considered as a missionary book to the extent that it uses secular language as a vehicle of confronting secular people with the Christian message. Therefore, missionary language and religious language do not always fit easily together. The linguistics of Christian mission has its links with the science of 'religious language', but also with 'secular' linguistics.

*GREGORY VON BREDA OFMCap. Die Muttersprache: eine missions- und religionswissenschaftliche
    Studie über die Sprachenfrage in den Missionsgebieten. Münster in Westfalen, &
    's Hertogenbosch, 1933.
*RICHTER, JULIUS. Das Buch der deutschen Weltmission. Gotha, 1935.
    P.152-157: Sprachforschung und Mission (Otto Dempwolff).
*RICHARDSON, ALAN (ed.). A dictionary of Christian theology. London, 1972.
    P. 188-189: Religious language (Alan Richardson).

5.3.2.7. CONCLUSION

Missionary theologians, missionaries, and missiologists have contributed substantially to the birth and growth of linguistics as an academic discipline. They have produced many grammars and dictionaries, especially in the 19th and the 20th centuries.

They are also responsible for Christianizing non-western languages. They created a Christian terminology, translated and published the Bible (in many cultures the first printed book!) and other Christian books, interpreted the message of the Bible to non-Christians, and are still doing so. Their ultimate goal is to functionalize the living 'Word of God' among people in all six continents.

The linguistics and hermeneutics of Christian mission reflect upon the interaction between the Christian mission and linguistics/hermeneutics. The study of missionary language which is closely related to the task of interpretating the biblical message to non-Christians (biblical hermeneutics, missionary hermeneutics) began in the 19th century (Graul, et al.) and has become a mature discipline in the 20th century (Nida, et al.). This study will never come to an end because the task of creating a Christian vocabulary and of translating and interpreting the Bible is an ongoing process in every culture and subculture: for the well-being of both religious and secular people.

5.3.3. THE HISTORY OF CHRISTIAN MISSION

> To ignore the history of missions leaves
> a defect in the best education...
> *Louise M. Hodgkins (1902:XI).*

5.3.3.1. INTRODUCTION

The 'history of Christian mission(s)' (Lat.: *historia missionum*) is the oldest branch of empirical mission studies.

Scholars have ascribed several names to this very broad discipline. Here I mention the following names: *history of the propagation of Christianity* (Millar 1731; et al.), *history of mission(s)* (Bock 1743: *Missionsgeschichte*; et al.), *history of the expansion of Christianity* (Volkmann 1823: *geschichtliche Übersicht der Ausbreitung des Christenthums*), *history of the expansion of Christ's kingdom on earth* (Gützlaff c. 1828: *geschiedenis der uitbreiding van Christus koninkrijk op aarde*), *history of the conversion of the heathen* (Brauer 1835-1839, 1841: *Geschichte der Heidenbekehrung*), *history of the apostolate* (Dally 1846: *histoire de l'apostolat*), *history of the planting and propagation of the gospel* (Schmidt 1857: *Geschichte der Pflanzung und Verbreitung des Evangeliums*), *history of humane progress under Christianity* (Brace 1900), *missionary history* (Goyau 1928-1936: *histoire missionnaire*; Warren 1945; Seumois 1952:278-313; et al.), *comparative history of missions* (Descamps 1932: *histoire comparée des missions*), *historical missiology* (Charles 1938:215-414: *missiologie historique*), *history of evangelism* (Scharpff 1966), etc. I prefer the term used by James A. Huie (1842), Stephen C. Neill (1986), et al.: *the history of Christian missions*, but *mission* in the singular.

This academic discipline uses the historical method which also is used in general history, the history of religions, and church history. The difference between this academic discipline and the other just-mentioned disciplines is not the method, but the object of research. Both general historians, historians of the world religions, church historians, and missiologists contribute to the progress of 'the history of Christian mission', i.e. 'the history of the subject and object of mission' (cf. Wiggers 1845-1846), including 'the history of the missionary societies' (Smith 1824-1825; De Groot 1830) and 'the history of missionary enterprise' (Pierson 1891-1901; World Missionary Conference 1910: Lecture memoranda). Some scholars, though not many, devote their whole life to the study of this field. In 1860 the General Missionary Conference held in Liverpool declared that a 'Professorship of missionary history and duties at the Universities and Colleges' (Myklebust 1955:I,133) was not necessary. However, today there are several chairs of 'missionary history'. For instance, at Utrecht University the chair of 'missiology' belongs to the Faculty of Theology, Department of Church History.

Most histories of the Christian mission have been produced in the West. They are usually written by western missionaries and missiologists. For instance, Karl F.A. Gützlaff (c. 1828) wrote his 'history of the expansion of Christ's kingdom on earth' in Dutch before he went to China; and John Foster (1961, 1963) and Stephen C. Neill (1986) published their histories of the Christian mission when they returned from their work as missionaries in China and India respectively. Alphonsus J.M. Mulders (1957), however, described this field as a missiologist who had never served abroad. A few handbooks on the history of the Christian mission have, however, been published in Asia and Latin America: e.g. Francisco J. Montalbán SJ (Shanghai 1935), Hermes Vieira (Sao Paulo 1938), Arie de Kuiper (Djakarta 1968:50-66), and Justo L. González (Buenos Aires 1970). Especially this last book is very important because it deals with the history of the Christian mission from the so-called 'third world' perspective.

There are many bibliographies of the history of the Christian mission which catalogue the relevant handbooks and monographs (cf. the following bibliography). Here, I can only refer to the *general* histories of the Christian mission. I omit all those historical studies which only deal with a *specific* period, a *specific* region or country, a *specific* denomination or church, a *specific* missionary order or society, and a *specific* missionary or missionary theologian. Therefore, the following titles occur in many bibliographies of mission history, but are not included in the bibliography of this study:

1. Adolf von Harnack, *The Mission and Expansion of Christianity in the First Three Centuries* (London 1904-1905; first Ger. ed.: 1902; second Ger. ed.: Leipzig 1906);
2. Kenneth S. Latourette, *A History of Christian Missions in China* (London 1929);
3. Gustav L. Plitt, *Geschichte der Lutherischen Mission...*; neu hrsg. und bis auf die Gegenwart fortgeführt von Otto Hardeland (Leipzig 1894-1895; first ed.: Erlangen 1871);
4. Arnold H. Rowbotham, *Missionary and Mandarin; the Jesuits at the Court of China* (Berkeley 1942); and
5. Theodor Bechler, *August Gottlieb Spangenberg und die Mission* (Herrnhut 1933).

Some specific titles, however, are mentioned in chapter 3.4.2.3.-3.4.2.5. and some exceptions are made in this section as well: the most important ones are the inclusion of the Roman Catholic and Protestant mission histories, general world surveys in the 19th and 20th centuries, general histories of missionary orders and societies, and collective missionary biographies.

Most missiological encyclopedias and journals publish articles on the history of the Christian mission among other items; but a few are devoted entirely to the study of this field. Here I refer to one journal and one encyclopaedia of this kind: *Revue d'Histoire des Missions; Éditée par 'les Amis des Missions'* (abbrev.: RHM), (Paris 1924-1938), and the forthcoming *Biographical Dictionary of Christian Missions* (abbrev.: BDCM) (ed.: Gerald H. Anderson).

*BLISS, EDWIN M. (ed.). The encyclopaedia of missions... New York, London, & Toronto, 1891.
    I, p. 637-647: Histories of missions (handbooks, cyclopaedias and gazetteers, manuals, Tract and Bible Societies, denominational and special missions). Bibliog.
*WARNECK. 1892-1903. 3 vols.
    I, p. 15-19: Allgemeine Missionsgeschichte.
    I, p. 272-290: Die geschichtliche Begründung.
*STRÜMPFEL, EMIL (ed.). Wegweiser durch die wissenschaftliche und pastorale Missions-litteratur... Berlin, 1898.
    P. 17-75: Missionsgeschichte. Bibliog.
HODGKINS, LOUISE M. Via Christi: an introduction to the study of missions. New York, 1902.
STRÜMPFEL, EMIL (ed.). Neuer Wegweiser durch die deutsche Missionsliteratur... Berlin, 1908.
    P. 23-68: Missionsgeschichte. Bibliog.
*DAUBANTON. 1911.
    P. 140-199: De zendingsgeschiedenis.
    P. 302-334: Zendingsgeschiedenis.
*STREIT, ROBERT, OMI. Führer durch die deutsche katholische Missionsliteratur. Freiburg im Breisgau, 1911.
    P. 9-98: Missionsgeschichte. Bibliog.

*LATOURETTE, KENNETH S. The study of the history of missions. In: IRM, XIV (1925), p. 108-115.

*SCHMIDLIN. 1925.
P. 53-95: Missionsgeschichte.

*STREIT, ROBERT, OMI. Die katholische Missionsliteratur... Aachen, & Immensee, 1925.
P. 30-40: Missionsgeschichte. Bibliog.

*BIBLIOGRAFIA MISSIONARIA. 1933-... I (1933)-...: 4. Storia generale delle missioni. Bibliog.

*SCHOMERUS. 1935.
P. 150-200: Missionsgeschichte.

CHARLES, PIERRE, SJ. Les dossiers de l'action missionnaire... I. Louvain, & Bruxelles, 1938.
P. 215-414: Missiologie historique.

*SEUMOIS. 1952.
P. 278-313: Partie historique: histoire missionnaire.

*HOLSTEN. 1953.
P. 61-67, 116-120: Missionsgeschichte.

*MYKLEBUST. 1955-1957. 2 vols.

*BAVINCK, JOHAN H. An introduction to the science of missions. Philadelphia, 1960.
P. 273-309: The history of missions.

*VRIENS. 1960.
P. 86-88: Mission history. Bibliog.

*ANDERSON. 1961.
P. 319-322: Historical studies. Bibliog.

*MULDERS. 1962.
P. 360-412: Missiegeschiedenis.

*SANTOS HERNANDEZ, ANGEL, SJ. Bibliografia misional. Santander, 1965. 2 vols.
II, p. 9-1203: Historia de las misiones. Bibliog.

*ANDERSON, GERALD H. (comp.). Bibliography of the theology of missions in the twentieth century: third ed., rev. and enl. New York, 1966.
P. 17-32: Historical studies. Bibliog.

*DICTIONARY CATALOG. 1968.
XI, p. 94-115: Missions-history. Bibliog.
XI, p. 172: Missions and history. Bibliog.
XI, p. 188: Missionsgeschichte. Bibliog.

*CUMING, GEOFFREY J. (ed.). The mission of the church and the propagation of the faith. Cambridge, 1970.
P. 149-170: The history of missions: an academic discipline (Stephen C. Neill).

*FROHNES, HEINZGÜNTER, HANS-WERNER GENSICHEN, & GEORG KRETSCHMAR (eds.). Kirchengeschichte als Missionsgeschichte. München, 1974.
I, p. LXXV-XC: Bibliographie zur Missionsgeschichte (Heinzgünter Frohnes). Bibliog.

*KRAUS, JOHANN, SVD. Missionswissenschaftliche Themen in Festschriften aus den Jahren 1960-1971. Immensee, 1974.
P. 29-44: Missionsgeschichte. Bibliog.

*BÜRKLE, HORST. Missionstheologie. Stuttgart, Berlin, Köln..., 1979.
P. 197-199: Die Geschichte der Mission und der Missionsidee. Bibliog.

5.3.3.2. HISTORY

In modern times, the history of the Christian mission has been described again and again. Already in the 16th, 17th, and 18th centuries Roman Catholic scholars published mission histories. Here I refer to the publications of Arnoldus Mermannius (1572), Alonso Fernandez OP (1611), Cornelius Hazart SJ (1667-1671), Urbano Cerri (1715), et al. The titles of these and similar studies are mentioned in *Bibliotheca missionum* (1916:I,862 under 'Allgemeine Missionsgeschichte').

François E. Daubanton was one of the first scholars to describe the history of doing historical studies of mission thoroughly. He started his survey with a reference to Arnoldus Mermannius (1572), on the Roman Catholic side, and a reference to Robert Millar (1723; second ed.: 1731) and Johann A. Fabricius (1731), on the Protestant side. He compared the studies of Millar (d. 1752) and Fabricius (1688-1731) and concluded that the former did indeed collect much material, but did not really master it because of a lack of method; while the latter is very important because he does mention his sources (1911:303).

In the 19th and 20th centuries, dozens of histories of the Christian mission have been published. Such studies can not only be divided into general and specific histories (cf. 5.3.3.1.) but also into (1) scientific and popular histories; (2) descriptive and normative histories; (3) denominational (or: ecclesiastical) and non-denominational histories; and (4) comprehensive and categorical histories. Since 1800 the history of doing historical studies of mission has been characterized by a continously increasing specialization. Therefore, I allow myself the use of the just- mentioned divisions as means of describing progress in this field after the studies of Millar and Fabricius.

Histories of Christian mission are either *scientific*, i.e. critical and empirical, or *popular*, i.e. furthering the interest of Christian mission on the home front. As examples of a scientific approach to the history of the Christian mission, I can refer to the studies of Joseph Schmidlin (1933) and Alphonsus J.M. Mulders (1957), on the Roman Catholic side, and the studies of Gustav Warneck (1902; tenth Ger. ed.: 1913) and Heinzgünter Frohnes, Hans-Werner Gensichen, & Georg Kretschmar (1974-1978), on the Protestant side. However, the study of Kenneth S. Latourette (1937-1945; reprint: 1971) can be considered to be the best scientific work in this field. Stephen C. Neill (1986:479) described his scholarly work as follows: 'Latourette handles temperately, charitably, and with immense erudition every part of Christian expansion - Roman Catholic, Protestant, and Orthodox. It is baffling to his successors that, when we think we have made some specially bright discovery of our own, we nearly always find that he has been there before us'. The main criticism of the seven volumes of Latourette's great work is the lack of an introductory chapter: he tells us nothing about the purpose, the method, the structure, and the general sources of his study. The number of scientific histories of the Christian mission is obviously larger than the afore-mentioned five studies; but the number of popular histories of the Christian mission is much larger. Here, I only refer to some popular works: the books of G. van den Berg (1887) and J.M. Wansink (1930) were written for primary schools; whilst the study of Hendrik A. Wiersinga (1959) was intended to provide secondary schools, youth organizations, and adults with information on the progress of Christian mission. Several popular histories are explicitly devotional; others only implicitly.

Further, histories of Christian mission are either *descriptive* or *normative*. Generally, we can state that scientific histories of mission are descriptive whilst popular histories are normative: but there are exceptions. If we analyse the scientific histories of Christian mission carefully, we can also find normative presuppositions. These are either rooted in worldviews or in Christianity: i.e. in the Christian theology and/or in the church (denomination). Joseph Schmidlin (1925:89) referred to the influence of Romanticism on Roman Catholic mission histories. In the Protestant mission histories, however, we can also find romantic tendencies: especially when describing the lives of missionaries. For instance, the Protestant Waldemar Augustiny (1962) did not make merely empirical sketches of the lives of the missionaries. Other very influential worldviews are colonialism and sexism: the role of non-western missionaries and evangelists as well as the role of women is repeatedly overlooked in mission histories. Theological influences are manifest in several works. Nicolas Poulain (1867), for example, sees God at work in the history of the Christian mission; whilst David Jenks (1926:5) offers 'a study of the way in which God speaks through history. *Voluntas Dei in factis revelata historia'*. Kenneth S. Latourette (1971) and Stephen C. Neill (1986) clearly exude confidence in the future of Christianity which can be compared with the theological optimism of previous missiologists who called attention to the following items:

1. *Progress* of the gospel, of missionary societies, of Christ's kingdom, and of (world-wide) missions (Pearson 1808; Smith 1838-1839; Aikman 1862; Croil 1883; Leonard 1913; Glover 1960);
2. *(Great) success(es)* of the various missionaries, of the gospel, and of Protestant/Christian missions (Smith 1824-1825; Historical collections 1854; Carroll 1883; Smith, & Choules 1884; Young 1890);
3. *Triumph(s)* of modern missions, of the church, and of the cross (Young 1884; Lasne 1891; Beets 1914); and
4. *Victory* of the gospel (Lilley 1910).

We also can find normative presuppositions in those Roman Catholic and Protestant histories of mission which are written from an ecclesiastical or denominational perspective (cf. 5.3.3.5.-5.3.3.6.).

Third, the histories of Christian mission are either *denominational* or *non-denominational* (cf. Bliss 1891:I,637-647: denominational missions). In conformity with chapter 3.4.2.3., the histories of the Christian mission can be divided into the following categories: Hebrew Christian, Eastern Orthodox, Roman Catholic, Protestant (Lutheran, Reformed, Anglican, Methodist, etc.), Ecumenical, Evangelical, and Pentecostal/Charismatic. However, here I only make a distinction between Roman Catholic and Protestant histories of mission (cf. 5.3.3.5. and 5.3.3.6.); because these are substantial categories in both the 19th and 20th centuries. Roman Catholic mission histories are usually denominational, while some Protestant mission histories are denominational and others are not. I have catalogued many non-denominational studies in the general category (cf. 5.3.3.4.). Some non-denominational studies emphasize 'Christianity' rather than 'the church' (cf. Latourette 1971), while others focus upon the Kingdom of God, the Kingdom of Christ, the conversion of the heathen, and human progress under Christianity (cf. 5.3.3.10.). There are also some denominational studies which focus on one or two of these items.

Finally, histories of Christian mission are either *comprehensive* or *categorical*. Comprehensive histories of the Christian mission do not limit the object of their mission studies, while categorical histories are engaged in special research. Here I mention as important examples of categorial histories of mission the histories of missionary orders and societies (cf. 5.3.3.7.) as well as missionary biographies (cf. 5.3.3.8.). However, other categorical histories of Christian mission must be mentioned as well. I have already referred to several studies which deal with the history of the philosophy of mission (cf. 3.2.), the history of the science of mission (cf. 3.3.), and the history of the theology of mission -including the history of (world) missionary conferences- (cf. 3.4.), and next I shall examine the history of the involvement of both the laity and women in the missionary enterprise (cf. 5.4.5.6.). A very special study is the monograph on 'the history of mission on stamps' (Anheuser 1962: *Missions-geschichte auf Briefmarken*). Surveys of world-wide mission (cf. 5.3.3.9.) are usually comprehensive.

I deal with the problem of chronology before I go into the problem posed by the general histories of mission (5.3.3.4.), and Roman Catholic and Protestant histories of mission (5.3.3.5.-5.3.3.6.), etc.

STREIT, ROBERT, OMI. Die Missionsgeschichte in ihrer gegenwärtigen Lage und der Plan einer Missions-Bibliographie... Freiburg im Breisgau, 1910.
*BIBLIOTHECA MISSIONUM. I-XXX. 1916-1974.
?SEMANAS ESPAÑOLAS DE MISIONOLOGIA DE BURGOS. Historia de la misiones y actualidad misionera. 1951.

*HISTORY'S LESSONS FOR TOMORROW'S MISSION; milestones in the history of missionary thinking. In: The student world, LIII (1960), p. 1-300.

*HARR, WILBER C. (ed.). Frontiers of the Christian world mission since 1938: essays in honor of Kenneth S. Latourette. New York, & London, 1962.

P. 171-188: The Christian mission since 1938: methods and techniques (Calvin H. Reber Jr).

P. 189-230: Faith missions since 1938 (Harold Linsell).

P. 231-280: Kenneth Scott Latourette: historian and friend (E. Theodore Bachmann).

*CONCISE DICTIONARY. 1971.

P. 252-253: History of missions (eds.).

*USTORF, WERNER. Missionsgeschichte als theologisches Problem. In: ZM, IX (1983), p. 19-29.

5.3.3.3. CHRONOLOGY

Johannes Dindinger OMI introduced the term *chronologia missionaria* (Seumois 1952:311). This term points to the science of listing or tabulating missionary events with their corresponding dates. Some histories of the Christian mission have an appended chart, table, or list containing the most important dates (e.g.: Pearson 1808: Ostertag 1858; Descombaz 1860; WCE 1982:21-32), but others (Ohm 1961; cf. Barrett 1987) only offer such a list. This last group of mission studies (which is very small) is another clear example of categorical histories of mission (cf. 5.3.3.2.).

Related to the problem of chronology is the problem of *the epochs of mission history* which cannot be identified with the problem of 'epochs of church history' or 'epochs of world history'. There is a great variety of opinions on establishing 'periods of mission' (Warneck 1892:I,277: *Missionsperioden*). In the 19th century other proposals were made than in the 20th century: which experienced both the advent of world missionary conferences (from Edinburgh 1910 to San Antonio and Manila 1989) and the shift from colonialism to post-colonialism. Here, I refer to three useful schemes for the division of the history of the Christian mission into epochs.

First, I call attention to the survey of Robert H. Glover (1924/25):

1. Rise and development
   1.1. Period of apostolic missions: from the ascension of Christ to the death of John (33-100)
   1.2. Period of the early church missions: from the death of John to Constantine (100-313)
   1.3. Period of early European missions: from Constantine to Charlemagne (313-800)
   1.4. Period of the Middle Ages: from Charlemagne to Luther (800-1517)

1.5. Period of the Reformation: from Luther to the Halle missionaries (1517-1650)
1.6. Period of the early missionary societies: from the Halle missionaries to Carey (1650-1792)
2. World-wide extension
  2.1. Period of modern missions: from Carey to the present day (1792-...).

Here, as well as in the historical studies of Lemuel C. Barnes (1906), Delavan L. Leonard (1913), George Smith (1913), and Victor R. Edman (1949), William Carey (1761-1834) is treated as the most important turning-point in mission history.

In his seven volumes on the 'history of the expansion of Christianity' (1937-1945; reprint: 1971), Kenneth S. Latourette divided the history of the Christian mission as follows:

1. The first five centuries (1-500) - volume 1
2. The thousand years of uncertainty (500-1500) - volume 2
3. Three centuries of advance (1500-1800) - volume 3
4. The great century (1800-1914) - volumes 4-6
5. Advance through storm (1914-...) - volume 7.

However, Latourette modified this division in his William Beldon Noble Lectures in Harvard University of 1940 (1948):

1. The initial stage (1-500)
2. The first and greatest recession (500-950)
3. The second great age of advance (950-1350)
4. The second major recession (1350-1500)
5. The third great age of advance (1500-1750)
6. The third major recession (1750-1815)
7. The fourth great age of advance (1815-1914)
8. The latest age (1914 to the present).

Whereas I can appreciate greatly the introduction of the idea of 'recession' into this scheme, I cannot approve the assumption that a period of advance will automatically be followed by a period of recession. William Carey (1792) actually becomes a victim of such schematic thinking: whereas Latourette puts him in a period of major recession, Glover places him at the beginning of 'modern missions' and 'world-wide extension'. In this case, I agree with Glover as well as with the earlier periodization in Latourette's original seven-volumes history (1937-1945).

My own periodization of the Christian mission, together with its related chronology, is as follows:

1. Period of mission by Jewish Christians (first century)
2. Period of mission by Jewish and western and non-western *goiim* Christians in a minority position: from the first century to the conversion of king Abgar in Edessa (c. 200), king Tiridates of Armenia (c. 285), emperor Constantine of Rome (315), king Clovis of France (496), etc.
3. Period of mission by non-western *goiim* Christians in a minority position (Nestorians, Monophysites); and by western *goiim* Christians in a majority position: from the establishment of the *corpus christianum* in Armenia, the Roman Empire, Europe, and the USA to the ending of the *corpus christianum* by the philosophy of the Enlightenment (17th-18th centuries), French Revolution (1789), Russian Revolution (1917), etc.
    3.1. Limitation of the *corpus christianum* by the rise and progress of Islam (7th century)
    3.2. Expansion of the *corpus christianum* during the period of western colonialism (Columbus 1492; Vasco da Gama 1498)
    3.3. Division in the *corpus christianum* following the rise of Protestantism (Luther 1517)
    3.4. Reorganization of Roman Catholic involvement in the *corpus christianum* by the establishment of the *Sacra congregatio de propaganda fide* (1622)
4. Period of mission by Jewish Christians and western and non-western *goiim* Christians in a global post-majority situation: from the ending of the *corpus christianum* to the present
    4.1. Reorganization of the western Protestant missionary movement by missionary societies (1792ff.) and world missionary conferences (1910ff.), emancipation of the non-western Protestant missions (New Delhi 1961), and advent of the so-called 'third world' missions (especially in Evangelical and Pentecostal/ Charismatic circles)
    4.2. Renewal of the Roman Catholic mission by the Second Vatican Council (1962-1965) and the Conferences of Asian, African, and Latin American bishops.

The main differences between the periodizations of Glover and Latourette, on the one hand, and my own, on the other, are: (1) the recognition of the Hebrew Christians as the subject of mission (cf. 3.4.2.3.); (2) the recognition of the difference between mission from a minority position (no political power) and mission from a majority position (confusion of throne and altar); and (3) the recognition of the difference between western and non-western mission

(Christian mission never was and never can be the sole prerogative of white western Christians).

*OHM, THOMAS, OSB. Wichtige Daten der Missionsgeschichte: eine Zeittafel: zweite, erw. und
    verb. Aufl. Münster in Westfalen, 1961.
    *First ed.: Münster in Westfalen, 1955.
    *Fr. tr.: 1961.
*WCE. 1982.
    P. 21-32: Chronology: a chronology of world evangelization, AD 27-1983.
BARRETT, DAVID B. Cosmos, chaos, and gospel: a chronology of world evangelization from
    creation to new creation. Birmingham, 1987.

5.3.3.4. THE HISTORY OF CHRISTIAN MISSION (GENERAL)

A 'general history of mission' (Ger.: *Allgemeine Missionsgeschichte*; cf. Blumhardt 1828-1837; Warneck 1892:I,15-19) deals with the history of the Christian mission from the beginning to the present day. It includes all denominations and all types of missionary work. However, a history of missions which limits itself to the description and analysis of one or two centuries can also be regarded as 'general'. In the bibliography of this section, I have catalogued books which belong to both groups: as well as books which do not belong to the specific items in chapter 5.3.3.5.-5.3.3.10.

In the 19th and 20th centuries, many good introductions to and handbooks of both the general history of Christian mission and the special histories of Roman Catholic and Protestant mission have been published: Johann C. Blumhardt (1846), William Brown (1864), Gustav E. Burkhardt (1876-1881), Just J.E. Roy (1880), Thomas Smith, & John O. Choules (1884), Schwarzkopf, & A. Petri (1887), Rufus Anderson (1889), John A. Graham (1899), Thomas W. Marshall (1901), Gustav Warneck (1902), Hermann Gundert (1903), W. Pakenham Walsh (1903), Henry W. Tucker (1904), Anthony Grant (1910), George Smith (1913), Henry Ussing (1924), William O. Carver (1928), Jakob E. Lundahl (1939), and Martin Schlunk (1951) wrote mission histories which were widely used for two or more decades. However, nearly all those studies which were published before the Second World War are now out of date. Today, we need a thorough evaluation of all the histories of the Christian mission which were written in the colonial period, parallel to the evalution of all the 'lives of Jesus' produced in the 19th century and at the beginning of the 20th century made by Albert Schweitzer in his famous study *The Quest of the Historical Jesus*, 1954 (*Geschichte der Leben-Jesu-Forschung*, vierte Aufl., Tübingen 1926).

The studies which still are useful date from the period after the Second World War and the onset of decolonization. The study of Stephen C. Neill (1964; rev. by Chadwick: 1986), who worked in India, is the best general

230

English survey we have at the moment. The best continental introduction is the study of Knut B. Westmann, & Harald von Sicard (1962). The ambitious history of mission by Heinzgünter Frohnes, Hans-Werner Gensichen, & Georg Kretschmar (1974-1978) is unfinished. The older study of Hans-Werner Gensichen (1976; first ed.: 1961) is best treated as an unplanned supplement to their unfinished study.

A modern comprehensive history of the Christian mission must draw the readers' attention to the contribution of both men and women, and western and non-western people, to the Christian mission. Therefore, the studies of Neill, of Westmann, & von Sicard, et al. must be supplemented by reading the following categorical works: Justo L. Gonzalez (1970), who wrote a modern mission history from the perspective of the so-called 'third world' (we still need an English translation of this book); and: Ruth A. Tucker, & Walter L. Liefeld (1987), who described the role of western and non-western women in the modern history of the Christian mission.

These studies of Neill, of Gonzalez, of Frohnes, Gensichen, & Kretschmar, of Gensichen, and of Tucker, & Liefeld also have an ecumenical perspective, while the studies of J. Herbert Kane (1982, 1983) are evangelical in outlook. In the last chapter of his concise history of Christian mission, 'Missions in prospect', Kane (1983:181) concludes: '... there is no cause for dismay. We are living in exciting times and our best days are ahead'.

*FABRICIUS, JOHANN A. Salutaris lux evangelii toti orbi per divinam gratiam exoriens, sive notitia historicochronologica literaria et geographica propagatorum per orbem totum Christianorum sacrorum... Hamburg, 1731.
MILLAR, ROBERT. The history of the propagation of Christianity, and the overthrow of paganism: wherein the Christian religion is confirmed: the rise and progress of heathenish idolatry is considered: the overthrow of paganism, and the spreading of Christianity in the several ages of the Church is explained: the present state of heathens is inquired: and methods for their conversion proposed: the third ed. corrected, with additions. London, 1731. 2 vols.
First ed.: Edinburgh, 1723.
*Dutch tr.: 1764. 2 vols.
BOCK, FRIEDRICH S. Kurzgefasste Missionsgeschichte, oder merkwürdige Nachrichten von den in neuern Zeiten angewandten Bemühungen die Heyden zum christlichen Glauben zu bekehren... Königsberg, 1743.
*SCHETS der middelen, waar aan het christendom deszelfs uitbreiding over den aardbodem te danken heeft: meerendeels naar het Hoogduitsch van Ludwig T. Spittler. Delft, 1801.
*PEARSON, HUGH N. A dissertation on the propagation of Christianity in Asia: in two parts: to which is prefixed, a brief historic view of the progress of the gospel in different nations since its first promulgation: illustrated by a chronological chart. Oxford, 1808.
WINSLOW, MIRON. A sketch of missions: or, history of the principal attempts to propagate Christianity among the heathen... Andover, 1819.
LEONHARDT, KARL G. Die gesegnete Ausbreitung des Christenthums unter Heyden, Muhammedanern und Juden in der neusten Zeit zur Beförderung des Missionswerks in einer kurzen

Übersicht dargestellt... Dresden, 1820.

(VOLKMANN, J.W.). Geschichtliche Uebersicht der Ausbreitung des Christenthums: mit besonderer Rücksicht auf das Missionswesen. Leipzig, 1823.

*BLUMHARDT, CHRISTIAN G. Versuch einer allgemeinen Missionsgeschichte der Kirche Christi. Basel, 1828-1837. 3 vols. (in 5 parts).

ZSCHOKKE, HEINRICH. Darstellung gegenwärtiger Ausbreitung des Christentums auf dem Erdball: ein geschichtlicher Umriss. In: (ausgewählte) Historische Schriften: zweite verb. Aufl. Aarau, 1830, V, p. 3-315.

    First ed.: Aarau, 1819.

    *Dutch tr.: 1823.

NOEL, BAPTIST W. Christian missions to the heathen nations. London, 1842.

HINKEL, KARL A.F. Die Bekehrung der Welt zu Jesus Christus und das christliche Missionswerk: ein Beitrag zur Apostolik und Apologetik des Christenthums, nach den Worten der Heiligen Schrift und den Zeugnissen der Reichsgeschichte. Berlin, 1843-1845. 3 vols.

CLARKE, ADAM. Christian missions: including an account of the introduction of the gospel into the British isles... London, 1844.

GESCHICHTE DER AUSBREITUNG DES CHRISTENTHUMS UNTER DEN HEIDEN. Colberg, 1844.

BLUMHARDT, JOHANN C. Christian missions: or, a manual of missionary geography and history. London, 1846. 2 vols.

    *Ger. ed.: Handbuch der Missionsgeschichte und Missionsgeographie: dritte, ganz neue Ausgabe. Calw, & Stuttgart, 1863. 2 vols.

    First Ger. ed.: Handbüchlein der Missionsgeschichte und Missionsgeographie... Calw, & Stuttgart, 1844.

    Fr. tr.: 1850. 2 vols. Cf. Descombaz. 1860. 2 vols.

    *Dutch tr.: 1851.

BURNS, JABEZ. Missionary enterprises in many lands: with a brief account of the rise and progress of missions...: third ed. London, 1854.

    First ed.: London, 1845.

HISTORICAL COLLECTIONS, relating to remarkable periods of success of the gospel. Glasgow, 1854.

*KINGSMILL, JOSEPH. Missions and missionaries: apostolic, Jesuit, and Protestant Christian: second ed. London, 1854.

    First ed.: London, 1853.

*REITSMA, ANNE T. Geschiedkundig overzigt van de vestiging en uitbreiding des christendoms op aarde. Groningen, 1856.

*HOFFMANN, F. (ed.). Missionsgeschichten. Potsdam, 1857-1861. 6 vols.

SCHMIDT, KARL C.G. Der Sieg des Christenthums: Geschichte der Pflanzung und Verbreitung des Evangeliums durch die Missionen: dritte verm. und verb. Aufl. Leipzig, 1857.

    First ed.: 1845.

    Dutch tr.: 1846.

AIKMAN, J. LOGAN. Christ's kingdom in progress: or, Christian missions, their rise, progress and present situation. London, 1862.

GUÉNOT, CHARLES. Les conquêtes du christianisme en Asie, en Afrique, en Amérique et en Océanie. Lille, 1866.

?KITTAN, GUST. Th. Missionsgeschichte: nebst einem Anhange enthaltend Versikel und Collekten zum Gebrauch bei Missionsstunden und Missionsfesten. Leipzig, 1866.

HASSELL, JOSEPH. From pole to pole: being the history of Christian missions in all countries of the world: new ed., greatly enl. London, 1872.

    *First ed.: London, 1866.

WALROND, FRANCIS P. Christian missions before the Reformation. London, 1877.
>   First ed.: London, 1873.
*KALKAR, CHRISTIAN A.H. Geschichte der christlichen Mission unter den Heiden... Gütersloh,
>   1879-1880. 2 vols.
>   First ed.: Den christelige mission blandt hedningerne. Kjobenhavn, 1879. 2 vols.
*LAURIE, THOMAS. The Ely volume... Boston, 1882.
>   P. 317-371: Contributions of history.
BAINBRIDGE, WILLIAM F. Self-giving: a story of Christian missions. Boston, 1883.
YOUNG, ROBERT. Modern missions: their trials and triumphs: third ed., rev. and enl. New
>   York, 1884.
>   First ed.: London, 1881.
>   *Second ed.: London, 1883.
*PIERSON, ARTHUR T. The crisis of missions: or, the voice of the cloud. London, 1886.
>   *Dutch tr.: n.d.
*BERG, G. VAN DEN. Personen en feiten uit de geschiedenis der zending: een leesboek,
>   hoofdzakelijk voor de Christelijke School. Zeist, 1887. 2 vols.
?(SCHWARZKOPF, & A. PETRI). Christliche Missionsgeschichte. Berlin, 1887. 3 vols.
>   First ed.: Missionsgeschichte in Heften. Berlin, 1867-1882. 12 vols.
*JOHNSTON, JAMES. A century of Christian progress and its lessons. London, 1888.
*TIEMERSMA, LIEUWE. De geschiedenis der zending. Nijmegen, 1888; Leiden, 1892; Ermelo,
>   1894. 3 vols.
ANDERSON, RUFUS. Foreign missions: their relations and claims. New York, 1889.
>   First ed.: New York, 1869.
TODD, ELBERT S. Christian missions in the nineteenth century. New York, & Cincinnati, 1890.
YOUNG, ROBERT. The success of Christian missions: testimonies to their beneficent results.
>   London, 1890.
*HANDBOEKJE VAN DE GESCHIEDENIS DER ZENDING: derde dr. Rotterdam, 1891.
>   First ed.: Rotterdam, 1879.
PIERSON, ARTHUR T. The miracles of missions: or, the modern marvels in the history of
>   missionary enterprise. New York, 1891-1901. 4 vols.
HODDER, EDWIN (ed.). Conquests of the Cross: a record of missionary work throughout the
>   world. London, 1893. 2 vols.
>   *First ed.: London, Paris, & Melbourne, 1890. 3 vols.
LOVETT, RICHARD. A primer of modern British missions, with references to American missions.
>   London, 1896.
BLISS, EDWIN M. A concise history of missions. New York, & Chicago, 1897.
LANG, JOHN M. The expansion of the Christian life. Edinburgh, & London, 1897.
*RICHTER, JULIUS. Vom grossen Missionsfelde: Erzählungen und Schilderungen aus der neueren
>   Missionsgeschichte. Gütersloh, 1900.
PIERSON, ARTHUR T. The new acts of the apostles: or, the marvels of modern missions: a
>   series of lectures. London, 1901.
>   First ed.: New York, 1894.
SPEER, ROBERT E. Missions and modern history: a study of the missionary aspects of some
>   great movements of the nineteenth century. New York, Chicago..., 1904. 2 vols.
TUCKER, HENRY W. Under his banner: papers on the missionary work of modern times...: eighth
>   ed.: with an appendix... London, 1904.
>   First ed.: London, 1872.
*STOSCH, J.E. GEORG. Der innere Gang der Missionsgeschichte in Grundlinien gezeichnet.
>   Gütersloh, 1905.
BARNES, LEMUEL C. Two tousand years of missions before Carey: based upon and embodying many

of the earliest extant accounts... Chicago, 1906.
First ed.: Chicago, 1900.
IHRMARK, A., & A. KARLGREN. Bilder ur missionshistorien jämte missionshistoriska öfversikter. Lund, 1907.
*BLISS, EDWIN M. The missionary enterprise: a concise history of its objects, methods, and extension. New York, Chicago, Toronto..., 1908.
VEDDER, HENRY C. Christian epoch-makers: the story of the great missionary eras in the history of Christianity. Philadelphia, New York..., 1908.
SMITH, HANS. Gaa ud i al verden! Kortfattet oversigt over missiones historie. Kristiana, 1909.
*WORLD MISSIONARY CONFERENCE. A brief history of missionary enterprise in ancient and modern times: lecture memoranda... Edinburgh, 1910. London, New York, Montreal..., 1910.
REED, EDWARD T. A world book of foreign missions: what they are, what they prove, how to help. London, 1911.
*SZABO, ALADAR. Külmisszioi kalauz: a kereszténység elterjedése a világon. Budapest, 1911.
*CREIGHTON, LOUISE. Missions: their rise and development. London, 1912.
*CARUS-WILSON, ASHLEY. The expansion of Christendom: a study in religious history; new and rev. ed. London, New York, & Toronto, 1913.
First ed.: London, 1910.
*SMITH, GEORGE. Short history of Christian missions from Abraham and Paul to Carey, Livingstone, and Duff. Edinburgh, 1913.
*First ed.: Edinburgh, 1884.
*BEETS, HENRY. Triumfen van het Kruis: schetsen der christelijke zending van alle eeuwen en allerlei landen. Kampen, 1914.
First ed.: 1909.
MOORE, EDWARD C. West and East: the expansion of Christendom and the naturalization of Christianity in the Orient in the XIXth century: being the Dale lectures, Oxford, 1913. London, 1920.
HUTCHINSON, PAUL. The spread of Christianity. New York, & Cincinnati, 1922.
MOORE, EDWARD C. The spread of Christianity in the modern world. Chicago, 1922.
*First ed.: Chicago, 1919.
HEILMANN, KARL. Die äussere Mission: ihre Geschichte und ihr gegenwärtiger Stand... 7. Aufl. Gütersloh, 1925.
*Fünfte und sechste Aufl.: Gütersloh, 1912.
*JENKS, DAVID. A study of world evangelisation. London, 1926.
*WHITE, EDWIN E. The story of missions: new and rev. ed. New York, 1926.
First ed.: New York, 1925.
CARVER, WILLIAM O. A syllabus of lectures on the outlines of the history of Christian missions: fifth rev. ed. Louisville, 1928.
First ed.: Louisville, 1909.
MASON, ALFRED DE WITT. Outlines of missionary history: rev. ed., with map. New York, 1929.
First ed.: New York, 1912.
MONTGOMERY, HELEN (BARRETT). From Jerusalem to Jerusalem. North Cambridge, 1929.
PÉTITE HISTOIRE DES MISSIONS CHRÉTIENNES: par un laïque. Paris, 1929.
First ed.: Paris, 1923.
*NOMES, J. Leerboekje der kerk- en zendingsgeschiedenis. Amsterdam, 1930.
ROBINSON, CHARLES H. History of Christian missions. New York, 1930.
*First ed.: Edinburgh, 1915.

*WANSINK, J.M. Kerk- en zendingsgeschiedenis voor de Lagere school. 's-Gravenhage, 1930. 2 vols.

*NORTIER, CARL W. Het christendom van West naar Oost: schetsen van kerk- en zendings-geschiedenis. I. Bandoeng, 1931.

PFEIFFER, EDWARD. Mission studies: historical survey and outlines of missionary principles and practice. Columbus, 1931.

USSING, HENRY. En lille missionshistorie for Born: 3 udg. Kobenhavn, 1931.
First ed.: Kobenhavn, 1908.
*Fr. tr.: 1912.

*SCHERMERHORN, WILLIAM D. The Christian mission in the modern world. New York, Cincinnati, & Chicago, 1933.

*BIRKELI, EMIL. Misjonshistorie: kristendommens utbredelse. Oslo, 1935-1937. 2 vols.

ROUSE, RUTH. God has a purpose: an outline of the history of missions and of missionary method. London, 1935.

CARVER, WILLIAM O. The course of Christian missions: a history and an interpretation: rev. ed. New York, Chicago..., 1939.
*First ed.: New York, Chicago, & London, 1932.

LANGE, POUL H. Morke og lys, i missionens historie. Kobenhavn, 1939.
Nor. tr.: 1946.

LUNDAHL, JAKOB E. Världmissionen: kortfatted översikt av missionens utveckling och nutidsläge jämte en framställning av de icke kristna folkens religioner. Stockholm, 1939.
First ed.: 1921.

HARDY, EDWARD R., Jr. Militant in earth: twenty centuries of the spread of Christianity. New York, London..., 1940.

*ABERLY, JOHN. An outline of missions. Philadelphia, 1945.

*WARREN, MAX A.C. The calling of God: four essays in missionary history; second impression. London, & Redhill, 1945.
First ed.: 1944.

*PHILLIPS, GODFREY E. The transmission of the faith. London, & Redhill, 1946.

MAHLSTROM, ALEX. Evangeliet til alverden. Copenhagen, 1947-1950. 3 vols.

*BAVINCK, JOHAN H. Zending in een wereld in nood: vierde uitgebreide dr. Wageningen, 1948.
P. 74-135: Kort overzicht der zendingsgeschiedenis.

*LATOURETTE, KENNETH S. The unquenchable light. London, 1948.

NIELSEN, ERIK W. Linier i missionens historie. Kobenhavn, 1948.

EDMAN, VICTOR R. The light in dark ages: eighteen centuries of missions from the giving of the Great Commission to the beginning of modern missions under William Carey. Wheaton, 1949.

AULEN, GERTRUD. Kristendomens vag till folken: missionshistoria: 4 uppl., delvis omarb. och pa alla punkter ford fram till nutiden. Stockholm, 1951.
First ed.: 1919.

?JUST, MARY. Immortal fire: a journey through the centuries with the great missionary. St. Louis, 1951.

SCHLUNK, MARTIN. Die Weltmission der Kirche Christi: ein Gang durch neunzehn Jahrhunderte: neue Ausgabe... Stuttgart, 1951.
*First ed.: Die Weltmission des Christentums: ein Gang durch neunzehn Jahrhunderte. Hamburg, 1925.

*ASCH VAN WIJCK, C.M. VAN. Gods werk gaat door: het grote hoofdstuk in de kerkgeschiedenis der laatste anderhalve eeuw. Amsterdam, 1952.

*SCHRUPP, ERNST. Blicke in die Weltmission. Wuppertal, 1953.

*PAYNE, ERNEST A. The growth of the world church: the story of the modern missionary movement. London, 1955.
   *New and rev. ed. of: The church awakes: the story of the modern missionary movement. London, 1942.
*LATOURETTE, KENNETH S. Christianity in a revolutionary age: a history of Christianity in the nineteenth and twentieth centuries. New York, 1958-1962. 5 vols.
*WIERSINGA, HENDRIK A. Geschiedenis van de zending. Kampen, 1959.
*GLOVER, ROBERT H. The progress of world-wide missions: rev. and enl. by J. Herbert Kane. New York, 1960.
   *First ed.: New York, & London, 1924-1925.
MATHEWS, BASIL J. Forward through the ages: with an epilogue by Kenneth S. Latourette...: new. ed. New York, 1960.
   *First ed.: Disciples of all nations: the story of Christian expansion. London, New York, & Toronto, 1952.
FOSTER, JOHN. To all nations: Christian expansion from 1700 to today. New York, 1961.
   *First ed.: London, 1960.
*ANHEUSER, P. CLEMENS, OFM. Missionsgeschichte auf Briefmarken: 383 Briefmarken auf 27 Tafeln. Münster in Westfalen, 1962.
*WESTMANN, KNUT B., & HARALD VON SICARD. Geschichte der christlichen Mission. München, 1962.
   First ed.: Den Kristna missionens historia. Stockholm, 1960.
FOSTER, JOHN. Beginning from Jerusalem: Christian expansion through seventeen centuries: rev. ed. London, 1963.
   *First ed.: London, 1956.
   Ger. tr.: 1958.
   Continuation: To all nations. 1961.
GORRÉE, GEORGES, & GERMAN CHAUVEL. L'église et sa mission... Paris, 1963.
*SUNDKLER, BENGT G.M. The world of mission. London, 1965.
   First ed.: Missionens värld: missionskunskap och missionshistoria. Stockholm, 1963.
*SCHARPFF, PAULUS. History of evangelism... Grand Rapids, 1966.
*COOK, HAROLD R. Highlights of Christian missions: a history and survey. Chicago, 1967.
*SYRDAL, ROLF A. To the end of the earth: mission concept in principle and practice. Minneapolis, 1967.
*KUIPER, ARIE DE. Missiologia (ilmu pekabaran indjil). Djakarta, 1968.
   P. 50-66: Penindjauan sedjarah PI.
*GONZALEZ, JUSTO L. Historia de las misiones. Buenos Aires, 1970.
*LATOURETTE, KENNETH S. A history of the expansion of Christianity. Exeter, 1971. 7 vols.
   First ed.: London, 1937-1945.
   *Ger. tr. (shortened version): 1956.
*FROHNES, HEINZGÜNTER, HANS-WERNER GENSICHEN, & GEORG KRETSCHMAR (eds.). Kirchengeschichte als Missionsgeschichte. München, 1974-1978. 2 vols.
   I: Die alte Kirche.
   II/1: Die Kirche des früheren Mittelalters.
   I, p. IX-LXXIV: Missionsgeschichte und Kirchengeschichte (Heinzgünter Frohnes).
*GENSICHEN, HANS-WERNER. Missionsgeschichte der neueren Zeit: dritte, verb. und ergänzte Aufl. Göttingen, 1976.
   First ed.: Göttingen, 1961.
*CAPELLE, M.C. Kruisgang van het Woord. Goes, 1977.
*ROSENKRANZ, GERHARD. Die christliche Mission: Geschichte und Theologie. München, 1977.
*WARREN, MAX A.C. I believe in the Great Commission. Grand Rapids, 1979.

P. 57-127: The church in history spells it out.

*First ed.: London, Sydney, Auckland..., 1976.

*KANE, J. HERBERT. A global view of Christian missions: from Pentecost to the present: rev. ed. Grand Rapids, 1982.

First ed.: Grand Rapids, 1971.

*KANE, J. HERBERT. A concise history of the Christian world mission: a panoramic view of missions from Pentecost to the present: rev. ed. Grand Rapids, 1983.

First ed.: Grand Rapids, 1978.

*MOSER, BRUNO (ed.). Gehet hin in alle Welt: Ereignisse und Gestalten christlicher Missionsgeschichte. München, 1984.

*NEILL, STEPHEN C. A history of Christian missions: rev. for the second ed. by Owen Chadwick. London, 1986.

First ed.: London, 1964. Several reprints.

*Ger. tr.: 1974.

*TUCKER, RUTH A., & WALTER L. LIEFELD. Daughters of the church: women and ministry from New Testament times to the present. Grand Rapids, 1987.

P. 291-327: Foreign missions.

P. 329-358: The non-western church.

*COMBY, JEAN. Deux milles ans d'évangélisation: histoire de l'expansion chrétienne. Tournai, & Paris, 1992.

5.3.3.5. THE HISTORY OF ROMAN CATHOLIC MISSION

Roman Catholic histories of mission date from the 16th to the 18th centuries (cf. 5.3.3.2.). This historical tradition was revived in the 19th and 20th centuries. Some of these publications give a detailed survey of the history of the *Congregatio de propaganda fide* which also is described in various monographies (Metzler 1971-1976; cf. the Protestant Mejer 1852-1853).

Many Roman Catholic histories of mission are based on the theological principle of *extra ecclesiam nulla salus est*: i.e. there is no salvation outside the (Roman Catholic) church. Most 19th century Roman Catholic mission histories are silent about or even hostile to Protestant missions. The worst example in this field is the study of Thomas W. Marshall who was himself converted from Protestantism to Roman Catholicism (1862; sixth ed.: 1901). Both Henry Venn (1862) and Gustav Warneck (1884-1885; 1888-1889) felt obliged to defend Protestant missions against his onslaughts. Joseph Schmidlin (1925:90-91) protested against the criticisms of Warneck. He also considered the Protestant mission histories of Johann H. Brauer (1835-1839, 1841), of Karl C.G. Schmidt (1857), of Gustav Leonhardi (1870-1873), and of H. Kypke (1875) as mission histories which are 'full of hateful attacks on the Catholic missions' (:91: *voll gehässiger Angriffe gegen den katholischen Missionen*; my tr.). The Ecumenical Movement, on the Protestant side, and the Second Vatican Council, on the Roman Catholic side, put an end to such hostilities.

The studies of Simon Delacroix (1956-1959) and of Alphonsus J.M. Mulders (1957) are still useful. Stephen C. Neill (1986:479-480) commented

on them as follows: 'Next to Latourette in range and thoroughness is the
four-volume composite work, edited by Mgr. S. Delacroix... The classic work
of J. Schmidlin (Eng. tr. 1933) has now been superseded by A. Mulders
(1957) which is balanced, factual, and notably accurate'. However, they date
from the period before the Second Vatican Council. At the present moment,
the study of Justo L. Gonzalez (1970) which was published a few years later is
the best Roman Catholic handbook in this field.

MAMACHI, THOMAS M., OP. Origines et antiquitates Christianae: ed. altera... Roma,
1841-1851. 6 vols.
    First ed.: Originum et antiquitatum christianarum libri XX. Roma, 1749-1755.
5 vols.
*WITTMANN, PATRICIUS. Die Herrlichkeit der Kirche in ihren Missionen seit der
Glaubensspaltung: eine allgemeine Geschichte der katholischen Missionen in den
letzten drei Jahrhunderten. Augsburg, 1841. 2 vols.
    It. tr.: 1842-1843. 2 vols.
HENRION, MATHIEU R.A. Histoire générale des missions catholiques depuis le XIIIe siècle
jusqu'à nos jours. Paris, 1844-1847. 4 parts in 2 vols.
    It. tr.: 1845-1846. 2 vols.
    Sp. tr.: 1845. Other Sp. trs.: 1848, 1856, 1863.
    Ger. tr.: 1846-1850. 2 vols. Other Ger. tr.: 1847-1852.
DALLY, NICOLAS. Histoire de l'apostolat: voyages des missionnaires catholiques dans toutes
les contrées du monde considerés au double point de vue de l'histoire de l'église
et de celle de la civilisation... Paris, 1846.
DIE MISSIONEN DER KATHOLISCHEN KIRCHE von der Entdeckung Amerika's bis auf unsere Tage.
Bonn, 1846.
WITTMANN, PATRICIUS. Allgemeine Geschichte der katholischen Missionen vom dreizehnten
Jahrhundert bis auf die neueste Zeit: mit besonderer Rücksicht auf Baron Henrion...
Augsburg, 1846-1850. 2 vols.
    Cf. Henrion. 1844-1847.
KARL VOM HEILIGEN ALOYS, CD. Die katholische Kirche in ihrer gegenwärtigen Ausbreitung auf
der Erde: oder, historische und statistische Nachrichten...: zweite, mit einem
Anhang verm. Ausgabe. Regensburg, 1847.
    First ed.: Regensburg, 1845.
*MEJER, OTTO. Die Propaganda: ihre Provinzen und ihr Recht... Göttingen, 1852-1853. 2 vols.
CHOWANETZ, JOSEPH (=CHOWNITZ, JULIAN F.J.). Die Missionen der katholischen Kirche: ihr
Begriff, ihr Wesen, ihre Geschichte und gegenwärtige Lage, ihre Behörden,
Institute, Vereine und ihre heutige Statistik: nebst einer Schilderung des Lebens
und Wirkens, der Leiden und Freuden in unseren neuesten Missionen, auch einem
bunten Anhang aus der Haupt- und Kehrseite des gesammten Missionswesens: nach
authenthischen Quellen, Berichten und den neuesten Briefen der katholischen
Missionäre. Neisse, 1855.
*HAHN, HEINRICH. Geschichte der katholischen Missionen seit Jesus Christus bis auf die
neueste Zeit: für die Mitglieder der katholischen Missions-Vereine und alle Freunde
der Missionen. Köln, 1857-1863. 5 vols.
PETRI, GIROLAMO. L'orbe cattolico ossia atlante geografico, storico, ecclesiastico...,
Roma, 1858-1859. 3 vols.
EINSIEDEL, JOHANNES. Spaziergänge durch Christen-, Türken- und Heidenwelt, vornämlich in

Sachen der Religion und Mission, Civilisation, Aufklärung, und mannigfaltiger Zeitgeisterei... Schaffhausen, 1860.

KÜLB, PHILIPP H. Die Reisen der Missionäre: ein Buch zur Belehrung und Unterhaltung. Regensburg, 1860-1863. 2 parts.

ARMOIRY, N. Histoire des missions célèbres dans tous les pays. Paris, 1862.

VENN, HENRY. The missionary life and labours of Francis Xavier, taken from his own correspondence: with a sketch of the general results of Roman Catholic missions among the heathen. London, 1862.
  *Rev. and enl. Ger. ed.: Venn, Henry, & Wilhelm Hoffmann. Franz Xavier: ein weltgeschichtliches Missionsbild. Wiesbaden, 1869.

*KALKAR, CHRISTIAN A.H. Geschichte der Römisch-katholischen Mission... Erlangen, 1867.
  First ed.: Den katolske missions historie. Kjobenhavn, 1862.

RIOU, ADOLPHE (pseud. le Père ANDRÉ). Les bons livres: histoires édifiantes: le christianisme jusqu'à nos jours: Europe, Asie, Afrique, Amérique, Océanie. Paris, 1869.

FOURCHEUX DE MONTROD, CLEMENT M.J.M. Les missions catholiques dans toutes les parties du monde. Lille, 1876.

?KATHOLISCHES MISSIONSBÜCHLEIN... Regensburg, 1877.

ROY, JUST J.E. Histoire abrégée des missions catholiques dans les diverses parties du monde dépuis la fin de XVe siècle jusqu'à nos jours. Tours, 1880.
  First ed.: Tours, 1855.

*WARNECK, GUSTAV. Protestantische Beleuchtung der Römischen Angriffe auf die evangelische Heidenmission: ein Beitrag zur Charakteristik ultramontaner Geschichtschreibung. Gütersloh, 1884-1885. 2 vols.

*WARNECK, GUSTAV. Der gegenwärtige Romanismus im Lichte seiner Heidenmission: I. Die Römische Feindschaft wider die evangelische Kirche; II. Das Römische Christentum; III. Die Römische Geschichtschreibung. Halle, 1888-1889.

LASNE, J. Le triomphe de l'église sur le protestantisme et dans les missions catholiques au XVIe siècle. Lille, 1891.

KLIMSCH, ROBERT. Merkwürdiges aus den Heidenländern: oder die Gnade Gottes unter den fernen Völkerschaften der Erde: gesammelt und zusammengestellt nach Briefen und Beschreibungen der Missionäre. Klagenfurt, 1896.

LOUVET, LOUIS-EUGÈNE. Les missions catholiques au XIXe siècle. Lille, 1898.
  First ed.: Lyon, 1896.

MARSHALL, THOMAS W. Christian missions: their agents, and their results: sixth ed. New York, 1901. 2 vols.
  First ed.: London, 1862. 3 vols. Several reprints.
  *Ger. tr.: 1863. 3 vols. Second Ger. tr.: 1863. 3 vols.
  Fr. tr.: 1865. 2 vols.
  It. tr.: 1868. 3 vols. Reprint: 1897.

BAUMGARTEN, PAUL M., & HEINRICH SWOBODA. Die katholische Kirche auf dem Erdenrund: Darstellung der Kirchenverfassung und kirchlichen Einrichtungen in allen fünf Erdteilen: in Verbindung mit zahlreichen Fachgenossen... München, 1907.
  First ed.: Das Wirken der katholischen Kirche auf dem Erdenrund, unter besonderer Berücksichtigung der Heidenmissionen. München, 1902.

SCHWAGER, FRIEDRICH, SVD. Die katholische Heidenmission der Gegenwart im Zusammenhang mit ihrer grossen Vergangenheit dargestellt. Steyl, 1907-1909. 4 vols.

GIERINGER, PAUL A. An outline history of Christian missions: a mission investigation. Cincinnati, 1925.

*SCHMIDLIN, JOSEPH. Die katholischen Missionen von der Völkerwanderung bis zur Gegenwart.

Berlin, & Leipzig, 1925.

HENDERSON, ALEXANDER, & ERNEST PARRY. A historical survey of Christian missions from the first to the end of the sixteenth centuries. London, 1927.

GOYAU, GEORGES. L'église en marche: études d'histoire missionnaire. Paris, 1928-1936. 5 vols.

LINDEBERG, GUSTAV W. Katolicismen i ljuset av dess missionsverksamhet. Lund, 1928.

DESCAMPS, BARON ÉDOUARD E.F. (ed.). Histoire générale comparée des missions... Paris, Bruxelles, & Louvain, 1932.

GOYAU, GEORGES. Missions and missionaries. London, 1932.
    First ed.: Missions et missionnaires. Paris, 1931.

SCHMIDLIN, JOSEPH. Catholic mission history. Techny, 1933.
    *First ed.: Katholische Missionsgeschichte. Steyl, 1924-1925.
    It. tr.: 1927-1929. 3 vols.

VIAN, CESCO. Le missioni cattoliche. Milano, 1933. 2 vols.

GOYAU, GEORGES. A la conquête du monde païen. Tours, 1934.

CENNI, ALFONSO, OSB. Le missioni cattoliche. Alba, Roma, & Messina, 1935.

MONTALBAN, FRANCISCO J., SJ. Manuale historiae missionum. Shanghai, 1935.
    Sp. ed.: 1938. Reprint: 1952.

OLICHON, ARMAND. Les missions: histoire de l'expansion du catholicisme dans le monde. Paris, 1936.

LESOURD, PAUL. Histoire des missions catholiques. Paris, 1937.

VIEIRA, HERMES. Historia das missoes. Sao Paulo, 1938.

ROSCHINI, GABRIELE M., OSM. Le missioni cattoliche... Torino, & Roma, 1939.

FREITAG, ANTON, SVD, & H. AHAUS SJ. Het Godsrijk, idee en plannen: verwezenlijking en planting, uitwerking en tegenwoordige toestand, christenplicht en medewerking. Steyl, 1940.
    First ed.: Steyl, 1932.

*(SACRA CONGREGATIO DE PROPAGANDA FIDE). Le missioni cattoliche...: storia, geografia, statistica. Roma, 1950.

ROCHE, ALOYSIUS. In the track of the gospel: an outline of the Christian apostolate from Pentecost to the present. New York, 1953.
    Fr. tr.: 1957.

*DELACROIX, SIMON (ed.). Histoire universelle des missions catholiques d'après la conception originale de J.L. Françoisprimo... Paris, 1956-1959. 4 vols.

MILLOT, RENÉ P. L'epopée missionnaire: aventures et missions au service de Dieu, de saint Paul à Grégoire XV... Paris, 1956.
    Ger. tr.: 1959.

ALZIN, JOSSE. La grande aventure des missions: 20.000 ambassadeurs de paix. Namur, 1957.

JUST, MARY. Digest of catholic mission history. New York, 1957.

*MULDERS, ALPHONSUS J.M. Missiegeschiedenis. Bussum, 1957.
    *Ger. tr.: 1960.

CONSTANTINI, CELSO. Die katholischen Missionen: kurze Missionsgeschichte: mit einem ergänzenden Kapitel über die Lage der Weltmission beim Beginn der neuen Missionsåra. Kaldenkirchen, 1960.
    It. ed.: Le missioni cattoliche. 1949.

VAULX, BERNARD DE. History of the missions. New York, 1961.
    First ed.: Les missions: leur histoire des origines à Benoit XV (1914). Paris, 1960.
    Ger. tr.: 1962.
    Also Sp. and It. trs.

240

CANOVESI, ANGELO. La diffusione geografica del Christianesimo: diario di vita missionaria della Chiesa. Torino, 1962.
?METZLER, JOSEF, OMI (ed). Sacrae Congregationis de Propaganda Fide memoria rerum: 350 Jahre im Dienste der Weltmission, 1622-1922. Rom, 1971-1976. 3 vols.

5.3.3.6. THE HISTORY OF PROTESTANT MISSION

Protestant histories of mission go back to the 18th century (Fabricius 1731; Millar 1731 [1723]). After the founding of Protestant missionary societies (1792ff.), such studies began to appear again. Here I refer to the works of Gustav Warneck (1882; 10th ed.: 1913; Eng. tr.: 1884/1902) and Julius Richter (1906-1932) as the 'classics'. True, Stephen C. Neill (1986:259) quoted Warneck in his own work but in his bibliography he only refered to Richter: 'Richter was a tremendous toiler, and much of his work is still of value' (:480).

In Germany, the Protestant mission histories of Warneck and Richter were followed by thorough studies of Carl Mirbt (1917), Heinrich Frick (1922), Horst R. Flachsmeier (1963), et al. In the Anglo-Saxon world, Kenneth S. Latourette (1971), Stephen C. Neill (1986), et al. came to the fore: they dealt with the history of Protestant mission in the framework of general mission history (cf. 5.3.3.4.).

Finally, I refer to the evaluation of the history of Protestant mission by Calvin H. Reber Jr, who wrote: 'During the 19th and 20th centuries, Protestant missions have been the primary concern of a part of the church. In Europe the separate structures of the missionary societies gave evidene of that. In America most mission boards were denominationally organized, but the whole church has never fully accepted missionary responsibility' (Harr 1962:177-178).

LORD, ELEAZAR (ed.). Compendious history of the principal Protestant missions to the heathen: selected and compiled from the best authorities. Boston, 1813. 2 vols.
?KNAPP, GEORG C. Abriss einer allgemeinen protestantischen Missionsgeschichte... In: Neuere Geschichte der evangelischen Missions-Anstalten zur Bekehrung der Heiden in Ostindien, Halle, LXVI (1816), p. 539-558.
*GÜTZLAFF, KARL F.A. Geschiedenis der uitbreiding van Christus koninkrijk op aarde, sedert de dagen der Kerkhervorming tot op den tegenwoordigen tijd: inzonderheid met betrekking tot de zendelingen en zendeling-genootschappen... Rotterdam, c. 1828. 2 vols.
*BRAUER, JOHANN H. Beiträge zur Geschichte der Heidenbekehrung. Altona, 1835-1839; Hamburg, 1841. 4 vols.
HUIE, JAMES A. History of Christian missions, from the Reformation to the present time: second ed. Edinburgh, 1842.
*WIGGERS, JULIUS. Geschichte der evangelischen Mission. Hamburg, & Gotha, 1845-1846. 2 vols.

*THE MISSIONARY GUIDE-BOOK: or, a key to the Protestant missionary map of the world: shewing the geography, natural history, climate, population, and government of the several countries to which missionary efforts have been directed: with the moral, social, and religious condition of their inhabitants: also, the rise and progress of missionary operations in each country: illustrated by forty-five wood-cuts, representing the costume of each people. London, 1846.

*BRAUER, JOHANN H. Das Missionswesen der evangelischen Kirche in seinem Bestande: Versuch einer Missions-Statistik. Hamburg, 1847-1851. 2 vols.

*HOFFMANN, WILHELM. Missions-Stunden: zweiunddreissig Vorträge über das evangelische Missionswerk...: zweiter unveränderter Abdruck. Stuttgart, 1848.
First ed.: Stuttgart, 1847.
*Neue Sammlung: Stuttgart, 1851.
Danish tr.: 1848-1849. 3 vols.
*Dutch tr.: 1851-1857. 2 parts in 1 vol.

*WALLMANN, JOHANN C. Die Missionen der evangelischen Kirche: ein Volksbuch: zweite veränderte Aufl. Quedlinburg, 1848.
First ed.: Quedlinburg, 1843.
*Dutch tr.: 1846. First Dutch ed.: 1844.

*LOWRIE, JOHN C. A manual of missions: or, sketches of the foreign missions of the Presbyterian church: with maps, showing the stations, and statistics of Protestant missions among unevangelized nations. New York, 1854.
Second ed.: New York, 1855.

*DE ZENDELINGSWEDUWE of geschiedenis en overzigt van het werk der evangelische zending op de geheele aarde, voor het opkomend geslacht: vrij bewerkt naar het Engelsch en met eene voorrede van Theodorus M. Looman. Amsterdam, 1856.

KALKAR, CHRISTIAN A.H. Den evangeliske missionshistorie. Kjobenhavn, 1857.

STEGER, BENEDICT St. Die evangelische Mission unter Heiden und Juden in ihrem gesegneten Wirken übersichtlich zusammengestellt: neue Ausgabe. Halle, 1857. 3 parts in 1 vol.
*Second ed.: Die protestantischen Missionen und deren gesegnetes Wirken: für alle, welche sich über die segensreiche Ausbreitung des Christenthums unter den Heiden durch die protestantischen Missionen belehren wollen...: zweite neu durchgesehene, theilweise verm. Aufl. Hof, & Wunsiedel, 1844-1851.
First ed.: Hof, & Wunsiedel, 1838-1843. Neue Folge: Hof, & Wunsiedel, 1843.

*OSTERTAG, ALBERT. Uebersichtliche Geschichte der protestantischen Missionen von der Reformation bis zur Gegenwart. Stuttgart, 1858.
*Dutch tr.: 1860.
*Second Dutch tr.: 1860.
Fr. tr.: 1860.

LEONHARDI, GUSTAV (ed.). Nacht und Morgen: Erzählungen aus der christlichen Missionsgeschichte: zweite Aufl. Leipzig, 1859-1860. 2 vols.
First ed.: Leipzig, 1849-1850. 2 vols.
*Dutch tr.: 1860. Danish tr.: 1862.

*DESCOMBAZ, SAMUEL. Histoire des missions évangéliques: deuxième éd. considérablement augmentée jusqu'à nos jours: avec carte. Paris, 1860. 2 vols.
First ed.: 1850. Cf. Blumhardt. 1846.

BROWN, WILLIAM. The history of the Christian missions of the 16th, 17th, 18th, and 19th centuries...: to which is added a list of the translations of the Holy Scriptures into the languages of heathen and Mohammedan nations...: third ed., greatly enl. and improved. London, 1864. 3 vols.
First ed.: The history of the propagation of Christianity among the heathen since

the Reformation... Edinburgh, & London, 1814. 2 vols.

*Second ed.: 1854.

*POULAIN, NICOLAS. L'oeuvre des missions évangéliques au point de vue de la divinité du christianisme. Genève, 1867.

Dutch tr.: 1868.

*Second Dutch ed.: 1882.

*LEONHARDI, GUSTAV (ed.). Die Missionsgeschichte der alten/christlichen Kirche in Cultur- und Lebensbildern aus dem Heidenthum und Christenthum: zweite völlig umgearbeitete Aufl. Leipzig, 1870-1873. 2 vols.

First ed.: Nacht und Morgen. II/1-2. Leipzig, 1860.

LANDGREN, LARS. Oefwersigt af de Protestantiska missionernes uppkomst och närwarande tillstand. Hudikswall, 1871-1872. 2 vols.

KYPKE, H. Missionsgeschichte für das christliche Volk. Berlin, 1875.

Danish tr.: 1890.

*BURKHARDT, GUSTAV E. Kleine Missions-Bibliothek, oder Land und Leute, Arbeiter und Arbeiten, Kämpfe und Siege auf dem Gebiete der evangelischen Heidenmission: zweite Aufl., gänzlich umgearbeitet und bis auf die Gegenwart fortgeführt von Peter R. Grundemann. Bielefeld, & Leipzig, 1876-1881. 4 vols. and Register.

*First ed.: Bielefeld, 1858-1861. 4 vols. Ergänzungsband: Bielefeld, & Leipzig, 1868.

Fr. tr.: 1884-1887. 4 vols.

Cf. Peter R. Grundemann. 1890.

CROIL, JAMES. The missionary problem: containing a history of Protestant missions in some of the principal fields of missionary enterprise, together with a historical and statistical account of the rise and progress of missionary societies in the 19th century: with map. Toronto, 1883.

SMITH, THOMAS, & JOHN O. CHOULES. The origin and history of missions: a record of the voyages, travels, labors, and successes of the various missionaries, who have been sent forth by Protestant societies and churches... compiled from authentic documents: forming a complete missionary repository... Boston, 1884. 2 vols.

First ed.: Boston, 1833.

Cf. 5.3.3.7.: Smith. 1824-1825. 2 vols.

ROBSON, JOHN. Outlines of Protestant missions. Edinburgh, 1885.

JOHNSTON, JAMES. A century of Protestant missions and the increase of the heathen during the hundred years: suggestive facts for thoughtful Christians: second ed. London, 1887.

*First ed.: London, & Edinburgh, 1886.

MITCHELL, JOHN M. Foreign missions of the Protestant churches: their state and prospects. London, & New York, 1888.

*VAHL, JENS. Laerebog i den evangeliske missionshistorie. Kjobenhavn, 1897.

GAY, TEOFILO. Breve storia della missioni evangeliche fra i pagani. Roma, 1899.

GRAHAM, JOHN A. Missionary expansion since the Reformation: third ed. Chicago, 1899.

Eng ed.: The missionary expansion of the Reformed churches... London, & Edinburgh, 1898.

First ed.: 1878.

GAREIS, REINHOLD. Geschichte der evangelischen Heidenmission, mit besonderer Berücksichtigung der deutschen: mit 11 Karten von Peter R. Grundemann: zweite durchgesehene und verm. Aufl. Konstanz, 1902.

*First ed.: Konstanz, & Emmishofen, 1901.

*WARNECK, GUSTAV. Outline of a history of Protestant missions from the Reformation to the present time... authorised tr. from the seventh German ed. by George Robson. New York, Chicago, & Toronto, 1902.

First Eng. tr. by Thomas Smith: Edinburgh, 1884.

*Ger. ed.: Abriss einer Geschichte der protestantischen Missionen von der Reformation bis auf die Gegenwart: mit einem Anhang über die katholischen Missionen: zehnte neu bearbeitete und verm. Aufl.: hrsg. von Johannes Warneck. Berlin, 1913.

First Ger. ed.: Leipzig, 1882.

Dutch tr.: 1882.

Swedish tr.: 1903.

*GUNDERT, HERMANN. Die evangelische Mission: ihre Länder, Völker und Arbeiten: vierte durchaus verm. Aufl. Calw, & Stuttgart, 1903.

*First ed.: Calw, & Stuttgart, 1881.

THOMPSON, AUGUSTUS C. Protestant missions: their rise and early progress. New York, 1903.

First ed.: New York, 1894.

*RICHTER, JULIUS. Allgemeine evangelische Missionsgeschichte. Gütersloh, 1906-1932. 5 vols.

Vols. 1-2: second ed. Also in English tr.: History of missions in India; History of Protestant missions in the Near East.

*STOCK, EUGENE. The story of church missions. London, 1907.

BAUDERT, SAMUEL. Die evangelische Mission: Geschichte, Arbeitsweise, heutiger Stand. Leipzig, & Berlin, 1913.

LEONARD, DELAVAN L. A hundred years of missions: the story of progress since Carey's beginning: third rev. ed. New York, & London, 1913.

First ed.: New York..., 1895.

*MIRBT, CARL. Die evangelische Mission: eine Einführung in ihre Geschichte und Eigenart: vierte unveränderte Aufl. Leipzig, 1917.

First ed.: Leipzig, 1917.

*FRICK, HEINRICH. Die evangelische Mission: Ursprung, Geschichte, Ziel. Bonn, & Leipzig, 1922.

USSING, HENRY. Illustreret missionshistorie: evangeliets sejrsgang ud over Jorden: en historisk oversigt over den evangeliske missions udvikling: tredie udgave. Kobenhavn, 1924.

First ed.: Kobenhavn, 1902.

*RICHTER, JULIUS. Evangelische Missionskunde: zweite erw. und umgearbeitete Aufl. Leipzig, 1927.

I: Evangelische Missionsgeschichte.

First ed.: Leipzig, & Erlangen, 1920.

*SCHICK, ERICH. Vorboten und Bahnbrecher: Grundzüge der evangelischen Missionsgeschichte bis zu den Anfängen der Basler Mission. Basel, 1943.

LINDEBERG, GUSTAV W. Den evangeliska missionen: fourth ed. rev. Stockholm, 1945.

First ed.: Stockholm, 1922.

*ANDERSON. 1961.

P. 95-111: The rise of Protestant missionary concern, 1517-1914 (William R. Hogg).

*FLACHSMEIER, HORST R. Geschichte der evangelischen Weltmission... Giessen, & Basel, 1963.

*VERSTEEG, JOHANNES P., CORNELIS GRAAFLAND, et al. Gij die eertijds verre waart...: een overzicht van de geschiedenis en taken van de zending. Utrecht, 1978.

*DIJKSTRA, H. Om de wereld: de protestantsche zending. Leiden, n.d.

5.3.3.7. THE HISTORY OF MISSIONARY ORDERS AND SOCIETIES

The church of Jesus is essentially
a missionary association.
J. Logan Aikman (1860:1).

The history of individual Roman Catholic missionary orders and Protestant missionary societies is rather well developed: there are (very) good studies of the mission history of the Dominicans, the Franciscans, the Augustinians, the Jesuits, et al. (cf. Mulders 1962:402-411), as well as of the history of the London Missionary Society, the Church Missionary Society, the Society for the Propagation of the Gospel in Foreign Parts, the Basel Mission, et al. (cf. Neill 1986:482).

I do not know comprehensive studies of Roman Catholic (monastic) orders but I know ones about Protestant missionary societies. Such studies were popular in last century (Smith 1824-1825; Gützlaff c. 1828; De Groot 1830; Sondermann 1846; Brauer 1847-1851; Aikman 1860; Carroll 1883; A handbook of foreign missions 1888; Gracey 1889). They either commence with the history of the missions of the United Brethren or Moravians (e.g. Smith 1824-1825), or with the New England Company (1649), the Society for Promoting Christian Knowledge (1698), and the Society for the Propagation of the Gospel in Foreign Parts (1701) (e.g. A handbook of foreign missions 1888). In the 20th century, those studies are out of date. They are being replaced by studies of the world mission conferences (Edinburgh 1910ff.) and the IMC (1921-1961) of which most Protestant missionary societies became members.

All comprehensive studies of the history of Protestant missionary societies have been written by westerners. Usually they either overlook non-western Christians, or mention them only in passing as assistants of the -white- missionaries. Another point of criticism is raised by Stephen C. Neill (Cuming 1970:151): they are '... written largely in terms of missionary societies and in connection with their special interests. This means that a vast amount is included which cannot be of any interest to either historian or theologian as such'.

*SMITH, THOMAS (comp.). The history and origin of the missionary societies, containing faithful accounts of the voyages, travels, labours, and successes of the various missionaries who have been sent out, for the purpose of evangelizing the heathen, and other unenlightened nations, in different parts of the habitable globe... London, 1824-1825. 2 vols.
Second ed.: History and progress of the missionary societies... London, 1838-1839. 2 vols.
*GROOT, DIRK A. DE. Beknopt overzigt over de geschiedenis der nieuwere zendeling-genootschappen en derzelver verrigtingen. Groningen, 1830.

*SONDERMANN, JOHANN S. (ed.). Tabellarische Übersicht über die protestantischen Missionsgesellschaften, Missionsstationen, und Missionare der Gegenwart: mit mehrfachen literarischen Verweisungen auf die Missionsgeschichte, einer Übersicht über die katholischen Missionen und drei Missionskarten. Nürnberg, 1846.

*AIKMAN, J. LOGAN. Cyclopaedia of Christian missions: their rise, progress, and present position. London, & Glasgow, 1860.

CARROLL, HENRY K. The world of missions: the societies, fields, agencies, and successes of Protestant missions. New York, 1883.

*A HANDBOOK OF FOREIGN MISSIONS: containing an account of the principal Protestant Missionary Societies in Great Britain, with notices of those on the Continent and in America: also an Appendix on Roman Catholic missions. London, 1888.

(GRACEY, JOHN T.) A manual of modern missions, containing historical and statistical accounts of the Protestant missionary societies of America, Great Britain, and the continent of Europe: also numerous maps and diagrams. New York, & Chicago, 1893.
First ed.: The missionary year-book for 1889/90, containing historical and statistical accounts of the principal Protestant missionary societies in America, Great Britain, and the continent of Europe: also numerous maps and diagrams. New York..., 1889.

*GRÜNDLER, JOHANNES. Lexikon der christlichen Kirchen und Sekten, unter Berücksichtigung der Missionsgesellschaften und zwischenkirchlichen Organisationen. Wien, Freiburg, & Basel, 1961.

5.3.3.8. MISSIONARY BIOGRAPHIES (COLLECTIVE WORKS)

> The story of world mission is more than
> the biography of missionaries.
> *Rolf A. Syrdal (1967:VIII)*

Both the historical surveys of Protestant missionary societies (cf. 5.3.3.7.) and the biographies of Roman Catholic and Protestant missionaries (cf. 3.4.2.5.: missionaries) were very popular in the 19th century. However, there is a significant difference between these categories of mission studies in the 19th and 20th centuries: only missionary biographies are still popular.

Collective works in this field deal either with the biographies of missionaries (Carne 1832-1835; Schmidt 1836-1842; Vormbaum 1849-1865; et al. in the second half of the 19th and the 20th centuries) or with the biographies of missionary Christians in the so-called 'third world' (Hübner 1880; Jarrett-Kerr 1972). Research into the former category is very well developed, but the study of the latter is still in its infancy.

The lives of the *great missionaries* (Thomson 1862) can be described as 'epoch makers of modern missions' (McLean 1912) and as 'heralds of the Cross' (Arnold-Foster 1893). The Missionary Research Library published *Missionary biography* (1965:114-135) in which other epithets of missionaries in book titles can be found as well: 'ambassadors for Christ', '(bridge) builders', 'Christ's expendables', 'couriers of the Cross', 'crusaders for God', '(missionary) explorers', 'giants of the missionary trial', '(missionary) heroes/ heroines', 'master workmen', 'messengers of the Cross', 'ministers of mercy', '(missionary) pathfinders', '(missionary) pioneers', 'saints', 'servants of the King', 'torchbearers', 'winners of the world', etc. I can agree with most of these religious and secular epithets, but I have difficulties with three of them.

First, I disagree with the epithet *heroes*: 'heroines of the missionary enterprise' (Eddy 1850), 'heroes of the modern missionary enterprise' (Smith 1857), 'heroines of the mission field' (Pitman 1880), 'heroes of the mission field' (Walsh 1890, 1903), 'missionary heroes' (Mathews 1922), 'heroes of the world mission' (Baeumker 1923: *Helden der Weltmission*), etc. The history of Christian mission is not at all a 'history of heroes' (Holsten 1953:64: *Heroengeschichte*). Stephen C. Neill (Cuming 1970:151) wrote: 'There was a natural desire, when so much real heroism and goodness were present, to touch up the narratives a little, and to suppress the shadows which in point of fact would have added so much life to page. The missionaries really made far more mistakes than was generally admitted...'. I fully agree with the intention of Neill's statement but I cannot follow him in maintaining the term 'hero(ism)'. This 'triumphalistic' term must be eliminated from the missiological vocabulary because it contradicts the biblical message: Jesus Christ, the apostles, and evangelists were not at all 'heroes'.

Second, I disagree with biographies in which the lives of the missionaries are described as the lives of *saints* (cf. Schamoni 1947). Missionary biography is not at all hagiography. The danger of describing the lives of missionaries as the lives of 'holy people' is especially present in Roman Catholic literature.

Finally, I disagree with the epithet *crusaders (for God)* (Schnittkind 1952; cf. Eddy 1945). This term must be dropped for the simple reason that Muslims always connect this term with the crusades of the Middle Ages.

Stephen C. Neill (Cuming 1970:158) has pointed out that 'almost all missionary biographies need to be rewritten'. This is not only due to the 'heroic', 'holy', and 'crusading' language which is used in many missionary biographies, but also -and primarily- because it is westerners who usually tell the story of missionary lives. Today, Christians from Asia, Africa, and Latin America also involve themselves in the study of western history: including the history of the western missionary enterprise. For example, Geoffrey Z. Kapenzi from Zimbabwe (1979) criticised western missionaries because of their link with European governments and bankers; he considered them as the *avant-garde* of the European traders, farmers, soldiers, and administrators. However, Mojola Agbebi from Nigeria (Ayandele 1971:8) distinguished them from other westerners who came to Africa, as well as to Asia and Latin America: 'Missionaries, and missionaries alone, are the real pioneers of African civilization. It was commercial Europe that invented slave labour and discovered the victims of slavery, but it was evangelical Europe that promulgated the edict of universal emancipation. It was adventurous Europe, under the title of "Anthropological Society", that placed us, the inhabitants of this good land, in the category of the brute creation; but it was Missionary Europe that proved us men. It is not and has never been the pleasure of commercial Europe to impart education in whatever scale to the natives of the soil, as this would lessen their hold over them and give them less scope to cheat, and enrich themselves from the product of the country. But Missionary Europe holds education as one of the important levers towards the amelioration of the people, and consider that without it their work is in vain. Whatever these pioneers of civilization are, whether they are Belgians, Frenchmen, Germans, Portuguese, English or American, tell them we shall ever hail them with delight...'.

A special category of missionaries are the *missionary martyrs* (Moister 1885; Croil 1894; cf. Smith 1857). They lived and died not only in the period of the New Testament and of the Early Church, but are of all ages (including the 20th century). Especially Asian mission history is full of missionary martyrs, both in 'the Vasco da Gama epoch of Asian history 1498-1945' (K.M. Panikkar 1967) and in the epoch before that era and thereafter. James Croil (1894) wrote a study of 130 Protestant missionary martyrs in which he introduced the doubtful term 'the noble army'. Nevertheless, scholars have not yet given enough attention to the study of missionary martyrs in modern times. The obligation to write missionary biographies is, first of all, an obligation to describe the lives and messages of the missionary martyrs *per crucem ad coronam* (Croil 1894).

*CARNE, JOHN. Lives of eminent missionaries. London, 1832-1835. 3 vols.
*SCHMIDT, KARL C.G. Kurzgefasste Lebensbeschreibungen der merkwürdigsten evangelischen Missionare: nebst einer Übersicht der Ausbreitung des Christenthums durch die Missionen. Leipzig, 1836-1842. 6 vols.
    Neue Folge: Leipzig, 1846 ff. 2 vols.
*VORMBAUM, REINHOLD. Evangelische Missionsgeschichte in Biographien. Düsseldorf, & Elberfeld, 1849-1865. 5 vols.
    I-II, zweite verb. und verm. Aufl.: 1859-1865.
    Swed. tr.: 1862-1877. 20 vols.
EDDY, DANIEL C. Heroines of the missionary enterprise: or, sketches of prominent female missionaries. Boston, 1850.
    *Dutch tr.: 1851.
SMITH, LUCIUS E. Heroes and martyrs of the modern missionary enterprise... Providence, 1857.
*THOMSON, ANDREW (MITCHELL). Great missionaries: a series of biographies. London, Edinburgh, & New York, 1862.
?HÜBNER. Lebensbilder bekehrter Heiden. 1880.
*JAPP, ALEXANDER H. Master-missionaries: chapters in pioneer effort throughout the world. London, 1880.

PITMAN, EMMA R. ... Heroines of the mission field: biographical sketches. New York, 1880.

MOISTER, WILLIAM. Missionary martyrs: being brief memorial sketches of faithful servants of God who have been put to death whilst endeavoring to propagate the gospel of Christ... London, 1885.

WALSH, W. PAKENHAM. Modern heroes of the mission field: third ed. New York, 1890.
First ed.: London, 1883.

*BLISS, EDWIN M. (ed.). The encyclopaedia of missions... New York, London, & Toronto, 1891.
I, p. 647-655: Biographies (collective, individual missionaries, missionary converts). Bibliog.

ARNOLD-FOSTER, FRANCES E. Heralds of the Cross: or, the fulfilling of the command: chapters on missionary work: second ed. London, 1893.
First ed.: London, 1882.

*CROIL, JAMES. The noble army of martyrs and roll of Protestant missionary martyrs from A.D. 1661 to 1891: 'per crucem ad coronam'. Philadelphia, 1894.

WALSH, W. PAKENHAM. Heroes of the mission field: links in the story of missionary work from the earliest ages to the close of the eighteenth century: fifth ed. New York, 1903.
First ed.: New York, 1879.

COMPARATIVE STUDIES IN MISSIONARY BIOGRAPHY. New York, 1905.

McLEAN, ARCHIBALD. Epoch makers of modern missions. New York, & Chicago..., 1912.

*KÖRNER, G. In alle Welt: Lebensbilder aus der evangelischen Mission. Berlin, 1918.

MATHEWS, BASIL J. The book of missionary heroes. New York, 1922.

BAEUMKER, FRANZ. Helden der Weltmission: 227 Lebensbeschreibungen hervorragender, um die Glaubensverbreitung verdienter Männer und Frauen. Aachen, 1923.

LINDEBERG, GUSTAV W. Märkesmän i missionshistorien. Stockholm, 1929.

SAILER, THOMAS H.P. Five missionary lives: a study in comparative biography... New York, 1929.

*SCHLUNK, MARTIN. Grosse Missionsführer der Kirchengeschichte. Leipzig, 1931.

*EDDY, GEORGE S. Pathfinders of the world missionary crusade. New York, 1945.

SCHAMONI, WILHELM. The face of the saints. New York, 1947.

SCHNITTKIND, DANA A. (pseud.: DANA THOMAS). Crusaders for God. New York, 1952.

HÜNERMANN, WILHELM. Geschichte der Weltmission: Lebensbilder grosser Missionare. Luzern, & München, 1960-1961. 3 vols.
Fr. tr.: 1961 ff. 2 vols.

*AUGUSTINY, WALDEMAR. Gehet hin in alle Welt: zwei Jahrtausende christliche Mission. Gütersloh, 1962.
*Dutch tr.: n.d.

*MISSIONARY RESEARCH LIBRARY. Missionary biography: an initial bibliography. New York, 1965. Bibliog.
P. 114-137: Collective biography.

*ROVER, PIET A. DE. De kerk op mars: zendingsgeschiedenis: vertel- en voorleesboek: tweede dr. Den Haag, 1968.
First ed.: Groningen, 1958.
Ger. tr.: 1960.

*AYANDELE, E.A. A visionary of the African church: Mojola Agbebi (1860-1917). Nairobi, 1971.

*JARRETT-KERR, MARTIN, CR. Patterns of Christian acceptance: individual response to the missionary impact 1550-1950. London, New York, & Toronto, 1972.

*MOORHOUSE, GEOFFREY. The missionaries. London, 1973.

*KAPENZI, GEOFFREY Z. The clash of cultures: Christian missionaries and the Shona of Rhodesia. Washington, 1979.

*TUCKER, RUTH A. From Jerusalem to Irian Jaya: a biographical history of Christian missions. Grand Rapids, 1983.

5.3.3.9. SURVEYS OF WORLD-WIDE MISSION

Finally, I would like to draw attention to the category of 'surveys of world-wide mission'. Such surveys also date from the middle of the 19th century and are still produced in the 20th century. Their main purpose is to present up-to-date information about the Christian mission. Some surveys give also a retrospective view (Lauterburg 1901: *Rückblick*), others are comparative (Vahl 1892), and yet others look at the future as an 'opportunity' (Lyall 1963).

Most surveys are very useful. Some, however, lack the necessary thoroughness because they were produced too quickly. Many books mentioned in chapter 5.3.3.4.-5.3.3.6. end with a 'survey' of the contemporary situation of the Christian/Roman Catholic/Protestant mission; such a survey can also be written too rapidly, reflecting more the (optimistic or pessimistic) view of the author concerning the future of Christian mission than the contemporary facts in six continents.

Theodor Christlieb (1880), Peter R. Grundemann (1880, 1890), Jens Vahl (1892), and James S. Dennis (1894, 1902) were professional writers of '(centennial) surveys' of foreign mission. Today David B. Barrett can be regarded as their successor. In chapter 5.3.5. on the statistics of Christian mission I shall pay attention to his (annual) surveys of 'global mission'.

*WILD, KARL. Umschau auf dem Arbeitsfelde der evangelischen Mission. Nördlingen, 1854.
?HÄRTING, R. Ueberblick der evangelischen Mission für jedermann. Leipzig, 1870.
?KOOY, F. VAN. Overzicht van de volken en godsdiensten der aarde: vooral op het gebied der zending: tweede dr. Groningen, 1871.
CHRISTLIEB, THEODOR. Protestant foreign missions: their present state: a universal survey. Boston, 1880.
　　*First ed.: Der gegenwärtige Stand der evangelischen Heidenmission: eine Weltüberschau. Gütersloh, 1880.
　　*First Ger. ed.: AMZ, VI (1879), p. 481-582.
　　Also trs. in Dutch, Fr., Nor., and Swed.
*GRUNDEMANN, PETER R. Overzicht van het christelijk zendingswerk over de geheele aarde...: bewerkt door Petrus van Wijk Jr. Amsterdam, 1880.
　　?First ed.: Orientirende Übersicht über den gegenwärtigen Stand des gesammten christlichen Missionswerkes....
*WIJK Jr, PETRUS VAN. Zendingskroniek. I. Amsterdam, 1882.
　　Continuation of: Peter R. Grundemann. 1880.
*BAINBRIDGE, WILLIAM F. Around the world tour of Christian missions: a universal survey...: third ed. Boston, 1882.
*ZAHN, FRANZ M. Der Acker ist die Welt: Blicke in das Arbeitsfeld der evangelischen Mission. Gütersloh, 1888.
*GRUNDEMANN, PETER R. Die Entwickelung der evangelischen Mission im letzten Jahrzehnt

(1878-1888): ein Beitrag zur Missionsgeschichte, zugleich als Ergänzungsband zur zweiten Aufl. der 'Kleinen Missionsbibliothek'. Bielefeld, & Leipzig, 1890. Cf. Burkhardt. 1876-1881. 4 vols.

*VAHL, JENS. Der Stand der evangelischen Heidenmission in den Jahren 1845 und 1890: eine vergleichende missionsgeschichtliche und missionsstatistische Rundschau... Gütersloh, 1892.
First ed.: 1891.

*DENNIS, JAMES S. Foreign missions after a century. Edinburgh, & London, 1894.

*LAUTERBURG, MORITZ. Rückblick auf die Geschichte der evangelischen Mission im 19. Jahrhundert. Basel, 1901.

*DENNIS, JAMES S. Centennial survey of foreign missions: a statistical supplement... New York, Chicago, & Toronto, 1902.

PISANI, PAUL. Les missions protestantes à la fin du XIX siècle: troisième éd. Paris, 1908.
First ed.: La Chapelle, & Montligeon, 1901.

*WHITLEY, WILLIAM T. Missionary achievement: a survey of world-wide evangelisation... London, 1908.

GRANT, ANTHONY. The past and prospective extension of the gospel by missions to the heathen...: reed. by Charles H. Robinson. London, 1910.
First ed.: London, 1844.

LILLEY, JAMES P. The victory of the gospel: a survey of worldwide evangelism... London, 1910.

*INTERCHURCH WORLD MOVEMENT OF NORTH AMERICA. World survey: rev. preliminary statement and budget. II: foreign volume and a statistical mirror: library ed. New York, 1920.

*LATOURETTE, KENNETH S., & WILLIAM R. HOGG. Tomorrow is here: a survey of the world-wide mission and work of the Christian church. London, 1948.

*DAIN, ARTHUR J. (ed.). Mission fields today: a brief world survey: repr. Chicago, 1957.
First ed.: Chicago, 1956.

BOER, HARRY R. The world missionary situation today. Grand Rapids, 1958.

*BRENNECKE, GERHARD (ed.). Weltmission in ökumenischer Zeit. Stuttgart, 1961.

MILLOT, RENÉ P. Missions in the world today. New York, 1961.
First ed.: Missions d'aujourd'hui. Paris, 1960.
Castilian tr.: 1962.

LYALL, LESLIE T. (ed.). Missionary opportunity today: a brief world survey. Chicago, 1963.

*RUF, WALTHER, & ERICH VIERING (eds.). Die Mission in der evangelischen Unterweisung: ein Arbeitsbuch. Stuttgart, 1964.
P. 28-130: Die Kirche Christi in den Ländern der Erde (Erich Viering, & Walther Ruf).

*THIESSEN, JOHN C. A survey of world missions: rev. ed. Chicago, 1968.
*First ed.: Chicago, 1955.

5.3.3.10. THE HISTORY OF CHRISTIAN MISSION AND WORLD HISTORY, THE HISTORY OF RELIGION, CHURCH HISTORY, AND THE HISTORY OF CONVERSIONS

As section 5.3.2. ends with a discussion of the relation between missionary linguistics and religious linguistics, so this section will be closed with an investigation of the link between mission history and the history of religion.

However, we also need to examine their link with world history, church history, and the history of conversions and acceptance of Christ.

Ernst Benz (1961) is one of the scholars who researched this broad field. He analysed the seven volumes of Kenneth S. Latourette (1937-1945) as a thorough contribution to 'world history - church history - mission history' (Ger.: *Weltgeschichte - Kirchengeschichte - Missionsgeschichte*). However, Latourette is certainly not the only missiologist to link world history, church history, and mission history. In the following section we will encounter others as well.

*BENZ, ERNST. Kirchengeschichte in ökumenischer Sicht. Leiden, & Köln, 1961.
    P. 13-38: Weltgeschichte-Kirchengeschichte-Missionsgeschichte: die Kirchen-geschichtsschreibung Kenneth Scott Latourettes.

MISSION HISTORY AND WORLD HISTORY

Several scholars have called attention to the relation between mission history and world history (Ger.: *Weltgeschichte*). Here I refer to the studies of Paul Tillich, Arend Th. van Leeuwen, and Stephen C. Neill.

In the 19th century Friedrich A.E. Ehrenfeuchter (1859; cf. Myklebust 1955:I,90) and Ernst F. Langhans (1875) had already linked Christianity and Christian mission with world history. In the 20th century this endeavour was repeated by Tillich who developed a Christocentric interpretation of history: Christ, the New Being, is the centre of world history; and Christian mission is 'that activity of the church by which it works for the transformation of its own latency into its own manifestation all over the world' (Anderson 1961:283).

Van Leeuwen (1964) developed a non-Christocentric concept. He considered world history as a process in which the (non-western) ontocratic models of understanding history are confronted with the (Christian) theocratic and (western) technocratic models. Western civilization, which is rooted in the Old Testament and New Testament, separates the 'holy' from the 'profane', both at home and abroad. Therefore, Christian mission promotes 'secularisation' by 'desacralizing' non-western cultures and religions. Karl Müller SVD (1987: 213) made a critical evaluation of this historico-theological and socio-cultural view: 'This is an imaginative yet controversial interpretation of Christianity's history in relation to the biblical faith, the world spread of western culture, the impact of technology and the meeting of the world religions'.

I agree more with Tillich than with Van Leeuwen. Therefore, I can consider the 'year of the Lord' (Lat.: *annus Domini*) as the main point of reference in world history. The Christian calendar is not only a good calendar to describe mission history and church history, but also to analyse world history and the history of world religions.

Neill (Cuming 1970:154) observed: 'Until very recently secular historians dealt with the missionary enterprises of the Christian church by simply ignoring them. It has often been noted that in the fourteen volumes of the first edition of the *Cambridge Modern History* there is only one reference to Christian missions, and that fortuitiously is connected with the great journeys in Africa of David Livingstone, who happened to be missionary as well as explorer. It is plain that that period of neglect is at an end'. Neill wellcomed the progress made in the *New Cambridge Modern History* but is still not satisfied. At the same time he criticized many historians of Christian mission: '... much of this writing failed to set the events recorded in the frame of contemporary history' (:152).

*PLATH, CARL H.C. Die Erwählung der Völker im Lichte der Missionsgeschichte... Berlin, 1867.
*LANGHANS, ERNST F. Das Christenthum und seine Mission im Lichte der Weltgeschichte. Zürich, 1875.
FOWLER, CHARLES H. Missions and world movements. New York, & Cincinnati, 1904.
    First ed.: Cincinnati, & New York, 1903.
MASON, CAROLINE (ATWATER). World missions and world peace: a study of Christ's conquest. West Medford, 1916.
*MIRBT, CARL. Missionsgeschichte und Kolonialgeschichte. In: NAMZ, IV (1927), p. 68-80.
*ANDERSON. 1961.
    P. 281-289: Missions and world history (Paul Tillich).
*LEEUWEN, AREND Th. VAN. Christianity in world history: the meeting of the faiths of East and West. London, & Edinburgh, 1964.
    *Dutch tr.: 1966.
*PANIKKAR, K. MADHU. Asia and western dominance: a survey of the Vasco da Gama epoch of Asian history (1498-1945). London, 1967.
    First ed.: London, 1953. Several impressions.
*LMG. 1987.
    P. 125-127: Geschichte (Hans-Werner Gensichen).
*MÜLLER, KARL, SVD. Mission theology... Nettetal, 1987.
    P. 207-213: Mission history.

MISSION HISTORY AND THE HISTORY OF RELIGION

The history of religion (Ger.: *Religionsgeschichte*) is also a frame of Christian mission.

The rise of the so-called 'Religious History School' (Bousset 1907: *religionsgeschichtliche Schule*) in Germany provoked considerable discussion on the relation between the history of mission and the history of religion. This school treated the Christian mission merely as a historical phenomenon, and not at all as a contemporary duty. This liberal school was vehemently criticized by Christian missiologists (e.g. Schomerus 1935:19-21) who, from their own profound understanding of the role of Christianity amidst the non-Christian world religions, refused to accept a non-normative interpretation of the Great Commission.

Some missiologists (Daubanton 1911:537-562; Mulders 1950:250-258; Santos Hernandez 1961:289,343-403; et al.) regarded the history of religion as an 'auxiliary science' of mission studies: but I am opposed to this view (cf. 5.3.1.2.). The 'history of religion' is an independent discipline. From one point of view I consider the history of Christian mission as merely a part of the history of religion (cf. the Religious History School), but from another point of view I regard it as a discipline which can never be separated from the normative theology of Christian mission and missionary theology.

BOUSSET, WILHELM. Die Mission und die sogenannte religionsgeschichtliche Schule...
     Göttingen, 1907.
     *First ed.: ZMR, XXIII (1907), p. 353-362.
*MÜHLHÄUSSER, L. Mission und Religionsgeschichte. In: EMM, LIII (1909), p. 413-421.
?MAUSBACH, J. Heidenmission und Religionsgeschichte. Münster in Westfalen, 1910.
*DAUBANTON. 1911.
     P. 537-562: De zendingswetenschap en de godsdienstwetenschap.
ANDRES, FRIEDRICH. Katholischer Missionare Verdienste um Völkerkunde und Religions-
     geschichte. In: HM, V (1923/24), p. 154-159.
MERKEL, FRANZ R. Quellen zur Missions- und Religionsgeschichte. In: ZMR, XXXIX (1924),
     p. 24-31.
ALTHAUS, PAUL. Theologische Aufsätze. I. Gütersloh, 1929.
     P. 153-205: Mission und Religionsgeschichte.
*SCHOMERUS. 1935.
     P. 19-21: Die Missionspädagogik und die Religionsgeschichte und Volkskunde.
*MULDERS, ALPHONSUS J.M. Inleiding tot de missiewetenschap... Bussum, 1950.
     P. 250-258: Godsdienstwetenschap.
*SEUMOIS. 1952.
     P. 416-423: Histoire des religions.
*HOLSTEN. 1953.
     P. 90-101: Geschichtlichkeit der Religion.
*RGG. 1960.
     IV, p. 969-971: Mission. I. Religionsgeschichtlich (Gerhard Rozenkranz).
*SANTOS HERNANDEZ. 1961.
     P. 289,343-403: La historia de las religiones.
*SANTOS HERNANDEZ, ANGEL, SJ. Bibliografia misional. Santander, 1965. 2 vols.
     I, p. 88-101: Historia de las religiones. Bibliog.
*CONCISE DICTIONARY. 1971.
     P. 253-254: History of religions (Stephen C. Neill).

MISSION HISTORY AND CHURCH HISTORY

> Church history ... should be ... the history
> of the missionary enterprise.
> *Theology and the Christian World Mission*
> *(1929:20; cf. Myklebust 1957:II,37)*

Church history (Ger.: *Kirchengeschichte*) is not in the same way a frame of mission history as world history and the history of religion. We can consider the history of mission as that part of church history which deals with 'the expansion of the church' (Mulders 1950:79), but we can also adopt the opposite position: the history of mission as frame of church history because Christian mission not only depends upon the church, but the church also -and primarily- depends upon mission (cf. the Acts of the Apostles). This last perspective was especially developed by Johannes C. Hoekendijk who introduced the slogan 'the church as function of the apostolate'.

Roman Catholic mission historians have related mission history and church history more closely than their Protestant colleagues. They regard the Roman Catholic church as the startingpoint and goal of mission. In their eyes, mission history is both history of 'the planting church' and history of 'the church which must be planted' (Streit 1910:11-13: *Geschichte der gründenden und der zu gründen Kirche*; my tr.). Especially the so-called Louvain school emphasized mission as church planting (cf. 3.4.2.3.) and consequently studied mission history as the history of *plantatio ecclesiae*. On the Protestant side, I regard the Church Growth Movement (cf. 2.2.4.) as a movement which strongly connects church history and mission history.

After the Second World War we begin to encounter new concepts; because mission history can no longer be described by dividing the world into a Christian part (the subject of mission) and a non-Christian part (the object of mission). In the *corpus christianum* era, scholars identified church history with the West, and mission history with the rest of the world. But today we observe that Christians in the non-western world write their own Asian, African, and Latin American church histories while Christians in Europe and the USA are starting to reflect on the history of their own mission, i.e. evangelism, at home.

Heinzgünter Frohnes, Hans-Werner Gensichen, & Georg Kretschmar (1974-1978) described the history of the early and mediaeval church *as mission history* (Ger.: *Kirchengeschichte als Missionsgeschichte*). This ecumenical study links both histories intimately. I can only agree to a certain extent with their view; because I also support the other position: i.e. mission history treated *as church history*. Moreover, I consider the history of the *conversio gentium* as prior to the history of the *plantatio ecclesiae*.

Both in the 19th and the 20th centuries we can find mission historians who did not choose to connect mission history and church history. They preferred, instead, to link mission history and the history of God's kingdom (Freitag, & Ahaus 1940); mission history and the history of Christ's kingdom (Gützlaff c. 1828; Aikman 1862); and mission history and the history of conversions.

*KILGER, LAURENZ, OSB. Missions- und Kirchengeschichte. In: ZM, XX (1930), p. 35-39.
KILGER, LAURENZ, OSB. Die Missionsgeschichte als Zeugnis für die Lebenskraft unserer Kirche. In: ZMR XXI (1931), p. 18-32.
*MORGAN, EDMUND R. The study of church history in relation to Christian missions. In: IRM, XXII (1933), p. 522-529.
*SCHOMERUS. 1935.
    P. 14-15: Die Missionsgeschichte und die Kirchengeschichte.
*DIBELIUS, OTTO. Die Epochen der Kirchengeschichte und die Mission. In: EMZ, IV (1943), p. 1-9, 33-42, 97-109, 129-134, 161-168.

MISSION HISTORY AND THE HISTORY OF CONVERSIONS

> Church history should be taught on a world basis
> as ... story of *gesta Christi per orbem*.
> *Edmund R. Morgan (IRM 1933:523).*

Most histories of mission centre either upon the church (Lat.: *plantatio ecclesiae*) or upon the kingdom of God. However, some histories of mission focus on the conversion of the heathens (Lat.: *conversio gentium*). Several historians of mission include the word 'conversion' into the title of their study (Millar 1731; Bock 1743; Brauer 1835-1839,1841; Hinkel 1843-1845).

Conversion can be understood as conversion to the Christian faith (Bock 1743), to Christianity, and to the church; but basically it is conversion to Jesus Christ (Hinkel 1843-1845). It implicates 'Christ acceptance' rather than 'Christian acceptance' (Jarrett-Kerr 1972). In the titles of some mission histories, Christ is mentioned (Gützlaff c. 1828; Aikman 1862; Mason 1916); but only in the title of the historical study of Charles L. Brace is Christ at the centre: *Gesta Christi*: or, a history of humane progress under Christianity (1900; first ed.: 1882). The definition of evangelism preferred by Johannes C. Hoekendijk (Wereld en zending 1976:323) is quite remarkable: i.e. 'to functionalize the *historia Jesu* among people'. This definition implies that the history of Christian mission must be described as the history of the way in which missionaries have functionalized the *historia Jesu* among people in six continents.

In the Great Commission, it is not the church but Christ that is central. Therefore, mission history must primarily be linked not with church history, but rather with 'the *historia Jesu* among people' and 'the history of *Christ acceptance*'. Jesus Christ is not only accepted by converts as Lord and Saviour, but also honoured outside the church in a great variety of ways. There are several studies which describe and analyse the 'Christ acceptance' by non-Christians: both generally (Pfannmüller 1939) and by special groups of non-Christians: Jews (e.g. Rottenberg n.d.), Muslims (e.g. Schumann 1975), Hindus (Panikkar 1964; Thomas 1969; Samartha 1974), secular philosophers (e.g. Le Cointre 1931: Pfannmüller 1939; Schönfelder 1949; Jongeneel 1971), Marxists (e.g. Fetscher, & Machovec 1974), etc. This literature has not yet been thoroughly examined by mission historians. I consider this a serious deficiency. Mission historians must be interested in the perception of Christ 'outside the gates' of the church. In most cases it is only a partial acceptance of Christ (e.g. Mani, Muhammed, Baruch de Spinoza, Martin Buber, Mahatma Gandhi, and Sarvepalli Radhakrishnan). However, we also know about exceptional cases in which non-Christians fully accepted Jesus as their Lord and Saviour but were never baptised. Christ-centred mission histories are mission histories which focus on conversions to Christ: i.e. partial or full 'acceptance' or 'reception' of Christ in world history.

Mission history clearly shows that Christian missions can reach persons and societies in places where the churches are not able to establish themselves. This history also demonstrates that -the unbound- Christ can reach persons and communities where not only the churches but also the Christian missions are not able to come or not allowed to operate.

BRACE, CHARLES L. Gesta Christi: or, a history of humane progress under Christianity: sixth
    ed., with new pref. and supplementary chap. New York, 1900.
    First ed.: London, 1882.
*COINTRE, W.M. LE. Het Jezusbeeld in de wijsgeerig-wetenschappelijke litteratuur.
    Amsterdam, 1931.
*COINTRE, W.M. LE. Het sociale Jezus-beeld. Amsterdam, 1931.
*PFANNMÜLLER, GUSTAV. Jesus im Urteil der Jahrhunderte: die bedeutendsten Auffassungen Jesu
    in Theologie, Philosophie, Literatur und Kunst bis zur Gegenwart. Berlin, 1939.
*SCHÖNFELDER, WALTER. Die Philosophen und Jesus Christus: ein Beitrag zur Geschichte des
    Gesprächs der neuzeitlichen Philosophie mit dem Christentum. Hamburg, 1949.
*PANIKKAR, RAIMUND. The unknown Christ of Hinduism... London, 1964. Several reprints.
*THOMAS, MADATHILPARAMPIL M. The ackowledged Christ of the Indian renaissance. London,
    1969.
*JONGENEEL, JAN A.B. Het redelijke geloof in Jezus Christus: een studie over de
    wijsbegeerte van de Verlichting. Wageningen, 1971. Diss. Leiden.
FETSCHER, IRING, & MILAN MACHOVEC (eds.). Marxisten und die Sache Jesu. München, & Mainz,
    1974.
    *Dutch tr.: 1975.
*SAMARTHA, STANLEY J. The Hindu response to the unbound Christ: towards a christology in
    India. Madras, 1974.
    *Ger. ed.: Hindus vor dem universalen Christus: Beiträge zu einer Christologie in
    India. Stuttgart, 1970.

*SCHUMANN, OLAF. Der Christus der Muslime: christologische Aspekte in der arabisch-islamischen Literatur. Gütersloh, 1975.
*HOEKENDIJK, JOHANNES C. Horizons of hope. In: Wereld en zending, V (1976), p. 323-324.
*ROTTENBERG, ALTER M.J. Joodsche stemmen over Christus en christendom. Rotterdam, n.d.

5.3.3.11. CONCLUSION

At the end of this exposition of the second branch of the empirical study of mission, I recapitulate and evaluate the main points of this section.

The history of Christian mission (cf. church history) is a well-developed academic discipline. Many general mission histories and general surveys of world mission have been written. And also many special studies of the history of Roman Catholic mission, of Protestant mission, of missionary orders and societies, and of missionary biography have been produced. In this discipline, we can also observe developments: e.g. the histories of missionary societies are largely replaced by the history of missionary conferences; and the participation of women and non-western Christians in doing historical mission studies leads to a reformulation of already-existing opinions as well. This also includes a redrafting of the relation between mission history and church history and a redrafting of the existing chronologies ('periods of mission').

A highly problematic point is the relation of mission history to world history and the history of religions. Most histories of mission are too narrowly focussed because they fail to locate the history of Christian mission in a broader framework. In history, the Christian mission is influenced by its environment; but, at the same time, it has contributed to the progress of most civilizations and even many religions and worldviews. For instance, Christian mission is a premise to understand the history of both Islam and communism.

The most crucial problem is the link between the history of the Christian mission, on the one hand, and the history of conversions and 'Christ acceptance' by non-Christians, on the other. The permanent neglect of the study of 'the *historia Jesu* among people' and 'the history of *Christ acceptance*' by most mission historians transformed Christian mission history into a non-Christ-centered field of study which is essentially alienated from the Great Commission ('discipling' the nations). Today we need post-colonial mission histories which are not primarily interested in the progress of (ecclesiastical) missionary institutions, but in the stories of conversions of both -Christian and non-Christian- individuals and communities to Christ and their -partial or full- acceptance of Christ as *guru*, Lord, and Saviour.

5.3.4. THE GEOGRAPHY OF CHRISTIAN MISSION

> The world is my parish.
> *John Wesley (Trueblood 1972:69).*

5.3.4.1. INTRODUCTION

In the fourth volume of *A History of the Expansion of Christianity* (1971), Kenneth S. Latourette deals with 'the great century'. In the first sentence of this volume we read: 'As our story moves into the 19th century we come to the age of the most extensive geographic spread of Christianity'.

His statement is quite correct. However, Christianity also extended rapidly in the first centuries. In the following centuries we can observe an amazing spread of Nestorianism in Asia which, unfortunately, was not permanent. The history of the Christian mission is the history of the expansion of Christianity in space: 'in Jerusalem, and in all Judaea, and in Samaria, and unto the uttermost part of the earth' (Acts 1:8). Although Latourette is right to treat the 19th century as 'the age of the most extensive geographic spread of Christianity', I would like to emphasize that the 20th century is the age of reaching 'the uttermost part of the earth' (Acts 1:8).

Several missiological handbooks (Daubanton 1911; Schmidlin 1925; Mulders 1962; et al.) devoted a separate section to the geography of Christian mission, i.e. the study of the 'extensive geographic spread of Christianity' (Latourette).

*DAUBANTON. 1911.
    P. 443-457: Zendingsgeografie en -statistiek.
*SCHMIDLIN. 1925.
    P. 95-117: Missionskunde (Missionsstatistik und Missionsgeographie).
*SEUMOIS. 1952.
    P. 321-322: La géographie ou cartographie missionnaire.
*SANTOS HERNANDEZ. 1961.
    P. 296: Geografia.
*MULDERS. 1962.
    P. 431-434: Missiecartografie.
    P. 434-438: Geografie en sociografie.

5.3.4.2. HISTORY

The discipline 'the geography of Christian mission' arose in the 19th century. In 1825/27 an Irish clergyman introduced the term *missionary geography*. Thereafter Johann C. Blumhardt (1805-1880) wrote his influential *Handbüchlein der Missionsgeschichte und Missionsgeographie* (1844; third ed.: 1863).

The translator of this book did not use the word 'geography of (Christian) mission', but 'missionary geography'. However, Harlan P. Beach (1901-1906) used the term *geography... of Protestant missions*. I prefer the term *geography of Christian mission*, which is parallel to the term 'history of Christian mission'.

After Johann C. Blumhardt, it was Peter R. Grundemann (1836-1924), a companion of Gustav Warneck, who came to the fore in Germany. He produced many missionary atlases (1867-1871, 1887, 1901, 1903, 1905), of which the *Allgemeiner Missions-Atlas* (1867-1871) is 'a work of first rank' (Myklebust 1955:I,297). None of these works was translated into English. In the 1890's preparations were made for the edition of a missionary atlas in English -Grundemann being responsible for the maps and Jens Vahl (1828-1898) for the text- but 'owing to lack of funds nothing came of it' (Myklebust 1955:I,297). In the 20th century, however, James S. Dennis, Harlan P. Beach, Samuel M. Zwemer, and Charles H. Fahs were able to publish the *Statistical Atlas of Christian Missions* (1910) which, after 15 years, was replaced by the *World Missionary Atlas*. It was Grundemann who founded single-handed the geography of the Christian mission as an academic discipline; but Dennis, Beach, Zwemer, and Fahs as a group developed this branch of mission studies further by their cooperation with others in the frame of the World Missionary Conference (1910) and the International Missionary Council (1921). This ecumenical cooperation enabled the editors to make the geography of Christian mission an accepted discipline world-wide.

In the Roman Catholic Church we can observe similar developments. Stephan J. Neher (1864-1868), Oscar Werner SJ (1890), and others established the geography of Roman Catholic missions. Karl Streit SVD, however, published the *Catholic World Atlas* (1929) which, in comparison with his earlier work, the *Katholischer Missionsatlas* (1906), did not use the word 'mission' in the title or subtitle of the book. After the Second World War a serious renewal of the geography of the Roman Catholic mission was initiated by Anton Freitag SVD, *The Universe Atlas of the Christian World* (1963), who in the subtitle referred to the 'expansion of Christianity'. Here, the term 'mission' is also avoided.

In the 19th century James Wyld (1839:V) complained: 'Maps have not hitherto been used to illustrate the labours of the Christian community...'. But in the 20th century there is no scholar who held the same opinion as Wyld. Both the *World Missionary Atlas* (1925) and the *Catholic World Atlas* (1929) 'illustrate the labours of the Christian community' (Wyld) remarkably.

Such comprehensive books are based upon studies of many scholars in previous centuries. Cosmas Indocopleustes (cf. Winstedt 1909), William of Rubruck (cf. Herbst 1925), and medieval monks and missionaries in general (cf. Bündgens 1889) already contributed to topography and geography in

260

general, and especially to the topography and geography of Christianity. The considerable scientific contribution of their successors in modern history also includes general geographical issues. Otto Zöckler (AMZ 1877:6-16) is right in typifying Christian missionaries as 'pioneers of the science of geography' (Ger.: *Pioniere geographischer Wissenschaft*). And Thomas Laurie (1882:3) proudly quoted the following pronouncement in the *Princeton Review*: 'Our missionaries have rendered more real service to geography than all the geographical societies of the world'. Therefore, both general geography and the geography of Christianity is indebted to the early, medieval, and modern missionaries.

After the Second World War, such standard works were replaced by David B. Barrett's *World Christian Encyclopedia* (1982). He too did not use the term 'mission' in the title and subtitle of his immense work.

*ZÖCKLER, OTTO. Die Missionare als Pioniere geographischer (und ethnologischer) Wissenschaft. In: AMZ, IV (1877), p. 6-16.
*LAURIE, THOMAS. The Ely volume... Boston, 1882.
    P. 1-93: Contributions to geographical science.
    P. 94-102: Geology.
*BÜNDGENS, CHRIST. J. Was verdankt die Länder- und Völkerkunde den mittelalterlichen Mönchen und Missionären? Frankfurt am Main, & Luzern, 1889.
*WALLROTH, E. Was hat die gegenwärtige Mission für die Geographie geleistet? In: AMZ, XVII (1889), p. 35-47, 70-80, 136-149, 231-237, 294-304, 356-370.
WINSTEDT, ERIC O. The Christian topography of Cosmas Indicopleustes: ed. with geographical notes. Cambridge, 1909.
*HERBST, HERMANN. Der Bericht des Franziskaners Wilhelm von Rubruk über seine Reise in das Innere Asiens in den Jahren 1253-1255. Leipzig, 1925.
*MYKLEBUST. 1955-1957. 2 vols.
*WESTMANN, KNUT B., & HARALD VON SICARD. Geschichte der christlichen Mission. München, 1962.
*LATOURETTE, KENNETH S. A history of the expansion of Christianity. Exeter, 1971. 7 vols.
*NEILL, STEPHEN C. A history of Christian missions: rev. for the second ed. by Owen Chadwick. London, 1986.

5.3.4.3. THE GEOGRAPHY AND CARTOGRAPHY OF CHRISTIAN MISSION

> Missionary geography has in some degree to include
> both these [physical and political geography],
> but is has more especially to consider the religious state
> of the inhabitants of the various countries
> of the world, and what has been done, and is doing,
> to enlighten those who are in error.
> *(Missionary geography 1865:1).*

Peter R. Grundemann regarded *missionary geography* as 'a branch of mission studies, not a branch of geography' (1901:9: *ein Zweig der Missionswissenschaft, nicht der Geographie*; my tr.). The first part of this statement is quite correct, but the second part is not. I also treat the geography of Christian mission as a branch of general geography; especially of the geography of world religions. There is a real link between both disciplines: missionaries have always used the expertise of general geographers and sometimes the latter have also contributed to progress in the field of the geography of Christian mission.

Some scholars pay special attention to *the cartography of Christian mission*. André V. Seumois (1952:321-322) did not distinguish between these disciplines because he wrote about 'missionary geography or cartography'. However, Alphonsus J.M. Mulders (1962:431-438) devoted one section of his handbook to 'missionary cartography' and another section to 'geography and sociography'. I follow Seumois. I regard cartography as a -very important- branch of geography which has a special interest in 'missionary atlases and maps'.

STÄUDLIN, CARL F. Kirchliche Geographie und Statistik. Tübingen, 1804.
MISSIONARY GEOGRAPHY: or, the progress of religion traced round the world: by an Irish clergyman...: second ed., enl. London, 1827.
    First ed.: London, 1825.
BLUMHARDT, JOHANN C. Christian missions: or, a manual of missionary geography and history. London, 1846. 2 vols.
    *Ger. ed.: Handbuch der Missionsgeschichte und Missionsgeographie...: dritte, ganz neue Ausgabe. Calw, & Stuttgart, 1863. 2 vols.
    First Ger. ed.: Handbüchlein der Missionsgeschichte und Missionsgeographie ... Calw, & Stuttgart, 1844.
    Fr. tr.: 1850. 2 vols.
    *Dutch tr.: 1851.
*NEWCOMB, HARVEY. A cyclopedia of missions: containing a comprehensive view of missionary operations throughout the world: with geographical descriptions ...: second rev. ed. New York, 1860.
    First ed.: New York, 1854.

BRAMMERZ, W. Die katholischen Bistümer des Erdkreises: eine geographisch-statistische Uebersicht. Bergheim, 1862.

NEHER, STEPHAN J. Kirchliche Geographie und Statistik: oder, Darstellung des heutigen Zustandes der katholischen Kirche mit steter Rücksicht auf die früheren Zeiten und im Hinblick auf die anderen Religionsgemeinschaften. Regensburg, 1864-1868. 3 vols.

*MISSIONARY GEOGRAPHY for the use of teachers and missionary collectors. London, 1865.

DOBBINS, FRANK S. A foreign missionary manual: geographical, synoptical, statistical, and bibliographical. Philadelphia, 1881.

WERNER, OSCAR, SJ. Orbis terrarum catholicus: sive, totius ecclesiae catholicae et occidentis et orientis conspectus geographicus et statisticus: ex relationibus ad sacras congregationes Romanas missis et aliis notitiis observationibusque fide dignis. Freiburg im Breisgau, 1890.

*BEACH, HARLAN P. A geography and atlas of Protestant missions: their environment, forces, distribution, methods, problems, results, and prospects at the opening of the 20th century. New York, 1901-1906. 2 vols.

*GRUNDEMANN, PETER R. Kleine Missions-Geographie und -Statistik zur Darstellung des Standes der evangelischen Mission am Schluss des 19. Jahrhunderts. Calw, & Stuttgart, 1901.

*STREIT, ROBERT, OMI. Führer durch die deutsche katholische Missionsliteratur. Freiburg im Breisgau, 1911.

    P. 99-102: Missionsgeographie und Missionsstatistik. Bibliog.

GARCIA, WENCESLAO, SJ. Geografía-atlas de las misiones católicas. Burgos, 1924.

*STREIT, ROBERT, OMI. Die katholische deutsche Missionsliteratur. Aachen, & Immensee, 1925.

    P. 104: Missionsstatistik und Missionsgeographie. Bibliog.

    P. 198: Missionsgeographie. Bibliog.

GRAMMATICA, LUIGI. Testo e atlante di geografia ecclesiastia. Bergamo, 1927.

*STREIT, KARL, SVD. Mission und Kartographie. In: ZM, XX (1930), p. 276-280.

*MULDERS, ALPHONSUS J.M. Missiegeschiedenis. Bussum, 1957.

    P. XVIII: Cartografische werken. Bibliog.

CANOVESI, ANGELO. La diffusione geografica del Christianesimo... Torino, 1962.

*SPINDLER, MARC R. Pour une théologie de l'espace. Neuchâtel, 1968.

    P. 19-36: La conception dite géographique de la mission.

    P. 47-58: La géographie du salut.

5.3.4.4. MISSIONARY ATLASES AND MAPS

GENERAL

Many missionaries, as well as many missiologists, strove mightily to produce scientific atlases and maps: with special attention to mission fields and mission stations. These *missionary atlases and maps* either deal with Christian missions in general -global atlases and maps (cf. WCE 1982)- or have a limited, denominational interest: i.e. the Roman Catholic church, Protestantism, Presbyterianism (Lowrie 1854), etc. in specific regions, countries, or areas.

    Missionary atlases and maps either stand on their own or are part of church atlases and maps (Jedin, Latourette, & Martin 1970; Chadwick, &

Evans 1987; cf. Stäudlin 1804). We can observe that, in the post-colonial era, the latter almost becomes a common place (cf. the trend to avoid the term 'mission' in the title and subtitle of atlases and maps which already started before the Second World War: Streit 1929).

MORSE, SIDNEY E., & Co. The cerographic missionary atlas. New York, 1848.

*GRUNDEMANN, PETER R. (ed.). Allgemeiner Missions-Atlas nach Originalquellen. Gotha, 1867-1871. 4 vols.

?GRUNDEMANN, PETER R. Erläuterungen zur Missions-Weltkarte. Halle, 1883.
    Dutch tr.: 1886.

VAHL, JENS. Missionsatlas: med tilhorende forklaring: utgivet af det Danske Missionsselskab... Kjobenhavn, 1883-1886. 4 vols.

?GRUNDEMANN, PETER R. Missions-Schulwandkarte in drei Blättern: nebst Erläuterungen. Calw, & Stuttgart, 1887.

*BLISS, EDWIN M. (ed.). The encyclopaedia of missions: descriptive, historical, biographical, statistical... New York, London, & Toronto, 1891.
    I, p. 575: Missionary atlases and maps. Bibliog.

?HEILMANN, KARL. Missions-Wandkarte der Erde für den Schulgebrauch. Leipzig, 1892.

*BLISS, EDWIN M. (comp.). Descriptive catalogue of books on missions and mission lands... Philadelphia, 1894. Bibliog.
    P. 3-4: Atlases.

HEILMANN, KARL. Missionskarte der Erde nebst Begleitwort: mit besonderer Berücksichtigung der deutschen Kolonien: dritte verb. Aufl. Gütersloh, 1897.
    *First ed.: Gütersloh, 1891.

*DENNIS, JAMES S., HARLAN P. BEACH, SAMUEL M. ZWEMER, & CHARLES H. FAHS (eds.). Statistical atlas of Christian missions: containing a directory of missionary societies, a classified summary of statistics, an index of mission stations, and a series of specially prepared maps of mission fields, compiled by Sub-Committees of Commission I..., as an integral part of its report to the World Missionary Conference, Edinburgh, June 14-23, 1910. Edinburgh, 1910.
    Cf.: World atlas of Christian missions... New York, 1911.

*BEACH, HARLAN P., & CHARLES H. FAHS (eds.). World missionary atlas: containing a directory of missionary societies, classified summaries of statistics, maps showing the location of mission stations throughout the world, a descriptive account of the principal mission lands, and comprehensive indices: maps by John Bartholomew. New York, 1925.

*FAHS, CHARLES H. On making a missionary atlas. In: IRM, XIV (1925), p. 260-273.

HEILMANN, KARL. Die äussere Mission: ihre Geschichte und ihr gegenwärtiger Stand: nebst Missionskarte der Erde... 7 Aufl. Gütersloh, 1925.
    *Fünfte und sechste Aufl.: Gütersloh, 1912.

DESPONT, JOSEPH. Nouvel atlas des missions. Paris, & Lyon, 1951.

*GEISSLER, HEINRICH. Mission in Karten: 2. Aufl. Wuppertal, & Barmen, 1956.

DELL, ROBERT S. An atlas of Christian history... London, 1960.

SPAETH, HAROLD J. (ed.). World mission map. Cincinnati, 1962.

*SANTOS HERNANDEZ, ANGEL, SJ. Bibliografia misional. Santander, 1965. 2 vols.
    II, p. 1209-1211: Atlas. Bibliog.

*DICTIONARY CATALOG. 1968.
    X, p. 758-759: Missionary atlas. Bibliog.
    XI, p. 81-83: Missions-atlases. Bibliog.

XI, p. 122-123: Missions-maps. Bibliog.
XI, p. 179-180: Missions-atlas. Bibliog.
*JEDIN, HUBERT, KENNETH S. LATOURETTE, & JOCHEN MARTIN (eds.). Atlas zur Kirchengeschichte:
die christlichen Kirchen in Geschichte und Gegenwart...: bearbeitet von Jochen
Martin. Freiburg im Breisgau, Basel, Wien..., 1970.
*CONCISE DICTIONARY. 1971.
P. 40-41: Missionary atlases (Burton L. Goddard).
*WCE. 1982.
P. 863-884: Atlas; atlas of Christianity and evangelization in the modern world.
CHADWICK, HENRY, & G.R. EVANS (eds.). Atlas of the Christian church. London, 1987.
*LM. 1992.
P. 53-55: Atlas zur Mission.

ROMAN CATHOLIC

In the Roman Catholic church we find specialists in cartography at both the
global and the local level: on the one hand, the missionary orders produced
atlases and maps of their own fields and stations, and, on the other hand, the
Congregatio de Propaganda Fide (1932; 1946; 1950; cf. Monticone 1948;
Emmerich 1958) published data on the world-wide spread of the Roman
Catholic church and her mission in modern history.

In the Roman Catholic church (cf. Brammerz 1862; Neher 1864-1868;
Werner 1890; Grammatica 1927) missionary cartography is more intimately
connected with church cartography than is the case in Protestantism.

PETRI, GIROLAMO. L'orbe cattolico ossia atlante geografico, storico, ecclesiastico... Roma,
1858-1859. 3 vols.
*WERNER, OSCAR, SJ. Katholischer Missions-Atlas: neunzehn Karten in Farbendruck mit
begleitendem Text: zweite, verb. Aufl. Freiburg im Breisgau, 1885.
First ed.: Freiburg im Breisgau, 1884.
Fr. tr.: 1886.
*STREIT, KARL, SVD. Katholischer Missionsatlas, enthaltend die gesamten Missionsgebiete des
Erdkreises... Steyl, 1906.
Fr. tr.: 1906.
BOUCHER, ANDRÉ. Petit atlas des missions catholiques: 2e éd. rev. et mise à jour. Paris,
1928.
STREIT, KARL, SVD. Catholic world atlas: containing a geographical and statistical
description with maps of the Holy Roman Catholic Church, with historical and
ethnographical notices... Paderborn, & New York, 1929.
*Latin ed.: Atlas hierarchicus: descriptio geographica et statistica Sanctae
Romanae Ecclesiae tum occidentis tum orientis juxta statum praesentem accedunt
nonnullae notae historicae necnon ethnographicae... Paderborn, 1929.
First ed.: Paderborn, 1913.
*(SACRA CONGREGATIO DE PROPAGANDA FIDE). Testo-atlante illustrato delle missioni: compilato
a cura dell'Agenzia Internazionale "Fides": con i dati cartografici e statistici
dell'Archivo della S. Congregazione di Propaganda Fide. Roma, Novara, & Parigi,
1932.

*Germ. tr.: 1932.

THAUREN, JOHANNES, SVD. Atlas der katholischen Missionsgeschichte: 49 Haupt- und Nebenkarten: mit erläuterndem Text und alphabetischem Register. Mödling bei Wien, 1932.
Kleinere Ausgabe: 1933.

*THAUREN, JOHANNES, SVD. Atlas der Geschichte der katholischen Missionen: mit einem kurzen Abriss der Geschichte der katholischen Missionen: dargestellt in geographischer und zeitlicher Folge. Mödling bei Wien, 1933.
First ed.: Steyl, 1925.

?(SACRA CONGREGATIO DE PROPAGANDA FIDE). Le missioni cattoliche...: cenni geographici et storici dati statistici. Roma, 1946.

MONTICONE, GIUSEPPE (ed.). Atlante delle missioni cattoliche dipendenti dalla Sacra Congregazione de 'Propaganda Fide'. Roma, 1947.

*(SACRA CONGREGATIO DE PROPAGANDA FIDE). Le missioni cattoliche...: storia, geografia, statistica. Roma, 1950.

EMMERICH, HEINRICH, SVD (ed.). Atlas missionum a Sacra Congregatione de Propaganda Fide dependentium... Mödling, 1958.

ATLANTINO MISSIONI. Venezia, 1960.

FREITAG, ANTON, SVD, HEINRICH EMMERICH SVD, & JAKOB BUYS SVD. The universe atlas of the Christian world: the expansion of Christianity through the centuries. London, 1963.
American ed.: The twentieth century atlas of the Christian world... New York, 1963.
First ed.: Atlas du monde chrétien: l'expansion du christianisme à travers les siècles... Paris, & Bruxelles, 1959.
Ger. tr.: 1960.
*Dutch tr.: 1960.

PROTESTANT

In Protestantism we find the same division as in the Roman Catholic church: some people are primarily interested in local developments, and others in general trends.

Most missionary atlases and maps have been produced by the missionary societies. They present information about the fields and stations where the societies work: the American Board of Commissioners for Foreign Missions (1843); the Basel Mission (Josenhans 1859); the Moravians (Reichel 1860; 1907); the Church Missionary Society (1879); the Rhenish Mission (1891); the Society for the Propagation of the Gospel in Foreign Parts (1894); the Christian and Missionary Alliance (1922; Snead 1950); the Conference of the Mennonite Brethren Church of North America (1957); etc. They are, depending upon the size of the societies involved, useful sources of information on special countries and continents. They also show that geography, cartography, and missionary policy are interrelated. For instance, we read in *The Church Missionary Atlas* (1879:VII), published by the Church Missionary Society, that there still 'remaineth very much land to be possessed'.

The missionary atlases and maps which go beyond the interests and needs of specific missionary societies were either produced in the universities or in the offices of international bodies. On the one hand, I refer to Harlan P. Beach (1854-1933) who published *A Geography and Atlas of Protestant Missions* (1901-1906) and thereafter became Professor of Missions at Yale University Divinity School; and, on the other hand, I refer to the *Statistical Atlas of Christian Missions* (1910), and the *World Missionary Atlas* (1925), which were born in the Ecumenical Movement. Stephen C. Neill (1986:487) dealt with the latter and pointed out that such a work is 'out of date, and it is unlikely that another of the same type will be published'. This view fits in with the conviction of Knut B. Westmann, & Harald von Sicard (1962:18-19) that 'the period of missionary atlases with their statistical data, however, comes to an end' (Ger.: *Die Zeit der Missionsatlanten mit ihren statistischen Angaben geht jedoch ihrem Ende zu*; my tr.).

After the integration of the IMC into the WCC (1961), we are not longer entitled to speak about the non-western world as the 'mission field' of the western world. The whole world became the mission field of the whole church. This implies that missionary geography and cartography must be shaped in a new way: i.e. in the framework of the concept of 'mission in six continents' (Mexico 1963). Missionary cartography can no longer be produced as a kind of extension of western missionary societies, but only as a function of *missionary* World Christianity (cf. WCE 1982).

This change of scope does not impede the historical study of missionary cartography (cf. Freitag 1963): a thorough study of the history of Christian mission always needs atlases and maps which give concrete information about mission lands, mission fields, mission stations, missionary travels, etc. in all six continents.

*WYLD, JAMES. An atlas of maps of different parts of the world: designed to show the stations of the Protestant missionaries. London, 1839.
*AMERICAN BOARD OF COMMISSIONERS FOR FOREIGN MISSIONS. Maps and illustrations of the missions ... Boston, 1843.
  First ed.: Boston, 1841.
  Reprint: N.p., 1846.
THE MISSIONARY GUIDE-BOOK: or, a key to the Protestant missionary map of the world: shewing the geography, natural history, climate, population, and government of the several countries to which missionary efforts have been directed: with the moral, social, and religious condition of their inhabitants: also, the rise and progress of missionary operations in each country...: illustrated by forty-five woodcuts, representing the costume of each people. London, 1846.
PROTESTANT MISSIONARY MAP OF THE WORLD: colored to shew the prevailing state of religion in the several countries, and containing all the stations mentioned in 'The missionary guide-book'. London, 1846.

HAWKINS, ERNEST. The colonial church atlas, arranged in dioceses; with some additional maps, geographical and statistical tables, and an index of places: third ed. ... London, 1853.

*LOWRIE, JOHN C. A manual of missions: or, sketches of the foreign missions of the Presbyterian church: with maps, showing the stations, and statistics of Protestant missions among unevangelized nations. New York, 1854.
Second ed.: 1855.

JOSENHANS, JOSEPH F. (ed.). Atlas der Evangelischen Missions-Gesellschaft zu Basel...: zweite Aufl. Basel, 1859.
*First ed.: Basel, 1857.

*REICHEL, LEVIN Th. (ed.). Missions-Atlas der Brüder-Unität: hrsg. vom Missions-Departement der Unitäts-Ältesten-Conferenz zum Besten der Brüder-Mission. Herrnhut, 1860.

*(CHURCH MISSIONARY SOCIETY). The church missionary atlas: containing an account of the various countries in which the Church Missionary Society labours, and of its missionary operations: with thirty-one maps, a chronological chart, etc.: new ed. (the sixth). London, 1879.
First ed.: London, 1859. Several reprints.

*RHEINISCHER MISSIONS-ATLAS: neun Karten nebst Text: zweite Ausgabe. Barmen, 1891.
First ed.: 1878.

SOCIETY FOR THE PROPAGATION OF THE GOSPEL IN FOREIGN PARTS. A collection of maps... London, 1894.

GAREIS, REINHOLD. Geschichte der evangelischen Heidenmission mit besonderer Berücksichtigung der deutschen: mit 11 Karten von R. Grundemann: zweite durchgesehene und verm. Aufl. Konstanz, 1902.
*First ed.: Konstanz, & Emmishofen, 1901.

?ATLAS OF PROTESTANT MISSIONS. 1903.

*GRUNDEMANN, PETER R. Neuer Missions-Atlas aller evangelischen Missionsgebiete mit besonderer Berücksichtigung der deutschen Missionen: zweite, verm. und verb. Aufl. Calw, & Stuttgart, 1903.
*First ed.: Calw, & Stuttgart, 1896.

*GRUNDEMANN, PETER R. Kleiner Missions-Atlas zur Darstellung des evangelischen Missionswerkes nach seinem gegenwärtigen Bestande: dritte, durchaus neu bearb. und verm. Aufl. Calw, & Stuttgart, 1905.
First ed.: Calw, & Stuttgart, 1883.

*(MISSIONSDIREKTION DER EVANGELISCHEN BRÜDER-UNITÄT) (eds.). Missions-Atlas der Brüdergemeine: achtzehn Karten mit erläuterndem Text. Herrnhut, 1907.
*First ed.: Herrnhut, 1895.

CHRISTIAN AND MISSIONARY ALLIANCE. Atlas showing mission fields... New York, 1922.

*SNEAD, ALFRED C. (ed.). Missionary atlas: a manual of the foreign work of the Christian and Missionary Alliance: illustrated with maps, charts and photographs. Harrisburg, 1950.
Rev. ed.: Harrisburg, 1964.
First ed.: Harrisburg, 1924.

(CONFERENCE OF THE MENNONITE BRETHREN CHURCH OF NORTH AMERICA). Missionary atlas: a compilation of maps and related data of the foreign mission fields... Hillsboro, 1957.

5.3.4.5. MISSION FIELDS AND MISSION STATIONS

> There is no country which is not a mission-field.
> *Max A.C. Warren (1948:137).*

Since Columbus and Vasco de Gama, the term *mission field* has been frequently used in the West. Most mission studies, however, do not give a proper explanation of this term. However, Harlan P. Beach and Charles H. Fahs (1925:15) applied the notion of the 'field' in their Directory 'not only to areas in which the societies have foreign missionaries and indigenous workers but also those areas to which there is a definite allocation of funds'. The use of this term changed after the Second World War: Hendrik Kraemer (1958) described the transition from the Columbus and Vasco da Gama era to the post-colonial era as a development 'from mission field to independent church'. Today the West no longer has its 'own' overseas mission fields; because the whole world is now considered to be one mission field of which God is the 'owner'. However, David B. Barrett (WCE 1982:834) still defines 'mission field' as 'the geographical region, country, or area in which foreign mission is undertaken'. Such a definition now belongs to the past.

Mission stations (cf. Oswald C. Fountain, in: Smalley 1978:824-833) were built in the mission fields. David B. Barrett (WCE 1982:834) described them as 'places of missionary residence in or from which local missionary activity is carried on'. In the period before and after the Second World War, we see that such stations were handed over by the 'sending' churches and societies in the West to the 'receiving' churches and organizations in the non-western world. In other words: western mission stations became independent church 'stations'; and western mission buildings -mission schools, mission hospitals, etc.- became non-western church institutions.

In the post-colonial era, several states closed their borders for western missionaries: travelling to mission fields and mission stations now becomes more difficult. Therefore Alfred C. Snead (1950:152-153) and others began to write about *closed lands* and *inadequately occupied lands*. This, however, is a very controversial vocabulary because religious liberty must be measured primarily in terms of the existence or non-existence of this right for 'indigenous' Christians who nowadays are first and foremost responsible for the preaching of the gospel in their own 'mission fields' and in their own 'mission stations'.

*SONDERMANN, JOHANN S. (ed.). Tabellarische Übersicht über die protestantischen Missionsgesellschaften, Missionsstationen und Missionare der Gegenwart... Nürnberg, 1846.
?GRAUL, KARL. Die christlichen Missionsplätze auf der ganzen Erde. Leipzig, 1847.
*ZAHN, FRANZ M. Der Acker ist die Welt: Blicke in das Arbeitsfeld der evangelischen Mission. Gütersloh, 1888.

*BLISS, EDWIN M. (ed.). The encyclopaedia of missions: descriptive, historical, biographical, statistical ... New York, London, & Toronto, 1891.
   II, p. 589-605: List of missionary stations.
*WARNECK. 1892-1903. 3 vols.
   III/1, p. 1-166: Das Missionsgebiet.
*DAUBANTON. 1911. P. 207-209: De agriek.
*ZWEMER, SAMUEL M. Missionslose Länder: ungelöste Missionsaufgaben. Basel, 1912.
?LAUKENAU, F.J. The world is our field: a missionary survey. St. Louis, 1928.
*WARREN, MAX A.C. The truth of vision: a study in the nature of Christian hope. London, & Edinburgh, 1948.
*DAIN, ARTHUR J. (ed.). Mission fields today: a brief world survey... Chicago, 1957.
*KRAEMER, HENDRIK. From mission field to independent church... The Hague, 1958.
*TRUEBLOOD, ELTON. The validity of the Christian mission. New York, Evanston, San Francisco..., 1972.
   P. 69-89: The field of mission.
*SMALLEY, WILLIAM A. (ed.). Readings in missionary anthropology II (enl. 1978 ed.). South Pasadena, 1978.
   P. 824-833: Some roles of mission stations (Oswald C. Fountain).

5.3.4.6. MISSIONARY TRAVELS

Jesus travelled with his disciples in Judaea, Samaria, and Galilee. The four gospels give us a lot of information about his going from place to place. The third gospel is especially interested in the geography of Jesus' ministry. This geographical interest is also clear in the Acts of the Apostles. It starts with the description of the missionary activities of the apostles in Jerusalem, Judaea, and Samaria (Acts 1:8), and finishes its survey in Rome, the capital of the Roman empire.

The three *missionary journeys* of Paul to Syria, Asia, Greece, and Italy, which are reported in the Acts of the Apostles, are described and analysed in special studies -with maps- on Paul (cf. 3.4.2.2.). Paul became the paradigmatic example of all Christian missionary travelling from *the 'sending' countries* to *the 'receiving' countries* (cf. Diffendorfer 1946), throughout the following centuries.

Paul was certainly not the only apostle who travelled to 'new fields'. In the New Testament we can also read about some of his companions who went their own way. The apocrypha, however, tell us stories about the twelve apostles dividing the whole world amongst themselves. The Acts of Thomas, for instance, tells us about the voyage of the apostle Thomas to India. The 'Thomas Christians' in India believe that he founded the Christian church in their own country. Stephen C. Neill (1986:45) investigated this claim and concluded: 'Two things we can affirm with certainty. First, we know that this church has existed from very early times... Secondly we can say that a voyage by St Thomas to South India in the first century would have been perfectly possible'.

During the first centuries, missionaries not only travelled to Asia: to India (Pantaenus and Cosmas Indocopleustes) and to Armenia (Gregory Thaumaturgus); but also travelled to Africa: to Ethiopia (Aedesius and Frumentius); and travelled to Europe: to the Goths (Ulfilas), Ireland (Patrick), and France (St Martin). In the Middle Ages the more remote parts of those three continents were reached. And, in modern times, we can observe missionaries travelling in Sub-Saharian Africa, America, Australia, and Oceania. Francis Xavier SJ (1506-1552) and Matthew Ricci SJ (1552-1610) in Asia, and David Livingstone (1813-1873) and Henry M. Stanley (1841-1904) in Africa travelled for thousands of miles and delivered reports on their experiences en route (cf. Livingstone 1857). Also in our era of trains and aircraft, travelling is still an important part of the missionary existence. However, 'a record of the voyages, travels, labors, and successes of the various missionaries, who have been sent forth by Protestant societies and churches' (Choules, & Smith 1851) has today a character which is entirely different from that in the previous centuries.

*CAMPBELL, JOHN. Maritime discovery and Christian missions, considered in their mutual relations. London, 1840.

CHOULES, JOHN O., & THOMAS SMITH. The origin and history of missions: a record of the voyages, travels, labors, and successes of the various missionaries, who have been sent forth by Protestant societies and churches...: ninth ed. New York, 1851. 2 vols.
First ed.: Boston, 1832. 2 vols.

*LIVINGSTONE, DAVID. Missionary travels and researches in South Africa: including a sketch of sixteeen years' residence in the interior of Africa. London, 1857.

KÜLB, PHILIPP H. Die Reisen der Missionäre: ein Buch zur Belehrung und Unterhaltung. Regensburg, 1860-1863. 2 parts.

*DIFFENDORFER, RALPH E. (ed.). Christian literature in the mission world: progress report. New York, 1946.

5.3.4.7. THE GEOGRAPHY OF CHRISTIAN MISSION AND THE GEOGRAPHY OF RELIGION

The geography of Christian mission is a branch of both mission studies and religious studies. It is also related to geography in general.

Jamie S. Scott and Paul Simpson-Housley (1991) dealt with the *geographics of religion* (Ger.: *Religionsgeographie*), especially with the geographics of Judaism, Christianity, and Islam. They considered their book as an 'interdisciplinary project in the study of religion and geography'. And they concluded: 'The study of religion has not been a major domain of human geography, even though the manifestations of religious experience express themselves with spatial variety on the landscape' (:XII). However, they did not link the 'geographics of religion' with '(Christian and/or non-Christian) mission'.

Other scholars consider the geography of Christian mission as just an 'auxiliary science' (cf. 5.3.1.2.). However, I regard it as an independent discipline which is closely related to the history of Christian mission. It not only studies the afore-mentioned cartographical topics, but also the interaction between 'mission' and 'the earth': the river Nile enabled missionaries to travel to Ethiopia in the fourth century, but the Sahara desert prevented them from reaching Sub-Saharian Africa in the following centuries. This branch also includes the study of Christian mission as a power which changed the 'face' of the earth: Christian mission allowed people to raise hogs but prohibited them from sacrificing animals; it preferred burials rather than cremation; and it introduced new methods in agriculture and fishing.

Usually scholars divide geography as an academic discipline into the physical and the social geography. The 'religious geography of the world' (Staples, in: News from the English churches 1982:100) is primarily related to the social geography because religion is not a physical, but a social phenomenon. This also concerns mission: including Christian mission. The study of the geography of Christian mission must be linked with the study of the geography of non-Christian religions (cf. Schlunk, & Quiring 1966), as well as with the study of 'human geography' (Roxby, in: IRM 1928:483-494) in general. Some missionaries and missiologists studied the geography of Christian mission in the context of other religions, but others went further: they described and analysed not only the social, but even the physical aspects of geography in their own mission fields.

*ROXBY, PERCY M. Human geography and some of its applications. In: IRM, XVII (1928), p. 483-494.
?SCHLUNK, MARTIN, & HORST QUIRING (eds.). Map of the world's religions and missions: explanations transl. by Stephen Neill: fourth ed.: including Roman catholic statistics brought up-to-date. Stuttgart, 1966.
    *Ger. ed.: Karte der Religionen und Missionen der Erde: hrsg. von Martin Schlunk und Horst Quiring in Verbindung mit IMC, London, und Missionary Research Library, New York: 3 verb. Aufl. Stuttgart, & Bern, 1960.
    First Ger. ed.: 1951.
    Reprint Ger. ed.: 1966.
*SCHWIND, MARTIN (ed.). Religionsgeographie. Darmstadt, 1975.
    P. 378: Missionsgeographie.
*STAPLES, PETER. Towards a genuinely ecumenical imagination. In: News from the English churches, I/4 (1982), p. 91-126.
*SCOTT, JAMIE S., & PAUL SIMPSON-HOUSLEY (eds.). Sacred places and profane spaces: essays in the geographics of Judaism, Christianity, and Islam. Westport, 1991.

5.3.4.8. CONCLUSION

The geography of Christian mission becomes more and more the geography of *missionary* World Christianity.

From a historical point of view, the geography and cartography of Christian (Roman Catholic and Protestant) mission must still be treated separately. From the decolonization point of view, however, missionary atlases and maps which are partly or totally western-centered cannot be accepted anymore. Mission fields and mission stations as western institutions are out of date: they became part of the 'enterprise' of the so-called 'third world' churches. Today, the voyages of non-western missionaries can be more important than the (expensive) voyages of white missionaries.

The concept of 'mission in six continents' is a good framework to rethink missionary geography. The expansion of the Christian faith in each continent continues: therefore the study of this global expansion is an ongoing responsibility of missionary geographers in both East and West, North and South. Missionary geography will only cease if Christianity becomes introverted and static: by neglecting the missionary obligation which Christ has given to the church to disciple 'all nations' (Matt. 28:19).

5.3.5. THE STATISTICS OF CHRISTIAN MISSION

> The dominant impression made upon one by
> a discerning study of the statistical tables and of
> the interpretative articles is
> one hopeful and reassuring.
> *John Mott (Parker 1938:9).*

5.3.5.1. INTRODUCTION

François E. Daubanton (1911:443-457), Joseph Schmidlin (1925:95-117), and also other writers of missiological handbooks have primarily connected the 'statistics of Christian mission' with the 'geography of Christian mission'. I follow these scholars because I like to emphasize that this discipline has grown up in the shadow of the 'history of Christian mission' and the 'geography of Christian mission'. The *statistics of Christian mission* (Ger.: *Missionsstatistik*), however, must be systematically related to the 'sociology of Christian mission' which as a discipline has grown up afterwards.

The statistics of Christian mission is not an auxiliary science (cf. 5.3.1.2.), but an independent science. It can be divided into *micro- and macro-statistics*: the former deals with the numbers of one (or more) missionary order(s), missionary society(s), mission field(s), mission church(es), etc., and the latter with global trends, for instance the *estimated* numerical growth of Islam as a missionary religion in comparison with the *estimated* numerical growth of Christianity as a missionary religion.

Some missiologists are more interested in statistics than others. I note that Roman Catholic and Evangelical scholars in general are more concerned about missionary statistics than their Ecumenical companions. The evangelical Church Growth Movement of Donald A. McGavran, with its strong emphasis on 'multiplying churches', combines a special interest in micro-statistics with the development of a missionary strategy (cf. 5.4.5.). The lack of interest in statistics which is demonstrated by the Ecumenical Movement (cf. DEM 1991, which has no article on statistics; even the index of this encyclopedia does not mention the word 'statistics'), must be understood in the light of its concern for the kingdom of God rather than for the size of the churches, and its struggling with the presence of Christ outside the 'gate' (Hebr. 13:12) of the churches rather than with the 'unreached people' who will be lost if they will not accept Christ as their personal Lord and Saviour.

Much -missionary- data can be expressed in statistical tables (for instance, the frequency of -missionary- prayers). But there are also many -missionary- data which cannot be expressed in numbers (for instance, the intensity of -missionary- prayers). The German scholar Rolf-Walter Becker (1968) made a distinction between *objective and subjective indicators*. Statistical tables are based upon objective indicators: numbers of church members and attendance at worship, amount of contributions to funds, frequency of Bible reading, etc. However, subjective indicators -e.g. religious convictions- are as important as the objective ones but usually they are not quantifiable. For example, a Christian who offers much money to mission funds (measurable) can be somebody who is lacking in basic missionary conviction (unmeasurable), and vice versa. Therefore, we must be very careful when interpreting the 'objective' micro- and macro-statistics of Christian mission because it does not clarify the -unmeasurable- personal 'convictions'. We must always be aware that there exists a 'beyond statistics' (Corey 1937).

Sadhu Sundar Singh (1929) in India divided humanity into four categories: 1. non-Christians without Christ; 2. non-Christians with Christ; 3. Christians without Christ; and 4. Christians with Christ. By and large we know the numbers of Christians and non-Christians; but the numbers of both non-Christians with Christ (secret believers, or crypto-Christians) and Christians with Christ (reborn Christians) are uncountable.

*DAUBANTON. 1911.
    P. 443-457: Zendingsgeografie en -statistiek.
*SCHMIDLIN. 1925.
    P. 95-117: Missionskunde (Missionsstatistik und Missionsgeographie).

*SEUMOIS. 1952.
    P. 332-339: Monographie d'enquête territoriale statistico-missiographique.
*MULDERS. 1962.
    P. 421-431: Missiestatistiek.

5.3.5.2. HISTORY

The statistical description and analysis of the Christian mission was initiated by the Sacra congregatio de propaganda fide (Corsi 1844; et al.) in the Roman Catholic church and by many missionary societies in Protestantism.

Olav G. Myklebust (1955:82) mentioned in passing the statistical studies of Carl F. Stäudlin (1804) and Julius Wiggers (1842-1843), but did nor refer to the works of Johann H. Brauer (1847-1851), John C. Lowrie (1854), and William B. Boyce (1863; 1874), who were the main founders of the statistics of Christian mission as an independent discipline in the middle of last century. Thereafter, Theodor Christlieb (1880), Peter R. Grundemann (1886; 1901), and Jens Vahl (1892; 1892-1897) on the Protestant side, and Stephan J. Neher (1864-1868; 1895), and Hermann A. Krose SJ (1906; 1908) on the Roman Catholic side searched for an academic level of this new discipline. François E. Daubanton (1911:455) considered Grundemann as 'the great master of missionary statistics' (Dutch: *de grote meester in de zendingsstatistiek*; my tr.); and Joseph Schmidlin (1925:115) characterisized Krose as the scholar who presented 'a methodology of missionary statistics' (Ger.: *eine Methodologie der Missionsstatistik*; my tr.).

Not only the geography of Christian mission but also the statistics of Christian mission was further developed in the context of the World Missionary Conferences. James S. Dennis (1902) published a 'statistical supplement' to his book on *Christian Missions and Social Progress* (1897-1906; 3 vols.), which was described by Gustav Warneck (AMZ 1902:327-343) as 'a giant statistics of mission' (Ger.: *eine gigantische Missionsstatistik*; my tr.). Dennis became famous as one of the editors of the *Statistical Atlas of Christian Missions* (1910). This work was followed by *World Statistics of Christian Missions* (1916), and two studies which are related to the International Missionary Council: *World Missionary Atlas: Containing... Classified Summaries of Statistics...* (1925), and *Interpretative Statistical Survey of the World Mission of the Christian Church* (1938). After the Second World War, these surveys were replaced by the *World Christian Handbooks* (1949-1968: five successive editions). In the last edition of these *Handbooks* (Coxill, & Grubb 1968:49) we read the following evaluation of the past by Frank W. Price: 'The *Interpretative Statistical Survey of the World Mission of the Christian Church* (IMC 1938), published just before the International Missionary Council conference in India, was a high-water mark in statistical research. It reflected, as the 1925 survey did not, the significant shifting of gravity from the western missionary societies established by them, and revealed many interesting contrasts and trends. This comprehensive and detailed study has been succeeded by the smaller but valuable *Handbooks* published by the World Dominion Press, in 1949, 1952, 1957, 1962, and now in 1967'. The *World Christian Encyclopedia* (1982) of David B. Barrett -and the yearly updates since 1982 by the same author- can be considered as the successor of these *Handbooks*. His name has already been mentioned in the Foreword of the 1968 edition of the *Handbooks*. Both the *Handbooks* and the *World Christian Encylopedia* offer micro- and macro-statistics, but the latter is more up-to-date and puts the collected materials in a larger frame.

In the Roman Catholic church we must honour Karl Streit SVD as 'the great master of missionary statistics' (cf. Daubanton on Grundemann). His *Catholic World Atlas; Containing a Geographical and Statistical Description with Maps...* (1929) is excellent. However, his work was not followed by other similar works immediately before or after the Second World War. Therefore, we can consider the *World Christian Encylopedia* (1982) of David B. Barrett as the successor of the *Catholic World Atlas* as well. At the same time we note that in this period the Sacra congregatio de propaganda fide (1930; 1932; 1946; 1950; cf. Schorer 1959) went on to collect, publish, and analyse statistical summaries of Roman Catholic missionary work.

HARNACK, ADOLF VON. The mission and expansion of Christianity in the first three centuries: second, enl. and rev. ed. London, & New York, 1908. 2 vols.
SINGH, SADHU SUNDAR. With and without Christ: being incidents taken from the lives of Christians and of non-Christians which illustrate the differences in lives lived with Christ and without Christ. New York, & London, 1929.
    *Dutch tr.: 1930.
*MYKLEBUST. 1955-1957. 2 vols.

5.3.5.3. THE STATISTICS OF CHRISTIAN MISSION

> Missionary statistics, to be sure, are mere figures,
> but they stand for immense and thrilling facts.
> *James S. Dennis (1902:1).*

The statistics of Christian mission is a branch of mission studies which needs much expertise. In *The Enylopaedia of Missions* (1891:II,606), edited by Edwin M. Bliss, we read: 'The preparation of the statistics has been perhaps the most perplexing part of the work of this *Encyclopaedia*'.

Alphonsus J.M. Mulders (1962:423) divided the statistics of Christian mission into *historical statistics* and *contemporary statistics*. The historical statistics of Christian mission describes and analyses the statistical data relating

276

to Christian mission in the past, from the Early Church to the end of the colonial period, with an emphasis on the eras of Columbus and Vasco da Gama. Adolf von Harnack (1908) had already collected statistical data on the Early Church. However, more statistical materials are available for the modern period. These cover a wide field of topics. Peter R. Grundemann (1901:11-12; my tr.) mentioned the following nine topics of which the numerical growth and strength must be studied:

1. Mission stations;
2. Missionaries;
3. Ordained indigenous people;
4. Other indigenous personnel;
5. Baptisms;
6. Indigenous Christians;
7. Participants in the Holy Communion;
8. Schools; and
9. Pupils.

In other books we can find other lists of topics. For instance, Ludwig Wolff SCJ (1920:146-147) also paid attention to the numbers of church buildings and charities. Usually, missionary finance is not included in the historical statistics of Christian mission.

Frank W. Price rightly says: 'It is relatively easy to collect data on institutions -number of Christian schools, hospitals, theological seminaries, social service centres, teachers, students, physicians, nurses, social workers, etc. ... It is far more difficult to secure complete and accurate data on the life and work of the national churches, the number of congregations, leaders, officers, members, and statistics on finances and the inclusive Christian community' (World Christian handbook 1968:49). The contemporary statistics of Christian mission (cf. WCE 1982) is only interested in these data on the life and work of national churches and national mission agencies which are difficult to find and verify.

STÄUDLIN, CARL F. Kirchliche Geographie und Statistik. Tübingen, 1804.
WIGGERS, JULIUS. Kirchliche Statistik oder Darstellung der gesammten christlichen Kirche nach ihrem gegenwärtigen äusseren und inneren Zustande. Hamburg, & Gotha, 1842-1843. 2 vols.
*GRUNDEMANN, PETER R. Zur Missionsstatistik. In: AMZ, II (1875), p. 49-58.
DOBBINS, FRANK S. A foreign missionary manual: geographical, synoptical, statistical, and bibliographical. Philadelphia, 1881.
*BLISS, EDWIN M. (ed.). The encyclopaedia of missions: descriptive, historical, biographical, statistical... New York, London, & Toronto, 1891.
    II, p. 606-634: Statistical tables.
*DWIGHT, HENRY O., HENRY A. TUPPER Jr, & EDWIN M. BLISS (eds.). The encyclopedia of

missions: descriptive, historical, biographical, statistical: second ed. New York, & London, 1904.

P. 835-847: Statistical tables.

*DENNIS, JAMES S., HARLAN P. BEACH, SAMUEL M. ZWEMER, & CHARLES H. FAHS (eds.). Statistical atlas of Christian missions: containing a directory of missionary societies, a classified summary of statistics, an index of mission stations, and a series of specially prepared maps of mission fields... Edinburgh. 1910.
Cf.: World atlas of Christian missions... New York, 1911.

BEACH, HARLAN P., & BURTON ST. JOHN (eds.). World statistics of Christian missions: containing a directory of missionary societies, a classified summary of statistics, and an index of mission stations throughout the world. New York, 1916.

*RICHTER, JULIUS. Eine neue Missionsstatistik. In: AMZ, XLIV (1917), p. 191-199.

*BOYNTON, CHARLES L. World statistics of Christian missions. In: IRM, VII (1918), p. 107-114.

*BEACH, HARLAN P., & CHARLES H. FAHS (eds.). World missionary atlas: containing a directory of missionary societies, classified summaries of statistics, maps showing the location of mission stations throughout the world, a descriptive account of the principal mission lands, and comprehensive indices: maps by John Bartholomew. New York, 1925.

COREY, STEPHEN J. Beyond statistics: the wider range of world missions. St. Louis, 1937.

*PARKER, JOSEPH I. (ed.). Interpretative statistical survey of the world mission of the Christian church: summary and detailed statistics of churches and missionary societies, interpretative articles, and indices. New York, & London, 1938.

*GRÜNDLER, JOHANNES. Lexikon der christlichen Kirchen und Sekten, unter Berücksichtigung der Missionsgesellschaften und zwischenkirchlichen Organisationen. Wien, Freiburg, & Basel, 1961. 2 vols.
II, p. 1-122: Statistik.

*ANDERSON, GERALD H. (ed.). Christian mission in theological perspective: an inquiry by Methodists. Nashville, & New York, 1967.
P. 261-262: Some statistics on Protestant and Roman Catholic missionary personnel.

*COXILL, H. WAKELIN, & SIR KENNETH GRUBB (eds.). World Christian handbook. London, 1968.
First ed.: London, 1949.

*DICTIONARY CATALOG. 1968.
X, p. 750: Missionaries-vital statistics. Bibliog.
XIV, p. 707: Statistics-missionaries. Bibliog.
XIV, p. 707-708: Statistics-missionary societies. Bibliog.
XIV, p. 708-712: Statistics-missions. Bibliog.

*LEXIKON ZUR WELTMISSION. 1975.
P. 3: Adressbücher und Statistiken der Mission (Niels-Peter Moritzen).

*VERKUYL, JOHANNES. De onvoltooide taak der wereldzending: afscheidscollege... Kampen, 1978.
P. 18-45: Enige statistische gegevens.

*WCE. 1982.
P. 773-812: Statistics: global, continental, and confessional statistical tables.

*BARRETT, DAVID B. Five statistical eras of global mission. In: Missiology, XII (1984), p. 21-37.

*BARRETT, DAVID B. Five statistical eras of global mission: a thesis and discussion. In: IBMR, VIII (1984), p. 160-169.

*JOHNSTONE, PATRICK. Operation world: a day-to-day guide to praying for the world: fourth ed. Bromley, & Bulstrode, 1986.

278

P. 498-499: Church statistics.
P. 500-501: Statistical sources.
First ed.: 1974.
*LMG. 1987.
P. 312-314: Missionsstatistik (Willi Henkel OMI).
*BARRETT, DAVID B. Annual statistical table on global mission: 1988. In: IBMR, XII (1988),
p. 16-17.
BARRETT, DAVID B., & TODD M. JOHNSON. Our globe and how to reach it: seeing the world
evangelized by AD 2000 and beyond. Birmingham, 1990.
*LM. 1992.
P. 388-390: Statistik.

5.3.5.4. THE STATISTICS OF ROMAN CATHOLIC MISSION

The historical development of Roman Catholic statistics has already been
mentioned. Today, the Roman Catholic church as institition is still very
interested in good statistical surveys but many Roman Catholic missiologists
have other priorities.

Karl Müller SVD (1987:194-203), for instance, dealt with statistics. He
did not talk about the statistics of the Roman Catholic church. He only paid
attention to the statistics of World Christianity in general: 'The numerical
analysis of Christianity is impressive even though the surprising growth does
not always keep pace with the general world population growth. There were
558.056.300 Christians in 1900, that is, 34,4 % of the world population. In
1980 there were 1.432.686.500 Christians, that is, 32,8 % of the world
population. In the year 2000 there will be an estimated 2.019.921.400, that is,
32,3 %. Thus, Christians make up about a third of humanity' (:194-195).
Müller based this statement upon David B. Barrett's *World Christian
Encyclopedia* (1982), which offered the following data on the Roman Catholic
church: in 1900: 271.990.700 (16.8 %); in 1980: 809.157.000 (18.5 %); and
in 2000: 1.169.462.600 (18.7 %). The Roman Catholic church has not only
more members than all the other churches combined, but is also still growing
while the Eastern Orthodox churches and Protestantism, for different reasons,
experience a serious decline.

(CORSI, OLIMPIADE). Notizie statistiche delle missioni di tutto il mondo dipendenti dalla
S.Congregazione di Propaganda Fide. Roma, 1844.
KARL VOM HEILIGEN ALOYS CD. Die katholische Kirche in ihrer gegenwärtigen Ausbreitung auf
der Erde: oder, historische und statistische Nachrichten... Regensburg, 1847.
First ed.: Regensburg, 1845.
*MEJER, OTTO. Die Propaganda: ihre Provinzen und ihr Recht... Göttingen, & Leipzig,
1852-1853. 2 vols.
I, Anhang: Notizia statistica delle missioni cattoliche in tutto il mondo. Roma,
1843.
*Dutch ed.: 1854.

CHOWANETZ, JOSEPH (=CHOWNITZ, JULIAN F.J.). Die Missionen der katholischen Kirche: ihr Begriff, ihr Wesen, ihre Geschichte und gegenwärtige Lage, ihre Behörden, Institute, Vereine und ihre heutige Statistik... Neisse, 1855.

KARL VOM HEILIGEN ALOYS CD. Statistisches Jahrbuch der Kirche: oder, gegenwärtiger Bestand des gesammten katholischen Erdkreises. Regensburg, 1860-1862. 2 vols.

BRAMMERZ, W. Die katholischen Bistümer des Erdkreises: eine geographisch-statistische Uebersicht. Bergheim, 1862.

NEHER, STEPHAN J. Kirchliche Geographie und Statistik: oder, Darstellung des heutigen Zustandes der katholischen Kirche mit steter Rücksicht auf die früheren Zeiten und im Hinblick auf die anderen Religionsgemeinschaften. Regensburg, 1864-1868. 3 vols.

SACRA CONGREGATIO DE PROPAGANDA FIDE. Missiones catholicae. Roma, 1886ff.

WERNER, OSCAR, SJ. Orbis terrarum catholicus: sive, totius ecclesiae catholicae et occidentis et orientis conspectus geographicus et statisticus... Freiburg im Breisgau, 1890.

NEHER, STEPHAN J. Conspectus hierarchiae catholicae in toto orbe terrarum: kirchlich-statistische Tabellen über die ganze katholische Welt. Regensburg, 1895.

?KROSE, HERMANN A., SJ. Notices statistiques pour les cartes de l'Atlas des missions catholiques. Steyl, 1906.

*STREIT, KARL, SVD (ed.). Statistische Notizen zum katholischen Missionsatlas. Steyl, 1906. Fr. tr.: 1906.

*KROSE, HERMANN A., SJ. Katholische Missionstatistik: mit einer Darstellung des gegenwärtigen Standes der katholischen Heidenmission. Freiburg im Breisgau, 1908.

*STREIT, ROBERT, OMI. Führer durch die deutsche katholische Missionsliteratur. Freiburg im Breisgau, 1911.
P. 99-102: Missionsgeographie und Missionsstatistik. Bibliog.

SCHWAGER, FRIEDRICH W., SVD. Vorschläge zur katholischen Missionsstatistik. In: ZM, I (1911), p. 158-172.

SCHWAGER, FRIEDRICH W., SVD (ed.). Der Düsseldorfer Missionskursus für Missionare und Ordenspriester 7-14 Oktober 1919: Vorträge, Aussprachen und Beschlüsse des Missionskursus. Aachen, 1919.
P. 207-219: Die Bedeutung der Statistik für den Missionsbetrieb (Hermann A. Krose SJ).

*WOLFF, LUDWIG, SCJ. Der Missionar als Forscher... Aachen, 1920.
P. 146-147: Statistik.

MIONI, UGO. Manuale di missionologia. Milano, 1921.

*STREIT, ROBERT, OMI. Die katholische deutsche Missionsliteratur. Aachen, & Immensee, 1925.
P. 41: Missionsstatistik. Bibliog.
P. 104: Missionsstatistik und Missionsgeographie. Bibliog.

*STREIT, ROBERT, OMI. Die Weltmission der katholischen Kirche: Zahlen und Zeichen auf Grund der Vatikan. Missionsausstellung 1925. Hünfeld, 1928.

STREIT, KARL, SVD. Catholic world atlas: containing a geographical and statistical description with maps of the Holy Roman Catholic Church, with historical and ethnographical notices... Paderborn, & New York, 1929.
*Latin ed.: Atlas hierarchicus: descriptio geographica et statistica Sanctae Romanae Ecclesiae tum occidentis tum orientis juxta statum praesentem accedunt nonnullae notae historicae necnon ethnographicae... Paderborn, 1929.
First ed.: Paderborn, 1913.

(SACRA CONGREGATIO DE PROPAGANDA FIDE). Missiones catholicae ... descriptae statistica, data statistica referentur ad diem 30 Iunii 1927. Roma, 1930.

ARENS, BERNARD, SJ. État actuel des missions catholiques. Louvain, 1932.

P. 11-32: Introduction: les exigences théoretiques de la statistique des missions.

(SACRA CONGREGATIO DE PROPAGANDA FIDE). Testo atlante illustrato delle missioni cattoliche: compilato a cura dell'Agenzia Internazionale Fides: con i dati cartografici e statistici... Roma, Novara, & Parigi, 1932.

?(SACRA CONGREGATIO DE PROPAGANDA FIDE). Le missioni cattoliche ...: cenni geografici et storici dati statistici. Roma, 1946.

*(SACRA CONGREGATIO DE PROPAGANDA FIDE). Le missioni cattoliche...: storia, geografia, statistica. Roma, 1950.

*SCHORER, EDGAR. Standort, Natur, Arten, Nutzen und Hauptprobleme der Missionsstatistik. In: NZM, X (1954), p. 161-179.

SCHORER, LUJO. Data statistica circumscriptionum ecclesiasticarum a Sacra Congregatione de Propaganda fide dependentium... Mödling, 1959.

*SANTOS HERNANDEZ, ANGEL, SJ. Bibliografia misional. Santander, 1965. 2 vols.

II, p. 1211-1213: Estadisticas. Bibliog.

5.3.5.5. THE STATISTICS OF PROTESTANT MISSION

David B. Barrett is the most outstanding contemporary scholar of the statistics of Christian mission. In one of his articles on this discipline (Jongeneel 1992: 189), he quoted Roger Schutz, founder of the Taizé Community in France: 'Statistics are signs from God' (Fr.: *Les chiffres sont les signes de Dieu*)'.

Barrett has a general interest in the 'statistical eras of global mission' (Missiology 1984:21-37; IBMR 1984:160-169) and the 'statistical tables on global mission' (IBMR 1988:16-17). He also has a special interest in the meteoric growth of the Pentecostal Movement and Charismatic Renewal in the 20th century: 'Its church members have risen from some 3 million in 1900 to 71 million by 1970, 158 million by 1980, and 372 million by 1990. Today the annual increase is 19 million: 54.000 new persons every day become Pentecostals/Charismatics' (Jongeneel 1992:190).

Barrett has yet another new area of special interest: the statistics of plans to evangelize the world. In *Seven Hundred Plans to Evangelize the World* (1988), Barrett and James W. Reapsome made a historical survey of 788 global plans to implement world evangelization and pointed out both the potential and the perils of these plans. Todd M. Johnson (Jongeneel 1992:197-198) commented as follows upon these plans: 'Though the potential to evangelize the world is evident, these plans are each almost entirely stand alone in their mentality. Various Christian traditions and agencies simply carve up the world in different, sometimes divergent, fashions and then each proceed to get on with the job with little or no reference to each other'.

In the post-colonial era, the statistics of the Protestant missionary societies (Boyce 1863; 1874) are less important. Today we need statistics of other missionary phenomena than in the past. Now the statistics of Two-Thirds World mission agencies and Two-Thirds World estimated missionaries is a first priority. Larry D. Pate (1989:54) analysed the Two-Thirds World mission trends and concluded: 'Denominational and missionary leaders around the world would do well to consider the implications of the growing missions movement in the Two-Thirds World. It is approximately 30% of the world Protestant missionary total. It is growing at a rate 5 times faster than the western missionary movement. The number of Two-Thirds World missionaries holds the very real promise of surpassing the number of western missionaries by the year 2000'.

HAWKINS, ERNEST. The colonial church atlas, arranged in dioceses: with some additional maps, geographical and statistical tables, and an index of places: third ed... London, 1853.

*BRAUER, JOHANN H. Das Missionswesen der evangelischen Kirche in seinem Bestande: Versuch einer Missions-Statistik. Hamburg, 1847-1851. 2 vols.

*LOWRIE, JOHN C. A manual of missions: or, sketches of the foreign missions of the Presbyterian church: with maps, showing the stations, and statistics of Protestant missions among unevangelized nations. New York, 1854.
    Second ed.: 1855.

BOYCE, WILLIAM B. (ed.). Statistics of Protestant missionary societies: 1861. London, 1863.

BOYCE, WILLIAM B. Statistics of Protestant missionary societies: 1872-3... London, 1874.

CHRISTLIEB, THEODOR. Protestant foreign missions: their present state: a universal survey. Boston, 1880.

CROIL, JAMES. The missionary problem: containing a history of Protestant missions in some of the principal fields of missionary enterprise, together with a historical and statistical account of the rise and progress of missionary societies in the nineteenth century: with map. Toronto, 1883.

*GRUNDEMANN, PETER R. Zur Statistik der evangelischen Mission. Gütersloh, 1886.

NORWEGIAN STUDENTS' MISSIONARY ORGANIZATION. Statistik oversigt over hedningemissionens stilling i nutiden. Kristiania, 1889.

VAHL, JENS. Missions to the heathen in 1889 and 1890: a statistical review. Copenhagen, 1892.
    Similar reviews in the years 1893-1898. 7 vols.

*VAHL, JENS. Der Stand der evangelischen Heidenmission in den Jahren 1845 und 1890: eine vergleichende missionsgeschichtliche und missionsstatistische Rundschau... Gütersloh, 1892.
    First Danish ed.: 1891.

(GRACEY, JOHN T.). A manual of modern missions, containing historical and statistical accounts of the Protestant missionary societies of America, Great Britain, and the Continent of Europe: also numerous maps and diagrams. New York, & Chicago, 1893.
    First ed.: New York, 1889.

DENNIS, JAMES S. Centennial statistics: paper prepared for the ecumenical conference on foreign missions: New York, City, April 21 - May 1, 1900. New York, (1900).

*GRUNDEMANN, PETER R. Kleine Missions-Geographie und -Statistik zur Darstellung des Standes der evangelischen Mission am Schluss des 19. Jahrhunderts. Calw, & Stuttgart, 1901.

*DENNIS, JAMES S. Centennial survey of foreign missions: a statistical supplement to 'Christian missions and social progress', being a conspectus of the achievements and results of evangelical missions in all lands at the close of the nineteenth century. New York, Chicago, & Toronto, 1902.

*WARNECK, GUSTAV. Eine gigantische Missionsstatistik. In: AMZ, XXIX (1902), p. 327-343.

*INTERCHURCH WORLD MOVEMENT OF NORTH AMERICA. World survey: rev. preliminary statement and budget: II: foreign volume and a statistical mirror: library ed. New York, 1920.

COMMITTEE OF REFERENCE AND COUNSEL (FOREIGN MISSIONS CONFERENCE OF NORTH AMERICA). The contemporary foreign missions of the Protestant churches of North America: a digest of statistical summaries, agencies, policies, and methods. New York, 1930.

BEAVER, R. PIERCE. Distribution of the American Protestant foreign missionary force in 1952. New York, 1953.

BARRETT, DAVID B., & JAMES W. REAPSOME. Seven hundred plans to evangelize the world: the rise of a global evangelization movement. Birmingham, 1988.

*PATE, LARRY D. From every people: a handbook of Two-Thirds World missions with directory/ histories/analysis. Monrovia, 1989.

*JONGENEEL, JAN A.B., et al. (eds.). Pentecost, mission, and ecumenism; essays on intercultural theology... Frankfurt am Main, Berlin, Bern..., 1992.
  P. 189-196: Signs, wonders, and statistics in the world of today (David B. Barrett).
  P. 197-206: Global plans in the Pentecostal/Charismatic tradition and the challenge of the unevangelized world, world A (Todd M. Johnson).

5.3.5.6. THE STATISTICS OF CHRISTIAN MISSION AND THE STATISTICS OF RELIGION

The statistics of Christian mission cannot be separated from the statistics of the world population, the statistics of world religions, and the statistics of church membership.

The world population is growing exponentially. Patrick Johnstone (1986:32) offers the following *statistics of world population*:

AD 1	170.000.000
1000	265.000.000
1800	900.000.000
1900	1.590.000.000
1950	2.525.000.000
2000	6.135.000.000

This growth differs from continent to continent: annual growth in general is 1,7 %; but the annual growth of Africa is 2,9%, and the annual growth of Europe is 0,4%. The development of Christian mission cannot be separated from that of the world population: in some continents or countries (for instance, South Korea) Christianity is growing faster than the population, and in other parts of the world (for instance, Western Europe) it is falling.

Second, the *statistics of world religions* concerns itself with statistical data on the adherence to religious communities (churches, synagogues, mosques, temples, etc.), on participation in rites, on receiving religious education, etc. It also includes data on Christianity. In China one and the same person can belong to more than one religion: a Chinese can be both a Confucian and a Buddhist. Christianity does not allow such a double religious life. However, there are exceptions: the secret believers, the syncretists, etc. The macro-statistics of the world religions reveal a decline of Buddhism and a growth of Islam. *World Christian Encyclopedia* (1982:6) presents the following data on these missionary religions: Buddhism goes down from 7,8 % of the world population (1900), to 6,3 % (1980), to 5,7 % (2000); while Islam increases from 12,4 % (1900) to 15,3 % (1975), to 16,5 % (1980), to 19,2 % (2000). The statistical development of Christianity and of Christian mission must be connected with the statistical development of non-Christian religions and worldviews which differ from one social context to the other.

Finally, there is an interrelation between missionary statistics and *church statistics*. In some parts of the world (for instance, Scandinavia) the government provides statistical surveys of church membership, etc., but in others (for instance, the USA) not at all. Sometimes the governmental statistical tables differ considerably from those made by churches: established churches and free churches can have a different relation to the administration which in one way or another influences statistical surveys. Many churches keep statistical data on missions. However, church statistics and missionary statistics are not identical. The statistics of churches and mission agencies not only differ because most mission agencies in the West and in the Two-Thirds World are interdenominational, but also because they collect different kinds of data: usually mission agencies will not provide tables of marriages, and churches do not distinguish between the baptisms of adults and children who came from inside or outside Christianity.

The statistics of Christian mission as an empirical discipline do not make predictions about the future of Christianity. However, Johannes C. Hoekendijk (Laity XI, 1961:5-19) referred to a very pessimistic prognosis of the future of Christianity amidst other religions and worldviews: from 34 % (1900), via 31% (1955), to 16% (2000). His opponents, Kenneth S. Latourette and David B. Barrett (WCE 1982:6), are rather optimistic: they agree with Hoekendijk that there is a decline of Christianity but they consider it as rather small: from 34,4 % (1900) to 32,3% (2000). Hans-Werner Gensichen (1971: 32) criticized Barrett because he has doubts about the exactness of Barrett's tables. On the one hand, scholars must not speculate on the future of a religion or worldview; and, on the other, they are obliged to interpret the statistical tables and to search for trends.

HOEKENDIJK, JOHANNES C. On the way to the world of tomorrow. In: Laity, XI (1961), p. 5-19.
*BECKER, ROLF-WALTER. Religion in Zahlen: Ursprung und Wege der quantifizierenden Erforschung religiöser Orientierungs- und Verhaltensweisen. Heidelberg, 1968.
*GENSICHEN, HANS-WERNER. Glaube für die Welt: theologische Aspekte der Mission. Gütersloh, 1971.

284

*MÜLLER, KARL, SVD. Mission theology: an introduction... Nettetal, 1987.
    P. 194-203: Christianity and the other religions.
*LM. 1992.
    P. 360: Religionsstatistik.

5.3.5.7. CONCLUSION

The statistics of Christian mission is a well-developed branch of mission studies. In the past, ecumenical scholars (IMC) took the lead in developing this discipline, but today evangelical scholars are in the vanguard.

Most churches and para-church agencies publish their own statistical tables, including mission tables. In the geography of the Christian mission as a discipline, there is a serious trend to replace 'the geography of Christian mission' by 'church geography' (cf. 5.3.4.). This trend can also be seen in the 'statistics of Christian mission', but here it is not as clear as in the geography of Christian mission. David B. Barrett, the leading statistician of World Christianity, does not replace missiological terms by ecclesiastical terms. 'Global mission' is a very characteristic term in his latest statistical studies.

The question whether Christianity in world history has already reached its zenith and from now onwards -the postcolonial period- will decline either rapidly (Hoekendijk) or slowly (Latourette, Barrett) is not merely a statistial question. It is related to the important question of the connection between numerical growth and spiritual growth. A numerical decline of Christianity can be caused by 'natural factors' -e.g. a larger population explosion in non-Christian communities than in Christian communities- but can also be caused by an earlier spiritual decline in its own ranks.

5.3.6. THE ETHNOLOGY AND CULTURAL ANTHROPOLOGY OF CHRISTIAN MISSION, MISSIONARY ANTHROPOLOGY

> A missionary is by his very vocation
> an 'anthropologist' - an 'applied anthropologist'.
> *Louis J. Luzbetak SVD (Müller 1962:63).*

5.3.6.1. INTRODUCTION

The term 'anthropology' is derived from the Greek noun *anthropos*=man, while the term 'ethnology' is derived from the Greek noun *ethnos*=nation, race, people.

In the 19th century anthropology as the 'science of man' was divided into 'physical anthropology' and 'cultural anthropology'. Physical anthropology as branch of 'human biology' was supposed to deal with 'the anatomy of man' and cultural anthropology was associated with 'ethnology'. Alfred C. Haddon (1945:VI-VII) presented the following scheme which is rooted in the 19th century:

1. Human biology
   Includes: Physical anthropology (Anthropology in some studies);
2. Cultural anthropology (Ethnology in some studies); and
3. Ethnography.

The modern scheme of Louis J. Luzbetak SVD (1970:26-27) is slightly different:

1. Physical anthropology (the study of man as a biological animal);
2. Cultural anthropology (the study of man as a rational animal):
   2.1. Archaeology;
   2.2. Linguistics;
   2.3. Etnology (understood in a broad sense):
      2.3.1. Ethnography;
      2.3.2. Ethnology (understood in a restricted sense); and
      2.3.3. Social anthropology.

Many contemporary scholars prefer the term 'cultural anthropology' to the term 'ethnology', and even the generic term 'anthropology' to the term 'cultural anthropology'.

Here, I employ the term *ethnology* (Ger.: *Völkerkunde*) as generally equivalent to the term 'cultural anthropology'. I do not eliminate the term 'ethnology' because of its etymological connection with terms such as 'ethnocentrism' and 'ethnotheology', as well as with biblical expressions such as 'all nations' (Gr.: *panta ta ethne*) in the Great Commission (Matt. 28:19). And I agree with William A. Smalley (1967:4) in the USA who wrote: '*Ethnology* is often the closest European equivalent to our *cultural anthropology*, although for us ethnology is a much more restricted word, referring to the description of individual cultures rather than the science of culture'. Richard J. Mohr (1956) and Thomas Ohm OSB (1962:678) introduced the term *Missionsethnologie*(=ethnology of mission), while Anton Pott SVD (ZMR 1956:301-310) wrote about *Ethnomissiologie* (=missiology of ethnic groups). In the English literature I did not come across these translations which I made.

Further, I like to use the broader term *cultural anthropology*, about which Smalley (1967:4) said: 'Because cultural anthropology is the largest and best known of the branches of anthropology in the USA, it tends to be called by the generic term *anthropology*'. I will not follow Smalley in this usage:

anthropology as a discipline is either 'cultural', or 'social', or 'philosophical', or 'theological', or 'missionary'. However, I agree with Smalley (1967:4) when he says that 'in Britain the term *social anthropology* refers to the cross-cultural study of societies. It, again, is a more restricted term than *cultural anthropology*'. The term 'cultural anthropology' seems best but I did not come across any publication which used the term *cultural anthropology of (Christian) mission(s)*.

I consider the terms 'ethnology of (Christian) mission' and 'cultural anthropology of (Christian) mission' as parallel to the already current terms 'linguistics of (Christian) mission', 'history of (Christian) mission', 'geography of (Christian) mission', etc. However, the specific terms *(applied) missionary anthropology* and *missiological anthropology* are now used by several authors in the USA (cf. 5.3.6.5.).

I disagree with François E. Daubanton (1911:503-519), Joseph Schmidlin (1925:172-174), Alphonsus J.M. Mulders (1950:242-250), and other scholars, who considered ethnology, or cultural anthropology, to be an 'auxiliary science' of mission studies (cf. 5.3.1.2.). I treat this as a totally independent discipline. Ethnology, or cultural anthropology, and missiology must surely respect one another as equals and illuminate each other's research.

*WARNECK. 1892-1903. 3 vols.
    I, p. 291-319: Die ethnologische Begründung.
    III/1, p. 31-42: Die volkliche Verschiedenartigkeit des Missionsgebiets.
*DAUBANTON. 1911.
    P. 503-519: De zendingswetenschap en de ethnologie.
*SCHMIDLIN. 1925.
    P. 172-174: Völkerkunde.
*SCHOMERUS. 1935.
    P. 19-21: Die Missionspädagogik und die Religionsgeschichte und Volkskunde.
*MULDERS, ALPHONSUS J.M. Inleiding tot de missiewetenschap: tweede om- en bijgew. dr.
    Bussum, 1950.
    P. 242-250: Volkenkunde.
*SEUMOIS. 1952.
    P. 412-415: Ethnologie et ethnographie.
*SANTOS HERNANDEZ. 1961.
    P. 283-341: Las misiones y etnologia.
*OHM. 1962.
    P. 678: Missionsethnologie.

5.3.6.2. HISTORY

The vast majority of early ethnologists or cultural anthropologists were missionaries. They were 'pioneers' (Zöckler, in: AMZ 1877:6-16) and men of 'merit' (Ger.: *Verdienste*; Andres, in: HM 1923/24:154-159) in this field.

In his historical survey of the growth of this new discipline, Alfred C. Haddon (1945:102-3) did not refer to the contribution of the mediaeval missionaries (cf. Bündgens 1889), but referred to the Jesuit missionaries of the 16th to the 18th centuries: José de Acosta (1539-1660); Joseph F. Latifau (1670-1740); Pierre F.X. de Charlevoix (1682-1761), who worked among the Canadian Indians; and Martin Dobrizhofer (1717-1791). He also included such 19th century missionaries as William Ellis (1794-1872), who laboured in Polynesia; John Williams (1796-1839); George Turner (1818-1891); W. Wyatt Gill (1826-1896), and others who also worked in the Pacific; Henry Callaway (1817-1890) in Africa; David Livingstone (1813-1873) in Africa; Evariste R. Huc (1813-1860) who worked in China and Tartary; and Jean Antoine Dubois (1770-1848) who described the manners, customs, and ceremonies of the Hindus. He concluded: 'In response to the modern requirements of ethnology, the contributions of missionaries for the past fifty years have been increasingly valuable, as can be seen by the use that students make of them. To mention but a few - Africa: Henri A. Junod (1863-1934), John Roscoe (1861-1932), Edwin W. Smith (1876-1957); Australia: Carl F.Th. Strehlow (1870-1922). Especially may be noted those missionaries trained by Father Wilhelm Schmidt (1868-1954), whose researches are published in *Anthropos*'.

Other historians of ethnology or cultural anthropology have mentioned other names. The name of Father Wilhelm Schmidt SVD, the founder of the *Vienna School* of Roman Catholic anthropologists, however, is always present (cf. Beckmann, in: NZM 1954:293-296). His journal *Anthropos* (cf. Henninger, in: NZM 1967:206-221) is commonly praised as 'weighty'. However, most anthropologists reject his hypothesis that primal peoples all over the world are characterized by a concept of a *high god* and that this belief goes back to an original monotheism (Ger.: *Urmonotheismus*).

*ZÖCKLER, OTTO. Die Missionare als Pioniere geographischer (und ethnologischer) Wissenschaft. In: AMZ, IV (1877), p. 6-16.

*BÜNDGENS, CHRIST. J. Was verdankt die Länder- und Völkerkunde den mittelalterlichen Mönchen und Missionären? Frankfurt am Main, & Luzern, 1889.

*ANDRES, FRIEDRICH. Katholischer Missionare Verdienste um Völkerkunde und Religionsgeschichte. In: HM, V (1923/24), p. 154-159.

*HADDON, ALFRED C. History of anthropology. London, 1945.
    First ed.: 1934.

*BECKMANN, JOHANNES, SMB. Mission und Ethnologie: zum Tode von P. Wilhelm Schmidt SVD (1868-1954). In: NZM, X (1954), p. 293-296.

*MYKLEBUST. 1955-1957. 2 vols.

*HENNINGER, JOSEPH, SVD. Im Dienste der Mission: 60 Jahre Anthropos (1906-1966). In: NZM, XXIII (1967), p. 206-221.

*WAARDENBURG, JACQUES. Classical approaches to the study of religion... I. The Hague, & Paris, 1973.
    P. 28-43: Anthropology.

5.3.6.3. ETHNOLOGY AND CHRISTIAN MISSION

> ... some of the best ethnological monographs were
> written by missionaries...
> *Ina C. Brown (Anderson 1946:183).*

The term *Ethnologie*, or *Völkerkunde* (Grösser, in: ZM 1913:29-53; Wolff 1920), is more popular in Germany than the term *Ethnology* in Great Britain and the USA. However, the terms *Gospel ethnology* (Pattison 1887) and *ethnology of missionary lands* (Bliss 1891:I,576-577) are of English and American origin.

In the 19th century, the term *ethnology* came into prominence. This term was chosen by William F. Edwards (1777-1842) as the title of the Société Ethnologique de Paris in 1839. The Ethnological Society was established in 1843 in London, which, after three decades, was united with the Anthropological Society of London (1863), bearing the new name Anthropological Institute of Great Britain and Ireland (1873). Missionaries and missiologists in the 19th and 20th centuries accepted this new term and applied it to their own field. They also discussed the theories of European and American ethnologists.

Missionaries and missiologists are interested in 'ethnology' (and 'ethnography') because they are interested in nations, races, and peoples. They are especially interested in the link between mission and the *goiim* in the Old Testament, between mission and the *ethne* in the New Testament, and between mission and all kinds of ethnic groups in mission and church history. Throughout the centuries many 'ethnic' churches were born. The 19th century gave birth to Romanticism (Ger.: *Romantik*), which lead to the glorification of *ethnicity* (Ger.: *Volkstum*). In Germany, terms such as *Volkskirche*(='ethnic' church), *Volkschristianisierung* (=Christianization of 'ethnic' groups), and *Völkerpädagogie* (=education of 'ethnic' groups) came to the fore in mission studies. Here, missionaries and missiologists distinguished between a 'pedagogical approach to ethnic groups' (Ger.: *volks-paedagogisch*), advocated by Christian Keysser (1877-1961) in Papua New Guinea, and an 'organic approach to ethnic groups' (Ger.: *volks-organisch*), propagated by Bruno Gutmann (1876-1966) in East Africa (cf. Hoekendijk 1948:135-187). They are unanimous, however, in emphasizing the notion that not individuals but rather ethnic groups must be approached to become Christian. Some German missionaries and missiologists combined this ethnicism in their missionary strategy with the ideology of the Nazis, but others (vehemently) refused to connect them. After the Second World War it was Johannes C. Hoekendijk (1948:268) who excoriated the error of glorifying ethnicity in church and mission: 'In no sense are *ethnos* or language constitutive of the church' (my tr.).

William A. Smalley (1967:256) defined *ethnocentrism* as follows: 'That point of view which we all have to varying degrees, that our own culture, our own way of doing things, is best'. Smalley advocates an ethnocentrism of 'respect' for other peoples. Paul A. Pomerville (1985:23-24) considered the 'latent ethnocentrism in western Christianity'. He criticized Gerardus C. Oosthuizen in South Africa who stated that local nativistic movements, being ethnocentric, are not churches. He wrote: 'Oosthuizen uses the term *ethnocentric* as synonymous with *ethnic identity*, which to him has the same pejorative connotation as does *ethnocentrism*. He does not admit that the western church is an expression of the Christian faith contextualized in western culture, having ethnic identity' (:32).

Donald A. McGavran (Glasser, & McGavran 1985:140-147) tackled the problem of *ethnos* in another way. He distinguished between acceptable and unacceptable *ethnotheologies* and considered every ethnotheology which departs from biblical revelation as a heresy; a really Christian ethnotheology will bring the *ethne* to Christ and will multiply (ethnic) churches.

Keith R. Crim (Phillips, & Coote 1993:101-102) wrote about *mission to ethnic groups* in the USA and Canada: 'The issues of ethnic diversity confronting Canada may take different forms than those of the United States, but they bring equal challenges to the churches'. Ethnic diversity, not only in the USA and Canada, but also in six continents, requires a large variety of missionary methods: each ethnic group needs its own specific approach.

The *ethnology of mission* (Ger.: *Missionsethnologie*) and the *ethnology of religion* (Ger.: *Religionsethnologie*) (LM 1992:359) are interrelated. Ethnology as a discipline not only deals with Christianity and Christian mission as a power which transforms peoples, but also with other religions and other missions which are transforming ethnic communities. Buddhism, Christianity, and Islam all have their own missionary frame of reference when they approach different peoples and races. Here, however, I only refer to Christianity and its mission to the *ethne* in six continents.

*LAURIE, THOMAS. The Ely volume: or, the contributions of our foreign missions to science and human well-being. Boston, 1882.
P. 197-203: Ethnography.
PATTISON, SAMUEL R. Gospel ethnology: new and cheaper ed. London, 1887.
*BLISS, EDWIN M. (ed.). The encyclopaedia of missions: descriptive, historical, biographical, statistical... New York, London, & Toronto, 1891.
I, p. 576-577: Ethnology of missionary lands. Bibliog.
GRÖSSER, MAX, PSM. Die Beziehungen der Missionswissenschaft und Missionspraxis zur Völker-, Sprachen- und Religionskunde. In: ZM, III (1913), p. 29-53.
*WOLFF, LUDWIG, SCJ. Der Missionar als Forscher: Anleitung für Missionare zum Beobachten und zum Sammeln von Material auf dem Gebiete der Missions- und Völkerkunde und deren Grenzgebieten. Aachen, 1920.

SCHMIDT, WILHELM, SVD. Die Bedeutung der Ethnologie und Religionskunde für Missionstheorie und -praxis. In: ZM, XVIII (1928), p. 117-131.

STREIT, KARL. SVD. Catholic world atlas: ... with historical and ethnographical notices... Paderborn, & New York, 1929.

*BIBLIOGRAFIA MISSIONARIA. 1933-...
> XXIX (1965)-XLI (1977): 8. Etnologia e missioni.
> XLII (1978)-XLIX (1985): 10. Missione e culture (antropologia, etnologia, sociologia). Bibliog.

MONDREGANES, PIO M. DE, OMCap. La etnologia y las misiones. N.p., 1933.

WINTHUIS, J. Neueste ethnologische Forschungen und Heidenmission. In: MR, I (1938), p. 158-169.

*HOEKENDIJK, JOHANNES C. Kerk en volk in de Duitse zendingswetenschap. Amsterdam, 1948. Diss. Utrecht.

*SCHORER, EDGAR. Bevölkerungswissenschaft und Missionskunde. In: NZM, VII (1951), p. 124-131.

*SCIENTIA MISSIONUM ANCILLA. 1953.
> P. 192-210: Die gegenwärtige Ethnologie in missionarischer Sicht (Richard J. Mohr).

MOHR, RICHARD J. Die christliche Ethik im Lichte der Ethnologie. München, 1954.

*MOHR, RICHARD J. Missionsethnologie: ein wissenschaftliches Programm. Nijmegen, & Utrecht, 1956. Address.

*POTT, ANTON, SVD. Vom Verhalten des Missionars zur modernen Zivilisierung: Einwände zu ethnomissiologischen Forschungen.
> In: ZMR, XL (1956), p. 301-310.

*GUSINDE, MARTIN, SVD. Die völkerkundliche Ausrüstung des Missionars. Kaldenkirchen, 1958.

MACONI, VITTORIO. Etnologia e missioni. Milano, 1962.

*SANTOS HERNANDEZ, ANGEL, SJ. Bibliografia misional. Santander, 1965. 2 vols.
> I, p. 82-87: Etnologia y misiones. Bibliog.

*SMALLEY, WILLIAM A. (ed.). Readings in missionary anthropology. New York, 1967.
> P. 255-257: Respect and ethnocentrism (William A. Smalley).
> P. 359-360: Etnographic questions for Christian missionaries (Joseph E. Grimes).

*DICTIONARY CATALOG. 1968.
> V, p. 757-770: Ethnology.

*BÜRKLE, HORST. Missionstheologie. Stuttgart, Berlin, Köln..., 1979.
> P. 62-72: Ethnos und Ekklesia.

*WCE. 1982.
> P. 105-115: Culture: peoples of the world: an ethnolinguistic classification.

*McGAVRAN, DONALD A. The priority of ethnicity. In: EMQ, XIX (1983), p. 14-23.

?STUDER, ERICH. Der Missionar und Ethnologe, Bruno Gutmann (1876-1966): seine volksorganische Missionsmethode. Basel, 1984.

*McGAVRAN, DONALD A., & ARTHUR F. GLASSER. Contemporary theologies of mission. Grand Rapids, 1985.
> P. 140-147: Acceptable and unacceptable ethnotheologies.

*POMERVILLE, PAUL A. The third force in missions... Peabody, 1985.
> P. 23-24: A latent ethnocentrism.

*BALZ, HEINRICH. Mission und Ethnologie: Anmerkungen eines Betroffenen. In: ZM, XII (1986), p. 226-234.

*ROSSEL, JACQUES. Mission und Ethnologie aus der Sicht eines Theologen. In: ZM, XII (1986), p. 235-240.

*SCHUSTER, MEINHARD. Religion und Mission in ethnologischer Sicht. In: ZM, XII (1986), p. 241-249.

*LMG. 1987.
   P. 92-94: Ethnologie (A. Quack).
   P. 94-96: Ethnologie und Mission (Louis J. Luzbetak SVD).
   P. 525-529: Volk (Werner Ustorf).
*LM. 1992.
   P. 359: Religionsethnologie.
*PHILLIPS, JAMES M., & ROBERT T. COOTE (eds.). Toward the twenty-first century in Christian mission. Grand Rapids, 1993.
   P. 101-102: North America: Mission to ethnic groups (Keith R. Crim).

5.3.6.4. CULTURAL ANTHROPOLOGY AND CHRISTIAN MISSION

> Missions and anthropology are closely related and the interaction between them has been characterized by the ambivalence -the love and hate- that accompanies intimate relationships.
> *Paul G. Hiebert (Missiology 1978:165).*

Both the term 'social anthropology' (Smith, in: IRM 1924:518-531; Newell, in: IRM 1947:253-257), and the terms 'applied anthropology' (Briggs, in: International Missionary Council 1935; Ewing, in: Worldmission 1951:105-107; Luzbetak, in: Anthropological quarterly 1961:165-176; idem, in: Müller 1962:63-83), and 'cultural anthropology' (Keesing 1958; Vriens 1960:98-103), are connected with 'missions'. I use the last term which is the best and most recent one.

   Here, I only refer to Paul G. Hiebert, Professor of Anthropology at Fuller Theological Seminary since 1977, who considered cultural anthropology as a discipline that emerged after the rejection of the theories of cultural evolution. He typified it as a new discipline which focuses its attention on 'systems of ideas and symbols'. He wrote: '*Culture* came to mean not merely the aggregates of human thought and behavior, but both the systems of beliefs that lie behind specific ideas and actions and the symbols by which those ideas and actions are expressed' (1987:21). Hiebert drew widely from cultural anthropology as an academic discipline: on the one hand, he sought to criticize its secular theories from the Christian perspective, and, on the other, he tried to integrate its insights into the 'systems of ideas and symbols' with missionary theology. Missionaries and missiologists must put the 'systems of ideas and symbols' on their agenda, in order to be able to bridge the gaps between cultures.

   Today the discussion is focused more on the relation between missionaries/missiologists and anthropologists than on the disciplines involved. Scholars paid attention to their 'love/hate relationship' (Hiebert, in: Missiology 1978:165-180) and their 'ambivalent relationship' (Salamone, in: Missiology

1986:55-70). These expressions can not only be used to determine the relationship between missionaries/missiologists and ethnologists/cultural anthropologists, but also between the first mentioned group and linguists, historians, geographers, statisticians, etc. Each of these parties has its own 'points of view' (Kornfield, in: EMQ 1973:201-204), 'perspectives' (Loewen 1975; Hvalkof, & Aaby 1981), 'presuppositions' (Stipe, in: Current anthropology 1980:165-179), and 'concepts' (Whiteman, in: Missiology 1981:223-239). Nevertheless, both parties can 'cooperate in research' (Loewen, in: Practical anthropology 1965:158-190) and can learn from one another. Eugene A. Nida (Practical anthropology 1966:276) referred to 'a real need for meaningful cooperation between missionaries and anthropologists'. And Elmer S. Miller (Anthropological quarterly 1981:125-133) suggested that anthropologists might learn from ecumenical missions in their response to 'Third World' criticisms of contemporary anthropology.

BULLOCK, CHARLES. Missionaries and anthropologists... London, 1865.
*STEVENSON, MARGARET. The study of anthropology on the mission field. In: IRM, IX (1920), p. 426-438, 581-591.
*SMITH, EDWIN W. Social anthropology and missionary work. In: IRM, XIII (1924), p. 518-531.
L'EVANGILE ET LE MONDE: congrès des missions protestantes, 9-11 juin 1931. Paris, 1931.
      P. 116-125: L'anthropologie et les missions (Paul Rivet).
*WESTERMANN, DIEDRICH, & RICHARD THURNWALD. The missionary and anthropological research. London, 1932.
      P. 3-15: The missionary as an anthropological field-worker (Diedrich Westermann).
*BIBLIOGRAFIA MISSIONARIA. 1933-...
      XLII (1978)-... : 10. Missione e culture (antropologia...).
INTERNATIONAL MISSIONARY COUNCIL. Conference on the training of the ministry of the younger churches abroad, Newark, N.J., October 7th - 8th, 1935. New York, 1935.
      Commission II: Applied anthropology and missions (George W. Briggs).
*JUNOD, HENRI P. Anthropology and missionary education. In: IRM, XXIV (1935), p. 213-228.
GRAHAM, JOHN M., & RALPH PIDDINGTON. Anthropology and the future of missions. Aberdeen, 1940.
DODGE, RALPH E. Missions and anthropology: a program of anthropological research for missionaries working among the Bantu-speaking peoples of Central and Southern Africa. Hartford, 1944. Thesis Hartford Theological Seminary.
SMITH, GORDON H. The missionary and anthropology: an introduction to the study of primitive man for missionaries. Chicago, 1945.
*ANDERSON, WILLIAM K. (ed.). Christian world mission. Nashville, 1946.
      P. 183-192: The anthropological approach (Ina C. Brown).
*NEWELL, WILLIAM H. 'Functional' social anthropology and Christian missionary method. In: IRM, XXXVI (1947), p. 253-257.
?EWING, J. FRANKLIN, SJ. Applied anthropology for the missionary. In: Worldmission, II (1951), p. 105-107.
NIDA, EUGENE A. Customs and cultures: anthropology for Christian missions. New York, 1954.
*LINDSELL, HAROLD. Missionary principles and practice. Westwood, 1955.
      P. 277-292: Anthropology and missions.
*KEESING, FELIX M. Cultural anthropology: the science of custom. New York, Chicago, San

Francisco..., 1958.
P. 296, 360, 413-414, 424: Missions.
*NIDA, EUGENE A. The role of cultural anthropology in Christian missions. In: Practical anthropology, VI (1959), p. 110-116.
ROSENSTIEL, ANNETTE. Anthropology and the missionary. London, 1959.
First ed.: Journal of the Royal Anthropological Institute, LXXXIX/1 (1959).
SMALLEY, WILLIAM A. Anthropological study and missionary scholarship. In: Practical anthropology, VII (1960), p. 113-123.
*VRIENS. 1960.
P. 98-103: Cultural anthropology. Bibliog.
*MÜLLER, KARL, SVD (ed.). Missionsstudien. Kaldenkirchen, 1962.
P. 63-83: An applied anthropology for Catholic missions (Louis J. Luzbetak SVD).
SMALLEY, WILLIAM A. Selected and annotated bibliography of anthropology for missionaries: rev. ed. New York, 1962.
First ed.: 1960. Bibliog.
*LOEWEN, JACOB A. Missionaries and anthropologist cooperate in research. In: Practical anthropology, XII (1965), p. 158-190.
*NIDA, EUGENE A. Missionaries and anthropologists. In: Practical anthropology, XIII (1966), p. 273-277, 287.
?CELAM. Anthropología y evangelización. Mexico, 1968.
CELAM=Conferencia Episcopal Latinoamericana.
*DICTIONARY CATALOG. 1968.
XI, p. 161-162: Missions and anthropology. Bibliog.
?TIPPETT, ALAN R. Anthropology: luxury or necessity for missions? In: EMQ, V (1968), p. 7-19.
*CONCISE DICTIONARY. 1971.
P. 25: Anthropology and missions (William A. Smalley).
*KORNFIELD, WILLIAM J. Looking at missions from an anthropological point of view. In: EMQ, IX (1973), p. 201-204.
*JACOBS, DONALD R., & JACOB A. LOEWEN. Anthropologists and missionaries face to face. In: Missiology, II (1974), p. 161-174.
*LOEWEN, JACOB A. Culture and human values: Christian intervention in anthropological perspective: selection from writings... South Pasadena, 1975.
P. 64-68: Anthropology in mission work.
*BOUTILIER, JAMES A., DANIEL T. HUGHES, & SHARON W. TIFFANY (eds.). Mission, church, and sect in Oceania. Ann Arbor, 1978.
P. 65-82: Mutual biases of anthropologists and missionaries (Daniel T. Hughes).
*HIEBERT, PAUL G. Missions and anthropology: a love/hate relationship. In: Missiology, VI (1978), p. 165-180.
FUCHS, STEPHEN. Anthropology for the missions. Allahabad, 1979.
*STIPE, CLAUDE E. Anthropologists versus missionaries: the influence of presuppositions. In: Current anthropology, XXI/2 (1980), p. 165-179.
*BARNEY, G. LINWOOD. The challenge of anthropology to current missiology. In: IBMR, V (1981), p. 172-177.
*HVALKOF, SOREN, & PETER AABY. Is God an American? An anthropological perspective on the missionary work of the Summer Institute of Linguistics. Copenhagen, 1981.
*MILLER, ELMER S. Great was the company of the preachers: the word of missionaries and the word of anthropologists. In: Anthropological quarterly, LIV (1981), p. 125-133.
*WHITEMAN, DARRELL L. Some relevant anthropological concepts for effective cross-cultural ministry. In: Missiology, IX (1981), p. 223-239.

294

*SALOMONE, FRANK A. (ed.). Missionaries and anthropologists. II. Williamsburg, 1983. Studies in third world soieties. XXVI.

*WHITEMAN, DARRELL L. (ed.). Missionaries, anthropologists, and cultural change. Williamsburg, 1983.

*KLOOS, PETER (ed.). Onderzoekers onderzocht: ethische dilemma's in anthropologisch veldwerk. Leiden, 1984.
P. 153-169: Van God en mensen verlaten? De relatie tussen antropologen en missionarissen, zendelingen en overige religieuze of kerkelijke functionarissen (Rien Ploeg).

*GEEST, SJAAK VAN DER. De antropoloog en de missionaris: een moeizame relatie. In: WenZ, XIV (1985), p. 215-220.

*TENNEKES, JOHANNES. Cultureel-anthropologische kanttekeningen bij een missiologische visie. In: WenZ, XIV (1985), p. 27-31.

*KLOOS, PETER. Het oordeel van een anthropoloog over zending en missie. In: WenZ, XV (1986), p. 199-205.

*SALAMONE, FRANK A. Missionaries and anthropologists: an inquiry into their ambivalent relationship. In: Missiology, XIV (1986), p. 55-70.

*HIEBERT, PAUL G. Anthropological insights for missionaries: second printing. Grand Rapids, 1987.
First ed.: Grand Rapids, 1985.

CASALEGNO, UGO. Antropologi e missionari a confronto... Roma, 1988.

*PIEPKE, JOACHIM G. (ed.). Anthropology and mission: SVD International consultation on anthropology for mission... Nettetal, 1988.
P. 68-81: Inculturation of the Christian message: claim, reality, consequences (Jon P. Kirby).

5.3.6.5. MISSIONARY ANTHROPOLOGY

Louis J. Luzbetak SVD (Anthropological quarterly 1961:165-176; 1963, second ed.:1970, revision: 1988) and William A. Smalley (1967; 1978) are the most outstanding advocates of a *missionary anthropology* and/or a *missiological anthropology*.

Luzbetak (1970) used both the term '(applied) missionary anthropology' (:23-55) and the term 'missiological anthropology' (:VIII,45,46). He preferred the first term. He considered 'applied missionary anthropology' as the discipline which examines the non-cultural aspects of missions in the light of culturological theory. A missionary course in applied anthropology consists of the following three parts:

1.   Basic anthropological concepts and principles;
2.   Ethnographic techniques for missionaries; and
3.   Missionary anthropology in action.

Applied missionary anthropology must not be confused with missiology. Luzbetak (:32) said: 'The relationship between missiology and applied missionary anthropology might perhaps be best viewed as a kind of syllogism: the major premise is set up by mission theology, mission history, mission law, and other non-culturological subfields of missiology; the minor premise consists of pertinent cultural anthropological theory. It is the task of applied missionary anthropology to bring together the pertinent culturological theory and to draw the logical conclusion from the premises'. I consider, however, 'mission law' (cf. 5.4.) as part of 'mission(ary) theology' (cf. 5.4.5).

In 1988, Luzbetak added: 'Missiological anthropology might best be regarded as a specialized form of applied anthropology. Its scope and purpose are missiological, while the procedures and analyses are anthropological' (:43).

Smalley (1967) treated Christian missionaries as the most frequent western observers of non-western cultures. He mentioned as famous European 'missionary anthropologists' the English Bishop Robert H. Codrington (1830-1922) who studied the Melanesians of the Pacific at first-hand as a missionary among them; Edwin W. Smith (1878-1957) from England who served as a missionary in South Africa; Maurice Leenhardt (1878-1954) from France who published on New Caladonia; and Father Wilhelm Schmidt (see above). In the USA, however, the Kennedy School of Missions (Hartford Seminary Foundation, Hartford) and Wheaton College (Wheaton) are very important institutions which pioneered courses in anthropology with the missionary group specifically in mind. Acording to Smalley (:11-12), there are at least two important situations in which missionary anthropologists are needed:

1.   the professional application of anthropology to missionary problems; and
2.   the anthropological study of the people with whom the missionaries are living and working.

Smalley (:13) regarded the afore-mentioned study of Luzbetak (1963) as 'essential in any reading course for the missionary'. Luzbetak concentrated on 'missionary/missiological anthropology' as a discipline, while Smalley focused on the 'missionary anthropologist' as a 'missionary scholar' (:9). Smalley neither used the term 'missiological anthropology' nor the term 'missiological anthropologist'.

Several scholars adopted the term 'missionary anthropology' from Luzbetak and Smalley and used it on occasions when dealing with its main problems:

1.   How do human cultures differ, and what effect do these differences have on the effective communication of the gospel?
2.   What is the church like in different cultures?

3.   What are the problems of a missionary in a culture different from his own?

4.   What is the place of anthropology, and its method, as applied to the problems of the church of Jesus Christ? (Smalley 1967:V-VI)

Jon P. Kirby, for instance, reflected upon the 'inculturation of the Christian message' and placed it in a post-colonial framework: 'Where formerly anthropology was used as a tool to communicate the meaning of the western church to the world, it is now freed to discover the essentials of the gospel in each of the world's ethnicities. Where the former role of missionary anthropology was apologetical and tactical, the new role of Christian anthropology must be dialogical and must promote communication in both directions' (Piepke 1988:74-75).

LUZBETAK, LOUIS J., SVD. Toward an applied missionary anthropology. In: Anthropological quarterly, XXXIV (1961), p. 165-176.
*SMALLEY, WILLIAM A (ed.). Readings in missionary anthropology. New York, 1967.
*SMALLEY, WILLIAM A. (ed.). Readings in missionary anthropology: II (enlarged 1978 ed.). South Pasadena, 1978.
*LUZBETAK, LOUIS J., SVD. The church and cultures: new perspectives in missiological anthropology. New York, 1988.
    First ed.: The church and cultures: an applied anthropology for the religious worker. Techny, 1963.
    *Second ed.: Pasadena, 1970.

5.3.6.6. CONCLUSION

The 'ethnology of Christian mission' (Ger.: *Missionsethnology*), or 'cultural anthropology of Christian mission', is an important branch of empirical mission studies. In the Anglo-Saxon world, however, the term 'missionary anthropology' (e.g. Luzbetak, Smalley, and Kirby) is more widely known. The term 'missiological anthropology' was mainly propagated by Louis J. Luzbetak SVD, the foremost Catholic missionary anthropologist in the English-speaking world.

Donald A. McGavran (EMQ 1983:17) maintained that 'Christ did not come to destroy *panta ta ethne*, but to disciple them'. This reference to the Great Commission makes very clear the interest of missionaries in the *ethne* and their cultures, which at the same time is the object of ethnological and anthropological studies. Missionaries have not only contributed to the rise and growth of ethnology and cultural anthropology as academic disciplines but also learnt from the studies of secular ethnologists and cultural anthropologists. Many ethnologists and cultural anthropologists 'report cordial relations with the missionaries' (Salamone, in: Missiology 1986:64), but we cannot ignore the fact that both 'anthropologist hostility' (:58) and 'missionary hostility' sometimes reveal themselves.

Missionary anthropology can be developed as an 'applied' discipline. However, it can also be treated as a discipline which is moving from an apologetical attitude to a more dialogical approach of peoples and cultures.

5.3.7. THE SOCIOLOGY OF CHRISTIAN MISSION

> The sociologist interprets missionary work as a form of motivated and goal-directed social behavior.
> *Quirinus J. Munters (1970:213).*

5.3.7.1. INTRODUCTION

Sociology must clearly be distinguished from cultural anthropology or ethnology. Emile Durkheim, who founded the *Année Sociologique* (1897) in France, and who considered religion to be a social reality, made in 1915 the following distinction between sociology, on the one hand, and history and ethnography, on the other: '... sociology raises other problems than history or ethnography. It does not seek to know the passed forms of civilization with the sole end of knowing them and reconstructing them. But rather, like every positive science, it has as its object the explanation of some actual reality which is near to us, and which consequently is capable of affecting our ideas and our acts: this reality is man, and more precisely, the man of to-day' (Waardenburg 1973:302). Therefore, the sociology of religion(s), and consequently the sociology of mission(s), raises other questions than the ethnology, or cultural anthropology, of religion (Ger.: *Religionsethnologie*), and consequently the ethnology, or cultural anthropology, of mission (Ger.: *Missionsethnologie*): it also deals with 'actual reality'.

Immediately after the establishment of sociology as an academic discipline at some universities in last century, the sociology of religion(s) came into being. Thereafter, the *sociology of mission(s)* -as a subdiscipline of both the sociology of religion and missiology- was born. As far as I know, James S. Dennis (1842-1914) was the first scholar to study missions from the sociological point of view; and George Zeegers and Corn. M. Thoen (Scientia missionum ancilla 1953:213) were the authors who introduced both the term *Missionssoziologie=sociology of mission(s)* and the term *Missionssoziografie= sociography of mission(s)*. Quirinus J. Munters (1970:213), however, preferred the term *sociology of missionary enterprise*.

298

*HOLSTEN. 1953.
    P. 135-204: Die Kirche als eschatologische und als soziologische Grösse.
*SANTOS HERNANDEZ. 1961.
    P. 296: Sociologia.

5.3.7.2. HISTORY

James S. Dennis, for many years an educational missionary in Syria with the Presbyterian Church in the USA, must be recognised as the founding father of *the sociology of mission(s)* as a distinct discipline. His main work *Christian missions and social progress* (1897-1906) is a broad 'sociological study of foreign missions'. Its first volume contains a chapter on 'the sociological scope of Christian missions' (I:21-69) which precedes substantial chapters on the social evils of the non-Christian world (both in the individual group and in the family group, the tribal group, the social group, the national group, the commercial group, and the religious group), on the ineffectual remedies of the non-Christian world, and on Christianity as 'the social hope of the nations'. The second volume includes a long chapter on 'the dawn of a sociological era in missions' (II:3-99), while the third volume declares that 'contributions to the comparatively recent science of sociology have also appeared from mission sources' (III:444). At the very beginning of this study we read the following personal 'message' from the author: 'Has sociology anything in common with Christian missions? This is a fair question, and deserves a candid and careful answer. We feel bound to advance the claim that Christian missions have already produced social results which are manifest, and that society in the non-Christian world at the present time is conscious of a new and powerful factor which is working positive and revolutionary changes in the direction of a higher civilization' (:I,31). Dennis supported whole-heartedly the so-called 'Social Gospel Movement' of Walter Rauschenbusch (1861-1918) who believed in the Kingdom of God as 'the first and most essential dogma of the Christian faith', in the '(lost) social ideal of Christendom', and in 'social progress'.
    In the interbellum further progress in developing a sociology of Christian mission was made: e.g. the concise study of Richard Thurnwald: *The Missionary's Concern in Sociology and Psychology* (Westermann, & Thurnwald 1932:16-31). But the most important event of this period was the publication of *Christian Missions and a New World Culture* (1934) by Archibald G. Baker (b. 1875), Associate Professor of Missions in the University of Chicago. He identified Christian mission as 'a cooperative quest for truth, and a cooperative activity for the good of mankind' (:300) which, in many ways, contributed to the birth and growth of 'a new world culture'. Olav G. Myklebust (1957:II,60) typified Baker as an 'exponent of the sociological method associated with the "Chicago School of Theology" ...' and Johannes C. Hoekendijk (1948:272)

characterized him as 'Troeltsch redivivus'. Baker built, in one way or another, on the insights of Dennis.

After the Second World War, however, the sociology of mission began to flourish enormously. Munters (1970) wrote a doctoral study on the proselytizing activities of Jehovah's Witnesses in the city of Utrecht, in which he also briefly described the history of the 'sociology of missionary enterprise'. He neither mentions Thurnwald nor Baker; but he did discuss the ideas of Rauschenbusch, Dennis, and Troeltsch. He paid attention to the few contributions of the classial sociologists (of religion) to mission studies and concluded: 'Authors such as Gustave le Bon, Emile Durkheim, Werner Sombart, William G. Sumner, Charles A. Ellwood, Georg Simmel, Edward A. Ross, and others were all active in the field of the sociology of religion; but it appears that they paid at most scant attention to the missionary enterprise' (:8; my tr.).

Maurice Leenhardt (1878-1954), Roger Bastide, and Roger Mehl revived this discipline in France. Mehl (1965:147), for instance, pointed out that the sociology of mission constitutes 'a still virgin territory' (Fr.: *un domaine encore vierge*; my tr.). In Germany, the Netherlands, England, the USA, etc. others were active in this field. David R. Heise (Journal for the scientific study of religion 1967:49-58) analysed the so-called 'diffuse or system-oriented' strategy, on the one hand, and the 'concentrated or personalistic' approach, on the other. He did not focus on missionary goals and missionary motives (cf. Munters 1970), but only on missionary strategies and missionary approaches. J. Boel (1975:9-10) described and evaluated the concepts of Mehl, Heise, and Munters, and concluded: '... these studies leave unanswered the basic question as to whether at all the very presence of Christian missions can be sociologically explained'.

Other important sociologists of the Christian mission in the post-war period are Paul E. Kraemer (Margull 1965:190-204), Pieter H. Vrijhof (Concept July 1965:25-31), Mary A. Thung (1976), and Alfred C. Krass (Coote, & Stott 1980:231-256). They examined the sociological presuppositions of missionary congregations in urban areas; mission in sociological perspective; sociological explorations of the church's mission and structure; and mission as an inter-cultural encounter - a sociological perspective.

After the Second World War, historical-sociological publications on the subject of Christian mission also appeared. Very influential are the studies of Gerd Theissen (NTS 1975:192-221; 1978) on the sociology of the New Testament period, including the sociology of the first Christian missionaries. Howard C. Kee (1980) and Richard A. Horsley (1994) also examined 'Christian origins' and the 'Jesus movement' sociologically.

*MYKLEBUST. 1955-1957. 2 vols.
*THEISSEN, GERD. Legitimation und Lebensunterhalt: ein Beitrag zur Soziologie urchristlicher Missionäre. In: New Testament Studies, XXI (1975), p. 192-221.

THEISSEN, GERD. The first followers of Jesus: a sociological analysis of the earliest Christianity. London, 1978.
*Ger. ed.: Soziologie der Jesusbewegung: ein Beitrag zur Entstehungsgeschichte des Urchristentums. München, 1977.
*KEE, HOWARD C. Christian origins in sociological perspective: methods and resources. Philadelphia, 1980.
*HORSLEY, RICHARD A. Sociology and the Jesus movement: second ed. New York, 1994.

5.3.7.3. THE SOCIOLOGY OF CHRISTIAN MISSION

> 'Applied Christianity' or 'Social Missions'.
> *Olav G. Myklebust (1955:1,250).*

The sociology of the Christian mission is still a relatively new discipline which covers a large number of problems. Here I can only mention a few key issues.

First of all, I refer to the important question of the context of the Christian mission which must be analysed sociologically. One of the most important contributions to this debate is made by George Zeegers and Corn. M. Thoen in Alphonsus J.M. Mulders' *Festschrift* (1953). They identified four specific areas of research in this very broad field:

1. Mission and the population problem (i.e. demographic development);
2. Mission and the economic problems (i.e. industrial and technical development);
3. Mission and national-political and racial-political development;
4. Mission and the development of ideological influence exerted by non-Christian powers in the western world (1. the influence of communism; 2. the influence of western humanism and capitalism) (Scientia missionum ancilla 1953:213ff.; my tr.).

Generally, I agree with this approach to contextual problems; but I would like to add another crucial issue: mission and the problem of religions. We cannot anymore be concerned about mainly or only the western context of Christian mission, but must also take into account its non-western -religious- context.

The second main object of the sociological study of Christian mission is the missionary enterprise itself; and its internal relation to mission societies and/or church institutions. Here I refer to the study of Mary A. Thung (1976:44-74) who raised the key question: 'the missionary church: what kind of organization?' She analysed the concept of 'missionary church' -in the thinking of the World Council of Churches- and considered this kind of church as a specific type of organized religion: 'it is a normative and a voluntary organisation...' (:74). She also dealt with its internal structure: subdivisions and unity; authority, influence, and leadership; and governmental structure: the incorporation of expertise, bureaucracy and oligarchy, democracy, ministry or leadership? And she concluded: 'The point of correct organising is, that one tries to obtain as great a coincidence as possible of the "manifest" and the "latent" church' (:325).

A third field of study is the impact of Christian missions on their 'context' or 'environment': both in the western and in the non-western world. Mary A. Thung (1976:125-156) dealt with the problem of 'operationalizing the church's mission in society'. This formulation reflects the aim of the project of the World Council of Churches entitled 'The Missionary Structure of the Congregation'. Some sociologists are pessimistic about the possibility and effectiveness of this structure in modern society, but others are rather optimistic. Pieter H. Vrijhof (Concept July 1965:31) clearly belongs to the first category: 'We must see the possibility that religion and the church in their present forms will disappear, or at least fade out as separate phenomena. We would then travel along the road towards a religion which is valid and true for the coming period of our civilization. It would be wise to take this into acount when reflecting about the structures of missionary congregations'. But the Evangelicals Tetsunao Yamamori and E. LeRoy Lawson (1975) belong to the latter category. They strongly emphasized that knowledge of sociology greatly aids church growth: 'Church growth is very much dependent upon an understanding of sociological factors within the societies in which the missionaries work. Some societal elements contribute to church growth while others hinder it. Sociology thus becomes an indispensable tool for those engaged in missionary work' (:79).

Fourth, the sociology of the Christian mission studies the linguistic, ethnic, national, denominational, etc. differences between the separate Christian missions in six continents. For instance, Roger Bastide (Archives de sociologie des religions 1959:47-51; Les missions protestantes et l'histoire 1971:47-62), Roger Mehl (1964; 1965:147-171), J.P. Willaime, et al. (1972:44-48) researched the separate Protestant missions sociologically while other scholars studied other fields of social divisions. The Ecumenical Movement paid little attention to these differences, but the Church Growth Movement wellcomed 'separate churches'. Donald A. McGavran (Yamamori, & LeRoy Lawson 1975:79) strongly criticized the neglect of peculiarities by Ecumenists: 'By ignoring social stratification and disregarding homogenous units and webbs of relationship, they constantly diminish the effectiveness of their presentation of Christ'.

Finally, I refer to the question of the relation between the sociology of Christian mission (an empirical discipline) and missionary theology (a normative discipline). Walter Holsten (1953:135) stated that 'the sociological understanding of the church can cause danger to missions' (my tr.). Also Hans J. Margull (1959:293-294) and Marc R. Spindler (1967:23-41) discussed this question. I maintain that the sociology of Christian mission can help the churches to rethink their missionary goals and motives, as well as their missionary strategies and approaches. But they can never usurp the responsibility of missionary ecclesiology (cf. 5.4.3.). The church as organization is a social phenomenon which can and must be researched sociologically; but the church as 'the body of Christ' can only be dealt with adequately by missionary ecclesiologists. Therefore, the sociology of Christian mission which is aware of its own limits will never 'cause danger to missions' (Holsten).

Derek Cook (Calver 1984:7-10) asked 'how can sociology help in evangelism', as well as in mission; and he answered:

1. It sees man in relation to man;
2. It identifies relationships;
3. It can give confidence; and
4. It analyses group functions.

*DENNIS, JAMES S. Christian missions and social progress: a sociological study of foreign missions. New York, Chicago, & Toronto, 1897-1906. 3 vols.

KEEN, WILLIAM W. The service of missions to science and society... Boston, 1906.

*SLATER, THOMAS E. Missions and sociology. London, 1908.

CAPEN, EDWARD W. Sociological progress in mission lands ... New York, Chicago..., 1914.

*WESTERMANN, DIEDRICH, & RICHARD THURNWALD. The missionary and anthropological research. London, 1932.

    P. 16-31: The missionary's concern in sociology and psychology (Richard Thurnwald). Reprint: London, 1948.

*BIBLIOGRAFIA MISSIONARIA. 1933-...

    XLII (1978)-...: 10. Missione e culture (... sociologia). Bibliog.

*BAKER, ARCHIBALD G. Christian missions and a new world culture. Chicago, & New York. 1934.

*HOEKENDIJK, JOHANNES C. Kerk en volk in de Duitse zendingswetenschap. Amsterdam, 1948. Diss. Utrecht.

    P. 269-276: The great society.

*ROUX, ANDRÉ. Maurice Leenhardt, pionier-socioloog in de zending. In: DH, X (1957), p. 259-260.

BASTIDE, ROGER. Sociologie des missions protestantes. In: Archives de sociologie des religions, IV/8 (1959), p. 47-51.

CONSIDINE, JOHN J. (ed.). The missionary's role in socio-economic betterment. Westminster, 1960.

*MARGULL, HANS J. Hope in action. Philadelphia, 1962.

    *Ger. original: Theologie der missionarischen Verkündigung: Evangelisation als oekumenisches Problem. Stuttgart, 1959.

    P. 293-294: Die soziologische Dimension der missionarischen Verkündigung (Evangelisation).

*POTEL, J. Mission et sociologie des religions: bibliographie. In: Parole et mission, VI (1963), p. 672-680. Bibliog.

*MEHL, ROGER. Décolonisation et missions protestantes. Paris, 1964.

    P. 21-40: Définition sociologique de la colonisation et de la mission.

*DOORN, CORNELIS L. VAN. Sociologisch documentatiebureau ten dienste van de zending. In: DH, XVII (1964), p. 314-316.

*THUNG, MARY A. Omzetting in een sociologisch studiesecretariaat. In: DH, XVII (1964), p. 316-322.

*MARGULL, HANS J. (ed.). Mission als Strukturprinzip: ein Arbeitsbuch zur Frage missionarischer Gemeinden. Genf, 1965.
P. 190-204: Soziologische Voraussetzungen für missionarische Gemeinden in den Grossstadträumen (Paul E. Kraemer).

*MEHL, ROGER. Traité de sociologie du protestantisme. Neuchâtel, 1965.
P. 147-171: Sociologie des missions.

SHORTER, AYLWARD, WF. Sociology and the missionary. In: Worldmission, XVI/1 (1965), p. 22-28.

*VRIJHOF, PIETER H. Mission in sociological perspective. In: Concept, X, July 1965, p. 25-31.

CARLETON, ALFORD. Comment on 'Prefatory findings in the sociology of missions'. In: Journal for the scientific study of religion, VI (1967), p. 59-60.

HEISE, DAVID R. Prefatory findings in the sociology of missions. In: Journal for the scientific study of religion, VI (1967), p. 49-58.

KATZ, ELIHU. Comment on 'Prefatory findings in the sociology of missions'. In: Journal for the scientific study of religion, VI (1967), p. 61-63.

*SPINDLER, MARC R. La mission, combat pour le salut du monde. Neuchâtel, 1967.
P. 23-41: La conception sociologique de la mission.

*DICTIONARY CATALOG. 1968.
XI, p. 174-176: Missions and sociology. Bibliog.

*MUNTERS, QUIRINUS J. Rekrutering als roeping: sociologische overwegingen met betrekking tot het missionaire handelen. Meppel, 1970. Diss. Nijmegen.

*CONCISE DICTIONARY. 1971.
P. 558-559: Sociology and missions (Harriet R. Reynolds).

*LES MISSIONS PROTESTANTES ET L'HISTOIRE: actes du deuxième colloque (4-9 octobre 1971). Paris, 1971.
P. 47-62: Sociologies (au pluriel) des missions protestantes (Roger Bastide).

*WILLAIME, J.P., et al. Bibliographie de sociologie du protestantisme. Paris, 1972.
P. 44-48: Les missions. Bibliog.

*BOEL, J. Christian mission in India: a sociological analysis. Amsterdam, 1975.

*YAMAMORI, TETSUNAO, & E. LeROY LAWSON. Introducing church growth: a textbook in missions. Cincinnati, 1975.
P. 79-80: Sociology in church growth studies.

*THUNG, MARY A. The precarious organisation: sociological explorations of the church's mission and structure. 's-Gravenhage, 1976. Diss. Leiden.

*COOTE, ROBERT T., & JOHN R.W. STOTT (eds.). Down to earth: studies in Christianity and culture: the papers of the Lausanne consultation on Gospel and Culture. Grand Rapids, 1980.
P. 231-256: Mission as inter-cultural encounter - a sociological perspective (Alfred C. Krass).

*CALVER, CLIVE, DEREK COPLEY, BOB MOFFETT, & JIM SMITH (eds.). A guide to evangelism. Basingstoke, 1984.
P. 7-10: The sociology of evangelism (Derek Cook).

*UKA, E.M. Missionaries go home? A sociological interpretation of an African response to Christian missions: a study in sociology of knowlegde. Berne, Frankfurt am Main, New York..., 1989.

304

*WAGNER. 1989.
    P. 299: Sociological strangulation.
    P. 299: Sociological tissue rejection.
*McGAVRAN, DONALD A., & C. PETER WAGNER. Understanding church growth: third ed. Grand
    Rapids, 1990.
    P. 151-192: The sociological foundation.
    First ed.: Grand Rapids, 1970.

5.3.7.4. THE SOCIOLOGY OF CHRISTIAN MISSION AND THE SOCIOLOGY OF RELIGION

Jacques Waardenburg (1973:43-50) mentioned as great sociologists: Emile Durkheim (1853-1917), Marcel Mauss (1873-1950), and Lucien Lévy-Bruhl (1857-1939) in France; and Ernst Troeltsch (1865-1923) and Max Weber (1864-1920) in Germany. All dealt with religion; some even included Christian missions in their sociological studies. Lévy-Bruhl (Waardenburg 1973:345), for instance, referred to 'a missionary's report'.

   Not only the great majority of sociologists, but also the great majority of missiologists neglected the study of mission as a social phenomenon. Olav G. Myklebust (1955-1957), for instance, did not refer to the studies of Durkheim, Mauss, and Lévy-Bruhl; he mentioned the name of Weber only in passing (I,96); and he dealt with Troeltsch as the scholar who treated the Christian mission merely as 'a phase of the general expansion of Europe' (I,243). Karl Müller SVD (1987:93) also referred only to Troeltsch: 'Troeltsch thought that Christianity is not only the climax but also the converging point of all recognizable streams of religion'. Alan R. Tippett (1987:13,160), however, only mentioned Durkheim. He disagreed with Durkheim's first corollary that 'all preconceptions must be eradicated' and made clear that Durkheim started his own research by 'an act of faith'. In fact, Tippett can be considered as having a keener eye for sociology than Myklebust and Müller: he also paid attention to the sociological problem of 'change processes', i.e. of the processes of modernization, urbanization, and mobility (:89-90), to the sociological problem of 'marginality' (:213), and to their relevance to the missionary enterprise.

   Both the *sociology of religion* (Ger.: *Religionssoziologie*) (LM 1992:359-360) and the *sociology of mission* (Ger.: *Missionssoziologie*) are not limited to Christianity. The non-Christian religions, religious movements (cf. Wilson 1973), and ideologies are the object of this branch of mission studies as well. Here, however, I only deal with the sociology of Christian mission.

   The discussion between the sociologists (of religion), on the one hand, and the sociologists of Christian mission, on the other, has already started but needs further development. In this discussion all those matters must be dealt with which are of mutual interest. Sociologists should no longer ignore the

Christian mission as a social phenomenon. And missiologists must have the courage to use sociological tools and insights, including Church Growth terms such as 'sociological strangulation' and 'sociological tissue rejection' (Wagner 1989:299), which respectively refer to 'a disease of church growth that is the result of overcrowded conditions due to lack of adequate physical facilities (occurs only in growing churches)' and to 'the sociological phenomenon in which some people would prefer the death of their social group rather than to see it infiltrated with people of a different homogenous unit'.

*HOLSTEN. 1953.
    P. 98, 100: Religionssoziologie.
*SCIENTIA MISSIONUM ANCILLA. 1953.
    P. 173-179: Die Religionswissenschaft im Dienste der Mission (Johannes P. Steffes).
    P. 211-242: Soziographische Forschung in der Missionierung (George Zeegers, & Corn. M. Thoen).
*NOTTINGHAM, ELIZABETH K. Religion: a sociological view. New York, 1971.
    P. 185-191: Christian missions and revolution.
*WAARDENBURG, JACQUES. Classical approaches to the study of religion: aims, methods and theories of research. I. The Hague, & Paris, 1973.
    P. 43-50: Sociology. Cf. Index of scholarly concepts.
*WILSON, BRYAN R. Magic and the millennium: a sociological study of religious movements of protest among tribal and Third-World peoples. London, 1973.
*MÜLLER, KARL, SVD. Mission theology: an introduction. Nettetal, 1987.
*TIPPETT, ALAN R. Introduction to missiology. Pasadena, 1987. Index of subjects: Sociology.
*LM. 1992.
    P. 359-360: Religionssoziologie.

5.3.7.5. CONCLUSION

As an empirical discipline, the sociology of Christian mission is (much) younger than the linguistics of Christian mission, the history of Christian mission, the geography of Christian mission, the statistics of Christian mission, and missionary anthropology which were discussed in previous sections. After the introductory studies of James S. Dennis (1897-1906) and Archibald G. Baker (1934), it began to establish itself. In the post-war period, it evolved into a mature discipline.

Today, the sociology of Christian mission is being researched by both sociologists and missiologists. Some scholars in both groups show a real interest in the link between 'society' and 'mission'. Quirinus J. Munters (1970:214), a sociologist, sketched in outline 'a sociology of missionary enterprise' which focusses on the following four issues: (1) the subject matter; (2) the methods of approach; (3) the possibilities; and (4) practical and theoretical relevance. Other scholars, however, occupied themselves with the

Christian mission in quite a different way, but on the same strictly sociological basis.

The points of contact between religion, including mission, and society are many. Therefore, a friendly and fruitful cooperation among sociologists and missiologists is required. It is to the interest of both parties to solve the basic methodological problems which have been raised and to obtain new perspectives. The 'sociology of Christian mission' is surely about to involve more and more scholars and to study even more topics.

5.3.8. THE LAW OF CHRISTIAN MISSION

> ... it is clear that 'Christian missions' and
> 'Law' belong to two distinct spheres of human life.
> *Carl T. Mirbt (IRM 1926:240).*

5.3.8.1. INTRODUCTION

Law -both national law and international law- and mission have their own spheres. In many law studies and mission studies the link between both fields is not dealt with. Alphonsus J.M. Mulders (1962:289-291), however, paid some attention to it. He referred to *mission law* (Dutch: *missierecht*), *international law* (Dutch: *volkenrecht*), and *state law* (Dutch: *staatsrecht*). The noun *mission law* is an old term but the adjective *mission juridical* (Ger.: *missionsjuristisch*) was only recently introduced by Max Bierbaum (Scientia missionum ancilla 1953:295).

I start my own explanation of the relation between law and mission with a discussion of the link between both the Christian and the non-Christian mission, on the one hand, and human rights in general and religious liberty especially, on the other. Thereafter I pay attention to the legal position of the Christian mission: both national law and international law will be dealt with. However, I start this survey with a short historical description.

*VRIENS. 1960.
    P. 52-67: Mission law (Anastasius Disch OFMCap.). Bibliog.
*MULDERS. 1962.
    P. 289-291: Hulpwetenschappen van het missierecht.

5.3.8.2. HISTORY

Only some lawyers and some missiologists have carefully studied the history of the link between (Christian) mission and law. In the excellent historical survey of Protestant mission studies by Olav G. Myklebust (1955-1957), for instance, this relation is not even dealt with.

Most scholars who entered this field specialised in the study of religious liberty: Margaret R. Seebach (Himes) (1917), for instance, studied the history of the influence of the Reformation on civil and religious liberty -including missionary freedom- in the USA.

M. Searle Bates (1945) wrote a substantial and influential study on religious liberty under the auspices of a Joint Committee appointed by the Foreign Missions Conference of North America and the Federal Council of the Churches of Christ in America. It was published by the International Missionary Council. The second part of this work deals with 'the problems of religious liberty in history', i.e. the history of liberty in both Christian and non-Christian societies (:132-293). The problem of 'missionary freedom' is not really explained in this part of the study; but, rather, in the systematic section. In the historical section, however, Bates refers to the following conviction of the Chinese presidential mandate of February 7, 1914: 'Freedom of religious belief is the common rule among all nations' (:278).

The acceptance of the *Universal Declaration of Human Rights* (1948) by the General Assembly of the United Nations is a milestone in the history of human rights: including the history of religious liberty. Nearly all historical, juridical, and theological studies of human rights and religious freedom published after 1948 refer to this declaration.

In the first centuries of modern history the Roman Catholic Church did not promote human rights and religious liberty (cf. the Inquisition). Today, however, it supports them in the same way as the World Council of Churches. Richard J. Regan (1967) studied the advent and growth of the dynamic view of the Second Vatican Council on religious liberty, including missionary freedom. He pointed out that Pope John XXIII started 'a veritable Copernican revolution in the theology of religious freedom' (:9; cf. Koshy 1992:87).

*MYKLEBUST. 1955-1957. 2 vols.

5.3.8.3. HUMAN RIGHTS AND CHRISTIAN MISSION

> To me the connection of the church's mission
> in the world and human rights is basic;
> it is part of our definition as the people of God.
> *John Perkins (IRM 1977:244).*

The French Revolution (1789) raised the serious question of *human rights* (Ger.: *Menschenrechte*). It produced the *Déclaration des droits de l'homme et du citoyen* (Eng.: *Declaration of the rights of man and the citizen*). The problem of religious liberty is dealt with in Article 10 of this declaration:

> No man may be disturbed for his opinions even in religion, provided that their mainfestation does not trouble public order as established by law (tr. Conscience and liberty 1989:I/2:71).

It is not our intention to describe the whole history of human rights thinking from the French Revolution -and the First Amendment of the American Constitution (1791)- to the United Nations *Universal Declaration of Human Rights* (1948) and its *Covenants on Human Rights* (1966). It is sufficient to state that, in these declarations and covenants, '(Christian) mission' is not dealt with explicitly, but only implicitly; it belongs to the realm of 'freedom of religion'.

Systematically we must emphasize that there are several links between *mission* -both Christian mission and non-Christian missions- and *human rights*: (1) mission is -and claims to be- a human right; (2) mission is 'free' where human rights are respected; and (3) mission promotes human rights. Maria R. Mendiola ICM (IRM 1977:225-230) puts the challenging question: 'human rights: content or context of mission?'

Most scholars consider mission to be a human right. They regard it as part of 'the right to freedom of thought, conscience, and religion' (Universal declaration of human rights, art. 18). And they criticize all those religions, worldviews, and ideologies which use their political power to suppress religious liberty, missionary freedom included.

There are also scholars who emphasize the link between respect for human rights in general and respect for missionary freedom in particular. Some even went so far to say that the degree to which nations recognize the freedom of mission is a very good indicator of the level of their respect for human rights in general.

Finally, scholars refer to religions and (secular) worldviews -such as humanism- as movements which demonstrate 'faith in human rights' (Traer 1991). Marcus Braybrooke (1992:10-16) questioned whether human rights are based upon religious traditions. The United Nations declarations and covenants do not base human rights, including religious liberty (and missionary freedom), upon religious traditions; but, rather, upon human dignity. However, the *Declaration of Principles* of the International Association for the Defence of Religious Liberty states: 'We believe that religious liberty is a God-given right'.

Christianity can be regarded as a missionary movement full of 'support for human rights' (Braybrooke 1992:17-20). Betty Stewart (1952), for instance, paid attention to the fact that 'home missions works for human rights'; and the Committee for East Asia and the Pacific, Division of Overseas Ministries of the National Council of the Churches of Christ in the USA (IBMR 1982:9-12), developed 'guidelines on missionary involvement in social-justice and human-rights issues'. This is why P.A. Liégé (Campbell 1965:167) observes: 'There can be no doubt of it: the efforts of a Christian community toward freedom have, of themselves, a missionary significance. First of all, because of the fact that the Church would appear as the place of true liberty-liberty combined with truth, need, love; as the place of fraternal respect for the real freedom of each one; as the place where this freedom is defended'.

Today, the issue of human rights is much more closely linked to the subject of 'dialogue' than to '(Christian) mission'. Now some authors are already examining the link between human rights and interreligious dialogue (Hollenbach, in: IBMR 1982:98-101); and others the link between human rights and the dialogue between the so-called First and Third Worlds (Evans, & Evans-Frazer 1983).

*BIBLIOGRAFIA MISSIONARIA. 1933-...
    L (1986)-... : 3. Canon law and human rights. Bibliog.
STEWART, BETTY (ed.). How! ... home missions works for human rights. New York, 1952.
*MENDIOLA, MARIA R., ICM. Human rights: content or context of mission? In: IRM, LXVI (1977), p. 225-230.
*MIGUEZ BONINO, JOSÉ. Whose human rights? A historico-theological meditation. In: IRM, LXVI (1977), p. 220-224.
*PERKINS, JOHN. What it means to be the church: reflections on mission and human rights. In: IRM, LXVI (1977), p. 244-247.
*ANDERSON, GERALD H., & THOMAS F. STRANSKY CPS (eds.). Mission trends. No. 4: Liberation theologies in North America and Europe. New York, Ramsey, Toronto..., 1979.
    P. 37-50: Human rights and the mission of the church (Richard A. McCormick SJ).
*COMMITTEE FOR EAST ASIA AND THE PACIFIC, DIVISION OF OVERSEAS MINISTRIES OF THE NATIONAL COUNCIL OF THE CHURCHES OF CHRIST IN THE USA. The development of guidelines on missionary involvement in social-justice and human-rights issues. In: IBMR, VI (1982), p. 9-12.
    Comments: W. Dayton Roberts (p. 12-13); and Simon E. Smith SJ (p. 13-14).
*HOLLENBACH, DAVID, SJ. Human rights and interreligious dialogue: the challenge to mission in a pluralistic world. In: IBMR, VI (1982), p. 98-101.
*EVANS, ROBERT A., & ALICE EVANS-FRAZER. Human rights: a dialogue between the First and

Third Worlds. New York, & Guildford, 1983.
SIEGHART, PAUL. The international law of human rights. Oxford, 1983.
*BOURDEAUX, MICHAEL. Mission and human rights. In: Mission studies, I/2 (1984), p. 13-17.
?SWIDLER, LEONARD J. (ed.). Religious liberty and human rights in nations and religions. Philadelphia, 1986.
*LHG. 1987.
    P. 270-274: Menschenrechte (W. Huber).
*DEM. 1991.
    P. 484-488: Human rights (Erich Weingartner).
*TRAER, ROBERT. Christian support for human rights in Latin America. In: IRM, LXXX (1991), p. 245-249.
?TRAER, ROBERT. Faith in human rights. Washington, 1991.
*BRAYBROOKE, MARCUS. Stepping stones to a global ethic. London, 1992.
    P. 10-16: Are human rights based on religious traditions?
    P. 17-20: Religious support for human rights.

5.3.8.4. RELIGIOUS LIBERTY, MISSIONARY FREEDOM

> Religious liberty is a universal human freedom.
> It is a human right.
> *Cecil Northcott (1948:6).*

Both governments and non-governmental organizations deal with the problem of *religious liberty* (Ger.: *Religionsfreiheit*): including the problem of *missionary freedom.*

Here, I deal with them one by one. However, I limit my explanation of government dealings with human rights problems to an analysis of the norms of the United Nations. And I divide my survey of the many non-governmental organizations into two sections: associations and churches.

UNITED NATIONS

In 1948, the United Nations adopted the *Universal Declaration of Human Rights*. Article 18 of this declaration states:

> Everyone has the right to freedom of thought, conscience, and religion; this right includes freedom to change his religion or belief, and freedom, either alone or in community with others and in public or private, to manifest his religion or belief in teaching, practice, worship, and observance.

As a member of the United Nations, Saoudi-Arabia voted against this article because it regarded this article as the result of 'a common plot of some missionary religions' (Koshy 1992:96). The Koran does not allow Muslims to change their religion or belief. However, the representative of Pakistan voted in favour of this declaration: 'Islam is a missionary religion. It claims the right and the freedom to persuade any man to change his faith and accept Islam. Surely and obviously, it must equally yield to other faiths the free right of conversion. It would be most unreasonable to claim (for oneself) the right of conversion and deny it to others' (Koshy 1992:96-97). So did Egypt, although it expressed the fear that 'by proclaiming man's freedom to change his religion or belief, the declaration would be encouraging, even though it might not be intentional, the machinations of certain missions, well known in the Orient... ' (Walkate, in: Conscience and liberty 1989:I/2:29).

The *International Covenant on Civil and Political Rights* (1966) deals with the problem of religious liberty in a slightly different way. Article 18 of this covenant says:

> Everyone shall have the right to freedom of thought, conscience, and religion: this right shall include freedom to have or to adopt a religion or belief of his choice, and freedom either individually or in community with others and in public or private, to manifest his religion or belief in worship, observance, practice, and teaching.

The formulation 'to change his religion or belief' (1948) was, at the request of a group of Muslim states, revised. It is replaced by the formulation 'to have or to adopt a religion or belief of his choice'. However, nothing fundamental has changed because the freedom 'to have or to adopt a religion or belief of his choice' implies the freedom 'to change his religion or belief' (cf. Van Boven 1967).

In 1981, the General Assembly of the United Nations adopted the *Declaration on the Elimination of All Forms of Intolerance and of Discrimination Based on Religion or Belief*, with only five socialist states abstaining. However, a group of Muslim states (Iraq on behalf of the organization of the Islamic Conference, Syria, and Iran) made a reservation as to the applicability of 'any provision or wording of the declaration which might be contrary to Islamic law (*shari'a*) or to any legislation or act based on Islamic law' (Walkate, in: Conscience and liberty 1989:I/2:27). Theodoor van Boven, the former moderator of the Commission of the Churches on International Affairs (WCC), commented on this statement that 'this example can be cited as the most outright case of a religious and legal system that challenges the validity of international human right standards' (ER 1985:351).

In 1984, there followed an United Nations seminar on 'the encouragement of understanding, tolerance, and respect in matters relating to freedom of religion or belief'. The United Nations also appointed a special 'Rapporteur' from the United Nations Commission on Human Rights for the implementation of the *Declaration on the Elimination of All Forms of Intolerance and of Discrimination Based on Religion or Belief.* In 1991 his report was submitted: *Implementations of the Declaration on the Elimination of All Forms of Intolerance and of Discrimination Based on Religion or Belief.*

ASSOCIATIONS

Several non-governmental organizations now deal with religious liberty: e.g. (1) the International Association for Religious Freedom (renamed in Boston 1969), which is the continuation of the (2) International Association for Liberal Christianity and Religious Liberty (renamed in St. Gall 1932) (cf. Braybrooke 1992:47-62); and (3) the International Religious Liberty Association (established in 1946 in Washington DC), which organized international forums in Amsterdam (1977), Rome (1984), and London (1989). This London Congress was co-sponsored by other international religious freedom organizations, among them (4) the International Association for the Defence of Religious Liberty (IADRL).

The last-mentioned organization was established after the Second World War. Today, it functions as a non-governmental organization in consultation with the United Nations, UNESCO, and the Council of Europe. Its in-house journal is *Conscience and Liberty: International Journal of Religious Freedom* (1989-...). It informs us about legislative concerns and applications, events and issues, congresses, texts of resolutions and recommendations, reports and documents, books and publications, etc. It deals with a great variety of issues; but '(Christian) mission' has not yet been discussed by even a single article in this journal.

CHURCHES

> The affirmation of religious liberty is
> inseparable from Christian witness.
> The defence of religious liberty is thus
> integral to the mission of the church.
> *Ninan Koshy (1992:115).*

In 1923 and 1930, the International Missionary Council dealt with the problem of religious liberty: more specifically: *Treaties, acts, and regulations relating to missionary freedom* and *Cases in which it is maintained that the principles of religious liberty have been violated.*

The Second Universal Christian Conference on Life and Work in Oxford (1937:85) recognised the 'freedom of Christian service and missionary activity, both home and foreign' as an essential condition necessary to the church's fulfilment of its primary duty. And the third World Missionary Conference at Tambaram (1938:VI,282) claimed the right 'to carry on Christian service and missionary activity both at home and abroad, and to organise local churches'.

In 1947, the Joint Committee on Religious Liberty, formed under the auspices of the British Council of Churches and the Conference of British Missionary Societies, issued a Statement on Religious Liberty which includes *A Charter of Religious Freedom*. It has the following seven clauses:

1. Freedom to choose and change;
2. Freedom to teach
   (includes the freedom to educate, to propagate, and to persuade);
3. Freedom to worship;
4. Freedom of association
   (also for the purposes of religious education, propagation, and persuasion);
5. Freedom of expression
   (includes the rights of expression of religious thought, of the propagation of religious belief, and of religious persuasion);
6. Freedom for religious education; and
7. Freedom under the law (Northcott 1948:7-28).

This charter contains phrases which can be compared with some of the formulations in the *Universal Declaration of Human Rights* (1948).

The World Council of Churches was founded in 1948. It not only influenced the text of the *Universal Declaration of Human Rights* (1948), but also accepted a *Declaration on Religious Liberty* at its first assembly at Amsterdam (1948). During the third assembly at New Delhi (1961) it adopted a report on *Christian Witness, Proselytism, and Religious Liberty in the Setting of the WCC* which treated religious liberty as 'fundamental for men every-where'. The treatise of Angel F. Carrillo de Albornoz, *The Basis of Religious Liberty* (1963), developed out of a study by the World Council of Churches's Secretariat for Religious Liberty. The fifth assembly at Nairobi (1975) once again dealt with this issue: it stated quite correctly that 'religious liberty should never be used to claim privileges' (cf. Koshy 1992:82).

In 1966, the World Council of Churches welcomed *Dignitatis humanae* (1965), i.e. the *Declaration on Religious Liberty* which was promulgated by the Roman Catholic Church during the Second Vatican Council (cf. Carrillo de Albornoz 1965). This declaration explicitly refers to Christian mission: 'If the church has a unique authority among people, a unique mission from God and a unique duty to fulfill that mission, it certainly has a uniquely well-grounded right to preach everywhere' (DEM 1991:862).

Alan R. Booth (Concise dictionary 1971:347) concluded, 'No similar rapprochement regarding religious liberty is in sight with Islam'. Because Islamic law divides the world into two parts: *the house of Islam* (Arab: *dar el Islam*) where Islam is the recognised religion, and *the house of war* (Arab: *dar el harb*) where Islam must be defended and propagated: if necessary by the declaration of a *holy war* (Arab: *Jihad*) (cf. Morrison 1948). Within 'the house of Islam', only Muslims are full citizens. Not only the rights of 'unbelievers' (Arab: *kafir*), but also the rights of the so-called 'People of the Book' -the Jews and the Christians- are limited.

Johannes Verkuyl (1948) examined the attitude of Christianity and Islam towards religious liberty (and missionary freedom); as well as the attitude of Hinduism, Buddhism, Confucianism, and Shintoism. He is very critical about their contributions; and especially about the contribution of Shintoism: 'Shintoism is in no way compatible with religious liberty; and not even with freedom of thought' (:160; my tr.). However, M. Frederico Mayor, Director General of UNESCO, insisted in his address during the 1989 international congress on the contribution of the world religions to the realization of human rights that: 'No one can deny that in the long, slow, and even painful emergence of human rights, religions have played a major role' (Conscience and liberty 1989:I/2:101).

SEEBACH, MARGARET R. (HIMES). Missionary milestones: a study of the Reformation in its influence on civil and religious liberty and home mission activities in America. New York, 1917.

ACHELIS, HANS, PAUL ALTHAUS, ALFRED BERTHOLET, et al. (eds.). Theologische Festschrift für G. Nathanael Bonwetsch. Leipzig, 1918.
P. 138-147: Die christliche Mission und der Gedanke der Religionsfreiheit (Carl T. Mirbt).

*INTERNATIONAL MISSIONARY COUNCIL. Treaties, acts, and regulations relating to missionary freedom. London, 1923.

*GRENTRUP, THEODORUS, SVD. Jus missionarium. Steyl, 1925.

GRENTRUP, THEODORUS, SVD. Die Missionsfreiheit nach den Bestimmungen des geltenden Völkerrechts. Berlin, & Leipzig, 1928.

INTERNATIONAL MISSIONARY COUNCIL. Cases in which it is maintained that the principles of religious liberty have been violated. New York, 1930.

*HOCKING, WILLIAM E. The ethical basis underlying the legal right of religious liberty as applied to foreign missions. In: IRM, XX (1931), p. 493-511.

*PADELFORD, NORMAN J. Religious liberty in international law and treaties. In: IRM, XXI (1932), p. 402-411.

*OLDHAM, JOSEPH H. The churches survey their task: the report of the conference at Oxford, July 1937, on church, community, and state: second impression. London, 1938.
P. 84-85: The freedom of the church.
First ed.: London, 1937.

*INTERNATIONAL MISSIONARY COUNCIL. Tambaram series. Oxford, & London, 1939. 7 vols.
VI:278-288: The church and the state.
*BATES, M. SEARLE. Religious liberty: an inquiry. New York, & London, 1945.
*MORRISON, S.A. Religious liberty in the Near East. London, 1948.
*NORTHCOTT, CECIL. Freedom of religion: a commentary on 'A Charter of Religious Freedom' issued by the Joint Committee on Religious Liberty. London, 1948.
*NORTHCOTT, CECIL. Religious liberty. London, 1948.
*VERKUYL, JOHANNES. Enkele aspecten van het probleem der godsdienstvrijheid in betrekking tot de plaats en arbeid van de christelijke kerken in Azië. Kampen, 1948. Diss. V.U. Amsterdam.
*FORMAN, CHARLES W. Freedom of conversion: the issue in India. In: IRM, XLV (1956), p. 180-193.
CARRILLO DE ALBORNOZ, ANGEL F. Ecumenical statements on religious liberty: a systematic analysis. Geneva, 1959.
*SYMPOSIUM on 'religious liberty'. In: ER, XIII (1961), p. 405-501.
*JANSEN SCHOONHOVEN, EVERT. Zending en tolerantie. 's-Gravenhage, 1962.
*CARRILLO DE ALBORNOZ, ANGEL F. The basis of religious liberty. London, 1963.
*CAMPBELL, ROBERT E., MM (ed.). The church in mission. New York, 1965.
P. 159-186: Religious liberty - a mission imperative (P.A. Liégé).
CARRILLO DE ALBORNOZ, ANGEL F. Comments on the last draft of the schema of a declaration on religious liberty submitted to the Second Vatican Council (November 1964). Geneva, 1965.
CARRILLO DE ALBORNOZ, ANGEL F. Religious liberty in the world; a general review of the world situation in 1965. Geneva, 1966.
*BOVEN, THEODOOR C. VAN. De volkenrechtelijke bescherming van de godsdienstvrijheid. Assen, 1967. Diss. Leiden.
MISSION ET LIBERTÉ RELIGIEUSE: rapports et compte-rendu de la XXXVIIe semaine de missiologie, Louvain, 1967. Bruges, 1968.
REGAN, RICHARD J. Conflict and consensus: religious freedom and the Second Vatican Council. New York, 1967.
*DICTIONARY CATALOG. 1968.
XIII, p. 449-455: Religious liberty. Bibliog.
*CONCISE DICTIONARY. 1971.
P. 346-347: Religious liberty (Alan R. Booth).
*SEDOS (ed.). Foundations of mission theology... New York, 1972.
P. 143-147: Mission work and freedom of conscience (José M. Gonzalez-Ruiz).
*BERKHOF, HENDRIK, & WESSEL E. VERDONK (eds.). Boeket voor Bolkestein... Leiden, 1979.
P. 189-217: Het universele recht van de kerk en de universele vrijheid van godsdienst (Jan A.B. Jongeneel).
*BOVEN, THEODOOR C. VAN. Religious liberty in the context of human rights. In: ER, XXXVII (1985), p. 345-355.
*LMG. 1987.
P. 508-511: Toleranz, Religionsfreiheit (F. Wolfinger).
*ISSACHAR FRONTIER MISSIONS STRATEGIES. Restricted world ministry handbook: a special report on the nations of the restricted-access world. Washington, 1989.
*MAYOR, M. FREDERICO. Religions in support of human rights. In: Conscience and liberty, I/2 (1989), p. 100-103.
*PERONNET, M. Freedom of worship and French Revolution (1789-1799). In: Conscience and liberty, I/2 (1989), p. 68-74.
*WALKATE, JAAP A. The U.N. Declaration on the Elimination of All Forms of Intolerance and

316

Discrimination Based on Religion or Belief (1981) - an historical overview. In: Conscience and liberty, I/2 (1989), p. 21-35.

*DEM. 1991.
P. 859-863: Religious liberty (Ninan Koshy).

*BRAYBROOKE, MARCUS. Pelgrimage of hope: one hundred years of global interfaith dialogue. London, 1992.
P. 47-62: The International Association for Religious Freedom.

*KOSHY, NINAN. Religious freedom in a changing world. Geneva, 1992.

5.3.8.5. THE LAW OF CHRISTIAN MISSION AND NATIONAL AND INTERNATIONAL LAW

Normally, both national law and international law deal with religious liberty. Sometimes they also refer to '(Christian) mission'.

Religious liberty and missionary freedom are primarily a matter which falls under *national law*. Surveying the constitutions of the various nations in the world we can find a great variety of legal provisions: in some nations the constitution is silent about religious liberty; in other nations the law only guarantees the freedom of one religion (and mission) as *the* religion (and mission) of the people; and in still other nations the law equates all religions and missions without exception. However, theory and practice are not the same. For instance, S.A. Morrison, Secretary of the Church Missionary Society Egypt Mission, wrote the following about the separation of religion and politics in Turkey: 'Constitutionally, there is complete religious freedom, but in practice it is not always realized' (1948:23).

International law (Ger.: *Völkerrecht*) is that body of rules, principles and customs accepted by the majority of (civilized) nations as governing their relations (cf. Mirbt, in: Festgabe Von Harnack 1921:342-361; Grentrup 1928; Delos 1932; idem, in: Revue générale de droit international public 1932:565-613; Padelford, in: IRM 1932:402-411; Bierbaum, in: ZM 1933:289-307; Müller, in: Katholisches Missionsjahrbuch der Schweiz 1944:71-75; Bierbaum, in: Scientia missionum ancilla 1953:290-295; Holsten, in: Hermelink, & Margull 1959:106-127; Higgins 1965; Van Boven 1967; Sieghart 1983). It permits nations to make international agreements: multi-lateral or bi-lateral treaties, acts, and regulations. Some of these agreements deal explicitly with '(Christian) mission'.

An interesting example is Article 11 of the revised form of the earlier multi-lateral Treaty of Berlin (1885) drawn up between those colonial powers having possessions or interests in Africa:

> Freedom of conscience and the free exercise of all forms of religion are expressly guaranteed to all nationals of the signatory powers and to those under the jurisdiction of States members of the League of Nations

which may become parties to the present convention. Similarly, missionaries shall have the right to enter into, and to travel and reside in, African territory with a view to prosecuting their calling (Padelford, in: IRM 1932:407).

Also famous is the following text of Article 438 of the multi-lateral Treaty of Peace between the Allied and Associated Powers and Germany after the First World War (1919):

> The Allied and Associated Powers agree that where Christian religious missions were being maintained by German societies or persons in territory belonging to them, or of which the government is entrusted to them in accordance with the present Treaty, the property which these missions or missionary societies possessed, including that of trading societies whose profits were devoted to the support of missions, shall continue to be devoted to missionary purposes.
>
> In order to ensure the due execution of this undertaking the Allied and Associated Governments will hand over such property to boards of trustees appointed by or approved by the Governments and composed of persons holding the faith of the mission whose property is involved. The Allied and Associated Governments, while continuing to maintain full control as to the individuals by whom the missions are conducted, will safeguard the interests of such missions.
>
> Germany, taking note of the above undertaking, agrees to accept all arrangements made or to be made by the Allied and Associated Governments concerned for carrying on the work of the said missions or trading societies and waives all claims on their behalf (International Missionary Council 1923:6-7).

Further, I quote Article 14 of the bi-lateral Treaty between the United States of America and China (1903):

> No restrictions shall be placed upon Chinese joining Christian churches. Converts and non-converts, being Chinese subjects, shall alike conform to the laws of China; and shall pay due respect to those in authority... Missionaries shall not interfere with the free exercise by the native authorities of their jurisdiction over Chinese subjects, nor shall the native authorities make any distinction between converts and non-converts, but shall administer the laws without partiality, so that both classes can live together in peace (Padelford, in: IRM 1932:408).

318

And, finally, I refer to the provisions of mandates. Article 8 of the British Mandate for the Tanganyika Terrritory (1922), for example, expresses something which is similar to that applied to the above-mentioned African possessions and interests:

> Missionaries who are nationals of States members of the League of Nations shall be free to enter the territory and to travel and reside therein, and to acquire and possess property, to erect religious buildings and to open schools throughout the territory... (Padelford, in: IRM 1932:409).

Norman J. Padelford (IRM 1932:411) concluded that, where such bi-lateral and multi-lateral agreements are present, 'the Christian worker has a right to insist on liberty to proclaim the Christian message within the limits of law and public order'.

All the above-mentioned texts belong to the colonial past. In the post-colonial era, neither national law nor international law treat missionary freedom as an important item. On the contrary, we observe that more and more nations, especiallly in the so-called Two-Third World, adopt regulations which in one way or another restrict (Christian) missionary activities: especially those which are undertaken by westerners. Issachar Frontier Missions Strategies published the *Restricted World Ministry Handbook* (1989). It made clear that 'Before the Second World War, and even for years after, Christian missionaries as well as national pastors and evangelists could move freely throughout most of the world and preach the gospel. Those days are now gone' (:1). The *Universal Declaration of Human Rights* and similar international declarations and covenants are not strong enough to reverse this negative trend. Those who drafted them have neither the right nor the power to apply sanctions against those nations which violate the rules of religious liberty: including missionary freedom.

*FISHER, GALEN M. Missionaries and international political questions. In: IRM, IX (1920), p. 517-530. FESTGABE von Fachgenossen und Freunden, Adolf von Harnack zum siebzigsten Geburtstag dargebracht. Tübingen, 1921.
   P. 342-361: Die christliche Mission in den völkerrechtlichen Verträgen der Neuzeit (Carl T. Mirbt).
*MIRBT, CARL T. Missions and law. In: IRM, XV (1926), p. 240-247.
?DELOS, JOSEPH T., OP. Les missions catholiques dans le droit international actuel. In: Revue générale de droit international public, (1932), p. 565-613.
?DELOS, JOSEPH T., OP. The situation of catholic missions in present international law. 1932.
   First ed.: La situation des missions catholiques dans le droit international actuel. In: Revue générale de droit international public, (1930), p. 671-703.
BIERBAUM, MAX. Mission und Völkerrecht. In: ZM, XXIII (1933), p. 289-307.

KATHOLISCHES MISSIONSJAHRBUCH DER SCHWEIZ. Freiburg, 1944.
  P. 71-75: Die Missionen im Lichte des Völkerrechts und der Weltgeschichte (J. Müller).
ROMMERSKIRCHEN, JOHANNES, OMI, & NIKOLAUS KOWALSKY OMI (eds.). Missionswissenschaftliche Studien: Festgabe Prof.Dr. Johannes Dindinger OMI... Aachen, 1951.
  P. 75-92: Mission und Naturrecht (Max Bierbaum).
*SCIENTIA MISSIONUM ANCILLA. 1953.
  P. 290-295: Mission und Rechtswissenschaft (Max Bierbaum).
*HERMELINK, JAN, & HANS J. MARGULL (eds.). Basileia... Stuttgart, 1959.
  P. 106-127: Die Mission in den völkerrechtlichen Verträgen und Verfassungen der Neuzeit (Walter Holsten).
HIGGINS, ROSALYN. Conflict of interests: international law in divided world: a background book. London, 1965.

5.3.8.6. CONCLUSION

The *Universal Declaration of Human Rights* (1948), the *International Covenant on Civil and Political Rights* (1966), and the *Declaration on the Elimination of All Forms of Intolerance and of Discrimination Based on Religion and Belief* (1981) are very clear about religious liberty. Nevertheless, many nations still violate the principles of religious liberty. There are not yet sanctions against such violators.

The rules of the United Nations do not explicitly refer to '(Christian) mission' as some treaties in the colonial past did. However, it is clear that missionary freedom is included in religious liberty (1948) and that discrimination against the (Christian) mission must be eliminated (1981).

Many national constitutions guarantee religious liberty. By doing so, they recognize missionary freedom. However, some nations do not maintain in practice what they have promised in theory in their law; and other nations possess constitutions and/or regulations which restrict missionary freedom.

Religions are supporters of human rights: including religious liberty. However, not only ideologies but also religions have repeatedly violated human rights and discriminated against people. The law of apostasy in Islam is one of the most extreme examples to illustrate this fact. However, Christians have also violated human dignity (for instance, the Crusades in the Middle Ages) and still are doing so (cf. Northern Ireland). Nevertheless, Christian mission is by nature a real champion of human rights in general, and of religious liberty in particular.

5.3.9. THE ECONOMICS OF CHRISTIAN MISSION

> Plan, at the earliest possible moment,
> as God prospers you, to make an *investment* in
> the foreign work of your domination, to become
> A CAPITALIST FOR CHRIST.
> *Cornelius H. Patton (1924:263).*

5.3.9.1. INTRODUCTION

In this section we will reflect upon the relationship between economics and mission: especially the Christian mission. Economics influences (Christian) mission, and vice versa. David M. Beckmann (Misssiology 1981:110), a student of William J. Danker, wrote: 'The challenge of Christian mission to economics remains for me more important than the challenge of economics to mission'. However, not all economists and all missiologists will agree with this view.

Many missiological handbooks are silent about the relationship between mission and economics. Gustav Warneck (1903:III/3:141-179) and Thomas Ohm OSB (1962:762-772), however, did devote some attention to this particular issue. In an article on 'Commerce and missions', Kenneth S. Latourette (Concise dictionary 1971:124) pointed out that 'No book appears to have been devoted exclusively to the subject of this article', but this is not true. The bibliography of this section actually demonstrates the opposite: some substantial monographs have already been published on this topic.

After a few lines on the history of the interaction between economics and (Christian) mission, we will discuss 'missionary economics' as a discipline; missionary finance; the whole issue of 'self-support'; the relation between mission and poverty/affluence; and the relation between missionary finance and the world economy. Other topics could be mentioned but we made this selection.

```
*WARNECK. 1892-1903. 3 vols.
     III/3, p. 141-179: Die finanzielle Selbstunterhaltung der heidenchristlichen
     Kirchen.
*OHM. 1962.
     P. 762-772: Die Finanzierung der Mission.
```

5.3.9.2. HISTORY

John S. Stone (1839), Carl H.C. Plath (1873: German ed.: 1868), Chapin H. Carpenter (1883; 1885; 1886), Franz M. Zahn (1886; AMZ 1891:355-373),

Julius Richter (AMZ 1890:495-505), and George C. Lorimer (1899) are 19th century scholars who already reflected upon the relationship between mission and economics. The phrase *mission economics* was coined by Carpenter (1886) who can be regarded as the founder of 'the economics of Christian mission' as a discipline.

Olav G. Myklebust (1955) neither referred to Stone, Carpenter, and Lorimer nor mentioned C.C. Thayer (The missionary review of the world 1903:516-520) who introduced the term *missionary economics*. We read the following explanation in Thayer's article on this topic: 'Missionary economics relate not only to the production and conservation of vital force, but to its sanctification and appropriation... Missionary economics require that the man of God be thoroughly furnished unto every good *word*... Missionary economics require that the missionary be furnished unto every good *work*... Missionary economics demand that an evangel must be furnished, not with a few notes and stories from the Holy Scriptures, for one can make of the Bible a museum or a university, but furnished with living, vital, and vitalizing truth burning in his bones... Missionary economics demand compensation for expenditure'. Therefore, Thayer considered the missionaries to be the vital and productive forces of the missionary movement. Mission boards must take care of the missionaries' health: missionary economics will be poor if the mission boards neglect the health of their missionaries both in the field and on furlough.

The world missionary conferences of Edinburgh (1910), Jerusalem (1928), and Tambaram (1938) dealt with economic matters: Edinburgh produced a small report on the 'Financial support of the missionary enterprise', Jerusalem dealt at length with 'missions and economics in Latin America', while the Tambaram Series even devoted a whole volume to 'the economic basis of the church'. In 1930, the International Missionary Council established a Department of Social and Economic Research in Geneva, which started research studies. Here we only mention *Mission Finance Policies and the Younger Churches* (1938) and *The Economic and Social Environment of the Younger Churches* (1939) by J. Merle Davis, director of the above-mentioned Department of Social and Economic Research. After the Second World War, such study programmes were not continued.

Vedanayagam S. Azariah (1874-1945), bishop of Dornekal (India), was one of the first Third World church leaders to reflect upon the use of money. In 1939 he wrote a small book in Tamil on *Christian Giving* which was published in the same year in an English version. We read in this study: 'We must not forget that most of the early converts of the missions were very poor... Even in those days, missionaries often spoke of the time when the younger churches would have to become independent; but by their actions they denied their words' (1956:29).

In the interbellum, a case-study was published on the early economic activities of the Moravians (Uttendörfer 1925). After 1945, other case-studies followed: on the missionary finance of the China Inland Mission (Thompson 1956); the Jesuits (Popescu 1967); the Moravians (Helman 1968; Danker 1971); the Basel Mission Trading Company (Danker 1971; Osafo 1972; cf. Rennstich 1978); and the Zambesi Missions (Rea 1976). William J. Danker (1971:133), Professor of Missions at Concordia Theological Seminary, compared the economic activities of the Moravians and Basel and concluded: 'Both the Moravians and Basel provided a matrix for economic activities that was pietistic, ecumenical, and international'.

In the post-colonial period, new issues were put on the agenda of the churches and the mission boards: poverty and affluence; the relation between missionary activities and economic development (Cole, in: Economic development and cultural change 1961:120-127); etc.

UTTENDÖRFER, OTTO. Alt-Herrnhut: Wirtschaftsgeschichte und Religionssoziologie Herrnhuts während seiner ersten zwanzig Jahre, 1722-1742. Herrnhut, 1925.

*MYKLEBUST. 1955-1957. 2 vols.

*AZARIAH, VEDANAYAGAM S. Christian giving: third impression. London, 1956.
    First ed.: London, 1954.

THOMPSON, PHYLLIS. Proving God: financial experiences of the China Inland Mission. London, 1956.

WRIGHT, LOUIS B. Religion and empire: the alliance between piety and commerce in English expansion, 1558-1625. New York, 1965.

POPESCU, ORESTE. El sistema económico en las misiones jesuíticas: un vasto experimento de desarrollo indoamericano. Barcelona, 1967.

*HELMAN, ALBERT. Zaken, zending en bezinning: de romantische kroniek van een tweehonderd-jarige Surinaamse firma. Paramaribo, 1968.

*DANKER, WILLIAM J. Profit for the Lord: economic activities in Moravian missions and the Basel Mission Trading Company. Grand Rapids, 1971.

OSAFO, ERNEST A. Der Beitrag der Basler Mission zur wirtschaftlichen Entwicklung Ghanas von 1828 bis zum Ersten Weltkrieg. Köln, 1972. Diss. Cologne.

REA, WILLIAM F., SJ. The economics of the Zambesi missions, 1580-1759. Roma, 1976.

RENNSTICH, KARL W. Mission und wirtschaftliche Entwicklung: biblische Theologie des Kulturwandels und christliche Ethik. München, 1978.

*JEURISSEN, RONALD. Gods kinderen en de machten: het Vaticaan en de Wereldraad van Kerken over internationale economische verhoudingen, ontwikkeling en bevrijding, 1965-1985. Utrecht, & Leiden, 1986.

5.3.9.3. THE ECONOMICS OF CHRISTIAN MISSION

That the missionary is a pioneer of commerce
is established beyond debate.
Cornelius H. Patton (1924:VII).

The main book of Chapin H. Carpenter (1835-1887), *Studies in mission economics* (1886), regarded mission societies as 'economical agencies for the propagation of the gospel' (:45) and compared their economy (:49). This study also questioned whether the subsidy system in missions should be extirpated (:75-152) and how self-supporting schools in missions may be escaped (:153-232). In this framework it discussed 'the promotion of parasitism an avowed policy' (:158-160).

Cornelius H. Patton (1924:287), Home Secretary of the American Board of Commissioners for Foreign Missions, used the term *missionary economy*. He pointed out that 'Under modern conditions sums of money are required beyond the dreams of the pioneers' (:142). He regarded mission as 'big business': 'finding the money' (:192-200); 'handling the funds' (:200-208); 'directing the work' (:208-209); etc. In the words of Frank M. North, quoted by Patton: 'From now on missions must be the *business*, not the *charity* of the church' (:252).

Richard Thurnwald (1932:19) greatly regretted that 'The observation of the economic life of native tribes has been deplorably neglected, even by authors who pay great attention to social institutions of all kinds'. Also several authors on 'missionary economics' underrated the importance of the economy of traditional societies -poor people; well-to-do families; chiefs; and commoners- and the impact which missions made on their financial resources.

In the post-World War situation, 'missionary economics' is more and more concerned about 'global economy' (Duchrow 1987). Especially the Commission on the Churches' Participation in Development (CCPD) of the World Council of Churches is very active in this broad field. Here I refer to the Sao Paulo meeting of Confessing Movements (1987) which was co-sponsored by CCPD. The statement of this important meeting, entitled: *Churches, Christians, and Economic Systems: A Call to Obedient Discipleship* (CCPD n.d.:8-11), dealt with the economic system, labour, capital, land, and theological convictions. CCPD also published seven Occasional Study Pamphlets, *Sacrifice and Humane Economic Life* (n.d.) being the last one. However, these publications, written by such outstanding scholars as Ulrich Duchrow, Julio de Santa Ana, and Franz J. Hinkelammert, do not use the term 'missionary economics' any more.

In the course of the last few decades, 'The Missionary's Role in Socio-Economic Betterment' (Considine 1960) has been transformed into 'the churches' participation in development'. It is now the CCPD -and no longer the Commission on World Mission and Evangelism of the World Council of Churches (as the successor of the International Missionary Council)- which is deeply involved in matters of world economy. Wilbert R. Shenk still referred to 'God's New Economy: Interdependence and Mission' (1988) but few ecumenical authors connect mission and economics. The same trend can be noted in the Roman Catholic Church (cf. Jeurissen 1986).

CARPENTER, CHAPIN H. The American Baptist Missionary Union: its present standing as an economical agency for propagating the gospel. Boston, 1885.

*CARPENTER, CHAPIN H. Studies in mission economics..., including 'Self-help in missions', by Franklin Johnson... Boston, 1886.

LORIMER, GEORGE C. Golden gate: or, the economics of missions... Boston, 1899.

*THAYER, C.C. Missionary health economics. In: The missionary review of the world, XVI (1903), p. 128-131.

*THAYER, C.C. Missionary economics: personal efficiency. In: The missionary review of the world, XVI (1903), p. 516-520.

*PATTON, CORNELIUS H. The business of missions. New York, 1924.
    P. 287: Missionary economy.

*INTERNATIONAL MISSIONARY COUNCIL. Report of the Jerusalem meeting. London, Melbourne, Cape Town..., 1928.
    V, p. 117-145: Missions and economics in Latin America (Samuel G. Inman).

*WESTERMANN, DIEDRICH, & RICHARD THURNWALD. The missionary and anthropological research. London, 1932.
    P. 19-22: Economics (Richard Thurnwald).

PHILIP, PUTHENVEETRE O. The Christian church and social and economic action in India... Calcutta, 1938.

*DAVIS, J. MERLE. The economic and social environment of the younger churches: the report of the Department of Social and Economic Research of the IMC to the Tambaram meeting - December 1938. London, 1939.

*INTERNATIONAL MISSIONARY COUNCIL. Tambaram series. London, 1939.
    V: The economic basis of the church (ed.: J. Merle Davis).
    V, p. 39-43: Economic determinism.

WISER, WILLIAM H. Building the social and economic foundations for an indigenous church in the United Provinces. Lucknow, 1940.

CONSIDINE, JOHN J., MM (ed.). The missionary's role in socio-economic betterment. Westminster, 1960.

?DANKER, WILLIAM J. Introduction to a theological, historical, and practical survey of economic activities in Protestant world missions. 1967. Diss. Heidelberg.

*DICTIONARY CATALOG. 1968.
    XI, p. 90-92: Missions-Economics. Bibliog.

*CONCISE DICTIONARY. 1971.
    P. 177-178: Economic problems and Christian missions (Eugene L. Stockwell).

*DANKER, WILLIAM J., & WI JO KANG (eds.). The future of the Christian world mission: studies in honor of R. Pierce Beaver. Grand Rapids, 1971.
    P. 155-161: A piece of the action: a new economic basis for the church.

*BECKMANN, DAVID M. The challenge of economics to the teaching of missiology. In: Missiology, IX (1981), p. 99-112.

?SHENK, WILBERT R. God's new economy: interdependence and mission. Elkhart, 1988.
*FORNET-BETANCOURT, RAúL (ed.). Verändert der Glaube die Wirtschaft? Theologie und Ökonomie in Lateinamerika. Freiburg, Basel, & Wien, 1991.
*COMMISSION ON THE CHURCHES' PARTICIPATION IN DEVELOPMENT (WCC). Economics: a matter of faith. Geneva, n.d.

5.3.9.4. MISSIONARY FINANCE

The object of 'missionary economics' as a discipline is *mission(ary) finance* (MacLennan, in: IRM 1912:488-497; Huntington 1918; Waddy 1930; Missionary council of the church assembly 1932; Davis 1938), or -more broadly conceived- *commerce and missions* (Zahn 1886; Concise dictionary 1971:124; Dennis n.d.). The key-issues are *missionary giving* (Fahs, in: IRM 1927:405-414; cf. Tampier, in: Bettray 1962:172-177), on the one hand, and the *costs* of the missionary enterprise (cf. Conservative Baptist Foreign Mission Society 1950), including *income taxes* (Mills 1953), on the other.

The report of the Edinburgh Missionary Conference (1910) on 'Financial Support of the Missionary Enterprise' pointed out that 'The success of foreign missions largely depends upon the financial support it receives...' (World missionary conference 1910:VI,146). This report also referred to the Apportionment Plan in the USA, which contemplated:

1. a decision on the part of the denomination as to what its immediate responsibility is for the support of its foreign missionary work;
2. the apportionment of that responsibility among the local churches in the different civil and ecclesiastical areas; and
3. the subdivision of this apportionment among the individual churches, so that each church will know its assigned share of the amount to be raised for the support of foreign missions for any particular year (:VI,147).

This report also raised the question of whether every church member should have a share in the financial support of the missionary enterprise.

The Edinburgh missionary conference was not the only missionary meeting which discussed 'raising mission funds'. Nearly every missionary conference in the 19th and 20th centuries discussed this. Also virtually every missionary conference dealt with the question of 'spending mission money'. In a chapter of their missiological textbook, entitled 'The Missionary Dollar: Where Should It Go?', Tetsunao Yamamori and E. LeRoy Lawson (1975:189) pointed out that 'Every dollar dedicated to foreign missions is divided into four unequal parts': the missionaries; the home base; the field; and research. They advised that 'It must be a unified dollar: that is, each part must contribute to the whole' (:192).

STONE, JOHN S. The bearings of modern commerce on the progress of modern missions: the annual sermon... New York, 1839.

PLATH, CARL H.C. The subject of missions considered under three new aspects: the church and missions: the representation of the science of missions at the universities: commerce and the church... Edinburgh, 1873.
*Ger. ed.: Berlin, 1868.

CARPENTER, CHAPIN H. The subsidy system in missions: shall it be extirpated? Boston, 1885.

?ZAHN, FRANZ M. Handel und Mission. Gütersloh, 1886.

*RICHTER, JULIUS. Der Unterhalt der Apostel während ihrer Missionsreisen. In: AMZ, XVII (1890), p. 495-505.

*ZAHN, FRANZ M. Mission und Geld. In: AMZ, XVIII (1891), p. 355-373.

*WORLD MISSIONARY CONFERENCE, 1910. Edinburgh, London, New York..., 1910.
VI, p. 146-160: Financial support of the missionary enterprise.

*GUNNING, JAN W. De financiën der zending. Baarn, 1911.

*HEADLAND, ISAAC T. Some by-products of missions. Cincinnati, & New York, 1912.
P. 25-34: By-products in trade.

*MacLENNAN, KENNETH. Ten years' missionary finance: a survey and some deductions. In: IRM, I (1912), p. 488-497.

*DAY, DWIGHT H. Some aspects of the work of a treasurer of a foreign mission board. In: IRM, IV (1915), p. 221-231.

HUNTINGTON, GEORGE B. The high cost of money: a problem of missionary finance. 1918.

*SELL, EDWARD. Financial administration in the mission field. In: IRM, VII (1918), p. 333-352.

*PATTON, CORNELIUS H. The business of missions. New York, 1924.

UTTENDÖRFER, OTTO. Wirtschaftsgeist und Wirtschaftsorganisation Herrnhuts und der Brüdergemeinde von 1743 bis zum Ende des Jahrhunderts. Herrnhut, 1926.

*FAHS, CHARLES H. Tendencies in missionary giving in the United States. In: IRM, XVI (1927), p. 405-414.

WADDY, PERCIVAL S. The piper and the tune (a study of missionary finance). London, 1930.

MISSIONARY COUNCIL OF THE CHURCH ASSEMBLY, MISSIONARY FINANCE COMMISSION. Missionary finance... London, 1932.

*DAVIS, J. MERLE. Mission finance policies and the younger churches: a study prepared for the Tambaram meeting of the IMC. Bangalore, 1938.

*GOODSELL, FRED F. The life of the indigenous church: finance. In: IRM, XXVII (1938), p. 393-402.

CONSERVATIVE BAPTIST FOREIGN MISSION SOCIETY. What a missionary costs. Chicago, 1950.

MILLS, WILSON P. Missionaries and income taxes. New York, 1953.

*HERMELINK, JAN, & HANS J. MARGULL (eds.). Walter Freytag. Reden und Aufsätze. München, 1961.
I, p. 269-286: Geld und Geist in der werdenden Kirche (1940).

BETTRAY, JOHANNES, SVD (ed.). Mission und Heimatseelsorge. Münster in Westfalen, 1962.
P. 172-177: Missionskollekten (Alois Tampier).

*RUF, WALTHER (ed.). Ihr werdet meine Zeugen sein: Georg F. Vicedom zum 60. Geburtstag. Nürnberg, 1963.
P. 119-130: Die Mission und ihr Geld (Arno Lehmann).

*DICTIONARY CATALOG. 1968.
XI, p. 93: Missions-Finance. Bibliog.

*CRAWFORD, JOHN R. Missionaries' giving through the local church. In: IRM, LVI (1967), p. 224-232.

*CONCISE DICTIONARY. 1971.
    P. 124: Commerce and missions (Kenneth S. Latourette).
    P. 208-209: Financial support for missions (eds.).
*YAMAMORI, TETSUNAO, & E. LeROY LAWSON. Introducing church growth: a textbook in missions. Cincinnati, 1975.
    P. 187-206: The missionary dollar: where should it go?
*COGGINS, WADE T., & E.L. FRIZEN Jr (eds.). Evangelical missions tomorrow. South Pasadena, 1977.
    P. 74-93: Financing missions in the future (Eldon J. Howard).
?SMITH, PAUL B. The senders: world missions conferences and faith promise offerings. Toronto, 1979.
DENNIS, JAMES S. Commerce and missions. New York, n.d.

5.3.9.5. SELF-SUPPORTING CHURCHES

> ... a church can exist without 'self-support',
> but it must die without the spirit of evangelism.
> *Vedanaiaken S. Azariah (IRM 1938:364).*

In the 19th and 20th centuries, many mission boards and missionaries discussed the highly contentious issue of raising funds and limiting costs in the mission fields. This issue became known as the question of *self-support*: *self-supporting schools* (Carpenter 1886), *self-supporting churches* (Dictionary catalog 1968: XIV:200-204), etc.

Renowned is the following formula: *self-extension, self-support, self-government* (these three terms are not always put in the same order). Rufus Anderson (1796-1880) and Henry Venn (1796-1873) are the well-known propagandists of this formula. They found almost general favour: both of individuals (cf. Tucker 1901), and of mission boards. We enounter this formula, for instance, in *The Principles of the Church Missionary Society*: 'All our evangelistic efforts are to aim, first, at the conversion of individual souls, and secondly, though contemporaneously, at the organization of the permanent native Christian church, self-supporting, self-governing, self-extending'. These *Principles* are quoted by Chapin H. Carpenter in his study on *Self-Support, Illustrated in the History of the Bassein Karen Mission from 1840 to 1880* (1883:86).

Carpenter considered the Bassein Karen missionary Elisha L. Abbott as a full supporter of the 'self-support'-idea. The Rev. Abbott's motto was: 'American support for Americans, Karen support for Karens'. 'Self-support' was not only put first in *The Principles of the Church Missionary Society*, but also became the leading principle of the whole Bassein Karen Mission. Carpenter argued that 'Individual missionaries there have been in every age sent forth by the home churches, and supported, to a greater or less extent, in heathen lands; but *in permanently successful missions, they never have subsidized their converts'* (:135). Neither 'self-extension', nor 'self-government', but 'self-support' became the keynote at home and abroad.

J. Merle Davis (1938:89) discussed the various definitions of 'self-support': some missions consider that the ability to pay the pastor's salary; others include widening areas of responsibility: such as support of evangelists; and still others require a regular contribution to the expenses of the central organization. Here, the crucial question is the extent of self-support.

After the Second World War, the 'ideology' of self-support was the subject of heated discussion. In 1971, African church leaders such as John Gatu, General Secretary of the Presbyterian Church of East Africa, called for a *moratorium* against missionary dollars as well as western personnel (DEM 1991:702-703). Harvie M. Conn (EMQ 1978:231-239), Associate Professor of Missions and Apologetics at Westminster Theological Seminary, Philadelphia, blamed the 'self-support myth' for the 'pillaging' or 'robbing' of Western and overseas churches of the joy of mutual giving. He quoted some Bible verses to support his contention that it is time to end the double standard of funding mission work, which is built on the distinction between the -rich- 'sending church(es)' and the -poor- 'receiving church(es)'.

*CARPENTER, CHAPIN H. Self-support, illustrated in the history of the Bassein Karen Mission from 1840 to 1880. Boston, 1883.

CARPENTER, CHAPIN H. Self-support: how far attained in our missions: a study in mission finance. Boston, 1885.

CARPENTER, CHAPIN H. Self-supporting schools in our missions... Boston, 1886.

TUCKER, ALFRED R. Self-extension, self-support, and self-government in missionary churches... London, 1901.

*CALKINS, HARVEY R. Foundation facts the ground of self-support. In: IRM, XII (1923), p. 421-433.

*AZARIAH, VEDANAIAKEN S. Self-support: false and true. In: IRM, XXVII (1938), p. 361-371.

*DAVIS, J. MERLE. The problem of aid to the younger churches: post-war reconstruction: a trained ministry and self-support. In: IRM, XXXIII (1944), p. 128-137.

*DICTIONARY CATALOG. 1968.
        XIV, p. 200-204: Self-supporting churches in the field. Bibliog.

*CONN, HARVIE M. The money barrier between sending and receiving churches. In: EMQ, XIV (1978), p. 231-239.

*DEM. 1991.
        P. 702-703: Moratorium (Gerald H. Anderson).

5.3.9.6. MISSION, POVERTY AND AFFLUENCE

> It is not easy to live simply in an affluent society
> and witness to the poor.
> *Keith R. Crim (Phillips, & Coote 1993:102).*

The issue of *poverty and wealth* was already debated in the colonial era (cf. MacVicar, in: IRM 1941:337-348), but became urgent in the post-colonial period: from the 1960s onwards. Not only Western scholars and Third World theologians contributed to the debate on this topic, but also church bodies. In 1979, the Third General Conference of Latin American Bishops, held in Puebla, dealt with 'the preferential option for the poor'; and, in 1982, the World Council of Churches followed with 'God's preferential option for the poor' (Mission and Evangelism: an Ecumenical Affirmation, 34).

Julio de Santa Ana, director of the Commission on the Churches' Participation in Development, wrote three (collective) studies on *poverty: Good News to the Poor: the Challenge of the Poor in the History of the Church* (1977); *Separation Without Hope? Essays on the Relation between the Church and the Poor during the Industrial Revolution and the Western Colonial Expansion* (1978); and *Towards a Church of the Poor: the Work of an Ecumenical Group on the Church and the Poor* (1979). They made clear that development is not *for* the poor; it can be achieved *by* the poor and *with* the poor when they become full participants in the processes which lead to justice and liberation. The last-mentioned volume also included a 'Letter to the Churches from the Contributors to this Book' in which the church *of* the poor is characterized as 'a community that is open towards the future... It is a community which in its poverty demonstrates *vigorous missionary activity*' (:207). However, none of these studies uses such terms as 'missionary economics' and 'missionary finance'. They are also absent in the study of Richard D.N. Dickinson (1983), who regarded the poor as 'agents of creative justice'.

Both Klaus Nürnberger (1978) and Jonathan J. Bonk (EMQ 1985:382-390; Missiology 1986:437-461; 1991) studied the difficult problem of *affluence*. Bonk warned the churches that affluence could well be 'the Achilles' heel of western missions' (in Greek mythology Achilles was invulnerable except for his heel). In his influential book on this topic (1991), Bonk discussed the context, the circumstances, and the challenge of Western missionary affluence. The African theologian Zablon Ntamburi wrote in the Foreword of this study: '... the *modus operandi* of Western missionaries reflects the increasing prosperity of their homelands in a world where the gap between rich and poor is widening. Such affluence cataclysmically isolates missionaries from the *cutting edge* of missionary endeavors, rendering their efforts futile' (:XV-XVI).

At the meeting of the Central Committee of the World Council of Churches in Moscow (1989), the issue of world poverty was discussed. There, Bishop Frederico J. Pagura (Argentina) presented a paper in which he referred to the 20th century idolatries: fascism turned the state into an idol; communism into a political party; and capitalism into a market (CCPD 1989:16).

*MacVICAR, NEIL. Poverty in the city of gold. In: IRM, XXX (1941), p. 337-348.

MERCIER, G., & MARIE-J. LE GUILLOU OP. Mission et pauvreté: l'heure de la mission mondiale. Paris, 1964.

*SANTA ANA, JULIO DE. Good news to the poor: the challenge of the poor in the history of the church. Geneva, 1977.

NÜRNBERGER, KLAUS (ed.). Affluence, poverty, and the Word of God... Durban, 1978.

*SANTA ANA, JULIO DE (ed.). Separation withour hope? essays on the relation between the church and the poor during the Industrial Revolution and the Western Colonial Expansion. Geneva, 1978.

    P. 137-154: The church and the poor in Asian history (C.I. Itty).

    P. 155-170: The Christian mission and the African peoples in the 19th century (Sam M. Kobia).

*SANTA ANA, JULIO DE (ed.). Towards a church of the poor: the work of an ecumenical group on the church and the poor: second printing. Geneva, 1982.

    P. 161-172: Evangelization, the Bible and liturgy in the church of the poor.

    First ed.: Geneva, 1979.

*DICKINSON, RICHARD D.N. Poor, yet making many rich: the poor as agents of creative justice. Geneva, 1983.

*SANTA ANA, JULIO DE. The mission of the church in a world torn between poor and rich. In: IRM, LXXII (1983), p. 20-29.

*BONK, JONATHAN J. Affluence: the Achilles' heel of missions. In: EMQ, XXI (1985), p. 382-390.

    Two responses: Nussbaum, Stan. Relationships may precede economic adjustments. In: EMQ, XXI (1985), p. 390-392.

    Plueddemann, James E. The issue is love, not affluence. In: EMQ, XXI (1985), p. 392-394.

*BONK, JONATHAN J. The role of affluence in the Christian missionary enterprise from the West. In: Missiology, XIV (1986), p. 437-461.

*NISSEN, JOHANNES. Poverty and mission: New Testament perspectives on a contemporary theme. Leiden, & Utrecht, 1984.

*LMG. 1987.

    P. 29-34: Armut (G. Reese).

*COMMISSION ON THE CHURCHES' PARTICIPATION IN DEVELOPMENT (WCC). Poor in the world economy: presentations at the Central Committee Moscow 1989. Geneva, 1989.

*BONK, JONATHAN J. Missions and money: affluence as western missionary problem. New York, 1991.

*PHILLIPS, JAMES M., & ROBERT T. COOTE (eds.). Toward the twenty-first century in Christian mission. Grand Rapids, 1993.

    P. 98-106: North America (Keith R. Crim).

5.3.9.7. THE ECONOMICS OF CHRISTIAN MISSION AND WORLD ECONOMY

> Making the economic system more just is possible
> but it will not happen until we want it to happen.
> *Michael Bradfield (IRM 1974:179).*

The Christian churches and missions have always regarded 'God's ownership' -cf. the Jerusalem missionary conference (1928)- as the startingpoint of their reflection upon local and global economy.

Missions have influenced economy: funds were raised at home and houses, churches, hospitals, schools, etc. were built on the mission fields. And economy has set its stamp upon Christian missions: in times of prosperity, people were able to contribute large sums to the mission societies; but, during times of economic depression, this was more difficult. In the 1930s, economic stringency caused considerable problems for the missionary societies: they were faced with a 20 %, 40 %, and even 60 % decline of their incomes (cf. Tambaram series 1939:V,42).

Today the problems are greater than in the colonial era. The world population is growing and economic attitudes and activities are not developing in the same quick way. The United Nations propagated a new economic order. The World Council of Churches discussed this new order and reflected upon concrete problems such as international trade relations; the availability of long term loans at reasonable terms; the stabilization of exchange rates; the reconsideration of decision-making in international financial circles; and the reconstruction of major world financial institutions such as the International Monetary Fund and the World Bank (cf. Advisory group on economic matters/ CCPD n.d.:VI).

In 1986, the National Conference of Catholic Bishops in the USA approved and published the pastoral letter *Economic Justice for All: Catholic Social Teaching and the US economy.* And in 1989, the San Antonio World Missionary Conference of the World Council of Churches accepted four section reports. The first report characterized the context of missions in the following way: 'In some parts of the world people face a total system of death, of monstrous false gods, of exploitative economic systems, of violence, of the disintegration of the fundamental bonds of society, of the destruction of human life, of helplessness of persons in the face of impersonal forces. We are called to exercise our mission in this context of human struggle and to keep the earth alive and to promote human dignity' (Scherer, & Bevans 1992:74).

Prophetic theologians such as Julio de Santa Ana, Arend Th. van Leeuwen, Ulrich Duchrow, Enrique Dussel, Franz J. Hinkelammert, et al. made a critical analysis of the modern world economy: some of them using Marxist vocabulary. Van Leeuwen (1984) wrote a large book about 'the dark night of capital' (Dutch: *De nacht van het kapitaal*). Duchrow (1987:186) identified 'possible ways whereby even Christians, congregations and churches from the rich countries can become an ecumenical covenant people of God and a church confessing its faith in face of the life and death issue of the global economy'. Dussel (1988:146-169) questioned the transnationals, international loans and armaments. And Hinkelammert (CCPD n.d.:41-80) dealt with the privatization of state industries and Western dominance. All these scholars avoid the terms 'missionary economics' and 'missionary finance'; however, their presentations can be characterized as 'a missionary dialogue with Marx' (cf. Jeroense 1994:167-205), and other world economists.

ROHRBACH, PAUL. Deutsche Kolonialwirtschaft: kulturpolitische Grundsätze für die Rassen und Missionsfragen. Berlin, 1909.

*RICHTER, JULIUS (ed.). Das Buch der deutschen Weltmission. Gotha, 1935.
P. 167-172: Weltwirtschaft und Weltmission (Otto Iserland).

COLE, ARTHUR H. The relations of missionary activity to economic development. In: Economic development and cultural change, IX (1961), p. 120-127.

*BRADFIELD, MICHAEL. Personal faith, social action, and the economic system. In: IRM, LXIII (1974), p. 176-179.

*LEEUWEN, AREND Th. VAN. De nacht van het kapitaal: door het oerwoud van de economie naar de bronnen van de burgerlijke religie. Nijmegen, 1984.
Second ed.: Nijmegen, 1985.

*GROENEN, HENNY. Economische theologie als omgekeerde missiologie: een gesprek met Arend Th. van Leeuwen. In: WenZ, XIV (1985), p. 339-344.

*DUCHROW, ULRICH. Global economy: a confessional issue for the churches? Geneva, 1987.
First ed.: Weltwirtschaft heute: eine Welt für bekennende Kirche? München, 1986.

*DUSSEL, ENRIQUE. Ethics and community. New York, 1988.
P. 111-232: Ten disputed questions.
First ed.: Etica comunitaria. Madrid, & Sao Paulo, 1986.

*SCHERER, JAMES A., & STEPHEN B. BEVANS SVD (eds.). New directions in mission and evangelization I: basic statements 1974-1991. New York, 1992.
P. 36-51: Ecumenical affirmation: mission and evangelism (WCC Central Committee).
P. 73-81: Mission in Christ's way: your will be done: San Antonio (World Conference on Mission and Evangelism).

*JEROENSE, P. JEROEN G. Theologie als zelfkritiek: een onderzoek naar de missionaire theologie van Arend Th. van Leeuwen. Zoetermeer, 1994.
P. 167-205: Van Leeuwens missionaire dialoog met Karl Marx.

*ADVISORY GROUP ON ECONOMIC MATTERS, COMMISSION ON THE CHURCHES' PARTICIPATION IN DEVELOPMENT (WCC). The international financial system: an ecumenial critique: report... Geneva, n.d.

*COMMISSION ON THE CHURCHES' PARTICIPATION IN DEVELOPMENT (WCC). Sacrifice and humane economic life. Geneva, n.d.
P. 41-45: Privatization of state functions in Latin America (Franz J. Hinkelammert)
P. 46-80: The sacrificial cycle as a justification for Western dominance: the western Iphigenia in Latin America (Franz J. Hinkelammert).

5.3.9.8. CONCLUSION

This section has briefly discussed the problems of 'missionary economics' and 'missionary finance'. In the past these terms were popular but today they receive little attention. However, the relationship between 'mission' and 'money' is still a burning issue.

The problem of 'self-support' has not yet been solved. Since 1971, the nature of this problem has largely been changed by the moratorium debate.

'Poverty and affluence' are key questions in contemporary economics and mission studies. 'God's preferential option for the poor', 'solidarity with the poor', and 'the poor as agents of the dawning Kingdom' (Nissen 1984:171-173) are crucial thoughts in the Christian (missionary) reflection upon (exploitative) economic systems.

The international financial system is the world in which the churches and mission agencies live and work. They cannot identify themselves with this global system because they are not 'from it', and at the same time they cannot withdraw from it because they are 'sent to it'. It is their missionary responsibility to protest -prophetically- against all institutions and persons who turn the global market into an idol, on the one hand, and to take pastoral steps to prevent, or at least to reduce, the dehumanization of poor people, on the other.

5.3.10. THE PSYCHOLOGY OF CHRISTIAN MISSION

> The new psychology is proving more and more
> clearly every day the healthiness of
> Christ's revolutionary teaching.
> *H. Mark (IRM 1931:118).*

5.3.10.1. INTRODUCTION

Very influential specialists in psychology and in the psychology of religion are William James (1842-1910), G. Stanley Hall (1846-1924), Edwin D. Starbuck (1866-1947), James H. Leuba (1868-1946), and Erich Fromm (b. 1900) in the Anglo-Saxon world; and Wilhelm Wundt (1832-1920), Sigmund Freud (1856-1939), Oskar R. Pfister (1873-1956), and Carl G. Jung (1875-1961) in Europe. None of these well-known psychologists are mentioned in the missiological handbooks of François E. Daubanton (1911), Joseph Schmidlin (1925), André V. Seumois (1952), Alphonsus J.M. Mulders (1962), and Thomas Ohm OSB (1962). Seumois (1952:417) referred to Freud and the Oedipus complex only in passing.

The term *Missionspsychologie=psychology of mission(s)* was coined by Dietrich Vorwerk (1914:6), and used thereafter by *Bibliotheca missionum* (1916:I,864), et al. The term *mission psychology* occurs in an article of the clinical psychologist Kelly S. O'Donnell (O'Donnell, & O'Donnell 1988:119). These terms must be carefully distinguished from the term *missionary care* which is a normative term (cf. 5.3.10.3.).

```
*WARNECK. 1892-1903. 3 vols.
*DAUBANTON. 1911.
*BIBLIOTHECA MISSIONUM. 1916.
        I, p. 864: Missionspsychologie.
*SCHMIDLIN. 1925.
*SEUMOIS. 1952.
*MULDERS. 1962.
*OHM. 1962.
```

5.3.10.2. HISTORY

Olav G. Myklebust (1955:I,296) discussed the criticisms of the missiological handbook of Gustav Warneck (1892-1903). He wrote: 'A third criticism concerns Warneck's failure to describe the psychology of conversion in its individual and social aspects and on the whole to develop a *Missions-Psychologie*'. This frank criticism can also be given to other missiological handbooks such as those mentioned in section 5.3.10.1.

The most important studies dealing with the interaction between psychology and ethnopsychology (Hesselgrave 1980:424-443), on the one hand, and Christian and non-Christian mission and propaganda, on the other, are monographs. Here I only refer to the publications of Oskar R. Pfister (1910; 1926), Dietrich Vorwerk (1914), and R. Schikora (ZM 1917:187-201), who can be regarded as the founders of the 'psychology of (Christian) mission(s)'. Pfister applied the psychoanalytical theory of Freud to the study of religion: including the study of Christian mission. He examined both the piety of Count Nikolaus L. von Zinzendorf and the religious experiences of Sadhu Sundar Singh in India (cf. Biehl 1990).

The discipline under discussion only came to maturity after the Second World War. Here, I only refer to the general article of Hubert Urban (Scientia missionum ancilla 1953:263-283), the handbook of Kelly S. O'Donnell, Michèle L. O'Donnell, et al., on missionaries (1988), and the book of Kelly S. O'Donnell, et al., on missionary care (1992). In the first-mentioned handbook of Kelly S. O'Donnell, William F. Hunter and Marvin K. Mayers stated that 'The involvement of psychology in missions is not altogether new. Daring and creative pioneers in the late 1920s began to use psychological and psychiatric services during the process of selecting missionaries for overseas service.

Those initial ventures were harbingers of what has been a slow but growing use of psychological services by missionary agencies and continuing efforts to create effective working relationships between mental health professors and mission agencies' (:8). And in the last-mentioned work of Kelly S. O'Donnell, Ruth Tucker and Leslie Andrews wrote 'historical notes on missionary care' (:24-36).

Some international missionary conferences were also interested in psychology: e.g. the Jerusalem conference of the International Missionary Council (1928) dealt with the 'psychological conditions for the growth of faith' (IMC 1928:VIII:138-161), and the Tambaram conference (1938) with the 'psychology of self-support' (IMC 1939:V:136-166). After the integration of the International Missionary Council into the World Council of Churches (1961) this broad concern disappeared.

*LAURIE, THOMAS. The Ely volume...: second ed. rev. Boston, 1882.
    P. 42-50: Sumatra.
*SCHARPFF, PAULUS (ed.). Mit der Seele erschaut: Briefe und Tagbuchblätter des Kabylenmissionars Dr. Fritz Rösch. Nürnberg, 1921.
PFISTER, OSKAR R. Die Frömmigkeit des Grafen Ludwig von Zinzendorf: ein psychoanalytischer Beitrag zur Kenntnis der religiösen Sublimierungs-Prozesse und zur Erklärung des Pietismus. Leipzig, 1910.
    Second rev. ed.: Leipzig, & Wien, 1925.
PFISTER, OSKAR R. Die Legende Sundar Singhs: eine auf Enthüllungen protestantischer Augenzeugen in Indien gegründete religionspsychologische Untersuchung. Bern, & Leipzig, 1926.
*MYKLEBUST. 1955-1957. 2 vols.
*BIEHL, MICHAEL. Der Fall Sadhu Sundar Singh: Theologie zwischen den Kulturen. Frankfurt am Main, Bern, New York..., 1990.

5.3.10.3. THE PSYCHOLOGY OF CHRISTIAN MISSION AND MISSIONARY POIMENICS(=MISSIONARY CARE)

> At first glance, bringing psychology in to to help
> with evangelism seems like bringing a man with his
> bare hands to do the job of a bulldozer.
> *James H. Jauncey (1972:11).*

The *psychology of mission(s)* is the academic discipline which deals empirically with the interaction between mission(s) and psychology: especially between Christian mission(s) and psychology. It studies missions; missionary societies; missionaries; etc. from the perspective of (secular) psychology.

However, *missionary poimenics(=missionary care)* is normatively concerned about the effective use of pastoral-psychological insights in missionary processes in order to make the Christian mission more successful.

For instance, Kelly S. O'Donnell (1992:XIII) entered this field and articulated the underlying convictions of 'missionary care' as a normative discipline:

1. A comprehensive, balanced approach to missionary care is an essential ingredient of mission strategy;
2. Member care resources must be prioritized to support those who are targeting and working among the least evangelized; and
3. A variety of cooperative, innovative endeavors, directed by the Lord, are needed to support the growing number of missionary personnel around the world.

In this section, we are only dealing with the empirical discipline: i.e. 'the psychology of Christian mission'. The normative discipline, i.e. 'the poimenics of mission(=missionary care)', will be discussed in the second volume of this study (5.4.9.). However, I must add that most scholars do not distinguish between these disciplines in the same precise way as I am trying to do.

HARTMANN, ANASTASIUS, OFMCap. Psychologia arti pastorali applicata in usum missionariorum totiusque cleri catholici utilitatem... Innsbruck. 1914.
*VORWERK, DIETRICH. Heidenmission und Kindesseele: eine psychologische und pädagogische Studie: zweite Aufl. Schwerin, 1914.
        First ed.: 1913.
SCHIKORA, R. Missionsarbeit und Psychologie. In: ZM, VII (1917), p. 187-201.
*BETTRAY, JOHANNES, SVD (ed.). Mission und Heimatseelsorge. Münster in Westfalen, 1962.
*DICTIONARY CATALOG. 1968.
        XI, p. 174: Missions and psychology. Bibliog.
*JAUNCEY, JAMES H. Psychology for successful evangelism. Chicago, 1972.
*O'DONNELL, KELLY S., & MICHELE L. O'DONNELL (eds.). Helping missionaries grow: readings in mental health and mission. Pasadena, 1988.
        P. 5-11: Psychology and missions: reflections on status and need (William F. Hunter, & Marvin K. Mayers).
        P. 118-125: A preliminary study on psychologists in missions (Kelly S. O'Donnell).

5.3.10.4. THE PSYCHOLOGY OF CHRISTIAN MISSION

The psychology of mission as an academic discipline deals with both the Christian mission and the mission and propaganda of non-Christian religions and ideologies as object of study.
        The *psychology of Christian mission* can be divided into three parts:

1. the psychology of mission boards;
2. the psychology of Christian missionaries; and

3.	the psychology of the people in six continents to whom the Christian message is addressed.

I prefer a survey which is slightly different, because I am not willing to separate the psychology of the people to whom the Christian message is addressed from the psychology of their religious environment. Furthermore, I would like to elaborate 'the psychology of missionary work'.

MISSION BOARDS

The psychology of *mission boards* studies the behaviour of the mission boards -and their individual members- towards both the home front and the overseas missionary personnel: as well as towards the leaders of the so-called 'third world' churches and 'third world' theologians.

Hans Finzel (O'Donnell 1992:219-234) is one of the few authors who seriously dealt with this broad field of study. He reflected upon the key provisions that the leaders of mission agencies must make to ensure a healthy and happy mission organization. He mentioned nine essentials for doing and enjoying missionary work (all beginning with the letter 'C'):

1.	Connection to Christ the Head;
2.	Commitment to members;
3.	Clear vision, goals, and strategies;
4.	Consistency with policies and procedures;
5.	Chain of command;
6.	Communication with staff;
7.	Credibility in financial stewardship;
8.	Care in crisis; and
9.	Concern for quality and excellence.

Other items (also beginning with the letter 'C') can be added: e.g. cross-cultural experiences of mission board leaders; crisis intervention in the mission community (Gardner, in: O'Donnell 1992:136-150); coaching missionary teams (Tim Lewis and Becky Lewis, in: O'Donnell 1992:163-170); career development and the mission agency (Shedlosky, in: O'Donnell 1992:247-259); etc.

MISSIONARIES

Paulus Scharpff (1921) and Geoffrey Z. Kapenzi (1979) have already reflected upon the *psyche*, or soul, of *Christian missionaries*. However, Ruth Tucker and

Leslie Andrews (O'Donnell 1992:24-36) researched the history of missionary adjustment and care, especiallly in the lives of several missionaries and their wives. They observed the mental breakdown of Georg Schmidt; the loneliness of Dorothy Carey; the depression of David Brainerd, J. Hudson Taylor, and Albert B. Simpson; the deep despair of Adoniram Judson; the mental disorder of Mary Morrison; and the outright neglect of Mary Livingstone. And they concluded: 'Indeed, some of the greatest names in the annals of mission history -including David Brainerd, David Livingstone, and Charles T. Studd- would not have survived the battery of psychological tests most candidates are now required to take. Other missionaries -both famous and obscure- suffered from serious depression and mental breakdowns' (:25).

The psychology of missionaries deals with several aspects of the lives and ministries of missionaries: especially 'missionary preparation' and 'missionary adjustment' (cf. O'Donnell, & O'Donnell 1988:13-136;303-443).

Missionary preparation deals with the personal 'call to mission'; candidate selection; and psychological screening. The modern missionary candidate has to go through a strict process of selection. In 1979, the Evangelical Foreign Missions Association (EFMA) invited several psychologists to organize a convention workshop on 'the place of psychological assessment in missionary candidate selection and rehabilitation' because it was observed that a significant number of missionary personnel were leaving the field after one term or less. These scholars made a survey and presented its results at the EFMA convention in 1980. This survey considered the following four items as the most important factors in the selection of candidates:

1. Depth of Christian commitment (personal resource);
2. Knowledge of the Bible (training factor);
3. Past performance in church work (background status factor); and
4. Overall emotional stability (validation factor).

The psychologists involved in this survey concluded: 'It is clear that much research and careful planning is necessary to improve the level of psychological services available to mission agencies' (Ferguson, Kliewer, Lindquist, Williams, and Heinrich, in: O'Donnell, & O'Donnell 1988:45).

Other scholars have discussed the problems of 'psychological adjustment': entering a new culture; cross-cultural stress; interpersonal relationships; and attrition. Dorothy Gish (O'Donnell, & O'Donnell 1988:379-389) investigated the main sources of stress in missionaries working abroad. She developed her own questionnaire: 970 copies were sent out and 566 were returned. Gish identified five major sources of stress in the mission field: confronting others; cross-cultural communication; support maintenance; overwork; and establishing work priorities.

Missionary martyrs are a special category. Thomas Laurie (1882) referred to missionary martyrdom at Sumatra (Indonesia) and concluded: 'This martyrdom also furnishes a contribution to psychology' (:50).

Community psychology emphasizes the significance of the group -the missionary team- 'to carry out activities and achieve goals that it holds to be important for itself and for others' (Ritschard, in: O'Donnell 1992:348). And psychopathology can help the missionary societies to overcome missionary stress, especially 'to destigmatize the psychological difficulties that missionary personnel may face' (Richardson, in: O'Donnell 1992:107).

In the publications which I examined no attention is paid to the contemporary 'third world' missionaries who are facing another kind of missionary stress than the western missionaries in the colonial past and the post-colonial present.

*KAPENZI, GEOFFREY Z. The clash of cultures: Christian missionaries and the Shona of Rhodesia. Washington, 1979.
P. 1-32: The psychology of the missionary.
*LINDQUIST, STANLEY E. Is the psychological test worth it? In: EMQ, XIX (1983), p. 114-119.
*O'DONNELL, KELLY S., & MICHELE L. O'DONNELL (eds.). Helping missionaries grow... Pasadena, 1988.
P. 35-45: Candidate selection criteria: a survey (Larry N. Ferguson, Dean Kliewer, Stanley E. Lindquist, Donald E. Williams, & Robert P. Heinrich)
P. 55-61: A rationale for psychological assessment of missionary candidates (Stanley E. Lindquist).
P. 62-69: Essentials and tools of psychological assessment (Larry N. Ferguson, Dean Kliewer, Brent Lindquist, & Stanley E. Lindquist).
P. 70-74: Misuses of psychological assessment with missionaries (Brent Lindquist).
P. 379-389: Sources of missionary stress (Dorothy Gish).
*O'DONNELL, KELLY S. (ed.). Missionary care: counting the cost for world evangelization. Pasadena, 1992.
P. XIII-XIV: Preface (Kelly S. O'Donnell).
P. 24-36: Historical notes on missionary care (Ruth Tucker, & Leslie Andrews).
P. 89-109: Psychopathology in missionary personnel (Jarrett Richardson).
P. 136-150: Crisis intervention in the mission community (Laura M. Gardner).
P. 163-170: Coaching missionary teams (Tim Lewis, & Becky Lewis).
P. 219-234: Nine essentials for organizational development (Hans Finzel).
P. 247-259: Career development and the mission agency (Peter Shedlosky).
P. 345-356: The member care consultation (Hans Ritschard).

MISSIONARY WORK

Several aspects of *missionary work* can be studied from the psychological point of view. I only refer to the complex topics of 'self-support' and 'oppression'.

In the colonial past, both mission boards and missionaries reflected upon 'the psychology of self-support'. The Tambaram Missionary Conference

340

(1938) dealt explicitly with it. The report of this conference declared that 'Dependence upon alien money violates the most elemental principles of self-respect and patriotism and forfeits the esteem of better-class neighbours in an oriental community' (IMC 1939:V,142).

This report also refers to the 'psychology of nationalism' which is 'common among the educated youth of Asia to-day and is a tremendous trend with which to reckon. This psychology is emptying the churches of China not only of modern Christian youth but of many of the older *intelligentsia* who called themselves Christians' (IMC 1939:V,145). In the post-colonial era, Asian, African, and Latin-American sensitivity became much more pronounced. The term 'psychology of a suppressed people' was coined by J.C. Heinrich in the colonial era, but became very significant in the post-colonial setting. Contemporary Christian missionary work has psychologically to deal with oppression, discrimination, etc.

*INTERNATIONAL MISSIONARY COUNCIL. Report of the Jerusalem meeting... London, Melbourne, Cape Town..., 1928.
  VIII, p. 138-161: Psychological conditions for the growth of faith (William E. Hocking).
WINTHUIS, JOSEPH, MSC. Zur Psychologie und Methode der religiös-sittlichen Heidenunterweisung, auf Grund eigener Erfahrungen in der Südsee-Mission. Feldkirch, 1930. Diss. München.
*MARK, H. A psychological justification for the Gospel message to India. In: IRM, XX (1931), p. 114-121.
*WESTERMAN, DIEDRICH, & RICHARD THURNWALD. The missionary and anthropological research. London, 1932.
  P. 16-31: The missionary's concern in sociology and psychology (Richard Thurnwald). Reprint: London, 1948.
HEINRICH, J.C. The psychology of a suppressed people. London, 1937.
*INTERNATIONAL MISSIONARY COUNCIL. Tambaram series. Oxford, & London, 1939.
  V, p. 136-166: The psychology of self-support.
*YAMAMORI, TETSUNAO, & E. LeROY LAWSON. Introducing church growth: a textbook in missions. Cincinnati, 1975.
  P. 76-78: Psychology, receptivity, and church growth.

5.3.10.5. THE PSYCHOLOGY OF THE CHRISTIAN ENCOUNTER WITH NON-CHRISTIAN RELIGIONS AND WORLDVIEWS

THE PSYCHOLOGY OF NON-CHRISTIAN RELIGIONS AND WORLDVIEWS

Only a few missionaries were trained in psychology, including *the psychology of non-Christian religions and worldviews*. Barend M. Schuurman (1937) and Johan H. Bavinck (1942) belong to this small but significant category. They researched the psychological background of the people with whom they were working.

The main studies in this field deal with 'the psychology of oriental religious experience' in Japan (Kato 1915), and the psychology of 'meditation and piety' in the Far East (Reichelt 1953). Comparative studies on religious experiences in other nations and regions will also be of great help to understand the context of the Christian mission.

Before the Tambaram World Missionary Conference (1938), Loofty Levonian (IRM 1940:236-240) visited important Muslim centres in Iran and India for the purpose of understanding the basic difficulties of the Muslim mind regarding the Christian faith which must be dealt with before any serious presentation of the Christian faith can be made. In his own words: '... the Muslim did not respond to the Christian Faith, because he could not understand it rightly; and he could not understand it rightly because he had initial psychological difficulties' (:237). This can also be said about the adherents of other non-Christian religions.

KATO, KATSUJI. The psychology of oriental religious experience: a study of some typical experiences of Japanese converts to Christianity. Menasha, 1915.
*LEVONIAN, LOOFFY. Muslim evangelization: a psychological study. In: IRM, XXIX (1940), p. 236-240.
*BAVINCK, JOHAN H. De psychologie van den Oosterling. Loosduinen, 1942.
*KRAEMER, HENDRIK, et al. Over alle bergen: geschriften van Barend M. Schuurman, zendeling-leraar op Java... 's-Gravenhage, 1952.
   P. 163-182: De psychologische achtergrond, waaruit de leerlingen voortkomen (1937).
*REICHELT, KARL L. Meditation and piety in the Far East: a religious-psychological study. London, 1953.
   First ed.: Oslo, 1947.

THE PSYCHOLOGY OF CONVERSION AND OTHER REACTIONS TO CHRISTIAN MISSION

> Psychologically, it is even more important to record
> alterations in attitudes and valuations than to portray
> in detail a character at some given moment.
> *Richard Thurnwald (Westermann, & Thurnwald 1932:31).*

The *reactions of non-Christians to Christian mission* are many. In the literature, most attention is devoted to conversion, but this is certainly not the only possible reaction or response.

Maurice T. Price (1924) made a profound psychological study of 'how non-Christians react to missions'. He distinguished between temporary and permanent, and active and passive responses to the Christian mission:

1. First impulsive reactions; or, initial temporary responses (:2,3-5,55-79);
2. Indifference; or, lack of any permanent response (:2,5-7,84-93);
3. Resistance; or, passive opposition (:3,7-8,93-97);
4. Counter-attack; or, active opposition (:3,8-22,97-103);
5. Connivance and tacit cooperation; or, passive receptivity (:3,22-27, 271ff.); and
6. Readiness to join the new group; or, active receptivity (:3,27-29, 271ff.).

Price paid much more attention to the positive reactions (5,6) than to the negative reactions (3,4). He rightly stated that 'The outright acceptance of Christianity -i.e., the formal joining of the recently introduced group- is the most frequently narrated and recorded of all the responses to propaganda' (:27).

Price referred to the studies of both Katsuji Kato (1915) and Campbell N. Moody (1920) on *conversion*. They have many companions and successors: Thomas L. Mainage (1913), Raoul S.P. Allier (1925), Alfred C. Underwood (1925), Ernest Harms (1939), Pedro G. de Escalante OFMCap (1950), Kurt Aland (1961), et al. Especially the study of Allier was influential. Henri A. Junod reviewed its volumes: 'It has come at the right time to refute the exaggerations of the school of philosophy or psychology inspired by the positivism of August Comte...' (IRM 1926:125).

Both in the 19th and in the 20th centuries many conversion stories (biographies and autobiographies) have been published. They need psychological analysis. Mass psychology can help us to understand the phenomenon of mass conversions which have sometimes occurred.

The psychology of conversion is related to the psychology of awakening. Elmer T. Clark (1929) studied 'the psychology of *religious awakening*'. In many cases a large religious awakening at home or abroad preceded and caused mass conversion. Raoul S.P. Allier talked about 'collective revivals' (French: *réveils collectifs*) as predecessors and initiators of mass conversion but the church growth school of Donald A. McGavran prefers to use the term 'people movements' (Wagner 1989:296).

*MAINAGE, THOMAS L. Introduction à la psychologie des convertis. Paris, 1913.
MOODY, CAMPBELL N. The mind of the early converts. London, 1920.
*PRICE, MAURICE T. Christian missions and oriental civilizations, a study in culture contact: the reactions of non-Christian peoples to Protestant missions from the standpoint of individual and group behavior: outline, materials, problems, and tentative interpretations. Shanghai, 1924.
*ALLIER, RAOUL S.P. La psychologie de la conversion chez les peuples non-civilisés. Paris, 1925. 2 vols.
UNDERWOOD, ALFRED C. Conversion, Christian and non-Christian: a comparative and psychological study. New York, 1925.

*JUNOD, HENRI A. The psychology of conversion among primitive people. In: IRM, XV (1926), p. 119-125.

CLARK, ELMER T. The psychology of religious awakening. New York, 1929.

HARMS, ERNEST. Psychologie und Psychatrie der Conversion. Leiden, 1939.

ESCALANTE, PEDRO G. DE, OFMCap. El problema psicológico de la conversión. Méjico, 1950.

*SCHÄR, HANS. Erlösungsvorstellungen und ihre psychologische Aspekte. Zürich, 1950.
    P. 361-389: Erlösung als Bekehrung.

*ALAND, KURT. Ueber den Glaubenswechsel in der Geschichte des Christentums. Berlin, 1961.

*HERMELINK, JAN, & HANS J. MARGULL (eds.). Walter Freytag. Reden und Aufsätze. München, 1961. 2 vols.
    I, p. 170-193: Zur Psychologie der Bekehrung bei Primitiven (1932).

*KOHLER, WERNER. Umkehr und Umdenken: Grundzüge einer Theologie der Mission: hrsg. von Jörg Salaquarda. Frankfurt am Main, Bern, New York..., 1988.
    P. 200-202: Zur Psychologie der Bekehrung.

*WAGNER. 1989.
    P. 296: People movement: types of people movements.

5.3.10.6. THE PSYCHOLOGY OF CHRISTIAN MISSION AND THE PSYCHOLOGY OF RELIGION

The *psychology of mission* is part of the discipline *psychology of religion(s)* (Ger.: *Religionspsychologie*), or *religious psychology*. At the same time it is part of missiology.

Most (religious) psychologists did not reflect upon 'mission' as an important item (cf. Waardenburg 1973:27-28,50-52). And only a few missiologists referred to religious psychology (cf. Schmidlin 1925:175; Holsten 1953:97,100-101); however, even they forgot to link missions with this discipline. Therefore, we still need considerable reflection upon the relation and the interaction between missiology and (religious) psychology before the psychology of mission can be regarded as a fully mature discipline.

A modern 'psychology of mission' must include a 'psychology of dialogue'. Today, most (religious) psychologists are more interested in interreligious dialogue than in the Christian mission. At the same time it is very clear that the psychologists who contributed to the above-mentioned studies edited by Kelly S. O'Donnell (and Michèle Lewis O'Donnell) prefer the term 'mission' to 'dialogue'.

*SCHMIDLIN. 1925.
    P. 175: Religionspsychologie.
*HOLSTEN. 1953.
    P. 97, 100-101: Religionspsychologie.
*SCIENTIA MISSIONUM ANCILLA. 1953.
    P. 263-283: Psychiatrie, Tiefenpsychologie, und Mission (Hubert Urban).
*WAARDENBURG, JACQUES. Classical approaches to the study of religion... I. The Hague, & Paris, 1973.

P. 27-28: Psychology.

P. 50-52: Depth psychology.

*HESSELGRAVE, DAVID J. Communicating Christ cross-culturally: third printing. Grand Rapids, 1980.

P. 424-443: Psychology, ethnopsychology, and mission.

First ed.: 1978.

5.3.10.7. CONCLUSION

The psychology of (Christian) mission, born in the 20th century, is a branch of both empirical psychology and empirical mission studies. However, missionary care, or missionary poimenics, also developed as late as the 20th century, is a normative discipline, which must carefully be distinguished from the psychology of (Christian) mission.

Only recently have psychologists and psychiatrists started to reflect systematically upon missionary phenomena such as missionary candidates, missionary assessment, missionary adjustment, missionary success, and missionary stress. They already contributed, each in their own way, to the maturity of the psychology of mission as an academic discipline.

Christian (and other) missiologists must overcome the suspicion that psychology in general, and especially religious psychology, is a real danger to the missionary enterprise. They certainly must not avoid the study of psychology, but make a good use of its various insights and integrate both disciplines as much as possible.

The psychology of the Christian mission is concerned about both the mission boards, the missionaries and their work, and the people in six continents to whom the Christian message is addressed. The psychology of conversion is the most developed part of the psychology of the Christian encounter with the adherents of the non-Christian religions and worldviews. In several contexts 'conversion' and 'religious awakening' are interrelated; therefore, the psychologists of religious awakening and the psychologists of conversion must cooperate.

A psychology of interreligious dialogue must be added to the older psychology of Christian mission.

5.3.11. THE PEDAGOGICS OF CHRISTIAN MISSION

> ... the aim of education is to glorify God.
> *R.A. Hodgkin (1957:146).*

5.3.11.1. INTRODUCTION

In the history of education and pedagogics, Johann A. Comenius (1592-1670), John Locke (1632-1704), Jean-Jacques Rousseau (1712-1778), Johann H. Pestalozzi (1736-1827), Johann F. Herbart (1776-1841), Friedrich Fröbel (1782-1852), John Dewey (1859-1952), and Maria Montessori (1870-1952), are great names. The missiological handbooks of François E. Daubanton (1911), Joseph Schmidlin (1925), André V. Seumois OMI (1952), and Alphonsus J.M. Mulders (1962), do not refer to these scholars but Jan M. van der Linde (1980:55) studied Comenius, who grafted all that has to do with schools and education into 'the verb *to teach* as it is used by Christ in the great commandment to his disciples at the end of Matthew 28' (my tr.). Karl Heilmann (NAMZ 1929:227) referred to Pestalozzi and Herbart. When Roland Allen discussed the Montessori methods of child education he said: 'It is clear then that our work is nearly akin to Dr. Montessori's. The results of false methods which we have to face are not unlike those with which she was familiar. May it not be that the means by which she succeeded in overcoming many of her difficulties may throw light on the path by which we may extricate ourselves from some of ours?' (IRM 1913:334).

The terms *Christian education, religious education*, and *missionary education* have strong ties but are not identical. Some definitions of 'Christian education' and 'religious eduation' refer to 'mission(s)' and others do not. Nevin C. Harner (1939:20), for instance, suggested a clear definition of 'Christian education' which, however, is unclear as far as 'mission(s)' is concerned: 'Christian education is a reverent attempt to discover the divinely ordained process by which individuals grow toward Christlikeness, and to work with that process'.

The terms 'Christian education' and 'religious education' are much more common than the term *mission(ary) education*. However, this last term became well-known by the publications and activities of both individual scholars and movements such as the Young People's Missionary Movement of the United States and Canada, and the Missionary Education Movement (which by and large emerged from the Student Volunteer Movement). Before the First World War, the General Secretary of the afore-mentioned movement already stated in his annual report *Missionary Education and the Evangelization of the World* (1910:15), that some fields of missionary work are 'fascinating to study, and full of promise for the future of missionary education'. A Mission

Secretary (1932:5), however, used the term in reverse in a quotation, i.e. *educational mission(s)*. The last term is also used by Henry P. Thompson (1938), Roger L. Shinn (1962), and J. Herbert Kane (1988:318-328).

The discipline which empirically reflects upon 'mission(ary) education' is *the pedagogics of mission* (Ger.: *Missionspädagogik*). Gustav Warneck (AMZ 1877:457) introduced this term which, in the 20th century, became popular in Germany (Vorwerk 1914:5-6; Heilmann, in: NAMZ 1929:225-235; Schomerus 1935:19-21; Thauren, in: ZMR 1952:23-28; et al.). In Italy, scholars introduced the term *pedagogia missionaria* (Bongioanni 1938); but, in the Anglo-Saxon literature, I did not come across the terms 'mission(ary) pedagogics' and 'the pedagogics of (Christian) mission'.

In the same way as I distinguished between 'the psychology of (Christian) mission' and 'missionary poimenics(=missionary care)' (cf. 5.3.10.), I distinguish between the terms 'the pedagogics of (Christian) mission' (Ger.: *Missionspädagogik*) and 'missionary catechetics'(Ger.: *Missionskatechetik*) as opposite terms: the first refers to an empirical treatment of 'mission(ary) education', and the last to a normative treatment of the same subject (cf. 5.3.11.3).

The 'pedagogics of mission' deals empirically and analytically with the link between education, on the one hand, and both the Christian mission and non-Christian missions and propaganda, on the other hand. In this section I pay more attention to the Christian mission as object of study than to the non-Christian missions and propaganda.

*WARNECK. 1892-1903. 3 vols.
*DAUBANTON. 1911.
*SCHMIDLIN. 1925.
*SCHOMERUS. 1935.
    P. 19-21: Die Missionspädagogik und die Religionsgeschichte und Volkskunde.
*SEUMOIS. 1952.
*HOLSTEN. 1953.
    P. 175-188: Erziehungsarbeit (Volkskirche und Volkserziehung).
*MULDERS. 1962.

5.3.11.2. HISTORY

> Education has always been
> an integral part of the missionary movement.
> *J. Herbert Kane (1988:319).*

Both individuals and movements have contributed to the genesis and growth of 'the pedagogics of (Christian) mission' as an academic discipline.

In the history of Christian missions, 'education' was always very important. The pietist August H. Francke (1663-1727) at Halle wrote a missionary program for the Danish-Halle missionaries in India -Bartholomew Ziegenbalg (1683-1719) and Heinrich Plütschau (1677-1746)- in which he embodied an instruction regarding school education. Karl Heilmann (NAMZ 1929:227) also pointed out that all missionaries of the Berlin Mission received a handbook of education before they went to their mission fields.

The philosophy of the Enlightenment emphasized the significance of global education. The tract of Gotthold E. Lessing (1729-1781), *The Education of the Human Race* (Ger.: *Die Erziehung des Menschengeschlechts*) (1780), challenged the Christian missions in a highly significant way. In Germany, Carl H.C. Plath (1829-1901), Ernst Busz (1843-1928), Ernst Troeltsch (1865-1923), et al., responded to this challenge by propagating 'the education of peoples' (Ger.: *Völkerpädagogie*). They considered 'mission' by and large as a means of the education of 'uncivilized' non-Christians by Western 'civilized' Christians. Christianization, civilization, westernization, education, and mission thus became virtually identical. Troeltsch regarded modern missions as 'the expansion of the world of European and American religious ideas in close connection with the expansion of the European sphere of influence' (my tr.; quoted by Hoekendijk 1948:81). On the mission field, the German missionary Christian Keysser (1877-1961) was an advocate of this liberal concept of mission: 'Educating the people (Ger.: *Volkserziehung*) must follow the awakening of the people (Ger.: *Volkserweckung*)' (my tr.; quoted by Hoekendijk 1948:179).

In the Anglo-Saxon world, parallel thoughts were developed. For instance, Alexander Duff (1806-1878), a 'pioneer of missionary education' (Paton 1923), was the first missionary in India to adopt the method of 'making use of higher education, given through the medium of the English language, as an instrument of evangelism' (Myklebust 1955:I,165). At home he called for the establishment of a chair 'of missions and education' (Myklebust 1955:I,173). And, in the USA, Harry W. Hicks, chairman of the Young People's Missionary Movement of the United States and Canada, not only talked about 'missionary education' but also about 'missionary cultivation' (Young People's Missionary Movement of the United States and Canada 1910:12).

Thomas H.P. Sailer linked 'missionary education' not so much with Western culture but with the universal church. He said: 'The great purpose of missionary education is to help the Church to discharge its responsibility of making disciples of all nations. The instruments needed in this work are prayer, money, and volunteers. Therefore missionary education must aim to create an adequate supply of prayer, money and workers for the field at home and abroad' (Young People's Missionary Movement of the United States and

348

Canada 1910:15). His ideas can be compared with those of Roland Allen (1868-1947). He wrote several publications on the link between education, church, and mission, especially on the church's application of educational principles to evangelism (IRM 1913:329-341; 1919; 1928). I quote: 'What is needed is a Christian education which is of the Church, by the Church, for the Church, a Christian education which depends in no sense upon the supply of men or money from a foreign country, but which lives in the life of the native church' (1928:18).

Modern missionaries also struggled against illiteracy. Frank C. Laubach (1884-1970), who for more than thirty years served as a missionary of the Congregational Christian Churches, was a pioneer in 'teaching the world to read' (1947). In 1930 he founded the Maranaw Folk Schools in the Filippines. Later he organized literacy campaigns in many parts of the world. He considered the Christian missionaries as people who play a vital role in the construction of a peaceful world. He was convinced that 'the great yearning love of the missionaries was doing more to rebuild the spiritual and educational life of India than any other single factor' (1945:175). He also stated that every outgoing missionary should know 'how important literacy is as a means of winning friends for the church and of winning people to Christ' (1947:X).

The World Missionary Conferences at Edinburgh (1910), at Jerusalem (1928), and at Tambaram (1938), also dealt with Christian, religious, and missionary education. Edinburgh (1910:III,383) concluded that 'The best educator is the best missionary'. Jerusalem (1928:II,239) added that 'In the whole range of religious education, emphasis should be laid upon the obligation resting upon all Christians to pass on to others the good news of salvation through Christ' (cf. Eberhard 1930). And Tambaram (1939:IV,151-152) regarded the school as a 'pioneer evangelistic agency'. The World Missionary Conferences after the Second World War paid less attention to 'missionary education'.

Significant post-War developments are: (1) the creation of the Theological Education Fund (TEF) by the Ghana Assembly of the International Missionary Council in 1958 (cf. DEM 1991:349); (2) the foundation and growth of Theological Education by Extension (TEE) as a form of contextual education (cf. Hogarth, Gatimu, & Barrett 1983); and (3) the establishment of 'ecumenical learning', i.e. 'development education', 'education for mission', 'education for justice, peace, and the integrity of creation' (DEM 1991:341). Especially in this last case pedagogics is moving 'from *teaching about* to *learning together with*' (DEM 1991:341).

PATON, WILLIAM. Alexander Duff: pioneer of missionary education. London, 1923.
*EBERHARD, OTTO. Der Erziehungsgedanke in der Weltmission: eine Umschau von den Höhen des Ölbergs. Langensalza, 1930.

*LAUBACH, FRANK C. The silent billion speak: new and expanded ed. New York, 1945.
First ed.: 1943.

*LAUBACH, FRANK C. Teaching the world to read: a handbook for literacy campaigns. New York, 1947.

*HOEKENDIJK, JOHANNES C. Kerk en volk in de Duitse zendingswetenschap. Amsterdam, 1948.
P. 76-82: Cultuurpropaganda: 'Volkerpädagogie'.
P. 174-187: De volks-paedagogische zendingsmethode; Christian Keysser (geb. 1877).

*MYKLEBUST. 1955-1957. 2 vols.

*RYCROFT, W. STANLEY, & MYRTLE M. CLEMMER. The struggle against illiteracy. New York, 1964.

LAIRD, MICHAEL A. Missionaries and education in Bengal 1793-1837. Oxford, 1972.

*LINDE, JAN M. VAN DER. Gods wereldhuis: voordrachten en opstellen over de geschiedenis van zending en oecumene. Amsterdam, 1980.
P. 47-69: Jan Amos Comenius, leraar der volken.

5.3.11.3. THE PEDAGOGICS OF CHRISTIAN MISSION AND MISSIONARY CATECHETICS

The discipline *pedagogics of Christian mission* is explained in some missiological handbooks (Schomerus 1935:19-21; Holsten 1953:175-188), and in many monographs.

Scholars express different opinions about the nature of this discipline. Hilko W. Schomerus (1935:21), for example, considered it to be 'the discipline which deals with the attitude of missions towards the religious and ethnic heritage of the people who must be evangelized' (my tr.). I disagree with this definition which consciously or unconsciously transforms the empirical 'pedagogics of Christian mission' into the normative 'apologetics of Christian mission'. I also disagree with Johannes Thauren SVD (ZMR 1952:23-28) who regarded the *catechetics of Christian mission* (Ger.: *Missionskatechetik*) as a branch of the *pedagogics of Christian mission* (Ger.: *Missionpädagogik*). However, I agree with the views of both Juan de Unzalu (1945) who wrote about the 'pedagogical value of the missionary ideal' (my tr.) and Johannes Hofinger SJ (Scientia missionum ancilla 1953:110-123) who dealt with 'pedagogics in the service of mission' (my tr.).

I maintain that the 'pedagogics of Christian mission' is that academic discipline which, in a strictly empirical way, describes and analyses the contribution of the Christian mission to education, and vice versa. And I treat the 'catechetics of Christian mission', or 'missionary catechetics', as a normative discipline which propagates and outlines Christian education as 'an integral part of the whole enterprise of the Church's witness' (IMC 1939:IV, 61). In exactly the same way as 'missionary poimenics(=missionary care)', 'missionary catechetics' is a task of the church both at home and abroad. In the second volume of this study, I will deal with this theological discipline (5.4.6.).

*WARNECK, GUSTAV. Die Missionslehre als 'Keryktik'. In: AMZ, IV (1877), p. 443-458.
P. 457: Missionspädagogik.

*DITSCHEID, HERMANN. Missionskunde: eine Forderung neuzeitlicher Pädagogik... Breslau, 1913.

MISSIONSPÄDAGOGISCHE BLÄTTER. 1913 ff.

*VORWERK, DIETRICH. Heidenmission und Kindesseele: eine psychologische und pädagogische Studie: zweite Aufl. Schwerin, 1914.
First ed.: 1913.

*HEILMANN, KARL. Missionspädagogik. In: NAMZ, VI (1929), p. 225-235.

*SCHWARTZ, HERMANN (ed.). Pädagogisches Lexikon. 1928-1931. 4 vols.
III, p. 701-704: Missionspädagogik (Otto Eberhard).

BONGIOANNI, FAUSTO M. Pedagogia missionaria. Torino, Milano, Padova..., 1938.

COLLECTION 'VITALIS' POUR FAIRE AIMER LES MISSIONS. Paris, 1939. 2 vols.
I: Éléments de pédagogie missionnaire.

UNZALU, JUAN DE. El valor pedagogico del ideal misionero: conferencia pronunciada en el Salón de Actos de la Catequesis de San Nicolás de Bari, de Bilbao. 1945.

*THAUREN, JOHANNES, SVD. Missionspädagogik und Missionskatechetik als Zweige der Missionswissenschaft. In: ZMR, XXXVI (1952), p. 23-28.

*SCIENTIA MISSIONUM ANILLA. 1953.
P. 110-123: Katechetik und Pädagogik im Dienste der Mission (Johannes Hofinger SJ).

VICEDOM, GEORG F. The mission of God. Saint Louis, 1965.
P. 108-110: The pedagogical boundary.
*Ger. ed.: Missio Dei... München, 1960.
P. 80-81: Die pädagogische Linie.

5.3.11.4. MISSIONARY EDUCATION

> ... Christian education and catechetical material
> must incorporate the missionary imperative.
> *CWME Consultation of Eastern Orthodox
> and Oriental Orthodox Churches, 1988
> (Scherer, & Bevans 1992:241).*

Hans-Werner Gensichen (1971:214) argued that missionary education takes place in the following three 'circles':

1. the catechumenate, or catechesis, in the life of the church (Ger.: *Glaubensunterweisung im innerkirchlichen Bereich*; my tr.);
2. religious education in public schools (Ger.: *Religionsunterricht im Rahmen des öffentlichen Schulwesens*; my tr.); and
3. participation in people's education (Ger.: *Mitwirkung in der Volksbildung*; my tr.).

This survey of the 'circles' makes abundantly clear that missionary education is not exclusively restricted to church buildings; both public schools and general

education structures can be used as well.
I make some comments upon these three 'circles', i.e. catechesis,
(mission)schools, and missionary participation in people's education.

*LAURIE, THOMAS. The Ely volume... Boston, 1882.
P. 372-405: Education.
HEILMANN, KARL. Der Missionsunterricht nach Theorie und Praxis. Breslau, 1895.
*THOMPSON, R. WARDLAW (ed.). Education in the mission field. London, 1908.
*YOUNG PEOPLE'S MISSIONARY MOVEMENT OF THE UNITED STATES AND CANADA. Missionary education
and the evangelization of the world: annual report... New York, 1910.
*YOUNG PEOPLE'S MISSIONARY MOVEMENT OF THE UNITED STATES AND CANADA. Report of conference
on missionary education, New York City, December 8-9, 1909. New York, 1910.
*WORLD MISSIONARY CONFERENCE. Edinburgh, London, New York..., 1910.
III: Education in relation to the Christianisation of national life.
SCHWAGER, FRIEDRICH, SVD. Die Erziehungs- und Bildungstätigkeit der katholischen Missionen.
In: ZM, III (1913), p. 53-66.
?WOOD, J.A. Missionary educational policy and a conscience clause. Ajmer, 1916.
*MONROE, PAUL. Mission education and national policy. In: IRM, X (1921), p. 321-350.
*STUDENT CHRISTIAN MOVEMENT. Christian education in Africa and the East. London, 1924.
MONROE, PAUL. Essays in comparative education: republished papers. New York, 1927.
Contents: Mission education and national policy; Problems of mission education;
etc.
*INTERNATIONAL MISSIONARY COUNCIL. Report of the Jerusalem meeting... London, Melbourne, &
Cape Town, 1928.
II: Religious education.
*DISCUSSION ON MISSION EDUCATION. London, New York, & Toronto, 1931.
*A MISSION SECRETARY. Education and the missionary task. London, New York, & Toronto, 1932.
MUSEUM LESSIANUM. L'éducation chrétienne aux missions: compte rendu de la onzième semaine
de missiologie de Louvain (1933). Louvain, 1933.
*JUNOD, HENRI P. Anthropology and missionary education. In: IRM, XXIV (1935), p. 213-228.
*THOMPSON, HENRY P. Educational missions at work: a sketch of the educational work of the
SPG in the mission field. Westminster, 1938.
?GREGORY VON BREDA OFMCap. Het godsdienst-onderricht in de missie. Tilburg, 1939.
*INTERNATIONAL MISSIONARY COUNCIL. Tambaram series. London, 1939.
IV, p. 54-172: Christian education.
*SAILER, THOMAS H.P. Christian adult education in rural Asia and Africa. New York, 1943.
HARNER, NEVIN C., & DAVID D. BAKER. Missionary education in your church: new and rev. ed.
New York, 1950.
First ed.: New York, 1942.
*HODGKIN, R.A. Education and change. London, 1957.
*SHINN, ROGER L. The educational mission of our church. Boston, & Philadelphia, 1962.
*ALL AFRICA CHURCHES CONFERENCE. Christian education in Africa: report of a conference...
London, 1963.
*DICTIONARY CATALOG. 1968.
X, p. 766-771: Missionary education. Bibliog.
*GENSICHEN, HANS-WERNER. Glaube für die Welt: theologische Aspekte der Mission. Gütersloh,
1971.
P. 213-216: 'Education'.

352

*KRAUS, JOHANN, SVD. Missionswissenschaftliche Themen in Festschriften aus den Jahren 1960-1971. Immensee, 1974.
    P. 61-64: Schule und Erziehung. Bibliog.
*BÜRKLE, HORST. Missionstheologie. Stuttgart, Berlin, Köln..., 1979.
    P. 203: Erziehung und Ausbildung. Bibliog.
*HOGARTH, JONATHAN, KIRANGA GATIMU, & DAVID B. BARRETT. Theological education in context: 100 extension programmes in contemporary Africa. Nairobi, 1983.
*McKINNEY, LOIS. Contextualizing instruction: contributions to missiology from the field of education. In: Missiology, XII (1984), p. 311-326.
*KANE, J. HERBERT. Understanding Christian missions: fourth ed. Grand Rapids, 1988.
    P. 318-328: Educational missions.
    First ed.: 1978.
*KOHLER, WERNER. Umkehr und Umdenken: Grundzüge einer Theologie der Mission: hrsg. von Jörg Salaquarda. Frankfurt am Main, Bern, & New York..., 1988.
    P. 198-200: Erziehung zur Grundidentität?
*DEM. 1991.
    P. 341-342: Ecumenical learning (Ulrich Becker).
    P. 347-352: Education and renewal (John S. Pobee).
*SCHERER, JAMES A., & STEPHEN B. BEVANS SVD (eds.). New directions in mission and evangelization, I: basic documents 1974-1991. New York, 1992.
    P. 232-241: Final report of CWME consultation of Eastern Orthodox and Oriental Orthodox Churches (Neapolis 1988).

CATECHESIS

From its inception, education was a basic task of the Christian community. Christ himself already gave an important place to teaching in his public ministry. Each new generation of Christians received lessons from church leaders in the Ten Commandments, the Lord's Prayer, the Articles of Faith, etc. This instruction was always and still is open to non-Christians. The pedagogics of the Christian mission analyses all missionary aspects of the 'catechumenate' or 'catechesis' through the centuries:

-     Who were and are the teachers: are they mission-minded?
-     Who were and are the pupils: are there non-Christians among them?
-     What were and are the teaching materials: do they clearly deal with non-Christian religions and worldviews?
-     In which way teaching has taken place and takes place: is it both problem-oriented and person-oriented, including non-Christians?
-     Did and does contextualization takes place: is the catechesis in the (secular) West different from the catechesis in the (religious) East and South?
-     Did and does the church after the Enlightenment make use of modern (secular) pedagogical methods and insights: does it also make use of non-western pedagogical methods and insights (Paulo Freire, etc.)?

*ALLEN, ROLAND. Education in the native church: second reprint. London, & New York, 1928. First ed.: 1925.

*HARNER, NEVIN C. The educational work of the church. New York, & Nashville, 1939.

*SOMASEKHAR, RENUKA M. The role of the church in education today. In: IRM, LIX (1970), p. 75-84.

*HOFINGER, JOHANNES, SJ. Evangelization and catechesis. New York, Paramus, & Toronto, 1976.

*EVANS, ROB, & TOSH ARAI (eds.). The church and education in Asia. Singapore, 1980.

MISSION SCHOOLS

Christians have always taught Christianity both inside and outside church buildings. The first Christians used several channels outside the church to educate non-Christians: public debates (Paul at the Areopagus), private discussions, etc.

The establishment of modern 'educational institutions' (Ripley 1865) -both primary and secondary schools as well as high schools- opened new opportunities for Christians to teach the Christian faith to non-Christians. Missiologists regarded them as 'missionary means' (Ger.: *Missionsmittel*) (Richter 1927:II,70), which could be used for the 'conversion' of non-Christians.

In the 19th and 20th centuries, Christian missionaries not only entered public schools but also built their own mission schools: in many cases the first schools in those areas. Thomas Laurie wrote in a long chapter on 'education' from which I only quote the beginning and the end: 'In the lands where they labor, our missionaries seldom find schools. Generally there are none...'; '...none of our missions can prosper in the conversion of men, without creating a demand at once for institutions to train up pastors for the churches, teachers for the schools, and intelligent men and women for every position in life' (1882:372,405). Thomas R. Batten (1959:6) affirmed this view, saying that 'most of the schools first started in the tropics were mission schools, controlled by Christian organizations and serving the purposes both of the missions and of the government'. Statisticians pointed out that between the First and the Second World Wars, about 100.000 mission schools were available in the mission fields: they offered Christian education to some 5.000.000 pupils: both Christians and non-Christians.

The influence of the mission schools was immense. However, we must also be aware of Floyd E. Hamilton's comment: '... it is a regrettable fact that some of the bitterest opponents of Christianity have received their education in mission schools' (A Mission Secretary 1932:19).

In the post-colonial period, mission schools were often nationalized: the mission schools became either secular schools, or Christian schools, runned either by indigenous churches or by local Christians. Renuka M. Somasekhar (IRM 1970:79) wrote: 'The big question for indigenous churches is that of finances. Missionary patterns of the Protestant churches have developed an excellent network of institutions and have trained a vast host of very capable teachers, but, except in some cases of school education, mission schools and colleges have remained dependent on grants from abroad for their year-to-year maintenance'. This problem of 'self-support' also occurs in the Roman Catholic church.

J. Herbert Kane (1988:325) does not consider the nationalization of mission schools in the post-colonial era as 'an unmitigated tragedy. Indeed, it may be a blessing in disguise. It relieves the missions of an enormous financial burden and the missionaries of onerous administrative chores, setting them free for work more directly connected with the spread of the gospel and the growth of the church'. Missionary education was given by, but is not at all bound to Western mission schools in the non-western world; today this form of Christian education must find its own post-colonial ways of expression in schools.

?RIPLEY, H.J. Missions in their relation to educational institutions. New York, 1865.
*WARNECK. 1892-1903. 3 vols.
    III/2, p. 130-171: Die missionarische Schule.
*COLIJN, HENDRIKUS. Onderwijspolitiek en zending. Groningen, 1910.
*GUNNING, JAN W. Zending en inlandsch onderwijs: een woord naar aanleiding van de laatste kamerdebatten. Utrecht, 1913.
*BOETZELAER VAN DUBBELDAM, CAREL W.TH. BARON VAN. De zendingsscholen en het volksonderwijs. Batavia, 1917.
*RICHTER, JULIUS. Evangelische Missionskunde. Leipzig, 1927. 2 vols.
    II, p. 70-73: Elementarschulen für Heidenkinder, Missions-Mittel- und Hochschulen.
HEILMANN, KARL. Mission und Schule: für Erzieher und Freunde der Mission. Berlin, 1929.
*RICHTER, JULIUS (ed.). Das Buch der deutschen Weltmission. Gotha, 1935.
    P. 129-134: Das Missionsschulwesen (Walter Freytag).
*BATTEN, THOMAS R. School and community in the tropics. London, 1959.
*CREDIC. École et missions chrétiennes extérieures: actes de la VIIIème session du CREDIC à Salamanque (24-27 Août 1987). Lyon, 1988.

MISSIONARY PARTICIPATION IN PEOPLE'S EDUCATION

The third and widest circle of missionary education is the people's education outside church and school buildings.

I already mentioned the struggle of Laubach against illiteracy. His very effective materials were translated into about 300 languages and used in about 100 nations. Today the Laubach Literacy Inc. is a fully secular organization; however, its roots lie in the Christian mission. W. Stanley Rycroft and Myrtle M. Clemmer (1964:20) said that 'Churches and missions have been pioneers in the struggle against illiteracy, but now the literacy campaign has been taken up by governments and by UNESCO'. Churches and missions must support the governments and UNESCO: without complaining that these institutions have taken the lead.

Churches and missions were also pioneers in the production of good books, relevant magazines, and effective radio and television programs. They have provided much Christian reading for all age groups: for the almost illiterate as well as the intelligentsia; for the church members as well as the adherents of other religions and worldviews. In each nation and each generation, the contextualization of Christian reading materials is an obligation (cf. McKinney, in: Missiology 1984:311-326). Today, both churches and missions are preparing reading materials not only for their own media but also for the mass media in order to reach enormous numbers of people. Radio and television can teach individuals and groups where no missionaries are allowed to be present.

*MATHEWS, BASIL J. Missions and the press: a study in educational practice. In: IRM, XII (1923), p. 389-402.

5.3.11.5. MISSIONARY METHODS

> Missionary work is educational work.
> *Roland Allen (1919:1).*

Gustav Warneck, Roland Allen, and others have reflected upon the use of 'missionary methods' in education. Olav G. Myklebust (1955:I,296) considered that part of Warneck's *Evangelische Missionslehre* (1892-1903) as the least satisfactory which dealt with 'the problem of *devolution*, i.e. the transfer of functions and powers from the foreign mission to the indigenous church. The author's treatment of this subject is dominated by a Western superiority complex which leaves but little scope for *native initiative and responsibility'*. Allen, however, compared Christian education given by missionaries with Christian education given by native churches and concluded: '... the thing of real importance is that we should establish the native Churches, and it is that work which we have yet to begin. The mission field is dotted with communities of Christians which are not churches and which are not native, dependent upon foreigners, in every possible way. Until these are native Churches there can be no education of native Churches' (1928:26).

The problem of missionary methods is not only connected with the problem of the indigenization of the Christian education but also with 'extension' (Young People's Missionary Movement of the United States and Canada 1910:105-113); with a 'comprehensive approach' and 'spirituality' (Student Christian Movement 1924:106-108); and with 'formal education'. The last-mentioned topic was dealt with by the All Africa Churches Conference

356

(AACC) on 'Christian education in Africa' (1963). This conference recommended that the African churches should review the provision for formal education in each country:

1. Where facilities are inadequate or non-existent the Church should seek to meet the need at whatever educational level provision is required;
2. where the Church is providing formal education and there is no reason for discontinuing this service, it should continue to provide it; but it should reassess the position with a view to rendering the best possible service to the nation and avoiding dissipation of resources through overlapping and competition with the State or other agencies doing the same work; and
3. whether or not the church continues formal education, new fields should be explored, such as pre-school education, adult education including literacy work, care of handicapped persons, youth work, running of Church hostels (All Africa Churches Conference 1963:51).

Finally, I refer to missionary reflection upon the educational methods of Fröbel, Montessori, and others which has incidentally taken place (cf. Allen, in: IRM 1913:329-341).

*ALLEN, ROLAND. The Montessori method and missionary methods. In: IRM, II (1913), p. 329-341.
*ALLEN, ROLAND. Educational principles and missionary methods: the application of educational principles to missionary evangelism. London, 1919.
WINTHUIS, JOSEPH, MSC. Zur Psychologie und Methode der religiös-sittlichen Heidenunterweisung, auf Grund eigener Erfahrungen in der Südsee-Mission. Feldkirch, 1930.
*THAUREN, JOHANNES, SVD. Die religöse Unterweisung in den Heidenländern: eine missionsmethodische Studie. Wien, 1935.
*ALLEN, ROLAND. Missionary methods: St. Paul's or ours? London, 1968.
    First ed.: 1912.
    Several reprints.
*CONCISE DICTIONARY. 1971.
    P. 182-184: Education as missionary method (A.J. Boyd).

5.3.11.6. THE PEDAGOGICS OF CHRISTIAN MISSION AND THE PEDAGOGICS OF RELIGION

The pedagogics of Christian mission as an academic discipline is a branch of both pedagogics and missiology. Missionaries and missiologists, on the one hand, and educationalists, on the other, have involved themselves in the birth and growth of this discipline. Hilko W. Schomerus (1935:19-21,122-149) and E. Schedl (1936) also connected this discipline with the history of religions and ethnology.

The pedagogics of religion, or 'religious pedagogics', deals with the interaction between the education of humanity and the religions and ideologies; whereas the pedagogics of mission is limited to the contribution of the (Christian) mission to the education of humanity and vice versa. On the one hand, Christian missions are challenged by the education of non-Christian religions and worldviews in their institutions; and, on the other, the Christian mission schools have challenged those religions and worldviews by the high standard of Christian reading materials and Christian discipline.

*SCHOMERUS. 1935.
    P. 19-21: Die Missionspädagogik und die Religionsgeschichte und Volkskunde.
    P. 122-149: Missionspädagogik: die Lehre von dem Verhalten der Mission gegenüber dem religiösen und völkischen Erbgut der Völker.
?SCHEDL, E. Die Völkerpädagogik und die katholische Missionspädagogik. 1936. Diss. Wien. Unpublished.

5.3.11.7. CONCLUSION

The pedagogics of Christian mission is an empirical discipline, as empirical as the linguistics of Christian mission, the history of Christian mission, the geography of Christian mission, the statistics of Christian mission, etc.

Teaching has always played an important role in the planting of churches and in church growth. Modern Roman-Catholic and Protestant missions have established schools of all kinds in most parts of the so-called 'third world'. These schools have functioned as tools for the conversion of non-Christians. However, missionary education is not bound to mission schools because the churches are responsible for their own catechesis; and churches and missions can also enter the wider circle of people's education through the mass media.

In the post-colonial era, the pedagogics of Christian mission has gone new ways and has invented new methods in order to reach even larger numbers of people, with at least Christian spirituality (the Lord's Prayer), Christian faith (the Twelve Articles), and Christian ethics (Ten Commandments, Sermon on the Mount).

5.3.12. CONCLUSION

I conclude this section of chapter 5 on *the science of mission* (Ger.: *Missionswissenschaft*) as the second concept of mission studies by making a chronological table of the names of its specific branches, and by making some final observations.

I start with the presentation of a short list of the dates when the names of the various empirical disciplines were mentioned for the first time:

1731: History of the propagation of Christianity (Robert Millar)
1743: *Missionsgeschichte*=history of mission (Friedrich S. Bock)
1825: Missionary geography (Irish clergyman)
1832: *MISSIONSWISSENSCHAFT*=SCIENCE OF MISSION (JOHANN T.L. DANZ)
1875: *Missionsstatistik*=statistics of mission (Peter R. Grundemann, in: AMZ 1875:49-58)
1877: *Missionspädagogik*=pedagogics of mission (Gustav Warneck, in: AMZ 1877:457)
1886: Mission economics (Chapin H. Carpenter)
1914: *Missionspsychologie*=psychology of mission (Dietrich Vorwerk)
1938: *Pedagogia missionaria*=missionary pedagogics (Fausto M. Bongianni)
1952: *Cartographie missionnaire*=missionary cartography (André V. Seumois OMI)
1953: *Missionsjuristisch*=adjective of 'mission law' (Max Bierbaum, in: Scientia missionum ancilla 1953:284-299)
1953: *Missionsphilologisch*=adjective of 'mission philology' (Max Bierbaum, in: Scientia missionum ancilla 1953:284-299)
1953: *Missionssoziografie*=sociography of mission (George Zeegers, & Corn. M. Thoen, in: Scientia missionum ancilla 1953:213)
1953: *Missionssoziologie*=sociology of mission (George Zeegers, & Corn. M. Thoen, in: Scientia missionum ancilla 1953:213)
1955: Missionary linguistics (Olav G. Myklebust)
1956: *Ethnomissiologie*=ethnomissiology (Anton Pott SVD, in: ZM 1956: 301-310)
1956: *Missionsethnologie*=ethnology of mission (Richard J. Mohr)
1961: (Applied) missionary anthropology (Louis J. Luzbetak SVD)
1970: Missiological anthropology (Louis J. Luzbetak SVD)
1993: Missiological hermeneutics (C. Timothy Carriker, in: Van Engen, & Gilliland 1993:45)

This list is necessarily provisional. Much research still remains to be done before a definite account of the advent of the branches of the science of mission can be given.

The main lines and issues of this third section of chapter 5 are very clear: there was a steady growth in the number of the branches of the science of mission. There is no doubt about the fact that the history of Christian mission is the oldest branch. Thereafter nine other branches came into existence, which relate mission studies to other academic disciplines in a way which is parallel to the link between the history of mission and world history, the history of religion, and church history. However, the linguistics of Christian mission is that branch of the science of mission which has fundamental significance.

The mission of the non-Christian religions and worldviews is in the same way an object of the science of mission as the Christian mission. However, in this study we have concentrated our thoughts upon the empirical study of Christian mission: this field is much more developed than the parallel study of the mission and propaganda of other religions and ideologies. And, within the framework of the empirical study of Christian mission, the history of Christian mission is the most elaborated branch.

In the second volume of this study we will deal with the ten branches of missionary theology as the third and last concept of mission studies (chapter 5.4.). A final review of all branches of mission studies (chapter 5.5.) will close the second and last volume of this missiological encyclopedia.

INDICES

1. Index of personal names

AABY, P., 292, 293
AAGAARD, J., 96, 154
ABBOTT, E.L., 327
ABE, Y., 32
ABERLY, J., 234
ABESAMIS, C.H., 124
ABGAR, 228
ABINENO, J.L.C., 46, 53, 55
ABRAHAM, W.J., 20, 23, 34, 35, 40, 43,
    44, 47, 179, 180
ACHELIS, H., 314
ACHILLES, 329
ACOSTA, J. DE, 59, 164, 192, 287
ADAM, D.S., 30
ADAMS, C., 35
ADRIANI, M.A., 105, 106
AEDESIUS, 270
AGBEBI, M., 246, 248
AHAUS, H., 239, 255
AICH, J.A., 113
AIKMAN, J.L., 7, 8, 224, 231, 244, 245, 255
ALAND, K., 342, 343
ALBRIGHT, L.S., 99, 103
ALCOTT, W.A., 129, 130
ALEXANDER, C., 55, 56, 142, 145
ALLAN, D.W., 123
ALLEN, G.F., 94
ALLEN, R., 127, 128, 129, 131, 197, 198,
    345, 348, 353, 355, 356
ALLIER, R.S.P., 63, 65, 70, 342
ALTHAUS, P., 253, 314
ALZIN, J., 239
AMALORPAVADASS, D.S., 44, 46, 48, 55
AMAYA, I.E., 42, 99, 104, 172
AMBROSE OF MILAN, 163, 164
AMSTUTZ, J., 96
ANDEL, H.A. VAN, 163
ANDERSEN W., 19, 20, 84, 86, 94
ANDERSON, G.H., xiii, xiv, 4, 5, 6, 7, 10,
    12, 42, 44, 46, 53, 54, 60, 62, 73, 75,
    89, 91, 92, 93, 95, 96, 99, 103, 107,
    109, 112, 115, 117, 119, 124, 126, 131,
    140, 145, 150, 165, 166, 168, 169, 170,
    171, 178, 180, 181, 221, 222, 243, 251,

252, 277, 309, 328
ANDERSON, R., 229, 232, 327
ANDERSON, W.K., 107, 108, 111, 112, 115,
    123, 288, 292
ANDRÉ, LE PÈRE, 238
ANDRES, F., 253, 286, 287
ANDRES, P., 163, 164
ANDREWS, L., 335, 338, 339
ANHEUSER, P.C., 225, 235
ANTES, P., 193, 194
ARAI, T., 353
ARCHIBALD, A.C., 37, 118
ARENS, B., 9, 10, 144, 279
ARIAS, M., 47
ARING, P.G., 89, 96
ARMOIRY, N., 238
ARMSTRONG, J., 39
ARMSTRONG, R.S., 34, 39
ARN, W., xv
ARN, W.C., 21, 22, 40
ARNOLD, F.X., 57
ARNOLD, W., 46
ARNOLD-FOSTER, F.E., 245, 248
AROZ, H.L.M. DE, 144
ASCH VAN WIJCK, C.M. VAN, 234
ASENSIO NIETO, F., 100, 104
ASHCRAFT, M., 104
AUFHAUSER, J.B., 85
AUGUSTINE, 135, 163, 164
AUGUSTINY, W., 224, 248
AULEN, G., 234
AUTREY, C.E., 37, 42, 128
AVILA, R., 46
AXENFELD, K., 25, 26, 82, 116, 117, 132,
    133
AYANDELE, E.A., 246, 248
AZARIAH, V.S., 321, 322, 327, 328

BAARDA, T., 180
BACHMANN, E.Th., 226
BACON, R., 208
BADER, J.M., 33, 35, 36
BADLEY, B.T., 94
BÄCHLI, O., 111

362

BAEUMKER, F., 246, 248
BAILEY, A.M., 36
BAINBRIDGE, W.F., 232, 249
BAIRD, W., 129, 131
BAKER, A.G., 73, 75, 91, 93, 94, 177, 178, 298, 299, 302, 305
BAKER, D.D., 351
BALZ, H., 217, 290
BALZARINI, M., 145
BANKS, W.L., 126
BARBERO, G., 65, 178, 180, 182
BARDY, G., 208, 209
BARION, H., 62
BARNES, L.C., 227, 232
BARNEY, G.L., 293
BARRETT, D.B., xv, 7, 13, 31, 35, 40, 43, 44, 47, 48, 49, 52, 192, 226, 229, 249, 260, 268, 275, 277, 278, 280, 282, 283, 284, 348, 352
BART, C. VAN, 48
BARTH, K., 19, 20, 94, 124, 126, 135, 147, 163, 164
BARTHOLOMEW, J., 263, 277
BARTON, J.L., 44, 45
BASSHAM, R.C., 97, 137, 141, 151, 154, 172
BASTIDE, R., 299, 301, 302, 303
BATES, M.S., 307, 315
BATTEN, T.R., 353, 354
BAUDERT, S., 243
BAUM, H., 132, 133
BAUMGARTEN, P.M., 238
BAUMGARTNER, J., 79, 83
BAUMGARTNER, W., 107, 108, 110
BAVINCK, J.H., 16, 23, 24, 51, 52, 60, 63, 78, 80, 83, 99, 102, 103, 207, 222, 234, 340, 341
BAXTER, R., 167
BEACH, H.P., 80, 82, 118, 130, 179, 180, 259, 262, 263, 266, 268, 277
BEAVER, R.P., 26, 53, 54, 56, 60, 62, 150, 282, 324
BECHLER, Th., 221
BECKEN, H.-J., 97
BECKER, J., 129, 132
BECKER, R.-W., 273, 283
BECKER, U., 352
BECKMANN, D.M., 320, 324
BECKMANN, J., 55, 83, 105, 106, 142, 145, 193, 287
BEEKMAN, J., 216

BEETS, H., 101, 224, 233
BEKER, J.C., 131
BELTON, R.H., 33, 37
BELTRAMI, S., 145
BEMMEL, H.A. VAN, 48, 132, 133
BENEDICT XV, 142, 145
BENGE, G., 40
BENGE, J., 40
BENNETT, M.A., 211
BENZ, E., 193, 251
BERG, G. VAN DEN, 224, 232
BERG, J. VAN DEN, 147, 150, 180
BERGEMA, H., 63, 65, 66, 93, 95
BERGER, G., 189
BERGMANN, L., 82, 93
BERKHOF, H., 52, 315
BERKHOF, L., 132
BERNHARDT, R., 170
BERTHOLET, A., 99, 100, 108, 114, 314
BERTSCH, L., 47
BETTRAY, J., 325, 326, 336
BEVANS, S.B., 137, 138, 139, 141, 143, 144, 151, 152, 154, 155, 331, 332, 350, 352
BEYERHAUS, P., 92, 96, 99, 103, 104, 116, 119, 121, 123, 149, 155, 157
BEYREUTHER, E., 46, 163, 164
BIEDER, W., 125, 126, 127, 128, 132, 133
BIEHL, M., 334, 335
BIERBAUM, M., 65, 203, 204, 209, 211, 306, 316, 318, 319, 358
BIERMANN, B.M., 88, 94
BIFET, J.E., 49
BIGELMAIR, A., 192
BILHEIMER, R.S., 42
BIRKELI, E., 234
BIRKELI, F., 8, 83
BISHOP, E.F.F., 132, 133
BJERKHEIM, T., 8, 83
BLACKMAN, C., 99, 103
BLACKWOOD, A.W., 36
BLAUW, J., 99, 100, 102, 103, 107, 108, 109, 110, 111, 112, 113, 114, 119, 120, 124, 125, 172
BLENK, C., 46
BLISS, E.M., 4, 5, 7, 8, 179, 180, 221, 225, 232, 233, 248, 263, 269, 275, 276, 288, 289
BLOESCH, D.G., 155
BLOW, N.J., 94, 147, 150
BLUMHARDT, J.C., 205, 229, 231, 241, 258,

259, 261
BOCK, F.S., 219, 230, 255, 358
BOCKMÜHL, K., 95, 96
BOEL, J., 299, 303
BOER, H.R., 250
BOER, P.A.H. DE, 112, 113
BOETZELAER VAN DUBBELDAM, C.W.Th. VAN, 354
BOFF, L., 47
BOHREN, R., 83
BOLKESTEIN, M.H., 315
BOLSHAKOFF, S., 140
BOLT, J., 56, 57
BONGIOANNI, F.M., 346, 350, 358
BONIFACE, 165
BONINO, J.M., xiii
BONK, J.J., 329, 330
BONWETSCH, G.N., 314
BOON-ITT, S.B., 32
BOOTH, A.R., 314, 315
BORAINE, A.L., 163, 164
BORCHERT, G.L., 35, 39
BORNEMANN, F.W.B., 106
BORNHÄUSER, K.B., 122, 125, 129
BORNKAMM, G., 21, 124, 126
BOSCH, D.J., xiii, 12, 21, 22, 32, 35, 39,
    40, 41, 43, 44, 47, 56, 57, 61, 62, 69,
    83, 89, 90, 92, 97, 98, 99, 104, 105,
    107, 108, 109, 117, 119, 121, 123, 124,
    125, 126, 127, 129, 132, 136, 137, 138,
    140, 141, 147, 149, 151, 152, 154, 155,
    157, 163, 164, 168, 170, 177, 178, 179,
    180, 181, 187, 188, 218
BOURDEAUX, M., 310
BOURITIUS, G.J.F., 140, 164
BOUSSET, W., 252, 253
BOUTILIER, J.A., 293
BOUW, W.J., 44, 47
BOVEN, Th.C. VAN, 311, 315, 316
BOYCE, W.B., 274, 280, 281
BOYD, A.J., 356
BOYNTON, C.L., 277
BRAAM, J., 59, 61
BRAATEN, C.E., 92, 97, 149, 172
BRACE, C.L., 219, 255, 256
BRADFIELD, M., 331, 332
BRADSHAW, M.R., 23, 34, 38
BRAINERD, D., 338
BRAMMERZ, W., 262, 264, 279
BRANCATI DE LAUREA, 164, 192
BRANNON, T.L., 103

BRAUER, J.H., 219, 236, 240, 241, 244, 255,
    274, 281
BRAUER, W., 46
BRAYBROOKE, M., 308, 309, 310, 312, 316
BREND, R.M., 210, 211
BRENNECKE, G., 250
BRIA, I., 38, 97, 139, 140, 176
BRIGGS, F.W., 129, 130
BRIGGS, G.W., 291, 292
BRILLENBURG WURTH, G., 54
BRING, E.G., 17
BRISBOIS, J., 53, 55, 165, 166
BROMILEY, G.W., xv
BROOMHALL, B., 42, 45
BROWN, F., 34, 38
BROWN, I.C., 288, 292
BROWN, O.E., 79, 80, 122, 130
BROWN, S.J.M., 6
BROWN, W., 229, 241
BROWNE, E.H., 129, 130
BRÜGGEMANN, W., 105
BRUNDIN, G., 118
BRUNE, R., 129, 130
BRUNNER, E., 68, 115, 116, 163, 164
BRYAN, D.C., 36, 37
BUBER, M., 135, 256
BUCHNER, C., 128
BUDDHA (GAUTAMA), 169, 194, 195
BÜHLMANN, W., 52, 53, 54, 55, 105, 106,
    214, 215
BÜNDGENS, C.J., 259, 260, 287
BÜRKLE, H., 4, 5, 7, 84, 86, 97, 104, 213,
    222, 290, 352
BULLOCK, C., 292
BULTMANN, R., 19, 124, 126
BUREN, P. VAN, 218
BURKE, T.J.M., 142, 145
BURKHARDT, G.E., 229, 242, 250
BURKHART, I.E., 102
BURNS, J., 231
BUSS, M.F.J., 127, 128
BUSSMANN, C., 129, 131
BUSZ, E., 347
BUYS, J., 140, 164, 265
BYRNES, P.A., 9, 10

CADOUX, C.J., 123
CAIRNS, D.S., 115, 116, 191, 192
CALKINS, H.R., 328
CALLAWAY, H., 287

CALLOW, J., 216
CALLOW, K., 216
CALVER, C., 40, 302, 303
CALVIN, J., 51
CAMARGO, G.B., 33
CAMPBELL, J., 270
CAMPBELL, R.E., 88, 89, 95, 142, 145, 309, 315
CAMPS, A., 176, 177, 182
CANOVESI, A., 240, 262
CAPELLE, M.C., 235
CAPEN, E.W., 302
CARALT, M. DE LOS SANTOS, 82
CAREY, D., 338
CAREY, W., 13, 20, 93, 147, 165, 192, 227, 232, 233, 234, 243
CARLETON, A., 303
CARMINATI, C., 65
CARNE, J., 245, 247
CARPENTER, C.H., 320, 321, 323, 324, 326, 327, 328, 358
CARRIKER, C.T., 216, 218, 358
CARRILLO DE ALBORNOZ, A.F., 313, 315
CARROLL, H.K., 224, 244, 245
CARUS-WILSON, A., 233
CARVER, W.O., 99, 102, 103, 120, 229, 233, 234
CASALEGNO, U., 294
CASSIDY, M., 34, 39
CASTRO, E., 41, 152, 154, 163, 165
CATARZI, D., 88, 95, 172
CAVE, S., 130
CENNI, A., 239
CERFAUX, L., 126
CERRI, U., 223
CHADWICK, H., 262, 264
CHADWICK, O., 62, 161, 208, 229, 236, 260
CHAMPAGNE, C., 45, 48
CHARLEMAGNE, 226
CHARLES, P., 17, 18, 56, 65, 70, 92, 94, 142, 144, 219, 222
CHARLEVOIX, P.F.X. DE, 287
CHAUVEL, G., 235
CHAVASSE, A., 54
CHEESMAN, G., 2, 154, 156
CHIRGWIN, A.M., 105, 106
CHO, J.C., 156
CHOULES, J.O., 224, 229, 242, 270
CHOWANETZ, J., 237, 279
CHOWNITZ, J.F.J., 237, 279

CHRISTLIEB, Th., 167, 190, 191, 249, 274, 281
CHRYSOSTOM, J., 163, 164
CLARK, E.T., 33, 36, 342, 343
CLARK, F.X., 142, 144
CLARKE, A., 231
CLEMMER, M.M., 349, 354
CLEWS, J.C., 193
CLOVIS, 228
CODRINGTON, R.H., 295
COFFELE, G., 68, 69, 165, 166
COGGINS, W.T., 34, 38, 327
COINTRE, W.M. LE, 256
COLE, A.H., 322, 332
COLEMAN, R.E., 22, 35, 38, 39, 40
COLENSO, J.W., 132, 133
COLIJN, H., 354
COLOMBO, D., 145
COLUMBUS, C., 228, 268, 276
COMBLIN, J., 92, 97, 143, 146
COMBY, J., 236
COMEE, L., 34, 39
COMENIUS, J.A., 163, 164, 345, 349
COMTE, A., 342
CONANT, J.E., 36
CONE, O., 129, 130
CONGAR, Y.M.J., 57, 92, 96, 143, 146
CONN, H.M., 35, 40, 97, 328
CONSIDINE, J.J., 302, 323, 324
CONSTANTINE, 163, 181, 226, 228
CONSTANTINI, C., 239
CONWAY, G.W., 165, 166
COOK, D., 302, 303
COOK, E.F., 99, 102
COOK, G., 46
COOK, H., 41, 42, 70
COOK, H.R., 108, 118, 235
COOLSMA, S., 106
COOTE, R.T., xiv, 12, 137, 143, 155, 157, 181, 199, 289, 291, 299, 303, 329, 330
COPLEY, D., 40, 303
CORDES, P.J., 146
COREY, S.J., 273, 277
CORSI, O., 274, 278
COSMAS INDICOPLEUSTES, 259, 260, 270
COSTAS, O.E., 20, 21, 22, 23, 44, 47, 48, 49, 63, 66, 155
COUCOUZES, A., 140
COXILL, H.W., 274, 277
CRACCO, A., 66

CRAFFORD, D., 84
CRAWFORD, J.R., 326
CREIGHTON, L., 233
CRIM, K.R., 289, 291, 329, 330
CROIL, J., 224, 242, 247, 248, 281
CULLMANN, O., 117, 119
CUMING, G.J., 222, 244, 246, 252
CURTIS, A.H., 123
CUSANUS, N., 74, 164
CUST, R.N., 42, 45

DABELSTEIN, R., 129, 132, 134, 135
DAGRAS, M., 48
DAHL, N.A., 129, 131
DAHLE, L.N., 112
DAHLMANN, J., 209, 210
DAIN, A.J., 250, 269
DALBERT, P., 114
DALLY, N., 54, 219, 237
DAMMANN, E., 213
DANBOLT, E.G., 132, 133
DANIÉLOU, J., 114, 115, 142, 144, 194, 195
DANKBAAR, W.F., 55
DANKER, W.J., 320, 322, 324
DANZ, J.T.L., 51, 67, 69, 79, 81, 171, 185, 358
DAPPER, H., 151, 154
DARWIN, C., 74
DAUBANTON, F.E., xiii, 3, 4, 11, 15, 16, 17, 18, 19, 20, 21, 22, 23, 24, 25, 26, 29, 30, 50, 51, 52, 60, 62, 63, 70, 72, 78, 79, 82, 84, 85, 98, 136, 137, 161, 162, 166, 167, 175, 176, 203, 204, 205, 207, 208, 209, 221, 223, 253, 258, 269, 272, 273, 274, 275, 286, 333, 334, 345, 346
DAVEY, F.N., 126
DAVIS, J.M., 321, 324, 325, 326, 328
DAY, A.E., 28
DAY, D.H., 326
DAYTON, E.R., 35, 39, 43, 44, 47
D'COSTA, G., 170
DECTER, M., 193
DELACROIX, S., 236, 237, 239
DELL, R.S., 263
DELOS, J.T., 316, 318
DEMPSTER, M.A., 157, 158, 159
DEMPWOLFF, O., 218
DENIS, H., 54
DENNIS, J.S., 249, 250, 259, 263, 274, 275,

277, 281, 297, 298, 299, 302, 305, 325, 327
DESCAMPS, E.E.F., 192, 219, 239
DESCOMBAZ, S., 226, 241
DESPONT, J., 263
DETWEILER, C.S., 102
DEVARANNE, Th., 115, 116
DEWAILLY, L.-M., 52, 70
DEWEY, J., 75, 345
DHAVAMONY, M., 46, 48, 66, 99, 104, 143, 146, 172, 190, 196
DIBELIUS, M., 131
DIBELIUS, O., 255
DICKINSON, R.D.N., 329, 330
DIFFENDORFER, R.E., 6, 269, 270
DIJKSTRA, H., 243
DILGER, W., 194, 195
DILLISTONE, F.W., 36, 166, 167
DINDINGER, J., xiii, 82, 226, 319
DINKLER, E., 21, 124, 126
DIRVEN, P.J., 146
DISCH, A., xv, 306
DITSCHEID, H., 350
DJUNKOVSKOY, E. DE, 7, 8
DOBBIE, R., 109, 116, 119
DOBBINS, F.S., 5, 9, 262, 276
DOBRIZHOFER, M., 287
DODD, C.H., 19, 20, 116, 118
DODDS, J.L., 37
DODGE, R.E., 292
DOEDES, J.I., 3, 4, 17
DÖLLER, J., 112
DOERNE, M., 83
DOMINIC, 160
DONAHUE, P., 131
DONALDSON, T.L., 114, 115
DOORN, C.L. VAN, 303
DOUGLAS, J.D., 44, 46, 156, 158
DOUMA, J., 30, 31
DOURNES, J., 95, 172
DRUMMOND, H., 33, 36
DRUMMOND, L.A., 33, 42
DUBOIS, J.A., 287
DUBOSE, F.M., 105, 111, 113, 134, 176, 185, 186, 187, 188, 197, 198, 200, 201, 202
DUCHROW, U., 323, 331, 332
DÜRR, J., 166, 167
DUFF, A., xiv, 25, 28, 29, 30, 31, 69, 93, 165, 233, 347, 348
DUMAS, N., 89, 95

DUNN, E.J., 69
DURAND, A., 94, 142, 144
DURKHEIM, E., 297, 299, 304
DURRWELL, F.X., 53, 55
DUSEN, H.P. VAN, 73, 75
DUSSELL, E., 331, 332
DWIGHT, H.O., 7, 8, 179, 180, 276
DYE, T.W., 73, 75, 171
DYRNESS, W.A., 99, 105, 172
DYROFF, A., 74, 75

EBERHARD, O., 348, 350
EBRARD, J.H.A., 17
EDDY, D.C., 246, 247
EDDY, G.S., 246, 248
EDMAN, V.R., 227, 234
EDWARDS, J., 167
EDWARDS, W.F., 288
EERENBEEMT, A. VAN DEN, 83
EGEDE, H., 159
EHRENFEUCHTER, F.A.E., 251
EICHRODT, W., 107, 108, 112
EINSIEDEL, J., 237
EISSFELDT, O., 108
EKLUND, J.A., 30
ELIOT, J., 167
ELLIGER, K., 108
ELLIS, W., 287
ELLWOOD, Ch.A., 299
ELY, A., 1, 2, 81, 209, 216, 232, 260, 289,
  335, 351
EMMERICH, H., 264, 265
ENGELEN, J.M. VAN, 146
ENGEN, C.E. VAN, 23, 136, 137, 168, 170,
  216, 218, 358
ERNST, C., 66
ESCALANTE, P.G. DE, 342, 343
ESCOBAR, S., 155
EVANS, F.B., 193
EVANS, G.R., 263, 264
EVANS, R., 353
EVANS, R.A., 309
EVANS-FRAZER, A., 309
EVERS, G., 90, 96, 146, 169
EWING, J.F., 291, 292
EXELER, A., 196, 202

FABER, E., 130
FABRI, F., 166, 167
FABRICIUS, J.A., 223, 230, 240

FACELINA, R., 7, 46
FACKRE, G.J., 34, 38, 42
FAHNER, C., 213
FAHS, C.H., 179, 180, 259, 263, 268, 277,
  325, 326
FELDMANN, F., 113, 114
FERGUSON, L.N., 338, 339
FERGUSON, R., 36
FERM, R.O., 37
FERNANDEZ, A., 223
FETSCHER, I., 256
FIEDLER, K., 156
FINDEIS, H.-J., 84
FINZEL, H., 337, 339
FISCHER, G.M., 318
FISCHER, H., 122
FLACHSMEIER, H.R., 240, 243
FORD, L., 158
FORMAN, C.W., 315
FORNET-BETANCOURT, R., 325
FORSYTH, P.T., 167
FOSTER, J., 220, 235
FOUNTAIN, O.C., 268, 269
FOURCHEUX DE MONTROD, C.M.J.M., 238
FOWLER, C.H., 252
FRANCIS OF ASSISI, 160
FRANCIS, J.E., 38
FRANCKE, A.H., 347
FRASER, D.A., 43, 44, 47
FRAZIER, W.B., 96
FREEMAN, D.H., 80
FREIRE, P., 352
FREITAG, A., 83, 129, 131, 239, 255, 259,
  265, 266
FRENCH, E.A., 36
FREUD, S., 333, 334
FREYTAG, W., 54, 60, 62, 95, 115, 116, 133,
  140, 150, 152, 153, 164, 166, 167, 326,
  343, 354
FRICK, H., 25, 26, 85, 240, 243
FRIDRICHSEN, A., 107, 116, 118, 121, 123,
  125
FRIEDRICH, G., xv, 20, 28
FRISQUE, J., 54
FRIZEN, E.L., Jr, 327
FRÖBEL, F., 345, 356
FROHNES, H., 25, 26, 96, 101, 119, 163,
  164, 222, 223, 230, 235, 254
FROMM, E., 333
FRUMENTIUS, 270

FUCHS, S., 293
FULLER, R.H., 123
FULTON, A., 169
FUNG, R., 152, 154

GADILLE, J., 177
GALL, J., 80, 81
GALLING, K., xiv
GANDHI, M., 135, 256
GANGI, M. DI, 99, 104
GARCIA, W., 262
GARDINI, W., 129, 131, 145
GARDNER, L.M., 337, 339
GAREIS, R., 242, 267
GASQUE, W.W., 73, 75, 117, 119, 171
GATIMU, K., 348, 352
GATU, J., 152, 328
GAUME, J.J., 42, 45
GAVENTA, B.R., 127, 128
GAY, P., 193
GAY, T., 242
GAZALBA, S., 26
GEEST, S. VAN DER, 294
GEFFRÉ, C., 97
GEISLER, N.L., 75
GEISSLER, H., 163, 164, 263
GÉLIN, P.A., 103
GENSICHEN, H.-W., 25, 26, 37, 83, 96, 97,
    101, 108, 109, 124, 142, 145, 194, 195,
    213, 222, 223, 230, 235, 252, 254, 283,
    350, 351
GHEDDO, P., 145
GIBSON, J.C., 30
GIERINGER, P.A., 238
GILHUIS, J.C., 132, 133
GILL, K.D., 158, 159
GILL, W.W., 287
GILLESPIE, R.T., 152, 153
GILLILAND, D.S., 129, 132, 137, 170, 189,
    190, 216, 218, 358
GILMORE, G.W., 5
GISH, D., 338, 339
GLASSER, A.F., 44, 46, 90, 92, 97, 137,
    149, 154, 156, 170, 217, 289, 290
GLAZIK, J., 66, 80, 83, 140, 142, 145, 146,
    193
GLOVER, R.H., 99, 100, 104, 224, 226, 227,
    228, 235
GODDARD, B.L., 7, 8, 264
GODDARD, D., 194, 195

GOERNER, H.C., 102, 104
GÖSSMANN, E., 83
GOFF, J.R., Jr, 159
GONZALEZ, J.L., 220, 230, 235, 237
GONZALEZ-RUIZ, J.M., 315
GOODSELL, F.F., 326
GOODWIN, J.F.B., xiii
GORDON, R., 28
GORRÉE, G., 235
GOULET, E., 144
GOYAU, G., 219, 239
GRAAFLAND, C., 97, 104, 213, 243
GRABMANN, M., 163, 164
GRACEY, J.T., 244, 245, 281
GRAF, A.E., 33, 38
GRAHAM, B., 37, 38, 39, 155
GRAHAM, J.A., 229, 242
GRAHAM, J.M., 292
GRAMBERG, Th.W.B.G., 129, 131
GRAMMATICA, L., 262, 264
GRANT, A., 229, 250
GRANT, C.A., 104
GRASSI, J.A., 129, 131
GRAUL, K., 29, 30, 70, 207, 209, 219, 268
GREEN, B., 37
GREEN, M., 38, 39, 41
GREENWAY, R.S., 22
GREGORY XV, 25, 59, 141, 239
GREGORY XVI, 142
GREGORY VON BREDA, 129, 131, 218, 351
GREGORY THAUMATURGUS, 270
GREINACHER, N., 47
GRENTRUP, Th., 61, 92, 93, 314, 316
GRIMES, J.E., 290
GROENEN, H., 332
GRÖSSER, M., 85, 211, 288, 289
GRÖSZEL, W., 54
GROOT, A. DE, 100, 103
GROOT, D.A. DE, 220, 244
GROSHEIDE, F.W., 45
GRUBB, K., 274, 277
GRÜNDLER, J., 7, 8, 245, 277
GRUNDEMANN, P.R., 2, 82, 205, 242, 249,
    259, 261, 262, 263, 267, 274, 275, 276,
    281, 358
GUBERNATIS, D. DE, 164, 192
GUÉNOT, C., 231
GÜNTHER, W., 152, 153
GÜTZLAFF, K.F.A., 219, 220, 240, 244, 255
GUIDES, D., 34, 39

GUNDERT, H., 74, 229, 243
GUNNING, J.W., 326, 354
GURGANUS, G.P., 32, 39
GURP, P. VAN, 165, 166
GUSINDE, M., 290
GUTIERREZ, G., 93, 96
GUTMANN, B., 165, 288, 290
GUZMAN, L. DE, 59

HAAS, O., 129, 131
HACKER, P., 49
HADDON, A.C., 285, 287
HÄRING, B., 44, 46
HÄRTING, R., 249
HAGEN, T.J., 45
HAHN, C.H., 165, 166
HAHN, F., 84, 86, 116, 119, 120, 125, 128
HAHN, H., 237
HALL, G.S., 333
HALLENCREUTZ, C.F., 121, 123, 165, 166
HAMILTON, F.E., 353
HAMMAN, G.A., 100, 103
HANSEN, J., 49
HARDELAND, O., 221
HARDY, E.R., Jr, 234
HARKNESS, G., 94
HARMS, E., 342, 343
HARNACK, A. VON, 121, 123, 125, 221, 275,
    276, 316, 318
HARNACK, T., 29, 30
HARNER, N.C., 345, 351, 353
HARPER, 128
HARR, W.C., 226, 240
HARRISON, E.F., 75, 119
HARTENSTEIN, K.W., 60, 91, 93, 94, 110,
    115, 116, 147, 163, 167
HARTMANN, A., 336
HARTT, J.N., 42
HASSELL, J., 231
HATTON, D.J., 66
HAUPT, E., 54, 99, 117
HAUSSLEITER, J., 26, 117, 125
HAWKINS, E., 267, 281
HAY, A.R., 118
HAYFORD, J.W., 158
HAYWARD, V.E.W., 151, 153
HAZART, C., 223
HEADLAND, I.T., 82, 212, 326
HEILER, F., 189
HEILMANN, K., 233, 263, 345, 346, 347, 350,

351, 354
HEIM, K., 116, 118, 164
HEINISCH, P., 114
HEINRICH, J.C., 340
HEINRICH, R.P., 338, 339
HEINRICHS, M., 169, 195
HEISE, D.R., 299, 303
HELMAN, A., 322
HEMPEL, J., 107, 108
HENDERSON, A., 239
HENGEL, M., 116, 119, 120
HENKEL, W., 5, 278
HENNINGER, J., 287
HENRION, M.R.A., 237
HENRY, A.-M., 88, 95
HENRY, C.F.H., 38, 156
HEPBURN, R.W., 76, 77, 186, 187
HERBART, J.F., 345
HERBST, H., 259, 260
HERING, H.W., 4, 6
HERMELINK, J., 53, 54, 62, 95, 115, 116,
    132, 133, 140, 148, 150, 151, 153, 316,
    319, 326, 343
HESS, W., 163, 164
HESSELGRAVE, D.J., 75, 97, 156, 165, 166,
    334, 344
HICK, J., 168, 169, 170
HICKS, H.W., 347
HIEBERT, P.G., 291, 293, 294
HIGGINS, R., 316, 319
HILLIS, D.W., 44, 46, 99, 103
HINKEL, K.A.F., 51, 231, 255
HINKELAMMERT, F.J., 323, 331, 332
HJERESSEN, A., 100, 102
HOCKING, W.E., 36, 91, 94, 168, 314, 340
HODDER, E., 232
HODGES, M.L., 92, 93, 97, 149, 157, 158
HODGKIN, R.A., 345, 351
HODGKINS, L.M., 219, 221
HOECKMAN, R., 96, 154, 172
HOEDEMAKER, L.A., 53, 56
HOEKENDIJK, J.C., 19, 20, 25, 26, 29, 31,
    37, 43, 45, 46, 48, 52, 53, 55, 56, 62,
    67, 68, 69, 70, 79, 82, 102, 162, 164,
    165, 166, 254, 255, 257, 283, 284, 288,
    290, 298, 302, 347, 349
HOEKSTRA, H.T., 39, 152, 154, 155
HOF, I.P.C. VAN 'T, 26, 152, 153, 163, 164
HOFFMAN, R., 88, 95, 142, 145, 164, 191,
    192

HOFFMANN, F., 231
HOFFMANN, W., 238, 241
HOFINGER, J., 46, 349, 350, 353
HOFSTEE, H., 91, 96
HOGARTH, J., 348, 352
HOGG, W.R., 142, 145, 150, 152, 153, 243, 250
HOLLENBACH, D., 309
HOLLENWEGER, W.J., 39, 47, 137, 194, 195
HOLMES, U.T., 49
HOLSTEN, W., xiii, 3, 4, 11, 19, 20, 25, 26, 78, 84, 86, 98, 128, 164, 166, 222, 246, 253, 298, 301, 302, 305, 316, 319, 343, 346, 349
HOLTEN, A.T. VAN, 176, 177
HONIG, A.G., 116, 118
HORNER, N.A., 150, 191, 192
HORSLEY, R.A., 299, 300
HORTON, R.F., 100, 101, 124
HOWARD, E.J., 327
HUBER, W., 310
HUC, E.R., 287
HÜBNER, 245, 247
HÜNERMANN, W., 248
HUGHES, D.T., 293
HUGHES, M.V., 127, 128
HUIE, J.A., 220, 240
HUMMEL, R., 193
HUMPHREYS, C., 193
HUNTER, W.F., 334, 336
HUNTER, G.G., III, 34, 40
HUNTINGTON, G.B., 325, 326
HUPPENBAUER, H.W., 109
HUSSERL, E., 189
HUTCHINSON, P., 233
HUTTEN, K., 193
HVALKOF, S., 292, 293

IGNACE OF LOYOLA, 59
IHMELS, C., 83
IHRMARK, A., 233
INMAN, S.G., 324
IQBAL, M., 193
ISERLAND, O., 332
ITTY, C.I., 330

JABAVU, D.T., 33
JACKSON, S.M., 5
JACOB, E., 109, 112
JACOBS, D.R., 293

JAFFRAY, G.R., Jr, 38
JAGER, O., 31
JAMES OF MELITA, 140
JAMES, W., 333
JANSEN SCHOONHOVEN, E., 43, 46, 53, 54, 55, 100, 101, 103, 110, 148, 150, 315
JAPP, A.H., 247
JARRETT-KERR, M., 245, 248, 255
JAUNCEY, J.H., 335, 336
JEDIN, H., 262, 264
JEFFERY, R.M.C., 96, 129, 131
JENKS, D., 44, 45, 224, 233
JEREMIAS, J., 121, 123
JEROENSE, P.J.G., 165, 166, 332
JESSOP, T.E., 36
JETTÉ, F., 65, 82
JEURISSEN, R., 322, 324
JOANNES A JESU MARIA, 59
JÖRGENSEN, S.E., 15
JOHN XXIII, 142, 145, 307
JOHN PAUL II, 143, 146
JOHN, B. ST., 277
JOHNSON, F., 324
JOHNSON, T.M., 278, 280, 282
JOHNSTON, A.P., 32, 38, 39, 41, 42, 152, 153
JOHNSTON, J., 232, 242
JOHNSTONE, P., 277, 282
JONES, E.S., 36
JONG, P. DE, 42
JONG, P.Y. DE, 31
JONGE, M. DE, 55
JONGENEEL, J.A.B., 9, 10, 31, 89, 98, 137, 158, 159, 163, 165, 166, 167, 172, 181, 182, 256, 280, 282, 315
JORDAN, W.G., 108
JOSENHANS, J.F., 265, 267
JOSEPHUS, F., 114
JOUBERT, H.L.N., 116, 118
JUDSON, A., 338
JUNG, C.G., 176, 203, 210, 333
JUNOD, H.A., 287, 342, 343
JUNOD, H.P., 292, 351
JUST, M., 234, 239
JUSTIN MARTYR, 163, 164

KAAJAN, H., 147, 149
KÄHLER, M., 25, 26, 96, 117, 119, 121, 122, 163, 164
KAGAWA, T., 32

KALKAR, C.A.H., 232, 238, 241
KANE, J.H., 76, 90, 91, 97, 104, 156, 211, 230, 235, 236, 346, 352, 354
KANG, W.J., 324
KANTONEN, T.A., 41, 42, 48
KAPENZI, G.Z., 246, 248, 337, 339
KARL VOM HEILIGEN ALOYS, 237, 278, 279
KARLGREN, A., 233
KARLSTRÖM, N., 153
KASBAUER, S., 66
KASDORF, H., 23, 166, 167
KASTING, H., 116, 119
KATO, K., 341, 342
KATO, Z., 124, 126
KATZ, E., 303
KEE, H.C., 299, 300
KEEN, W.W., 82, 302
KEESING, F.M., 291, 292
KELLERHALS, E., 128
KENNEDY, D.J., 35, 38
KERTELGE, K., 116, 119, 122, 124, 127, 129, 132
KESSELRING, H., 149
KESSLER, W., 115, 116
KETTNER, E.A., 37
KEYSSER, C., 288, 347, 349
KILGER, L., 255
KILPATRIC, T.B., 36, 118
KILPATRICK, G.D., 124, 126
KIM, S., 129, 132
KIMBANGU, S., 194
KINGSMILL, J., 231
KIRBY, G.W., 38
KIRBY, J.P., 294, 296
KIRBY, R., 193
KIRKPATRICK, L., 79, 81
KISTE, R., 170
KITTAN, G., 231
KITTEL, G., xv
KIVENGERE, F., 155
KLAUS, B.D., 159
KLEINPAUL, B., 99, 100, 101
KLERK, J.J. DE, 30, 31
KLIEWER, D., 338, 339
KLIMKEIT, H.-J., 86
KLIMSCH, R., 238
KLINGSEIS, R., 75
KLOOS, P., 294
KLOOTWIJK, E., 170
KLOSTERMANN, F., 55

KNAK, S., 82, 94, 117, 118, 163, 164
KNAPP, G.C., 240
KNITTER, P.F., 168, 169, 170
KOBIA, S.M., 330
KÖBERLE, A., 94
KOENIG, J., 134, 135
KÖRNER, G., 248
KÖSTER, H., 83
KÖSTER, H.M., 97
KOHLER, W., 343, 352
KOHNSTAMM, P.A., 75, 91, 96, 138
KOLB, R., 42, 187, 188
KOLLBRUNNER, F., 142, 146
KOLMODIN, A., 99, 102
KOOY, F. VAN, 249
KOPER, J., 108, 216, 217
KORNFIELD, W.J., 292, 293
KORTHALS, R.G., 34, 39
KORTZFLEISCH, S. VON, 193
KOSHY, N., 307, 311, 312, 313, 316
KOWALSKY, N., 82, 142, 144, 319
KOYAMA, K., 165, 166
KRAEMER, H., 19, 20, 21, 53, 54, 55, 81, 83, 91, 93, 94, 147, 162, 165, 166, 168, 199, 268, 269, 341
KRAEMER, P.E., 299, 303
KRAMM, T., 89, 97, 196
KRASS, A.C., 21, 22, 39, 199, 299, 303
KRAUS, J., 7, 84, 97, 104, 222, 352
KRAUS, N.C., 23, 35, 39
KRETSCHMAR, G., 101, 222, 223, 230, 235, 254
KRISHNA, 169
KRISTOFFERSEN (LIER), A., 131
KRITZINGER, J.J. (DONS), 3, 4, 89, 97
KROSE, H.A., 274, 279
KUBIK, W., 163, 164
KÜBLER, O., 149, 162, 163
KÜLB, P.H., 238, 270
KUHL, J., 125, 126
KUHN, K.G., 116, 118
KUIPER, A. DE, 63, 66, 99, 104, 220, 235
KUIPER, R.B., 42
KUNZE, W., 162, 163
KUYPER, A., 3, 4, 17, 18, 19, 20, 21, 22, 23, 24, 29, 30, 51, 52, 70, 147
KVIST, G., 103
KYPKE, H., 236, 242

LAAN, D.W. VAN DER, 46

LABIN, S., 193
LACROIX, M., 7, 8
LAIRD, M.A., 349
LAMARCHE, P., 114, 115
LANDGREN, L., 242
LANEY, J.T., 39
LANG, A., 164
LANG, J.M., 232
LANG, J.R., 143, 146
LANGE, J.P., 17
LANGE, P.H., 234
LANGE, R., 93, 142, 144
LANGHANS, E.F., 251, 252
LAPHAM, H.A., 100, 101, 102, 112
LARKIN, W.J., 217
LA ROCHE, F., 2, 93
LASNE, J., 224, 238
LA SOR, W.S., 73, 75, 117, 119
LATIFAU, J.F., 287
LATOURETTE, K.S., 2, 35, 36, 74, 75, 152,
    153, 208, 209, 221, 222, 223, 224, 225,
    226, 227, 228, 234, 235, 237, 240, 250,
    251, 258, 260, 262, 264, 283, 284, 320,
    327
LAUBACH, F.C., 37, 348, 349, 354
LAUBE, J., 77
LAUKENAU, F.J., 269
LAURENTIN, R., 46
LAURIE, T., 1, 2, 13, 81, 207, 208, 209,
    216, 232, 260, 289, 335, 339, 351, 353
LAUTERBURG, M., 249, 250
LAWRENCE, J.B., 100, 102
LAZZARINI, D.M.P., 67, 68
LEAVELL, R.Q., 37
LE BON, G., 299
LECHNER, J., 164
LEENHARDT, M., 295, 299, 302
LEES, H.C., 129, 130
LEEUW, G. VAN DER, 189, 194, 195, 196
LEEUWEN, A.Th. VAN, 53, 55, 162, 165, 166,
    251, 252, 331, 332
LEFEBVRE, P., 166, 167
LEGRAND, L., 105, 119
LE GUILLOU, M.-J., 330
LEHMANN, A., 326
LEIBNIZ, G.W. VON, 74, 75
LEIPOLD, H., 68, 163, 164
LEIPOLDT, J., 123
LEMAITRE, A., 116, 118
LEMOPOULOS, G., 139, 140

LENNOX, W.G., 192
LENWOOD, F., 197, 198
LEO XIII, 142, 145
LEONARD, D.L., 224, 227, 243
LEONHARDI, G., 236, 241, 242
LEONHARDT, K.G., 230
LEPSIUS, R., 208
LERLE, E., 117, 119
LEROY LAWSON, E., 301, 303, 325, 327, 340
LESOURD, P., 239
LESSING, G.E., 347
LEUBA, J.H., 333
LEVONIAN, L., 341
LÉVY-BRUHL, L., 304
LEWIS, B., 337, 339
LEWIS, E., 42
LEWIS, T., 337, 339
LIAGRE-BÖHL, F.M.Th. DE, 107, 108, 110, 112
LIECHTENHAN, R., 116, 118
LIEFELD, W.L., 230, 236
LIÉGÉ, P.A., 309, 315
LIGHTFOOT, J.B., 190, 191
LIGHTFOOT, R.H., 126
LILLEY, J.P., 125, 224, 250
LIN, J.J.E. VAN, 152, 154, 168, 169
LINDBLOM, J., 122
LINDE, J.M. VAN DER, 84, 345, 349
LINDEBERG, G.W., 239, 243, 248
LINDQUIST, B., 339
LINDQUIST, S.E., 338, 339
LINDSELL, H., 73, 75, 95, 154, 156, 171,
    172, 226, 292
LINSSEN, G., 132, 133
LINTON, J.H., 36
LINZ, M., 83, 95
LITTELL, F.H., 147, 149, 150, 171
LIVINGSTONE, D., 1, 93, 165, 192, 233, 252,
    270, 287, 338
LIVINGSTONE, M., 338
LLOYD, R., 94, 147, 150
LOCKE, J., 345
LÖHR, M.R.H., 99, 100, 108
LOEWEN, J.A., 292, 293
LOFFELD, E., xiv, 12, 59, 61, 65
LOHFF, W., 84, 86
LOHFINK, G., 124
LOHMEYER, E., 20, 124, 126
LOHSE, E., 125, 126
LOOMAN, Th.M., 241
LOPEZ, J., 59

LORD, E., 240
LORIMER, G.C., 321, 324
LOSSKY, N., xiii
LOTZ, D., 43, 46
LOUVET, L.E., 238
LOVE, J.P., 99, 102
LOVETT, R., 232
LOWRIE, J.C., 241, 262, 267, 274, 281
LUBAC, H. DE, 94, 142, 144
LÜCKE, G.C.F., 2, 79, 81, 99
LÜTGERT, W., 26, 77
LULL, R., 165, 208
LUM, A., 99, 104
LUM, G., 99, 104
LUNDAHL, J.E., 229, 234
LUTHER, M., 135, 226, 227, 228
LUZBETAK, L.J., 284, 285, 291, 293, 294,
    295, 296, 358
LYALL, L.T., 249, 250

MA, J.T., 9, 10
MABIE, H.C., 73, 74, 171, 191
MACAULEY, J.C., 33, 37
MACHOVEC, M., 256
MACKAY, J.A., 36, 88, 94
MACKICHAN, D., 68
MACLENNAN, K., 325, 326
MACONI, V., 290
MACVICAR, N., 329, 330
MÄRKER, O., 42, 45
MAHFUZ, N., 135
MAHLSTROM, A., 234
MAINAGE, Th.L., 342
MAJOR, H.D.A., 123
MALLO, E., 53, 55
MAMACHI, T.M., 237
MANECKE, D., 163, 164, 165, 166
MANI, 256
MANN, U., 83
MANSON, T.W., 120, 123
MANSON, W., 103
MARGOT, J.C., 213
MARGULL, H.J., 25, 26, 33, 37, 46, 53, 54,
    62, 92, 95, 115, 116, 133, 140, 148, 149,
    150, 151, 153, 172, 299, 301, 302, 303,
    316, 319, 326, 343
MARK, H., 333, 340
MARKHOFF, G., 53, 55
MARMY, E., 142, 145
MARSHALL, T.W., 229, 236, 238

MARTIN, bishop of Tours, 270
MARTIN, H., 99, 100, 102, 120
MARTIN, J., 262, 264
MARTIN-ACHARD, R., 107, 109, 112, 113, 114
MARTYN, H., 165
MARX, K., 194, 332
MASON, A. DE WITT, 233
MASON (ATWATER), C., 252, 255
MASSON, J., 5, 6, 38, 48, 143, 146, 172
MASUTANI, F., 194, 195
MATHER, C., 167
MATHEWS, B.J., 21, 235, 246, 248, 355
MATHEWS, J.K., 125, 126
MATTHEY, J., 21, 124, 126
MAUNU, J.A., 122
MAUR, I. AUF DER, 142, 145, 146
MAUSBACH, J., 253
MAUSS, M., 304
MAYERS, M.K., 34, 35, 38, 334, 336
MAYOR, M.F., 314, 315
MCCLUNG, F., Jr, 33, 40
MCCLUNG, L.G., Jr, 158, 159
MCCORMICK, R.A., 309
MCDILL, W., 39
MCGAVRAN, D.A., 22, 23, 33, 40, 73, 75, 90,
    92, 97, 103, 137, 149, 156, 156, 217,
    273, 289, 290, 296, 301, 304, 342
MCGEE, G.B., 157, 158, 159
MCGLASSON, R.T., 158
MCKINNEY, L., 352, 355
MCLEAN, A., 101, 245, 248
MCLEISH, A., 44, 45, 123
MCPHEE, A.G., 39
MEHL, R., 299, 301, 302, 303
MEIDEN, A. VAN DER, 25, 26, 55
MEIJER, B.F., 124
MEINERTZ, M., 82, 100, 102, 121, 122
MEINHOF, C., 209, 210, 212
MEIRING, P.G.J., 3, 4, 89, 97
MEJER, O., 236, 237, 278
MELZER, F., 212
MENASCE, J.-P. DE, 165
MENDIOLA, M.R., 308, 309
MERCIER, G., 330
MERENSKY, A., 165
MERKEL, F.R., 74, 75, 82, 253
MERMANNIUS, A., 223
MERWE, W.J. VAN DER, 83
MESOT, J., 163, 164
MESTOKO, D., 21, 54

METZGER, G., 163, 164
METZLER, J., xiii, 5, 236, 240
MEYENDORFF, J., 140
MEYER, R.P.M., 132, 133, 134, 163, 165
MICHAELIS, W., 118
MICHEL, O., 20, 124, 126
MIDDELKOOP, P.R., 20, 27, 105
MIGNE, J.P., 7, 8
MIGUEZ BONINO, J., 309
MILES, D., 35, 40
MILLAR, R., 219, 223, 230, 240, 255, 358
MILLER, D.G., 131
MILLER, E.S., 292, 293
MILLER, H., 39
MILLOT, R.P., 239, 250
MILLS, W.P., 73, 75, 325, 326
MINEAR, P.S., 132, 133
MINOR, E., 129, 130
MIONI, U., 63, 65, 279
MIRANDA, J.P., 125, 126
MIRBT, C.T., 240, 243, 252, 306, 314, 316, 318
MISSELBROOK, L.R., 34, 37
MITCHELL, J.M., 242
MITTERHÖFER, J., 115, 119
MÖLLER, C., 49
MOFFETT, B., 40, 303
MOHR, R.J., 285, 290, 358
MOHRMANN, C., 208, 209, 214, 215
MOISTER, W., 7, 8, 247, 248
MOLLENKOTT, V.R., 33, 40
MONDREGANES, P.M. DE, 65, 290
MONLOUBOU, L., 132
MONNIER, H., 54, 122
MONROE, P., 351
MONSMA, M., 37
MONTALBAN, F.J., 220, 239
MONTESSORI, M., 345, 356
MONTGOMERY, H.B., 102, 200, 233
MONTGOMERY, J., 21, 22
MONTICONE, G., 264, 265
MOODY, C.N., 342
MOONEN, W.M.M., 46
MOONEYHAM, W.S., 38, 156
MOORE, E.C., 233
MOORHOUSE, G., 248
MOREAU, J.L., 213
MORGAN, E.R., 94, 147, 150, 255
MORITZEN, N.-P., xiii, 277
MORRISON, M., 338

MORRISON, S.A., 314, 315, 316
MORSE, S.E., 263
MOSER, B., 236
MOTT, J.R., 32, 36, 43, 45, 88, 272
MOTTE, M., 143, 146, 147
MOULTON, H.K., 104, 117, 118, 213
MOURANT, J.A., 76, 77
MÜHLHÄUSER, L., 253
MÜLLER, A., 47
MÜLLER, F.M., 209
MÜLLER, G., 26, 117, 132, 133
MÜLLER, J., 104, 316, 319
MÜLLER, K., xiv, 2, 79, 84, 92, 98, 129, 131, 132, 133, 143, 147, 196, 197, 214, 215, 251, 252, 278, 284, 291, 293, 304, 305
MUGAMBI, J.N.K., 47, 99, 105
MUHAMMED, 169, 194, 256
MULDER, J., 45
MULDERS, A.J.M., xiv, 3, 4, 5, 6, 9, 10, 11, 13, 16, 65, 66, 71, 72, 78, 82, 85, 88, 93, 94, 98, 136, 137, 166, 169, 172, 175, 178, 180, 203, 204, 205, 207, 208, 209, 220, 222, 223, 236, 237, 239, 244, 253, 254, 258, 261, 262, 274, 275, 286, 300, 306, 333, 334, 345, 346
MUNTERS, Q.J., 297, 299, 303, 305
MURPHY, E.L., 21, 66
MURRAY, I., 41
MURRAY, J.L., 6
MUSSCHENGA, A.W., 181
MUURLING, W., 31, 35, 51
MYKLEBUST, O.G., xiv, 10, 12, 28, 29, 31, 72, 73, 75, 76, 77, 79, 80, 83, 95, 99, 103, 128, 190, 207, 208, 209, 210, 220, 222, 251, 254, 259, 260, 274, 275, 287, 298, 299, 300, 304, 307, 321, 322, 334, 335, 347, 349, 355, 358

NACPIL, E.P., 215, 216
NASH, R.H., 33, 37
NEHER, S.J., 259, 262, 264, 274, 279
NEILL, S.C., xiii, 13, 23, 38, 55, 61, 62, 152, 153, 160, 161, 196, 207, 208, 220, 222, 223, 224, 229, 230, 236, 240, 244, 246, 251, 252, 253, 260, 266, 269, 271
NEMBRO, M. DA, 53, 55, 66, 83
NEUHÄUSLER, E., 83
NEURDENBURG, J.C., 60, 78
NEWBIGIN, J.E.L., 69, 123

NEWCOMB, H., 7, 8, 179, 261
NEWELL, W.H., 291, 292
NICHOLLS, B.J., 35, 40, 156
NICOLAI, P., 163, 164
NIDA, E.A., 209, 210, 211, 212, 213, 216, 217, 219, 292, 293
NIEDEN, E. ZUR, 162, 163
NIELSEN, E.W., 234
NILES, D.T., 32, 37, 152, 153
NINEHAM, D.E., 124, 126
NINOMIYA, T., 163, 165
NIPPOLD, F.W., 77
NISSEN, J., 116, 117, 119, 330, 333
NISSEN, K., 152, 154
NOEL, B.W., 231
NÖSGEN, K.F., 129, 130
NOMES, J., 233
NOMMENSEN, L.I., 165
NOORDEGRAAF, A., 23, 24, 127, 128
NORTH, F.M., 323
NORTHCOTT, C., 310, 313, 315
NORTIER, C.W., 21, 54, 234
NOTTINGHAM, E.K., 305
NTAMBURI, Z., 329
NÜRNBERGER, K., 329, 330
NUNNENMACHER, E., 143, 146
NUSSBAUM, S., 330

O'CONNOR SLOANE, C., 100, 102
O'DONNELL, K.S., 334, 335, 336, 337, 338, 339, 343
O'DONNELL, M.L., 334, 336, 338, 339, 343
OBER, C.K., 106
OEHLER, Th., 42, 45, 116, 117
OEHLER, W., 125
OEPKE, A., 125, 129, 130
OESTERLEY, W.O.E., 108, 112
OHM, Th., xiv, 3, 4, 9, 10, 11, 13, 20, 21, 26, 52, 53, 53, 55, 62, 71, 72, 78, 83, 87, 88, 95, 98, 109, 119, 136, 137, 163, 164, 207, 226, 229, 285, 286, 320, 333, 334
OLDHAM, J.H., 75, 197, 198, 314
OLICHON, A., 239
OLLROG, W.-H., 129, 131
OOSTERZEE, J.J. VAN, 17, 29, 30, 162
OOSTHUIZEN, G.C., 289
ORCHARD, R.K., 60, 62, 151, 153
ORME, W., 67, 69, 72, 73, 171, 185, 202
OSAFO, E.A., 322

OSPINA, E., 66
OSTERTAG, A., 226, 241
OSTWALD, Th., 129, 130
OTTO, R., 189, 194
OUSSOREN, A.H., 165, 191, 192

PACKER, J.I., 37
PADELFORD, N.J., 314, 316, 317, 318
PADILLA, R., 155
PAGURA, F.J., 330
PAK, J.Y.-S., 129, 132, 195
PANIKKAR, K.M., 247, 252
PANIKKAR, R., 168, 169, 256
PANNENBERG, W., 180, 181
PANTAENUS, 270
PARHAM, C.F., 157, 159
PARKER, J.I., 272, 277
PARRY, E., 239
PASCAL, B., 74
PASSERI, V., 45
PATE, L.D., 156, 280, 282
PATERSON, J., 107, 107, 108, 111, 112, 115
PATHRAPANKAL, J., 46, 119
PATON, W., 36, 347, 348
PATRICK, 270
PATTISON, S.R., 288, 289
PATTON, C.H., 320, 323, 324, 326
PAUL VI, 43, 143
PAUL, C., 26, 117, 133
PAUNU, U., 125
PAVENTI, S., 16, 31, 52, 65, 70
PAWSON, H.C., 33, 38
PAYNE, E.A., 23, 235
PEARSON, H.N., 224, 226, 230
PELACH, E., 144
PENNELL, Th., 192
PENNOYER, F.D., 34, 41
PENSTONE, M.M., 127, 128
PENTECOST, E.C., 63, 66, 86, 124, 126
PERBAL, A., 65, 67, 68, 142, 144, 145
PERKINS, J., 308, 309
PERONNET, M., 315
PERRY, E.T., 31, 36
PERSON, L., 4, 5, 6
PESCH, R., 116, 122, 127
PESTALOZZI, J.H., 345
PETERS, G.W., 34, 38, 99, 104
PETERSEN, J., 34, 40
PETERSON, D., 159
PETERSON, P.D., 7

PETRI, A., 229, 232
PETRI, G., 237, 264
PFANNMÜLLER, G., 256
PFEIFFER, E., 2, 234
PFISTER, O.R., 333, 334, 335
PFLEIDERER, O., 77
PHILIP, P.O., 33, 324
PHILLIPS, G.E., 91, 94, 115, 116, 234
PHILLIPS, J.M., xiv, 12, 137, 143, 155,
    157, 181, 289, 291, 329, 330
PHILO OF ALEXANDRIA, 114
PICKERING, E.D., 42
PICKERING, J., 208
PIDDINGTON, R., 292
PIEPER, K., 129, 130
PIEPKE, J.G., 294, 296
PIERSON, A.T., 42, 220, 232
PIERSON, P., 137, 170
PIET, J.H., 95
PIETSCH, J., 79, 83
PIKE, K.L., 209, 210, 211
PISANI, P., 250
PITMAN, E.R., 246, 248
PIUS X, 144
PIUS XI, 142, 144, 145, 264
PIUS XII, 142, 144, 145
PLATH, C.H.C., 2, 29, 30, 74, 79, 81, 252,
    320, 326, 347
PLATT, W.J., 106
PLATVOET, J.G., 85, 86
PLESSIS, H. DU, 63, 66
PLITT, G.L., 221
PLOEG, J.P.M. VAN DER, 100, 102
PLOEG, R., 294
PLUEDDEMANN, J.E., 330
PLÜTSCHAU, H., 347
POBEE, J.S., xiii, 152, 154, 352
POETSCH, H.L., 48
POMERVILLE, P.A., 157, 158, 159, 172, 217,
    289, 290
PONDER, J.A., 39
POP, F.J., 53, 55
POPE-LEVISON, P., 47
POPESCU, O., 322
PORTMANN, J.R., 153
POST, G.E., 101
POTEL, J., 302
POTT, A., 285, 290, 358
POTTER, P., 38, 42
POULAIN, N., 182, 224, 242

POULTON, J., 38
POUSSON, E.K., 159
POWER, J., 96, 100, 104
PREEZ, J. DU, 134
PRESSENCÉ, E.D. DE, 52, 54
PRICE, F.W., 274, 276
PRICE, M.T., 341, 342
PRINS, J.J., 81
PROBST, M., 97

QUACK, A., 291
QUIRING, H., 271

RABANOS ESPINOSA, R., 129, 131
RADHAKRISHNAN, S., 256
RAEN, G., 99, 104
RAGUIN, Y., 67, 68, 108
RAHNER, K., 66, 134, 163, 165
RATSCHOW, C.H., 170
RATTENBURY, J.E., 36
RAUPP, W., 147, 150
RAUSCHENBUSCH, W., 298, 299
RAYAN, S., 44
REA, W.F., 322
REAPSOME, J.W., 47, 280, 282
REBER, C.H., Jr, 226, 240
REED, E.T., 233
REESE, G., 330
REGAN, R.J., 307, 315
REICHEL, L.Th., 265, 267
REICHELT, K.L., 341
REILLY, W.S., 100, 102
REIMARUS, H.S., 123
REITSMA, A.T., 231
RENAUD, R., 131
RENDTORFF, H., 46
RENGSTORF, K.H., 50, 54, 109, 120, 134, 135
RENNSTICH, K.W., 322
RÉTIF, A.V., 67, 68, 100, 103, 113, 114,
    115, 128, 142, 143, 144, 145, 209, 210,
    211
REYBORN, W.D., 217
REYNOLDS, H.R., 303
RHINELANDER, P.M., 102
RICCI, M., 1, 270
RICHARDSON, A., 76, 77, 96, 186, 187, 188,
    189, 197, 216, 217, 218
RICHARDSON, J., 339
RICHARDSON, W.J., 35, 39, 53, 55
RICHMOND, J., 188, 189, 197

RICHTER, J., 15, 25, 26, 45, 75, 93, 99, 102, 131, 190, 211, 212, 218, 232, 240, 243, 277, 321, 326, 332, 353, 354
RICHTER, M., 93, 147, 149
RIDDER, R.R. DE, 22, 25, 26, 109, 124, 126
RIDDERBOS, H.N., 118
RIEDEL-SPANGENBERGER, I., 59, 62
RIEHM, E.K.A., 108
RIIS, J., 192
RIJCKEVORSEL, L.J. VAN, 61, 63, 65, 70
RIOU, A., 238
RIPLEY, H.J., 353, 354
RITSCHARD, H., 339
RITSON, J.H., 100, 102
RIVET, P., 292
RIVIERE, L. LA, 47
ROBERT, D.L., 43, 47
ROBERTS, W.D., 309
ROBINSON, C.H., 233, 250
ROBINSON, Th.H., 108, 112, 113
ROBSON, G., 243
ROBSON, J., 125, 242
ROCHE, A., 54, 239
ROEHRICH, H., 149
ROELS, E.D., 132, 133
RÖSCH, F., 335
ROHRBACH, P., 332
ROMMERSKIRCHEN, J., xiii, 4, 82, 142, 144, 319
ROOY, S.H., 150, 167
ROSALES, R.S., 33, 38
ROSCHINI, G.M., 239
ROSCOE, J., 287
ROSEN, G., 114
ROSENKRANZ, G., 83, 97, 146, 168, 169, 235, 253
ROSENSTIEL, A., 293
ROSIN, H.H., 60, 62, 147, 150, 214, 215
ROSS, E.A., 299
ROSSEL, J., 290
ROTTENBERG, A.M.J., 256, 257
ROUSE, R., 152, 153, 234
ROUSSEAU, J.-J., 345
ROUX, A., 302
ROVER, P.A. DE, 248
ROWBOTHAM, A.H., 221
ROWLEY, H.H., 108, 110, 112, 113
ROXBY, P.M., 271
ROY, J.J.E., 229, 238
RÜTTI, L., 89, 92, 96, 97, 143, 146

RUF, W., 250, 326
RULER, A.A. VAN, 53, 56, 57
RUSCHE, H., 117, 118
RUSSELL, B.A.W., 193
RWEYEMAMU, R., 143, 146
RYANG, J.S., 32
RYCROFT, W.S., 349, 354
RZEPKOWSKI, H., xiv, 143, 146, 161

SAAYMAN, W.A., 3, 4, 89, 97
SAILER, T.H.P., 191, 192, 248, 347, 351
SALAMONE, F.A., 211, 291, 294, 296
SALAQUARDA, J., 343, 352
SAMARTHA, S.J., 70, 93, 168, 169, 170, 180, 181, 192, 195, 216, 217, 256
SAMUEL, V., 40
SANNEH, L., 215, 216
SANTA ANA, J. DE, 323, 329, 330, 331
SANTOS HERNANDEZ, A., xiv, 3, 4, 5, 6, 10, 11, 16, 31, 52, 59, 62, 63, 66, 78, 98, 99, 100, 103, 137, 142, 145, 150, 172, 175, 178, 180, 203, 204, 205, 207, 208, 211, 222, 253, 258, 263, 280, 286, 290, 298
SARAVIA, A., 51
SCHÄR, H., 343
SCHÄRER, H., 82, 144, 149, 171
SCHAFF, P., 29, 30, 80, 82
SCHAMONI, W., 246, 248
SCHARPFF, P., 38, 43, 219, 235, 335, 337
SCHEDL, E., 356, 357
SCHELBERT, G., 143, 146
SCHELER, M., 189
SCHEMANN, A., 140
SCHERER, J.A., 58, 60, 61, 62, 137, 138, 139, 141, 143, 144, 149, 150, 151, 152, 154, 155, 157, 191, 192, 331, 332, 350, 352
SCHERMERHORN, W.D., 234
SCHICK, E., 103, 243
SCHIKORA, R., 334, 336
SCHILLE, G., 116, 119
SCHILLING, W., 84
SCHINDELIN, F., 166, 167
SCHIRRMACHER, T., 167
SCHLATTER, A., 118
SCHLEIERMACHER, F.E.D., 15, 29, 69, 88, 99, 149, 162, 163
SCHLETTE, H.R., 92, 97, 143, 146
SCHLIER, H., 134, 135

SCHLÖSSER, F., 47
SCHLUNK, M., 6, 102, 129, 131, 165, 229, 234, 248, 271
SCHMAUCH, W., 21, 124, 126
SCHMAUS, M., 164
SCHMIDLIN, J., xiv, 3, 4, 5, 6, 9, 10, 11, 15, 53, 54, 61, 63, 65, 71, 72, 78, 79, 82, 84, 85, 92, 93, 98, 136, 137, 142, 166, 171, 175, 192, 200, 203, 204, 207, 208, 209, 222, 223, 224, 236, 237, 238, 239, 258, 272, 273, 274, 286, 333, 334, 343, 345, 346
SCHMIDT, G., 338
SCHMIDT, K.C.G., 219, 231, 236, 245, 247
SCHMIDT, M., 163, 164
SCHMIDT, O.H., 132, 133
SCHMIDT, W., 287, 290, 295
SCHMIDT, W.R., 166, 167
SCHMITT, J., 113, 114
SCHMITZ, J., 96
SCHMITZ, O., 129, 130
SCHNEEMELCHER, W., 116, 118
SCHNEIDER, J., 42, 45
SCHNITTKIND, D.A., 246, 248
SCHÖNFELDER, W., 256
SCHOLEY, C.H., 18
SCHOMERUS, H.W., xiv, 3, 4, 11, 16, 61, 72, 78, 98, 108, 117, 118, 120, 123, 136, 137, 194, 195, 207, 222, 252, 253, 255, 286, 346, 349, 356, 357
SCHORER, E., 280, 290
SCHORER, L., 275, 280
SCHRAM, P.L., 53, 55, 56
SCHREITER, R., 170
SCHRENK, G., 116, 118, 132, 133
SCHRUPP, E., xiii, 234
SCHÜTTE, J., 143, 145
SCHULTE, A., 47
SCHULZ-ANKERMANN, F., 152, 153
SCHUMANN, O., 256, 257
SCHUSTER, M., 290
SCHUTZ, R., 280
SCHUURMAN, B.M., 21, 53, 54, 340, 341
SCHWAGER, F.W., 84, 238, 279, 351
SCHWARTZ, H., 350
SCHWARZ, G., 167
SCHWARZKOPF, A.H.Th., 229, 232
SCHWEITZER, ALBERT, 121, 123, 229
SCHWEITZER, ALEXANDER, 17, 51
SCHWIND, M., 271

SCOTT, J.S., 270, 271
SCOTT, R.W., 35, 37
SCOTT, W., 163, 164
SEEBACH (HIMES), M.R., 307, 314
SELL, C.M., 152, 153
SELL, E., 326
SELLIN, E., 107, 108, 112
SENIOR, D., 99, 100, 105, 113
SEUFERT, W., 54
SEUMOIS, A.V., xv, 3, 4, 5, 6, 9, 10, 11, 16, 31, 52, 53, 54, 57, 58, 59, 61, 63, 65, 67, 68, 71, 72, 78, 91, 98, 99, 103, 128, 140, 142, 144, 145, 164, 172, 175, 178, 179, 180, 182, 193, 207, 219, 222, 226, 253, 258, 261, 274, 286, 333, 334, 345, 346, 358
SEVERIJN, J., 51, 52, 190, 202
SEYMOUR, W.J., 157
SHEDLOSKY, P., 337, 339
SHENK, W.R., 21, 109, 124, 126, 324, 325
SHIBLEY, D., 158, 159
SHILLITO, E., 116, 118
SHINN, R.L., 346, 351
SHIVUTE, T., 41, 42, 97, 152, 154
SHORTER, A., 95, 303
SIBBES, R., 167
SICARD, H. VON, 230, 235, 260, 266
SICKEL, G.A.F., 17, 69
SIDER, R.J., 35, 39
SIEFFERT, F., 114
SIEGHART, P., 310, 316
SIEPEN, K., 145
SILVA REGO, A. DA, 66
SIMMEL, G., 299
SIMON, G., 99, 102, 131
SIMPSON, A.B., 338
SIMPSON-HOUSLEY, P., 270, 271
SINGH, SADHU SUNDAR, 273, 275, 334, 335
SIRCAR, B.C., 18
SISSON, R., 39
SKI, M., 8, 83
SLATER, T.E., 73, 74, 302
SLESSOR, M., 192
SMALLEY, W.A., 211, 212, 215, 268, 269, 285, 286, 289, 290, 293, 294, 295, 296
SMART, W.A., 123
SMITH, B.E., 39
SMITH, E.W., 287, 291, 292, 295
SMITH, G., 88, 93, 227, 229, 233
SMITH, G.H., 292

SMITH, H., 233
SMITH, J., 40, 303
SMITH, K., 66
SMITH, L.E., 246, 247
SMITH, P.B., 327
SMITH, R., 33, 36
SMITH, R.P., 167
SMITH, S.E., 309
SMITH, T., 220, 224, 229, 242, 243, 244, 270
SMITH, W.C., 168, 169, 170
SNAITH, N.H., 112, 113
SNEAD, A.C., 265, 267, 268
SOMASEKHAR, R.M., 353
SOMBART, W., 299
SOMERVILLE, A.N., 30, 31, 35, 36
SONDERMANN, J.S., 244, 245, 268
SOPER, E.D., 73, 75, 91, 94, 103, 120, 123, 171
SPAETH, H.J., 263
SPANGENBERG, A.G., 221
SPECKER, J., 53, 55, 105, 106
SPEER, R.E., 43, 45, 80, 82, 177, 178, 194, 195, 232
SPIETH, J., 85, 165
SPINDLER, M.R., 20, 27, 56, 57, 63, 66, 105, 147, 150, 176, 177, 189, 190, 262, 301, 303
SPINOZA, B. DE, 256
SPITTA, F., 121, 122
SPITTLER, L.T., 230
SPITTLER, R.P., 159, 200
SPRINGER, K., 34, 40, 159
STÄHLIN, G., 123
STAERK, W., 108
STÄUDLIN, C.F., 261, 263, 274, 276
STAMOOLIS, J.J., 138, 139, 140, 172
STANGHETTI, G., 141, 144
STANLEY, H.M., 270
STAPLES, P., 271
STARBUCK, E.D., 333
STEFFES, J.P., 77, 85, 86, 196, 305
STEGEMANN, W., 124
STEGER, B.S., 241
STEIN, P.E., 132, 133
STEINMANN, A.A., 132, 133
STENDAHL, K., 131
STEPHENS, K., 39
STEVENSON, M., 292
STEWART, B., 309

STEWART, M., 39
STIER, R., 18, 19, 69
STIPE, C.E., 292, 293
STIRNIMANN, H., 142, 146
STOCK, E., 243
STOCK, K., 124
STOCKWELL, E.L., 152, 153, 324
STOEVESANDT, H., 121, 123
STOLL, D., 17, 18, 210, 211
STONE, J.S., 320, 321, 326
STORR, V.F., 102
STOSCH, J.E.G., 130, 232
STOTT, J.R.W., 39, 40, 62, 156, 199, 299, 303
STRACHAN, R.K., 33, 34, 37
STRANSKY, T.F., 42, 44, 46, 96, 140, 165, 166, 169, 309
STREHLOW, C.F.Th., 287
STREIT, K., 259, 262, 263, 264, 275, 279, 290
STREIT, R., xiii, 4, 5, 6, 9, 79, 82, 83, 92, 93, 100, 101, 171, 175, 221, 222, 225, 254, 262, 279
STRÖBEL, A., 113, 114
STRÜMPFEL, E., 5, 6, 221
STUDD, C.T., 338
STUDER, E., 290
STUHLMÜLLER, C., 99, 100, 105, 113
SUENENS, L.J., 56
SUGDEN, C., 40
SUMNER, W.G., 299
SUNDERMEIER, T., xiv, 86, 97, 165, 166
SUNDKLER, B.G.M., 107, 116, 118, 121, 123, 125, 235
SWAN, W., 73
SWEAZEY, G.E., 33, 37
SWIDLER, L.J., 170, 310
SWIGCHEM, D. VAN, 31, 132, 133
SWOBODA, H., 238
SYRDAL, R.A., 235, 245
SZABO, A., 233

TABER, C.R., 213
TAFT, W.H., 200
TAMPIER, A., 325, 326
TAN, K.-S., 32, 39, 152, 154, 155
TANABE, H., 77
TARGET, G.W., 34, 38
TAYLOR, C.W., 34, 38
TAYLOR, J.H., 165, 338

TAYLOR, M., 35, 38, 42
TAYLOR, R.B., 211
TAYLOR, V., 37
TAYLOR, W.M., 129, 131
TEINONEN, S.A., 166, 167
TEMPLE, W., 35, 36, 151
TEMPLETON, C.B., 37
TENNEKES, J., 294
TESTA, E., 105
THAUREN, J., 53, 54, 265, 346, 349, 350, 356
THAYER, C.C., 321, 324
THEISSEN, G., 117, 119, 299, 300
THIESSEN, J.C., 250
THOEN, C.M., 297, 300, 305, 358
THOMAS, C.L.H., 35, 37
THOMAS, D., 248
THOMAS, J., 55
THOMAS, M.M., 256
THOMAS, N.E., 5
THOMAS, W., 34, 35, 39
THOMAS AQUINAS, 163, 164
THOMAS A JESU, 59, 164, 192
THOMPSON, A.C., 243
THOMPSON, H.P., 346, 351
THOMPSON, P., 322
THOMPSON, R.W., 351
THOMPSON, W.J., 33
THOMSON, A.M., 245, 247
THOMSON, D.P., 38
THUNG, M.A., 299, 300, 301, 303
THURNWALD, R., 292, 298, 299, 302, 323, 324, 340, 341
TIDEMAN, J., 25, 69
TIEMERSMA, L., 232
TIFFANY, S.W., 293
TILLICH, P., 87, 92, 94, 189, 197, 198, 251, 252
TILSON, E., 95, 147, 150
TING, K.H., 135
TIPPETT, A.R., 63, 64, 67, 73, 76, 92, 96, 99, 104, 149, 156, 293, 304, 305
TIRIDATES, 228
TISDALL, W.St.C., 194, 195
TITIUS, A., 85, 129, 130
TODD, E.S., 232
TOTTIE, H.W., 29, 30
TOWNS, E.L., xv, 34, 40
TOYNBEE, A.J., 81, 83
TRAER, R., 308, 310

TRAGELLA, G.B., 2, 65, 144
TRICOT, A.E., 129, 131
TRIEBEL, J., 166, 167
TRILLHAAS, W., 76, 77
TROELTSCH, E., 168, 299, 304, 347
TROMPF, G.W., 176
TRUEBLOOD, E., 53, 55, 96, 189, 190, 191, 192, 258, 269
TUCKER, A.R., 327, 328
TUCKER, H.W., 229, 232
TUCKER, R.A., 230, 236, 249, 335, 337, 339
TUPPER, H.A., Jr, 7, 8, 179, 180, 276
TURNER, F.S., 68
TURNER, G., 287

ULFILAS, 207, 270
UKA, E.M., 303
ULRICH, H.H., 46
UNCITI, M. DE, 66
UNDERWOOD, A.C., 195, 342
UNDERWOOD, B.E., 44, 47, 116, 119
UNZALU, J. DE, 349, 350
URBAN, H., 334, 343
URQUHART, J., 72
USSING, H., 229, 234, 243
USTORF, W., 226, 291
UTTENDÖRFER, O., 322, 326

VACCARO DE PETRELLA, L.S., 159
VAHL, J., 190, 191, 242, 249, 250, 259, 263, 274, 281
VASCO DA GAMA, 228, 247, 252, 268, 276
VAULX, B. DE, 239
VEDDER, H.C., 233
VELARDE, B.L., xv
VELLANICKAL, M., 48, 99, 104, 119, 172
VENN, H., 208, 236, 238, 327
VERDONK, W.E., 315
VERKUYL, J., 16, 23, 30, 31, 51, 52, 53, 56, 60, 63, 66, 71, 72, 78, 79, 87, 150, 152, 169, 180, 277, 314, 315
VERSTEEG, J.P., 97, 99, 104, 213, 243
VERSTRAELEN, F.J., 66, 67, 181
VERWER, G., 37
VIAN, C., 239
VICEDOM, G.F., 21, 22, 56, 57, 62, 92, 93, 95, 149, 193, 326, 350
VIEIRA, H., 220, 239
VIERING, E., 250
VISCHER, L., 148, 150

380

VISSER 'T HOOFT, W.A., 153, 168, 169
VOETIUS, G., 88, 98, 163, 165
VOLKMANN, J.W., 219, 231
VOLZ, P., 112, 113
VORMBAUM, R., 245, 247
VORWERK, D., 334, 336, 346, 350, 358
VOULGARAKIS, E., 139, 140
VRIENS, L., xv, 4, 5, 6, 10, 11, 83, 86,
  99, 103, 145, 172, 175, 209, 211, 222,
  291, 293, 306
VRIEZEN, Th.C., 107, 108, 112
VRIJHOF, P.H., 299, 301, 303

WAARD, J. DE, 216
WAARDENBURG, J., 176, 177, 189, 190, 194,
  195, 196, 199, 203, 210, 211, 287, 297,
  304, 305, 343
WACH, J., 189
WADDY, P.S., 325, 326
WAGNER, C.P., xv, 9, 12, 21, 22, 23, 33,
  34, 35, 40, 41, 43, 52, 56, 63, 64, 67,
  76, 157, 304, 305, 342, 343
WAGNER, F., 95
WAGNER, H., 23
WALD, S.N., 214, 215
WALDENFELS, H., 193, 196
WALKATE, J.A., 311, 315
WALKER, A., 33, 39
WALKER, T., 128
WALLIS, E.E., 211
WALLMANN, J.C., 241
WALLROTH, E., 210, 260
WALLS, A., 67
WALROND, F.F., 232
WALSH, J., 47
WALSH, J.E., 180
WALSH, W.P., 229, 246, 248
WALTER, G., 163
WANG, T., 22
WANKO, P., 142, 146
WANSINK, J.M., 224, 234
WARD, M., 2, 94
WARMAN, F.S.G., 112
WARNECK, G., xv, 3, 4, 9, 11, 13, 15, 17,
  18, 19, 26, 29, 30, 43, 45, 60, 61, 67,
  70, 71, 72, 78, 79, 82, 87, 88, 89, 93,
  101, 108, 116, 117, 120, 121, 122, 125,
  129, 130, 133, 137, 166, 167, 168, 171,
  185, 207, 208, 209, 212, 221, 223, 226,
  229, 236, 238, 240, 242, 259, 269, 274,
  281, 286, 320, 334, 346, 350, 354, 355,
  358
WARNECK, J., 130, 166, 243
WARREN, M.A.C., 117, 119, 132, 133, 166,
  167, 219, 234, 235, 268, 269
WASHINGTON, B.T., 192
WATSON, C.R., 101
WATSON, D.C.K., 35, 39
WATSON, D.L., 34, 35, 40
WAYLAND, F., 190, 191
WEAD, D.W., 73, 75, 117, 119, 171
WEBBER, R., 155
WEBER, H.E., 129, 131, 132, 133
WEBER, H.-R., 126
WEBER, M., 304
WEBER, N., 75
WEBSTER, D., 38, 103, 104, 166, 167
WEDEL, Th.O., 19, 20, 37
WEINEL, H., 116, 117, 191
WEINGARTNER, E., 310
WEISMANN, G., 101, 108
WEISS, G.C., 69
WEIST, H., 165
WEITBRECHT, H.U., 4, 6
WERNER, O., 259, 262, 264, 279
WERNLE, P., 129, 130
WESLEY, J., 163, 164, 258
WESSELS, A., 135, 181, 182
WESTERMANN, D., 292, 298, 302, 324, 340,
  341
WESTMANN, K.B., 230, 235, 260, 266
WHALING, F., 188, 190, 194, 195, 202
WHITE, E., 67, 68, 70
WHITE, E.E., 233
WHITE, H.V., 75, 88, 91, 93, 94, 171
WHITE, J., 194, 195
WHITEMAN, D.L., 73, 75, 171, 292, 293, 294
WHITLEY, W.T., 45, 250
WIEBE, F., 94
WIEDENMANN, L., 147, 150, 164
WIEGERAAD, B.J., 46
WIERSINGA, H.A., 103, 108, 116, 119, 224,
  235
WIESER, T., 52, 55, 62
WIESKE, G., 47
WIGGERS, J., 220, 240, 274, 276
WIJK, P. VAN, Jr, 249
WIJSSEN, F., 47
WILCKENS, U., 127, 128
WILD, K., 249

WILDER, R.P., 105, 106
WILLAIME, J.P., 301, 303
WILLEKE, B.H., 97, 193
WILLIAM OF RUBRUCK, 259, 260
WILLIAMS, D.E., 338, 339
WILLIAMS, J., 287
WILLIAMS, S.W., 214, 215
WILS, J., xiv, xv, 12, 209, 210, 211
WILSON, B.R., 304, 305
WILSON, S.G., 125, 126
WIMBER, J., 34, 35, 40, 159
WIND, A., 152, 154
WINN, A.C., 125, 126
WINSEN, G.A.C. VAN, 62, 86, 140, 164
WINSLOW, M., 230
WINSTEDT, E.O., 259, 260
WINTHUIS, J., 290, 340, 356
WISER, W.H., 35, 37, 324
WITTMANN, P., 237
WOLFENSBERGER, G.H., 106, 115, 116
WOLFF, L., 203, 276, 279, 288, 289
WOLFINGER, F., 315
WOOD, J.A., 351
WOODSON, L.H., 35, 38
WOOLSEY, R.H., 38
WREDE, W., 123
WRIGHT, C.J., 123
WRIGHT, G.E., 107, 109, 112, 115, 116
WRIGHT, L.B., 322

WÜLLNER, W.H., 17, 18
WÜRZ, F., 116, 118
WUNDT, W., 333
WYK, A.J. VAN, 54
WYLD, J., 259, 266

XAVIER, F., 13, 165, 238, 270

YAMAMORI, T., 301, 303, 325, 327, 340
YANNOULATOS, A., 138, 139, 140
YOUNG, R., 224, 232

ZAHN, F.M., 106, 117, 166, 167, 212, 249, 268, 320, 325, 326
ZAHN, Th., 99, 116, 117
ZAMESA, J., 142, 144
ZANGGER, C.D., 74, 75
ZANOTTO, A., 145
ZEEGERS, G., 297, 300, 305, 358
ZELLER, D., 129, 132, 133
ZEZSCHWITZ, C.A.G. VON, 18, 19, 51
ZIEGENBALG, B., 165, 347
ZINZENDORF, N.L. VON, 147, 163, 164, 334, 335
ZÖCKLER, O., 29, 30, 81, 210, 260, 286, 287
ZSCHOKKE, H., 231
ZWEMER, S.M., 32, 33, 35, 36, 37, 102, 190, 259, 263, 269, 277
ZYCHLINSKI, P. VON, 99, 100, 101

2. Index of subjects

Abbreviations:
      evm = evangelism
      evn = evangelization
      hi. = history
      m. = mission
      mgy = missiology
      mry = missionary
      ph. = philosophy
      r. = religion
      rs = religious
      sc. = science
      th. = theology

Absolutism, 189
Acceptance (see also Reception), 188, 210, 255, 342

- of Christ (full/partial) (hi.of), 251, 255, 256, 257
Accommodation, 215
Accumulation, 176
Activity/ies, 1, 43, 44, 48, 60, 61, 73, 76, 90, 107, 121, 136, 138, 142, 159, 179, 187, 199, 205, 211, 251, 268, 269, 298, 299, 313, 318, 322, 329, 331, 339
Action, social, 35
ACTS OF THE APOSTLES, 22, 27, 100, 127, 181, 269
AD GENTES, 60, 142
Adaptation, 177
Adding (th. of), 24, 27
Adjustment, 338, 344
Adoration, 68

Advance (see also Progress), 22, 227
Aesthetics, 74, 186, 199, 201, 202
AFFIRMATION, ECUMENICAL, 32, 152, 329
Affluence, 320, 322, _329-330_, 333
AGAPE (see Evm)
Agency/ies, 60, 280, 323, 348, 356
- M(ry)/of m., 3, 7, 16, 24, 89, 276, 280,
  283, 333, 335, 337, 338
- Para-church, 147, 284
Age of mission(s), 61
Ages, middle, 25, 50, 74, 136, 160, 208,
  226, 246, 270, 319
Agnosticism, 41
Agrics, 16
Agriculture, 271
Altar, 228
Amnesty International, 2
Animals, 271, 285
Anthropocentric, 93
Anthropology (hi. of), 86, 93, 204, 284,
  285, 286, 291, 292, 295, 296
- Applied, 286, 291, 294, 295, 358
- Christian, 296
- Cultural, 81, 205, 206, _284-297_
- Missiological, 286, 294, 295, 358
- Mry, _284-297_, 305, 358
- Philosophical, 286
- Physical, 284, 285
- Social, 285, 286
- Theological, 286
Anti-Semitism, 138
Apologetics, 173
- Mry/of m., 173, 349
Apostacy, 319
APOSTELLEIN/APOSTOLE/APOSTOLOS, 32, _50_, 57,
  58, _120_
Apostle(s), 18, 28, 50, 99, 106, 115, 120,
  129, 181, 208, 246, 269
Apostolate (see also Morality), 21, 25, 50,
  51, _52-54_, 56, 57, 58, 120, 254
- Apostolate of the church, 51, 53, 148
- Apostolate of morality, 201
- Direct/indirect, 53
- Heathen, 53,
- Hi. of the apostolate, 219
- Hierarchical/lay, 53
- Last, 53
- Mry, 52, 53
- Th. of the apostolate, 50, 52, _56_, 58,
  70, 120

- Universal/world apostolate, 53, 56
Apostolics, 50, _51_, 57, 58, 62, 69, 120
Apostolo(lo)gy, 50, _52_, 57, 58, 63, 64, 65,
  69, 70, 120
Appearance (see also Phenomenology), _191_,
  127
Approach(es), 1, 34, 93, 101, 179, 183,
  187, 189, 194, 223, 288, 289, 297, 299,
  302, 305, 336, 355
Archeology, 1, 285
Articles of faith (see Faith)
Articles, twelve, 357
Art(s), 2, 216, 217
Ascetics (mry), 173
Assembly/ees (WCC), 136, 149, 311, 348
- Amsterdam (1948), 41, 313
- Evanston (1954), 33, 41
- New Delhi (1961), 138, 139, 149, 151,
  152, 154, 228, 313
- Uppsala (1968), 177
- Nairobi (1975), 313
Assessment, 338, 344
Association(s), 244, 310, _312_
Atlas(es), 179, 262, 263, 264, 266
- Church, 262, _264-266_
- Mry, 259, 261, _262-266_, 272
Augustinians, 244
Authority (see also Bible, Church, Jesus),
  151, 162, 314, 317
Auxanics, 16, _22-23_, 24, 27, 70
Awakening (rs) (see also Revival), 342,
  344, 347
Axiology (see also Value), 74, 173, 199,
  200
- Axiology of m. (hi. of), 173, _199-201_
- Axiology of r., 173
- Normative, 199

Baptism(s), 18, 122, 147, 214, 276
- Adults/children, 283
- Baptism with Spirit, 158
Base/basis of mission, 3, 12, 60, 64, 89,
  99
Beauty (see also Value, aesthetic), 199,
  201
Belief, 29, 44, 310, 311, 312, 319
- Rs, 2, 307, 313
Believers, secret (see also Christians-
  Crypto), 273, 283
Bible/biblical (see also Faith, Foundation,

Hermeneutics, Interpretation, Language, Mgy, M., M. studies, Personalism, Realism, SCRIPTURA, Scripture, Th., Th. of m., Translation, Witness), 2, 29, 42, 64, 92, 93, 99, 100, 101, 105, 106, 115, 134, 136, 159, 161, 170, 174, 178, 187, 207, 212, 214, 215, 217, 219, 273, 321, 328, 338
- Authority, 161, 200
- Bible in m., 105-106
- Division of Bible, 106-107
- M. in Bible, 99-101
Biblicism, 91, 107, 162
Bibliography/ies, 4-5, 7, 8, 9, 10, 12, 13, 100, 204, 220, 229, 240, 320
Biography/ies, 190, 191, 221, 225, 245-247, 257, 342
Biology, 285
Blessing(s), 114, 188, 354
Boards, mission, 73, 151, 240, 321, 322, 327, 336, 337, 339, 344
Branch(es), 3, 29, 42, 72, 74, 76, 81, 169, 174, 175, 176, 179, 183, 185, 189, 202, 204, 205, 207, 219, 257, 259, 261, 270, 271, 275, 285, 296, 304, 344, 349, 356, 358, 359
- Branches of mgy, 3, 12, 71, 76, 77, 182, 185-359
- Branches of sc. of m., 174, 202, 204-206, 357, 358, 359
Buddhism/buddhist (see also M., Worldview), 106, 187, 194, 283, 289, 314
Buildings
- Church, 350, 353
- School, 354
Burials, 271
Business, 27, 323

Call/calling, 2, 24, 100, 110, 111, 112, 129, 162, 179, 317, 323, 338
Candidate(s), 28, 338, 344
Capitalism/capitalist, 300, 320, 330
Care, missionary (see also Poimenics), 334, 335-336, 37, 338, 344, 346, 349
Cartography, 261, 264, 265
- Church, 264
- Mry/of m., 204, 261-266, 272, 358
Catalogues, 179
Catechesis/catechumenate, 18, 44, 350, 351, 352, 357

Catechetics, 15, 173
- Mry/of m., 173, 346, 349
Centrifugal/centripetal, 107, 108, 117, 171
Challenge(s), 12, 105, 188, 289, 329, 347
Charismatic (see Renewal, Th. of m.),
Charity/ies, 276, 323
Christ (see also Acceptance, Christlikeness, Christology, GESTA, Hi. of m., Jesus, M., Mgy, MISSIO, Paradigm, Reception, Uniqueness), 19, 21, 24, 32, 33, 34, 43, 44, 50, 58, 61, 73, 90, 91, 93, 100, 106, 115, 120, 125, 127, 135, 139, 143, 144, 148, 157, 158, 161, 169, 182, 198, 214, 226, 245, 246, 251, 255, 256, 257, 272, 273, 289, 296, 301, 302, 320, 334, 345, 348, 352
- Christ's kingdom, 224, 225, 255
- Christophany, 129
- Christ outside the gate(s), 256, 273
- Unbound, 256
Christendom, 298
Christian(s), 2, 20, 23, 32, 33, 58, 60, 70, 71, 73, 99, 105, 115, 132, 144, 149, 156, 161, 169, 194, 206, 254, 173, 278, 288, 314, 319, 323, 332, 340, 348, 352, 353, 355
- 'Civilized', 347
- Crypto (see also Believers), 273
- Hebrew/Jewish (see also Jew), 138, 228
- Heroic, 100
- Indigenous, 268, 276
- Local, 353
- Mry, 245
- Non-Jewish, 136
- Non-western, 32, 228, 244, 257
- Reborn, 273
- Western, 32, 228, 229, 347
Christianity (see also Expansion, Propagation), 12, 19, 29, 44, 81, 91, 135, 138, 168, 187, 189, 191, 194, 196, 199, 206, 219, 224, 225, 251, 253, 255, 258, 270, 272, 273, 278, 282, 283, 284, 289, 300, 304, 314, 342, 353
- Future, 2, 224, 283
- Mry, 266, 272
- Western, 289
- World, 7, 266, 272, 278, 284
Christianization, 21, 53, 210, 212, 288, 347
Christlikeness, 345

Christology, 122, 181
- Bullock-cart/helicopter, 180, 181
- From above/from below, 180
Chronology/ies, 205, 225, 226-229, 257
Church(es) (see also Apostolate, Atlas,
    Buildings, Cartography, Church Growth,
    Economics, Epochs, Evm, Expansion, EXTRA
    ECCLESIAM, Hi., M., Map, Mgy, MISSIO,
    Orthodox, Para-church, People,
    Protestant, PROVINCIAE, Roman Catholic,
    Statistics, Witness), 1, 2, 17, 23, 33,
    51, 53, 58, 60, 61, 68, 73, 93, 99, 105,
    107, 112, 116, 117, 120, 134, 136, 138,
    139, 142, 143, 144, 148, 149, 151, 152,
    156. 159, 161, 170, 174, 179, 200, 206,
    208, 210, 220, 224, 225, 236, 240, 251,
    252, 254, 255, 256, 266, 269, 272, 278,
    282, 283, 284, 288, 289, 295, 296, 300,
    301, 302, 305, 309, 310, 312-314, 317,
    322, 323, 324, 325, 327, 329, 331, 332,
    333, 340, 347, 348, 349, 350, 352, 353,
    354, 355, 356, 357
- Authority, 178, 300
- Church's m./m. of church, 19, 32, 100,
    139, 148, 155, 299, 301, 308, 312
- Church work, 24
- Early, 23, 28, 52, 106, 115, 117, 125,
    128, 134, 136, 158, 208, 247, 276
- Established/free, 158, 283
- 'Ethnic', 288, 289
- Growing (see also Church Growth), 22, 305
- Implantation (PLANTATIO ECCLESIAE)
    /planting (hi. of), 53, 142, 143, 254,
    255, 357
- Independent, 268, 321
- Indigenous, 353, 355
- Latent/manifest, 301
- Local, 34, 313, 325
- Membership, 34, 282, 283
- Mry (nature/function), 29, 135, 143, 300
- Mission, 273
- Mission-centric, 56
- Multiplying, 273
- National/native, 276, 327, 348, 355
- Order, 51, 53, 148
- Overseas, 328
- Poor/rich, 328
- Self-supporting, 327-328
- 'Sending'/'receiving', 268, 328
- 'Third World', 272, 337

- Western, 289, 296, 328
- Universal, 347
- Younger, 321
Church growth (th. of) (see also School),
    22, 27, 127, 301, 305, 357
- Church Growth Movement, 21, 22, 24, 35,
    254, 173, 301
Circumcision, 122, 127, 136
Civilization(s), 115, 246, 247, 251, 257,
    297, 298, 301, 347
Claim(s), 186, 187, 188, 298
Classification, 176, 187
Climatology, 63
Colleagues, missionary, 129
Colonial(ism)/colonialistics   (see   also
    Decolonization, Post-colonialism), 69, 90,
    204, 216, 224, 226, 228, 229, 276, 316,
    318, 319, 329, 331, 339, 340
Commandment(s), 148
- Great, 135, 345
- Ten (see also Decalogue), 352, 257
Commerce (see also M.), 2, 320, 323, 325
(Com)mission, 50, 120, 134, 196
Commission, Great, 20, 21, 53, 124, 253,
    255, 257, 285, 296
Communication(s), 19, 30, 41, 64, 86, 196,
    210, 215, 295, 296, 337, 338
Communion, holy (see also Eucharist), 276
Communism (hi. of) (see also M.,
    Propaganda), 257, 300, 330
Community/ies (see also Psychology), 2, 19,
    24, 27, 60, 114, 130, 134, 139, 144, 160,
    170, 181, 188, 206, 215, 256, 257, 259,
    276, 280, 282, 284, 289, 309, 310, 311,
    329, 337, 340, 352, 355
Comparison (see also Hi., Phenomenology,
    Philology, Th.), 192-195, 208, 259
- External/internal, 191
Complex (see Guilt, Superiority),
Concept(s) (of mgy, evm, m. studies, mry),
    3, 19, 35, 64, 67, 76, 122, 125, 127,
    138, 171, 172, 185, 202, 203, 207, 266,
    272, 287, 292, 299, 300, 347, 357, 359
Conference(s) (hi. of mry), 28, 32, 80,
    138, 139, 143, 151, 152, 153, 155, 171,
    20, 225, 226, 228, 244, 257, 265, 274,
    313, 325, 329, 331, 335, 340, 348, 355,
    356
- Edinburgh (1910), 29, 80, 147, 151, 200,
    226, 228, 259, 321, 325, 348

- Jerusalem (1928), 32, 151, 321, 331, 335, 348
- Tambaram (1938), 22, 32, 56, 151, 313, 321, 335, 339, 341, 348
- Whitby (1947), 33, 56, 151
- Willingen (1952), 60, 61, 151
- Achimota/Ghana (1957/58), 151, 348
- Mexico City (1963), 60, 151, 266
- Bangkok (1973), 151
- Melbourne (1980), 151
- San Antonio (1989), 151, 153, 226, 331
Confession, 148
Confucian(ism), 106, 187, 283, 314
CONGREGATIO
- SACRA CONGREGATIO PRO GENTIUM EVANGELIZATIONE (sacred congregation for the evangelization of the peoples), 25, 43, 143
- SACRA CONGREGATIO DE PROPAGANDA FIDE (sacred congregation for the propagation of the faith) (hi. of), 25, 43, 59, 136, 141, 178, 228, 236, 264, 274, 275
Congregation(s), 21, 23, 53, 68, 127, 147, 276, 299, 301, 332
Congress(es), 155, 156, 157, 158, 312, 314
- Wheaton (1966), 155
- Berlin (1966), 155, 156
- Lausanne (1974) (see also Lausanne), 155, 156
- Manila (Lausanne II) (1989) (see also Manila Manifesto), 153, 155, 158, 226
Connivance, 342
Conscience, 90, 308, 310, 311, 316
Consciousness, 107, 116, 189
Conservatism, 90
Consultation(s), 138, 155, 350
- Lausanne (1991), 138
- Neapolis (1988), 139
- Pattaya (1980), 155
Context(s) (see also Education, Evn, Mgy, Th., Th. of m.), 11, 27, 34, 63, 93, 99, 117, 142, 152, 163, 177, 185, 198, 214, 271, 283, 300, 301, 308, 329, 331, 341
Contextualization/contextualizing, 89, 90, 139, 217, 352, 355
Continents, six (see M., People)
Conversion(s) (see also Hi., Psychology, Reconversion), 32, 152, 155, 160, 228, 255, 256, 257, 311, 327, 341, 342, 344, 353, 357

- Conversion of the heathen(s) (hi. of), 219, 225, 255
- Conversion stories, 342
- CONVERSIO GENTIUM, 254, 255
- Mass conversions, 342
Converts, 81, 129, 256, 317, 321
Conviction(s), 57, 149, 152, 177, 266, 273, 323, 336
- Mry/about m., 73, 273
- Rs, 273
- Universalistic, 121
Cooperation (see also Method), 259, 292, 306, 342
CORAM DEO, 2
CORPUS CHRISTIANUM, 163, 228, 254
Costs, missionary (see Finance)
Council(s), 136, 141, 142, 143, 151, 152, 155, 178
- Council of Jerusalem, 136
- Council of Nicea, 136
- Second Vatican Council, 5, 43, 92, 141, 142, 228, 236, 237, 307, 313
Counter-attack, 342
Country/ies, 13, 21, 58, 220, 247, 261, 262, 265, 268, 269, 282
- Foreign, 60, 348
- Islamic, 58
- Mission (TERRAE MISSIONIS), 59
- 'Receiving'/'Sending', 269
- Rich, 332
- Western, 90
- Whole, 21
Covenant(s) (see also Lausanne), 30, 114, 124, 308, 309, 311, 318, 319, 332
Creation, 2, 18, 113, 139, 149, 179, 247, 348
- Integrity of creation, 348
Cremation, 271
Criminology, 205
Cross (see also Red Cross), 115, 135, 224, 245, 246
Crusader/crusades (see also Evm), 246, 319
Cultivation, missionary, 347
Culture(s) (see also Anthropology, Evn, Inculturation, Mandate, Ph., Stress), 64, 139, 148, 155, 192, 219, 285, 291, 295, 296, 297
- Culture-centered, 92, 93
- Cultures of the book/non-oral/oral, 106, 207

- Indigenous, 215
- Local, 139
- New, 338
- Non-western, 64, 215, 217, 251, 295
- Oriental, 1
- Sc., 285
- Subculture, 219
- Traditional, 214
- Western, 64, 251, 289, 347
- World, 298
CWME, 32, 61, 90, 138, 139, 144, 151, 152, 158, 324, 350
Cybernetics, (mry), 173, 179

DAWN (see also Discipling), 21
Decalogue (see also Commandment), 115
Declaration(s), 142, 143, 307, 308, 309, 311, 313, 314, 318, 319
- Frankfurt, 155
- Universal (1948), 307, 308, 310, 313, 318, 319
Decolonization, 229, 272
Deduction, 79, 177, 178
Dehumanization, 333
Democracy, 301
Denomination(s)/denominational(ism) (see also Hi., Interdenominationalism), 89, 91, 92; 93; 147, 149, 220, 224, 225, 229, 262, 281, 301, 325
Development (see also Education), 12, 112, 120, 122, 127, 147, 202, 226, 259, 265, 268, 273, 278, 282, 283, 300, 304, 322, 324, 329, 337, 348
Devolution, 355
Devotion (see Piety)
DIAKONIA, 19
Diakonics, (mry), 173
Dialogue (see also Mgy, Psychology), 53, 76, 90, 93, 138, 143, 153, 168, 174, 309, 343
- Dialogue-centrism, 93
- GUIDELINES, 152
- Intercultural, 196
- Interreligious, 143, 309, 343, 344
- Theological, 196
Dictionary/ies, 1, 4, 5, 7-8, 9, 10, 208, 218
DIDACHE, 19
Discipleship, 21, 117, 124, 323
Discipling (the nations) (th. of), 21, 24,

27, 257
Discrimination, 311, 312, 319, 340
Divisions, 59
Doctrine (see also Norm, Statement), 15, 17, 59, 91, 142, 157, 158, 177
- Doctrine of m., 15, 70, 88
Document(s), 136, 139, 141, 142, 143, 144, 152, 155
- Church/ecclesiastical, 136, 143, 147
- Mry, 117
Dogma, 298
Dogmatics, (mry), 173
Dominicans, 160, 244
Doxology, 139

Eastern Orthodoxy (see Orthodoxy)
Ecclesiasticism, 162
Ecclesiology, (mry), 23, 140, 169, 302
Economics/economy, 173, 205, 206, 320, 321, 323, 324, 331, 333
- Economic basis of the church, 321
- Econonomic problems, 300
- Economics/y of m./m(ry) (hi. of), 81, 173, 176, 320-333, 358
- Economy of r., 173
- Global/world/local economy, 320, 323, 324, 331-332
Ecumenical(s)/Ecumenists (see also Mgy, M., Th. of m.), 153, 161, 177, 254, 273, 284, 301, 324
- Ecumenical Movement, 11, 32, 90, 92, 149, 158, 178, 217, 236, 266, 273, 301
Education (hi. of) (see also M., Method, Pedagogics, Value), 2, 28, 81, 206, 247, 288, 345, 346, 347, 348, 349, 352, 353, 355, 357
- Adult/child, 345, 356
- Christian, 345, 348, 349, 350, 353, 354, 355, 356
- Contextual, 348
- Development, 348
- Formal 355, 356
- General 350/351
- Global, 347
- Higher, 347
- Mry, 345, 346, 347, 348, 350-351, 354, 357
- People's, 347, 350, 351, 354-355, 357
- Pre-school, 356
- Rs, 282, 313, 345, 348, 350

- School, 347, 354
- Theological Education by Extension, 348
- Theological Education Fund, 348
Emancipation, 168, 170, 228, 247
Empiricism (see also Methodology, Method,
  M. studies, Mgy, Sc.), 81, 176, 187, 203,
  210
Encounter, 117, 217, 299, 340-342, 344
Encyclical (see Letters)
Encyclopedia(s), 1, 3, 4, 7-8, 10, 12, 13,
  15, 29, 87, 88, 179, 185, 221, 273, 359
Endeavour(s), mission(ary), 33, 73, 86,
  329, 336
Enlightenment, 74, 162, 193, 203, 228, 347,
  352
Enterprise (see also Sociology), 3, 60,
  181, 272, 349
- Mry (hi. of), 25, 28, 81, 89, 120, 220,
  225, 246, 252, 254, 299, 300, 304, 321,
  325, 344
Episcopalism, 51
Epistemology, 74, 173, 186, 187, 188, 202
- Epistemological break, 188
- Epistemology of m. (hi. of), 74, 173,
  186-188, 202
- Epistemology of r., 173
- New epistemology, 188
- Traditional western epistomology, 188
Epistles (NT), 132-133, 135, 181
Epochs
- Epochs of church hi., 226
- Epochs of m(ry) hi., 226
- Epochs of world hi., 226
Eschatology, 92, 93, 117, 140
Essence(s) (see also Ontology), 87, 124,
  186, 189, 197, 198, 206
Esthetics (see Aesthetics)
Ethic(s) (see also Morality, Th. of m.),
  74, 91, 173, 186, 199, 201, 202, 202,
  204, 357
- Ethic of the sending, 201
ETHNE/ETHNOS (see Gentiles)
Ethnicity/ies, 288, 296
Ethnic group(s) (see also Mgy), 81, 288,
  289
Ethnicism, 288
Ethnocentrism, 285, 289
Ethnography, 2, 204, 285, 288, 297
Ethnology, 81, 173, 203, 205, 206, 284,
  285, 286, 287, 288, 296, 356

- Ethnology of mry lands, 288
- Ethnology of m./m(ry) (hi. of), 173, 176,
  284-297, 358
- Ethnology of r., 173, 289, 297
- Gospel, 288
Ethnomissiology, 358
Ethnopsychology, 334
Ethnotheology/ies, 217, 285, 289
EUANGELION/EUANGELISTES/EUANGELIZEIN,
  27-28, 49, 57
EUANGELIZESTHAI, 32, 49
Eucharist (see also Communion), 214
Eudaemonism, 91
Evangel (see also Thought, Value), 44, 48,
  321
Evangelical(s) (see also Mgy, Th. of m.),
  153, 155, 156, 161, 177, 273, 284, 301
- Evangelical Movement(s), 92, 149, 154,
  157, 158, 178
EVANGELII NUNTIANDI, 43, 143
Evangelism (see also Method, Principles,
  Least evangelized), 19, 21, 30, 31-35,
  41, 42, 43, 44, 49, 53, 57, 58, 60, 105,
  117, 155, 158, 161, 179, 254, 255, 302,
  327, 329, 335, 347, 348
- Agape evm, 34
- Church evm, 34
- Contagious evm, 34
- Cross-cultural evm, 34
- Crusade evm, 34
- Dynamics of evm, 35
- Effective evm, 33
- Engagement evm, 34
- Evm explosion, 35
- Evm-in-depth, 33, 34
- Expectant evm, 33
- Goals of evm, 35
- Hi. of evm, 219
- Incarnational evm, 34
- Itinerant evm, 33
- Jewish evm, 138
- Lifestyle evm, 34
- Mass evm, 34
- New evm, 33
- Personal evm, 33, 34
- Persuasion evm, 35
- Power evm, 34, 35
- Presence evm, 34
- Proclamation evm, 34
- Prophetic evm, 34

- Public evm, 34
- Saturation evm, 34
- Secular evm, 34
- Service evm, 34
- Th. of evm, 31, 41-42, 48, 49, 58, 70, 99, 172
- World evm, 32, 44, 280
Evangelist(s), 28, 34, 51, 99, 106, 158, 208, 224, 246, 318, 328
Evangelistic theology (see Th.)
Evangelistics, 28-30, 33, 41, 49, 51, 62, 70
Evangelistology, 28, 31, 70
Evangelization (see also CONGREGATIO, Lausanne, Least evangelized), 29, 31, 42-45, 49, 61, 107, 143
- Contextual evn, 44
- Co-responsible evn, 44
- Direct/indirect evn, 44, 54
- Evn of the world in this generation, 42, 43
- Inculturated evn, 44
- Integral evn, 44
- New evn, 44
- Ongoing evn, 44
- Preevn, 44
- Th. of evn, 28, 31, 48, 49, 70, 99, 172
- World evn, 44, 155, 158
Evolutionism/evolutionary/evolutionist,74, 107, 121, 291
Exclusivism, 169
Exegesis, 101, 108
Existentialism, 216
Exodus (see Paradigm)
Exorcisms, 157
Expansion (hi. of), 223, 228, 272, 304, 347
- Expansion of Christ's kingdom, 219, 220
- Expansion of the Christian Faith, 272
- Expansion of Christianity, 2, 219, 227, 258, 259
- Expansion of the church, 254
- (Global) expansion of the Christian m., 206
Experience(s), 86, 170, 176, 189, 200, 270
- Christian, 32
- Cross-cultural, 337
- Human, 162, 182
- Mry, 71, 76, 165
- Overseas, 167
- Rs, 76, 270, 334, 341

EXTRA ECCLESIAM NULLA SALUS EST, 236

Faith(s) (see also Communication, CONGREGATIO, Expansion, PROPAGATIO), 12, 21, 25, 28, 52, 58, 61, 116, 139, 149, 158, 161, 187, 188, 192, 196, 200, 216, 304, 308, 311, 317, 335
- Articles of faith (see also Articles), 352
- Biblical, 251
- Catholic, 160
- Change of faith, 311
- Christian, 25, 64, 139, 161, 174, 196, 215, 217, 255, 289, 298, 341, 353, 357
- Faith missions, 162
- Israel's, 113
- People of Living Faiths, 90, 152
- Saving, 41
Fascism, 330
Field(s), mission (see also Method), 16, 28, 59, 134, 165, 166, 196, 208, 209, 262, 264, 265, 266, 268, 269, 271, 272, 273, 321, 325, 327, 331, 338, 347, 353, 355
Finance(s) of mission/missionary (see also Fund, Money, Support), 205, 276, 320, 322, 325, 329, 332, 333, 354
Fishers of men, 17, 125
Fishing (th. of), 17, 27
Focus of attention (-centeredness), 89, 92, 93
Follow-up, 34
Forgiveness, 125
Foundation(s) of mission (biblical), 2, 99, 116, 121
Franciscans, 159, 160, 244
FRANKFURT DECLARATION (see Declaration)
Freedom, 44, 76, 307, 309, 310, 311, 313, 316
- Freedom of r./rs (th. of), 307, 308, 310, 311, 312, 313, 316
- Mry/of m., 307, 308, 309, 310-314, 316, 318, 319
Free-thought (see M., Propaganda)
Fullness, 158
Fund(s) (see also Education, Finance), 74, 191, 259, 268, 273, 323, 325, 327, 331
- International Monetary Fund, 331
Fundamentalism/fundamentalist, 91, 210

Gentiles (ETHNE, GOIIM; see also Heathen, Lands, M., Pagan), 18, 27, 50, 91, 106, 107, 114, 120, 121, 122, 127, 129, 134, 148, 228, 285, 288, 289, 296
Geographics/geography, 1, 173, 203, 204, 205, 206, 259, 260, 261, 265, 269, 270, 271
- Church, 284
- Geography of Christianity, 206, 272
- Geography of m./m(ry) (hi. of), 7, 13, 81, 173, 176, 204, 205, 206, 258-272, 274, 284, 286, 305, 357
- Geography of r./r(s), 173, 261, 270-271
- Human/political/social, 261, 270, 271
- Physical, 261, 271
- Sc. of geography, 260
Geology, 1
GESTA CHRISTI PER ORBEM, 255
Ghettoism, 174
Giving
- Mry, 325
- Mutual, 328
Glad Tidings (see also EUANGELION, Gospel, Good news), 31
Glossaries, 4, 9
Glossolalia, 157
Gnosticism, 187
Goal(s), (mry/of m.) (see also Evm), 21, 32, 41, 49, 149, 169, 210, 219, 254, 299, 302, 337, 339
God (see also MAGNALIA DEI, Mgy, People), 18, 22, 24, 28, 33, 41, 51, 68, 73, 100, 107, 110, 111, 112, 113, 114, 120, 122, 128, 133, 134, 148, 161, 169, 182, 186, 187, 188, 197, 198, 200, 201, 206, 211, 212, 214, 216, 219, 224, 245, 268, 280, 287, 309, 320, 321, 329, 331, 333
- Existence of God, 76
- Glory of God, 64
- God-centered, 93
- God's free good pleasure, 24
- God's image (IMAGO DEI), 198
- God's kingdom, 43, 120, 139, 149, 151, 152, 225, 255, 273, 298
- God's mission (MISSIO DEI), 25, 60, 61, 70, 99, 149, 151, 152, 188, 192, 196, 198
- God's name(s), 198, 214
- God's reign, 121
- God's will, 139, 151, 177
- God's (mry) work (see also MAGNALIA DEI), 24, 41, 70, 179
- God the Creator, 149
- 'Jealous God', 81
- Mry God, 188, 200
- Nature of God, 200
- Triune God, 60
GOIIM (see Gentiles)
Good news (see also EUANGELION, Glad Tidings, Gospel), 18, 27, 32, 43, 112, 152, 201, 348
Gospel(s) (see also Ethnology, EUANGELION, Glad Tidings, Good news, Proclamation, PROPAGATIO, Propagation), 19, 20, 24, 27, 30, 31, 32, 33, 34, 35, 43, 44, 49, 50, 53, 58, 59, 64, 73, 91, 106, 107, 129, 135, 142, 143, 152, 155, 181, 205, 210, 212, 214, 224, 268, 269, 295, 318, 354
- Essentials of the gospel, 296
- Hi. of the planting of the gospel, 219
- Mry gospels, 125
- Social Gospel Movement, 298
- Whole gospel, 60
Government(s) (see also Self-government), 27, 246, 283, 310, 317, 353, 354, 355
Grace (see also GRATIA), 23, 41, 149
Grammars, 1, 208, 218
GRATIA, SOLA (see also Grace), 194
Growth (see also Church growth), 22, 70, 81, 116, 136, 162, 166, 169, 218, 278, 280, 282, 283, 287, 296, 298, 307, 335, 346, 348, 354, 356, 358
- External/internal, 23
- Miraculous, 158
- Numerical/spiritual, 23, 206, 273, 276, 284
Guilt (complex), 215

Hagiography (see also Saint), 246
Halieutics, 16-17, 27, 69
Healing(s) (th. of), 42, 61, 157
Heathen (see also Apostolate, Conversion, Gentiles, Land, Pagan, People), 29, 113, 114, 147
Heresy/heretics, 160, 289
Hermeneutic(s)/hermeneutical (see also Method), 216, 217, 219
- Biblical, 213, 217, 219
- Gap, 215
- Issue, 217
- Key, 177

- Missiological, 216, 358
- Mry/of m., 216, 217, 219
- Philosophical, 216
- Revolt, 217
- Task, 217
Heroes/heroism, 100, 246
Hinduism/hindus, 106, 187, 256, 287, 314
HISTORIA JESU (see Jesus)
HISTORIA MISSIONUM (see Hi.)
Histori(ci)sm, 91, 216
Historiography, 203
History/ies (see also Communism, Conversion
   of the heathen, Education, Epochs, Hi. of
   m., Islam, Method, Mgy, Pedagogics,
   Progress, Sociology), 1, 2, 35, 74, 107,
   110, 112, 127, 136, 152, 173, 182, 188,
   205, 206, 210, 224, 225, 227, 246, 251,
   252, 254, 256, 260, 264, 297, 307, 308
- Church, 101, 127, 137, 165, 220, 250,
   251, 254-255, 257, 288, 359
- Hi. of conversions, 250, 251, 255-256,
   257
- Cultural, 204
- Hi. of r./rs (see also Schools), 173,
   207, 220, 250, 251, 252-253, 254, 257,
   356, 359
- Human, 139, 148, 182
- Salvation (see also Mgy), 149
- Theory (circular/linear) (see also
   Centrifugal/centripetal), 115
- World, 135, 250, 251-252, 254, 256, 257,
   284, 359
History/ies of mission/mission(ary) (see
   also Acceptance, Apostolate, Axiology,
   Church, Conference, CONGREGATIO,
   Economics, Education, Enterprise,
   Epistemology, Evm, Expansion,
   Geographics, Gospel, Law, Linguistics,
   M., M. studies, Ontology, Order,
   Pedagogics, Philosophy, Progress,
   Propagation, Psychology, Society,
   Sociology), 7, 12, 29, 64, 81, 101, 127,
   173, 176, 182, 203, 204, 205, 206, 207,
   209, 219-257, 258, 259, 266, 271, 272,
   286, 295, 305, 338, 347, 357, 358, 359
- Categorical/comprehensive, 223, 225, 226,
   230
- Catholic, 221, 225, 236
- Christ-centered, 256
- Comparative, 209

- Denominational/ecclesiastical/non-
   denominational, 223, 225
- Descriptive/normative, 223, 224
- General/specific, 220, 223, 225, 229-230,
   240, 257
- HISTORIA MISSIONUM, 219
- Popular/scientific, 223, 224
- Protestant, 221, 225, 240
Holiness, 114
Holy Spirit (see Spirit)
Home front, 223, 337
Homiletics, 17, 18, 173, 191
Hope(s), 115, 200, 298
Hospital(s), 268, 276, 331
Hospitality, 117, 134
Humanism, 44, 300, 308
Humanization (see also Mgy), 44
Hygiene, 204
Hymnody, 113

Ideal(ism), 91, 298, 349
Idea(s), 113, 121, 134, 170, 291, 297, 299,
   327, 348
- Mry, 101, 112, 124, 142, 165, 191, 199
- Rs, 347
Ideology/ies (see also Worldviews), 91,
   192, 193, 194, 211, 288, 304, 308, 319,
   328, 336
Idol(s), 114, 115, 330, 333
Idolatry/ies, 64, 330
Illiteracy/illiterate, 348, 354, 355
IMAGO DEI (see God)
IMC (see also Conference), 32, 33, 41, 61,
   88, 90, 99, 138, 151, 152, 154, 155, 244,
   259, 266, 274, 284, 307, 312, 317, 321,
   324, 335, 348, 349
Immanence/immanentism, 74, 187
Imperative, missionary, 350
Imperialism, 90
Incarnation (see also Evm), 148, 180, 212
Inclusiveness/inclusivism, 143, 169
Inculturation (see also Culture, Evm), 296
Indifference, 342
Indigenization, 355
Indigenous (see Christians, Church,
   Culture, Language, Personnel)
Individuality (see also Th. of m.,
   Witness), 160, 162
Induction, 79, 177, 178
Innovation, 177

Inscriptions, 2
Integrity (see Creation)
Intellectualism (see also Value), 189
Intelligentsia, 340, 355
Intercession, 134
Interdenominational(ism), 92, 283
Interpretation(s)/interpreting, 25, 43, 73,
   76, 107, 111, 122, 127, 182, 215, 216,
   217, 219, 251, 253
- Bible interpretation, 216-217
- Sc. of interpreting, 213-217
- Th. of interpreting, 217
Intolerance, 311, 312, 319
Involvement, social, 35, 42
Islam/muslim(s) (hi. of) (see also Country,
   Law, M., Propaganda, Th. of m., Th. of
   r.), 81, 105, 135, 187, 194, 206, 228,
   246, 256, 257, 270, 273, 283, 289, 311,
   314, 319, 341
Israel (see also Faith, Light, M.), 53, 99,
   107, 110, 111, 112, 113, 114, 121, 124,
   127

Jehovah's Witnesses, 299
Jesuit(s), 59, 159, 160, 244, 287, 322
Jesus (see also Christ, M.),17, 18, 19, 27,
   33, 43, 50, 58, 61, 99, 106, 107, 115,
   125, 127, 128, 129, 134, 135, 161, 182,
   194, 198, 215, 244, 246, 255, 256, 269,
   296
- Authority of Jesus, 124
- HISTORIA JESU, 255, 256, 257
- Historical Jesus, 180
- 'Jesus Movement', 299
- Lives of Jesus, 229
- Mry features of Jesus, 121
Jew(s) (see also Christian, Evm, Judaism,
   M.), 28, 106, 120, 138, 148, 256, 314
- Christian, 134
JHWH, 110, 111, 112, 113, 214
John (see also Revelation), 20, 125, 132,
   134, 181, 226
John the Baptist (see M.)
Journal(s), (mry), 5, 78, 79, 84, 138, 143,
   221, 312
Journey, (mry) (see also Travels), 129, 252
Joy, 160
Judaism/jewish (see also Christians, Evm,
   Jew, M., Propaganda, Th. of m., Th. of r.),
   81, 91, 107, 115, 116, 120, 122, 134,

187, 240
Judgement (see also Sending), 74, 111, 113,
   121, 187
Juridical/jurisdiction, 306, 316, 317
Jurisprudence, 205, 206
Justice, (social) (th. of), 35, 41, 61,
   101, 113, 329, 348
Justification, 149, 186, 199

KERYGMA, 18, 19, 20, 215
Keryg(ma)tics, 18
Keryktics, 16, 18-19, 27, 69
Kingdom (see also Christ, Expansion, God),
   61, 93, 139, 169, 333
Knowledge, (theory of) (see Epistemology)
KOINONIA, 19
Koran, 311

Land(s) (see also Ethnology), 194, 247,
   265, 266, 323, 353
- Closed, 268
- Heathen, 328
- Occupied, 268
- Sending, 191
Language(s) (see also Tongue), 56, 59, 60,
   76, 81, 105, 115, 134, 135, 139, 205,
   206, 208, 210, 211, 212, 214, 215, 216,
   219, 246, 288, 347, 354
- Biblical, 212
- Christian, 210, 212, 218
- Foreign, 207
- Indigenous/local, 210, 212
- LINGUA FRANCA, 211
- Literary/oral/written, 207, 214
- Mry/of m., 205, 206, 211-212, 218, 219
- Pagan, 212
- Rs, 218
- Sc. of language, 208, 218
- Secular, 218
- Vernacular (see also Vernaculars), 211
Lausanne (see also Congress, Consultation,
   MANILA MANIFESTO)
- Lausanne Committee of World Evn, 43, 154,
   155, 158
- LAUSANNE COVENANT, 155, 156, 158
- Lausanne Movement, 90, 93, 155, 157
Law (see also Moses), 59, 81, 173, 205,
   206, 306, 307, 308, 313, 316, 317, 318,
   319
- Ecclesiastical, 178

- (Inter)national, 178, 306, <u>316-318</u>
- Islamic (see also SHARI'A), 311, 314
- Law of m./m(ry) (hi. of), 81, 173, 176, 295, <u>306-319</u>, 358
- Law of r., 173
Lay (see Apostolate)
Leaders, (mry), 59, 165, 281, 337
Least evangelized, 336
Letter(s), 28, 132, 133, 153, 329, 331
- Apostolic, 134, 142
- Encyclical, 142, 143
Liberalism, 90, 160
Liberation (th. of) (see also Mgy, Th. of m.), 93, 143, 217, 329
- Liberation-centrism, 93
- Movement, 92
Liberty, 112, 307, 309, 318
- Civil, 307
- Rs, 142, 268, 306, 307, 308, 309, <u>310-312</u>, 316, 318, 319
Library, Missionary Research (MRL), 5, 80
Light to the nations, 114
Linguistics (see also Summer Institute), 173, 203, 205, 209, 210, 217, 218, 219, 285
- Linguistics of m./mry (hi. of), 81, 173, 176, 205, 206, <u>207-219</u>, 250, 286, 305, 357, 358, 359
- Linguistics of r./rs, 173, <u>218</u>, 250
- Secular, 218
Literacy, 106, 348, 354, 356
Literature, 2, 5, 13, 21, 32, 35, 43, 44, 52, 53, 59, 60, 63, 71, 84, 100, 110, 114, 136, 138, 167, 176, 201, 246, 285, 341, 346
Liturgics, 173, 191, 201
Liturgy, 59, 139, 196
Love (see also AGAPE), 33, 100, 148, 200, 291, 309, 348
Lutheranism, 149

Magazines (see also Periodicals), 9, 355
MAGNALIA DEI, 24, 182
Majority, 228, 304, 316
Mandate(s), 307, 318
- Cultural, 124
- M(ry), 25, 51
- Spiritual, 124
MANILA MANIFESTO, 155
Map(s), 1, 259, 262, 263, 264, 266, 269

- Church, 262
- Mry, 261, <u>262-266</u>, 272
Marginality/marginalized, 181, 304
Marriage, 63, 283
Martyr(s), 165, 247, 339
Martyrdom, 339
MARTYRIA, 70
Martyriology, 70
Marxism/marxist, 216, 331
Mass (see Conversion, Evm, Media, Psychology),
Matheteutics, 16, <u>20-21</u>, 24, 27, 70
Meaning(s), 25, 31, 35, 44, 71, 73, 109, 114, 186, 188, 189, 210, 214, 296
Means, missionary, 191, 353
Media, mass, 355, 357
Medical (see M., Sc.)
Meditation, 187, 341
Membership (see Church)
Message, 18, 24, 27, 34, 99, 100, 101, 107, 111, 116, 125, 129, 158, 180, 214, 218, 219, 246, 247, 296, 298, 318, 337, 344
Metaphysics, <u>176</u>, 203
Metereology, 1, 12
Method(s), 25, 34, 79, 81, 175, 178, 179, 223, 224, 296, 345, 347, 357
- Deductive/inductive, <u>177-178</u>
- Educational/pedagogical, 352, 356
- Empirical, 175, 203
- Hermeneutical, 217
- Historical, 220
- Methods of cooperation, 175
- Methods of evangelism, 19, 35
- Methods on the field, 175
- Methods of presentation at the home base, 175
- Methods of realisation, 175
- Methods of witnessing, 148
- Methods of mgy/m. studies, 3, 29, 71, 74, 77, <u>175-183</u>, 203, 223, 224
- Mry/of m., 2, 64, 112, 116, 129, 148, 289, <u>355-356</u>
- Montessori, 345
- Phenomenological, 189, 191
- Philosophical, 175
- Theological, 175
Methodology, 3, 183, 274
- Ecclesiastical, 175
- Empirical, 176
- Missiological, 175, 182

- Scientific, 175
Mind(s), 28, 73, 112, 148, 162, 205, 341
Ministry/ies, 21, 28, 50, 79, 121, 129,
  158, 161, 215, 269, 301, 338, 352
Miracles, 158
Minority, 194, 228
MISSIO(NES), 1, 58-61, 64, 69
- MISSIO CANONICA, 59, 147
- MISSIO CHRISTI, 60, 99, 188
- MISSIO DEI (see God's mission)
- MISSIO ECCLESIAE, 60, 70, 188
- MISSIO HOMINUM, 60, 70, 188
- MISSIONES ECCLESIAE, 61
- MISSIONES EXTERAE, 60
- SACRAE MISSIONES, 60
- TERRAE MISSIONIS (see Country)
Missiography, 204, 205
Missiologist(s), 1, 3, 9, 19, 22, 57, 62,
  67, 73, 74, 76, 77, 78, 80, 81, 88, 91,
  92, 99, 107, 109, 115, 136, 139, 149,
  162, 166-167, 170, 174, 178, 179, 181,
  182, 185, 187, 190, 196, 199, 200, 206,
  212, 217, 218, 220, 224, 251, 252, 253,
  262, 271, 273, 278, 288, 291, 292, 304,
  305, 306, 307, 320, 343, 344, 353,
  356
Missiology/nology (see also Branches,
  Concepts, Methodology, Names), passim
- Biblical, 98, 99, 172
- Church-centered, 181
- Conciliar ecumenical, 151
- Context-centered, 181
- Deductive/inductive, 178, 182
- Descriptive/normative/prescriptive,
  178-179, 182
- Dialogical, 181
- Eastern Orthodox, 138
- Empirical, 176, 182
- Evangelical, 154, 157
- From above/from below, 180-181, 182, 188
- Fundamental, 179
- God/Christ/Spirit-centered, 181
- Historical, 219
- Humanizing, 181
- Liberationist, 181
- Mgy of ethnic groups, 285
- Patristic, 98
- Protestant, 12,147, 172
- Roman Catholic, 141
- Salvation hi.-centered, 181

Mission(s), passim
- Ancient, 191
- Apostolic, 226
- Biblical, 18
- Buddhist, 80, 193, 194
- Charismatic (hi. of), 157, 225
- Christian, passim
- Church, 136, 226
- Church-centric, 56
- Commercial, 64
- Critical, 194
- Denominational, 225
- Diplomatic, 64
- (Eastern) Orthodox (hi. of), 139, 225
- Ecumenical (hi./th. of), 151, 157, 225,
  292
- Educational, 346
- European/western, 226, 228, 329
- Evangelical (hi. of), 225
- Faith (see Faith)
- Foreign (th. of), 60, 105, 11, 172, 200,
  247, 268, 298, 325, 355
- Future of m., 249
- Gentile, 121, 122, 124, 127, 129, 134
- Global, 247, 280, 284
- Goodwill, 64
- Hebrew Christian (hi. of), 225
- Holistic (th. of), 99
- Home, 60, 309
- Islam/muslim, 80, 193, 194
- Israel's, 110
- Jewish, 121, 127, 134
- M. in Christ's way, 151, 152
- M. in six continents, 60, 152, 266, 272,
  301
- M. in the west, 163
- M. of communism/communist ideology, 193,
  194
- M. of Free-Thought, 193
- M. of ideologies, 336, 359
- M. of Jesus, 120, 122, 125
- M. of John the Baptist, 122
- M. of non-Christian/other religions/
  worldviews, 80, 192, 193, 206, 359
- M. outside the gates, 68
- Modern (hi. of), 25, 191, 224, 227, 230,
  245, 347, 357
- Non-Christian, 76, 176, 186, 187, 192,
  194, 197, 199, 203, 206, 271, 306, 308,
  334, 336, 346

394

- Non-western, 228
- Parliamentary, 64
- Pentecostal (hi. of), 157, 162, 200, 225
- Prophetic, 194
- Protestant (hi. of), 147, 191, 221, 224, 225, 228, 229, 236, 240, 249, 257, 272, 280-281, 301, 307, 357
- Roman Catholic (hi. of), 25, 191, 221, 224, 225, 228, 229, 236-237, 249, 257, 259, 272, 278, 357
- Secular meaning, 2
- Social, 300
- Society-centric, 56
- 'Third world'/'two-thirds world', 228, 280
- World/universal, 61, 64, 100, 112, 117, 120, 157, 171, 185, 245, 257
- World-wide, 127, 155, 224, 225, 249
Mission studies/study of mission (see also Concept, Hi., Method), 1-2, 3, 4, 11, 12, 13, 15, 17, 18, 19, 24, 25, 27, 28, 30, 35, 49, 50, 57, 63, 67, 68, 69, 70, 71, 72, 77, 81, 84, 85, 89, 93, 107, 116, 120, 132, 165, 166, 167, 174, 175, 176, 177, 182, 183, 185, 187, 191; 199, 200, 201, 206, 207, 209, 225, 226, 245, 253, 259, 268, 270, 271, 275, 286, 288, 299, 304, 306, 307, 333, 334, 359
- Biblical, 100, 107
- Comparative (see also Phenomenology of m.), 190, 202
- Empirical(=scientific), 1, 2, 8, 10, 67, 71, 72, 80, 81, 85, 86, 173, 174, 175, 176, 177, 179, 182, 183, 185, 202, 203, 204, 205, 206, 207, 219, 257, 296, 344, 359
- Formal/material, 3
- Historical (hi. of), 223-225, 257
- Philosophical, 1, 2, 8, 10, 72, 74, 173, 174, 175, 177, 182, 183, 185, 187, 189, 197, 202
- Sociological, 300
- Theological, 1, 2, 8, 10, 72, 85, 87, 90, 92, 93, 173, 174, 175, 176, 177, 182, 183, 185, 202
MISSIONARIUS, 58-61
Missionary/ies (see also Personnel, Psychology), 1, 9, 13, 24, 50, 81, 89, 90, 91, 105, 106, 107, 110, 111, 115, 125, 127, 129, 130, 162, 166, 170, 174,

189, 196, 199, 201, 203, 207, 208, 209, 210, 212, 214, 215, 216, 218, 220, 224, 227, 244, 245, 246, 247, 252, 255, 259, 260, 261, 262, 268, 270, 271, 272, 276, 280, 281, 284, 286, 287, 288, 291, 292, 294, 295, 296, 298, 299, 317, 318, 321, 323, 325, 327, 329, 334, 335, 336, 339, 340, 344, 347, 348, 353, 354, 355, 356
- Epithets, 245, 246
- 'Original', 120
Missioners, 127
Missionics, 58, 62, 63, 69, 70
Missio(no)logy, passim
Mission theory (see Theory)
MITTERE, 32, 58-61
Mobility, 304
Modernization, 304
Money, (mry) (see also Finance, Fund, Support), 273, 321, 323, 325, 333, 340, 347, 348
Monks, 259
Monophysite(s), 163, 228
Monotheism/monotheistic, 81, 107, 115, 287
Morality (see also Apostolate, Ethics), 201
- Morality of the apostolate, 201
Moratorium, 152, 328, 333
Moravian(s), 13, 15, 147, 159, 162, 244, 265, 322
Moses, 110, 111, 113
- Law of Moses (thora), 99, 106, 109, 110-111, 115, 121, 122
Mosques, 282
Motive(s), (mry), 100, 101, 116, 120, 299, 302
Movement(s) (see also Church Growth, Ecumenical, Evangelical, Gospel, Jesus, Lausanne, Liberation, Pentecostal, People, Philology, Prophetic, Religion, Renewal, Translation), 157, 189, 289, 308, 323, 345, 346
- M(ry), 112, 204, 216, 228, 281, 309, 321, 346
Music, 2
Muslim (see Islam)
Mysticism, 204

Names of God (see God)
Names of missiology, 3, 15-70, 71, 77, 172
Nation(s) (see also Discipling, Gentiles, Light), 18, 20, 100, 110, 112, 113, 114,

115, 129, 134, 148, 200, 206, 272, 284, 285, 288, 298, 307, 308, 316, 318, 319, 341, 347, 354, 355, 356
- League of Nations, 316, 318
- United Nations, 307, 309, 310-312, 319, 331
Nationalism, 90, 340
Nationality (see also Church), 191
Nationalization, 354
Naturalism, 91
Nestorian(ism), 163, 228, 258
New Testament, 16, 18, 19, 20, 22, 23, 27, 28, 50, 99, 100, 101, 106, 107, 108, 114, 115, 116, 117, 120, 121, 132, 134, 135, 136, 137, 206, 208, 214, 215, 247, 251, 269, 288, 299
- M. in NT, 116-117
- NT in m., 135
Non-Christians,34, 41, 135, 142, 212, 217, 219, 256, 273, 341, 347, 352, 353, 357
Non-converts, 317
Non-Jews, 106, 120, 121, 129, 134, 138
Norm (see also Axiology, Hi., Th.), 179
- Norms of doctrine, 178, 179
- Ultimate norm, 91, 182

Obedience, 19, 160
Obligation(s), (mry), 28, 151, 247, 272, 348, 355
Observance, 310, 311
Old Testament (see also R.), 81, 99, 100, 101, 106, 107, 108, 109, 110, 112, 113, 114, 115, 116, 134, 206, 214, 251, 288
- M. in OT, 107-108, 109
- OT in m., 115-116
Ontocratic, 251
Ontology, 63, 74, 173, 186, 189, 197, 204
- Ontology of m. (hi. of), 173, 197-198, 202
- Ontology of r., 173
Oppression, 339, 340
Orality (see also Culture, Language), 200
Order(s) (see also Church), 159, 160, 161, 170, 244, 308, 318, 331
- Mry (hi. of), 160-161, 220, 221, 225, 244, 257, 264, 273
Organics, 16
Organization(s), 27, 148, 155, 178, 179, 224, 268, 300, 302, 310, 312, 327, 328, 337, 353, 354

Ornithology, 63
Orthodox Church(es)/Orthodoxy, Eastern (see also Mgy, Th. of m.), 92, 138, 139, 140, 151, 278, 350
Orthodox Churches, Oriental, 350
Otherworldliness, 200
Outreach, 53
Overseas (see also Church, Experience), 1, 35

Pagan(s) (see also Gentiles, Heathen, Language), 114, 160, 204
Para-church (see Agency)
Paradigm, 125, 149
- Christ paradigm, 198
- Exodus paradigm, 198
- Mry, 124, 130, 138, 141, 147, 151
Parasitism, 323
Particularism, 107, 115, 120, 121
Passion, missionary, 32, 101
Patriotism, 340
Paul, 18, 27, 32, 50, 106, 125, 127, 129-130, 132, 135, 162, 165, 181
Peace, 58, 317, 348
Pedagogics/pedagogy (hi. of) (see also Education, Method, Value), 173, 205, 248, 249, 256
- Empirical, 349
- Pedagogics of m./mry, 81, 173, 176, 206, 345-357, 358
- Pedagogics of r./rs, 173, 356-357
- Social, 206
PEMPEIN, 58, 120
Pentecostal Movement (see also M., Th. of m.), 92, 157, 158, 280
People(s) (see also Education), 1, 4, 17, 21, 24, 25, 32, 34, 44, 50, 53, 59, 60, 74, 89, 90, 112, 113, 120, 143, 148, 158, 162, 163, 166, 180, 196, 210, 212, 214, 246, 247, 255, 257, 265, 271, 284, 288, 289, 295, 297, 305, 314, 316, 319, 331, 337, 340, 341, 347, 348, 349, 355, 357
- All, 120, 125, 169
- Asean/non-European/non-western, 210, 215, 230
- Christian, 200
- Heathen, 29
- Indigenous, 276
- Mry, 112
- Non-rs, 64

- People in (all) six continents, 219, 255, 337, 344
- People Movements, 342
- People of God/His people, 107, 111, 308, 332
- People of Living Faiths (see Faith)
- 'People of the Book', 314
- People outside the church, 135
- Poor, 323, 333
- Primal, 209, 287
- Rs, 219
- Secular, 218, 219
- Unreached, 273
- Western, 230
Perfecting, 21
Period(s) of m. (see Chronology)
Periodicals, 4, 9
Personalism/personalistic (see also Th. of m.), 91, 299
Personnel, (indigenous) (see also Missionary), 59, 276, 328, 336, 337, 338, 339
Persuasion (see also Evm), 313
Peter, 16, 27, 127, 128, 132
Phenomenology (see also Method, School), 74, 173, 186, 188, 189, 197
- Phenomenology of m. (hi. of), 173, 188-196, 202
- Phenomenology of r., 173, 189, 196
Phenomenon/a of mission/missionary phenomenon/a, 1, 2, 49, 74, 76, 186, 189, 191, 205, 252, 280, 344
Philanthropy, 2
Philology, 2, 205, 207, 216
- Comparative, 208
- Philological Movement, 209
- Philology of m./m(ry), 209-210, 216, 358
Philosophy (see also Hermeneutics, Method, M. studies), 34, 49, 73, 74, 173, 181, 185, 186, 188, 228, 342, 347
- Mry, 73, 171
- Ph. of cultures, 204
- Ph. of m. (hi. of), 1, 58, 64, 67, 69, 71, 72-77, 80, 84, 87, 88, 117, 168, 169, 171, 172, 173, 174, 185-202, 225
- Ph. of r., 72, 76-77, 84, 168, 169, 173, 204
Pietist(ic)/piety, 322, 334, 341, 347
Plan(s), 73, 280
PLANTATIO ECCLESIAE (see Church)

Plausibility, 188
PLEROMA, 158
Plethunics, 16
Pluralism, religious (see also Society), 168
Pneumatocentrism, 93
Pneumatology, 127, 157
Poimenics, (mry) (see also Care), 173, 335-336, 344, 346, 349
Policy, 265, 323
Politics, 27, 316
Polytheism, 107
Poor (see Poverty)
Pope, 25, 43, 59, 136, 160, 162, 178, 307
Population, 282
- Explosion, 106, 284
- Problem, 300
- World population, 278, 282, 331
Populism, 216
POREFTHENTES, 138
Positivism, 342
Post-colonial(ism), 69, 148, 206, 226, 257, 263, 268, 280, 284, 296, 318, 322, 329, 339, 340, 353, 354, 357
Poverty/poor (see also People, Solidarity), 117, 152, 160, 181, 320, 322, 329-330, 333
- Preferential option for the poor, 329, 333
Power(s) (see also Evm), 19, 28, 33, 50, 116, 124, 138, 139, 148, 157, 158, 161, 205, 228, 271, 289, 300, 308, 316, 317, 318, 355
Practice, 44, 49, 64, 139, 149, 158, 159, 160, 162, 179, 213, 310, 311, 316, 319
Praise, 113, 134
Prayer(s), 111, 134, 157, 196, 198, 206, 273, 347
- The Lord's prayer, 208, 214, 352, 357
- Mry, 273
Praxis, 188
Preaching (th. of), 17, 18, 24, 31, 61, 101, 116, 129, 160, 172, 194, 205, 268
Preevangelization (see Evn)
PREPARATIO EVANGELICA, 107
Preparation, 28, 100, 101, 107, 116, 275, 338
Presbyterianism, 262
Presence (see also Evm), 107, 139, 169, 273, 299

Presentation(s) (mry) (see also Method),
44, 301, 341
Principles, (mry), 35, 49, 64, 116, 170,
177, 179, 191, 198
Proclamation (see also Evm), 18, 19, 149,
196, 217
- Proclamation of the gospel, 18, 32, 34
- Th. of proclamation, 27
Progress (hi. of), 2, 33, 41, 208, 209,
223, 224, 228, 257, 261
- Human, 219, 225
- Mry/of m., 191, 220, 224
- Social, 298
Promise, 188
Proof, 188, 215
Propaganda (see also CONGREGATIO), 25, 27,
342
- Christian, 334
- Communist/of communism, 80, 193
- Jewish, 25
- Mry, 25, 27
- Muslim, 25
- Non-Christian, 206, 334, 346
- Propaganda of Free-Thought, 193
- Propaganda of (non-Christian)
ideologies/religions/worldviews, 193,
206, 336
Propagandics, 16, 24-25, 27, 69
PROPAGATIO
- PROPAGATIO CHRISTIANAE RELIGIONIS, 50
- PROPAGATIO EVANGELII, 50
- PROPAGATIO FIDEI, 50
Propagation (hi. of), 25, 313
- Gospel, 25, 29, 219, 323
- Propagation of Christianity, 29, 219, 358
Prophecy, 157
Prophetic/prophetism (see also Evm, M.),
111, 115
- Prophetic Movement, 112
Prophets (NEBIIM), 99, 106, 109, 111-112,
115
Proselytism, 116, 117, 313
Prosperity, 329, 331
Prosthetics, 16, 24, 27, 70
Protestant churches, 92, 147, 158, 270, 354
Protestantism (see also M., Mgy, Th. of
m.), 53, 100, 147, 160, 178, 228, 236,
262, 264, 265, 274, 278
Providence (see Sending)
PROVINCIAE ECLESIASTICAE, 59

Psychology (see also Ethnopsychology,
Psychopathology), 86, 173, 205, 333, 334,
335, 336, 339, 340, 341-342, 343, 344
- Community, 339
- Empirical, 344
- Mass, 342
- M. psychology/psychology of m. (hi. of),
81, 173, 176, 206, 333-344, 346, 358
- Psychology of Christian encounter (see
Encounter)
- Psychology of (Christian) missionaries,
336, 337-339
- Psychology of conversion(s), 334,
341-342, 344
- Psychology of dialogue, 343, 344
- Psychology of mry work, 337, 339-340
- Psychology of m. boards (see Boards)
- Psychology of r./rs, 173, 204, 333, 343,
344
- Secular, 335
- Social, 206
Psychopathology, 339
Purpose(s) of mission/missionary, 2, 87,
100, 112, 117, 160, 353

Race(s)/racism, 90, 101, 120, 284, 288, 289
Radio, 355
Rational(ism), 187, 216, 285
Reactions to Christian mission, 341-342
Realisation (see Method)
Realism, biblical, 91
Reality, 76, 189, 197, 198, 297
- Actual, 297
- Immanent, 187
- Transcendent, 187, 194
- Ultimate, 71, 187, 197
Reason (see also Rationalism), 187, 199
Reborn (see Christians, Regeneration)
Reception of Christ (see also Acceptance),
256
Receptivity, 342
Recession, 227
Reconversion, 160
Red Cross, 2
Redemption, 112, 149, 179, 188
REDEMPTORIS MISSIO, 143
Reference books/reference works, 4, 5, 9,
10-12, 13
Reformation, 53, 147, 227, 307
Regeneration, 2, 161

Rejection, 51, 210, 291
Rejection, tissue, 305
Relationship(s), 19, 33, 187, 188, 196,
   198, 201, 291, 292, 294, 301, 302, 320,
   321, 333, 335, 338
Relativism, 189
Religion(s) (see also Ethnology, Freedom,
   Geography, Hi., Linguistics, M.,
   Pedagogics, Ph., Phenomenology,
   Psychology, Sc., Sociology, Statistics,
   THEOLOGIA RELIGIONUM, Th., Th. of r.),
   76, 81, 85, 91, 148, 149, 168, 174, 178,
   187, 189, 193, 194, 198, 199, 257, 270,
   271, 283, 289, 297, 299, 300, 301, 304,
   306, 308, 310, 311, 312, 314, 316, 319,
   334, 355, 357
- Asian, 81
- Christian, 25, 29
- Comparative, 196, 207
- Future of a religion, 283
- Mry, 29, 112, 187, 193, 194, 197, 206,
   273, 283, 311
- Non-Christian, 73, 80, 91, 143, 168, 169,
   189, 192, 193, 194, 196, 199, 206, 253,
   271, 283, 304, 336, 340-341, 344, 352,
   357
- Non-western, 251
- Old Testament, 110
- Rs Movements, 304
- Traditional, 1, 187
- World, 220, 251, 252, 253, 261, 282, 283,
   314
Religious studies, 78, 84, 85, 168, 176,
   270
Renewal, Charismatic, 157, 158, 280
Research(es) (see also Library), 1, 35, 68,
   166, 172, 202, 225, 274, 286, 287, 292,
   300, 304, 321, 325, 338, 358
Resistance, 342
Respect, 289, 311
Responses to Christian mission (see
   Reactions)
Responsibility/ies, 34, 35, 41, 84, 112,
   141, 147, 155, 240, 272, 302, 325, 328,
   333, 347, 355
Revelation, 76, 92, 110, 112, 182, 187,
   214, 289
REVELATION OF JOHN, 134
Revivals, collective, 342
Revolution (see also World)

- Copernican, 307
- French, 228, 308
- Russian, 228
Rights, 309, 310, 311, 313, 314, 317, 318
- Civil/political, 311, 319
- Human (see also Declaration), 2, 306,
   308-309, 314, 319
- Mry/of m., 191, 205, 268
Rites, 282
Roman Catholic Church (see also M., Mgy,
   Th. of m.), 25, 43, 67, 88, 90, 100, 143,
   158, 177, 236, 254, 259, 262, 264, 265,
   274, 275, 278, 307, 313, 324, 354
Roman Catholicism, 236
Romanticism, 224, 288

Saint(s) (see also Hagiography), 68, 246
Salary, 117, 328
Salvation (see also EXTRA ECCLESIAM, Hi.,
   Sending, Universalism), 28, 58, 93, 112,
   121, 139, 151, 161, 236, 348
Sanctification, 179, 321
Sceptics, 186, 187
School(s) (see also Building, Education),
   35, 224, 276, 318, 331, 342, 345, 348,
   351, 353, 354, 357
- Belgian/Louvain, 142, 143, 254
- Christian, 276, 353
- Church Growth (see also Church Growth),
   9, 342
- French, 142
- German, 142, 143
- High/primary/secondary, 353
- Missiological, 142
- Mission schools, 268, 351, 353-354, 357
- Phenomenological, 190
- Public, 350, 353
- Religious History, 252, 253
- Secular, 353
- Self-supporting, 323, 327
- Spanish, 142
Science(s) (see also Branch, Geographics,
   Language, Methodology, M. studies, Sc. of
   m.), 29, 49, 51, 79, 85, 86, 173, 175,
   178, 185, 199, 226, 272, 284, 298
- Auxiliary, 3, 4, 176, 203, 204, 209, 253,
   271, 272, 286
- Deductive, 176
- Empirical, 176
- Inductive, 176

- Medical, 2
- Natural, 1, 13
- Positive, 297
- Prescriptive, 176
- Sc. of interpreting (see Interpretation)
- Sc. of r., 78, <u>84-85</u>, 86, 168, 169, 173, 196, 203, 209
- Sc. of translating (see Translating)
- Social, 1, 176, 181
Science(s) of mission/mission(ary) science (see also Branch, M. studies), 1, 3, 24, 29, 30, 51, 58, 60, 63, 64, <u>67</u>, 69, 71, 72, 87, 88, 168, 169, 171, 172, 173, 174, 176, 185
- Comparative (see also Phenomenology of m.), 190, 202
- Hi. of sc. of m., 3, <u>203-204</u>, 225
- Sc. of the home base, 80
- Sc. of the mry societies, 80, 171
SCRIPTURA, SOLA, 159, 178
Scripture(s), 27, 105, 107, 108, 115, 177, 181, 217, 321
Sects, 181
Secular (see also Evm, Language, Linguistics, M., People, Psychology, School, Worldview), 64, 67, 74, 84, 256, 291, 296
- Secularism, 44, 218
- Secularization, 44, 251
Self-extension, 327, 328
Self-government, 327, 328
Self-support (see also Church, School), 320, 327, 328, 333, 335, 339, 354
Seminary/ies (see also University), 1, <u>28</u>, 276
Sending (see also Church, Country, Ethics, Land), 53, 60, 111, 120, 125, 134, 135, 186, 187, 197, 198, 200
- Judgmental, 113
- Providential, 113
- Salvific, 113
Septuagint, 115
Sermon on the Mount, 135, 357
Service(s) (th. of) (see also Evm), 1, 2, 19, 33, 35, 41, 52, 61, 160, 196, 260, 276, 313, 334, 335, 338, 349, 356
Sexism, 224
SHALACH/SHALIACH, <u>109</u>, 110, 111, 113, 120
SHARI'A (see also Law), 311
Shintoism, 314

Signs and wonders, 158, 280
Simplicity, 160
Slave labour/slavery 111, 246, 247
Sociation of the mission, 205
Society/ies (see also M.), 24, 44, 48, 59, 74, 79, 148, 159, 160, 161, 170, 206, 212, 256, 260, 265, 268, 270, 286, 298, 301, 305, 306, 307, 317, 323, 329
- M(ry), (hi. of) (see also Sc. of m.), 7, 13, 138, 147, <u>160-161</u>, 167, 220, 221, 224, 225, 227, 228, 240, <u>244</u>, 257, 265, 266, 273, 274, 275, 280, 300, 317, 323, 331, 335, 339
- Pluralistic, 148
Sociography (of m.), 204, 261, 297, 358
Sociology (hi. of), 63, 86, 173, 204, 205, 206, 297, 298, 299, 301, 304
- Sociology of m., 81, 176, 206, 272, <u>297-306</u>, 358
- Sociology of the mry enterprise, 297, 299, 305
- Sociology of r., 297, 299, <u>304-305</u>
Solidarity (with the poor) (see also Poverty/poor), 125, 333
Soteriocentrism, 93
Soteriology, 140
Spirit, (Holy) (see also Baptism, Mgy, Pneumatology), 20, 33, 93, 99, 111, 139, 155, 157, 158, 161, 188, 214
Spirituality (see also Growth, Mandate, Value), 159, 355, 357
- Mry, 159
Spontaneity, 200
Spread (of m.), 52, 53, 81, 194, 258, 264, 354
Stamps, 225
Statement(s), 60, 138, 139, 143, 149, 151, 152, 158, 161, 170, 178, 246, 261, 311, 313, 323
- Doctrinal, 160, 161
- Missiological/mry, 136, 157, 178
Station, mission, 81, 262, 264, 265, 266, <u>268</u>, 272, 276
Statistics, 173, 179, 203, 204, 205, 273, 278, 280, 282
- Church statistics, 283
- Contemporary/historical, 275, 276
- Macro/micro, 272, 273, 275, 283
- Statistics of m./mry, 7, 81, 173, 176, 191, 204, 205, 247, <u>272-284</u>, 305, 357, 358

- Statistics of r., 173, 207, <u>282-283</u>
Strangulation, 305
Strategy/ies, 21, 35, 129, 158, 191, 273, 288, 299, 302, 336, 337
Stratification, 301
Stress, cross-cultural/missionary, 338, 339, 344
Structuration of the mission, 205
Structure(s), 3, 63, 71, 74, 155, 189, 197, 205, 210, 214, 224, 299, 300, 301, 351
Study of mission(s) (see M. studies)
Success(es), 139, 215, 224, 270, 325, 344
Suffering, 134
Summer Institute of Linguistics, 210
Superiority (complex), western, 355
Supernatural, 158
Supplication, 134
Support, financial (see also Finance, Fund, Money), 317, 321, 325
Survey(s) (of m.), 2, 4, 5, 9, 92, 100, 147, 149, 155, 157, 173, 221, 223, 225, 236, 245, <u>249</u>, 255, 274, 278, 280, 283, 306, 307
Syllogism, 295
Synagogue(s), 18, 134, 138, 282
Syncretism/syncretists, 189, 283

Taoism, 106
Task(s), (mry) (see also Hermeneutics), 19, 51, 59, 61, 151, 215, 219
Teaching (see also DIDACHE, Education), 19, 21, 61, 205, 215, 310, 311, 352, 357
Team(s), missionary, 337, 339
Technocratic/technology, 251
Television, 355
Temple(s), 27, 113, 121, 282
Terminology, 17, 32, 205, 213, <u>214-215</u>, 217, 219
Territory/ies, 59, 299, 317, 318
Testimony, 50, 134, 214
Text(s), 16, 50, 78, 100, 101, 109, 111, 112, 117, 139, 143, 144, 213, 217, 259, 312, 313, 317, 318
Thanksgiving, 134
Theocentrism, 93
Theocratic, 251
Theologian(s), 1, 15, 19, 29, 31, 41, 44, 52, 53, 56, 93, 99, 129, 139, 158, 169, 174, 182, 186, 244, 329, 331
- Mry/of m., 90, 91, 92, 149, 152, 156,

158, 159, 162, <u>163</u>, 169, 170, 174, 176, 178, 196, 199, 218, 220
- 'Third-world', 90, 329, 337
THEOLOGIA RELIGIONUM, 168
Theology (see also Dialogue, Ethnotheology, Freedom, Method, M., M. studies, Preaching, Th.,mry, Th. of m., Thinking), 3, 15, 29, 32, 41, 48, 49, 91, 117, 129, 147, 159, 160, 163, 172, 173, 179, 181, 182, 188, 196
- Adoring (see Adoration)
- Biblical, 99, 101, 172
- Christian, 11, 35, 68, 135, 173, 185, 214, 224
- Communal, 68
- Comparative, <u>196</u>, 202
- Contextual, 181
- Ecumenical, 152
- Evangelistic, <u>28-30</u>, 31, 33, 49, 69
- From above/from below, 181
- Normative, 253
- Orthodox, 139, 140
- Phenomenological, 196
- Practical, 15, 29, 68, 79, 163
- Systematic, 68, 163
- 'Third world', 90
- Western/non-western, 180
Theology, missionary, 41, 42, 49, 58, <u>67-68</u>, 69, 70, 71, 72, 87, 89, 90, 91, 92, 101, 165, 178, 179, 189, 191, 253, 291, 295, 301, 359
- (Eastern) Orthodox, 91
- Practical, 179
- Protestant, 91, 92
- Roman Catholic, 91
- Systematic, 179
- 'Third world', 90
Theology of adding (see Adding)
Theology of adoration (see Adoration)
Theology of the apostolate (see Apostolate)
Theology of church growth (see Church growth)
Theology of discipling (the nations) (see Discipling)
Theology of evangelism (see Evm)
Theology of evangelization (see Evn)
Theology of healing (see Healing)
Theology of interpreting (see Interpretation)
Theology of liberation (see Liberation)

Theology of mission/mission theology (see
  also M., Th., Th.,mry), 56, 58, 64, <u>67</u>,
  69, 70, 71, 72, 79, 86, <u>87-171</u>, 172, 173,
  174, 179, 185, 217, 295
- Biblical, 88, 91, 93, <u>98-135</u>, 159, 161,
  172
- Charismatic, 136, <u>157-158</u>
- Communitarian, 159, 172
- Conciliar, 92, 151, 154
- Contextual, 132
- Corporate, 88, 91, 93, <u>159-161</u>, 170, 172
- Denominational, 91, 136
- (Eastern) Orthodox, 91, 92, 136, <u>138-140</u>,
  153
- Ecclesiastical, 88, 91, 93, 98, <u>136-158</u>,
  159, 161, 172
- Ecumenical, 92, 136, 138, <u>151-153</u>, 154,
  172
- Ethical, 172
- Evangelical, 92, 136, 153, <u>154-156</u>, 172
- Existential, 172
- General, 88, 89
- Global, 152
- Hebrew Christian, 91, 136, <u>137-138</u>
- Hi. of th. of m., 225
- Individual, 88, 91, 93, 159, 160, 161,
  <u>162-167</u>, 172
- Interdenominational, 137
- Jewish, 168
- Jewish Christian, 137
- Liberationist, 92
- Muslim, 168
- Non-Jewish, 138
- Patristical, 172
- Pentecostal, 92, <u>157-158</u>
- Personal, 159, 162, 172
- Practical, 88
- Protestant, 91, 92, 136, <u>147-149</u>, 172
- Roman Catholic, 91, 92, 136, 138,
  <u>141-144</u>, 147, 153, 162, 172
- Special, 88, 89, 91
- 'Third world', 90
- Traditional, 136, 172
- Transdenominational, 137
- Western, 152
Theology of proclamation (see Proclamation)
Theology of religion, (see also THEOLOGIA
  RELIGIONUM), 87, <u>168-169</u>, 170, 171, 173
- Christian, 168, 171, 173
- Jewish, 168

- Muslim, 168
- Pluralistic, 169
Theology of (social) justice (see Justice)
Theology of (social) service (see Service)
Theology of (social) witness (see Witness)
Theory/ies of hi. (see Hi.)
Theory/ies of mission/mission(ary), 12, 15,
  18, 29, 30, 63, 64, 69, 73, 88, 139, 158,
  159, 160, 162, 170, 171, 172, 191, 207
Thetics, 16
Thinking, 71, 149, 177, 227
- Christian, 71
- M(ry), 20, 56, 61, 90, 139, 140, 162,
  170, 198
- Theological, 68
Thought(s), 174, 189, 194, 215, 291, 308,
  310, 311, 314, 333, 347
- Evangel, 41, 44, 48
- Free (see M., Propaganda)
- Mry/of m., 64, 74, 108, 116, 129, 165,
  191
- Rs, 313
Throne, 228
Tolerance, 311
Tongue(s) (mother) (see also Language),
  211, 212
Topography, 259, 260
Tradition(s) (see also Culture,
  Epistomology, R., Th. of m.), 13, 136,
  159, 161, 170, 181, 191, 215, 236, 280,
  309
Transcendence/transcendentism (see also
  Reality), 187
Transformation, 176, 214, 216, 251
Translating (Sc. of), <u>213-217</u>
Translation(s), 13, 43, 50, 58, 60, 64, 78,
  79, 80, 115, 206, 208, 210, 213, 214,
  215, 230, 285
- Bible translation(s)/of the Bible, 2, 52,
  58, 213, <u>215-216</u>, 217
- Translation movement, 216
Travels, missionary (see also Voyage), 266,
  <u>269-270</u>
Trinity, 139, 158, 214
Triumph(s)/triumphalistic, 224, 246
Truth, 140, 148, 149, 168, 169, 188, 189,
  199, 298, 309, 321

Ultimacy (see also Norm, Reality), 186
Unbelief, 58, 124

UNESCO, 312, 314, 354, 355
Uniqueness of Christ, 168
Unit(s), homogenous, 301, 305
United Nations (see Nation)
Unity, 125, 143, 149, 152, 161, 300
Universal Declaration (see Declaration)
Universalism (see also Conviction), 107,
  108, 115, 121
- Explicit, 121
- Intensive, 121
- Salvation, 125
University/ies (see also Seminary), 84,
  167, 220, 266, 297, 321
Unsaved, 35
Urbanization, 304

Value(s) (see also Axiology), 74, 194, 199,
  200-201, 210, 240
- Aesthetic, 186, 199, 201
- Educational/pedagogical, 200, 349
- Evangel, 41, 44, 48
- Intellectual, 200
- Mry, 199
- Moral, 199, 200, 201
- Rs, 199
- Spiritual, 200
- Theoretical/practical, 200
Vatican, 141
- Second Vatican Council (see Council)
Vengeance, 112, 121
Vernaculars (see also Language), 215
Victory, 224
Violence, 331
Vocabulary (see also Terminology), 29, 32,
  33, 59, 106, 107, 212, 214, 219, 246,
  268, 331
Vocation, 42, 110, 111, 284
Volunteers, 347
Voyage(s), 59, 269, 270, 272

Wave, third, 157
WCC (see also Assembly), 32, 33, 41, 49,
  61, 90, 92, 99, 138, 139, 144, 151, 152,
  154, 155, 158, 217, 266, 300, 301, 307,
  311, 313, 323, 324, 330, 331, 335
Wealth (see also Affluence), 329
Western-centered, 272
Westernization, 347
Will of God (see God)
Witness/witnessing, 58, 61, 70, 127, 134,

  139, 152, 157, 169
- Biblical/of the Bible, 99, 100
- Christian, 144, 151, 312, 313
- Church's, 349
- Common, 60, 152
- Communitarian, 144
- Individual, 144
- Mutual, 169
- Social (th. of), 35, 41
Witnessology, 70
Wonders (see Signs)
Work, (foreign) missionary (see also
  Church, God, Psychology), 13, 53, 70,
  100, 105, 120, 128, 129, 160, 169, 179,
  191, 200, 201, 229, 275, 297, 301, 317,
  320, 323, 325, 328, 337, 344, 345, 355
World(s) (see also Apostolate,
  Christianity, Culture, CWME, Economics,
  Epochs, Evm, Evn, Hi., Lausanne, M.,
  Population, R.), 27, 29, 68, 99, 100,
  101, 107, 112, 117, 121, 125, 127, 133,
  134, 135, 139, 148, 169, 174, 191, 192,
  194, 197, 216, 221, 246, 251, 254, 255,
  260, 261, 271, 280, 281, 282, 283, 287,
  296, 308, 314, 316, 318, 329, 331, 333,
  336, 347, 348
- All (over) the world, 18, 251, 287
- Anglo-Saxon, 73, 78, 79, 80, 88, 240,
  296, 347
- Christian (part), 60, 160, 254
- Contemporary/modern, 43, 64, 143, 178
- First, 309
- Non-Christian (part), 17, 19, 254, 298
- Non-western, 32, 212, 216, 254, 266, 268,
  301, 354
- Protestant, 60, 93
- Revolutionary, 151
- 'Third world' (see also Church, M., R.,
  Theologian, Th., Th., mry, Th. of m.),
  32, 90, 152, 220, 230, 245, 292, 321, 357
- 'Two-Third world' (see also M.), 280,
  281, 283, 318
- Western, 32, 90, 152, 212, 266, 300, 301
- Whole, 60, 113, 139, 143, 266, 268, 269
- World provides the agenda, 177
- World-wide, 227, 259, 264
World Bank, 331
World Evangelical Fellowship, 154, 157
Worldliness (see also Otherworldliness), 32
Worldview(s) (see also Ideologies, M.,

Propaganda), 89, 90, 91, 93, 178, 187, 193, 194, 224, 257, 283, 308, 355, 357
- Buddhist, 194
- Future of a worldview, 283
- Mry, 187, 193, 197
- Non-Christian, 80, 192, 193, 206, 283, 340-341, 344, 352, 357
- Secular, 308

Worship, 115, 273, 310, 311
Writings (KETUBIM), 99, 106, 109, 113, 115

YHWH (see JHWH)
Youth, 340, 356

Zoroastrianism, 187

STUDIEN ZUR INTERKULTURELLEN GESCHICHTE DES CHRISTENTUMS
ETUDES D'HISTOIRE INTERCULTURELLE DU CHRISTIANISME
STUDIES IN THE INTERCULTURAL HISTORY OF CHRISTIANITY

Begründet von/fondé par/founded by
Hans Jochen Margull †, Hamburg

Herausgegeben von/edité par/edited by

Richard Friedli   Walter J. Hollenweger   Theo Sundermeier
Université de Fribourg   University of Birmingham   Universität Heidelberg

Jan A.B. Jongeneel
Universiteit Utrecht

Band   1   Wolfram Weiße: Südafrika und das Antirassismusprogramm. Kirchen im Spannungsfeld einer Rassengesellschaft.

Band   2   Ingo Lembke: Christentum unter den Bedingungen Lateinamerikas. Die katholische Kirche vor den Problemen der Abhängigkeit und Unterentwicklung.

Band   3   Gerd Uwe Kliewer: Das neue Volk der Pfingstler. Religion, Unterentwicklung und sozialer Wandel in Lateinamerika.

Band   4   Joachim Wietzke: Theologie im modernen Indien - Paul David Devanandan.

Band   5   Werner Ustorf: Afrikanische Initiative. Das aktive Leiden des Propheten Simon Kimbangu.

Band   6   Erhard Kamphausen: Anfänge der kirchlichen Unabhängigkeitsbewegung in Südafrika. Geschichte und Theologie der äthiopischen Bewegung. 1880-1910.

Band   7   Lothar Engel: Kolonialismus und Nationalismus im deutschen Protestantismus in Namibia 1907-1945. Beiträge zur Geschichte der deutschen evangelischen Mission und Kirche im ehemaligen Kolonial- und Mandatsgebiet Südwestafrika.

Band   8   Pamela M. Binyon: The Concepts of "Spirit" and "Demon". A Study in the use of different languages describing the same phenomena.

Band   9   Neville Richardson: The World Council of Churches and Race Relations. 1960 to 1969.

Band   10   Jörg Müller: Uppsala II. Erneuerung in der Mission. Eine redaktionsgeschichtliche Studie und Dokumentation zu Sektion II der 4. Vollversammlung des Ökumenischen Rates der Kirchen, Uppsala 1968.

Band   11   Hans Schöpfer: Theologie und Gesellschaft. Interdisziplinäre Grundlagenbibliographie zur Einführung in die befreiungs- und polittheologische Problematik: 1960-1975.

Band   12   Werner Hoerschelmann: Christliche Gurus. Darstellung von Selbstverständnis und Funktion indigenen Christseins durch unabhängige charismatisch geführte Gruppen in Südindien.

Band   13   Claude Schaller: L'Eglise en quête de dialogue. Vergriffen.

Band   14   Theo Tschuy: Hundert Jahre kubanischer Protestantismus (1868-1961). Versuch einer kirchengeschichtlichen Darstellung.

Band   15   Werner Korte: Wir sind die Kirchen der unteren Klassen. Entstehung, Organisation und gesellschaftliche Funktionen unabhängiger Kirchen in Afrika.

Band   16   Arnold Bittlinger: Papst und Pfingstler. Der römisch katholisch-pfingstlerische Dialog und seine ökumenische Relevanz.

Band   17   Ingemar Lindén: The Last Trump. An historico-genetical study of some important chapters in the making and development of the Seventh-day Adventist Church.

Band 18 Zwinglio Dias: Krisen und Aufgaben im brasilianischen Protestantismus. Eine Studie zu den sozialgeschichtlichen Bedingungen und volkspädagogischen Möglichkeiten der Evangelisation.

Band 19 Mary Hall: A quest for the liberated Christian. Examined on the basis of a mission, a man and a movement as agents of liberation.

Band 20 Arturo Blatezky: Sprache des Glaubens in Lateinamerika. Eine Studie zu Selbstverständnis und Methode der "Theologie der Befreiung".

Band 21 Anthony Mookenthottam: Indian Theological Tendencies. Approaches and problems for further research as seen in the works of some leading Indian theologicans.

Band 22 George Thomas: Christian Indians and Indian Nationalism 1885-1950. An Interpretation in Historical and Theological Perspectives.

Band 23 Essiben Madiba: Evangélisation et Colonisation en Afrique: L'Héritage scolaire du Cameroun (1885-1965).

Band 24 Katsumi Takizawa: Reflexionen über die universale Grundlage von Buddhismus und Christentum.

Band 25 S.W. Sykes (editor): England and Germany. Studies in theological diplomacy.

Band 26 James Haire: The Character and Theological Struggle of the Church in Halmahera, Indonesia, 1941-1979.

Band 27 David Ford: Barth and God's Story. Biblical Narrative and the Theological Method of Karl Barth in the Church Dogmatics.

Band 28 Kortright Davis: Mission for Carribean Change. Carribean Development As Theological Enterprice.

Band 29 Origen V. Jathanna: The Decisiveness of the Christ-Event and the Universality of Christianity in a world of Religious Plurality. With Special Reference to Hendrik Kraemer and Alfred George Hogg as well as to William Ernest Hocking and Pandipeddi Chenchiah.

Band 30 Joyce V. Thurman: New Wineskins. A Study of the House Church Movement.

Band 31 John May: Meaning, Consensus and Dialogue in Buddhist-Christian-Communication. A study in the Construction of Meaning.

Band 32 Friedhelm Voges: Das Denken von Thomas Chalmers im kirchen- und sozialgeschichtlichen Kontext.

Band 33 George MacDonald Mulrain: Theology in Folk Culture. The Theological Significance of Haitian Folk Religion.

Band 34 Alan Ford: The Protestant Reformation in Ireland, 1590-1641. 2. unveränderte Auflage.

Band 35 Harold Tonks: Faith, Hope and Decision-Making. The Kingdom of God and Social Policy-Making. The Work of Arthur Rich of Zürich.

Band 36 Bingham Tembe: Integrationismus und Afrikanismus. Zur Rolle der kirchlichen Unabhängigkeitsbewegung in der Auseinandersetzung um die Landfrage und die Bildung der Afrikaner in Südafrika, 1880-1960.

Band 37 Kingsley Lewis: The Moravian Mission in Barbados 1816-1886. A Study of the Historical Context and Theological Significance of a Minority Church Among an Oppressed People.

Band 38 Ulrich M. Dehn: Indische Christen in der gesellschaftlichen Verantwortung. Eine theologische und religionssoziologische Untersuchung politischer Theologie im gegenwärtigen Indien.

Band 39 Walter J. Hollenweger (Ed.): Pentecostal Research in Europe: Problems, Promises and People. Proceedings from the Pentecostal Research Conference at the University of Birmingham (England) April 26th to 29th 1984.

Band 40 P. Solomon Raj: A Christian Folk-Religion in India. A Study of the Small Church Movement in Andhra Pradesh, with a Special Reference to the Bible Mission of Devadas.

Band 41 Karl-Wilhelm Westmeier: Reconciling Heaven and earth: The Transcendental Enthusiasm and Growth of an Urban Protestant Community, Bogota, Colombia.

Band 42 George A. Hood: Mission Accomplished? The English Presbyterian Mission in Lingtung, South China. A Study of the Interplay between Mission Methods and their Historical Context.

Band 43 Emmanuel Yartekwei Lartey: Pastoral Counselling in Inter-Cultural Perspective: A Study of some African (Ghanaian) and Anglo-American viewes on human existence and counselling.

Band 44 Jerry L. Sandidge: Roman Catholic/Pentecostal Dialogue (1977-1982): A Study in Developing Ecumenism.

Band 45 Friedeborg L. Müller: The History of German Lutheran Congregations in England, 1900-1950.

Band 46 Roger B. Edrington: Everyday Men: Living in a Climate of Unbelief.

Band 47 Bongani Mazibuko: Education in Mission/Mission in Education. A Critical Comparative Study of Selected Approaches.

Band 48 Jochanan Hesse (Ed.): Mitten im Tod - vom Leben umfangen. Gedenkschrift für Werner Kohler.

Band 49 Elisabeth A. Kasper: Afrobrasilianische Religion. Der Mensch in der Beziehung zu Natur, Kosmos und Gemeinschaft im Candomblé - eine tiefenpsychologische Studie.

Band 50 Charles Chikezie Agu: Secularization in Igboland. Socio-religious Change and its Challenges to the Church Among the Igbo.

Band 51 Abraham Adu Berinyuu: Pastoral Care to the Sick in Africa. An Approach to Transcultural Pastoral Theology.

Band 52 Boo-Woong Yoo: Korean Pentecostalism. Its History and Theology.

Band 53 Roger H. Hooker: Themes in Hinduism and Christianity. A Comparative Study.

Band 54 Jean-Daniel Plüss: Therapeutic and Prophetic Narratives in Worship. A Hermeneutic Study of Testimonies and Visions. Their Potential Significance for Christian Worship and Secular Society.

Band 55 John Mansford Prior: Church and Marriage in an Indonesian Village. A Study of Customary and Church Marriage among the Ata Lio of Central Flores, Indonesia, as a Paradigm of the Ecclesial Interrelationship between village and Institutional Catholicism.

Band 56 Werner Kohler: Umkehr und Umdenken. Grundzüge einer Theologie der Mission (herausgegeben von Jörg Salaquarda).

Band 57 Martin Maw: Visions of India. Fulfilment Theology, the Aryan Race Theory, and the Work of British Protestant Missionaries in Victorian India.

Band 58 Aasulv Lande: Meiji Protestantism in History and Historiography. A Comparative Study of Japanese and Western Interpretation of Early Protestantism in Japan.

Band 59 Enyi Ben Udoh: Guest Christology. An interpretative view of the christological problem in Africa.

Band 60 Peter Schüttke-Scherle: From Contextual to Ecumenical Theology? A Dialogue between Minjung Theology and 'Theology after Auschwitz'.

Band 61 Michael S. Northcott: The Church and Secularisation. Urban Industrial Mission in North East England.

Band 62 Daniel O'Connor: Gospel, Raj and Swaraj. The Missionary Years of C. F. Andrews 1904-14.

Band 63 Paul D. Matheny: Dogmatics and Ethics. The Theological Realism and Ethics of Karl Barth's Church Dogmatics.

Band 64 Warren Kinne: A People's Church? The Mindanao-Sulu Church Debacle.

Band 65 Jane Collier: The culture of economism. An exploration of barriers to faith-as-praxis.

Band 66 Michael Biehl: Der Fall Sadhu Sundar Singh. Theologie zwischen den Kulturen.

Band 67 Brian C. Castle: Hymns: The Making and Shaping of a Theology for the Whole People of God. A Comparison of the Four Last Things in Some English and Zambian Hymns in Intercultural Perspective.

Band 68 Jan A. B. Jongeneel (Ed.): Experiences of the Spirit. Conference on Pentecostal and Charismatic Research in Europe at Utrecht University 1989 .

Band 69 William S. Campbell: Paul's Gospel in an Intercultural Context. Jew and Gentile in the Letter to the Romans.

Band 70 Lynne Price: Interfaith Encounter and Dialogue. A Methodist Pilgrimage.

Band 71 Merrill Morse: Kosuke Koyama. A model for intercultural theology .

Band 73 Robert M. Solomon: Living in two worlds. Pastoral responses to possession in Singapore.

Band 74 James R. Krabill: The Hymnody of the Harrist Church Among the Dida of South Central Ivory Coast (1913-1949). A Historico-Religious Study.

Band 75 Jan A. B. Jongeneel a.o. (Eds.): Pentecost, Mission and Ecumenism. Essays on Intercultural Theology. Festschrift in Honour of Professor Walter J. Hollenweger.

Band 76 Siga Arles: Theological Education for the Mission of the Church in India: 1947-1987. Theological Education in relation to the identification of the Task of Mission and the Development of Ministries in India: 1947-1987; with special reference to the Church of South India.

Band 77 Roswith I.H. Gerloff: A Plea for British Black Theologies. The Black Church Movement in Britain in its transatlanctic cultural and theological interaction with special reference to the Pentecostal Oneness (Apostolic) and Sabbatarian movements. 2 parts.

Band 78 Friday M. Mbon: Brotherhood of the Cross and Star. A New Religious Movement in Nigeria.

Band 79 John Samuel Pobee (ed.): Exploring Afro-christology.

Band 80 Frieder Ludwig: Kirche im kolonialen Kontext. Anglikanische Missionare und afrikanische Propheten im südöstlichen Nigeria.

Band 81 Werner A. Wienecke: Die Bedeutung der Zeit in Afrika. In den traditionellen Religionen und in der missionarischen Verkündigung.

Band 82 Ukachukwu Chris Manus: Christ, the African King. New Testament Christology.

Band 83 At Ipenburg: 'All Good Men'. The Development of Lubwa Mission, Chinsali, Zambia, 1905-1967.

Band 84 Heinrich Schäfer: Protestantismus in Zentralamerika. Christliches Zeugnis im Spannungsfeld von US-amerikanischem Fundamentalismus, Unterdrückung und Wiederbelebung "indianischer" Kultur.

Band 85 Joseph Kufulu Mandunu: Das "Kindoki" im Licht der Sündenbocktheologie. Versuch einer christlichen Bewältigung des Hexenglaubens in Schwarz-Afrika.

Band 86 Peter Fulljames: God and Creation in intercultural perspective. Dialogue between the Theologies of Barth, Dickson, Pobee, Nyamiti and Pannenberg.

Band 87 Stephanie Lehr: "Wir leiden für den Taufschein!" Mission und Kolonialisierung am Beispiel des Landkatechumenates in Nordostzaire.

Band 88 Dhirendra Kumar Sahu: The Church of North India. A Historical and Systematic Theological Inquiry into an Ecumenical Ecclesiology.

Band 89 William W. Emilsen: Violence and Atonement. The Missionary Experiences of Mohandas Gandhi, Samuel Stokes and Verrier Elwin in India before 1935.

Band 90 Kenneth D. Gill: Toward a Contextualized Theology for the Third World. The Emergence and Development of Jesus' Name Pentecostalism in Mexico.

Band 91 Karl O. Sandnes: A New Family. Conversation and Ecclesiology in the Early Church with Cross-Cultural.

Band 92 Jan A.B. Jongeneel: Philosophy, Science and Theology of Mission in the 19th and 20th Centuries. A Missiological Encyclopedia. Part I: The Philosophy and Science of Mission.